Software Testing in the Cloud:

Perspectives on an Emerging Discipline

Scott Tilley
Florida Institute of Technology, USA

Tauhida Parveen
Independent Consultant, USA

T0338704

Managing Director:	Lindsay Johnston
Editorial Director:	Joel Gamon
Book Production Manager:	Jennifer Romanchak
Publishing Systems Analyst:	Adrienne Freeland
Development Editor:	Austin DeMarco
Assistant Acquisitions Editor:	Kayla Wolfe
Typesetter:	Alyson Zerbe
Cover Design:	Nick Newcomer

Published in the United States of America by
Information Science Reference (an imprint of IGI Global)
701 E. Chocolate Avenue
Hershey PA 17033
Tel: 717-533-8845
Fax: 717-533-8661
E-mail: cust@igi-global.com
Web site: http://www.igi-global.com

Library of Congress Cataloging-in-Publication Data

Software testing in the cloud: perspectives on an emerging discipline / Scott Tilley and Tauhida Parveen, editors.
    p. cm.
  Includes bibliographical references and index.
  ISBN 978-1-4666-2536-5 (hbk.) -- ISBN 978-1-4666-2537-2 (ebook) -- ISBN 978-1-4666-2538-9 (print & perpetual access) 1. Cloud computing. 2. Computer software--Testing. I. Tilley, Scott R. (Scott Robert), 1964- II. Parveen, Tauhida, 1978-
  QA76.585.S625 2013
  004.67'82--dc23
                                    2012033729

British Cataloguing in Publication Data
A Cataloguing in Publication record for this book is available from the British Library.

All work contributed to this book is new, previously-unpublished material. The views expressed in this book are those of the authors, but not necessarily of the publisher.

To my parents.
– Scott Tilley

To Rafique.
– Tauhida Parveen

You see, but you do not observe. The distinction is clear.
– Sherlock Holmes, *A Scandal in Bohemia*

Table of Contents

Detailed Table of Contents

Chapter 1
Alan W. Brown, IBM Rational and University of Surrey, UK

In enterprise software delivery, the pursuit of software quality takes place in the context of a fundamental paradox: balancing the flexibility that drives speed of delivery with the rigor required to verify that what is being delivered is complete, correct, and appropriate for its intended use. One common approach to address this concern is to create "software testing factories" with the aim of increasing testing efficiency by standardizing and speeding up delivery of testing services. To achieve this balance, software testing factories are turning to cloud-based infrastructures as an essential delivery approach. Cloud technology exhibits characteristics that make adoption of software testing factories particularly attractive: elasticity of resources, ease of deployment, and flexible pricing. In this chapter, the author examines the role and structure of software testing factories and their realization using cloud technology, illustrates those concepts using real world examples, and concludes with some observations and a discussion on future directions.

Chapter 2
Bharat Shah, Lockheed Martin Corporation, USA

Recent years have seen the rapid growth of on-demand, flexible, low-cost cloud-based information technology services. Government and business organizations around the world have started transforming their traditional in-house data center environments to cloud-based outsourced data centers. This transformation is opening doors to new risks given that the cloud computing delivery models, related services, and technologies are still maturing and evolving. Before deployment, organizations must implement cloud environment assessment methodologies to comply with the applicable standards and regulations. They must evaluate the environment's quality attributes of Internet connectivity, user access control, privacy and confidentiality, asset protection, multiple platforms locality, availability, reliability, performance, and scalability. The purpose of this chapter is to assist organizations that are considering providing and consuming cloud-based services in developing an assessment plan specific to organizational policies, strategies and their business and applicable legal and regulatory requirements; and assessing the cloud environment controls for infrastructure, platform, and software services.

#### Chapter 3

Cloud computing provides an innovative technology that enables Software as a Service (SaaS) to its customers. With cloud computing technologies, a suite of program understanding tools is suggested to be deployed in a cloud to aid the generation of test cases for software testing. This cloud-enabled service allows customers to use these tools through an on-demand, flexible, and pay-per-use model. Lastly, the issues and challenges of cloud computing are presented.

#### Chapter 4

Cloud-based applications like email services or office suites enable real-time collaboration and traceability for shared data from nearly anywhere by using a modern web-browser. Thus, a significant shift has happened to these common applications to focus only on their usage than on their maintenance. However, today's software development projects spend a noteworthy amount of resources to setup and maintain necessary development tools—over and over again. Thus, a similar shift for these development tools in the future would enable to spend valuable resources more on the actual project's goals than on the tools' maintenance. Especially development projects for cyber-physical systems, which interact with the real life's surroundings by relying on sensors and actuators, have specific needs when using cloud-based solutions. In this contribution, preconditions, design decisions, and limitations of a cloud-based testing approach for CPS are outlined and discussed on the example "Hesperia." "Hesperia" bases on the experiences from the development of "Caroline"–an autonomously driving vehicle for the 2007 DARPA Urban Challenge. "Hesperia" as a cloud-based testing approach was tested 2009 during the development of an autonomously driving vehicle at the University of California, Berkeley.

HadoopUnit is a software testing framework that integrates Hadoop and JUnit to facilitate the distribution of unit tests to the nodes of a cluster for concurrent execution. It was conceived of the need to reduce test execution time for large collections of tests and has been shown to successfully accomplish this in a medium-size cluster of 150 nodes. This work considers its effectiveness on a small cluster (4 nodes) to determine any inefficiency present in the system and attempts to overcome them with the purpose of increasing performance. It was found that naïve use of HadoopUnit on a small cluster was slower than the best times achieved on a single machine, but by properly configuring the number of tests executed by each Hadoop Map task, a 75% reduction in execution time was achieved. These results show that, on a small scale, the original implementation of HadoopUnit may not be the best solution, but with the addition of a new feature, a significant increase in performance can be achieved.

Sergio Di Martino, University of Naples Federico II, Italy

Filomena Ferrucci, University of Salerno, Italy

Valerio Maggio, University of Naples Federico II, Italy

Federica Sarro, University of Salerno, Italy

Search-Based Software Testing is a well-established research area, whose goal is to apply meta-heuristic approaches, like Genetic Algorithms, to address optimization problems in the testing domain. Even if many interesting results have been achieved in this field, the heavy computational resources required by these approaches are limiting their practical application in the industrial domain. In this chapter, the authors propose the migration of Search-Based Software Testing techniques to the Cloud aiming to improve their performance and scalability. Moreover, they show how the use of the MapReduce paradigm can support the parallelization of Genetic Algorithms for test data generation and their migration in the Cloud, thus relieving software company from the management and maintenance of the overall IT infrastructure and developers from handling the communication and synchronization of parallel tasks. Some preliminary results are reported, gathered by a proof-of-concept developed on the Google's Cloud Infrastructure.

Harry M. Sneed, Independent Consultant, Germany

Cloud Computing makes it possible for users to access a wide range of web services in the public domain and to embed these global services in their local applications. This promises to save a significant amount of individual development cost. The biggest obstacle to using this technology is the problem of trust. To gain trust in the services offered they have to be extensively tested, either by the user himself or by a trusted agent. This chapter deals with the testing of web services in the cloud. There are many similarities to testing web services in a local service-oriented architecture, but there are also significant differences. In a company specific SOA, testers can gain access to the source. This is not true of the cloud. There is no possibility of accessing the source. Therefore, testers must rely solely on the specification contained in the service level agreement – SLA – and the web service interface definition – WSDL or REST – to base their test upon. Testing in the cloud is strictly a black-box test. The goal of a cloud service test is also not to find errors but to assess the suitability of the service to the purpose of the user. It may be necessary to test several services in order to find that one best suited to the requirements of the user. To judge suitability it is necessary to define an ideal usage profile, including performance, security and other non-functional criteria, and to compare that with the actual profile of each potential service. For this both static and dynamic analysis methods must be applied. The chapter presents an automated approach to assessing cloud services and selecting that one most suitable to the user's application.

James H. Hill, Indiana University-Purdue University Indianapolis, USA

Douglas C. Schmidt, Vanderbilt University, USA

It is critical to evaluate the quality-of-service (QoS) properties of enterprise distributed real-time and embedded (DRE) system early in their lifecycle—instead of waiting until system integration—to minimize the impact of rework needed to remedy QoS defects. Unfortunately, enterprise DRE system developers and testers often lack the necessary resources to support such testing efforts. This chapter discusses how test clouds (i.e., cloud-computing environments employed for testing) can provide the necessary testing resources. When combined with system execution modeling (SEM) tools, test clouds can provide the necessary toolsets to perform QoS testing earlier in the lifecycle. A case study of design and implementing resource management infrastructure from the domain of shipboard computing environments is used to show how SEM tools and test clouds can help identify defects in system QoS specifications and enforcement mechanisms before they become prohibitively expensive to fix.

Chapter 9

Leah Riungu-Kalliosaari, Lappeenranta University of Technology, Finland

Ossi Taipale, Lappeenranta University of Technology, Finland

Kari Smolander, Lappeenranta University of Technology, Finland

This chapter describes a qualitative study whose aim was to explore and understand the conditions that influence software testing as a service. Interviews were conducted with software professionals from 16 organizations. The study used qualitative grounded theory as its research method. The level of domain knowledge required by testers was an initial indication of whether testing could be delivered as a service. The benefits of software testing as a service included flexibility and cost effectiveness. Among top requirements were security and pricing. Cloud computing was envisaged as the delivery model for software testing as a service. Some potential research areas suggested were pricing models and handling of test data. There was an indication that the demand for software testing as a service was on the rise, albeit with mixed feelings. Organizations would have to make careful considerations before embarking on testing their systems and applications over the internet.

Chapter 10

W. Morven Gentleman, Computers for People, Canada

Software testing, whether performed by the software development organization itself or on behalf of the software development organization by an independent testing organization, is typically described in the literature as part of the development or maintenance process for the purpose of improving the quality of the software product (i.e. finding and removing defects). Nevertheless, interested parties other than the software development organization perform software testing for reasons other than finding and removing defects, and such testing can be facilitated when the software is available as a service in the cloud. Unfortunately, access to software only as a service in the cloud can inhibit certain kinds of testing. In this chapter, the author discusses who such other interested parties might be, what they intend to learn from software testing, and what some of the techniques are they might use.

Chapter 11

Nikolai Kosmatov, CEA LIST, France

Software testing in the cloud can reduce the need for hardware and software resources and offer a flexible and efficient alternative to the traditional software testing process. A major obstacle to the wider use of testing in the cloud is related to security issues. This chapter focuses on test generation techniques that combine concrete and symbolic execution of the program under test. Their deployment in the cloud leads to complex technical and security issues that do not occur for other testing methods. This chapter describes recent online deployment of such a technique implemented by the PathCrawler test generation tool for C programs, where the author faced, studied, and solved many of these issues. Mixed concrete/symbolic testing techniques not only constitute a challenging target for deployment in the cloud, but they also provide a promising way to improve the reliability of cloud environments. The author argues that these techniques can be efficiently used to help to create trustworthy cloud environments.

Chapter 12

Anjan Pakhira, University of Newcastle upon Tyne, UK
Peter Andras, University of Newcastle upon Tyne, UK

Testing is a critical phase in the software life-cycle. While small-scale component-wise testing is done routinely as part of development and maintenance of large-scale software, the system level testing of the whole software is much more problematic due to low level of coverage of potential usage scenarios by test cases and high costs associated with wide-scale testing of large software. Here, the authors investigate the use of cloud computing to facilitate the testing of large-scale software. They discuss the aspects of cloud-based testing and provide an example application of this. They describe the testing of the functional importance of methods of classes in the Google Chrome software. The methods that we test are predicted to be functionally important with respect to a functionality of the software. The authors use network analysis applied to dynamic analysis data generated by the software to make these predictions. They check the validity of these predictions by mutation testing of a large number of mutated variants of the Google Chrome. The chapter provides details of how to set up the testing process on the cloud and discusses relevant technical issues.

Chapter 13

Philipp Zech, University of Innsbruck, Austria
Philipp Kalb, University of Innsbruck, Austria
Michael Felderer, University of Innsbruck, Austria
Ruth Breu, University of Innsbruck, Austria

Today's increasing trend towards outsourcing IT landscapes and business processes into the Cloud is a double-edged sword. On the one side, companies can save time and money; however, on the other side, moving possible sensitive data and business processes into the Cloud demands for a high degree of information security. In the course of this chapter, the authors give an overview of a Cloud's various vulnerabilities, how to address them properly, and last but not least, a model-driven approach to evaluate the state of security of a Cloud environment by means of negative testing. Besides, the authors incorporate the idea of living models to allow tracking and incorporating of changes in the Cloud environment and react properly and, more important, in time on evolving security requirements throughout the complete Cloud Life Cycle.

Chapter 14

Tanja Vos, Universidad Politécnica de Valencia, Spain
Paolo Tonella, Fondazione Bruno Kessler, Italy
Joachim Wegener, Berner & Mattner, Germany
Mark Harman, University College London, UK
Wishnu Prasetya, University of Utrecht, The Netherlands
Shmuel Ur, Bristol University, UK

The cloud will be populated by software applications that consist of advanced, dynamic, and largely autonomic interactions among services, end-user applications, content, and media. The complexity of the technologies involved in the cloud makes testing extremely challenging and demands novel approaches and major advancements in the field. This chapter describes the main challenges associated with the testing of applications running in the cloud. The authors present a research agenda that has been defined in order to address the testing challenges. The goal of the agenda is to investigate the technologies for the development of an automated testing environment, which can monitor the applications under test and can react dynamically to the observed changes. Realization of this environment involves substantial research in areas such as search based testing, model inference, oracle learning, and anomaly detection.

In cloud computing, applications are hosted, deployed, and delivered as services over the Internet. New cloud application services can be developed by tailoring existing ones, while hiding the complexity of the underlying implementation. Cloud applications may be able to adapt to changes in their environment, which should be secure and reliable. The infrastructure on which cloud applications are built is characterized by power, storage, and virtualization. But how does all of this affect the ability to adequately test cloud applications? This chapter investigates the testability of cloud application services. It focuses on the specific problem of reduced controllability and observability of software services hosted in the cloud, and proposes a novel solution referred to as Test Support as-a-Service (TSaaS). A prototype of TSaaS is also presented, and is used to discuss the feasibility, challenges, and benefits of the approach.

Various information systems are widely used in the information society era, and the demand for highly dependable system is increasing year after year. However, software testing for such a system becomes more difficult due to the enlargement and the complexity of the system. In particular, it is often difficult to test parallel and distributed systems in the real world after deployment, although reliable systems, such as high-availability servers, are parallel and distributed systems. To solve these problems, the authors propose a software testing environment for dependable parallel and distributed system using the cloud computing technology, named D-Cloud. D-Cloud consists of the cloud management software as the role of the resource management, and a lot of virtual machine monitors with fault injection facility in order to simulate hardware faults. In addition, D-Cloud introduces the scenario manager, and it makes a number of different tests perform automatically. Currently, D-Cloud is realized by the use of Eucalyptus as the cloud management software. Furthermore, the authors introduce FaultVM based on QEMU as the virtualization software, and D-Cloud frontend that interprets test scenario, constructs test environment, and dispatches commands. D-Cloud enables automating the system configuration and the test procedure as well as performing a number of test cases simultaneously and emulating hardware faults flexibly. This chapter presents the concept and design of D-Cloud, and describes how to specify the system configuration and the test scenario. Furthermore, the preliminary test example as the software testing using D-Cloud is presented. As the result, the authors show that D-Cloud allows easy setup of the environment, and to test the software testing for the distributed system.

#### Chapter 17

Cloud computing introduces a new paradigm for software deployment, hosting, and service renting. Based on the XaaS architecture, a large number of users may share computing resources, platform services, and application software in a multi-tenancy approach. To ensure service availability, the system needs to support an advanced level of massive scalability so that it can provide necessary resources on demand following the pay-per-use pricing model. This chapter analyzes the unique requirements of cloud performance and scalability, compared with traditional distributed systems. Measurements are proposed with performance indicators, meters, and metrics identified from different perspectives. To support scalability testing in a dynamic environment, an agent-based testing framework is proposed to facilitate adaptive load generation and simulation using a two-layer control architecture.

#### Chapter 18

A proliferation of mobile smartphone platforms, including Android devices, has triggered a rise in mobile application development for a diverse set of situations. Testing of these smartphone applications can be exceptionally difficult, due to the challenges of orchestrating production-scale quantities of smartphones such as difficulty in managing thousands of sensory inputs to each individual smartphone device. This work presents the Android Tactical Application Assessment and Knowledge (ATAACK) Cloud, which utilizes a cloud computing environment to allow smartphone-based security, sensing, and social networking researchers to rapidly use model-based tools to provision experiments with a combination of 1,000+ emulated smartphone instances and tens of actual devices. The ATAACK Cloud provides a large-scale smartphone application research testbed.

#### Chapter 19

Cloud-based applications offer great value and benefits to businesses and other application consumers. However, unlike traditional in-house developed systems or commercial-off-the-shelf (COTS) applications, the customer has little or no control over when and how functionality may change. The cloud consumer also has little or no control over how the data controlled by the application is processed, stored, and secured. This chapter explores how the testing of cloud applications is fundamentally different from other contexts where the customer has a greater degree of control. The limitations of risk mitigation are discussed as well as cloud computing models that may also reduce the cloud consumer's risk.

Foreword

A few years ago I co-wrote the book *How We Test Software at Microsoft*, along with Alan Page and BJ Rollison. As the author with the most experience with online services it fell to me to write the chapter on "Software Plus Services." The book was published in 2009 – just a few years ago – and it may be surprising that many of the techniques in that chapter are already a bit dated. The root of the challenge was that cloud computing wasn't strongly on my radar at the time.

We had an internal Microsoft memo on cloud computing and a project code named RedDog (now Windows Azure) that leaked to the press as early as 2008, but at the time the cloud wasn't real for us testers. As test engineers, we always dealt with what needed to be shipped in the next few weeks or months. The techniques we used were the tried and true ones we had at hand to simply get the job done and release the product with good quality. At that time, the approach we used for software testing was very hands on and very lab centric, where you could deploy your service to a machine under your desk and test away or maybe even push the bits down the hall to a test lab. The thought that the service would run as a virtual machine in the cloud or that the storage would be a separate cloud service wasn't even part of the equation.

In this new book, *Software Testing in the Cloud: Perspectives on an Emerging Discipline*, Scott Tilley and Tauhida Parveen have gathered together some of the top researchers in software testing with an eye to answer the question, "What changes when you test in the cloud?" If you are new to cloud, don't worry; the book's chapters cover all the core concepts, from defining what is meant by Software as a Service (SaaS), Platform as a Service (PaaS), and Infrastructure as a Service (IaaS) to many other basics such as virtualization and cloud storage.

Readers will learn from practical examples that are well researched and documented for techniques such as leveraging cloud-based testing services or Testing as a Service (TaaS) along with performance and scale testing in the cloud and even how to improve the testability of your cloud-based application. Some chapters tap into the rise of Big Data and the use of techniques such as MapReduce to analyze and produce test data as well as dealing with the rapid growth of mobile device applications. Another chapter, one of my favorites from a conceptual angle, is about building effective and efficient software testing factories. I love this idea because it embraces agile development and mixes in concepts of organizational and architectural isolation with an eye toward speed of delivery.

In just the past few years I've noticed that organizations that move to the cloud either adopt agile development or they build on top of and extend their current use of these development practices. With agile development and the cloud we are seeing projects that used to run for months and years before releasing anything cut down, modularized, and released over weeks up to months. Add to that the shift toward speed as a massively important competitive advantage both for software companies and other industries that are tapping into technology for a competitive edge and we can now see why the factory metaphor is useful for framing and managing process changes for organizations that are moving to the cloud.

As the wheels of software innovation speed up, we have to ask ourselves, how do we optimize for throughput instead of simply output? How do we maximize value shipped to the customer, at the right quality, that truly delights them? Of course one key answer is the cloud, but the other more germane answer is optimizing our use of the cloud both as a release platform for services and as a tool to help us test those services more effectively.

The last point I want to make is that *Software Testing in the Cloud: Perspectives on an Emerging Discipline* is meant to be a reference and as such you'll want to rough it up a bit. Tom Peters, author of *In Search of Excellence* and several other great business books, wrote that he loved it when folks would give them their personal copy of one of his books to autograph. He'd flip through the first few pages of the book and note all the dog-eared pages, the yellow highlights and the notes in the margins. He commented though that he would keep flipping all the way to the end of the book and he noticed that the number of underlines and bent page corners would often drop off to nil. To be honest I have a number of books I use as references where my diligent reading and note taking dropped off long before the final chapter.

Each chapter in *Software Testing in the Cloud: Perspectives on an Emerging Discipline* is a great standalone case study but as a collection they become an invaluable reference for anyone goaled on ensuring quality of cloud-based solutions. Enjoy the book, mark it up, flag key concepts for quick recall and then when you've beaten your copy into a personal reference put it on the shelf about hand high; then, when that young engineer is in your office and not quite understanding your point you can reach over, grab the book, and flip right to that critical illustration.

Please enjoy.

Ken Johnston
Microsoft Corp., USA

Ken Johnston *is a frequent presenter, blogger, and author on software testing and services. Currently, he is the Principal Group Program Manager for the Bing Big Data Quality and Measurements team at Microsoft Corp. Since joining Microsoft in 1998, Ken has filled many other roles, including test lead on Site Server and MCIS, and test manager on Hosted Exchange, Knowledge Worker Services, Net Docs, MSN, Microsoft Billing and Subscription Platform service, and Bing Infrastructure and Domains. He has also been the Group Manager of the Office Internet Platforms and Operations team (IPO). For two and a half years (2004-2006) he served as the Microsoft Director of Test Excellence. Ken earned his MBA from the University of Washington in 2003. His is a co-author of the book How We Test Software at Microsoft and contributing author to Experiences of Test Automation: Case Studies of Software Test Automation.*

Preface

Software testing is an important part of the software engineering life cycle. Testing requires resources that are often not readily available, contributing to an inefficient testing process. Running large test suites of test cases can consume considerable time and resources, often precluding their use in an interactive setting.

Cloud computing has gained a significant amount of attention in the last few years. It includes virtualized hardware and software resources that are hosted remotely and made available on-demand using a services model (e.g., SOA). Instead of running or storing applications locally, one can host their application in the cloud and access it from anywhere using a thin client application such as a Web browser. Cloud computing promises efficiency, flexibility, and scalability.

Software testing in the cloud (STITC) lies at the intersection of three key areas: software testing, cloud computing, and system migration. According to the National Defense Industrial Association (NDIA), STITC is an area that will grow in importance in the next few years. It is an emerging discipline with the potential to significantly change the way software testing is done, and as such deserves the attention of researchers, practitioners, and managers alike.

WHAT IS UNIQUE ABOUT THIS BOOK?

The book *Software Testing in the Cloud: Perspectives on an Emerging Discipline* addresses three distinct facets of STITC:

1. Migrating testing **to** the cloud: Moving the testing process, test assets, and test infrastructure from their current state for testing in the cloud or testing of the cloud.
2. Testing **in** the cloud: Leveraging the resources provided by a cloud computing infrastructure to facilitate the concurrent execution of test cases in a virtualized environment.
3. Testing **of** the cloud: Testing applications that are hosted and deployed in a cloud environment.

This genesis for this book began with a workshop held on April 10, 2010 in Paris, France as part of the *3rd IEEE International Conference on Software Testing, Verification, and Validation* (ICST 2010). The STITC 2010 workshop was a full-day event that attracted a truly international group of participants. The workshop sessions were structured along the same lines as the three central themes of the book. Each presenter had written a position paper in preparation for workshop. Several of the chapters included in the book are much expanded and updated versions of these papers.

The book has 19 chapters of material that discuss various facets of STITC from multiple perspectives. Each chapter is written by leading experts in the field. The experts come from varied backgrounds, including academia, industry, and government. The experts also come from a dozen different countries, providing unique insight into current work in STITC across the world.

WHO SHOULD READ THIS BOOK?

Testing is one of the most important areas of software engineering. It is also one of the most underemphasized areas – particularly in academia. When software testing is coupled with a rapidly changing area like cloud computing, the potential interest in the topic crosses many disciplines. There is something in the book for academics and advanced practitioners alike with an interest in STITC.

For anyone who has an interest in the challenging research problems of software testing in the cloud, this book provides invaluable information. Similarly, for those dealing with difficult practical problems of software testing in the cloud, this book provides real-world solutions through case studies and experience reports with various technologies. The book also provides enough overview material that someone simply looking to gain more of an understanding of the STITC landscape should find considerable background information.

STITC is such a new area that the book's chapters could easily serve as the basis for a graduate special topics course. The material offers the opportunity for in-class discussions. Many of the chapters outline possible avenues for further work, which could be the starting point for future theses and dissertations.

Scott Tilley
Florida Institute of Technology, USA

Tauhida Parveen
Independent Consultant, USA

Melbourne, FL
September 2012

Acknowledgment

This book would not have been possible without the efforts of all 50 authors who contributed material. We are grateful for their efforts in revising their work for publication. We all benefit from them sharing their knowledge and experience with us.

We would like to extend our deepest thank to the members of the Editorial Advisory Board (EAB). The 10 EAB members carefully reviewed all submissions to the book, provided detailed feedback and comments to the authors, and often re-checked the work as it went through the editorial process. Without the tremendous efforts of the EAB, this book would not have been possible.

We are extremely grateful for the wonderful personnel at IGI Global who helped make this book a reality. In particular, we'd like to thank Austin DeMarco and Hannah Abelbeck for their patience and encouragement.

This book is one element of a developing community of interest in the area of STITC. The website www.STITC.org is the hub for these efforts. Please contact us if you are interested in getting involved.

Chapter 1
Experiences with Cloud Technology to Realize Software Testing Factories

Alan W. Brown
IBM Rational and University of Surrey, UK

ABSTRACT

In enterprise software delivery, the pursuit of software quality takes place in the context of a fundamental paradox: balancing the flexibility that drives speed of delivery with the rigor required to verify that what is being delivered is complete, correct, and appropriate for its intended use. One common approach to address this concern is to create "software testing factories" with the aim of increasing testing efficiency by standardizing and speeding up delivery of testing services. To achieve this balance, software testing factories are turning to cloud-based infrastructures as an essential delivery approach. Cloud technology exhibits characteristics that make adoption of software testing factories particularly attractive: elasticity of resources, ease of deployment, and flexible pricing. In this chapter, the author examines the role and structure of software testing factories and their realization using cloud technology, illustrates those concepts using real world examples, and concludes with some observations and a discussion on future directions.

INTRODUCTION

Enterprise organizations are looking to enterprise software delivery as a core capability to bring efficiency and stability in delivery of services to the business, and the driving force for innovation and differentiation for new services or new products to the market. To achieve this, they are enhancing their own enterprise software delivery organization with systems integrators and technology partners to create centers of excellence and capability centers specialized in delivering value to the business. We call this a "software factory" approach.

At the same time, enterprise organizations are demanding rapid innovation and evolution of existing enterprise software solutions to support deployment to new platforms, to address

DOI: 10.4018/978-1-4666-2536-5.ch001

new market needs, and to overcome competitive threats. While standardization using software factories helps reduce cost and improve predictability of enterprise software delivery, agile ways to approach innovation are essential for solution differentiation and to enhance the value delivered to the enterprise's clients. Significant invention, adaptation, and flexibility is essential in research and development activities to drive forward the solutions brought to market, and to improve the services made available. Yet often these aspects are viewed as being in conflict with the needs for efficiency and control.

This clash between rigor and flexibility is often most clearly seen in the area of software testing. It is in the pursuit of software quality that we frequently see challenges in the balance between speed of delivery and rigor in verifying that what is being delivered is complete, correct, and appropriate for its intended use. In creating "software testing factories," many organizations are looking to increase testing efficiency at the same time that they improve software quality and accelerate their time to market.

To achieve this balance they are not only adopting new processes and techniques, they are also deploying more flexible technology infrastructures, notably based on cloud technologies. Cloud technology exhibits characteristics that make adoption of software testing factories particularly attractive: elasticity of resources, ease of deployment, and flexible pricing. As a result, many organizations are making investments in cloud technology to support their implementation of software testing factories.

In this chapter we examine the role and structure of software testing factories and their realization using cloud technology. We first explore the idea of the "software factory" and the characteristics of the software factory approach as it applies to software testing. We then discuss cloud technologies and examine how they help realize a software testing factory. We illustrate

those concepts using real world examples, and conclude with some observations and directions.

BACKGROUND

Over 40 years ago, the original NATO reports (Naur & Randell, 1968; Randell & Buxton, 1969) focused attention on some of the core elements of an industrialized approach to enterprise software delivery; increasing productivity and quality of software delivery in the face of severe skills shortages, the importance of standardized processes to improve predictability, and the role of measurement and metrics in gaining insight into project progress and for optimizing development and delivery activities.[1] In the succeeding years there was a great deal of attention turned toward these themes, particularly in understanding how different forms of software process improvement could raise the quality and consistency of software delivery (Hunter & Thayer, 2001; Humphrey, 1991). This resulted in "spiral" and "iterative" models of software development (Boehm, 1988; Krutchen, 2002), and measured improvement schemes such as the Capability Maturity Model (CMM) (CMU, 2010).

More recent work on the industrialization of software has focused attention towards automation and verification aspects of software production (Clements & Northrop, 2001). From one perspective, component-based design techniques and reuse libraries were seen to be the central elements to create catalogs of parts for assembly of systems from pre-developed pieces (Brown, 2000). While from another perspective the key to automation was the role of more formal modeling languages amenable to improved analysis techniques from which working systems could be generated (Greenfield et al., 2004).

In fact, many existing texts have discussed the scope of enterprise software, and the many challenges faced in their delivery into production, and their on-going maintenance. Broadly speaking, we see that delivering quality enterprise software is challenging as a result of many factors. But it is useful to highlight three of these for particular attention:

- **Increasing Complexity:** The scope and capability of software and systems has increased significantly in recent years. Plus, many products containing software must now be integrated with other software or subsystems, including multiple subassemblies, in-house developed code, supplier-created code, and packaged application elements.
- **Geographically Distributed Teams:** The advent of distributed delivery teams and a global supply chain of IT and engineering talent have made managing an enterprise software delivery organization more challenging. Geographic dispersion introduces communication challenges and effective stakeholder collaboration is often overlooked.
- **Lack of Standardization:** Many teams operate with little standardization or without a common foundation, resulting in a lack of shared processes and little automation.

Ultimately, the proliferation of interconnected devices and the globalization of software delivery have highlighted how software is increasingly seen as a strategic business asset, key to unique customer value and sustained business differentiation. Best-in-class product and service companies are those that have built a strong competency in enterprise software delivery – approaching this as a core business process (Harmon, 2007). Their attention is placed on enabling innovation, lowering costs, and managing change. All these tasks are critical to this global view of effective enterprise software delivery, and must be industrialized to deliver the services necessary with the speed,

quality, and flexibility essential to meet the new demands.

These factors are significant because they draw attention to an aspect of enterprise software delivery that is becoming increasingly dominant in today's interconnected world. Specifically, we see many organizations that have begun to re-think the delivery model of enterprise software to move away from a series of discrete islands of activity that are visible and under the control of a single organization, to consider it a "distributed integrated supply chain" where parts of that supply chain may be delivered by partners and 3rd party suppliers (Fredendall & Hill, 2000; Geunes & Pardalos, 2010).

A SOFTWARE FACTORY APPROACH TO ENTERPRISE SOFTWARE DELIVERY

We have seen how today organizations are facing an unparalleled rate of change in their business environments. And they are often doing so while managing and lowering operating costs across the organization. The direct implication is that they must not only minimize waste and inefficiency, but increase productivity. As the software and systems industry evolves, it is changing from a craft-based process focused on individuals to a mature, repeatable process that produces consistent high-quality output and is not hostage to variances in individual practitioner nuances.

In defining a software factory approach to enterprise software design, development and delivery, we see key characteristics that are analogous to those from the industrial sector (Hotle & Landry, 2009; IBM, 2009). We can apply these characteristics to enterprise software delivery to reduce time to market, increase flexibility and agility, and reduce costs while increasing quality and end-user satisfaction. An integrated approach can help to achieve business agility, collaborate more effectively and deliver higher quality products and services.

Aligning Business and Engineering

A software factory approach to enterprise software delivery requires a well-established, multiplatform process with tooling that aligns business strategy with engineering and system deployment. Critical in building applications that meet the needs of the customer, such processes can help to identify business needs and stakeholder requirements, and drive those business goals into enterprise software delivery projects and solutions, ensuring that the final product meets the business objectives with the lowest possible cost and highest possible quality.

Executives and management teams need to focus their attention on making appropriate strategic decisions, selecting the "right" products to execute and choosing the "right" assets to retain in their infrastructure. Factors that are key to enabling organizations to be leaner, more agile and more profitable include: identifying and prioritizing potential areas of consolidation, reducing redundancy and recurring costs, and improving operational efficiency.

To fine-tune the organization requires better enterprise decision-making and an understanding of business/technology dependencies. This requires access to an easily searchable, corporate-wide repository of related business and technical information that can support enterprise analysis, planning and execution.

Automating Processes and Tasks

Automating the enterprise software delivery lifecycle can help reduce errors and improve productivity, leading to higher quality products. An integrated portfolio of tools can help teams automate specific, labor-intensive tasks—similar to the way automation is used to perform repetitive manual tasks in manufacturing. Using automation, practitioners are able to focus on creating more innovative solutions with industry-leading design and development environments that help support the delivery of high-quality, secure and scalable products. Companies that invest in automation and a more efficient means of production and delivery can experience a sizeable jump in productivity, quality, time to market and scalability.

Leveraging Assets Across the Enterprise

Modern architectural and product development frameworks can introduce complexity, as they often include third-party, custom, off-the-shelf or outsourced or components in the overall software or system. There are several ways of coping with this, including:

- Service-oriented architecture (SOA) frameworks, which can help promote re-use across the enterprise. However, to achieve significant value from an SOA approach, applications must be assembled from standardized software components (Bieberstein et al., 2005);
- Product line engineering (PLE), an approach to achieving strategic reuse in developing portfolios of similar products that share many components but are differentiated by variations in features and functions (Clements & Northrop, 2001).

To truly achieve the benefit from reuse, organizations must be able to understand what assets they already have and leverage those assets to create reusable, flexible components that can be applied to extend architectural frameworks in meaningful, predictable ways.

Supporting Lean Processes and Integrated Infrastructures

Today's enterprise software delivery teams can be highly distributed geographically. Consequently, they need flexible and agile processes with real-time collaboration, integrated across disparate platforms, roles and geographies to reap the benefits of modern software and systems frameworks. Globally distributed development can be facilitated through defined, customizable processes and best practices to support flexibility, mitigate risk with comprehensive quality management and enhance developer productivity through task and process automation.

Automating Operational Measurement and Control

To help ensure predictable outcomes, the enterprise software delivery process must be governed so it can be continuously measured and improved. A fundamental aspect of this is the definition and codification of processes for developing products. These processes and best practices are corporate assets, and need to be captured in an actionable form so teams can be guided to adhere to appropriate best practices through automated workflows.

Relevant metrics should be gathered automatically at each step, including after software and systems are delivered into production. By constantly, automatically measuring the specific key value aspects of processes, these metrics can provide insight into the efficacy of existing processes and identify areas for improvement. Automated measurement and control is also critical in tightly regulated industries, such as government, aerospace, medical or financial sectors.

Ultimately, it is return on investment (ROI) that justifies introducing these concepts in a dynamic factory approach to software and systems delivery. The productivity achieved through more efficient methods, and the quality improvements in the resulting software and systems, have quantifiable monetary value.

THE SOFTWARE FACTORY MODEL AND SOFTWARE TESTING

The changing pressures on enterprise software delivery have led to many advances in software delivery approaches. Important changes have taken place in areas such as agile development, lean thinking, and model-driven code generation. But in the area of software quality, the basic approaches to software testing have been slower to evolve. The primary approach remains a traditional model that involves dedicating large numbers of full-time testing staff to projects, use of expensive enterprise testing tools, acquisition of large amounts of infrastructure to validate all possible deployment configurations, and so on. More recently, however, organizations have made efforts to curtail the heavy expense and cyclic nature of many of the testing and quality management aspects. Initial approaches have involved pooling testing staff and resources across collections of projects and departments to share costs and smooth the resource loading on test teams. More recently, organizations have broadened this approach to allow variable staffing, using specialist quality assurance (QA) consulting companies to supply talented and experienced help for specialized needs and to augment resources during peak periods.

The natural extension of these approaches is to separate large parts of the test and quality management process into a more factory-oriented model: the software testing factory. The goal of a software testing factory is to provide a highly organized facility that performs various tests using standardized frameworks and processes with well-trained test professionals. The scope and delivery of those testing capabilities can vary based on several factors. It's helpful to distinguish between different kinds of specialized software testing

Figure 1. Contrasting traditional and factory-based software testing approaches

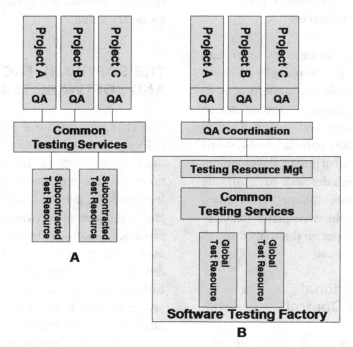

factories and the more general software testing factories. As illustrated in Figure 1, a software testing factory identifies and externalizes common testing capabilities and practices with the goal of optimizing their effective use.

The traditional software testing approach (shown on the left-hand side of Figure 1) duplicates testing capabilities on a per project basis, at best supported by a basic set of common testing services to be shared by those projects and delivered through subcontracted testing specialists. While in such an approach testing resources and infrastructures can be optimized to the specific project needs, it frequently leads to redundancy, inconsistency, and high management costs for testing capabilities across the organization as a whole. In effect, the factory-based approach (shown on the right-hand side of Figure 1) focuses on consistent, standardized approaches to common activities in the software testing life cycle. In a factory-based software testing approach the focus is on three key activities:

1. Test Planning, Design and Execution
   a. Using common approaches to define, document, and manage all test assets (excluding Unit & UAT).
   b. Establishing predefined test processes that support organizational or industry best practices (e.g., CMMI based).
   c. Configuring a workbench of shared test tools for automation, performance testing, regression testing, etc.
   d. Agreeing organization-wide KPIs for testing to enable data sharing, comparison across projects and divisions, and to benchmark against competitors and industry norms.
2. Test Environment and Data Management
   a. Establishing common test environment management procedures to make most efficient use of test resources.
   b. Coordinating cross-product and cross-project integration test planning to

avoid costly communication and mis-configuration errors.

c. Planning resource utilization across projects and teams to optimize use of scarce skills and resources.

d. Defining effective test data with adequate coverage and privacy protection, and managing that test data as it evolves.

3. Infrastructure Management

a. Building, managing and supporting the variety of test infrastructure instances that are required to ensure they are appropriate and stable.

b. Coordinating infrastructure availability according to test plans and organizational priorities.

c. Supporting the test infrastructure as a service to the organization, ensuring its availability, upgrade, and accessibility.

Of course, both models of software testing have advantages and disadvantages typical of any categorization that contrasts a specialized versus a centralized approach to operation. As a result, hybrid approaches between these two extremes are possible in which some aspects of the software testing process are shared while others may be on a per-project basis. Hence, we can distinguish between specialized software testing factories focused on a subset of testing needs, and the more general software testing factories.

Many organizations have adopted software testing factory approaches to overcome challenges due to the limited availability of specialized services for specific kinds of testing, analysis, or validation that more clearly benefit from a shared services approach. Typical examples of specialized software testing factories are those that focus on areas such as:

-   Performance and load testing (using pre-configured dedicated server farms)

-   Security testing (running a battery of security scans, and ensuring that they frequently update those scans to include checks for the latest reported operating system flaws and hacker trends)

-   Compliance testing (providing analysis and certification of compliance against government and industry standards)

An example of a specialized software testing factory is shown in Figure 2. This depicts the operational workflow for a specialized software testing factory for a global system integrator (SI). The SI has created several specialized software testing factories for different kinds of testing needs. One of these, illustrated in Figure 2, serves a large group of clients who are deploying enterprise solutions based on the SAP packaged applications. Such packaged applications are large, complicated enterprise systems, and they play a core function in an organization. These applications contain a large number of features, divided into a number of business areas. Typically such packaged applications are heavily customized and extended during deployment, and they must be carefully tested and validated before their release into production. However, deep, specialized skills are frequently needed to validate the correct operation of these packaged applications. Such skills are expensive and difficult to find. In this context, a specialized software testing factory approach becomes very attractive.

In this example of a specialized software testing factory, the client of the SI and the software testing factory agree to a set of work packets and acceptance criteria to initiate the complete testing process. The software testing factory executes a complete set of tests on the system and returns the results to the client for their review.

While many kinds of specialized software testing factories have emerged to meet different needs, the concept of a specialized software testing factory is still expanding. Hosting a com-

Figure 2. An example workflow for a specialized software testing factory

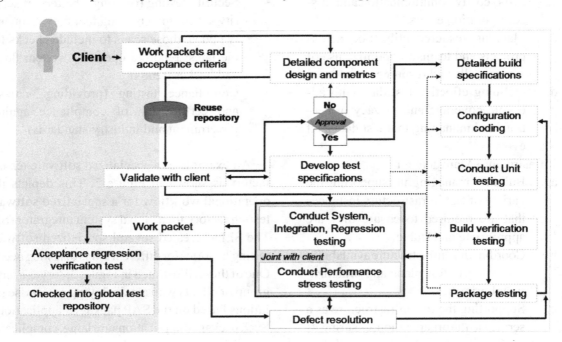

plete virtualized testing facility is now possible, driven by greater availability of high-bandwidth networks, cheap data storage, and fast servers. The result is the emergence of general software testing factories. These can perform wide varieties of software quality functions as services to client organizations. The advantages they offer to their clients is that they create specialized work centers where high levels of particular testing skills are matured, they maintain extensive databases of analytical data to improve the quality of their testing, and they invest in research to advance their testing practices to be more predictive, accurate, and efficient.

From an organizational and financial viewpoint, software testing factories are being created within organizations as a way to pool costs across a series of departments and lines of business. Additionally, a separate testing industry is also emerging in which SIs and third-party companies are creating independent software testing factory offerings that can be used by a variety of clients. Furthermore, costs can be further reduced by locating software testing factories in locations where there is greater access to skills and lower labor rates. Consequently, many organizations have made major investments in software quality improvements by deploying global software testing factories in locations such as India, China, and Latin America.

As illustrated in Figure 3, the use of independent software testing factories provides the opportunity to create different business models for the delivery of testing services. Initially, the role of software testing factories was viewed from a staff-augmentation approach based on reducing costs. Now that role is evolving and software testing factories are viewed as centers of excellence in important areas of software quality delivery. Ultimately, the evolution of the role of the software testing factory is toward a utility view of testing as a service that can be readily acquired on a pay-per-usage model or a results-based scheme.

Figure 3. Evolution of the software testing factory

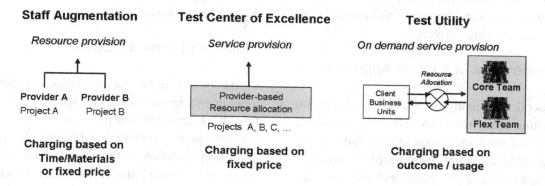

THE SOFTWARE FACTORY IN THE CLOUDS

The arrival of cloud computing is by far the most conspicuous trend in recent times, and it's likely to have the most wide-scale impact on enterprise software delivery in the coming years. Whether viewed as a natural extension of Internet-based computing or a completely new phenomenon, high-bandwidth global interconnectivity and cheap processors and storage have fueled moves to create large computing centers that can act as massive computing hubs to serve organizations that may be distributed around the globe. These centralized computing centers can be created by a single organization, shared between organizations, or be provided by third parties as a resource that can be acquired as necessary. All these give rise to the possibility that enterprise software delivery can be coordinated more effectively via shared service centers and can be supported more efficiently using a flexible set of hardware and software services that can expand and contract as the organization's needs evolve.

This move toward a centralized approach for greater flexibility and efficiency in enterprise software delivery is not new. Enterprise software delivery organizations have been on a multiyear journey toward greater efficiency and effectiveness. From the earliest days of computing, there have been moves to centralize computer resources,

share access to costly infrastructure, increase flexibility of access to common services, and improve responsiveness to peak demands for capabilities. In recent years, this journey has taken the enterprise software delivery organization from a focus on simplification toward greater sharing and virtualization of its delivery infrastructure. What is new in the recent trend around cloud computing is the technology infrastructure that now makes the next step possible, driven by a business environment that is forcing efficiencies across enterprise software delivery, by the expanding global nature of our organizations and their supply chains, and by a broader business reevaluation of the role of IT services in support of the organization's value to its stakeholders.

There are many primers on cloud computing (e.g., [Reese, 2009; Rhoton, 2009]), and there have been several insightful analyses published on cloud computing and its impact (e.g., [Mather, Kumaraswamy, & Latif, 2009; Bennioff, 2009]). Rather than replay those themes here, I'll provide a short contextual review of cloud computing and then focus on the most important implications of this trend for enterprise software delivery.

Understanding the Cloud

The broad notion of cloud computing is composed of many different elements, and several different perspectives are possible. We highlight three dimensions of cloud computing that help understand the breadth and impact of this approach on enterprise software delivery.

Characteristics of a Cloud Approach

In general, the main characteristics of a cloud computing approach is to deliver "convenient, on-demand network access to a shared pool of configurable computing resources (e.g., networks, servers, storage, applications, and services) that can be rapidly provisioned and released with minimal management effort or service provider interaction."[2] The value of this approach is that it offers a great deal of flexibility to consumers of those resources. In particular, capabilities can be rapidly and elastically provisioned to scale up when demands for those capabilities increase, and similarly, they can be rapidly released to scale down when demand reduces.

Supporting this elasticity of capabilities are two key enablers that are essential to make the approach practical. The first is to allow the consumers of the resources to be able to self-provision the capabilities they need and to obtain (near) immediate access via a set of provision automation services. The second is a monitoring and measurement approach that allows pay-per-use accounting for those resources being consumed. The richness of these two enablers helps to distinguish cloud computing from previous attempts to offer pooled virtualized services that typically were restricted to a very limited set of options and required expensive and time-consuming interventions from a service provisioning team for the majority of changes to the configuration.

In enterprise software delivery, the flexibility that is possible with cloud computing approaches is critical. Not only does this flexibility encourage the kinds of dynamic relationships that characterize supply chain approaches; it also provides much more explicit ways to look at infrastructure costs and assign those costs to the role of each organization and team, and it encourages global

delivery approaches more suited to today's highly diverse enterprises.

Cloud Deployment Models

Cloud computing services are made available to users in a variety of ways. Two significant variations have emerged that polarize two ends of a delivery spectrum: Private and Public clouds.

For organizations with many teams requiring access to common capabilities, it can be effective to create a private cloud computing solution that serves those teams and is managed by the enterprise software delivery organization. The technologies and processes necessary for creating a cloud solution are acquired and dedicated to that organization's needs. The main advantages of a private cloud computing approach are clear: teams are quickly given access to the cloud services, teams have elasticity of use of those services, and metering provides accurate accounting (and even allows cross-charging) of those services to their consumers. Private cloud computing services can be created by organizations when they require the flexibility offered by shared, virtualized capabilities but are not able (or are unwilling) to accept the implications of sharing those capabilities with other organizations.

In contrast, one of the most compelling directions for cloud computing is the emergence of public cloud capabilities. Several organizations provide cloud-based capabilities that are readily accessible over a public infrastructure such as the Internet. Multiple organizations share the use of that infrastructure (so-called multi-tenancy) and thereby reduce costs for both the cloud users and cloud supplier. The use of a third-party provider of resources over a public infrastructure can offer great cost savings to the consumer, increases the flexibility and availability of the services, and eliminates wasted investment in infrastructure acquisition, setup, and service administration.

However, public cloud solutions also have significant disadvantages for many organizations that require the security, privacy, and reassurance of a privately owned cloud-base solution. As a result, various hybrid models of cloud computing are also possible. For example, some organizations use private cloud capabilities for key aspects of their business, and they make use of public cloud services where there are less concerns about performance and data privacy. Similarly, many public cloud-computing providers are able to offer dedicated infrastructure capabilities to clients to ensure their availability and increase confidence about security and privacy of data.

Service Models for the Cloud

With respect to the capabilities being made available through cloud computing, there is a huge array of offerings and a wide variety of ways of packaging, delivering, and charging for those capabilities. I'll highlight three clear categories of capabilities being offered through cloud computing models.

The first involves infrastructure as a service (IaaS). A starting point for offering cloud-based services is to provide the organization with dependable, scalable, and expandable hardware (CPU, storage, networking). These capabilities may be offered directly as the service that the end users consume or be used as the foundation for building virtualization layers and higher-level services. For example, if a team requires an additional terabyte of disk space to manage the temporary data needed for a series of system tests, a cloud-based solution would be able to accommodate that request (whether implicitly or explicitly made) rather than having the team to look for an available machine or go through any complex acquisition approval process.

A number of services must support the IaaS, including supplying the abilities to pool highly available CPUs and storage (perhaps differentiated by particular kinds of hardware characteristics), meter the capacity and utilization of resources,

bill and chargeback for consumed services, audit and analyze for compliance to specific norms and standards, and so on. The IaaS services must guarantee particular functional and nonfunctional requirements will be met in areas such as performance, response time, availability, and so on. One example of this approach is IaaS applied to large-scale development and test teams across the IBM Tivoli organization. In IBM Tivoli, there are more than six thousand software practitioners in thirty-eight labs around the world responsible for a wide variety of software delivery tasks. A recent analysis revealed that they were using more than 30,000 servers, with typical utilization between 5–9 percent per server. By introducing a cloud-based IaaS solution, IBM Tivoli has been able to deliver to all practitioners a set of common desktop images housed in a central set of managed systems running IBM's own cloud software. Within two years of this switch, IBM was able to demonstrate vastly reduced services, provisioning times for new projects, and capital expense reductions of more than $10 million, and it accumulated operation expense savings of more than $11.5 million.

The second category, platform as a service (PaaS) delivers a more complete computing platform for developing and delivering applications. In particular, a PaaS offering will include operating-system and other middleware capabilities typically with the latest versions of the software, updates, and patches applied. For example, often when an organization wants to test a new application, it needs to acquire and configure each computer platform on which the application must be tested. This may mean several different platform variations with combinations of operating system, database, web server, and so on. In a PaaS approach, specific platform combinations are requested and provisioned using a cloud computing model. Typically, a limited set of PaaS solutions is available for use by default. In addition, users may be able to define specialized stacks of software that combine the available platform elements to provision a specific PaaS solution that meets their needs.

An important variation on the PaaS approach is that the platform may itself be a development and delivery platform for new cloud-based services. For example, the Amazon web services platform (AWS) is a PaaS offering that delivers a fully functional development and delivery capability for organizations wanting to deliver solutions that run on the Amazon IaaS offering called the Amazon elastic compute cloud (EC2) and that integrate with a set of solution components they have created to execute on that infrastructure. Similarly, Salesforce.com provides Force.com as the PaaS offering for creating new solutions that integrate with its Salesforce.com solution elements.

The PaaS approach is very appealing to two kinds of organizations. First, smaller organizations can take advantage of PaaS to access a wide set of platform variations without the capital investment necessary for each of them. Second, for larger organizations, the PaaS approach offers standardization to ensure that teams use the same technology base with appropriate versions of each component of the platform installed there.

An interesting illustration of the application of this approach is within a large financial institution that has almost five thousand people in its enterprise software delivery organization spread across local sites and three different systems integrators (SIs). These included substantial offshore teams located in India. The organization was struggling with the challenges of maintaining an effective software development and delivery workbench across the organization. Failings due to inconsistencies across development and test tools had been identified as major factors in several high-profile software delivery delays. As a result, the organization created a standard corporate-wide development and delivery workbench as a PaaS offering that it mandated across the global enterprise software delivery organization. Due to its

cloud-based foundation, this provided a consistent solution with easy management and configuration essential for the business to match its diverse organizational structure.

The third category is SaaS. Most organizations interested in the cloud computing model are not software development companies. Rather, they use the enterprise software as a means to support and differentiate their businesses. They are looking to have business or domain-specific capabilities offered as a service whereby they simply make use of that service when and as they need it and in the quantity they need at the time. This has resulted in a very large set of offerings now available in a SaaS model.

Again, both public and private cloud approaches are possible. In the public cloud category there are now some very well-established examples of SaaS. One example is Gmail, Google's e-mail service that provides a SaaS e-mail capability that is widely used by individuals and increasingly deployed in businesses. Another well-known example is the cloud-based sales management service from Salesforce.com. Both of these examples exhibit the key characteristics of today's SaaS offerings: Internet-based access to a core organizational capability that is provided on a pay-per-use model with a great deal of elasticity in the underlying technology. This kind of simplification of service provisioning is very appealing to organizations that see no value in the investment and administration required to maintain close control of that capability in house.

Many examples of SaaS offerings for software development and deployment are already commercially available. For example, at least one software vendor[3] offers several cloud-based software delivery workbenches aimed at different sizes of teams and different blends of software delivery roles. These offerings are available in a variety of pay-per-use schemes according to different operational needs.

Summary

There is a high level of excitement about cloud computing and the promises that it brings to enterprises to reduce cost and increase flexibility of service delivery. Many organizations are already involved in pilots, or are actively using cloud technologies and cloud-based services. Over the coming years the massive excitement will be tempered with the reality that in some respects cloud is "just another deployment platform." Hence, the use of this platform will require a wealth of supporting capabilities to both create enterprise solutions *for* the cloud, and to take advantage of solutions and services *on* the cloud.

Initially, we have seen many traditional enterprise software solutions ported to the cloud platform, and included in platform images that can be uploaded to a cloud infrastructure. This is an important starting point for enterprise system use on the cloud. However, it is very limited in terms of many of the important usage scenarios for cloud technology. There is less understanding of which new enterprise software capabilities, services, and approaches will be needed in much more complex scenarios. For example, we already are seeing interesting scenarios that are raising new challenges for enterprise software delivery organizations:

- Several teams are deploying business application onto a public cloud infrastructure for access by clients around the world. How do those teams collaborate to share information to ensure that they do place sensitive data on the public infrastructure? What coordination is given to the teams to ensure the management of shared images is handled effectively?
- Multiple System Integrators and specialist vendors must deliver different parts of key enterprise solutions as part of a software supply chain that must be integration to be delivered into production. How can the cloud be used as the delivery platform to coordinate and govern delivery and integration of these components?

These, and many more such scenarios, are stretching conventional processes, skills and technologies for enterprise software delivery. Software delivery organizations are actively working on new deployment approaches that provide the additional governance, visibility, and control that is demanded in such situations.

SOFTWARE TESTING FACTORIES AND THE CLOUD

The general capabilities of cloud computing – elasticity of resources, instant access to services, and flexible accounting for resource use – have opened up a wide variety of potential uses in many domains. Perhaps the most prominent examples of cloud computing in use today involve archiving of data in the cloud (e.g., photo archives, email backups, etc.) and hosting common personal and business functions in the cloud (e.g., email management, contact and sales management, etc.). However, supporting software development and testing activities is also being seen as a highly appropriate application area for cloud technologies.

In considering the application of cloud computing to software development and test activities, we can identify several ways in which the characteristics cloud computing can be of most value.

As illustrated in Figure 4, there are several uses of cloud technologies for software development and test. The first is that applications may be developed and tested to operate within a cloud infrastructure. We can refer to this as software development and test *for* the cloud. For example, a company wants to develop a new sales management application that will be deployed on a public cloud infrastructure such as Amazon EC2 to make it available to its sales people across the organization. In such cases it is likely that new

Figure 4. An overview of software develop/test scenarios in the cloud

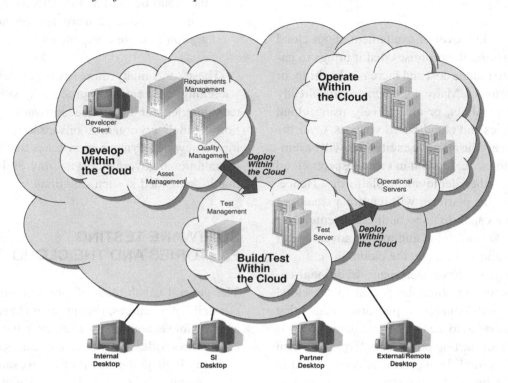

testing approaches may be needed to ensure the application operates effectively in such an environment, test coverage procedures may have to be adjusted, and effective ways to test the application with respect to the characteristics of the selected public cloud infrastructure need to be determined (e.g., with respect to security and availability).

The second use of cloud technologies is when the software development and test teams deploy their own tools and assets on a cloud infrastructure. We can refer to this as software development and test *on* the cloud. In this case, for example, a software tester may access their testing tools, scripts and test data by connecting to a cloud-based environment that their company has set up, or by using publically-offered cloud-hosted testing services.

The third use of cloud technologies is when the software development and test teams require specific capabilities or services that can be more effectively supplied using cloud technologies. We can refer to this as software development and test *leveraging* the cloud. Here, for example, a software test team would like to run a series of performance stress tests on a complex application to simulate simultaneous operation of the application by a large number of users. In that case, it may be much more effective to provision a large number of machines using the elasticity of a cloud infrastructure provided by a 3rd party cloud technology supplier rather than the team having to acquire, configure, and manage a large amount of software testing infrastructure for themselves.

In summary, we note that there is a clear distinction that can be drawn between cloud capabilities applied to three distinct areas: Software development and testing *on, for*, and *leveraging* the cloud.

Focusing on the software testing aspects, we now consider each of these in more detail.

Software Development and Testing on the Cloud

Managing and governing the supporting tools and assets presents one of the key challenges for any software development and test organization. Typically a significant set of resources (people and technology) is dedicates to this task. In particular, such teams face difficulties such as:

- The high cost of coordination and collaboration across teams that are organizationally dispersed (e.g., across projects, programs, and divisions) and geographically dispersed (e.g., based in offshore and nearshore delivery centers).
- The complexity of managing a variety of software development and test tools for different software delivery environments, often requiring support for multiple versions of tools from many software vendors, coordinating the maintenance and support of those tools, ensuring integration across those tools, and ensuring the currency of appropriate patches, fixes and upgrades.
- The high cost of acquiring new software development and testing infrastructure at the start of new projects. This is exacerbated in short projects with tight deadlines.
- The wide variety of infrastructure needs across the software development and test teams increases the pressure on costs and can make predictable resource planning impossible. For example, while most projects follow a well defined lifecycle and require standard testing environments, emergency situations often arise in which urgent performance, load, and security testing may be needed on core business applications.

As a result of these needs, use of cloud technologies is particularly attractive to software development and test teams to operate their day-to-day environment. In line with other uses of cloud technologies, software development and test teams can take advantage of a cloud infrastructure to improve access to the tooling, reduce costs for acquisition and maintenance of hardware and software, and increase standardization of tools and processes in use. Specifically focusing on software test activities, experiences from companies taking a cloud based approach to deliver a software testing factory have identified a number of distinct differences and corresponding benefits to testing on the cloud. In particular, the key benefits have been found to be:

- **Flexibility:** Easier provisioning of standard testing environments has encouraged "catalogs" of test environment to be created. This allows different levels or grades of tests to be available in separate environments that can be executed based on the organization's assessment of risk, cost, and value. Furthermore, testing issues are being addressed much earlier in the project lifecycle as testers no longer need to wait until the end of the testing phase to move to a "production-like" environment for planning performance, load and stress tests. Instead a production-like environment is available early in the project as it can be reused from the existing catalog, or can be designed and configured in the early stages of the project and used for continuous validation as the project evolves toward delivery.
- **Simplicity:** More explicit and accurate test environment configurations for cloud deployment are simplifying the test management process. Organizations are experiencing a reduction in test environment configuration errors, and a greater confidence that applications are being tested in

appropriate contexts. Additionally, using cloud infrastructure offers increased simplicity in terms of ensuring the testing tools and practices are up-to-date with vendor upgrades and fixes.

- **Cost Reduction:** Utilization of test equipment is typically very uneven – often long periods of low utility, with short bursts of intense activity. Historically, internal testing environments have been set up on a project-by-project basis and are deployed throughout the life of the project regardless of their use. Cloud environments have had a major impact in cost reduction as they are more easily enabled and disabled as needed, elasticity of resources allow the testing environment to be sized for the needs, and charges for cloud infrastructure can be more closely aligned to usage patterns.

- **Greener Testing:** A major issue in many data centers is to improve the use of resources by reducing the power consumption, physical footprint, and CO_2 emissions. This not only saves cost to the company, but also has positive impact in the physical environment by eliminating waste. By sharing cloud resources for their test infrastructure, companies have been able to demonstrate improvements in all of these areas. A number of studies make broad claims about the financial impact of cloud computing in helping companies to achieve their environmental goals.[4]

- **Transparency and Traceability:** A specific issue for many software testing teams is how to organize, share, align, and compare test data and test results. In many companies they have found that use of cloud technology for software testing has led to associated improvements in the visibility, transparency, and traceability of test assets across projects. For example, cloud-hosted shared repositories of test results have al-

lowed direct comparison of project results, and for application of various analytics and trending techniques across the data.

- **Test Environment Standardization:** Many companies see the adoption of cloud technology as one step in the goal of increased standardization and reuse across many important business activities. In particular, for software testing organizations, the switch to cloud technologies has frequently been a catalyst for improvements in test processes, and is a component of a change in how the larger IT organization operates to improve efficiency and accountability to the business it serves.

Software Development and Testing for the Cloud

Particularly important for software testing is to ensure that the applications under test will perform effectively and predictably in the final operating environment. In moving to running applications on cloud technologies, software testing teams face three specific issues:

- Poor understanding and management of the cloud infrastructure as a deployment environment. While deploying an application to a cloud infrastructure is "just another environment" that needs to be tested. There are some specific issues that must be addressed in this case. Notably, the openness, flexibility, and elasticity of cloud infrastructures complicate testing application to be deployed there. Additional testing techniques and test cases will be required.

- Inconsistent and manual hand-off from software development and testing teams to the operations teams. Poor communication and collaboration means that development and testing teams do not have a complete understanding of the target operating environment, and the operating teams do not receive clear guidance on what has been tested, and what known faults remain. Such misunderstandings can have profound implications when applications are deployed instantly for immediate worldwide access in a cloud infrastructure. Increased attention to this communication gap is essential.

- Design and development of application components that do not match the cloud infrastructure characteristics. Most applications require early knowledge of key characteristics of the target operating environment as a critical input into requirements and design activities. For example, many non-functional requirements of an application can only be met if the specific operating environment is explicitly defined and controlled. However, in many companies the cloud infrastructure on which applications will be deployed are defined and operated by 3rd party organizations (either via a public cloud, or a privately managed cloud). This increases the complexity of all aspects of software development and delivery, including all test activities.

As a result, in software testing factories that make use of a cloud infrastructure we see specific attention paid to deployment planning and automation capabilities. The goal is to ensure that the right deliverables are deployed on the cloud infrastructure, with the right deployment plan, using automation capabilities wherever possible to increase the communication across the different teams.

Several interesting approaches toward improving cloud deployment are in use as part of the more general increase in activity to better align development and operation (the so-called

Figure 5. An example deployment model for a cloud infrastructure

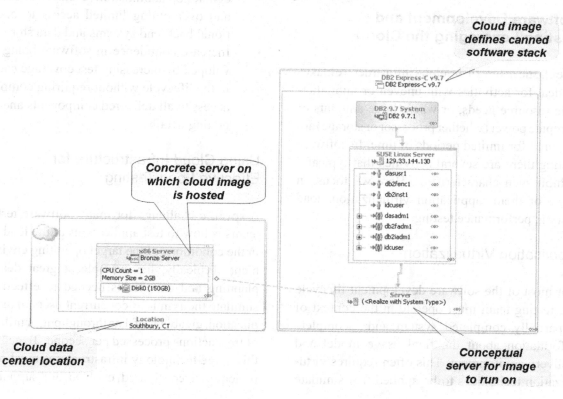

"devops" challenge[5]). As illustrated in Figure 5, one approach being investigated in IBM involves how the deployment environment can be explicitly defined as part of the component modeling phase of a software project.[6]

Using such approaches to deployment modeling for cloud infrastructure allows the software development and test team to gain control over:

- **Deployment Workflow:** To manage sharing of deployed components across the development/test and operations teams.
- **Policies:** To enforce deployment rules to the cloud infrastructure.
- **Access Permissions:** To restrict who can deploy applications to the cloud infrastructure.
- **Traceability and Auditing:** For plans and automations to assist testing teams in auditing their practices, and for diagnosis of errors when fixing applications deployed to the cloud infrastructure.

Software Development and Testing Leveraging the Cloud

The elastic nature of the cloud infrastructure makes it ideal for activities with uneven or unpredictable resource needs, or where large amounts of compute power (whether processor or storage) are required for limited periods of time. In software testing there are several activities that typically exhibit such characteristics. Here we focus on three of them: application virtualization, load testing, performance testing.

Application Virtualization

For most of the software development lifecycle the testing team must operate in the context of a partially completed system and incomplete information about the final usage model and delivery environment. This often requires virtualization techniques to be applied that simulate

the complete application or the planned operating context for that application. In essence, application virtualization allows simulation of the behavior of a component (hardware or software). It may require handling of missing capabilities and features, or emulation of undefined or inaccessible operating capabilities. A crucial role of application virtualization is to deliver realistic simulated development and test environments to allow test teams to complete tasks earlier in the software development lifecycle, and with more completeness and depth.

Many companies have moved toward the use of a cloud infrastructure to support application virtualization Services. This enables software test teams to:

- Rapidly create multiple virtual test environments customized for each specific operating environment.
- Obtain instant, 24/7 availability to testing environments as needed without dependencies on administrative staff availability, and overcoming limited access to operational back-end systems and data stores.
- Increase confidence in software being developed by increasing test coverage earlier in the lifecycle without requiring complete access to all delivered components and operating details.

Using Cloud Infrastructure for Effective Load Testing

A specific challenge for many software testing teams is how to test applications at the load and in the conditions of the target operating environment. Typically, for example, a great deal of planning and expense is needed to effectively simulate thousands of concurrent users of an application, gigabytes of data throughput, or millions of transactions processed per second. To achieve this, large technology infrastructures must often be acquired, configured, evolved, and supported.

Use of a cloud infrastructure to support effective load testing is highly attractive to many organizations. In a cloud-based approach, test agents running in a cloud infrastructure can simulate large loads against specific test profiles to exercise an application running in a native or simulated operating environment. Hence, to affordably implement large scale load testing, use of a cloud infrastructure allows test teams to:

- Build a schedule of load tests to be applied to the application under test with broad coverage for different loads and different behavior profiles.
- Automatically provision virtual agents during the test either on existing infrastructure or the cloud infrastructure (or a combination).
- Account for load testing activities using pay-per-use mechanisms for infrastructure and load generation agents to reduce up-front costs, eliminate on-going wasted resource maintenance, and increase project cost predictability.

Cloud-Based Performance Testing

Performance testing on critical applications provides insights into performance related bottlenecks when the application is deployed in typical usage contexts. The primary objective is to accurately simulate situations that will stress the application at its extreme performance limits, instrument the application to receive accurate data on its execution, and analyze how performance bottlenecks can be overcome.

Hosting performance tests in a cloud infrastructure brings together automation and performance testing tools to significantly reduce the time required to complete such tasks. Figure 6 illustrates a cloud-based performance testing scenario using IBM Rational technologies.

Figure 6. Performance testing using the IBM cloud technologies

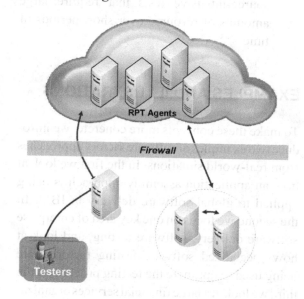

In the scenario illustrated in Figure 6, a testing team uses local hardware to host the Rational Performance Test (RPT) tool. This has the ability to spawn and control an arbitrary number of RPT agents to a cloud infrastructure (such as the IBM Smart Cloud). Each of these agents can then drive load to an application under test, receive the results, and return them to the controlling RPT instance for local analysis.

In summary, cloud–based performance testing provides dynamic, robust, large-scale performance testing services to enterprises when teams need to:

- Minimize infrastructure set-up time to run performance tests.
- Provision all necessary infrastructure components to execute the performance tests in a controlled, standardized fashion.
- Gain access to shared bodies of knowledge on instrumentation and performance metrics of importance in key application categories, and to obtain the latest advice on techniques to improve application performance based on the returned results.

- Deliver a cost effective solution to resource-intensive tests that require large amounts of resource over short periods of time.

EXAMPLES AND ILLUSTRATIONS

To make these concepts more concrete, we introduce two examples of software factory approaches from real-world situations. In the first we look at how an application assembly approach is being applied to global software delivery in IBM. In the second we focus on one key area of enterprise software delivery, software testing, and look at how specialized software testing factories are being used to optimize the testing process. In the third we look at a large financial services organization that is delivering a major insurance solution platform for deployment in locations around the world using a software factory approach to delivery and maintenance.

Example: IBM Application Assembly Optimization (AAO) Approach

Application assembly optimization (AAO) is a recently initiated delivery approach and a key component of IBM's globally integrated capabilities strategy (IBM, 2009). The approach was launched to introduce an industrialized approach to enterprise software delivery by aligning responsibilities, strategies, and priorities across a number of worldwide "competency centers." With these centers, supported by a centralized governance model, IBM can quickly assemble critical expertise for substantial opportunities across key industries to bring the right skills to each situation, as needed without unnecessary duplication or delays. This more integrated, repeatable approach is aimed at increasing operational efficiencies through global deployment of application assembly techniques across IBM global business services teams.

In terms of a software factory approach to enterprise software delivery, AAO enables the following process transformations:

- **Delivery:** From a skills- and time-based model to a reusable assets- and automation-based model.
- **Cost:** From an hourly rate-based model to an outcome-based model.
- **Metrics:** From utilization measures to performance-based value measures.
- **Control:** From direct line of management to a more centralized pool of shared resources.
- **Workflow:** From location-based global delivery centers to a virtual workflow distributed among centers and geographic locations.

Fundamental to the AAO approach is a collaborative environment with strong global management disciplines, automation techniques, and innovative approaches to measurements and incentives. To realize this, the AAO solution has four basic components:

- **Centers of Competency:** These are concentrations of skills around specific industry or domain needs that form a network of expertise and asset libraries to be rapidly aligned and used as needed in specific client situations.
- **Technology Assembly Centers (TACs):** TACs apply factory-floor concepts and automated processes to enterprise solution delivery at IBM global delivery centers. The TACs are specialized service areas (e.g., testing, web-based architectures) that form a virtual global team of highly skilled practitioners to deliver work products in their areas of expertise.
- **Collaboration and Measurement:** Using real-time, in-context team collaboration, distributed teams can think and work in

unison. AAO uses tools with deep collaboration functions and supports them with social networking sites, wikis, blogs, and mobile offerings specifically targeted at business interests of the practitioners. The measurement framework for AAO is a dynamic system with automation, extensibility, and flexibility. The framework supports multiple dimensions of measurements that include customer value, strategy, operations, risk, quality, and governance.

- **Lean Processes:** Each AAO process is developed using a lean approach and is regularly reviewed to provide continuous operational improvement by addressing any bottlenecks and waste proactively.

The operating model of the AAO approach uses "work packets" as the key mechanism to deliver enterprise software. A work packet is a prescriptive, self-contained unit of work that can include instructions, assets to be reused, schedules, exit criteria, and any input work products needed. The receiver of the packet designs, plans, and executes the work requested. Application optimization is the umbrella term for the processes, procedures, tools, metrics, and governance management, and multisite locations where work is performed.

As illustrated in Figure 7, to deliver on these work packets, virtual teams are created and organized into "cells." These cells allow flexible configurations of people and resources to come together with a collection of deep expertise in the service or solution being delivered, armed with appropriate tools and reusable assets and frameworks to accelerate delivery and maintain high quality in delivery. Governance, measurement, and control of software delivery are optimized around this flexible organizational model to allow each delivery to be composed of the appropriate cells, as required to complete a specific work packet.

In summary, we see that the AAO approach can be viewed as the software and services equivalent of a traditional manufacturing approach, applied to enterprise software delivery in an organization consisting of thousands of people delivering software-based solutions to its clients. Work packets form the heart of an assembly-line

Figure 7. Organization of delivery centers in the IBM application assembly optimization (AAO) approach

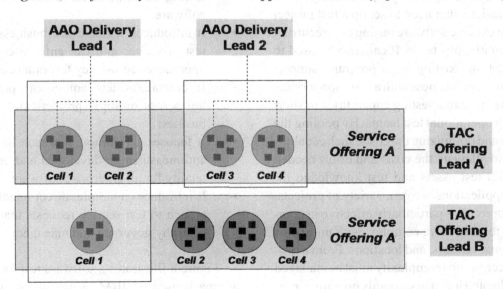

approach with real-time measurement across work packet progress and delivery. The underlying supporting tool platform provides information on in-progress and completed work, gives the status of resource utilization, and helps identify bottlenecks in software delivery. In this way, real-time optimization of key delivery processes is possible.

Example: IBM Test Factory Approach

A key objective for many organizations is to maintain high levels of quality while reducing costs in enterprise software delivery. Most testing solutions available today have focused on the test execution and test management functions in areas such as functional and performance testing, automatic regression testing, and test defect management. Currently, market pressures are driving significant improvements in enterprise software quality and cost reduction by forcing a consolidation of many expensive testing capabilities into specialist centers of excellence, where skills, tools, and practices can be centralized as common services across an organization. In several organizations, these testing-focused centers are referred to as software testing factories.

A software testing factory is particularly suited to organizations that need to set up a test project quickly or execute software testing on a recurring but non-continuous basis. It can also be used to supplement an existing large program, support multiple lines of business with a common service, or provide specialist testing capabilities in short demand in operational test teams. By pooling the resources and optimizing the costs, such capabilities help to alleviate the costs and effort needed to maintain test assets and test knowledge for existing applications across a variety of projects.

The approach is particularly effective in organizations that are more complex, with numerous departments, vendors, and locations. From a testing perspective, this complexity must be managed and coordinated into one smoothly operating, reliable test management system with automation of

key practices and a clear measurement framework to govern its activities. A software testing factory provides a basis for effective standardization and communication across the testing organizations and business units to, ultimately, the end users and clients.

System integrators (SI) such as IBM Global Business Services, Sogeti, Atos Origin, and Accenture have all created specific practices based on the software testing factory model. They are coordinated around a common governance structure, methodology, and set of tools and processes, and they use a factory approach toward execution and delivery of results to maintain efficiency in the face of highly fluctuating consumer demand for their services. As a result, the SI acts as the focal point for all change management into the test cycle and takes responsibility for best practices in test management and test execution areas such as test planning, cost estimation, and various forms of code analysis.

In summary, a software testing factory approach is considered useful in many organizations for the following reasons:

- It provides cost-efficient and effective testing on-demand for different kinds of software.
- It introduces standardized business-driven test processes and can enforce consistent approaches across key test practices.
- It centralizes test equipment provisioning across multiple projects and lines of business.
- It focuses a common approach to metrics and measures on developed and delivered quality for all enterprise software.
- It introduces a simple, direct handling approach to test service requests that can be centrally governed and managed.

Figure 8 illustrates a software testing factory approach used by IBM in one of its European regions. IBM's testing solution provides managed

Figure 8. An example software testing factory

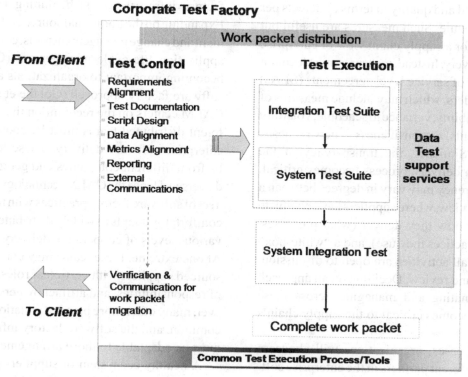

testing services via a software testing factory in a two-tier model using teams in Europe and Asia. It provides an accelerated and phased method for transforming current methods, processes, and tools into an industrialized approach. The solution aims to achieve the following kinds of target results with clients:

- On-demand resource model (typically up to 40 percent core team, 60 percent flexible resources).
- Optimized onshore–offshore resource profile, with often 90 percent of work performed off-shore.
- Productivity improvements resulting from high levels of test automation (50 percent to 70 percent).
- Unit-based pricing using a test-case-based approach or focused on testing as a service for its clients.

- Transparency of factory performance metrics through shared dashboards containing as many as twenty service level measures that are continuously assessed by the test provider and the client.

OBSERVATIONS AND COMMENTARY

The move toward software testing factories is seen as fundamental to cost control and efficiency in enterprise software delivery. Software factory situations such as those described here provide important insights for an industrialized view of enterprise software delivery, from which several observations can be made.

A different set of ideas is needed for monitoring progress and effective status management in software factory approaches. Most traditional metrics highlight two kinds of measures: productivity in terms of function points or source lines of code delivered and quality in terms of defects per delivered module. Such measures are useful but insufficient for a supply chain view of enterprise software delivery. Instead, measures must focus on a broader set of service level agreements (SLAs) across providers, which may include measures of cost, predictability, variance to schedule, volatility in requirements, responsiveness to new requests, and so on. Similarly, the transparency of the supply chain delivery process becomes critical. This transparency may vary in degrees between a "black-box" view, where suppliers have complete control over how they deliver (what processes, tools, and practices they use), and a "white-box" view where all activities are open to discussion, inspection, and review. Deciding on an approach (and coordinating and managing across these activities) becomes critical to the supply chain's operation.

In many cases, organizations will choose a variety of different partners in the enterprise software delivery process. Organizations will not only choose different suppliers for different specialist tasks, they'll also implement multisourcing in some areas to reduce risk, increase flexibility, and enhance competition. While such schemes can provide value, they also significantly increase the management costs across such complex supply chains.

An extreme version of multisourcing is the use of crowd sourcing for component delivery. Some organizations are already experimenting with delivery approaches in which new demands are essentially "put up for auction," with the goal of finding the cheapest supplier that can meet the stated needs. This is an extension of the typical request for proposals (RFP) approach in which a more open marketplace is used to increase the flexibility of component suppliers to a much wider constituency. Of course, organizations must address many challenges with such an approach, particularly those around security, intellectual property, and quality.

A more standardized approach to the software factory infrastructure is beginning to emerge. Expanding on the traditional source code management and change management tools, collaborative application life-cycle management (CALM) is becoming important to organizations adopting a software factory approach (Goethe et al., 2008). CALM centers on the recognition that many different distributed teams must be coordinated in enterprise software delivery. These teams may be from different companies and geographically dispersed. Hence the CALM technology reinforces a set of software factory practices with tooling that comfortably adapts to widely distributed teams in various levels of cooperative delivery scenarios. At one extreme, these teams may consist of out-sourced suppliers with very clear roles, handover of responsibilities, and artifact ownership. However, many other more blended situations are also common, and the software factory infrastructure must be adaptable to those arrangements.

A healthy ecosystem of suppliers of components in a supply chain proves critical. Supplier organizations in a software factory must be able to optimize the delivery of components, often for many potential consumers. One of the most interesting approaches we see today involves model-driven architectures (MDA) and PLE techniques (Frankel et al., 2004).

In these approaches, abstract models of system characteristics are used to generate components and subassemblies. Organizations can analyze and customize these models for different usage contexts more easily than they can with system-specific delivered code. With these approaches, specialist suppliers of components and component tooling have emerged. For example, some financial services organizations choose to start with a third-party core-banking framework and adapt it to their operating context by modifying its data and process models, rather than develop it from scratch themselves.

Virtualized technology platforms are particularly attractive for organizations adopting a software factory approach. Analogous to other industries, a widely distributed, flexible supply chain requires an automation framework well matched to those characteristics. A natural extension of CALM technology is to look to supply those automation capabilities "on-demand" using cloud technologies (Reese, 2009). Cloud-hosted services have advantages for the organization delivering the enterprise software (in terms of flexibility of infrastructure across the peaks and troughs of the life cycle, opening up the supply chain as widely as possible) and for the suppliers (in terms of permitting easy access to their services without expensive infrastructure investment).

The move to cloud-hosted services has encouraged a growing number of software-as-a-service offerings as a way to deliver software factory capabilities (Geothe et al., 2008). For example, in software testing, many SIs and third-party companies have announced "testing on the cloud" approaches that enable enterprise software delivery organizations to obtain testing activities such as performance testing as a service. Rather than invest in significant infrastructure, organizations can provision load testing of an enterprise software system using cloud infrastructure as needed, and a variety of load tests can be configured and run on demand.

SUMMARY

Enterprise software delivery organizations are facing the challenges of developing more software more quickly with higher quality. Looking to the experiences in other industrial domains, we can learn from their engineering and manufacturing approaches to apply key concepts to the software supply chain.

The software factory vision focuses on approaches specifically aimed to improve software delivery capability, helping teams to understand how they scale lean practices, deliver more for

less, correlate business outcomes with investments in processes and tools, and produce higher quality in faster delivery times.

As applied to software testing services, we have found that using the characteristics of cloud technologies – elasticity, instant access, and pay-per-use accounting – delivers significant benefits when realizing this approach. The result is a structured approach to helping enterprise software delivery teams drive business innovation through measured and continuous process improvement by delivering a dynamic factory approach to software and systems delivery.

ACKNOWLEDGMENT

This chapter includes several sections adapted with permission from the recently-published book, *Brown, Alan W., Enterprise Software Delivery: Bringing Agility and Efficiency to the Global Software Supply Chain, 1st, ©2012*. Printed and Electronically reproduced by permission of Pearson Education, Inc., Upper Saddle River, New Jersey.

REFERENCES

Bennioff, M. (2009). *Behind the cloud: The untold story of how Salesforce.com went from idea to billion-dollar company and revolutionized an industry*. Jossey-Bass.

Bieberstein, N., et al. (2005). *Service-oriented architecture (SOA) compass: Business value, planning, and enterprise roadmap*. IBM Press, 2005.

Boehm, B. (1988, May). A spiral model of software development and enhancement. *Computer*, *21*(5). doi:10.1109/2.59

Brown, A. W. (2005). *Large-scale component-based development*. Prentice-Hall.

Clements, P., & Northrop, L. (2001). *Software product lines: Patterns and practices* (3rd ed.). Addison Wesley.

CMU. (2010, November). *CMMi for development,* Version 1.3. (CMU/SEI-2010-TR-033, November 2010).

Frankel, D. S. (Eds.). (2004). *The MDA journal: Model driven architecture straight from the masters.* Meghan Kiffer Press.

Fredendall, L., & Hill, E. (2000). *Basics of supply chain management.* CRC Press. doi:10.1201/9781420025767

Geunes, J., & Pardalos, P. (2010). *Supply chain optimization.* Springer Verlag.

Goethe, M. (2008). *Collaborative application lifecycle management with IBM rational products.* IBM Redbook.

Greenfield, J. (2004). *Software factories: Assembling applications with patterns, models, frameworks, and tools.* Wiley Press.

Harmon, P. (2007). *Business process change,* 2nd ed. OMG Press, Morgan Kaufman.

Hotle, H., & Landry, S. (2009). *Application delivery and support organizational archetypes: The software factory.* (Gartner Research Report G00167531, May 2009).

Humphrey, W. (1991). Software process improvement at Hughes Aircraft. *IEEE Software, 8*(4). doi:10.1109/52.300031

Hunter, R., & Thayer, R. (Eds.). (2001). *Software process improvement.* Wiley-IEEE Computer Society Press.

IBM. (2009, August). *Application assembly optimization: A new approach to global delivery.* IBM White paper.

IBM. (2009, September). *Give your software factory a health check: Best practices for executing with reduced risk and cost for real results.* IBM White paper.

Krutchen, P. (2002). *Rational unified process.* Addison Wesley, 2002.

Mather, T., Kumaraswamy, S., & Latif, S. (2009). *Cloud security and privacy: An enterprise perspective on risks and compliance (theory in practice).* O'Reilly.

Naur, P., & Randell, B. (Eds.). *Software engineering: Report of a conference sponsored by the NATO Science Committee.* Garmisch, Germany, 7-11 Oct. 1968. Retrieved from http://homepages.cs.ncl.ac.uk/brian.randell/NATO/nato1968.PDF

Randell, B., & Buxton, J. N. (Eds.). (1969). *Software engineering techniques: Report of a conference sponsored by the NATO Science Committee.* Rome, Italy, 27-31 Oct. 1969. Retrieved from http://homepages.cs.ncl.ac.uk/brian.randell/NATO/nato1969.PDF

Reese, G. (2009). *Cloud application architectures: Building applications and infrastructures in the cloud.* O'Reilly Press.

Rhoton, J. (2009). *Cloud computing explained: Implementation handbook for enterprises.* Recursive Press. [1]

ENDNOTES

[1]   It is remarkable how, 40 years later, the reports from those workshops remain a touchstone for the move from software delivery as a "craft" to an "engineering" approach. Their coining of the term "software engineering" was explicitly aimed as a provocation and as a vision for the future – and so it remains.

2   The US National Institute of Standards and Technology (NIST) definition of cloud computing http://csrc.nist.gov/groups/SNS/cloud-computing/cloud-def-v15.doc.

3   For an interesting commercial example, see www.oncloudone.net.

4   See, for example, the *Cloud Computing - the IT Solution for the 21st Century* study, carried out by Verdantix for the "Carbon Disclosure Project," (www.cdproject.net).

5   For further discussion on devops issues see http://devops.com/ and http://www.dzone.com/mz/devops.

6   For more on the IBM approach to devops, see http://www.ibm.com/software/rational/devops/.

Chapter 2
Cloud Environment Controls Assessment Framework

Bharat Shah
Lockheed Martin Corporation, USA

ABSTRACT

Recent years have seen the rapid growth of on-demand, flexible, low-cost cloud-based information technology services. Government and business organizations around the world have started transforming their traditional in-house data center environments to cloud-based outsourced data centers. This transformation is opening doors to new risks given that the cloud computing delivery models, related services, and technologies are still maturing and evolving. Before deployment, organizations must implement cloud environment assessment methodologies to comply with the applicable standards and regulations. They must evaluate the environment's quality attributes of Internet connectivity, user access control, privacy and confidentiality, asset protection, multiple platforms locality, availability, reliability, performance, and scalability. The purpose of this chapter is to assist organizations that are considering providing and consuming cloud-based services in developing an assessment plan specific to organizational policies, strategies and their business and applicable legal and regulatory requirements; and assessing the cloud environment controls for infrastructure, platform, and software services.

INTRODUCTION

The new wave of innovation has grown in Internet-based cloud computing in recent years. The usages of infrastructure, platforms, and software applications at large data centers through a pay-per-use leasing model have increased. Because of its ease and speed of deployment, geographic distribution capability, and financial advantages, cloud computing has emerged as one of the fastest-growing segments of the Information Technology (IT) industry. Organizations throughout the world are considering providing or consuming cloud-based application delivery models for their business growth Robinson, 2009). According to Gartner (Petty, 2010), the worldwide cloud services revenue has increased by 21.3 percent from $46.4 billion in 2008 to $58.6 billion in 2009, and

DOI: 10.4018/978-1-4666-2536-5.ch002

the market is expected to reach $148.8 billion in 2014. Cloud application services evolving from Software-as-a-Service (SaaS) offerings are poised to jump from $13.1 billion in 2008 to $40.5 billion by 2014 as business models mature.

The interconnectivity between cloud services makes seamless exchange of information and availability of user services any time at any place possible. This often presents unique challenges and new risks because of a lack of basic security mechanisms, especially when interconnected via a heterogeneous environment. Experience has shown that as new technologies are developed, they become a major source of new vulnerabilities and increased exposure to potential attackers. With easy-to-use and low-cost hacking tools downloadable from the Internet, attackers are capable of launching organized, disciplined, and sophisticated attacks on the cloud computing environments. The successful attacks can result in severe or catastrophic damage to the organization and nation's critical information infrastructure and ultimately threaten the nation's economy and security. In short, all information created, modified, transmitted, or received via cloud service communications must adhere to the required security goals of confidentiality, integrity, availability, sensitivity, and criticality. Organizations require a methodical approach to safeguard the cloud computing environment. Without proper safeguards, a cloud computing environment is vulnerable enabling the individuals and groups with malicious intentions to intrude and use their access to obtain and manipulate sensitive information, commit fraud, disrupt operations, or launch attacks. The objectives of this chapter are to:

- Provide an understanding of the cloud environment related services and delivery models.
- Outline benefits and challenges for deploying cloud-based service models.
- Provide the framework for assessment of cloud environment controls.

BACKGROUND

The advent of World Wide Web in the 1990s has contributed to an exponential growth in Internet-based tools and technologies. In recent years, the availability of open-source and low-cost hardware and software, and the telecommunications infrastructure has given recognition to cloud computing. The cloud concept is not new. In 1961, John McCarthy, an American computer scientist from Massachusetts Institute of Technology (Wordpress.com, 2008) had proposed a time-sharing computing model that organizations can use to sell and centrally manage computing power, hardware, software and applications like a utility (water and electricity) business models. A half a century later, cloud computing is emerging as utility-based computing that relies on Internet-based computing resources to provide services to all sizes of organizations, their business partners, and customers, while freeing them from the burden and costs of maintaining the underlying infrastructure.

Definitions

There is no one definition for cloud computing in circulation. The United States National Institute of Science and Technology (NIST) defines cloud computing as "A model for enabling ubiquitous, convenient, on-demand network access to a shared pool of configurable computing resources that can be rapidly provisioned and released with minimal management effort or service provider interaction" (Mell, 2011).

Gartner (Petty, 2009) defines "cloud computing" as "A style of computing that characterizes a model in which providers deliver a variety of IT-enabled capabilities to consumers." Forrester (Torrens, 2008) defines "cloud computing" as "A pool of abstracted, highly scalable, and managed compute infrastructure capable of hosting end-customer applications and billed by consumption." Armbrust et al. (Armbrust, 2009) refers to "cloud computing" as "Both the applications delivered as services over the Internet and the hardware and systems software in the datacenters that provide those services." In addition, Armbrust et al. (Armbrust, 2009) outlines three new aspects of cloud computing listed below:

1. *"The illusion of infinite computing resources available on demand."*
2. *"The elimination of an up-front commitment by Cloud users."*
3. *"The ability to pay for use of computing on a short-term basis as needed."*

In simple terms, "cloud computing" is "personalized computer recourses that are scalable on demand and accessible anytime from anywhere. These resources can be geographically distributed and available using Internet technologies."

Cloud Computing Actors

NIST defines five actors (Reference Architecture Working Group (RAWG), March 2011) responsible for performing set of activities and functions in cloud computing environment.

- **Cloud Providers:** Person, organization or entity responsible for providing service capabilities available to cloud consumers.
- **Cloud Consumers:** Person or organization that uses services provided by cloud providers and maintains a business relationship with them.
- **Cloud Auditors:** An assessment team responsible for conducting independent assessment of cloud services, information system operations, performance, and security of the cloud environment controls.
- **Cloud Broker:** An organization that integrates and manages the use, performance and delivery of cloud services, and negotiates relationships between cloud providers and cloud consumers.

- **Cloud Carrier:** The intermediary that provides connectivity and transport of cloud services from cloud providers to cloud consumers.

Advantages of Cloud Computing

Cloud computing provides an organization the ability to access a location-independent pool of computing resources owned and maintained by another organization(s) using Internet-based technologies. Cloud computing services allow users to access these resources without the knowledge or expertise to support them. The computing resources that are part of the cloud computing environment include servers, software, storage, networks, communications, and interfaces. The computing resources provide the means through which users can access services and applications for processing information at any time from any location. The distinct advantages to using Cloud computing technologies include (Cloud Security Alliance (CSA), 2009; Catteddu et al, 2009A; Jansen, 2011):

- **Portability:** Many organizations are doing business in various geographic locations throughout the world and require availability of data to a number of end-user devices (e.g., portable computers, personal digital assistants (PDA), pagers, wireless telephones). Cloud computing network provides the ability to send and receive critical data at any given location.
- **Flexibility:** The consumers of the cloud service do not require a fixed infrastructure to establish cloud services. Consumers can lease and modify service capabilities by scaling up or down depending on the specific business missions with usage-based payment mechanisms.
- **Low Installation Costs:** Cloud service installation is possible at a very less cost and in a short time. The cloud service provider

offers complete IT server with the underlying computing infrastructure including servers, operating systems, Commercial off-the-Shelf (COTS) software, communication devices and mechanisms, operating systems, data storage, etc. It frees the cloud consumers from the need to acquire or spend capital to build and maintain their own systems.

- **Business Continuity:** To ensure the continuity of business communications, cloud computing resources offer the consumer an infrastructure with diversity and redundancy to avoid service disruptions and single points of failure.

- **Streamlined Data Center:** The ability to perform on-demand provisioning of data center resources enables developers to quickly provision development environments for any of their required tasks. This can also enable provisioning parallel streams of development with multiple environments for development in multiple branches, or for running multiple test runs concurrent with development.

Cloud Computing Reference Architecture

The cloud reference architecture (RAWG, 2011) represents three service models, four deployment models, and five essential characteristics. Figure 1 relates them to the overall model.

Cloud Computing Service Models

NIST defines three service models of cloud computing. They are Infrastructure as a Service (IaaS), Platform as a Service (PaaS), and Software as a Service (SaaS) as described below (Jansen, 2011; CSA, 2009)

- **Infrastructure as a Service (IaaS):** Provides cloud provider organizations capability to lease data-center with infrastructure components such as servers, storage, networks communications components, and power systems with infrastructure management and support where cloud consumers can install operating systems, databases, and applications with full control over them. Examples include Amazon WebService, VMWare, Xen, Xcalibre, Nirvanix, Akamai, Savvis.

Figure 1. Cloud computing reference architecture

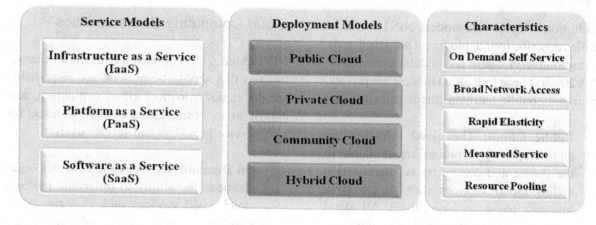

- **Platform as a Service (PaaS):** Provides cloud provider organizations capability to lease platform environment resources including development tools, programming languages, middleware, and database software for the development of applications. cloud consumers can develop their applications and host them to run over an underlying infrastructure accessible using Internet-based connectivity and a web browser. Examples of PaaS include Google App-Engine and Akamai Content Delivery Network.
- **Software as a Service (SaaS):** Provides cloud provider organizations capability to lease applications hosted in a cloud environment including software application maintenance and underlying infrastructure maintenance. Multiple cloud consumers can access and interact with these software applications over the Internet using a web browser from various devices without the need for upfront investment in infrastructure and software application licenses. Examples of SaaS include Microsoft Office Live, Google Docs, SalesForce, Google-Mail, Yahoo! Mail, e-Commerce Carts, and financial management software and payroll services.

Cloud Computing Deployment Models

In addition to the service models, NIST and other entities describe four deployment models that relate to cloud service delivery models (Jansen 2011; CSA 2009). These four cloud models are private, community, public, and hybrid as described below:

- **Public Cloud:** The cloud infrastructure and computing resources are available to the public and owned by an organization selling cloud services with an attractive low-cost pay-as-you-go model. All cloud consumers share off-site cloud computing

resources in a multi-tenancy environment with limited security protection.
- **Private Cloud:** A private cloud gives the organization greater control over the infrastructure security and computational resources than does a public cloud. The owning organization operates solely and manages the cloud infrastructure on-site or off-site, delivering IT enabled services to internal users through Internet technologies.
- **Community Cloud:** The cloud infrastructure is similar to the private cloud, but several organizations (cloud consumers) of a specific community shares infrastructure and computing resources and shared workflows, such as design and supply chain. The organizations in the community or an independent third-party organization manages the community cloud on premise or off premise.
- **Hybrid Cloud:** The cloud infrastructure is a composition of two or more clouds (Public, Private, and Community) and traditional IT delivery services. The clouds remain unique entities but bound together by standardized or proprietary technology. An example of a hybrid cloud is keeping data locally but off-loading related computations to a public cloud resource thus increasing the flexibility of computing.

Cloud Computing Characteristics

NIST (Mell, 2009) defines five essential characteristics that should be present, are responsible for the rapid growth of cloud computing, and contribute to its success as a business model for both service providers and service users:

1. **On Demand Self-Service:** Provides organizations the ability to order and manage cloud-based services such as server time, a web portal application, and data storage

as needed automatically without requiring human interaction with each cloud service provider.

2. **Broad Network Access:** Provides organizations the ability to order cloud services such as accessibility to organization's network via Internet-based network protocols by heterogeneous thin or thick client platforms including desktops, notebooks, smart phones, and personal digital assistants (PDA).

3. **Resource Pooling:** Provides organizations (cloud providers) to lease homogeneous infrastructure (physical and virtual) resources to multiple organizations (cloud consumers) using a multi-tenancy model that are dynamically assigned and reassigned according to consumer demand.

4. **Rapid Elasticity:** Provides organizations (cloud providers) capability to rapidly and elastically scale up or down the type of the cloud service leased such that organizations (cloud consumers) can purchase needed services at any time in any quantity.

5. **Measured Service:** Provides organizations (cloud providers) metering capability to automatically control and optimize resource use at level appropriate to the type of service consumed by an organization (cloud consumer) providing transparency for both the provider and consumer of the service.

Cloud Computing Technologies

Cloud computing is not a single technology but combines a number of computing concepts, architecture approaches, and software design approaches as depicted in Figure 2. It is a set of technologies and business practices for enabling convenient, on-demand network access to a shared pool of configurable computing resources (e.g., networks, servers, storage, applications, and services) that organization can rapidly provision and release with minimal management effort or service provider interaction.

CLOUD COMPUTING CONCERNS

Cloud computing has grown out of an amalgamation of technologies, with that it also has brought potential areas of concern related to the privacy

Figure 2. Cloud computing technologies

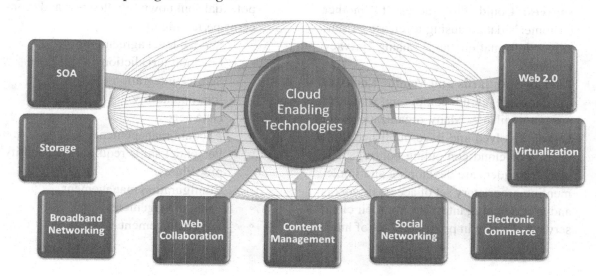

and security. This section describes some of the more fundamental concerns.

Cloud Computing Deployment Concerns

With the astonishing growth of cloud computing evolution, cloud computing delivery and service models promises potential benefits over current IT environment. However, along with these benefits are the potential issues and threats of adopting a new model for delivering cloud services. They include (Janson, 2011; Catteddu, 2009B; CSA, 2009; Government Accounting Office (GAO), 2010):

- **Loss of Governance:** Cloud consumers are completely dependent on the services provided by the cloud provider, which may include issues with security and service level agreements.
- **Reliability and Performance:** Loss of governance means that organizations lose control over IT environment and may not be able to maintain and monitor performance and reliability of mission critical systems and applications in a timely fashion.
- **Multi-Tenancy and Use of Shared Resources:** Could allow access to another customer's data, causing a release of sensitive information and raising privacy concerns.
- **Lack of Standards and Vendor Lock-In:** To date, the cloud computing standards are not available. Many organizations are getting involved and have published draft version of cloud computing controls. The cloud providers are developing and implementing proprietary set of access protocols and programming interfaces for their cloud services. Failure in proprietary set of inter-

faces may expose cloud consumers to data protection risks related to confidentiality, integrity, availability, and accountability of data, and situation could lead to legal ramifications.

- **Service Termination:** If a cloud provider is not able to continue service operation due to unforeseen reasons, including financial constraints, the cloud consumer may not get the required service causing interruption in business operations.
- **Data Privacy Protection:** The interconnectivity between cloud providers causes transfer of data multiple times from one cloud provider to another until the data reaches its final destination. If the cloud provider has improperly implemented data processing and data handling practices, the data during transit may get lost, corrupted, or modified compromising confidentiality and privacy of data.
- **Unknown Challenges:** The adoption of cloud computing concept is still new. The processes and technologies used are not mature and the standards are not available for enforcement. In addition, during cloud service design, implementation, deployment, and operation, the cloud providers and cloud consumers may face numerous potential unknown challenges and concerns pertaining to:
  ○ Service level agreements
  ○ Location jurisdiction
  ○ Service integration
  ○ Interoperability
  ○ Data access
  ○ Account management
  ○ Personnel skills required for security procedures
  ○ Configuration management
  ○ Patch management
  ○ Log management

Cloud Computing Security Concerns

The proliferation of cloud computing technologies poses significant risks to IT infrastructures of an organization. News reports are becoming more frequent about the security threats plaguing government and commercial organization's IT environment and websites. Identity theft from hospitals and financial institutions is evidence that it is more important than ever to secure and safeguard an organization's information. The cloud computing environment is susceptible to similar threats and attacks against cloud computing IT infrastructure due to the vulnerabilities found in Internet-based technologies, design flaws in implementation, poor security control processes, and lack of security awareness and education. Hackers and intruders are finding ways to tap into the signals communicated over the Internet communication infrastructure and are focusing their efforts on hacking cloud environment. It is likely that the security issues of cloud computing will introduce a new series of vulnerabilities and challenges described below (Janson, 2011; CSA 2009; Henna 2009):

- **Improper Configuration:** The cloud computing communications technologies are relatively new. If the security settings for cloud computing resources are not properly established or lack the necessary security controls, it can create an open invitation for hackers to access these resources. If the hackers get access to these resources, by employing malicious code or virus, they can threaten the confidentiality of information and integrity of the cloud networks.

- **Inadequate Physical Security:** Because of its nature of multi-tenancy, cloud computing can pose risks that are more substantial. If the proper physical security controls are not in place, access to unauthorized cloud resources can cause its misuse, un-

authorized access to the network, and loss of information stored on the network.

- **Inadequate Management of Passwords and Keys:** Many computing resources use Public Key Infrastructure-based (PKI) mechanism that uses shared keys. Improper use of these keys can leave a cloud computing network vulnerable to attack and allow unauthorized persons to access user names and passwords.

- **Insecure Application Programming Interfaces:** The nature of cloud computing architecture requires cloud providers and consumers to interact with each other using Application Programming Interfaces (API). The cloud providers and consumers need to consider properly securing and implementing interface authentication mechanisms to prevent attackers find ways to identify vulnerabilities and compromise the cloud computing network.

- **Session Highjack:** An attack against the integrity of a session where an attacker uses network packet sniffing technique to steal the session cookie to gain access to the cloud service network. If the cloud computing communications implementation does not employ strong encryption, then by using the known vulnerability of the cloud computing resources, the attacker can take control of an authorized and authenticated session from its original owner and thereby gain access to the cloud network resources.

- **Internet Protocol Vulnerabilities:** Many Internet protocols have well-publicized vulnerabilities including eavesdropping, unauthorized access, password sniffing, masquerading, replay, and message modification. These vulnerabilities potentially threaten system availability, confidentiality, and integrity of the cloud computing network. By using freely available tools on the Internet, hackers can crack the key code to gain access to the network.

- **Wireless Network Vulnerabilities:** A key component of the transformation taking place in this global business world is the use of wireless communication solutions in data enabled cellular phones, two-way pagers, Personal Digital Assistants, and handheld or laptop computers with wireless connectivity capabilities. The use of wireless network devices in the cloud computing network infrastructure raises critical security issues for organizations. Hackers can tap into the signals communicated over a Wireless Local Area Network (WLAN), even if they are not in the physical proximity of the transmission due to the vulnerabilities found in wireless standards, wireless firmware, design flaws in technology implementation, poor security control processes, and lack of security awareness and training.

- **Denial of Service:** The Internet-based interconnectivity between location-independent cloud service providers and the growth of readily available hacking and virus/worm spreading tools and spamming tools such as Botnets and social networking provides attackers an opportunity to attack cloud computing resources to create denial of service attacks causing disruption in availability of the cloud service.

SECURING THE CLOUD ENVIRONMENT

Experience has shown that as new technologies are developed, they become a major source of new vulnerabilities for which it is important to have strong encryption, strong mutual authentication, and other controls that work together to provide layered security. The Information System (IS)

hosted in the cloud environment must comply with the necessary security regulations and standards to support the security principles of Confidentiality, Integrity, and Availability (CIA). The definitions of the confidentiality, integrity, and availability objectives are as follow: (Joint Task Force (JTF), 2008):

- **Confidentiality:** Information system security controls must protect data during transmission and receipt, and must not disclose any data to unauthorized individuals or parties. For Personally Identifiable Information (PII), the information system must comply with applicable privacy laws to protect the privacy of an individual. Disclosure of such data without authorization might result in economic hardship and inconvenience to customer.

- **Integrity:** Information system must protect data from accidental or unauthorized change, corruption, or removal. Failure to maintain the integrity of data can result in economical impact to both the cloud provider and the cloud consumer. It will also require extensive resources to correct and validate data affected.

- **Availability:** Information system provided services must be available at all times to all authorized users. The information must be available on products and services in a timely manner. Slow response times may result in loss of business opportunities.

The system security principles are useful for assessing the potential impact of an exploited vulnerability. Additional security-related objectives or services, such as accountability, non-repudiation assurances, or authentication services, might be required for specific cloud service application.

Cloud Computing Controls

As organizations start migrating to the cloud, they are looking for ways to obtain necessary assurances for successful deployment. The risks to the cloud computing resources and operations, business partners, individuals, and the nation arising from the use of the cloud services must be acceptable. Standards are critical to ensure risks are acceptable and complying with the standards provides a clear picture of safeguards and countermeasures used as the controls for cloud services to protect the confidentiality, integrity, and availability of the cloud service environment.

Because of the lack of established standards, multiple industry groups have developed and published requirements and controls for securing cloud environment. They include information security practitioners from federal, commercial, and international organizations, and the regulators of the security policies and standards listed here:

- Cloud Security Alliance (CSA), a nonprofit international organization
- European Network and Information Security Agency (ENISA)
- National Institute of Science and Technology (NIST)
- General Services Administration (GSA)
- Federal Chief Information Officer (CIO) Council
- Information Security and Identity Management Committee (ISIMC)
- Federal Risk and Management Program (FedRAMP) Council

For the ease of use and assessment, these organizations have recommended requirements and controls frameworks grouped by classes and categorized into specific controls as summarized in Figure 3 and defined below (JTF 2009; CSA 2009; Kundra, 2010). As market for cloud technologies matures and industry develops new tools

Figure 3. Cloud computing environment controls

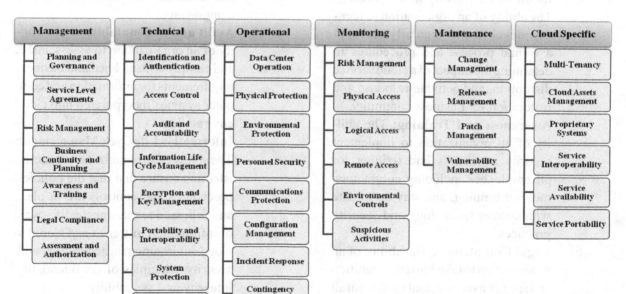

and standards for various cloud service models, organizations may consider adding specific additional security controls, or implement other compensating controls as additional security measures.

Control Class: Management Controls

1. **Planning and Governance:** The ability of an organization to control and oversight over policies, procedures, regulations and standards for system and application design, implementation, testing, and maintenance and monitoring of deployed cloud services.

2. **Service Level Agreements:** The ability of an organization to define cloud services outsourced or subcontracted including legal requirements to protect the cloud computing resources, and to define, implement and monitor service level performance measurements.

3. **Risk Management:** The ability of an organization to manage risks of cloud service environment.

4. **Business Continuity and Planning:** The ability of an organization to identify, develop, and regularly maintain a formal process and procedures to determine the impact of a cloud service disruption, and activate response and restoration for business continuity.

5. **Awareness and Training:** The ability of an organization to implement security awareness and training for all employees including contractors, monitor training, and stay up to date with current technology and security practices.

6. **Legal Compliance:** The ability of an organization to take into consideration and specify as contractual agreement all applicable business specific standards, regulations and laws, privacy laws, international laws and security breach disclosure laws to protect cloud service environment resources.

7. **Assessment and Authorization:** The ability of an organization to support certification and accreditation of cloud service computing resources including information systems and interconnected systems and ability to develop and update the plan of action and milestones based on assessment findings.

Control Class: Technical Controls

8. **Identification and Authentication:** The ability of an organization to implement and manage access to cloud services including identification, authorization, authentication, and auditing for all user types of cloud provider and cloud consumer.

9. **Access Control:** The ability of an organization to support multi-level security by implementing access control measures on cloud infrastructure components.

10. **Audit and Accountability:** The ability of an organization to assess, audit, and comply with all legal and business requirements for information and computer systems incorporated into cloud environment.

11. **Information Life Cycle Management:** The ability of an organization to administer and ensure that that the policies, procedures and controls are in place and followed to manage the life-cycle of information in-transit and stored in cloud environment in accordance with security principles of confidentiality, integrity and availability.

12. **Encryption and Key Management:** The ability of an organization to identify proper encryption usage and manage encryption keys, security cer-

tificates and credentials for protection of cloud computing resources and data.

13. **Portability and Interoperability:** The ability of an organization to develop and provide cloud service interfaces that is interoperable with other cloud service providers to enable seamless transfer of data and services with each other.

14. **System Protection:** The ability of an organization to protect routing and network management infrastructure against both passive and active attacks.

15. **Application Security:** The ability of an organization to understand challenges associated with the security threats related to cloud-based Internet technologies used, identify safeguards and protection measures, and incorporate them in design, development, and deployment of cloud service-based applications.

Control Class: Operational Controls

16. **Data Center Operation:** The ability of an organization to manage data center that complies with the operational requirements.

17. **Physical Protection:** The ability of an organization to implement controls necessary for physical access to the building and information systems, visitor access, and preventative measures for physical damage to information systems components.

18. **Environmental Protection:** The ability of an organization to develop and implement policies and procedures to ensure environmental issues such as fires, floods, and power failures do not cause an interruption of cloud service.

19. **Personnel Security:** The ability of an organization to develop, disseminate, review and update periodically a for-

mal, documented, personnel security policy that addresses purpose, scope, roles, responsibilities, and compliance; and formal, documented procedures to facilitate the implementation of the Personnel Security Policy and associated personnel security controls.

20. **Communications Protection:** The ability of an organization to protect data and voice communications against Internet attacks and establish trusted communication between designated endpoints for message confidentiality, and integrity.

21. **Configuration Management:** The ability of an organization to document configuration information, monitor changes, and restrict access to information systems.

22. **Incident Response:** The ability of an organization to understand the complexity of cloud service environment, stakeholders involved and manage incident handling program.

23. **Contingency Planning:** The ability of an organization to plan, train, test, and review all contingency plans as well as providing alternative storage and processing sites.

24. **Capacity Planning:** The ability of an organization to manage network bandwidths, storage, and processing power to accommodate current and future business requirements.

Control Class: Monitoring Controls

25. **Risk Management:** The ability of an organization to continuously manage risks with changes in cloud service environment.

26. **Physical Access:** The ability of organization to control all physical access points (including designated entry/exit points) to facilities containing informa-

tion systems and verifies individual access authorizations before granting access to the facilities. The organization also controls access to areas officially designated as publicly accessible, as appropriate, in accordance with the organization's assessment of risk.

27. **Logical Access:** The ability of an organization to implement tools to monitor access to cloud services including identification, authorization, authentication for all user types of cloud provider and cloud consumer.

28. **Remote Access:** The ability of organization to document, monitor, and controls all methods of remote access (e.g., Wireless, Internet, VPN) to the information system including remote access for privileged functions. Appropriate organization officials authorize each remote access method for the information system and authorize only necessary users for each access method.

29. **Environmental Controls:** The ability of an organization to implement tools to monitor policies and procedures to ensure environmental issues such as fires, floods, and power failures do not cause an interruption of cloud service.

30. **Suspicious Activities:** The ability of an organization to provide needed support and resources necessary to monitor and audit cloud computing resources to ensure the delivery of the cloud service provided in accordance with the agreed contractual terms, established service level agreements and compliance requirements.

Control Class: Maintenance Controls

31. **Change Management:** The ability of an organization to ensure that all changes (implementations, modifications, upgrades, decommissioning etc.) to cloud service environment are planned, communicated, recorded, and implemented successfully.

32. **Release Management:** The ability of an organization to ensure that all releases for cloud environment applications are planned, communicated, recorded, and implemented successfully.

33. **Patch Management:** The ability of an organization to ensure that all required patches for cloud environment components are planned, communicated, recorded, and implemented successfully.

34. **Vulnerability Management:** The ability of an organization to have a systematic, accountable, and documented process for proactively managing exposure to vulnerabilities through the timely deployment of patches and prevent exploitation of IT vulnerabilities.

Control Class: Cloud Specific Controls

35. **Multi-Tenancy:** The ability of an organization to mitigate risks associated with items such as multi-tenancy, or the sharing of computing resources by different organizations.

36. **Cloud Assets Management:** The ability of an organization to maintain an inventory of the cloud computing environment assets.

37. **Proprietary Systems:** The ability of an organization to manage their proprietary system and interfaces that is secured and trustworthy in cloud service environment.

38. **Service Interoperability:** The ability of an organization to deploy services in cloud service environment that is interoperable amongst different types of computing hardware, operating

systems, and application software in Internet-based technologies and protocols environment.

39. **Service Availability:** The ability of an organization to deploy services in cloud service environment that is available for use in accordance with organization's business requirements.

40. **Service Portability:** The ability of an organization to seamlessly port cloud service applications from one cloud service provider to another.

Cloud Application Domain Specific Standards

For applications deployed in cloud service environment, cloud actors are accountable for the protection and privacy of information as one component of an effective security management program. The increased frequency of security and data privacy related incidents has resulted in new legislation at both the federal and state level. The cloud actors need to comply with the applicable laws and regulations specific to cloud applications as listed below:

- **Confidentiality of Healthcare Information (HIPAA):** Congress passed HIPAA (Health Insurance Portability and Accountability Act) in 1996 to increase the protection of healthcare related information that patients can transfer from one insurer to other. As part of HIPAA, Congress required the development of privacy regulations to protect the confidentiality of individually identifiable health care information. The final Privacy Rule issued on August 14, 2002 comprises of four parts (Office for Civil Rights, 2003):
  - Privacy
  - Security of Electronic Signature
  - Security of Healthcare Transactions
  - Security of Healthcare Provider Identifier

- **International Information Security Standards (ISO/IEC 17799):** The International Standards Organization (ISO) recognized a comprehensive set of controls and best practices in information security. The standards known as ISO 17799 now replaced by ISO 27002 comprises of twelve prime sections (ISO 17799, n.d.):
  - Risk Assessment and Treatment
  - Security Policy
  - System Access Control
  - System Development and Maintenance
  - Physical and Environmental Security
  - Compliance
  - Personnel Security
  - Security Organization
  - Asset Classification and Control
  - Business Continuity Management (BCM)
  - Communications and Operations Management
  - Information Security Incident Management

- **Sarbanes-Oxley Compliance (SOX):** The Sarbanes-Oxley Public Company Accounting Reform and Investor Protection Act of 2002 (Oxley, 2002) require the Chief Executive Officer (CEO) and the Chief Financial Officer (CFO) of publicly held company certify each annual and quarterly report filed with the Securities and Exchange Commission. The act introduced stringent new rules with the stated objective: "to protect investors by improving the accuracy and reliability of corporate disclosures made pursuant to the securities laws".

- **Homeland Security Presidential Directive (HSPD-7):** President Bush signed this directive in December 2003 to establish a national policy to identify, prioritize, and protect United States critical infrastructure and key resources (Bolton, 2004).

- **Homeland Security Presidential Directive/HSPD-12:** President Bush signed this directive in August 2004 to establish a mandatory, Government-wide standard for secure and reliable forms of identification issued by the Federal Government to its employees and contractors (Homeland Security, 2004).

Solutions and Recommendations

The new wave of cloud computing has added new challenges for organizations planning to build and deploy applications using cloud technologies. The deployment platforms and ownership of the supporting IT infrastructure have changed significantly in recent years. In addition, these Internet-based cloud computing applications also necessitate the need for several types of test and evaluation of the cloud computing environment controls. Organizations are looking for ways to implement sound test and evaluation methodologies to assess the state of cloud computing environment

controls. However, if the guidelines for assessing them are not available or widely publicized, organizations may face serious problems in their successful development, deployment, operation, and maintenance of cloud computing-based applications. This section provides the guidelines for

- Planning and assessing the cloud computing environment controls.
- Determining if the controls are operating as intended.
- Identifying the gaps between the implemented controls and the required controls.
- Capturing, documenting, and retaining information sufficient to prove the existence or non-existence of vulnerabilities discovered through the assessment process.

Cloud Computing Controls Assessment Life Cycle

The goal of an assessment is to examine the cloud computing controls both internal and external as applicable for the cloud service environment. Figure 4 provides the cloud service actors with a standardized approach for scoping, planning,

Figure 4. Cloud computing controls assessment life cycle

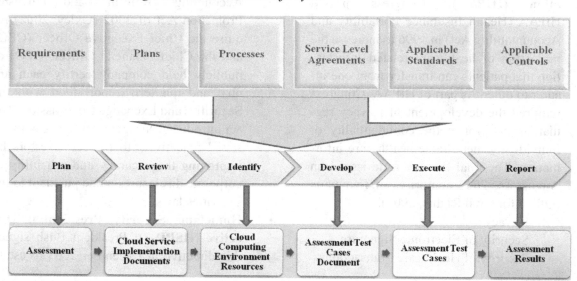

performing, documenting, and assessing cloud service environment controls. The assessment cycle described helps evaluating whether the controls minimize risks that could result in fraud and/or loss of integrity of the cloud service operation.

Plan Phase

A wide range of activities is involved in assessment planning as described below.

- Set Assessment Objectives
  - Determine the adequacy of security mechanisms, assurances, and other properties that enforces organization's security policy.
  - Ensure the confidentiality, integrity, and availability of all information the cloud service environment resources creates, processes, receives, maintains, or transmits.
  - Ensure compliance to legislative and regulatory standards.
  - Ensure that the system responsibilities and roles are properly assigned.
  - Provide reasonable resolution options for problem areas identified.
  - Ensure that the responsible entity gets all needed support during mitigation planning.
  - Ensure the protection against security vulnerabilities and threats.
  - Ensure cloud service environment is reliable, recoverable and resilient.
- Determine Assessment Scope
  - Verify the existence of documentation (e.g., system security plan, risk assessment, service level agreements) and determine the consistency between documentation and its implementation.
    - Assess the degree of inconsistency between the cloud service objectives and its implementation.
    - Assess whether cloud service implementation specification is a reasonable and appropriate.
    - Assess the policies and procedures and its compliance to applicable laws and regulations.
    - Uncover the flaws in design, implementation, and operations that violate security policy.
    - Review physical, personnel, operational, and environmental protection controls.
    - Review disaster recovery and continuity plans in the event of unexpected system failures.
    - Conduct penetration tests to assess vulnerabilities or exposures to the cloud computing environment.
    - Assess protection against any anticipated threats due to these vulnerabilities to the integrity of cloud computing.
- Identify Assumptions
  - All actors that are involved in cloud computing environment design, implementation, and deployment will make the appropriate documentation and system(s) available to conduct complete analysis and potentially on-site assessment.
- Acquire Resources
  - **People:** To ensure that there is adequate education, awareness, and skill to support and conduct assessment activity.
  - **Process:** To ensure that the process and techniques for controls assessment are appropriate and effective.

○ **Technology:** To ensure that the applicable and required test tools, technologies and test environment are available.

cloud computing environment assessment is a new phenomenon. Organizations are implementing any one or all cloud computing delivery models depending on the organization needs and the information processing requirements. The assessment team lead must have the managerial and technical skills to plan the assessment in close collaboration with the stakeholders of cloud providers and cloud consumers involved in implementation and deployment of the cloud service environment. Unexpected events may occur due to circumstances beyond anyone's control. The assessment team lead must have ability to adapt the plan, reschedule tasks, and reallocate resources to fit reality. The assessment team must perform the following:

- Have understanding of the challenges for this new concept.
- Know the relationships, and dependencies between delivery and service models, the integrated features between them.
- Understand the complexity vs. openness (extensibility) of model.
- Know the physical location of assets, resources, information owners and consumers.
- Understand the applicable security requirements.
- Be objective and independent.
- Apply traditional assessment processes and methods for ensuring a reliable, manageable, and secure cloud computing service.

The actual employment of these security activities and evaluations is dependent upon many additional factors including adequately addressing requirements in contract documents, service level agreement, and the development schedules.

Review Phase

This phase starts with collecting all possible information about the cloud service to help the assessment activities. The assessment team reviews and analyzes policies, procedures, plans and other relevant documentation related to the protection of the cloud service environment against the defined assessment objectives. The review process must include analyzing the cloud service requirements to address issues associated with effectiveness, efficiency, and reliability of the cloud service environment. Undefined or unidentified requirements are particularly problematic in the cloud service availability and security arena since the omission may compromise the cloud service environment. The review resources must include any additional documentation containing security controls descriptions and requirements, including, but not limited to:

- Mission Statements
- Organization Charts
- Organization Policies
- Service Level Agreements
- System Requirements
- System Architecture
- Network Architecture
- Technical Design
- System Interfaces
- Information Flows and Storage
- Security Architecture
- System Security Controls Specifications
- Environment Specific Physical Security Plans
- Environment Specific Operations Manuals
- Standard Operating Procedures
- Configuration Documentation
- System Logs and Rule sets
- Risk Register
- Disaster recovery and Incident Management Procedures
- Processes used to monitor and enforce policy compliance

Data collected from documentation must be reviewed and analyzed to determine the system boundaries, functionality, and security requirements and identifying and mitigating the threats and vulnerabilities. In addition to reviewing the system boundaries for each cloud provider and cloud consumer, an understanding of all relevant controls and how they are integrated between the cloud service is required to evaluate their effectiveness in protecting the confidentiality, integrity and availability of the cloud service environment's data. Finally, the review report must include identifying the discrepancies between documentation and implemented controls. The cooperation of all stakeholders and the support personnel for the cloud service environment is critical to the success of the review phase.

Identify Phase

This phase forms the foundation for all subsequent assessment activities and includes identifying cloud computing environment assets, information sensitivity, the documented security control requirements, and the known business risks. After reviewing the documents in "Review Phase", the assessment team must perform following activities in this phase:

- Identify policies, functions, plans, processes, and procedures that support cloud service environment.
- Identify cloud service environment requirements and critical components.
- Identify cloud service communication including protocols, services and data sensitivity.
- Identify applicable service level agreements between the cloud provider and the cloud consumer.
- Identify support provided by any external partners for cloud service.

- Evaluate the weaknesses associated with the critical resources and information, thus resulting in a list of potential vulnerabilities.
- Identify new risks based on possible threats due to vulnerabilities identified.

Develop Phase

In this phase, the assessment team must design and develop the assessment techniques and procedures to confirm the presence or absence of specific controls. The team must evaluate the effectiveness of controls as applicable for the cloud service environment, and identify vulnerabilities after the implementation of safeguards. The assessment techniques must consider the threat and vulnerability information from both the government and the industry sources to evaluate a comprehensive range of attack methods. The assessment procedures must include the evaluation or testing of each control with expected results. Each procedure at a minimum must verify that the control is in effect and correctly implements the identified functional criteria in the control statement. The assessment activities can exercise the following methods to evaluate the existence of security controls:

- **Interview:** Focused discussion with individuals or groups to facilitate understanding, achieve clarification, or obtain evidence.
- **Examine:** The physical examination of the object including configuration, version and patch level to facilitate understanding, achieve clarification or obtain evidence.
- **Demonstration:** Of security control implemented.
- **Test:** The execution of steps to verify and validate implementation of security control.

In absence of the specific cloud computing standards and regulations, this document is a good start for developing assessment procedures for security controls for the information system assets hosted in cloud computing environment. In addition, it is necessary to develop the assessment procedures for each cloud service delivery models to ensure that the service level agreement exists between the cloud provider and the cloud consumer with clearly defined responsibility of the items listed in Table 1, Table 2, and Table 3.

Execute Phase

The assessment team with support from assigned system and network administrators will execute the assessment procedures developed to establish a high degree of confidence in cloud comput-

Table 1. IaaS controls assessment

No.	Consumer (Responsible for Platform and Software)	Provider (Responsible for Underlying Infrastructure)
1	Verify that the physical support infrastructure components (facilities, rack space, power, cooling, cabling, etc) are secured and available	Procure, install and configure the physical support infrastructure components (facilities, rack space, power, cooling, cabling, etc) for security and safety
2	Verify that the information technology infrastructure components (servers, storage, networking, etc) are secured and safe	Procure, install and configure the information technology infrastructure components (servers, storage, networking, etc) for security and safety
3	Verify that the communication connection pools are configured in accordance with the desired service levels	Procure, install and configure the communication connection pools in accordance with the desired service levels
4	Verify that the network bandwidth is configured in accordance with the desired service levels	Configure the network bandwidth in accordance with the desired service levels
5	Verify that the available security platform (Firewall rules, IDS/IPS tuning, etc) in accordance with security policy	Procure, install and configure the security platform (Firewall rules, IDS/IPS tuning, etc) in accordance with security policy
6	Verify that the Web application firewalls (WAFs) are configured properly to prevent unauthorized access or denial-of-service attacks	Procure, install and Configure the Web application firewalls (WAFs) are configured properly to prevent unauthorized access or denial-of-service attacks
7	Verify that the systems monitoring and log collection processes are implemented	Implement systems monitoring and log collection processes
8	Procure, install and configure the operating systems and virtual images for security	Verify that the operating systems virtual images are hardened for security
9	Implement the OS patch management and hardening procedures in accordance with organization and IaaS provider security policy	Verify that the OS patch management and hardening procedures exists and check any conflict between consumer hardening procedure and provider security policy
10	Procure, install and configure the required middleware, database and tools for protecting against vulnerabilities	Verify that the middleware, database and tools used are optimally configured for protecting against vulnerabilities
11	Configure authentication and password mechanism in accordance with the security policy	Verify that the authentication and password policy is enforced in accordance with the security policy
12	Procure, install, configure and maintain identity management system in accordance with security policy	Verify that the identity management system is maintained in accordance with security policy
13	Ensure that each web application developed and installed is performing to the desired service levels for performance, security and availability	Verify that each web application is secured and does not provide vulnerability to compromise IaaS components
14	Ensure compliance with applicable standards and regulations	Ensure compliance with applicable standards and regulations
15	Ensure required service level agreement is met	Ensure required service level agreement is met

Table 2. PaaS controls assessment

No.	Consumer (Responsible for Software)	Provider (Responsible for Underlying Platform Infrastructure)
1	Verify that the physical support infrastructure components (facilities, rack space, power, cooling, cabling, etc) are secured and available	Procure, install and configure the physical support infrastructure components (facilities, rack space, power, cooling, cabling, etc) for security and safety
2	Verify that the information technology infrastructure components (servers, storage, networking, etc) are secured and safe	Procure, install and configure the information technology infrastructure components (servers, storage, networking, etc) for security and safety
3	Verify that the communication connection pools are configured in accordance with the desired service levels	Procure, install and configure the communication connection pools in accordance with the desired service levels
4	Verify that the network bandwidth is configured in accordance with the desired service levels	Configure the network bandwidth in accordance with the desired service levels
5	Verify that the available security platform (Firewall rules, IDS/IPS tuning, etc) in accordance with security policy	Procure, install and configure the security platform (Firewall rules, IDS/IPS tuning, etc) in accordance with security policy
6	Verify that the Web application firewalls (WAFs) are configured properly to prevent unauthorized access or denial-of-service attacks	Procure, install and Configure the Web application firewalls (WAFs) are configured properly to prevent unauthorized access or denial-of-service attacks
7	Verify that the systems monitoring and log collection processes are implemented	Implement systems monitoring and log collection processes
8	Verify that the operating systems virtual images are hardened for security	Procure, install and configure the operating systems and virtual images for security
9	Verify that the OS patch management and hardening procedures exists and check any conflict between consumer hardening procedure and provider security policy	Implement the OS patch management and hardening procedures in accordance with organization and IaaS provider security policy
10	Verify that the middleware, database and tools used are optimally configured for protecting against vulnerabilities	Procure, install and configure the required middleware, database and tools for protecting against vulnerabilities
11	Configure authentication and password mechanism in accordance with the security policy	Verify that the authentication and password policy is enforced in accordance with the security policy
12	Procure, install, configure and maintain identity management system in accordance with security policy	Verify that the identity management system is maintained in accordance with security policy
13	Ensure that each web application developed and installed is performing to the desired service levels for performance, security and availability	Verify that each web application is secured and does not provide vulnerability to compromise IaaS components
14	Ensure compliance with applicable standards and regulations	Ensure compliance with applicable standards and regulations
15	Ensure required service level agreement is met	Ensure required service level agreement is met

ing environment. The assessment procedures execution must involve scrutiny of the entire cloud computing environment system design and implementation and identify vulnerabilities and weaknesses that authorized or unauthorized users of the cloud provider and consumer organization could exploit.

The assessment team member performing assessment must document the results of each assessment and make a note of anomalies observed or found. Certain assessment procedures will require re-execution to confirm the results. The completed and signed assessment procedure document serves as a written record of the test assessment process and acceptance of the results. The results of the assessment are a major consideration in recommending the cloud computing environment-based system deployment into a production environment.

Table 3. SaaS controls assessment

No.	Consumer (Responsible for Using Software Leased)	Provider (Responsible for Underlying Infrastructure, Platform Software)
1		Procure, install and configure the physical support infrastructure components (facilities, rack space, power, cooling, cabling, etc) for security and safety
2		Procure, install and configure the information technology infrastructure components (servers, storage, networking, etc) for security and safety
3		Procure, install and configure the communication connection pools in accordance with the desired service levels
4		Configure the network bandwidth in accordance with the desired service levels
5		Procure, install and configure the security platform (Firewall rules, IDS/IPS tuning, etc) in accordance with security policy
6	Verify that required software is installed and available for use.	Procure, install and Configure the Web application firewalls (WAFs) are configured properly to prevent unauthorized access or denial-of-service attacks
7		Implement systems monitoring and log collection processes
8		Procure, install and configure the operating systems and virtual images for security
9		Implement the OS patch management and hardening procedures in accordance with organization and IaaS provider security policy
10		Procure, install and configure the required middleware, database and tools for protecting against vulnerabilities
11		Configure authentication and password mechanism in accordance with the security policy
12		Procure, install, configure and maintain identity management system in accordance with security policy
13		Ensure that each software application installed is performing to the desired service levels for performance, security and availability
14	Ensure provider is in compliance with applicable standards and regulations	Ensure compliance with applicable standards and regulations
15	Ensure required service level agreement is met	Ensure required service level agreement is met

The assessment team member must verify and validate that all required controls are in place and working properly.

Report Phase

The purpose of the assessment report is to document the degree and effectiveness of the controls implemented in the cloud computing environment. To achieve the benefits of assessment, the assessment lead must document results and brief to the appropriate stakeholders of the cloud provider and the cloud consumer responsible for taking necessary and/or corrective actions listed below to improve the effectiveness of the cloud computing environment:

- Identifying new problem areas
- Identifying the need for new controls

- Monitoring recommended follow-up actions
- Redirecting subsequent assessment activities
- Reassessing the appropriateness of existing controls and related activities
- Reassessing previously identified risks
- Holding managers accountable for compliance

The assessment report must include a full description of the assessment process, specific technical information related to each cloud computing environment component assessed. In addition, the report must include the following:

- Cloud computing environment description
- Assessment objectives
- Assessment method(s) used to assess/evaluate the control
- Assessment procedure(s) for each control
- The expected results of each assessment procedure
- The actual results of each assessment procedure
- Assessment findings
- Effectiveness of control assessed
- Analysis and evaluation of assessment results and findings
- Recommendations for resolving discrepancies

The report must end with a summary or conclusion of overall assessment. The detailed assessment procedures and details of results must be included in appendixes.

FUTURE RESEARCH DIRECTIONS

The market for the cloud computing services has expanded rapidly in the past few years. The number of vendors providing cloud service will also continue to increase (Sharp, 2011). With that, the cloud consumers will continue to rely on cloud computing for developing, testing, and hosting new applications because of their ability to access infrastructure, platform, and business application services at a fraction of the cost and management of traditional on-site systems.

In a worldwide Chief Information Officer (CIO) survey conducted by Gartner (McDonald, 2011), almost half of all CIOs expect to deploy the enterprise applications and infrastructures in cloud environment using cloud technologies. According to Pew Research (Anderson et all, 2010), cloud computing will continue to expand and become more dominant for computing and communicating activities through connections to servers operated by outside firms.

However, this new emerging technology is still in development. To benefit from the cloud computing, there is a need to research questions about data encryption, access control and authentication issues, multi-tenancy agreements, liabilities, and data storage jurisdictions. There needs to be standards and guidelines for cloud deployment and an equally urgent need to develop and provide guidelines for testing and evaluating cloud requirements and controls to assess the effectiveness of the cloud environment before deployment into production. Continuous and consistent security and private assessment of constantly changing infrastructure components and technologies is necessary. cloud computing assessment presents an opportunity for IT evaluators, auditors, and assessors to emerge as an important and necessary stakeholder to help address these challenges.

CONCLUSION

The cloud computing assessment framework described in this chapter introduces cloud computing environment, provides an overview on cloud computing architecture components, the implementation challenges and the security issues and threats that organizations considering cloud computing deployment may face. The assessment life cycle framework of the cloud computing controls is presented next for assessing the environment to verify the compliance with applicable standards, laws, regulations, and to determine the extent to which the controls are implemented correctly, operating as intended, and producing the desired outcome with respect to meeting the cloud computing requirements. Successful execution of the assessment life cycle described in this chapter will enable the organization management create strategies to effectively address potential security protection and threats prevention measures for cloud computing infrastructure. The assessment plan when executed will help determine the overall effectiveness of the controls implemented for cloud computing environment. Organizations must assess the effectiveness based on the specific type of cloud service considered before making final decisions for deployment and use.

REFERENCES

Anderson, J. Q., & Rainee, L. (2010, June). *The future of cloud computing.* Pew Research Center Publications. Retrieved June 26, 2011, from http://pewresearch.org/pubs/1623/future-cloud-computing-technology-experts

Armbrust, M., Fox, A., Griffith, R., Joseph, A., Katz, R., & Konwinski, A. ... Stoica, I. (2009, February). *Above the clouds: A Berkeley view of cloud computing.* University of California, Berkeley. Retrieved from http://www.eecs.berkeley.edu/Pubs/TechRpts/2009/EECS-2009-28.pdf

Bolton, J. (2004, June). *Development of Homeland Security Presidential Directive (HSPD) - 7.* The Executive Office of the President. Retrieved April 13, 2011, from http://www.whitehouse.gov/sites/default/files/omb/assets/omb/memoranda/fy04/m-04-15.pdf

Catteddu, D., & Hogben, G. (2009A, November). *Cloud computing: Information assurance framework.* The European Network and Information Security Agency. Retrieved April 23, 2011, from http://www.usccu.us/documents/US-CCU%20Cyber-Security%20Check%20List%202007.pdf

Catteddu, D., & Hogben, G. (2009B, November). *Cloud computing risk assessment.* The European Network and Information Security Agency. Retrieved April 23, 2011, from http://www.enisa.europa.eu/act/rm/files/deliverables/cloud-computing-risk-assessment

Cloud Security Alliance. (2009, December). *Security guidance for critical areas of focus in cloud computing* V2.1. Cloud Security Alliance. Retrieved April 23, 2011, from http://www.cloudsecurityalliance.org/csaguide.pdf

Cloud Security Alliance. (2010, March). *Top threats to cloud computing* V 1.0. Cloud Security Alliance. Retrieved April 23, 2011, from https://cloudsecurityalliance.org/topthreats/csathreats.v1.0.pdf

Government Accounting Office. (2010, May). *Federal guidance needed to address control issues with implementing cloud computing.* Government Accounting Office. Retrieved April 23, 2011, from http://www.gao.gov/new.items/d10513.pdf

Hanna, S. (2009, December). A security analysis of Cloud Computing. *Cloud Computing Journal.* Retrieved April 24, 2011, from http://cloudcomputing.sys-con.com/node/1203943

Homeland Security. (2004, August). *Homeland Security Presidential Directive (HSPD) -12*. The US Department of Homeland Security. Retrieved April 13, 2011, from http://www.dhs.gov/xabout/laws/gc_1217616624097.shtm

ISO 17799. (n.d.). *What is ISO 17799?* ISO 17799 Information and Resource Portal. Retrieved April 13, 2011, from http://17799.denialinfo.com/whatisiso17799.htm

Jansen, W., & Grance, T. (2011, January). *Guidelines on security and privacy in public cloud computing* (800-144). National Institute of Standards and Technology. Retrieved April 24, 2011, from http://csrc.nist.gov/publications/nistpubs/800-144/SP800-144.pdf

Joint Task Force. (2004, May). *Guide for the security certification and accreditation of federal information systems* (800-37). National Institute of Science and Technology. Retrieved April 23, 2011, from http://csrc.nist.gov/publications/nistpubs/800-37-rev1/sp800-37-rev1-final.pdf

Joint Task Force. (2009, August). *Guide for assessing security controls publication 800-53A Rev 3*. National Institute of Standards and Technology. Retrieved April 24, 2011, from http://csrc.nist.gov/publications/nistpubs/800-53-Rev3/sp800-53-rev3-final.pdf

Kundra, V. (2011, February). *Federal cloud computing strategy*. The U.S. CIO. Retrieved April 23, 2011, from http://www.cio.gov/documents/Federal-Cloud-Computing-Strategy.pdf

McDonald, M., & Aron, D. (2011, June). *Reimagining IT: The 2011 CIO agenda*. Gartner Technology Research. Retrieved June 26, 2011, from http://www.gartner.com/DisplayDocument?id=1524714

Mell, P., & Grance, T. (2011, January). *The NIST definition of cloud computing* (800-145). National Institute of Standards and Technology. Retrieved April 24, 2011, from http://csrc.nist.gov/publications/nistpubs/800-145/SP800-145.pdf

Office for Civil Rights. (2003, May). *Summary of the HIPAA privacy rule*. US Department of Health and Human Services. Retrieved April 13, 2011, from http://www.hhs.gov/ocr/privacy/hipaa/understanding/summary/privacysummary.pdf

Oxley. (2002, July). Sarbanes-Oxley Act of 2002. *Sarbanes-Oxley Act Community Forum*. Retrieved April 13, 2011, from http://frwebgate.access.gpo.gov/cgi-bin/getdoc.cgi?dbname=107_cong_reports&docid=f:hr610.107.pdf

Pettey, C. (2009, October). *Gartner identifies the top 10 strategic technologies for 2010*. Gartner Technology Research. Retrieved April 24, 2011, from http://www.gartner.com/it/page.jsp?id=1210613

Pettey, C. (2010, June). *Gartner says worldwide cloud services market to surpass $68 billion in 2010*. Gartner Technology Research. Retrieved April 24, 2011, from http://www.gartner.com/it/page.jsp?id=1389313

Reference Architecture Working Group. (2011, March). *Cloud computing reference architecture*. National Institute of Standards and Technology. Retrieved May 24, 2011, from http://collaborate.nist.gov/twiki-cloud-computing/pub/CloudComputing/ReferenceArchitectureTaxonomy/NIST_CC_Reference_Architecture_v1_March_30_2011.pdf

Robinson, J. (2009, April). Cloud computing spending leaps 21%. *Information Age*. Retrieved April 24, 2011, from http://www.information-age.com/channels/data-centre-and-it-infrastructure/perspectives-and-trends/1017852/cloud-computing-spending-leaps-21.thtml

Sharp, D. (2011, June). Will cloud computing be the future of IT? *Online Magazine and Writer's Network*. Retrieved June 26, 2011, from http://www.suite101.com/content/will-cloud-computing-be-the-future-for-it-a327753

Torrens, H. (2008, October). Coming to terms with cloud computing. *Application Development Trends* Retrieved April 23, 2011, from http://adtmag.com/articles/2008/10/02/coming-to-terms-with-cloud-computing.aspx

Wordpress.com Weblog. (2008, September). *Life in the cloud, living with cloud computing.* Wordpress.com. Retrieved April 23, 2011, from http://computinginthecloud.wordpress.com/2008/09/25/utility-cloud-computingflashback-to-1961-prof-john-mccarthy/

ADDITIONAL READING

AWS Security and Compliance Center. (n.d.). *Amazon Web services*. Retrieved April 23, 2011, from http://aws.amazon.com/security/

Badger, L., & Grance, T. (2010, May). *Standards acceleration to jumpstart adoption of cloud computing*. National Institute of Standards and Technology. Retrieved April 23, 2011, from http://www.nist.gov/itl/cloud/upload/nist_cloud_computing_forum-badger_grance.pdf

Baumgartner, J., & Borg, S. (2007). *The US-CCU cyber-security check list.* The U.S. Cyber Consequences Unit, Washington. Retrieved April 23, 2011, from http://www.usccu.us/documents/US-CCU%20Cyber-Security%20Check%20List%202007.pdf

Cloud Security Alliance. (2010). *Domain 10: Guidance for application security* v.2.1. Cloud Security Alliance. Retrieved April 23, 2011, from http://www.cloudsecurityalliance.org/guidance/csaguide-dom10-v2.10.pdf

Privacy Committee. (2010, August). *Privacy recommendations for the use of cloud computing by federal departments and agencies.* The U.S. CIO. Retrieved April 23, 2011, from http://www.cio.gov/Documents/Privacy-Recommendations-Cloud-Computing-8-19-2010.docx

SANTA FE Group. (2010, October). *Evaluating cloud risk for the enterprise: A shared assessments guide.* The Shared Assessments Program. Retrieved April 23, 2011, from http://www.sharedassessments.org/media/pdf-EnterpriseCloud-SA.pdf

Stoneburner, G., Goguen, A., & Feringa, A. (2002, July). *Risk management guide for information technology systems* (800-30). National Institute of Science and Technology. Retrieved April 23, 2011, from http://csrc.nist.gov/publications/nistpubs/800-30/sp800-30.pdf

Swanson, M., Hash, J., & Bowen, P. (2004, May). *Guide for developing security plans for federal information systems* (800-18). National Institute of Science and Technology. Retrieved April 23, 2011, from http://csrc.nist.gov/publications/nistpubs/800-18-Rev1/sp800-18-Rev1-final.pdf

Swanson, M., Wohl, A., Pope, L., Grance, T., Hash, J., & Thomas, T. (2002, June). *Contingency planning guide for information technology systems* (800-34). National Institute of Science and Technology. Retrieved April 23, 2011, from http://csrc.nist.gov/publications/nistpubs/800-34-rev1/sp800-34-rev1_errata-Nov11-2010.pdf

KEY TERMS AND DEFINITIONS

Accreditation: Decision by a senior agency official to authorize operation of an information system based on the implementation of an agreed-upon set of security controls.

Assurance: A confidence that the set of intended controls are effective in an information system environment.

Certification: A comprehensive assessment of the security controls in an information system to determine the extent of the correct implementation and operation of the controls, and if it produces the desired outcome with respect to meeting the security requirements for the system.

Grid Computing: The use of processing power and cycles of many computers in a network to process large amount of data at the same time to solve a scientific or technical problem.

Middleware: Set of software components and utilities that sit between operating systems, COTS, database and custom applications providing set of services that enable passing data between heterogeneous networks.

Multi-Tenancy: An enterprise environment that hosts applications and data from different organizations on same physical infrastructure.

Non-Repudiation: Assurance that the sender will receive proof of delivery and recipient will receive proof of sender's identity for information sent by sender to recipient so neither can later deny having processed the information.

Risk: The level of impact on organizational operations, assets, or individuals resulting from a threat and the likelihood of that threat on the operation of an information system.

Risk Management: The process of managing risks resulting from the impacts of changes in people, process, technologies, environments, policies, standards, and regulation on the operation of an information system environment.

Service Level Agreement (SLA): A contractual agreement between a service provider and a service consumer about responsibilities of each for providing services that guarantees availability and performance of the Cloud environment in accordance with required service levels.

Threat: Any circumstance or event such as unauthorized access, destruction, disclosure, modification of information, and/or denial of service that can adversely affect organizational operations, assets, and individuals.

Vendor Lock-In: Dependency on proprietary middleware including Application Programming Interface (API), protocols and data formats, and service interfaces developed and provided by Cloud vendor and difficulty in moving from one Cloud provider to another Cloud provider.

Virtualization: The use of software that allows running multiple operating system images at the same time on hardware (server, workstation).

Vulnerability: A weakness in an information system internal controls or procedures that any threat actors can exploit or trigger to comprise the information system environment.

Chapter 3
Cloud–Enabled Software Testing Based on Program Understanding

Chia-Chu Chiang
University of Arkansas at Little Rock, USA

Shucheng Yu
University of Arkansas at Little Rock, USA

ABSTRACT

Cloud computing provides an innovative technology that enables Software as a Service (SaaS) to its customers. With cloud computing technologies, a suite of program understanding tools is suggested to be deployed in a cloud to aid the generation of test cases for software testing. This cloud-enabled service allows customers to use these tools through an on-demand, flexible, and pay-per-use model. Lastly, the issues and challenges of cloud computing are presented.

INTRODUCTION

The quality of software testing lies in the use of effective test cases. Creating effective test cases requires the in-depth study of the application for which test cases are being generated. In this chapter, a suite of tools developed to aid the understanding of programs is suggested to be hosted on a cloud with the innovative technology of cloud computing. This suite of tools on the cloud provides a cloud-enabled service to customers without the need to purchase the tools.

Most importantly, customers can use the service through the on-demand, flexible, and pay-per-use model. The purpose of this chapter is to propose a technical solution for designing a cloud-based environment that enables detailed understanding of the programs in the portfolio and further aids the generation of test cases for software testing.

This chapter is organized as follows: First, the needs of program understanding for software testing are explained. Following that, reverse engineering techniques for program comprehension are briefly overviewed. A suite of automated

DOI: 10.4018/978-1-4666-2536-5.ch003

program understanding tools is presented. Then, a cloud-based platform with its implementation alternatives for hosting the tools is given. Later, the issues and challenges of cloud computing are presented. Customers should be aware that cloud computing has limitations. They should carefully evaluate these trade-offs before making decisions to migrate their proprietary programs into cloud computing.

BACKGROUND ON PROGRAM COMPREHENSION

Software testing serves to discover defects in the software where the outputs do not meet the expected results or fail to meet the user requirements. One essential activity of software testing is creating test cases. Two major software testing techniques that include white-box and black-box testing are used to generate test cases. The white-box testing generates the test cases from the programs. The black-box testing generates the test cases from the specifications and designs. Test cases are not created from the source code. For both software testing techniques, program (specification) understanding is a key activity in the testing process. Programmers can understand a program by reading its documentation (such as specification and design documents), reading the source code, or just executing the program. Reading the documents can either be effective or misleading. Unfortunately, one of the major problems of documentation is keeping the documents current to reflect the changes of the code. If the documents are outdated, reading the documentation for program understanding is not a good idea. Executing a program to understand the program's dynamic behavior can dramatically improve understanding which cannot be assimilated from reading the source code alone. However, the knowledge of the program mainly lies in the source code. Currently, programmers still count on reading the source code to gain knowledge about a program.

Several reverse engineering techniques and tools have been developed to help automate knowledge extraction from the programs used for program understanding (Bellay & Gall, 1997; Chikofsky & Cross, 1990; Gannod & Cheng, 1999; Zvegintzov, 1997). The techniques of reverse engineering are applied to automate program understanding by analyzing a system (1) to identify the system's components, their interrelationships, and (2) to create representations of the system in another form or at a higher level of abstraction (Chikofsky & Cross, 1990). The outputs of reverse engineering include structure chart, module calling hierarchy, data dictionary, data flow dependence, and control flow dependence. The knowledge about the programs is embedded in these artifacts. Programmers gain the understanding of programs by reading these artifacts.

Existing reverse engineering techniques mainly work on code for white-box testing. These reverse engineering techniques can be classified into two categories: static and dynamic analyses. Static analysis relies on code and its associated documentation that can be broken down into formal and informal methods. A formal method generates a formal specification in mathematical notations such as logic, set, and axioms from source code (Gannod & Cheng, 1996). An informal method for reverse engineering can be classified into two categories: plan-based and parsing-based approaches. The plan-based approaches automate the recognition of abstract concepts in source code using a library of programming plan templates and concepts with top-down and bottom-up search strategies (Abd-El-Hafiz & Basili, 1996; Woods & Yang, 1996). To date, industrial adoption of formal methods is still limited. In addition, many legacy systems have the problems of delocalized plans caused by enhancements and patches as the systems evolve (Bennett, 1995; Rugaber, Stirewalt, & Wills, 1995). Therefore, most plan-based approaches are limited as well. The parsing-based approach is usually applied to most programming languages. A parsing-based approach analyzes the syntactic structure of a program using a parsing-based technique to produce a variety of outputs for program understanding (Zvegintzov, 1997).

Dynamic analysis focuses on program execution where the visualization of program execution helps understand a system's entities with their calling relationships and the system's dynamic behaviors. However, understanding a program by viewing its execution behavior is often overwhelmed with a large amount of traces. Several methods have been developed to reduce the traces and make the traces more tractable and visualization more manageable (Cornrlissen, Zaidman, & Van Deursen, 2011; Lanza & Ducasse, 2003; Mesbah, Van Deursen, & Lenselink, 2012).

Very few reverse engineering techniques are developed to support black-box testing. Without the formality of specification and design, it would be difficult to automate the analysis on them. Nevertheless, some researchers working on formal specifications have devoted their efforts to the automated generation of test cases from a formal specification (Edwards, 2001).

SOFTWARE ARCHITECTURE WITH TOOLS FOR PROGRAM COMPREHENSION

The architecture of a software system defines the system in terms of components and relationships among the components (Shaw & Garlan, 1996). A software architecture with a suite of tools presented to automate program understanding is shown in Figure 1. A centralized repository is designed where the knowledge of the tested programs via reverse engineering is populated into the repository. The centralized repository serves as a coordination tool for sharing the information. The information in the repository can be queried using a database query language. Automated test case generation is based on the information in the repository. The reverse engineering tools are the software components for program understanding.

Figure 1. Repository-based software architecture

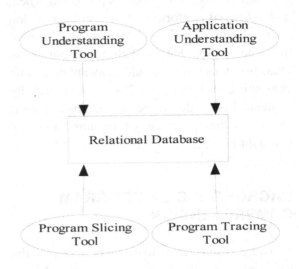

A commercial software vendor has implemented these tools using the parsing-based approach to support the understanding of tested programs. These tools mainly target legacy applications in COBOL, PL/1, and Assembly.

The program understanding tool identifies all the program structures, control flows, execution paths, data usages and relationships of a program. The information can be used to expose program anomalies including data items not used in logic paths, recursive logic, non-executable logic, and fall-through logic between labels. The application understanding tool identifies all the entities of an application and the relationship between those entities. The entities may include programs, files, databases, JCL (Job Control Language), load modules, copybooks, and data items. The cross reference information helps determine which files and databases need to be accessed in which programs for test case generation. The tool also provides the list of data items that are affected by the change of a data item. The program tracing tool allows users to step through the code one statement or paragraph at a time, run to breakpoints, and execute entire perform ranges with a single command. The tool also allows the users to apply the changes to the original source code or alter program logic. In the test session, the tool enables the users to review program execution and pinpoint the locations where erroneous data values were set. The program slicing tool divides large, complex programs into small, single-function programs or callable modules based on functionality. Instead of trying to understand a whole program, this tool helps users understand the program in a modular fashion.

A parsing-based approach is used to implement the tools in Figure 1. A program is parsed into a tree structure where the control flow graph, control dependence graph, and data dependence graph are generated. From these three graphs, a program structure, control flow dependency, execution flow, and data dependency are extracted from a program.

A control flow graph (CFG) is a directed graph where the vertices represent basic blocks and edges represent a possible transfer of control flow from one basic block to another. A basic block is a sequence of contiguous statements without branches or labels in the block. A CFG represents an algorithmic solution to a given problem. A CFG is denoted a quadruple CFG = <V, E, Entry, Exit>, where <V, E> represents a directed graph consisting of a set of nodes (statements) V and a set of edges E, where each edge $e \in E$ is an ordered pair of nodes with a direction. Entry $\in$ V is a single entry that reaches every other node in the CFG. Exit is a single exit node in V that is reachable from every other node in the CFG. A CFG represents a program while edges represent the flow of the control. A conditional branch is represented by a node with two or more successors.

A control dependence graph (CDG) is a directed graph CDG = <V, E>, where V is a set of nodes (statements) and E is a set of edges, where each edge $e \in E$ is an ordered pair of nodes. A CDG shows the presence of branch statements, when the Boolean value is used in a branch statement can determine whether or not the statement is executed. An edge $e \in E$ denoted as X →^{CD} Y

indicates Y is control dependent on X, where X $\in$ V and Y $\in$ V. A control dependence graph is used to capture the conditions controlling the execution code in the program.

A data dependence graph (DDG) is a quadruple DDG = <CFG, V, D, U>, where CFG is a control flow graph representing a program P. Each node n in CFG corresponds to a statement in Program P. V is the set of variables that appear in the program P. Then, D is a subset of V whose values are defined at node n. A variable $d \in D$ (definition) is defined at node n, if an execution of n assigns a value to d. U is also a subset of V whose values are used at node n. A variable $u \in U$ (use) is used at node n if an execution of n requires the value of u to be evaluated. A use-definition chain (UD chain) consists of a use, u, of a variable, and all the definitions, d, of that variable that can reach that use without any other intervening definitions. A definition-use chain (DU chain) consists of a definition, d, of a variable and all the uses, u, reachable from that definition without any other intervening definitions.

Reverse engineering for program understanding is performed by constructing a combined data and control dependence graph of the program and then traversing the graph to select the interest of statements and data via control and/or data dependence edges. The results of data and control dependence analysis are a set of statements within sequence, selection or repetition structures that directly or indirectly create, use, or modify output data values. The collection of outputs is populated into a database as a repository for storing program knowledge. An example of the data and control dependence is shown in Figure 2.

Figure 2 shows a UD chain of C where UD, STMT, and SYM represent use-definition chain, statement number, and the symbol index to the symbol table. The variable C defined in statement 22 depends on the value of B (use B) where B is defined in statement 19 or 16 depending on the value of I.

Figure 2. An example of data and control dependence with respect to <22, C>

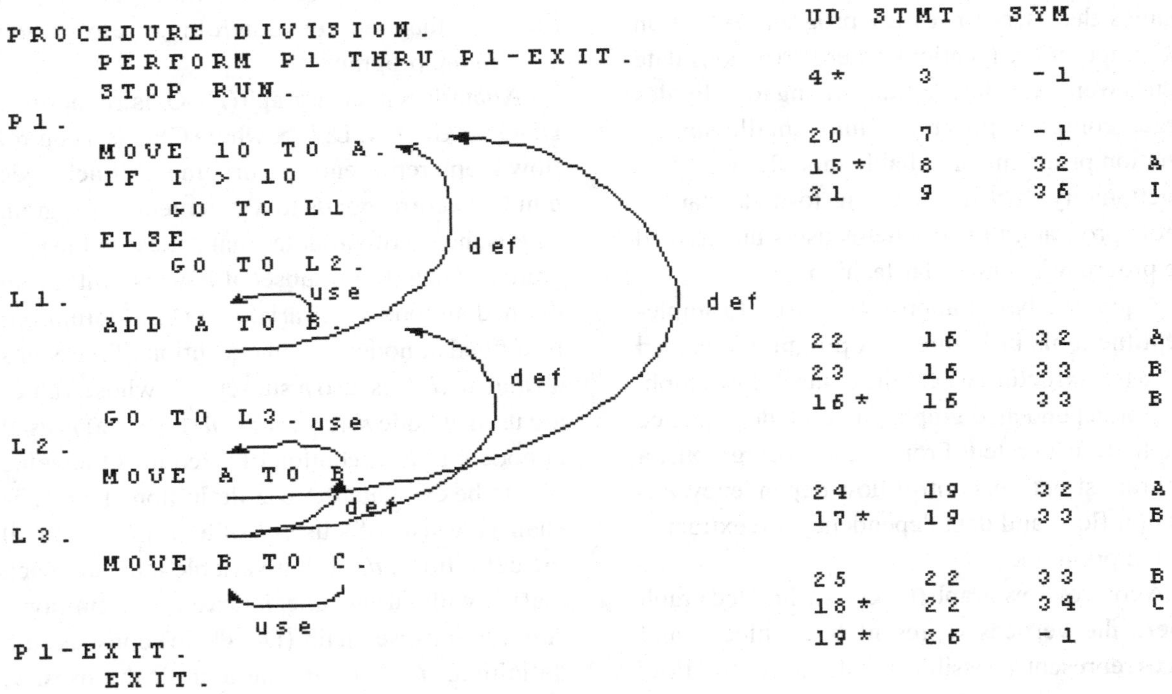

```
PROCEDURE DIVISION.                          UD  STMT    SYM
     PERFORM P1 THRU P1-EXIT.
     STOP RUN.                                4 *    3      -1
P1.
     MOVE 10 TO A.                           20      7      -1
     IF I > 10                               15 *    8      32    A
          GO TO L1                           21      9      36    I
     ELSE
          GO TO L2.
L1.                                          22     16      32    A
     ADD A TO B.                             23     16      33    B
                                             16 *    16      33    B
     GO TO L3.
L2.
     MOVE A TO B.                            24     19      32    A
                                             17 *    19      33    B
L3.
     MOVE B TO C.                            25     22      33    B
                                             18 *    22      34    C
P1-EXIT.                                     19 *    26      -1
     EXIT.
```

CLOUD COMPUTING

Cloud computing is an innovative IT computing model which is a collection of entities including humans, equipments, and software capable of providing required services to users with the pay-per-use strategy. A definition of could computing is given by Mell and Grance:

Cloud computing is a model for enabling ubiquitous, convenient, on-demand network access to a shared pool of configurable computing resources (e.g., networks, servers, storage, applications, and services) that can be rapidly provisioned and released with minimal management effort or service provider interaction (Mell & Grance, 2011).

Cloud computing exhibits five essential features (Mell & Grance, 2011): on-demand self-service, broad network access, resource pooling, rapid elasticity, and measured service. Today, many companies are striving to cope with rapid business changes such as changes in user requirements and business operations. Competitiveness requires companies to be able to modify or improve their IT systems in a relatively short period of time. Traditional computing fails to address this issue. Cloud computing offers a potential solution to companies for dealing rapid changes to their IT systems. Companies can use the cloud to rapidly scale up or down by the pay-per-use model without having to purchase equipments that are often underutilized.

A cloud can be public or private. In a public cloud, the cloud services are available to the public over the Internet. A company may build a private cloud for its proprietary use. Cloud computing can be classified into three categories based on the service provided: infrastructure cloud, platform cloud, and application cloud. The infrastructure cloud provides virtual server instance APIs (Application Program Interfaces) to start, stop, access, and configure the virtual servers and storage. Amazon EC2 (Elastic Computing Cloud) is an example of the infrastructure as the service that allows a company to gain the computing and storage capacity as is needed (Amazon Web Services, 2012). The platform cloud provides a service that allows companies to create and install the software and products on the provider's infrastructure. Companies might be required to follow the standards of creation and installation in the cloud. Force.com is an example of the platform cloud as a service. The application cloud provides a service that allows companies to use an application. Salesforce.com is an example of the application cloud as a service.

TOOLS ON A CLOUD FOR PROGRAM UNDERSTANDING

The suggested tools depicted in Figure 1 can be installed on a platform cloud provided by a cloud computing service provider. Amazon platform cloud provides the services such as elastic computing cloud, simple DB, and simple storage solution

(S3) for the testing activities. First, companies can create an Amazon EC2 instance and save it as a permanent server image called Amazon Machine Image (AMI). Elastic computing cloud allows companies to launch new servers from the image to create virtual machines to carry out the computing activities. Elastic computing cloud provides computing resources as needed to process data. SimpleDB provides a Web service for storing, processing, and querying data in a database. Simple storage service allows companies to access or retrieve the data from the storage. Figure 3 shows a diagram of Amazon EC2 instances for program comprehension tasks.

Implementation Feasibility

There are several alternatives for deploying the proposed tools shown in Figure 1 to a cloud. Several research projects provide open source for the development of clouds. OpenStack (OpenStack, 2012) is an Infrastructure as a Service (IaaS) that offers hardware level virtualization and provides for bare computing and storage resources on demand. StackOps (StackOps, 2012) is a Platform as a Service (PaaS) that provides an improved OpenStack option for developing and managing

Figure 3. Tools for program understanding on Amazon EC2 instances

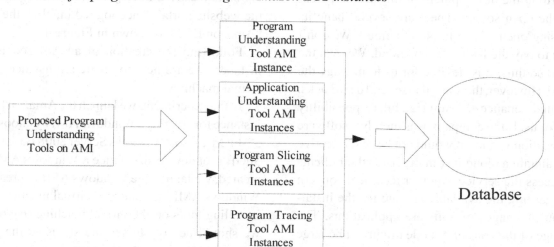

cloud computing applications. Other open source cloud computing options for the construction and management of clouds include Eucalyptus (Nurmi et al., 2009), Nimbus (Nimbus, 2012), and OpenNebula (OpenNebula, 2012). Eucalyptus implements an IaaS private cloud that is accessible via an API compatible with Amazon EC2 and Amazon S3. Nimbus implements an IaaS which is compatible with Amazon EC2 and Amazon S3. Nimbus mainly targets scientific applications such as batch schedulers, best-effort allocations, and support for proxy credentials. OpenNebula implements an IaaS cloud based on VMware (VMware, 2012), Xen (Xen, 2012), and KVM (KVM, 2012) for virtualized data storages. In order to study the feasibility of successfully implementing a cloud using open source, we have implemented a prototype using OpenStack. This prototype successfully demonstrates the possibility of application executions on both Windows and Linux operating systems. This experimental cloud hosts two computers with the virtualization technology where one is configured as the cloud controller node and the other one is the compute node. An image of Windows XP is uploaded to the controller node. With the XP, the images of applications are then uploaded to the system including Word and Microsoft Visual Studio. We have experienced some positives and negatives regarding the development of this prototype using the open source. There are several benefits of using open source to build a cloud. We don't have to pay the fee to use the cloud. We own the cloud so thus, it is flexible for us to manage the cloud. However, there are also several drawbacks. The maintenance of a cloud is a full responsibility job for us. If the company was merely a software application vendor, it would not be cost effective to maintain a cloud just in order for their clients to access the service. Another technical concern is regarding the available storage for the installation of images of software applications. The storage of the controller node might not be large enough to host the images of the applications you

want to upload to the node. Therefore, we recommend another alternative to deploy the tools to a commercial cloud and pay the nominal fee to the cloud provider.

Commercial clouds provide different kinds of virtual machine instances. For example, Amazon AMIs are preconfigured with an increasing list of operating systems such as Windows Server and variants of Linux system. Installing the suggested tools on selected AMIs makes no difference with installing other applications. With the tools available for use, companies can use applications that are hosted online (enabling them to lower their costs by paying only for what they use), enjoy seamless and painless upgrades in functionality, and integrate easily with their existing data and systems.

We conducted an experiment for installing a program understanding tool called Source Insight (Source Insight, 2012) on Amazon EC2 for its feasibility. Source Insight parses an object-oriented program and presents reference trees, class inheritance diagrams, and call trees to the users. A centralized repository is maintained to store the artifacts. The steps to deploy the tool are described in the following sections and the same steps can be applied to install the suggested tools depicted in Figure 1. First, we are required to create an Amazon EC2 instance. To do this, we log on to the AWS management console through the website portal. Once logged in, click the tab "Amazon EC2" as shown in Figure 4.

Following the creation of an Amazon EC2 instance, we are next to create an instance of a virtual machine.

In the experiment, we launch the Amazon EC2 instance for creating a Windows AMI by choosing 32-bit Microsoft Windows Server 2008 Base with 30GB root device size. Once a Windows AMI is created, we launch the Windows AMI to create a Windows AMI instance as a virtual machine for installing tools on the virtual machine. By now, we should be able to see the status of the just launched Windows AMI instance indicated as

Figure 4. Amazon EC2 management console

"running" on the AWS EC2 management console. Once the Windows AMI instance is running, we then set a login password for this Windows AMI instance. This Windows AMI instance is now up and running and ready for the installation of tools. See Figure 5 and Figure 6.

In this experiment, we demonstrate the installation of Source Insight to the virtual machine for its technical feasibility. We log on to the Windows AMI instance and download the executable installation package of Source Insight from the software's website. By double clicking the executable

Figure 5. List of AMIs

Figure 6. Screen shot of remotely logged on windows AMI

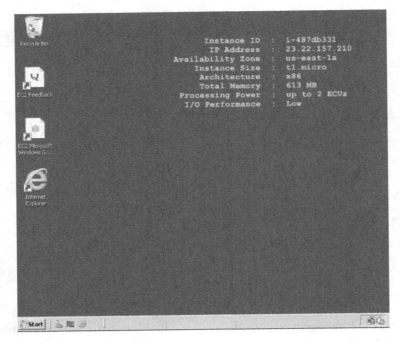

icon, we start the installation process. After the installation of the tool is done, we can launch the image of Source Insight for use.

From the results of this experiment, the steps of installation of Source Insight can be applied to deploy the suggested tools to the AMI instance. To deploy the suggested tools to Amazon EC2, we can start multiple virtual machine instances on Amazon EC2. These virtual machine instances will host the images of the suggested tools for program comprehension as shown in Figure 3. This is similar to making images of our local operation system, but the process of duplicating such images in the cloud is much more convenient. Compared to the experiment of building a cloud from open source, this task saves us a lot of effort and there is no need to maintain the cloud. The cloud provider is responsible for the maintenance of the cloud. However, we are paying the fee to use the cloud.

Challenges and Recommendations

There are several trade-offs that companies need to be aware of when planning a migration of software testing activities into a cloud computing environment (Hofmann & Woods, 2010). Companies will no longer have control of the infrastructures and platforms controlled by the cloud providers. Furthermore, current cloud providers offer unique and proprietary data storages, creating problems when companies attempt to transfer data from one cloud provider to another. Systems running on the cloud are not guaranteed to meet performance stability and longer delay may occur and create problems for performance. The lack of well-defined service-level agreements between cloud providers is another problem. Thus said, the biggest concern for a company is cloud security which includes the abuse of cloud computing, insecure software, malicious insiders, technological vulnerabilities, data loss, traffic hijacking, and unknown risk profiles. Software testing services hosted by a cloud are subject to system Byzantine failures and/or malicious attacks. The quality of the testing results can potentially be compromised. Moreover, the integrity of the database that stores program knowledge shall be assured for correct software testing. Existing solutions for data integrity protection (Wang et al., 2009) are usually based on cryptographic primitives and applicable for static data. Their applicability to applications like software testing, which involves dynamic transactional data with frequent data read/write operations, is still limited. Companies should carefully evaluate these trade-offs before making decisions to migrate their programs into cloud computing for software testing.

We proposed a suite of tools for program understanding to be hosted in a cloud in this chapter. The suggested tools for program understanding help the generation of test cases for software testing. These cloud-enabled tools provide companies with services through a pay-per-use model. However, there may be challenges that software testing tool vendors must initially overcome (Wei & Blake, 2010). First, the quality of services depends on both service providers and cloud providers. What happens when a service needs to cross different clouds? Current cloud providers provide proprietary APIs for cloud computing. Thus, testing tool vendors are unable to deploy their testing services to different clouds. The future development of standard cloud APIs should allow testing tool vendors to deploy their services to different clouds owned by different cloud computing providers. Second, it is difficult for testing tool vendors to ensure a certain level of security in public cloud computing environments. Providing confidentiality of tested programs might be a challenge. Nevertheless, companies can keep their tested programs confidential by running a private cloud. Third, current cloud computing providers do not provide services to monitor the services running on their clouds. Companies are responsible for monitoring their own services. Fourth, interpretation of testing services and data may be defined differently by different test tool

vendors. Ontologies would help clarify the syntax and semantics of different testing services and the stored data in nodes by testing tool vendors and cloud providers.

FUTURE RESEARCH DIRECTIONS

Since the cost reduction is the primary benefit of cloud adoption, it is expected to see growth in cloud adoption among business companies; especially for large companies (Lockheed Martin, 2010). We are also expecting to see growth in cloud-based software testing. However, the lack of cloud awareness and understanding mostly hampers cloud adoption. In addition, very few commercial tools are deployed to the cloud. We suggest that cloud-based test beds for software testing activities may be created to pave the way for more awareness. The increasing awareness of cloud computing for software testing will pave the way for more cloud adoptions. We would like to see more vendors that are willing to deploy their tools to the cloud that allows companies to have hands-on experience in cloud computing and discover the value from it. We also expect further progress in research on automated software testing (Candea et al., 2010) with which automated software testing can be provided as services in the cloud. In addition, it is imperative to have practical security solutions that efficiently support applications such as software testing which involves dynamic transactional data.

CONCLUSION

Business companies usually face the many challenges of rapid change and increase in business and technology complexity. Thus, business companies are often required to modify their business operations in order to respond to new needs. In addition, the changes need to be made without compromising the quality of the services. Cloud computing can help companies deal with changes quickly and cost effectively.

Cloud computing for software testing activities, including automated test case generation and automated software testing, ensures rapid and immediate feedback while creating business values rather than incurring costs. Companies can perform software testing economically in terms of resources, time, and cost. This paper discussed economical practices in software testing via cloud computing. A suit of tools for program understanding were suggested to be installed on a cloud that extracts the knowledge of programs into a centralized repository. The knowledge about programs helps programmers generate test cases for software testing. These cloud-enabled tools provide services on a pay-per-use basis. The implementation methods of a cloud were presented to build a private or public cloud. A build of a private cloud was illustrated with the use of open source. A build of a public cloud was presented with the application of Amazon EC2. The concerns of building a private or public cloud were discussed. The advantages and disadvantages of using a private or public cloud were also presented.

REFERENCES

Abd-El-Hafiz, S., & Basili, V. (1996). A knowledge-based approach to the analysis of loops. *IEEE Transactions on Software Engineering*, *22*(5), 339–360. doi:10.1109/32.502226

Amazon Web Services. (2012). *Amazon elastic compute cloud* (Amazon EC2). Retrieved from http://aws.amazon.com/ec2/

Bellay, B., & Gall, H. (1997). A comparison of four reverse engineering tools. In I. Baxter & A. Quilici (Eds.), *Working Conference on Reverse Engineering* (pp. 2-11). Los Alamitos, CA: IEEE Computer Society Press.

Bennett, K. (1995). Legacy systems: Coping with success. *IEEE Software*, *12*(1), 19–23. doi:10.1109/52.363157

Candea, G., Bucur, S., & Zamfir, C. (2010). Automated software testing as a service. *ACM Symposium on Cloud Computing* (pp. 155-160). New York, NY: ACM.

Chikofsky, E. J., & Cross, J. H. II. (1990). Reverse engineering and design recovery: A taxonomy. *IEEE Software*, *7*(1), 13–17. doi:10.1109/52.43044

Cornelissen, B., Zaidman, A., & van Deursen, A. (2011). A controlled experiment for program comprehension through trace visualization. *IEEE Transactions on Software Engineering*, *37*(3), 341–355. doi:10.1109/TSE.2010.47

Edwards, S. H. (2001). A framework for practical, automated black-box testing of component-based software. *Software Testing, Verification, and Reliability*, *11*(2), 97–111. doi:10.1002/stvr.224

Gannod, G., & Cheng. (1996). Strongest postcondition semantics as the formal basis for reverse engineering. *The Journal of Automated Software Engineering*, *3*(1-2), 1–27.

Gannod, G., & Cheng, B. (1999). A framework for classifying and comparing software reverse engineering and design recovery techniques. In F. Balmas, M. Blaha, & S. Rugaber (Eds.), *Working Conference on Reverse Engineering* (pp. 77-88). Los Alamitos, CA: IEEE Computer Society Press.

Gruber, T. (2009). Ontology. In Liu, L., & Özsu, M. T. (Eds.), *Encyclopedia of database systems*. New York, NY: Springer-Verlag.

Hofmann, P., & Woods, D. (2010). Cloud computing: The limits of public clouds for business applications. *IEEE Internet Computing*, *14*(6), 90–93. doi:10.1109/MIC.2010.136

KVM. (2012). *Website*. Retrieved from http://www.linux-kvm.org/page/Main_Page

Lanza, M., & Ducasse, S. (2003). Polymetric views – A lightweight visual approach to reverse engineering. *IEEE Transactions on Software Engineering*, *29*(9), 782–795. doi:10.1109/TSE.2003.1232284

Lockheed Martin. (2010). *Awareness, trust and security to shape government cloud adoption*. Retrieved from http://www.lockheedmartin.com/data/assets/isgs/documents/CloudComputingWhitePaper.pdf

Martin, B. (1996). Technological vulnerability. *Technology in Society*, *12*(4), 511–523. doi:10.1016/S0160-791X(96)00029-2

Maybury, M. (2009). *How to protect digital assets from malicious insiders*. Retrieved from http://www.thei3p.org/research/mitremi.html

Mell, P., & Grance, T. (2011). *The NIST definition of cloud computing. Special publication 800-145, National Institute of Standards and Technology (NIST)*. Information Technology Laboratory.

Mesbah, A., Van Deursen, A., & Lenselink, S. (2012). Crawling Ajax-based web applications through dynamic analysis of user interface state changes. *ACM Transactions on the Web*, *6*(1), 3:1-3:29.

Nimbus. (2012). *Website*. Retrieved from http://workspace.globus.org

Nurmi, D., & Wolski, R. Grzegorczyk, Graziano Obertelli, G., Soman, S., Youseff, L., & Zagorodnov, D. (2009). The eucalyptus open-source cloud-computing system. *IEEE International Symposium on Cluster Computing and the Grid*, (pp. 124-131). Los Alamitos. CA: IEEE Computer Society Press.

OpenNebula. (2012). *Website*. Retrieved from http://www.opennebula.org

OpenStack. (2012). *Website*. Retrieved from http://openstack.org/

Rugaber, S., Stirewalt, K., & Wills, L. (1995). The interleaving problem in program understanding. In E. Chikofsky, L. Wills, & P. Newcomb (Eds.), *Working Conference on Reverse Engineering*, (pp. 166-175). Los Alamitos, CA: IEEE Computer Society Press.

Scott, M. (2008). *Tort liability for vendors of insecure software: Has the time finally come?* Retrieved from http://www.law.umaryland.edu/academics/journals/mdlr/print/articles/67-425.pdf

Shaw, M., & Garlan, D. (1996). *Software architecture: Perspectives on an emerging discipline*. Upper Saddle River, NJ: Prentice Hall.

Source Insight. (2012). *Website*. Retrieved from http://www.sourceinsight.com/

StackOps. (2012). *Website*. Retrieved from http://www.stackops.org/

VMware. (2012). *Website*. Retrieved from http://www.vmware.com/

Wang, Q., Wang, C., Li, J., Ren, K., & Lou, W. (2009). *Enabling public verifiability and data dynamics for storage security in cloud computing*. European Symposium on Research in Computer Security, Saint Malo, France.

Wei, Y., & Blake, M. B. (2010). Service-oriented computing and cloud computing. *IEEE Internet Computing*, *14*(6), 72–75. doi:10.1109/MIC.2010.147

Woods, S., & Yang, Q. (1996). The program understanding problem: Analysis and a heuristic approach. In T. Maibaum & M. V. Zelkowitz (Eds.), *International Conference on Software Engineering*, (pp. 6-15). Los Alamitos, CA: IEEE Computer Society Press.

Xen. (2012). *Website*. Retrieved from http://xen.org/

Zvegintzov, N. (1997). A resource guide to year 2000 tools. *Computer*, *30*(3), 58–63. doi:10.1109/2.573662

KEY TERMS AND DEFINITIONS

AMI (Amazon Machine Image): A pre-configured operating system and virtual application software which is used to create a virtual machine within the Amazon Elastic Compute Cloud (EC2).

API (Application Programming Interface): An interface format that a program provides to support requests for services to be made of it by another program.

Black-Box Testing: Test cases generated from specification or design for software testing.

Cloud Computing: Mell and Grance (Mell & Grance, 2011) define cloud computing as "A model for enabling ubiquitous, convenient, on-demand network access to a shared pool of configurable computing resources (e.g., networks, servers, storage, applications, and services) that can be rapidly provisioned and released with minimal management effort or service provider interaction."

Copybooks: Source code that can be copied or included into other programs.

Data Loss: Information in information systems is destroyed by failures or neglect in storage, transmission, or processing.

Elastic Computing Cloud (EC2): An infrastructure as a service that allows a company to gain the computing and storage capacity in the cloud as is needed.

Infrastructure as a Service (IaaS): A platform in which a company outsources the equipment used to support operations, including hardware, servers, storage, and networking components at pay-per-use service. The service provider owns the equipment and is responsible for housing, running, and maintaining it.

Insecure Software: Contains flaws that could allow violations of security policy. It requires the use of patches to fix known vulnerabilities (Scott, 2008).

Malicious Insider: Has legitimate access, privilege, or knowledge of information systems to adversely impact an organization's mission by taking action that compromises information confidentiality, integrity, and/or availability (Maybury, 2009).

Ontology: Defines a set of representational primitives with which to model a domain of knowledge or discourse (Gruber, 2009).

Platform as a Service (PaaS): Provides a computing service model to its clients including operating system, programming language execution environment, database, and web server. Developers can develop and run their applications on a cloud platform without buying and managing the underlying hardware and software layers.

Program Slicing: A technique for abstracting from program statements relevant to an interest of computation.

Reverse Engineering: Chikofsky and Cross (Chikofsky & Cross, 1990) define reverse engineering as "Reverse engineering is the process of analyzing a subject system to identify the system's components and their relationships and create representations of the system in another form or at a higher level of abstraction."

Software as a Service (SaaS): Software hosted by a service provider is made available to customers over the Internet.

Software Testing: The process of validating and verifying that the software meets its requirements.

Technological Vulnerability: Refers to the chance of failure of an entire technological system due to outside events (Martin, 1996).

Traffic Hijacking: Traffic on a network is intercepted and read by attackers on the network other than the sender and receiver.

Unknown Risk Profile: The threats are not listed in any order of severity.

White-Box Testing: Test cases generated from the code for software testing.

Chapter 4
Cloud-Based Testing for Context-Aware Cyber-Physical Systems

Christian Berger
University of Gothenburg, Sweden

ABSTRACT

Cloud-based applications like email services or office suites enable real-time collaboration and trace-ability for shared data from nearly anywhere by using a modern web-browser. Thus, a significant shift has happened to these common applications to focus only on their usage than on their maintenance. However, today's software development projects spend a noteworthy amount of resources to setup and maintain necessary development tools–over and over again. Thus, a similar shift for these development tools in the future would enable to spend valuable resources more on the actual project's goals than on the tools' maintenance. Especially development projects for cyber-physical systems, which interact with the real life's surroundings by relying on sensors and actuators, have specific needs when using cloud-based solutions. In this contribution, preconditions, design decisions, and limitations of a cloud-based testing approach for CPS are outlined and discussed on the example "Hesperia." "Hesperia" bases on the experiences from the development of "Caroline"–an autonomously driving vehicle for the 2007 DARPA Urban Challenge. "Hesperia" as a cloud-based testing approach was tested 2009 during the development of an autonomously driving vehicle at the University of California, Berkeley.

INTRODUCTION

Nowadays, cloud-based applications are *in vogue* for services, which were operated separately and individually in the past. Cloud computing bases on the fundamental idea that today's servers are sufficiently powerful so that the underlying hardware can be entirely encapsulated through

DOI: 10.4018/978-1-4666-2536-5.ch004

special CPU instructions. Thus, it is possible to run several instances of any major operating system (OS) independently without significant losses in their overall performance. This basic concept is called Infrastructure-as-a-Service (IaaS).

The separation of the OSes from the hardware CPU enables the migration from one real computation node to another node at run-time. Thus, the underlying computing power can be extended or reduced to match the required computation load–manually or even automatically as a software layer in terms of Platform-as-a-Service (PaaS). Therefore, the applications, which are running inside this environment, can react in an elastic manner on changing system loads.

Very popular applications are web-based email solutions or entire office suites, which are running on top of the PaaS. These applications realize the Software-as-a-Service (SaaS) principle. Furthermore, cloud-based office solutions often provide collaborative features to track changes or to work simultaneously. Thus, traditional workflows are not only simplified but also accelerated by using SaaS in public or private clouds.

However, the most popular experience for cloud-based solutions is focusing on end-user-related services. But, how can the modern software development benefit from those cloud-based approaches? To answer this question, the processes of today's software engineering must be analyzed to identify potential use cases. Some classical services, which are mandatory for any software development project nowadays, could already be successfully migrated into the cloud. Such services are for example a software artifacts' versioning system to track changes over time; furthermore, "build farms" are also available where computing nodes are compiling a set of source files with different configurations or even on different OSes and platforms to identify interoperability errors. Both services were successfully realized for example at "SourceForge" (Korecki, 2005) or by the "openSUSE Build Service" (Schroeter, 2009).

Nevertheless, the aforementioned services can be regarded as the backbone of a modern software development project for which a fully cloud-based solution is not necessarily required (low/none cloud-based solution). The other extreme is the developer's experience at the front-end site: Mandatory tools for editing source code are directly migrated into the cloud like Cloud9 IDE for JavaScript editing (von Wedel, 2011). These solutions also allow the execution of the created artifacts (full cloud-based solution). Thus, any

developer can participate by using a modern web browser only.

The former situation is the minimal tool support for a collaborative software development project and the latter is a cloud-based-only solution for a very specific problem domain. Between both extremes of cloud-based support, the cloud's potential must be evaluated for today's software engineering projects of any industrial sector. While there are projects whose development and especially testing processes can already migrated into the cloud with manageable effort, there are many other development projects whose software-driven functions rely mainly on sensors to perceive information about their surroundings to perform actions. These systems are called cyber-physical systems (CPS) whose required computation time is not an issue of performance but of correctness (Lee & Seshia, 2011). For using the cloud to support testing processes of these CPS for example, special requirements and conditions must be kept in mind.

On the example of car manufacturers, which are increasingly equipping their vehicles with software-intense functions to protect passengers, pedestrians, and bicyclists by using cameras, radars, and the like, their specific testing processes must be revised to be ready for the cloud. However, these processes base mainly on real vehicle test-drives, which are insufficient due to the following circumstances:

- The test processes depend on the system's surroundings, i.e. various, representable, and repeatable context situations are necessarily required.
- The system's overall complexity is still increasing for which an also increasing testing effort is mandatory.
- The quality assurance has to deal with variants in the system's setup due to changing sensors' and actuators mounting positions, software modules' deployments, and evolutions in the algorithms.

Regarding these circumstances, today's testing processes will be insufficient in the near future. The logical and consequent next step to test these CPS is to extend real vehicle test-drives by virtual test-drives which base on a simulation environment. For this step, some success stories already exist (Gietelink, Ploeg, Schutter, & Verhaegen, 2004).

However, problems remain with a simulation-based testing process. First, the initial setup is specific to a given project and its continuous maintenance is time-consuming. Next, the quality of questions, which can be answered by using simulations, depends directly on the quality of the modeled CPS together with its specific system's context. For example, a certain level of accuracy for the sensors' and surroundings' models is required to approve a specific release of a software function on simulative results only. But this level of accuracy is barely to achieve during a regular project's development process. Thus, only rudimentary simulations are used from which only simplified questions can be answered in the end.

However, the aforementioned limitations can be overcome by a cloud-based testing process, which is not only elastic to different simulation loads, but which also provides sound models for a CPS' interfaces and its surroundings. Thus, a cloud-based testing solution can simply be reused for similar development projects on the one hand and can easily be maintained centrally on the other hand.

On the example of the development of an autonomously driving vehicle for the 2007 DARPA Urban Challenge (Rauskolb et al., 2010; Berger, & Rumpe 2010) and its succeeding project at the University of California, Berkeley (Berger, 2010; Berger, & Rumpe, 2012a), preconditions, design decision, experiences, and results for a cloud-based testing solution are presented and discussed to extend real vehicle test-drives. Therefore, this contribution is structured as follows: First, the background of testing processes for CPS on the example of autonomously driving vehicles is given; next, architectural considerations for CPS

are discussed, which are mandatorily required to realize a cloud-based testing process. Afterwards, the development framework "Hesperia" for CPS is outlined on the example of the autonomously driving vehicle from the University of California, Berkeley; furthermore, results from its application within a cloud-based testing process are outlined and discussed.

As the running example in this contribution, software test processes on the example of autonomously driving vehicles are of major interest. These complex systems are still in the focus of research and development in academia and industry (Berger, & Rumpe, 2012b). Thus, experiences from the international competition 2007 DARPA Urban Challenge (Rumpe, Berger, & Krahn, 2006; Basarke, Berger, & Rumpe, 2007; Basarke, Berger, Homeier, & Rumpe, 2007; Rauskolb et al., 2010) are utilized to derive preconditions, requirements, and design decisions for the CPS development environment "Hesperia." "Hesperia" was used during the development of an autonomously driving vehicle at the Center of Hybrid and Embedded Software Systems (CHESS) at the University of California, Berkeley (Berger, 2010; Biermeyer et al., 2010). Results from that cloud-based testing process, which was enabled by "Hesperia," are discussed.

BACKGROUND

To foster the research in autonomously driving vehicles, DARPA carried out several major international competitions. In the 2005 Grand Challenge, the autonomously driving robot "Stanley" from Stanford University won the first prize (Montemerlo, Thrun, Dahlkamp, Stavens, & Strohband, 2006). During that challenge, participants had to demonstrate that they could safely handle stationary obstacle in rough environments. Having successfully demonstrated that robots could drive safely in stationary environments, DARPA announced in 2006 the Urban Challenge. Contrary to its preceding ones, the robotic vehicles had to deal safely with moving objects within an urban-like environment.

From the results of the site visit in April 2007 and due to their performance at the semi-finals, only eleven teams from initially 89 teams were selected to compete in the 2007 DARPA Urban Challenge Final Event, which was held on November 3, 2007. The final event was carried out at the former George Airforce Base in Victorville, CA. Besides all finalists, human drivers were additionally on the course at the same time to evaluate a robot vehicle's performance and to observe the overall safety. Team "Tartan Racing" from the Carnegie Mellon University with their vehicle "Boss" won the final event followed by "Junior" from Stanford University and "Odin" from Virginia Tech. Team "CarOLO" with their autonomously driving vehicle "Caroline" from the Technische Universitaet Braunschweig, Germany was among these finalists. Experiences and results from "Caroline" are discussed in the following (Rauskolb et al., 2010).

Due to similar sensors' setup of all contestants, the competition was mainly a software challenge to tackle unsafe and unreliable sensors' data for deriving robust driving decisions. Moreover, the software modules had to be developed in parallel in a very tight schedule but with high quality in the end. However, nearly every team had only one vehicle for testing purposes, and furthermore, real vehicle tests were time consuming, error-prone in their particular initial setup, and a test's repeatability could not be easily ensured to enable comparability between different software versions to track the software quality over time.

The above-mentioned observations, which are gathered from this international competition, are very similar to challenges with which all major vehicle manufacturers are faced today when they are developing vehicle functions, which rely on sensors to perceive information from a vehicle's surroundings. The main problem is that real vehicle tests are nowadays not sufficient anymore

to release safely complex and safety-critical vehicle functions. Instead, a paradigm shift can be observed (Pretschner, Broy, Krueger, & Stauner, 2007), which explicitly embraces virtual vehicle tests to evaluate a software function already at early stages and during the entire development with the goal to extend real vehicle test-drives.

As shown in Figure 1, different services during the software development for CPS can be identified. These services can be sorted qualitatively regarding their particular syntactic and semantic dependence on an artifact's particular content on the one hand and with respect to the level of the cloud-based solution on the other hand. For example, some tools are completely independent from an artifact's specific content like a versioning service, some depend only on its syntactic structure like a compiler, while tools which evaluate the implementation's conformance to a given requirements specification rely not only on the artifact's syntax but also on its semantics. While the next sections outline in greater detail achievements, experiences, and results for a cloud-based unit testing and simulation environment, a brief description of the other underlined services is given in the exemplary project for the development of an autonomously driving vehicle.

One of the most rudimentary services is a sound versioning solution to enable a unique identification of artifacts and their particular evolvement over time. On the one hand, this is important to support the packaging process to create installation bundles with the latest artifacts. On the other hand, every developer must be able to track changes easily, which are made to the source code to locate potentially faulty areas within the source code as quickly as possible. As shown in Figure 2, Subversion (Collins-Sussman, Fitzpatrick, & Pilato, 2004) was chosen for the "CarOLO" project as the centrally maintained versioning system due to its capabilities of transactional commits of entire change sets. Nowadays, alternatives like git (GIT, 2012) would also be appropriate.

Figure 1. Various services, which are used during a software development project, are classified wrt. Their level of semantic dependence from the artifact's particular content on the one hand and to the level of the cloud-based solution on the other hand. The underlined services and tools were used for the development of the autonomously driving vehicle "Caroline."

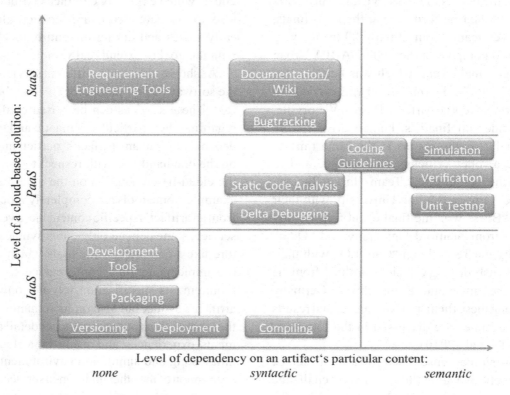

The versioning service was not only used to uniquely track changes of single source code files over time but also to track changes, which were made to all OSes of the autonomously driving vehicle. Therefore, we used FSVS (Tigris.org, 2011) to monitor changes, which were made to the OS' configuration and to backup them safely on the versioning service. However nowadays, we would consider using a file-system, which is able to take snapshots like Btrfs or ZFS, which we did not consider mature enough at that time.

Besides the aforementioned versioning system to track changes uniquely and independently from a particular artifact's content over time, we also wanted to monitor their quality at syntactic and semantic levels. While the latter is described in the following sections, the former relies only on

the compiler and a sound software construction description to generate the binary code. Because we used C and C++ to meet real-time requirements on the one hand, and to avoid drawbacks of Make on the other hand, we decided to rely on Cook (Miller, 2010) to build our artifacts in a parallelized and distributed manner.

Within the CarOLO project, a centralized server-based compilation to check the syntactic quality was carried out on a single host without any virtualization. In a succeeding project (Berger, 2010), the compilation service itself was hosted on the IaaS-layer which was realized by Xen (von Hagen, 2008) on an Ubuntu Dom0 and a Debian DomU. Thus, we were able to check OS updates before rolling them out on developer's and vehicle computers on the one hand. On the other hand,

Figure 2. Architecture of our cloud approaches to implement various services during the CarOLO project and a succeeding project at the University of California, Berkeley. During the former project, a single centralized server was used to host mandatory project's services; the latter project relied on a split approach which is depicted on the right hand side of the dashed vertical line.

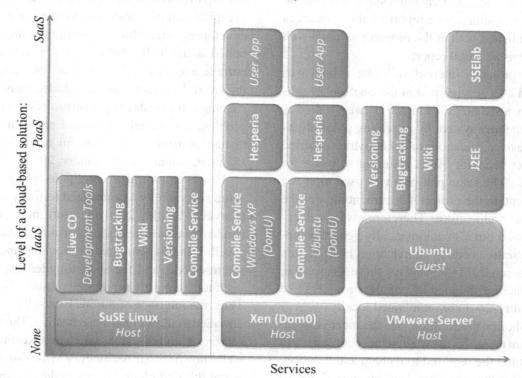

we could simply revert malfunctioning alternative libraries. Furthermore, we could simply migrate the software construction service to a more powerful hardware platform with nearly no downtime for the service and without any changes to the guest system itself. Moreover, the reporting front-end, which was used to publish results from the compilation service, could be separated from the build service and moved to a SaaS system. The entire setup of the virtualized services is shown in Figure 2. We used Xen (von Hagen, 2008) to realize all project's core services, which require semantic information about the artifacts. The development environment "Hesperia" provided this semantic information as part of the cloud. We used VMware to realize all semantically independent cloud-based services–for example the version-ing and reporting system. These semantically independent services were bundled to "SSELab" (SSELab, 2011), which is a content-independent platform to enable software engineering concepts and services.

Nowadays, nearly every major compiler is able to perform some rudimentary checks with the source code by evaluating the abstract syntax tree (AST). Together with our compilation service, we realized some quality monitoring measures already at the artifacts' syntax. Amongst others, potentially faulty code fragments like the usage of assignment over comparison operators within an if-statement could be identified at no significantly additional costs. Furthermore, coding guidelines as proposed by (Meyers, 1996; Meyers, 1997) were checked easily by the open source compiler g++

by using the corresponding arguments on the command line. Thus, the quality of software artifacts was improved significantly with ease whenever a developer added or changed some code on the central repository. The report of these changes was published both at the project's internal web site and as an email report.

The project's internal web site, which was realized as a service within the SaaS-layer provided by SSELab (SSELab, 2011), also served as a bug tracking system by providing possibilities to add, assign, and monitor tickets which describe incorrect behavior of the resulting software for example. The same platform was used to create and maintain the project's documentation of the software architecture. Therefore, we used not only a wiki but also automatically generated up-to-date source code documentation by Doxygen (van Heesch, 2011). Nowadays, these services can also either be obtained by popular providers like (Assembla, 2011) or maintained locally.

To shorten the duration, which is necessary for new team members to install, setup, configure, and understand the required tool chain and therefore to increase the individual learning curve's gradient, we modified the popular Ubuntu live DVD distribution by installing and setting up all required tools and applications. Thus, we provided a preconfigured development environment, which was ready to use for new team members without modifying their computers. Furthermore, we preserved the live DVD feature so that it could be installed easily including all our changes and configuration alongside with any already existing OS on a computer's hard drive. Furthermore, we also installed the live DVD into a VMware image, which was also included in our distribution, to enable the usage of the development environment parallel to a developer's regular system by simply using the popular VMware player application. Thus, we saved valuable time during the initial phase of our project and enabled individual team members to focus on the actual algorithms' challenges.

Besides these infrastructural services, a system for the testing artifacts during the development is required–for both the developers and at the central site as part of a build system. The former is required to rapidly test new features and functionalities at developers' site, which is configured and maintained individually, but the latter is required to enforce a regular and unattended testing to meet the overall project's quality goals. Thus, when running software development projects for related problems, a centrally provided and maintained testing platform is meaningful as outlined by (Riungu, Taipale, & Smolander, 2010).

However, several preconditions must be met to setup successfully a centralized testing platform. (Parveen, & Tilley, 2010) therefore mention independence between test cases, which are executed in a well-defined operational environment including the test code, and the system-under-test (SUT) itself together with its required run-time libraries. Thus, the interface of the SUT must be carefully designed to allow cloud-based testing. The authors refer to JUnit test cases, which are executed on a well-known virtual machine (JVM); however, Java is not the first choice for embedded systems or CPS. This aspect is elaborated in greater detail in the section *Cyber-Physical Systems in the Cloud*.

When regarding testing approaches for the running example of automotive applications, some frameworks are available to support the quality assurance. First, the Automotive Data and Time Triggered Framework (ADTF) as described in (Schabenberger, 2007) is an approach, which is inspired by Microsoft's Component Object Model to model the system under development (SUD) as interconnected and interoperating algorithms, which themselves are implemented C++. Following the criteria mentioned by (Parveen, & Tilley, 2010), this framework provides a well-known operational environment. Especially for CPS however, an approach is missing to support developers to model sensors, actuators, and the surroundings in an adequate manner, which is sufficiently detailed to answer questions posed to such a simulation environment.

The simulation environment *Virtual Test Drive*, which is provided by VIRES Simulationstechnologie GmbH, could be used to address the aforementioned drawbacks. This environment is already used by prominent automotive OEMs like AUDI AG or Daimler AG to drive virtually through a vehicle's environment. Furthermore, there exist some approaches, which use this environment to evaluate driver-assisting systems by providing synthetically generated data (von Neumann-Cosel, Nentwig, Lehmann, Speth, & Knoll, 2009). These approaches however rely on very rudimentary models for sensors, which restrict their parameters to viewing angle, direction, range, update frequency, and an arbitrarily chosen error model. Thus, only basic evaluations can be carried out, which are limited by these assumed simplifications.

To support the development of automotive applications, popular tools are available for simulating the environment of control algorithms especially for algorithms for the driving dynamics—for example CarMaker from IPG Automotive (IPG, 2011) and DYNAware from TESIS (TESIS DYNAware, 2011). However, these applications focus only on evaluating control algorithms, which base on differential equations, and which therefore require only a limited simulation of the surroundings. Thus, they are not applicable to virtualize the evaluation of complex CPS algorithms including their sensors in general.

Besides these toolkits with a focus on automotive applications, several other frameworks exist to support the development of algorithms especially for robot platforms, which are used for teaching purposes or for the RoboCup competition. An open source approach is Player/Stage/Gazebo (Gerkey, Vaughan, & Howard, 2003), which provides a simulation and development environment for experimental robotic platforms with standard sensors like sonar, laser, and cameras. A commercial alternative is Microsoft's Robotics

Developer Studio (Jewett, 2009) which provides a similar development environment with the focus on.Net and C# development. Both frameworks exhibit a clearly defined application programming interface (API), which enables their integration with cloud-based testing approaches as mentioned by (Parveen, & Tilley, 2010). Though, modeling a CPS' surroundings with appropriate sensors' and actuators' interfaces has only limited support.

However, the quality of virtual approaches for testing algorithms is the limiting factor for questions to be answered by such a simulation. Thus, not only a framework is required, which provides a clear API to allow transparent re-usage in various technical environments; even more the modeling of aspects, which are inherently coupled with CPS, must be supported properly. In the case of automotive functions, which rely on data from a vehicle's surroundings, not only sensors' and actuators' models must be specified with different details and physical properties but also the actual surroundings must be modeled with a sufficient quality to serve a function's sensors.

Besides these technical aspects, simulation environments are installed and configured over and over again for every new project. Thus, substantial re-use of gathered experiences is barely possible to increase the level of questions, which can be posed to simulations. Therefore, a centralized approach for testing and evaluating related algorithms of CPS is required to reduce maintenance efforts, to realize synergies between several projects, and to enhance the quality of the simulation by modeling sensors and actuators in a more realistic and thus physically correct manner.

Even recent publications like (Bertolino, 2007; Christie, 1999; Masticola, & Gall, 2008; Underseth, 2007) state that improved concepts as well as methods for integrating development and testing processes for realizing software-intensive embedded systems are necessary to assure the quality in the resulting systems. Referring to these, selected challenges for the software engineering especially for the field of embedded systems, which interact with their surroundings using sensors and actuators, can be summed up to the following demands:

Methodologies for Software Testing

Completing the actual development of software-intensive embedded systems, system tests are crucial for examining the SUD's quality by identifying malfunctions and errors. However, standardized organizational processes dealing with software testing including the integration of subsystems are partly unsuccessful often due to errors, which are detected often lately. According to Underseth (2007), one reason is the wrong allocation of resources between development and product testing. Thus, a centrally provided and maintained testing environment like a cloud-based approach would enable the standardization of testing processes among different but related projects.

Compositional Testing Using Test Oracles

According to (Bertolino, 2007), one major problem is to reuse previously generated test results to design or control further test cases. Moreover, for complex embedded systems, which do not rely only on continuous input data for computing continuous or discrete output data, but which also depend on time or previous computation cycles, even more complex test oracles including simulated elements from the embedded system's surroundings are necessary to evaluate the software and system quality correctly.

Rigorous Integration of Simulation

Referring to Christie (1999) in conjunction with Masticola, & Gall (2008), simulations shall be the major part during system development. Nowadays, MATLAB/Simulink for designing control algorithms allows the stepwise execution of models even at early development stages. However, complex systems require appropriate

testing methodologies because they rely heavily on concepts and patterns of modern programming languages like elements of object-oriented software engineering (Gamma, Helm, Johnson, & Vlissides, 1994) or processing of embedded domain specific languages (DSL) for example. Thus, a centrally provided testing approach reduces the individual project's effort in setting up and configuring a complex simulation environment by sharing and growing common knowledge.

Automation

Finally, the aforementioned aspects must be automatable to support not only the developer's daily work. Moreover, any tooling must be capable to get technically integrated in any software construction process to allow an automated execution before deployment. On the other hand, the tool chain shall be part of a continuous integration system, which periodically evaluates the software quality in an unattended manner to produce valuable reports.

In the next section, requirements and design decisions for the SUT to be simulated by a cloud-based testing approach are elaborated. These aspects are validated by a case study with the development environment "Hesperia," which was carried out at the University of California, Berkeley with the Autonomous Vehicle Group (AVG) from the Center of Hybrid and Embedded Software Systems (CHESS) during the development of an automotive software function for an autonomously driving vehicle.

CYBER-PHYSICAL SYSTEMS IN THE CLOUD

Architecture of Cyber-Physical Systems

In Figure 3, the general system architecture of a context-aware cyber-physical system is depicted. At the highest level, three consecutive data pro-

Figure 3. General system architecture of a context-aware cyber-physical system which consists of three layers: the perception layer to gather information from the system's surroundings, the decision layer for interpreting the perceived information, and the action layer to perform actions in the system's environment. The support layer is used to monitor and evaluate the CPS.

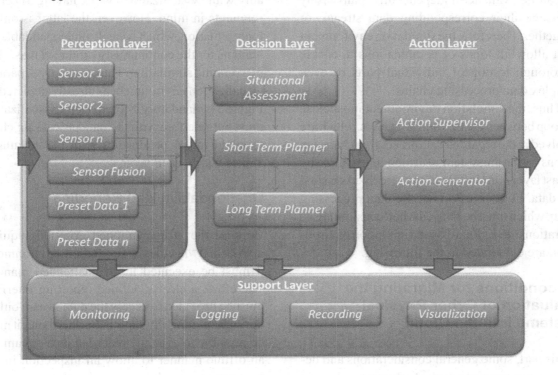

cessing layers can be identified, which process incoming data from the system's surroundings. The incoming data is perceived by sensors to derive decisions for actions to be performed in the environment. Sensors do not include only cameras, radars, and the like, but also receivers for data, which is transferred wirelessly for example. The gathered raw data from the system's sensors could also be preprocessed and even a priori available static data can be subsumed within the perception layer.

The preprocessed data is provided to the next layer, which evaluates the continuously incoming data to derive the next decision, which shall be performed by the action layer. The actual evaluation is carried out in the situational assessment part, which is feeding its information to the short and an optional long-term planner: For example,

if the current traffic situation would allow the overtaking of a vehicle, which is driving in front (short term planner), but within a few minutes the vehicle should turn right, the proposed maneuver would be rejected by the long term planner.

The new and updated decision is passed to the action layer, which realizes the decision using the system's actuators. Therefore, necessary set values are calculated, continuously observed, and adjusted by the control algorithm to act within the system's surroundings.

An additional layer is also depicted in Figure 3: The support layer. Using the components in this layer, all three aforementioned layers can be inspected during the development of a CPS. Thus, internal data streams can be logged or interactively monitored for visualization purposes. However, this inspection must be carried out in a non-reactive manner to prevent interdependencies with the actual data processing.

As depicted by Figure 3, the three main layers can be evaluated independently, pair-wisely alongside their corresponding data stream, or altogether. Therefore, the simulation environment must allow all kinds of combinations to enable a thorough testing of individual parts or even complex data processing chains.

Thus, the simulation environment must close the loop between the first and last layers, which are involved in the regarded data processing chain, i.e. actions within the system's surroundings caused by the last layer must influence the perceived sensors' raw data. Further aspects of the data processing chain, which must be obeyed when considering its migration into a cloud-based simulation environment, are elaborated in the following.

Preconditions for Migrating the Evaluation of Cyber-Physical Systems into the Cloud

In this part, some general considerations and design criteria are discussed which must be kept in mind when realizing a cloud-based simulation and testing approach for CPS. The following aspects base on (Broekman, & Notenboom, 2003) and (Schaefer, & Wehrheim, 2007) and are adapted for cloud-based related issues.

Decoupled Simulation Time from Real Time

The simulated system time and the time actually elapsing for executing the simulation need to be entirely decoupled to enable a repeatable schedulability for deterministic executions. Therefore, the cloud-based approach must not only provide an entirely virtualized system time for the SUT but also for its surroundings to get repeatable results—especially for continuous algorithms.

No Integrated Visualization

The term "simulation" is often used interchangeably with "visualization" while having 3D environments in mind. However, the latter is only a representation, which is easily understandable for humans for the continuously produced mass data of a running simulation. Thus, a strictly separated visualization environment as already depicted by Figure 3 is mandatory. Moreover, the visualization must not interfere with the data processing chain to avoid interdependencies with the calculated values within each layer.

Unattendability and Reporting

Because the aforementioned criterion requires a so-called "headless" simulation environment, it must be executed in an unattended manner. Therefore, a clearly defined reporting interface must be provided to access the data stream online during a running simulation. Furthermore, it must be possible to evaluate recorded data streams in an offline manner to allow an inspection in the post-processing phase.

Composability

As shown in Figure 3, a CPS is continuously evaluating the perceived data from its surroundings to continuously validate its decisions for adjusting its actions. Thus, the internal structure realizes a pipe consisting of layers, which are filtering incoming data. To support the individual evaluation of all layers, the simulation environment must provide layer-dependent stimuli data and also layer-dependent evaluation criteria. However, these criteria must also be composable to enable more complex evaluations of several parts of the data processing chain.

Extensibility

Another aspect is extensibility, which can be derived from the aforementioned aspect. Due to the fact that a CPS may consist of several sensors or sensors, which provide data with different details, the simulation components in the cloud-based testing approach must be extendable and even exchangeable where it is necessary.

Reusability

A large amount of simulation test suites is necessary to evaluate an embedded system's behavior especially on specific input data to deal with the system's physical limitations. Therefore, the cloud-based testing approach must be reusable at different stages during the development on the one hand; but on the other hand, also individual components of the simulation itself shall be reusable.

After the discussion of design criteria, which are relevant for a successful cloud-based testing approach for CPS, the development and evaluation environment (DEE) "Hesperia" is outlined in the following. This development environment realizes the aforementioned design criteria to allow the development of CPS on the one hand. On the other, a cloud-based evaluation approach according to Figure 2 was realized at the Center of Hybrid and Embedded Software Systems at the University of California, Berkeley. Thus, a navigation function as a CPS was realized for an autonomously driving vehicle, which was entirely evaluated in a cloud-based virtualized environment before its first real operation on the vehicle.

Hesperia: An Approach for Evaluating CPS in the Cloud

In the following, "Hesperia"[1] is outlined which enables the development of a CPS with ease due to its clear API and internal design. It was also used to realize a cloud-based evaluation approach to evaluate a CPS in an unattended manner. While the latter is outlined later on, some general considerations and design decisions are provided at first.

Abstraction and Virtualization of the SUT

To evaluate a running SUT at any time of its entire run-time, its main control flow must be supervisable on the one hand; on the other hand, the entire communication between all SUT's components must be controllable. However, it should be avoided to modify the application and to realize a non-invasive inspection instead.

Decoupled Simulation Time from Real Time

As already identified as an important design driver for a cloud-based testing approach, the simulated system time and the time necessary for executing simulations must be entirely decoupled to realize repeatable and also efficient simulations. Thus, the DEE "Hesperia" provides an entirely virtualized system time and enforces a repeatable schedulability to enable deterministic execution of tests.

Providing Reusable, Robust, and General Purpose Programming Patterns

Today's complex embedded applications rely on basic services like communication and concurrency control which can be error-prone and hard to debug if implemented manually over and over again. Thus, composable patterns for these programming tasks are provided in a fast, robust, and portable manner to shorten the development time and to focus on the actual programming task.

Integrated Support for Modeling an Embedded System's Surroundings

To use the development environment for evaluating a CPS, a DSL to model aspects from an autonomously driving vehicle's environment is seamlessly integrated in the DEE "Hesperia." Therefore, instances from this DSL found also the base for the system simulations, which is necessary to evaluate a CPS in a cloud-based testing approach.

The aforementioned design drivers were kept in mind during the development of the DEE Hesperia as shown in Figure 2. As already described briefly, Hesperia is on the one hand a development environment consisting of an API which provides a robust but at the same time light-weight software framework which is written in portable ANSI C++ with strict object-oriented concepts. The framework runs on 32bit and 64bit platforms including Microsoft Windows XP, Windows Vista, Windows 7, all major Linux distributions, and FreeBSD. The main focus during its implementation was to hide all programming pitfalls like endianness or low-level I/O.

On the other hand, the same framework is also the enabling technology to realize a cloud-based evaluation approach for testing a CPS, which was successfully shown at the University of California, Berkeley. Thus, it is possible that a developer can realize a CPS's function in a well-designed object-oriented framework and evaluate it later on. In the following, the most important concepts of the DEE "Hesperia" are described.

The first major concept enabling non-reactive inspection of a data processing chain is the avoidance of directed communication links between components. Instead, an undirected, non-blocking, filterable, and strictly typed, bus-like communication is the main communication principle in "Hesperia." Another advantage of a bus-like communication is the reduced overhead of consumed bandwidth by relying on the publisher-subscriber pattern to send a datum only once–regardless how many recipients are listening. Additionally, a receiving component can easily discard unwanted information on the one hand before actually processing it, and on the other hand, merging data from different types is necessary. For example,

Hesperia can automatically merge position data from GPS with perceived distances from an ultra sonic sensor to create an environmental map while considering correctly the associated timestamps.

Next, Hesperia follows a principle also demanded by (Parveen, & Tilley, 2010). Besides the already mentioned platform-independence, Hesperia reduces the coupling between developed components and 3rd-party libraries to preserve reusability of a specific component or algorithm in different contexts. But instead of re-implementing algorithms from 3rd-party suppliers inside the framework, which are required by autonomously driving vehicles for example, Hesperia exhibits only the necessary interfaces to the developer's application by using the factory pattern (Gamma, Helm, Johnson, & Vlissides, 1994), which describe the syntactic interface of an algorithm by hiding its concrete implementation at the same time. Thus, algorithms and components, which rely on certain libraries, can simply be reused in various contexts to enable exchangeability without modifications. For example, algorithms from the *OpenCV* library (Bradski, & Kaehler, 2008) are provided to developers by factories to allow fast image and matrix processing.

As already briefly mentioned, Hesperia is not only used for the actual development of a CPS' algorithm by providing a convenient design. It is also the framework to realize simulations for the CPS. Therefore, Hesperia also includes a formal modeling language to describe the surroundings of a CPS. From these instances, stimuli data for all three layers and even combinations thereof can be derived to feed data from the environment into a CPS and to evaluate its reactions afterwards. Moreover, this process is carried out in an unattended manner as required by the preconditions as mentioned before.

In the following, the aspect of evaluating a CPS is described in greater detail. Further information especially on implementation details can be found in (Berger, 2010).

Virtualizing a Cyber-Physical System

In Figure 4, the general software architecture to control the execution and communication of the SUT *MyApplication* is depicted. Realized by the fundamental design of Hesperia, this application automatically receives all distributed data by the bus-like communication of so-called *Containers*, which encapsulate strictly typed objects. The bus-like communication is implemented by a *Conference*, which is responsible for receiving incoming *Containers* and for the delivery of outgoing *Containers* from the user-developed application. Thus, the developer does not need to bother with a concrete communication implementation; instead, his application simply joins in an actually ongoing conversation between already running components.

Exactly one *RuntimeControl* controls each simulation for a CPS by using a *RuntimeEnvironment*, which describes the SUT together with its associated surroundings. The former is described by at least one instance of *ConferenceClientModule*, the latter by instances of *SystemFeedbackComponent* and optionally *SystemReportingComponent*, which both derive from *SystemContextComponent*.

A *SystemFeedbackComponent* is used both to model missing parts from the embedded system itself and to model aspects from its surroundings to feed data back to the SUT. Thus, an instance of a *SystemFeedbackComponent*'s subclass can contain a mathematical model, which describes the vehicle's motion or a sensor for example.

Contrary to this interface, which contains an instance of *SendContainerToSystemsUnderTest* to actually send data to an inspected SUT, *SystemReportingComponent* is a read-only interface, which can only be used to continuously and non-reactively evaluate a running SUT. Therefore, it derives from *SystemContextComponent* to join an ongoing conversation to automatically receive *Containers* for a continuous evaluation.

To control the entire communication within a conversation by exchanging *Containers*, *ContainerConferenceFactory* is inherited to *ControlledContainerConferenceFactory*, which exchanges the concrete sending and receiving implementations. Thus, a centrally controlled data routing implementation is used to handle the exchange of *Containers*. For sending data from *SystemFeedbackComponents* to an SUT, the interface *SendContainerToSystemsUnderTest* is used, which synchronously distributes a *Container* to all SUTs within a *RuntimeEnvironment*.

Additionally to the control of the entire communication, *RuntimeControl* encapsulates the valid time system-widely. Therefore, it uses *ControlledTimeFactory*, which derives from *TimeFactory* to return the controlled system-time to the SUT up on request. Thus, the exchanged *TimeFactory* is used transparently for all SUTs belonging to this *RuntimeEnvironment* to prevent interdependencies.

To control the SUT itself, it is wrapped into a *ConferenceClientModuleRunner*, which also derives from *Periodic* and *Runner* comparable to *SystemContextComponents*. The former interface provides information about the required run-time frequency while the latter actually provides a method to perform a time-dependent step during the simulation. Additionally, the wrapping class *ConferenceClientModuleRunner* uses instances of *RunModuleBreakpoint* and *BlockableContainerReceiver*. The former instance is necessary to interrupt a concurrently running SUT, which is the core concept for the virtualization of an embedded system. Therefore, it calls automatically and regularly its *Breakpoint* to indicate the begin of a new computation cycle, which in turn enables *RuntimeControl* to suspend the SUT's execution. The latter instance is used to restrict the communication initiated by an SUT only to its unsuspended phase. Both concepts within a complete sequence are shown in Figure 5. In this sequence chart the control flow over time is shown during one computation cycle in the SUT together with its surround-

Figure 4. System architecture for a virtualized CPS. On the left hand side, the SUT "MyApplication" is shown, which is realized with the DEE "Hesperia." Therefore, it automatically provides a so-called "Breakpoint," which is the key concept to interrupt the application periodically at run-time for a controlled execution, which is realized by RuntimeControl. This class also supervises the global valid system time and the entire communication from and to the SUT to enable a non-reactive inspection.

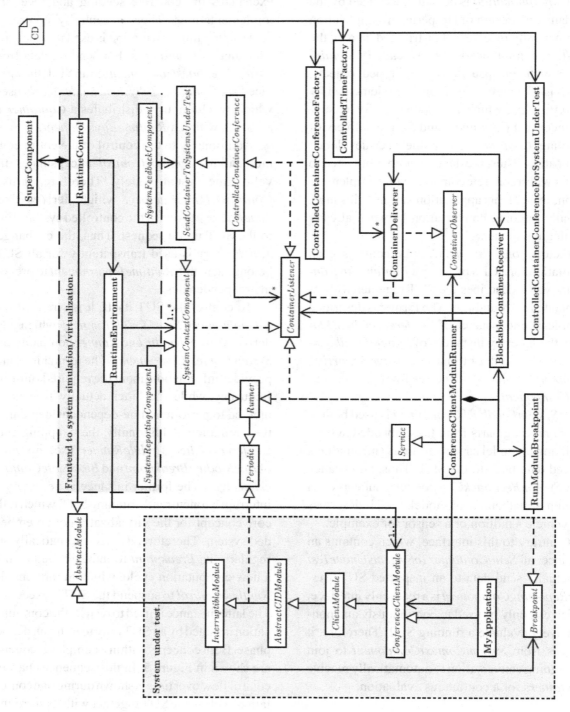

ings. The SUT indicates by calling *reached()* that it has completed its previous computation cycle successfully and that it is ready for the next step. Thus, every communication, which is initiated in the meanwhile, is blocked as shown by the lifeline at the instance of *BlockableContainerReceiver*. Next, *RuntimeControl* increments the overall valid system-time and updates subsequently the SUT's surroundings, which are realized by an instance of *SystemContextComponent*. For example, this could be a feedback component to provide updated data from the surroundings to the SUT or an evaluation component to validate an SUT's actions. Afterwards, the suspended Breakpoint is released to continue the SUT's execution and to unblock any meanwhile suspended communication for the next computation cycle.

In Figure 5, starting on the right hand side, the SUT indicates the completion of its previous computation cycle by calling the method *reached()* from the interface *Breakpoint*. This call is blocked until the computation is resumed later to indicate the next cycle. Thus, the control flow returns to *RuntimeControl*, which can trigger the next computation cycle by incrementing the system's time first.

Because *ControlledContainerConferenceFactory* exchanges the concrete implementation for the communication automatically, the SUT uses transparently *BlockableContainerReceiver* for sending a *Container* within an ongoing conversation to other SUTs. While the SUT is suspended, all calls for sending a *Container* are blocked by *BlockableContainerReceiver* and are released not until the next computation cycle is triggered. Therefore, the entire communication can be restricted to an unsuspended phase during a running computation of the SUT.

Next, *RuntimeControl* runs *SystemContextComponent* when it is necessary for the current time value. As mentioned before, a *SystemContextComponent* is either a feedback component to produce updated data within the surroundings or an evaluation component to validate the

SUT's actions. After executing all registered instances, the control flow, which is supervised by *RuntimeControl*, returns to the SUT by calling *ConferenceClientModuleRunner*. However, the call does not return either until the SUT has completed its computation cycle, a malfunction in the SUT is detected by catching an exception, which is thrown by the SUT, or after a timeout has occurred. Thus, the overall control flow still remains under control of *RuntimeControl*.

At the beginning of a new computation cycle, *ConferenceClientModuleRunner* releases the blocked SUT by unlocking all calls to *BlockableContainerReceiver*, which are blocked from sending a *Container*. Additionally, the suspended *Breakpoint* is resumed until the SUT indicates the completion of the actual computation cycle by calling the *Breakpoint* again. Afterwards, the call finally returns to *RuntimeControl*, which continues the simulation by incrementing the time for the next cycle. Otherwise, if the call does not return to *RuntimeControl* within a specified maximum duration for one computation cycle, it cannot be excluded that an error during the SUT's execution has occurred; then, the execution of the SUT is canceled and a report is created automatically.

Testing an Autonomously Driving Vehicle with Hesperia in the Cloud

For demonstrating the applicability of the concepts and software, which are presented in the previous sections, a simple algorithm for navigating a vehicle using a given digital map was designed and implemented on an experimental vehicle from the University of California, Berkeley, which is shown in Figure 6. Before the software was put into operation for the first time, it was extensively testing during its development with the DEE "Hesperia" in a cloud-based testing approach as outlined in Figure 2.

The experimental vehicle based on a 2008 Ford Escape Hybrid–ByWire XGV, which was modified by TORC Technologies to be control-

Figure 5. Sequence chart for complete computation cycle for one time step

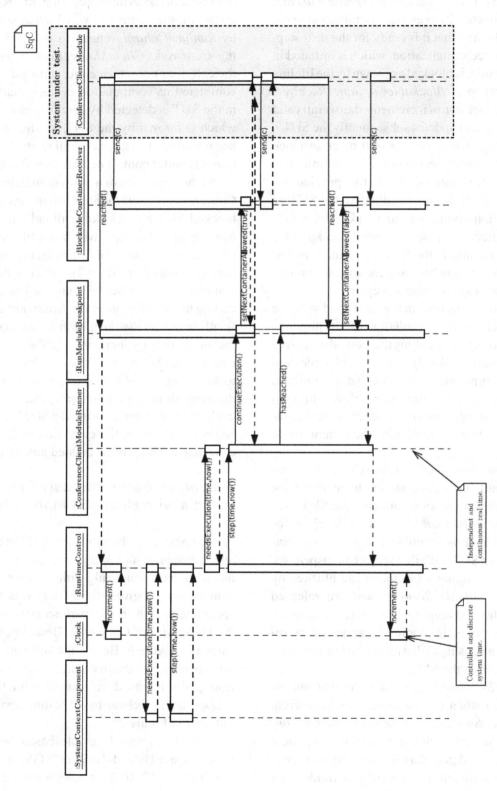

Figure 6. Experimental vehicle from the University of California, Berkeley, which is based on 2008 Ford Escape Hybrid–ByWire XGV

lable completely by software. On the left hand side in Figure 6, the sensor setup of the vehicle is depicted. The vehicle perceives its surroundings using a stereovision system combined with a single layer laser scanner. On the right hand side of the same figure, the vehicle's trunk is shown. The stereovision system is synchronized by hardware using a waveform generator. For getting localization data, a GPS receiver together with the inertial measurement unit (IMU) HG-1700 from NovAtel are used. The software itself is running on a Debian Linux system, which is running on an Intel Core 2 Quad.

The vehicle tests were carried out at the Richmond Field Station, a test facility, which is located for about 6 miles northwest of the University of California, Berkeley. For planning a route to a given destination, a digital map was created using a highly precise GPS receiver to provide a digital representation of the course on which the vehicle should navigate. This data was also used as the basis to create the world's model, which contains the modeled roads from the raw GPS data and an aerial image for an intuitional understanding by using the DSL, which is provided by the DEE Hesperia. The instance of the DSL, which is describing the stationary surroundings for the

autonomously driving vehicle, was not only used to visualize the current vehicle's position and orientation during the interactive development, but also for virtualizing its surroundings to create "headless" cloud-based system simulations.

For testing the aforementioned concepts, a navigation algorithm was developed to compute a steering angle, a desired velocity, and a braking force. This algorithm was inspired by (Montemerlo, 2008) but modified for usage in rural to suburban environments. Its principles are outlined briefly in the following; the full description can be found at (Berger, 2010). The main idea is to choose an arbitrary but constant point S, which lies on the elongated center axis in front of the vehicle. The goal for the steering algorithm is to minimize the distance between S and its perpendicular point on the skeleton line of the actual lane's segment.

Additionally to determine the necessary steering angle, the algorithm uses a similar approach for computing the desired velocity and braking force. Hereby, the reciprocal distance to the path is used: The smaller the distance between a constant point V and its perpendicular point on the skeleton line, the greater is the resulting velocity and vice versa. Thus, the vehicle reduces its velocity right before a curve because the distance is

Figure 7. Performance of the algorithm in the simulation for v = 3.0m/s, which was carried out by the DEE "Hesperia." The red line denotes the planned route on the previously recorded digital map, the blue line is the vehicle's performance without optimization, and the grey line shows its performance using a Bézier curve, which is reducing significantly the absolute distance to the initially planned route. During the development, the algorithm's performance was evaluated interactively or in an unattended manner by using the "headless" testing approach in the cloud-based evaluation approach.

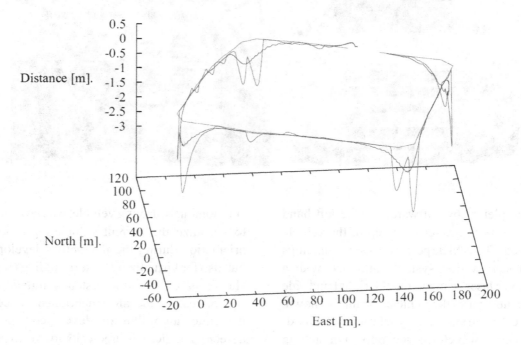

increasing before passing the curve's apex. Right after passing the apex, this distance is decreasing again, which is resulting in an increasing velocity. Complementary to the desired velocity, a braking force is computed proportionally to the distance between V and the associated perpendicular point to reduce actively the vehicle's velocity.

Before trying the algorithm on the real vehicle, it was extensively tested using the DEE Hesperia for system simulation. In Figure 7, the algorithm's performance compared to the actually planned route on the Richmond Field Station marked as red is depicted. The blue solid line shows the actually driven path without optimization. In the X-Y-layer, the position of the autonomously driving vehicle on the ground relative to the route is shown, while the Z-dimension shows the distance to the route. The grey solid line shows its performance using

Bézier curves, which were introduced to optimize the navigation algorithm.

First, it can be observed that the vehicle is not only following the initially planned route but it also tends to reduce the distance of S converging to 0 as expected. However, especially in curves, the distance from the vehicle's center to the initially planned route increases up to 2.73m depending on the vehicle's velocity before the navigation algorithm is adjusting the vehicle's steering angle to follow the route again.

To reduce significantly the distance to the planned route, the linearly connected points from the route are optimized using Bézier curves. Thus, the vehicle tends to steer earlier towards the next point of a route. Moreover, the distance to the initially planned route is significantly smaller

Figure 8. Performance of the navigation algorithm in reality observed from the bird's eye view from the upper left corner of the course. Compared to the aforementioned figure, the red line also represents the planned route on the digital map while the grey line represents its optimization by a Bézier curve. The dashed blue line represents the actually driven path by the vehicle in reality for v = 4.1m/s.

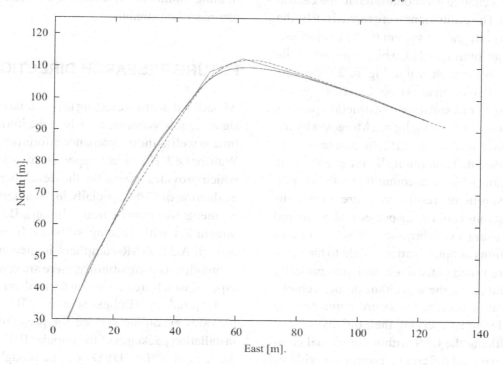

compared to the non-optimized variant–especially in curves.

After purely virtually testing and evaluating the algorithm's performance, the software was integrated in the 2008 Ford Escape Hybrid–ByWire XGV. The component's setup was identical to the virtualized one except for the virtualized sensors and actuators, and thus, no modifications to the algorithmic components were necessary at all.

In Figure 8 depicts the algorithm's performance in reality. Comparable to the prior diagrams, the red graph shows the planned route and the grey line denotes the optimized route using Bézier curves. The dashed blue line shows the path, which was actually driven by the vehicle. Despite an increasing distance to the optimized route in the curve, the autonomously driving vehicle was following the initially planned route pretty well in reality.

To evaluate the performance of the navigation algorithm systematically, we simply re-used the same interfaces and concepts from the DEE Hesperia, which were already used for the interactive simulations. Therefore, subclasses of the *System-ReportingComponent* were used to monitor and evaluate continuously the reactions of the SUD according to predefined stimuli in an unattended manner. These subclasses of *SystemReporting-Component* were embedded into the assert-macros from the unit test environment CxxTest (Tigris.org 2011) within a test-driven development. Thus, no further scripting language was necessary to automate the execution of unattended system evaluations and developers could simply carry out these unit tests interactively on the one hand.

On the other hand, we set up a cloud-based solution according to Figure 2 to carry out unattended evaluations of the navigation algorithm whenever a change was committed to the central repository. The evaluations were carried out by the continuous integration system (CIS) CruiseControl (CruiseControl, 2011), which was part of the compile service as shown in Figure 2. Thus, the already available unit tests from CxxTest could be run as part of our software construction process within our cloud-based solution. Moreover by using CruiseControl as our CIS, the unit tests were not only executed automatically for every single modification, which was committed to the version server. Even more, results from previous unattended test runs could be inspected and compared easily by using a web browser. Thus, even small modifications or optimizations made to the algorithm were tested extensively and automatically before evaluating the algorithm on the vehicle. Hence, time consuming tests were automated and shortened while preserving their quality.

To evaluate the CPS within our virtual environment, we used different reporting algorithms, which were realized easily by using the DSL for getting information from the stationary surroundings. These reporting algorithms formed a test oracle to continuously evaluate the SUD's behavior. Therefore, the reporting algorithms were simply added to the *RuntimeEnvironment* as shown in Figure 4, which executed them automatically by *RuntimeControl*. For evaluating the navigation algorithm, the *DestinationReachedReport* was used to ensure that the vehicle would finally reach the last point of a given route; next, *ChoosingShortestRouteReport* was supervising if the vehicle would choose and drive the shortest possible route to the given destination. Moreover, *DistanceToRouteReport* was continuously measuring the vehicle's distance to the planned and optimized route. All aforementioned reporters consisted of no more than 30 lines to check the mentioned conditions. Thus, different scenarios could be set up easily to ensure the navigation

algorithm's quality. Furthermore, the same reporters could be composed and reused for different virtual driving scenarios both online during a running simulation and offline to evaluate already recorded data streams.

FUTURE RESEARCH DIRECTIONS

As outlined, software testing in the cloud provides significant advantages to reduce the initial setup time as well as the maintenance efforts per project. With the DEE Hesperia, an approach was described which provides means for the development and evaluation of CPS especially in "headless" environments like cloud-based solutions. Besides its integration with existing software frameworks or with AUTOSAR-compliant implementations to broaden its compatibility, there are some more aspects, which are interesting for further research.

Inspired by (EclipseSource, 2011), which provides an online service for pre-configuring installation packages of the popular IDE Eclipse, the idea of a "LiveDVD" can be thought ahead to reduce the familiarization time for team members who are newly involved in an already running project. As shown by Figure 1 that the LiveCD's concrete dependence on an artifact's particular content is nearly none, enterprises should rethink their supply and maintenance of development environments as a first step. These infrastructural services can either migrated into the cloud where possible e.g. like the aforementioned Cloud9 IDE for JavaScript editing (von Wedel, 2011), or pre-configured IDEs can be provided for download from a company's intranet to save valuable developer resources both as installation package and as entirely preconfigured and ready to use OS-containers with an installed tool-chain.

Especially for CPSs, which are the running example in this contribution, the modeling for the CPS' interfaces to its surroundings must be significantly improved to extend tests for these CPS considerably. Acting interfaces of a CPS–and especially in the case of vehicles–are actuators whose models are better understood compared to the sensing interfaces; they consist not only of a specific sensor's model but even more of a model from the CPS' environment. For autonomously driving vehicles, their surroundings are urban environments, highways, and so on, which must be modeled in greater detail than today's approaches to be useful for virtual evaluations. Opening angle, viewing direction and range, and update frequency are necessary but in the end insufficient. A specific sensor's characteristics like "ghost objects" or impacts from environmental conditions like weather and sunlight depend directly on the environmental model. Thus, these aspects must be kept in mind when simulation approaches should be successful–regardless whether they are operated in a cloud-based environment or not.

But not only technical aspects for software testing in the cloud must be adapted. Even traditional development methodologies like the V-model must be adapted for using cloud-based testing approaches. By using AUTOSAR to ensure clearly defined interfaces for algorithms, testing processes should not be started after the implementation and thus late during the development, but they should be used at the earliest possible stage instead. Therefore, established development processes must be evolved and best practices should be developed to provide guidelines when and how algorithms and components can be or should be evaluated within a cloud-based testing approach. Moreover, best practices can be supplied by testing patterns in the cloud.

But the discussion about aspects for software artifacts, which should be tested in the cloud, leads to a more fundamental rethinking of the way, how software for CPS is created nowadays. AUTOSAR already separates the hardware from the automotive functions, which are realized in software, but why do we have to decide the programming language to be used for realization of the function right at the beginning and thus,

restricting the developers to the expressiveness of that chosen language? A shift during the implementation phase is not economic when the provided means of the chosen programming language are insufficient to solve the problem in an elegant or reusable way. Thus, the future reuse of the developed components is endangered. Here, the cloud-based development and testing approach offers good prospects by completely abstracting from the underlying hardware including specific sensors together with its surroundings to enable a more problem-centric modeling approach, which is focusing on the algorithmic aspects while preserving the future reuse of algorithms.

An already existing tool-chain points in this direction: Automotive functions even for safety-relevant systems are modeled with MATLAB/ Simulink from which the concrete source code in a general purpose language like C is generated later on. Here, a domain specific modeling approach, which accompanies the cloud-based development and evaluation environment, would enable the developers to focus more on the solution of the actual problem, while they are supported by the results from an automated cloud-based testing approach.

Moreover, model checking approaches or even verification (Siegl, Hielscher, German, & Berger, 2011) can be carried out at such an abstract level: After completion of a function's development and after its evaluation in the cloud, the concrete required source code artifacts, which are used to create the object code that is flashed on ECUs, can be derived automatically using model transformation and code generation. These generators in turn can consider concrete hardware limitations like sensor characteristics. Such an approach would lead to a development and evaluation, which considers a specific sensor's characteristics and limitations during the transformation phase of the algorithmic model from the abstract cloud-based environment to the real environment to be executed on a CPS.

CONCLUSION

In this contribution, requirements, preconditions, and design decisions to evaluate a CPS within a cloud-based testing approach were outlined and discussed. The most important precondition is a clear design of a CPS' interfaces to use its components within another context than originally intended. Therefore, the CPS or the software framework, which should be used for the CPS' realization, must fulfill several important criteria as previously outlined.

First, the time, which is used inside the simulation, must be independent from the time, which is actually elapsing during the execution of the simulation. This is fundamentally important to ensure a deterministic and repeatable schedulability during the execution of an SUT. When this requirement is violated, simulations could produce different results for the same input conditions.

Because a cloud-based testing approach is strictly separated in a front-end and a back-end part, the actual simulation environment must be "headless." Only thereby, the computation power, which is necessary to simulate even complex physical models for sensors and actuators, can be extended or reduced in an elastic manner by migrating seamlessly to a more powerful IaaS. A pretty visualization of mass data is only required to enable an easier understanding or analysis by human beings. Thus, the front-end can be separated from the running simulation and connected to it when necessary. Therefore, the simulation's core must provide a clearly defined reporting interface, which enables the developers both to inspect data during a running simulation as mentioned before, and to analyze the data afterwards in the post-processing phase.

Additionally, the cloud-based testing approach must consist of several loosely coupled components for the simulation of a CPS' surroundings on the one hand, and of components for its evaluation on the other hand. Only thereby, the following goals can be achieved:

- Individual simulations to evaluate different parts of the data processing chain.
- Gather and improve common knowledge about physical aspects for a CPS' sensors and actuators.
- Create and provide increasingly complex simulation environments, which were not thought of at the beginning.
- Ensure the overall reusability for several related projects, which rely on a common cloud-based testing approach.

One approach is the DEE Hesperia, which relies on the aforementioned aspects to support the development and evaluation of distributed, complex embedded systems. It provides concepts for virtualizing an embedded system by modeling its surroundings for unattended and automated system simulations. Hesperia demonstrated its applicability within a cloud-based testing approach for CPS according to Figure 2 during the development of a steering angle and velocity control navigation algorithm for an autonomously driving vehicle. Therefore, the algorithm was developed while relying only on the cloud-based testing approach at first, before it was set into operation for the first time on the experimental vehicle. Thus, it was demonstrated successfully that a cloud-based testing process, which consisted of several unit tests to test different aspects of the navigation algorithm, is applicable even for the development of a CPS, which relies on sensors' data to interact with its surroundings.

Besides unattended evaluations using a DSL for modeling an embedded system's surroundings, the DEE Hesperia can also be used to develop hardware independent algorithms for virtualized environments. For example, the steering angle and velocity control algorithm could be applied on another vehicle with similar sensors by slightly adjusting the parameters of the mathematical model only. Thus, the approach supports to analyze and understand physical interrelations and impacts of different sensors and actuators.

Moreover, "Hesperia" can be used to evaluate machine-learning algorithms like reinforcement learning algorithms by providing a safe sandbox for evaluation to derive optimal settings. Thus, it provides an easily extensible approach, which addresses challenges of the software engineering for embedded systems.

ACKNOWLEDGMENT

I am very grateful the entire team from the Center of Hybrid and Embedded Software Systems (CHESS) at the University of California, Berkeley for giving me the opportunity to evaluate "Hesperia." Furthermore, I would like to thank team CarOLO for a great time during our participation in the 2007 DARPA Urban Challenge.

Trademarks appear throughout this contribution without any trademark symbol; they are the property of their respective trademark owner. There is no intention of infringement; the usage is to the benefit of the trademark owner.

REFERENCES

Assembla, L. L. C. (2011). *Assembla*. Retrieved April 27, 2011, from http://www.assembla.com

Basarke, C., Berger, C., Homeier, K., & Rumpe, B. (2007). Design and quality assurance of intelligent vehicle functions in the "virtual vehicle.". In *Proceedings of the 11 (vol. 9)*. Automobiltechnische konferenz –virtual vehicle creation.

Basarke, C., Berger, C., & Rumpe, B. (2007). Software & systems engineering process and tools for the development of autonomous driving intelligence. *Journal of Aerospace Computing, Information, and Communication, 4*(12), 1158–1174. doi:10.2514/1.33453

Berger. C., & Rumpe, B. (2012b). Autonomous driving – 5 years after the urban challenge: the anticipatory vehicle as a cyber-physical system. In *Proceedings of the INFORMATIK 2012*.

Berger, C. (2010). *Automating acceptance tests for sensor- and actuator-based systems on the example of autonomous vehicles. Aachener Informatik-Berichte (Vol. 6)*. Aachen, Germany: Shaker Verlag.

Berger, C., & Rumpe, B. (2010). Supporting agile change management by scenario-based regression simulation. *IEEE Transactions on Intelligent Transportation Systems, 11*(2), 504–509. doi:10.1109/TITS.2010.2044571

Berger, C., & Rumpe, B. (2012a). Engineering autonomous driving software. In Rouff, C., & Hinchey, M. (Eds.), *Experience From The Darpa Urban Challenge* (pp. 243–271). London, UK: Springer-Verlag. doi:10.1007/978-0-85729-772-3_10

Bertolino, A. (2007). Software testing research: Achievements, challenges, dreams. In *Proceedings Of The Future Of Software Engineering At Icse 2007* (pp. 85 – 103).

Biermeyer. J. O., Templeton, T. R., Berger, c., Gonzalez, H., Naikal, N., Rumpe, B., & Sastry, S. (2010). Rapid integration and calibration of new sensors using the berkeley aachen robotics toolkit (bart). In *Proceedings of the 11. Braunschweiger Symposiums "Automatisierungssysteme, Assistenzsysteme und eingebettete Systeme für Transportmittel"*.

Bradski, G., & Kaehler, A. (2008). *Learning Opencv*. Sebastopol, CA: O'Reilly Media.

Broekman, B., & Notenboom, E. (2003). *Testing Embedded Software*. Upper Saddle River, NJ: Addison-Wesley.

Christie, A. M. (1999). *Simulation: An enabling technology in software engineering* (pp. 25–30). Crosstalk-The Journal Of Defense Software Engineering.

Collins-Sussman, B., Fitzpatrick, B. W., & Pilato, C. M. (2004). *Version control with subversion.* Sebastopol, CA: O'Reilly Media.

CruiseControl. (2011). *Cruisecontrol.* Retrieved April 27, 2011, from http://cruisecontrol.source-forge.net

EclipseSource. (2011). *Yoxos Ondemand.* Retrieved April 27, 2011, from http://ondemand.yoxos.com/geteclipse/start

Gamma, E., Helm, R., Johnson, R., & Vlissides, J. (1994). *Design Patterns: Elements Of Reusable Object-Oriented Software.* Upper Saddle River, NJ: Addison-Wesley.

Gerkey, B., Vaughan, R. T., & Howard, A. (2003). The Player/Stage Project: Tools for multi-robot and distributed sensor systems. In *Proceedings Of The 11th International Conference On Advanced Robotics* (pp. 317–323).

Gietelink, O., Ploeg, J., Schutter, B. D., & Ver-haegen, M. (2004). Testing advanced driver as-sistance systems for fault management with the VEHIL test facility. In *Proceedings Of The 7th International Symposium On Advanced Vehicle Control* (AVEC'04) (pp. 579 – 584).

GIT. (2012). *Git Source Code Management.* Retrieved May 17, 2012, from http://git-scm.com

IPG GmbH. (2011). *Carmaker 3.0.* Retrieved April 27, 2011, from http://www.ipg.de/CarMaker.609.0.html

Jewett, E. (2009). *Robotics Developer Studio 2008r2. Technical Report.* Microsoft Corp.

Korecki, J. (2005). *Sourceforge.Net: Cvs ~ Com-pile Farm.* Retrieved April 27, 2011, from http://www.nd.edu/~oss/Papers/Korecki_Sourceforge.pdf

Lee, E. A., & Seshia, S. A. (2011). *Introduction To Embedded Systems – A Cyber-Physical Systems Approach.* Retrieved April 27, 2011, from http://LeeSeshia.org

Masticola, S., & Gall, M. (2008). Vision: Testing of mechatronics software using agile simulation. In *Proceedings Of The 3rd International Workshop On Automation Of Software Test* (pp. 79 – 84).

Meyers, S. (1996). *More Effective C++: 35 New Ways To Improve Your Programs And Designs.* Upper Saddle River, NJ: Addison-Wesley.

Meyers, S. (1997). *Effective C++: 50 Specific Ways To Improve Your Programs And Design.* Upper Saddle River, NJ: Addison-Wesley.

Miller, P. (2010). *Cook-A file construction tool-reference manual.* Retrieved April 27, 2011, from http://miller.emu.id.au/pmiller/software/cook/cook-2.34.rm.pdf

Montemerlo, M., Becker, J., Bhat, S., Dahlkamp, H., Dolgov, D., & Ettinger, S. … Thrun, S. (2008). Junior: The Stanford entry in the urban challenge. In M. Buehler, K. Iagnemma, & S. Singh (Eds.), *Journal Of Field Robotics, 25*(9), 569–597.

Montemerlo, M., Thrun, S., Dahlkamp, H., Stavens, D., & Strohband, S. (2006). Winning the DARPA Grand Challenge with an AI robot. In *Proceedings Of The National Conference On Artificial Intelligence* (pp. 982–988). Menlo Park, CA: AAAI Press.

Parveen, T., & Tilley, S. (2010) When to migrate software testing in the cloud? In *Proceedings Of The 2nd International Workshop On Software Testing In The Cloud* (STITC'10) (pp. 13 – 16). Melbourne, FL: Florida Institute of Technology.

Pretschner, A., Broy, M., Krueger, I. H., & Stauner, T. (2007). Software engineering for automotive systems: A roadmap. In *Proceedings Of 2007 Future Of Software Engineering* (FOSE'07) (pp. 55 – 71). Washington, DC: IEEE Computer Society.

Rauskolb, F. W., Berger, K., Lipski, C., Magnor, M., Cornelsen, K., & Effertz, J. … Rumpe, B. (2010). Caroline: An autonomously driving vehicle for urban environments. In M. Buehler, K. Iagnemma, & S. Singh (Eds.), *The Darpa Urban Challenge - Autonomous Vehicles In City Traffic, Springer Tracts In Advanced Robotics, Volume 56* (pp. 441 – 508).

Riungu, L. M., Taipale, O., & Smolander, K. (2010). Software testing as an online service: Observations from practice. In *Proceedings of the 2nd International Workshop on Software Testing in the Cloud* (STITC'10) (pp. 7 – 12). Melbourne, FL: Florida Institute of Technology.

Rumpe, B., Berger, C., & Krahn, H. (2006). Software engineering methods for quality management of intelligent automotive systems. In *integrierte sicherheit und fahrerassistenzsysteme, no. 1960* (pp. 473 – 486).

Schabenberger, R. (2007). ADTF: Framework for driver assistance and safety systems. In *vdi wissensforum iwb gmbh (ed.), integrierte sicherheit und fahrerassistenzsysteme* (pp. 701–710).

Schaefer, W., & Wehrheim, H. (2007). The challenges of building advanced mechatronic systems. In *Proceedings Of Fose '07: 2007 Future Of Software Engineering* (pp. 72–84). Washington, DC: IEEE Computer Society. doi:10.1109/FOSE.2007.28

Schroeter, A. (2009). *Kiwi Imaging With Opensuse Build Service*. Retrieved April 27, 2011, from http://en.opensuse.org/images/b/be/OBS-Imageing.pdf

Siegl, S., Hielscher, K.-S., German, R., & Berger, C. (2011). Formal specification and systematic model-driven testing of embedded automotive systems. In *Proceedings Of The Conference On Design, Automation, And Test In Europe* (DATE 2011), (pp. 1530 – 1591).

SSELab. (2011). *SSELAB*. Retrieved April 27, 2011, from http://sselab.de

TESIS DYNAware GmbH. (2011). *DYNA4*. Retrieved April 27, 2011, from http://tesis-dynaware.com

Tigris.org. (2011a). *CXXTEST*. Retrieved April 27, 2011, from http://cxxtest.tigris.org

Tigris.org. (2011b). *FSVS*. Retrieved April 27, 2011, from http://fsvs.tigris.org

Underseth, M. (2007). The complexity crisis in embedded software. In *Embedded Computing Design* (pp. 31-33).

van Heesch, D. (2011). *Doxygen*. Retrieved April 27, 2011, from http://www.stack.nl/~dimitri/doxygen/index.html

von Hagen, W. (2008). *Professional Xen Virtualization*. Indianapolis, IN: Wiley Publishing Inc.

von Neumann-Cosel, K., Nentwig, M., Lehmann, D., Speth, J., & Knoll, A. (2009) Preadjustment of a vision-based lane tracker. In *Proceedings On Driving Simulation Conference*.

von Wedel, X. (2011). *Cloud9 Ide Launches Paas For Javascript And Html5*. Retrieved April 27, from http://cloudexpo-europe.com/node/1733520/print

ADDITIONAL READING

Bacha, A., Bauman, C., Faruque, R., Fleming, M., Terwelp, C., & Reinholtz, C. ... Webster, M. (2008). Odin: Team VictorTango's entry in the DARPA Urban Challenge. In M. Buehler, K. Iagnemma, & S. Singh (Eds.), *Journal of Field Robotics, 25*(9), 467–492.

Bartels, A., Berger, C., Krahn, H., & Rumpe, B. (2009). Qualittsgesicherte Fahrent scheidungsunsterttzung fr automatisches Fahren auf Schnellstraßen und Autobahnen (Quality Assurance for a Component for Driving Decisions to Drive Automatically on Highways). In *Proceedings of the Braunschweiger Symposiums "Automatisierungssysteme, Assistenzsysteme und eingebettete Systeme für Transportmittel,"* Vol. 10 (pp. 341 – 353).

Basarke, C., Berger, C., Homeier, K., & Rumpe, B. (2007). Design and quality assurance of intelligent vehicle functions in the "virtual vehicle.". In *Proceedings of 11th Automobiltechnische Konferenz*. Virtual Vehicle Creation.

Berger, K., Lipski, C., Linz, C., Stich, T., & Magnor, M. (2008). The area processing unit of Caroline - Finding the way through DARPA's Urban Challenge. In *Proceedings of the 2nd Workshop Robot Vision* (pp. 260 – 274).

Dickmanns, E., Behringer, R., Dickmanns, D., Hildebrandt, T., Maurer, M., Thomanek, F., & Schiehlen, J. (1994). The seeing passenger car "VaMoRs-P." In *Proceedings of the Intelligent Vehicles Symposium* (pp. 68 – 73).

Dupuis, M., & Grezlikowski, H. (2006). OpenDRIVE - An open standard for the description of roads in driving simulations. In *Proceedings of the Driving Simulation Conference* (pp. 25 – 36).

Effertz, J. (2008). Sensor architecture and data fusion for robotic perception in urban environments at the 2007 DARPA Urban Challenge. In *Robot Vision* (pp. 275–290). Berlin, Germany: Springer. doi:10.1007/978-3-540-78157-8_21

Fennel, H., Bunzel, S., Heinecke, H., Bielefeld, J., Fuerst, S., & Schnelle, K.-P. ... Kunkel, B. (2006). *Achievements and exploitation of the AUTOSAR development partnership*. Technical report, Society of Automotive Engineers.

Franke, U., Gavrila, D. M., Goerzig, S., Lindner, F., Paetzold, F., & Woehler, C. (1998). Autonomous driving goes downtown. In *Proceedings of IEEE Intelligent Systems* (pp. 40 - 49).

Franke, U., Goerzig, S., Lindner, F., Mehren, D., & Paetzold, F. (1997). Steps towards an intelligent vision system for driver assistance in urban traffic. In *Proceedings of the IEEE Conference on Intelligent Transportation System* (pp. 601–606).

Franke, U., & Heinrich, S. (2002). Fast obstacle detection for urban traffic situations. In *Proceedings of the IEEE Transactions on Intelligent Transportation Systems* (pp. 173 – 181)

Franke, U., & Joos, A. (2000). Real-time stereo vision for urban traffic scene understanding. In *Proceedings of the IEEE Intelligent Vehicles Symposium* (pp. 273 – 278).

Frischkorn, H.-G., Negele, H., & Meisenzahl, J. (2000). *The need for systems engineering: An automotive project perspective*. In Key Note at the 2nd European Systems Engineering Conference.

Gavrila, D. M., Franke, U., Woehler, C., & Goerzig, S. (2001). Real-time vision for intelligent vehicles. *IEEE Instrumentation & Measurement Magazine*, 22–27. doi:10.1109/5289.930982

Groenniger, H., Krahn, H., Rumpe, B., Schindler, M., & Voelkel, S. (2008). MontiCore: A framework for the development of textual domain specific languages. In *Companion Of The 30th International Conference On Software Engineering* (ICSE'08) (pp. 925 – 926). New York, NY: ACM.

Heinecke, H., Schnelle, K.-P., Fennel, H., Bortolazzi, J., Lundh, L., Leflour, J., … Scharnhorst, T. (2004). *Automotive open system architecture–An industry-wide initiative to manage the complexity of emerging automotive E/E-architectures.*

Kornhauser, A. L., Atreya, A., Cattle, B., Momen, S., Collins, B., & Downey, A. … Yu, D. (2007). *DARPA Urban Challenge.* Princeton University– Technical Paper. Technical report, Department of Operations Research and Financial Engineering, Princeton University.

Lee, E. A. (2007). *Computing foundations and practice for cyber-physical systems: A preliminary report.* Technical Report UCB/EECS-2007-72, University of California, Berkeley.

Lee, S. J., Lee, D. M., & Lee, J. C. (2008). Development of communication framework for unmanned ground vehicle. In *Proceedings on Control* (pp. 604–607). Automation and Systems.

Lipski, C., Scholz, B., Berger, K., Linz, C., Stich, T., & Magnor, M. (2008). A fast and robust approach to lane marking detection and lane tracking. In *Proceedings of IEEE Southwest Symposium on Image Analysis and Interpretation.*

MISRA. (2004). *Misra-c: guidelines for the use of the c language in critical systems.* Motor Industry Software Reliability Association.

Nothdurft, T., Hecker, P., Ohl, S., Saust, F., Maurer, M., Reschka, A., & Böhmer, J. R. (2011). Stadtpilot: First fully autonomous test drives in urban traffic. In *Proceedings Of The International Ieee Conference On Intelligent Transportation Systems* (pp. 919 – 924).

Olstam, J. J., Lundgren, J., Adlers, M., & Matstoms, P. (2008). A framework for simulation of surrounding vehicles in driving simulators. *ACM Transactions on Modeling and Computer Simulation, 18*(3), 1–24. doi:10.1145/1371574.1371575

Siegl, S., Hielscher, K.-S., German, R., & Berger, C. (2011b). Automated testing of embedded automotive systems from requirement specification models. In *Proceedings of the 12th IEEE Latin-American Test Workshop.*

Urmson, C., Duggins, D., Jochem, T., Pomerleau, D., & Thorpe, C. (2008). From automated highways to urban challenges. In *Proceedings on IEEE International Conference on Vehicular Electronics and Safety* (pp. 6 – 10).

KEY TERMS AND DEFINITIONS

Cyber-Physical System (CPS): Continuously processes perceived data from its surroundings to generate actions.

Development and Evaluation Environment (DEE): Supports the development of CPS.

Domain Specific Language (DSL): Provides an intuitional syntax to describe relations or problems of a specific domain in a compact and well-known manner to the developer.

System Under Test (SUT): Evaluated by a testing approach.

ENDNOTES

[1] "Hesperia" was named according to a town in California where the team "CarOLO" was accommodated during the 2007 DARPA Urban Challenge.

Chapter 5
Performance Analysis of a Distributed Execution Environment for JUnit Test Cases on a Small Cluster

Eric Bower
ENSCO, Inc., USA

Tauhida Parveen
Independent Consultant, USA

Scott Tilley
Florida Institute of Technology, USA

ABSTRACT

HadoopUnit is a software testing framework that integrates Hadoop and JUnit to facilitate the distribution of unit tests to the nodes of a cluster for concurrent execution. It was conceived of the need to reduce test execution time for large collections of tests and has been shown to successfully accomplish this in a medium-size cluster of 150 nodes. This work considers its effectiveness on a small cluster (4 nodes) to determine any inefficiency present in the system and attempts to overcome them with the purpose of increasing performance. It was found that naïve use of HadoopUnit on a small cluster was slower than the best times achieved on a single machine, but by properly configuring the number of tests executed by each Hadoop Map task, a 75% reduction in execution time was achieved. These results show that, on a small scale, the original implementation of HadoopUnit may not be the best solution, but with the addition of a new feature, a significant increase in performance can be achieved.

DOI: 10.4018/978-1-4666-2536-5.ch005

INTRODUCTION

Testing is a process that includes evaluation of a software product to assess its quality. Proper testing increases the level of confidence in the quality of a product. Testing is a challenging activity for many software engineering projects and is one of the five main technical activity areas of the software engineering lifecycle (Sommerville, 2010) that still poses substantial challenges, especially for large-scale systems. Because testing can be such a difficult, expensive, and labor-intensive process, there is always high demand for better testing support.

For large, complex systems, the number of test cases can range from a few hundred to several thousand. Even computers with substantial processing capacity may require an excessive amount of time to execute such a large quantity of tests. Furthermore, test suites may need to be executed several times over the course of a day. This adds even more challenge to the problem of properly testing a system and identifying errors early in the development lifecycle. In addition, regression testing is often performed as a part of the software maintenance process, and the inability to provide test results in a timely manner to the software engineers involved can have a negative impact on system maintenance.

Testing also requires considerable resources that are often not readily available, contributing to an inefficient testing process. Imagine a scenario where an application needs to be tested for multiple configurations: different operating systems, multiple browsers, several database clients, and complex server interactions. A tester running thousands of test cases each day is required to manage the configuration for these machines, incurring considerable cost associated with setting up and tearing down the test configurations every time testing needs to be done.

One way to add efficiency to the testing process is through faster test execution, leading to better and faster feedback to programmers and testers.

Our solution to this problem is HadoopUnit, which integrates JUnit with Hadoop and has proven to be an effective means of reducing unit test runtime (Parveen, Tilley, Daley, & Morales, 2009). The initial work on HadoopUnit looked at testing the benefit of using Hadoop as a platform for distributed JUnit test case execution. It looked specifically at using Hadoop to reduce the runtime of JUnit tests of the Hadoop project, which was successfully accomplished. Using a medium-size cluster of 150 nodes, the total runtime was reduced 30 times.

As impressive as the results are, not everyone has access to even a medium-sized cluster such as this. To increase the adoption rate of HadoopUnit for software engineers and testers who may lack IT support for larger clusters, but who have access to a limited set of personal computers that can be formed into a small-scale cluster with relatively little effort, this work considers the performance of HadoopUnit on a small cluster of four nodes.

Execution runtimes of a single machine with varying amounts of processes are compared to those of HadoopUnit on the cluster, using test suites of processor-intensive and I/O-intensive tests at counts of 100 and 1000. Through experimentation, an adjustment to HadoopUnit was made providing a significant reduction of the total execution time, resulting in a benefit that can still be realized by engineers and testers working in highly resource-constrained environments.

The remainder of the chapter is structured as follows. The next section provides background information on software testing and the components used to create HadoopUnit. Section 3 describes the high-level design of HadoopUnit. Section 4 details the experiments conducted with a modified version of HadoopUnit on a 4-node cluster. Section 5 analyzes the results of the experiments and discusses the broader impact of this form of distributed execution for regression testing during software maintenance. Finally, Section 6 summarizes the work and outlines possible avenues for future investigation.

BACKGROUND

The following subsections provide background information on some of the fundamental topics related to this research. Included among them are software testing, JUnit, and Hadoop. These topics represent the core technologies and areas of study that were combined to advance the distributed test execution environment of HadoopUnit.

Software Testing

Three levels of testing are commonly applied to software: unit, integration, and system. Among those, unit testing focuses on individual functions, objects, or modules in insolation from the rest of the program. The rise of agile methodologies has put more emphasis on the need for unit testing in software engineering. Unit testing is a fundamental practice and a central tenet of agile methodologies, particularly Extreme Programming (XP) (Beck, 1999) and Test-Driven Development (TDD). This research focuses on execution of unit test cases, specifically running large regression suites of unit test cases.

Regression testing is the testing of software after modifications have been made (Wahl, 1999). It involves execution of existing test cases and any new test cases that may have been created due to the modification of the program. Regression testing is a critical activity of software engineering because it helps to validate modifications made to a program and it ensures that the modifications have not introduced any new bugs into previously tested code.

Although an important activity, regression testing can be very costly due to the large amount of test cases that build up over time. Specifically, the cost lies in the execution of a large number of test cases. In fact, lengthy run times associated with regression testing have become such a problem that it has been a topic of ongoing research in an attempt to reduce this expense.

JUnit

Unit testing is performed during the development of individual units (modules or functions) and are primarily created and executed by developers. This type of testing is also known as "developer's tests." Since every unit created should be accompanied by a test, the number of unit test cases grows very fast. Thus creating, executing, and maintaining unit testing requires the help of a framework.

Since unit tests need to be automated and they should be executed in batch, a common way of creating and executing unit test cases is by using automated testing frameworks. Various open source unit testing frameworks are available today which are collectively known as xUnit (Fowler, 2010). From the xUnit family, the JUnit testing framework is used for unit testing of Java code. JUnit supports the build-and-test approach of incremental testing, extreme programming, and the continuous testing approach. Regardless of the methodology, tests can be re-run following changes whether to the software directly or to configuration settings. The JUnit testing framework helps developers write test cases at the unit level, and provides functionality for running the test cases and presenting the results.

The main features of the JUnit framework are as follows:

- **Test Case:** The test case contains all test logic. These are composed of statements that invoke the code of the unit under test and verify its results. The test cases are represented by Java classes containing one or more test methods. Each test method is called a unit test and they embody the minimal unit of test code. The setUp and tearDown functions can optionally be implemented and are called automatically by the framework before and after each unit test runs. It is within these two functions that the test environment is intended to be created and then returned back to its default state.

- **Test Suite:** A test suite is an aggregation of one or more test cases. Multiple test cases can be run together in a test suite.
- **Test Result:** A test may pass, fail, or have an error. A test result contains information about the final state of the test execution.
- **Test Runner:** JUnit consists of test runners, which are responsible for executing test cases or test suite and thereby producing test results.

The JUnit framework facilitates the creation of test cases with minimal dependencies. Each test case is contained in a Java class file consisting of one or more tests. Each test may have dependencies between them but the test cases (classes) are independent and can be executed separately (JUnit, 2012).

JUnit provides assertions to verify test results. Assertions can be used to check many different data types, such as integer, Boolean, and string, and are applied within each test method. Test execution continues as long as the assertions pass. Upon assertion failure, the test method will halt execution and report the cause of the failure (JUnit, 2012).

Another feature available within JUnit is the ability to setup and tear down application state for each test method before running. This is accomplished by implementing setUp() and tearDown() functions that are executed immediately before and after each test method runs regardless of assertion results. In addition to supporting test creation and execution, JUnit also seamlessly integrates with Ant (Apache Ant, 2010) to further aid in the development lifecycle. With the execution of a single Ant command, an entire Java project can be built and tested (JUnit, 2012).

Hadoop

Google's MapReduce programming model, built on top of the distributed Google File System (Dean and Ghemawat, 2004), provides a parallelization framework that has acquired considerable attention for its ease-of-use, scalability, and fault-tolerance. MapReduce was created from a need to process large amounts of Web-based data, though its use is not restricted to this domain. The success at Google prompted the development of the Hadoop project (Apache Hadoop, 2010), hosted as a subproject of the Apache Software Foundation (Apache Software, 2010), an open-source attempt to reproduce Google's implementation of MapReduce. Although in early stages of development, the popularity of Hadoop is increasing rapidly. Hadoop has seen adoption by companies such as Amazon.com, Facebook, Google, IBM, Twitter, and Yahoo, to name a few. Hadoop is also available for use as a service from several companies, such as Amazon.com's Elastic MapReduce (EMR) web service running on the Elastic Compute Cloud (EC2) (Amazon, 2012).

Hadoop supplies both storage and data processing capability all in one framework and is intended for use on commodity hardware; there is no requirement for high-end servers to take advantage of the services provided. Hadoop consists of the Hadoop Distributed File System (HDFS), which stores data as well as intermediate results, and MapReduce for data processing. HDFS is a typical hierarchical file system where data is organized in files and directories. Hadoop provides the ability to divide data into discrete blocks, distribute them for processing, and then join the results back together as output, which is accomplished using MapReduce.

MapReduce is a programming model that applies a computation over a large number of records to generate partial results that are then aggregated in a way to provide an ultimate solution. The computation takes a set of input key/value pairs <key,value>, and produces a set of output key/value pairs. The Map function, written by the user, takes an input pair and produces a set of intermediate key/value pairs. The Reduce function, also written by the user, accepts an intermediate key and a set of values for that key. It merges together these values to form a possibly smaller set of values. More information on Hadoop and the MapReduce programming model can be found at the Apache Hadoop website.

HADOOPUNIT

HadoopUnit is a distributed execution framework for JUnit test cases that was developed as a Hadoop MapReduce job. HadoopUnit was developed in order to execute large numbers of unit tests in a timely fashion and has accomplished this by combining the divide and conquer technique employed by Hadoop with the unit test execution framework JUnit. HadoopUnit, like Hadoop, does not require expensive, high-end computers. Instead, it is intended to run on cheap, commodity hardware to perform its function.

HadoopUnit was designed as a browser based solution that interacts with the application server bundled with Hadoop thereby reducing the requirements of installation. Through the browser, users are provided with all the necessary controls for executing, monitoring, and reviewing test results via its dashboard. To facilitate understanding the manner in which unit test cases are executed concurrently as realized by the design of HadoopUnit, the following scenario may be considered:

A software engineer is working on a large project where the application is constantly evolving. This software is tested using JUnit test cases and the result of their execution is required as soon as possible to provide confidence to the software engineer about the changes being made.

The software engineer is aware of the distributed framework called HadoopUnit and would like to use this service every time there is a need to execute the regression suite. However, to use HadoopUnit, the engineer must have the projects production code, test cases (test code), and any other libraries for which there are dependencies, defined in an Apache Ant build script.

Assuming both Hadoop and HadoopUnit have already been installed, the engineer uses a Web browser to create a HadoopUnit project that references the software project, and starts the execution of its tests.

Behind the scenes, a list of all the test cases to be executed is constructed. Once this is complete, the list and all libraries required by the project's classpath are provided to Hadoop where they are loaded into the HDFS and the job is started. Hadoop splits the list of test cases and each test case is executed by a predefined Map function. By default, every piece of this split is a single test case.

Each Map is provided the fully qualified class name of the test case to execute. Using the test class and the current classpath of the map function, a command string is constructed to execute the test cases. The command string is executed as an external process to the map function which allows it to run within a new JVM. As tests complete, the results are sent back to the HadoopUnit server where they are accessible by the user.

Following Map execution, a Reduce function is called which takes a <key, value> pair as input. In this case it receives the <test name, test result> pair from each map, combines the pairs, and outputs them to a file. Since it was more sensible from a user point of view to have one aggregated output consisting of all the test execution results, only one reducer is used. The Reducer collects all the results and stores them on the HDFS. From either location, the engineer can view the results of the test execution.

The high level design for HadoopUnit that supports this scenario is shown in Figure 1. More details on the implementation of HadoopUnit and preliminary results from its use on a 150-node cluster can be found in (Parveen, Tilley, Daley, & Morales, 2009).

Figure 1. High level design of HadoopUnit

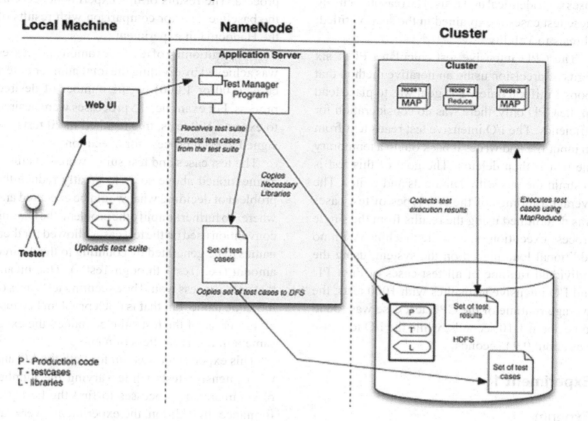

EXPERIMENTS AND RESULTS

The original work with HadoopUnit, achieved a reduction of the total execution time of a regression test suite by a factor of 30. However, not everyone has access to even medium-size clusters (150 nodes) such as that used in earlier work. The current research considers the performance of HadoopUnit on a much smaller cluster (4 nodes), attempts to determine when it is appropriate for use in this context, and provides guidance for further reducing execution time.

Toward this goal, to test the benefit of using HadoopUnit as a platform for distributed JUnit test case execution, several experiments were setup to run test cases. These experiments included running test suites both with and without HadoopUnit in order to compare the execution times. Both se-

quential and concurrent execution strategies were used on a single machine to provide a baseline for comparison, since this closely resembles a typical testing environment for software engineers.

The experiments were conducted on a small cluster of four nodes. The nodes were running a Unix OS with 64-bit SparcV9 processors and 1 GB of RAM each. All nodes were single processor, single core systems with two operating at 1 GHz and two operating at 1.5 GHz. The experiments were conducted using two different test suites, executed at separate times: one that was processor (CPU) intensive and the other that was I/O intensive. The two test suites were homogenous in that they contained a single test case duplicated 1,000 times. The test cases both contained a single unit test either CPU or I/O intensive. The end result was two test suites, each composed of 1,000 test cases with identical unit tests. The reason for using these test cases is explained in the section titled: Threats to Validity.

The CPU intensive test calculates PI to six digits of precision using an iterative method that loops 3 million times. The goal was to place load on the CPU only, there was no consideration for efficiency. The I/O intensive test reads text from an input file and writes it back out to a temporary file that is then deleted. The goal of this test is to strain the bus with data reads and writes. The average runtimes of the two types of test cases was determined using the results from the single process execution on a single machine. With no additional load placed on the system, using the individual runtime of all test cases of the CPU and I/O intensive test suites with 1000 tests, the average runtime of the CPU test case was found to be about 1.10 seconds, while the I/O test case was about 0.94 seconds.

Experiment 1

Experiment

The first experiment was conducted to determine the performance of JUnit test execution on a single machine without the aid of HadoopUnit. This was accomplished by running the two test suites in multiple processes to find the lowest achievable execution time. The experiment was controlled by a Java program that calculated the number of test cases to be executed by each process, given the desired number of concurrent processes. These processes were then executed (as external processes to the JVM) using the Runtime.exec command. Each process ran the test cases by executing Ant and specifying the number of tests to run. Given the set of concurrent processes executing the tests of a test suite, the reported runtime was that of the longest running process. In other words, the time taken to execute a test suite in multiple concurrent processes is the run time of the longest running

process. The results of this experiment serve as the baseline data for comparison with results of the HadoopUnit experiments.

The partitioning of test cases among processes was achieved by dividing the total number of test cases (100 or 1,000) by the number of desired process. For example, if 5 processes were desired to execute 100 tests, this resulted in 20 tests assigned to each process for execution.

The test cases and test suites were structured as mentioned above so as to greatly reduce the problem of deciding what would be executed and where. To further simplify the problem, the naming convention used on the test cases allowed for their names to be generated by counting to the desired amount (i.e., Test1 through TestN). This means that each process would be executing test cases of the same name, but that is not a problem because all test cases of the test suite contained the exact same unit test regardless of name.

This experiment was run for both the I/O and CPU intensive tests while varying the number of simultaneous processes to find the best performance. In addition, the experiments were run using 100 and 1,000 test cases to determine if the execution time scaled linearly with the number of test cases.

Results

With the setup mentioned above, a series of experiments were conducted and the execution times recorded. The goal was to determine what the execution time of the test suites would be when the test cases were run both sequentially and concurrently. Sequential execution of the tests means that all tests were run in a single process, one after another. The runtime for this case is reported because it is the typical manner that regression tests are run. The purpose of running the tests concurrently is to determine the peak performance that can be attained on one machine. It is expected that sequential execution

Table 1. Sequential and concurrent execution of 100 test cases

100 Test Cases	CPU Intensive	I/O Intensive
Sequential Runtime (s)	247	215
Multi-process Runtime (s)	164	143
Process Count	5	5

Table 2. Sequential and concurrent execution of 1,000 test cases

1000 Test Cases	CPU Intensive	I/O Intensive
Sequential Runtime (s)	2567	2240
Multi-process Runtime (s)	1567	1337
Process Count	7	10

will not produce the fastest runtimes. The results of the experimental runs are shown in Table 1 and Table 2.

The 100 test case suites ran in 247 seconds for the CPU tests and 215 seconds for the I/O tests. The 1,000 test case suites reported times of 2567 and 2240 seconds for the CPU and I/O test cases respectively. The fastest concurrent runtimes of the 100 test case suite were 164 seconds for the CPU intensive and 143 seconds for the I/O intensive and were achieved by each while running the tests in 5 processes. In the 1,000 test case suite, the best times were found to be 1567 and 1337 seconds, running 7 and 10 processes, for the CPU and I/O test cases respectively.

Analysis

These results show that a ten-fold increase in the number of test cases resulted in an increase, nearly the same, in execution time for the sequential execution and also for the concurrent execution. The variation in process count for the test suites of 1,000 tests can be attributed to slight variations in performance. At about 5 simultaneous processes, the graphs depicting runtime for both the CPU and I/O tests approached an asymptote where they fluctuated within 5% of the reported minimum while trending upwards. These numbers represent the best runtimes achieved by a single machine and will serve as a baseline when comparing the runtime of the tests using HadoopUnit.

Experiment 2

Experiment

The second series of experiments was a re-creation of the first set with the addition of HadoopUnit to coordinate the four available nodes in the cluster. Within Hadoop, a map task is a process run on one of its nodes; therefore the total number of concurrent processes would be equal to the number of map tasks per node multiplied by the number of nodes. Note that each node was assigned the same number of map tasks to execute concurrently, which does not mean that each node will run the same amount of map tasks. Setup required starting Hadoop and HadoopUnit, as well as creating a project for each of the four test suites in HadoopUnit. The four cases being: CPU test suites at counts of 100 and 1000 tests, and I/O test suites at counts of 100 and 1000 tests. Controlling the number of tests included in each scenario was done using a build.xml provided to Apache Ant. See Table 3 and Table 4.

Result

The test execution results for 100 test cases show that while HadoopUnit was able to improve the runtime as compared to the sequential execution of the test suites, it came in slightly behind the best times found on an individual machine. The fastest times returned from HadoopUnit were 179 and 164 seconds for the CPU and I/O tests which translate to running approximately 9% (15 seconds) and 15% (21 seconds) slower than when

Table 3. Test execution using HadoopUnit for 100 test cases

100 Test Cases	CPU Intensive	I/O Intensive
Sequential Runtime (s)	247	215
Multi-process Runtime (s)	164	143
Hadoop Unit Runtime (s)	**179**	**164**

Table 4. Test execution using HadoopUnit for 1000 test cases

1000 Test Cases	CPU Intensive	I/O Intensive
Sequential Runtime (s)	2567	2240
Multi-process Runtime (s)	1567	1337
Hadoop Unit Runtime (s)	**1657**	**1638**

run as multiple processes on a single machine. Running three map tasks on each of the Hadoop nodes produced these results.

The 1,000 test case suite resulted in similar numbers showing that HadoopUnit does provide some improvement over the sequential execution of the tests, but that a single machine can actually produce better results than a cluster of four nodes by partitioning the tests for execution as multiple concurrent processes. HadoopUnit ran about 6% (90 seconds) slower when running the CPU tests while the I/O tests work out to be 23% (301 seconds) slower than multiple processes on a single machine. The best times produced by HadoopUnit were done so running 2 map tasks per node, which corresponds to 8 tasks running throughout the cluster.

Analysis

The results from experiment 2 show that given a small Hadoop cluster of four nodes, the execution of JUnit tests is actually better suited for multiple concurrent processes on a single machine rather

than via HadoopUnit. Moreover, the observed performance of HadoopUnit did not provide a significant improvement over sequential execution of the test suites either.

The answer to the question of why the numbers returned from the execution of Hadoop with four nodes are larger than what was found on a single machine running the tests in multiple processes was found by further investigation into the Hadoop framework. The Hadoop documentation claims that "Task setup takes a while, so it is best if the maps take at least a minute to execute" (How Many, 2009). Going back to the average runtime of the two types of unit tests used in this research, each CPU test runs on average 1.10 seconds and the I/O test in about 0.94 seconds. This suggests that the workload per map task is significantly less than is prescribed by Hadoop and may be dwarfed by the amount of overhead required to setup and execute the map function, which is running our JUnit test cases.

To confirm this hypothesis, Equation 1 was used to provide a close approximation of the overhead of the map function:

$$\bar{t}_{MO} = (T - \sum_{1}^{n} t_M) / N_m \tag{1}$$

where:

$\bar{t}_{MO}$ = Average map overhead time

T = Total runtime of the test suite

$\sum_{1}^{n} t_M$ = Sum of the runtime of each test case

N_m = Number of map tasks

This equation does not take into consideration the following issues:

- The project startup time, the time taken for HadoopUnit to distribute the classpath libraries required by the tests, out to the HDFS. For the tests used in these experiments, this time is negligible due to minimal required classpath libraries.
- The overhead time introduced by HadoopUnit to perform the setup, execution, and reporting of results of the test cases within the map task. This value will ultimately be included in the map overhead and is expected to also be small.

To remove as much error as possible when collecting this data, HadoopUnit was reduced to using a single data node executing a single map task. In doing so, the possibility of one node running faster than another was removed. Solving for the average map overhead, it was discovered that there are approximately 5.5 seconds of overhead time associated with each map task. As mentioned above, there are portions of this number that can be attributed to other tasks.

However, this is a significant amount of time needed to setup a map task as compared to the average time taken to execute the unit tests used in these experiments. The overhead reported here would not be the same for every installation of Hadoop as the specifications of the available nodes will differ from those used in these experiments; however this should serve to highlight the importance of properly loading each map task. In fact, this is a lesson that all users of Hadoop can benefit from regardless of the type of work being performed using the Hadoop framework.

Experiment 3

Experiment

The analysis of Experiment 2 led to the conclusion that it is important to ensure an appropriate amount of work for each map task; otherwise its overhead can play a significant role in the overall

performance of the job. The initial implementation of HadoopUnit called for one test case to be executed in one map task, and experiments showed that for certain test cases (e.g., test cases whose execution time is very short), this can significantly increase the execution time of a test suite. The proposed solution to this problem is to increase the workload of each Map task by setting up multiple test cases for execution by each, thereby reducing the number of Maps and the overhead imposed. In doing so, there are a few factors to consider:

- **Average Runtime of Test Cases in a Test Suite:** As this average run time becomes larger, the influence of the map overhead on the overall run times of the test suite becomes smaller. The test cases used in these experiments have relatively short run times, which translate to a greater influence due to map overhead.
- **Number of Nodes Available for Execution:** As the number of available nodes approaches the number of test cases, the map overhead will become less important due to the large number of map functions executing at the same time. However with a small cluster, the number of maps executed sequentially on each node becomes much larger which translates to longer runtimes.

The need to control the number of JUnit test cases sent to each map task was handled by making this a configurable parameter passed to HadoopUnit via the Ant build file. The test cases were then executed using HadoopUnit in two ways: (a) sequentially, and (b) concurrently within each map. The concurrent execution of test cases within a Map task was accomplished in a fashion similar to what was done in Experiment I to execute multiple, concurrent processes on a single machine. Each test case is executed as an external process (separate from the JVM of the Map) by using Runtime.exec. In order to obtain the results of each test case, a reader is setup on the process. Due to the blocking of thread execution that occurs while reading the output of a process, the only way to run the external processes concurrently is to start them from a separate thread that is executed by the Map. The Map is then required to wait for all to finish before it can emit the results and return.

Once properly setup, experiments were again conducted using test suites of 100 and 1,000 test cases distributed to multiple nodes, this time varying the number of test cases executed by each Map task. The number of Map tasks per node was held constant at 2, the default value, in order to reduce the complexity.

Result

The results of executing multiple test cases concurrently within a single map task for the suite of 100 tests are also shown in Table 5. The best CPU execution time was found to be 106 seconds (executing four test cases concurrently per map). The best I/O execution time was 85 seconds (executing 11 test cases per map). Comparing these numbers against the sequential execution on a single machine it was found that the CPU tests ran 57% faster and the I/O tests ran 60% faster. As compared to the concurrent execution on a single machine, the CPU tests ran 35% faster and the I/O tests ran 41% faster.

The results of running multiple test cases sequentially within each Map for the suite of 1,000 test cases can be seen in Table 6. The fastest sequential execution of multiple tests by a Map task ran in 646 and 551 seconds for the CPU and I/O cases respectively and the times for both test suites were achieved by running 15 test cases per map. Comparing these numbers against the sequential execution of tests on a single machine, both the CPU and I/O tests ran approximately 75% faster. As compared to the concurrent execution on a single machine, the CPU and I/O tests both finished 59% faster.

Table 5. Test execution of multiple tests per map (100 tests)

100 Test Cases	CPU Intensive	I/O Intensive
Sequential Runtime within one map (s)	93	87
Concurrent Runtime within one map (s)	106	85

Table 6. Test execution of multiple tests per map (1,000 tests)

1000 Test Cases	CPU Intensive	I/O Intensive
Sequential Runtime within one map (s)	646	551
Concurrent Runtime within one map (s)	793	753

The results acquired while running multiple test cases concurrently within each Map task for the test suite of 1000 tests can also be seen in Table 6. It was found that the fastest time for the CPU tests was 793 seconds and for the I/O tests was 753 seconds. Comparing against the sequential execution time on a single machine, the CPU tests were 69% faster and the I/O tests were 66% faster. Examining the differences with the concurrent process execution on a single machine, it was found that the CPU tests ran 49% faster and the I/O tests ran 44% faster.

Analysis

While the execution times of the test suites by the initial implementation of HadoopUnit were not faster than what could be produced on a single machine, there was a significant reduction in run time achieved by properly loading the Map tasks regardless of whether the test cases were executed sequentially or concurrently. Surprisingly, the execution times of these test suites ran nearly 2 to 3 times faster than the times recorded when a 1-to-1 ratio between map tasks and test cases existed and 1.5 to nearly 2.5 times faster than a single machine executing them in multiple concurrent processes.

The numbers are also impressive when considering the performance as the number of test cases scaled up by a factor of 10. As found in the results of execution on a single machine running the tests in single and multiple concurrent processes, as well as the results of the original implementation of HadoopUnit, the runtimes scaled up roughly by a factor of 10 following that of the number of tests. However, the scale factors when executing multiple test cases sequentially within each map task for the CPU and I/O tests were 6.9 and 6.3 respectively.

Analyses of these results are very promising. They suggest that even in a small-scale implementation such as used in these experiments (i.e., a four-node cluster), a significant improvement in runtime can be expected even as the number of tests begins to grow large. This implies that considerable, measurable benefits can be realized when running regression test suites during software maintenance even with very limited resources.

DISCUSSION

As described above, several experiments were conducted under various setups to analyze the performance of distributed execution of test cases on a small cluster using HadoopUnit. In the discussion below, the experimental setup included the following five configurations:

1. Single machine, sequential execution
2. Single machine, concurrent execution
3. Original HadoopUnit, one test case per Map task
4. Revised HadoopUnit, multiple test cases per Map, executed sequentially
5. Revised HadoopUnit, multiple test cases per Map, executed concurrently

This section provides an analysis of the results across all three experiments and also discusses threats to validity of the results, application to the cloud, and compares this research to related work.

Analysis of Experimental Results

The charts in Figure 2 and Figure 3 illustrate the best results obtained from conducting the experiments under various setups. In each of these charts, the first grouping represents the results of the CPU tests and the second grouping, the I/O tests. The data points appear as the experimental setups mentioned above, with test suites of 100 and 1,000 test cases. In all cases, the benefit obtained by creating a many-to-one ratio of test cases to Map tasks is evident.

As compared to the sequential execution on a single machine, the revised HadoopUnit was able to complete test suite execution from 2.3 to 4 times faster, with the most significant improvements in the 1,000 test case suite.

When considering the results of the multi-test per Map of the updated HadoopUnit as compared to the multiple concurrent process execution on a single machine, the revised HadoopUnit provided a speed up of 1.5 to nearly 2.5 times. These numbers are compared to the slower performance of the original HadoopUnit. This may not be overly impressive, but considering the original operation of HadoopUnit was actually slower than the execution in multiple concurrent processes on a single machine, the improvement is notable.

Comparing the improved operation of the revised HadoopUnit to its original, a reduction in run time of between 1.7 and 3 times was found. With the original implementation of HadoopUnit, which maintained a 1-to-1 ratio between Map tasks and test cases, the CPU tests ran 48% faster and the I/O tests ran 47% faster by executing multiple test cases in each Map task for execution of 100 test cases running sequentially in a map. For execution of 100 test cases running concurrently within each map, the CPU tests ran 41% faster

Figure 2. Best performance attained for 100 tests

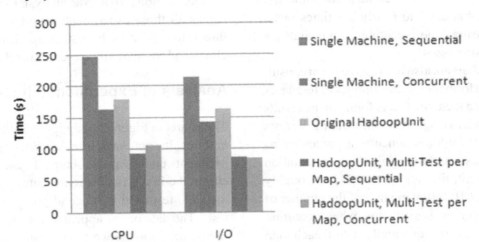

Figure 3. Best performance attained for 1,000 tests

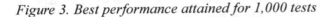
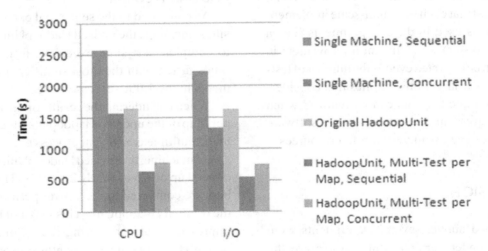

and the I/O tests ran 48% faster. For 1,000 test cases executing sequentially within one map, the CPU tests ran 61% faster while the I/O tests ran 66% faster than the original of 1-to-1 test to map implementation of HadoopUnit. Lastly, the CPU tests ran 52% faster while the I/O tests ran 54% faster for execution of 1000 test cases running concurrently within each map.

This is probably the most noteworthy of the results, as it represents the recognition of a problem within the original HadoopUnit implementation and its correction. This in no way should diminish the results as compared to the single machine, single process execution. However, what has been shown amounts to a potentially great increase in performance of HadoopUnit.

In summary, when analyzing the execution times scaled as the size of the test suites increased 10 fold, we have found that the sequential execution of multiple tests by a Map task provided the best performance increasing by a factor as small as 6.3 times. This may be the most significant discovery of these experiments because it shows that execution times of regression test suites executed by the revised HadoopUnit will scale very well as the number of tests increase, even on a very small cluster of 4 nodes.

Threats to Validity

Like all applications, HadoopUnit has limitations and it is not meant to be applied to all types of testing. Some of the decisions that were made regarding experimentation drew concerns that could threaten the validity of the data and conclusions that were drawn. The following are the threats to validity for this research:

Constraints on Types of Testing

It is very important to note that this paper and the experiments mentioned are conducted on unit test cases, specifically JUnit test cases. Therefore the following assumptions are considered:

- There are no dependencies among the test cases (test classes). JUnit provides such an environment to create test cases that are not dependent on each other. Therefore, the results or execution of previous test cases does not affect the execution of the next test case.
- It is assumed that there are no temporal or resource dependencies which may lead to deadlock or memory problems. We acknowledge that this might be the case for some test cases and we consider that to be something that needs to be addressed in future work.
- Since these are unit test cases, there are no databases or other external interaction or connections involved in executing these JUnit test cases. (Usually such connectivity and module integration is assumed for integration testing which is not the focus of this research at its current stage.)

- In its current state, HadoopUnit does not provide support for the ordering or prioritizing of test cases. There is other research on methods to minimize regression test suites, such as test case selection (Graves, Harrold, Kim, Porter, & Rothermel, 2001; Rothermel, & Harrold, 1997), test case prioritization (Rothermel, Untch, & Chu, 2001; Rothermel, Untch, Chu, & Harrold, 1999), and test suite reduction (Harrold, Gupta, & Soffa, 1993; Black, Melachrinoudis, & Kaeli, 2004). Our technique is complementary to these traditional approaches; they can be used as pre-processing before test cases are executed using HadoopUnit.

Choice of Test Cases for Research

For the performed experiments, two categories of tests were selected: CPU and I/O intensive. Within each category, a single test was duplicated to create suites of 1000 tests. The decision to use only two different unit tests, 1 of the CPU intensive type and 1 of the I/O intensive type, was made for several reasons and they are as follow:

- The goal was to load each process with the same amount of work and populating the test suite with the same test case allows for this. If each test case were different, there would be no expectation on the runtime or the type of load placed on the machine.
- It removes any ambiguity over what tests were executed and on which node.
- Execution times can be directly compared regardless of how many maps or processes were used when running a test suite.

Despite this reasoning, the option of using a real world test suite could have been exercised to produce data with direct application. Working in this direction may have provided more validity to the results, but it would also have introduced variables that may not have been fully understood due to a lack of familiarity with the software being tested. For example, test execution time could potentially have been affected by a variable value such as the date or time of day. If this were the case, runtime could change depending on when the tests were executed. Using a controlled suite of tests, variables such as this could be guaranteed not to influence the performance of the system and thus not threaten the validity of the results.

False Negatives

False negatives can result when the test execution environment fails, but the application under test may be fine. For example, any code (test or production) reading or writing a file to the file system may not be able to find the desired location resulting in false failures of tests due to exceptions being thrown. Thus, there is no guarantee what node each test will be executed on, so unless a network location or common path that exists everywhere is used, such failures may occur even though the software may be running free of bugs.

Cluster Size

Previous work with HadoopUnit was performed using a cluster of 150 nodes, so a question that may come to mind is: Why reduce the cluster size to only 4 nodes? The answer is to better determine the efficiency of the system. Using a cluster of 150 nodes likely masked the overhead issues that became obvious in the small scale implementation. Without a significant reduction in cluster size, the problem may have never been found. In doing so, we have found a way to further reduce test execution time which is at the core of this research.

SUMMARY

Large companies such as Google are purported to have over 3 million test cases, with over 120 million tests run on a daily basis (Copeland, 2010). This is a truly impressive scale of regression testing, and perhaps not one that every company shares. Nevertheless, the allure of reducing the execution time for regression testing during software maintenance for most organizations is very strong. It is only possible to achieve quality in such a torrential environment by moving to a faster execution and rapid feedback environment. HadoopUnit offers such potential.

HadoopUnit has the potential to change the way software engineers look at unit testing and running large regression test suites. By providing a solution that can quickly execute large test suites, users of HadoopUnit can put the lengthy intervals of test execution in the past. The excuse of having too many tests will no longer be usable as this scalable solution can grow with the number of tests. With the addition of every new node, HadoopUnit provides test results faster and faster up to the point where there is a single test per node to be executed. The ability to quickly provide management with the current state of a project in short order, regardless of the number of tests, may prove to be an invaluable asset.

Our previous experience with HadoopUnit has shown it to be an effective means of reducing the execution time of JUnit tests on a medium-size cluster (150 nodes) of commodity computers. However, not everyone has access to even medium-size clusters such as this. This paper presented the performance of a revised version of HadoopUnit on a much smaller cluster (four nodes). The results show that even in the constrained environment of a 4-node cluster, HadoopUnit can significantly outperform single-machine execution (sequential or parallel) of regression tests.

REFERENCES

Amazon. (2012). *Elastic MapReduce*. Retrieved from http://aws.amazon.com/elasticmapreduce/

Apache. (2010). *Ant*. Retrieved from http://ant.apache.org/

Apache. (2010). *Hadoop*. Retrieved from http://hadoop.apache.org/

Apache Software Foundation. (2010). Retrieved from http://www.apache.org/

Beck, K. (1999). *Extreme programming explained: Embrace change*. Addison-Wesley Professional.

Black, J., Melachrinoudis, E., & Kaeli, D. (2004). Bi-criteria models for all-uses test suite reduction. In *International Conference on Software Engineering* (pp. 106-115). Washington, DC: IEEE Computer Society.

Copeland, P. (2010). Google's innovation factory: Testing, culture, and infrastructure. In *3rd IEEE International Conference on Software Testing, Verification, and Validation* (pp.11-14). Los Alamitos, CA: IEEE CS Press. doi:10.1109/ICST.2010.65

Dean, J., & Ghemawat, S. (2004). MapReduce: Simplified data processing on large clusters. *Communications of the ACM, 51*(1), 107–113. doi:10.1145/1327452.1327492

Fowler, M. (2010). *Xunit*. Retrieved from http://www.martinfowler.com/bliki/Xunit.html

Graves, T., Harrold, M., Kim, Y., Porter, A., & Rothermel, G. (2001). An empirical study of regression test selection techniques. *ACM Transactions on Software Engineering and Methodology, 10*(2), 184–208. doi:10.1145/367008.367020

Hadoop Wiki. (2009). *How many maps and reduces*. Retrieved from http://wiki.apache.org/hadoop/HowManyMapsAndReduces

Harrold, M., Gupta, R., & Soffa, M. (1993). A methodology for controlling the size of a test suite. *ACM Transactions on Software Engineering and Methodology, 2*(3), 270–285. doi:10.1145/152388.152391

JUnit. (2012). Retrieved from http://junit.org

Parveen, T., Tilley, S., Daley, N., & Morales, P. (2009). Towards a distributed execution framework for JUnit test cases. In *Proceedings of the 25th IEEE International Conference on Software Maintenance* (pp. 425-428). Los Alamitos, CA: IEEE Computer Society. doi:10.1109/ICSM.2009.5306292

Rothermel, G., & Harrold, M. (1997). A safe, efficient regression test selection technique. *ACM Transactions on Software Engineering and Methodology, 6*(2), 173–210. doi:10.1145/248233.248262

Rothermel, G., & Untch, R. Chu, C., & Harrold, M. (1999). Test case prioritization: An empirical study. In *IEEE International Conference of Software Maintenance* (pp. 179–188). Los Alamitos, CA: IEEE Computer Society. doi:10.1109/ICSM.1999.792604

Rothermel, G., Untch, R., & Chu, C. (2001). Prioritizing test cases for regression testing. *IEEE Transactions on Software Engineering, 27*(10), 929–948. doi:10.1109/32.962562

Sommerville, I. (2010). *Software engineering* (9th ed.). Addison Wesley.

Wahl, N. (1999). An overview of regression testing. *ACM SIGSOFT Software Engineering Notes, 24*(1), 69–73. doi:10.1145/308769.308790

KEY TERMS AND DEFINITIONS

Distributed System: A collection of computers that are organized to work together toward the goal of reducing processing time.

Hadoop: An open-source software framework for distributing vast amounts of data to a cluster of computers for processing.

HadoopUnit: A software testing framework that integrates Hadoop and JUnit to facilitate the distribution of unit tests to the nodes of a cluster for concurrent execution.

JUnit: A framework for unit testing Java code.

Software Testing: The process of exercising software to ensure it behaves as designed.

Chapter 6
Towards Migrating Genetic Algorithms for Test Data Generation to the Cloud

Sergio Di Martino
University of Naples Federico II, Italy

Filomena Ferrucci
University of Salerno, Italy

Valerio Maggio
University of Naples Federico II, Italy

Federica Sarro
University of Salerno, Italy

ABSTRACT

Search-Based Software Testing is a well-established research area, whose goal is to apply meta-heuristic approaches, like Genetic Algorithms, to address optimization problems in the testing domain. Even if many interesting results have been achieved in this field, the heavy computational resources required by these approaches are limiting their practical application in the industrial domain. In this chapter, the authors propose the migration of Search-Based Software Testing techniques to the Cloud aiming to improve their performance and scalability. Moreover, they show how the use of the MapReduce paradigm can support the parallelization of Genetic Algorithms for test data generation and their migration in the Cloud, thus relieving software company from the management and maintenance of the overall IT infrastructure and developers from handling the communication and synchronization of parallel tasks. Some preliminary results are reported, gathered by a proof-of-concept developed on the Google's Cloud Infrastructure.

DOI: 10.4018/978-1-4666-2536-5.ch006

INTRODUCTION

The software testing encompasses a range of different activities that are critical for software quality assurance. For each activity, depending on the testing objective, specific test cases need to be devised to check the system (Bertolino, 2007). Since an exhaustive enumeration of software inputs is unfeasible for any reasonable-sized system (McMinn, 2004), a careful selection of test data must be performed to obtain a high testing effectiveness. This task is often difficult, time-consuming, and error-prone. Thus, the need to decrease time and costs of software testing, while increasing its effectiveness has motivated the research for advanced techniques able to automatically generate test data. This is an active research area and a number of different approaches has been proposed and investigated in the literature (e.g., (Ali, 2010; Bertolino, 2007; De Millo, 1991; Miller, 1976)).

Among them, Search-Based techniques (Harman, 2007) are promising approaches to increase testing quality, by automatically generating relevant test data (Harman, 2001). Search-Based techniques include a variety of meta-heuristics, such as Local Search (i.e., Hill Climbing, Tabu Search, Simulated Annealing, etc.), Evolutionary Algorithms (i.e., Genetic Algorithms, Evolution Strategies, Genetic Programming, etc...), Ant Colony Optimization, or Particle Swarm Optimization. All these meta-heuristics search for a suitable solution in a typically large input space guided by a fitness function which expresses the goals and leads the exploration into potentially promising areas of the search space. Thus, using these approaches, test data generation is treated as a search or optimization problem whose goal is to find the most appropriate input data conforming to some adequacy criteria (i.e., test goals/objectives), such as maximizing the code coverage. Thus, moving from conventional manual test data definition to Search-Based test data generation essentially consists in defining a suitable fitness function to determine how good a test input is.

The generic nature of these metaheuristics let them to be fruitful for different testing goals and issues, simply by redefining the solution representation and the fitness function. Thus, in the last decades there has been an explosion of researches on the use of Search-Based techniques for software testing that have addressed a range of testing problems, giving rise to a very active research field, known as Search-Based Software Testing (SBST). These techniques have been used for structural testing (both static and dynamic) functional testing (both for generating test data and testing the conformance of the implementation to its specification), non-functional testing (e.g., testing for robustness, stress testing, security testing, gray-box testing (e.g., assertion testing and exception condition testing), state–based testing, mutation testing), regression testing interaction testing, integration testing, test case prioritization, and so on (McMinn, 2004; Ali, 2010). Despite all such efforts, so far these investigations have produced limited impact in industry (Bertolino, 2007). Maybe the main reason for that lies in the fact that few attempts have been made to improve performance of these techniques and make them more scalable. On the other hand, while several empirical studies have been carried out showing that Search-Based testing can outperform other automated testing approaches (e.g., random testing), little attention has been deserved to the scalability and effectiveness issues for real world applications (Ali, 2010). One of the few experimentation with complete open source applications reported that there are still many challenges to be addressed to make existing Search-Based test data generation tools robust and with a significant level of code coverage that can be useful for industrial use (Lakhotia, 2009).

The use of Cloud Computing can provide a significant impulse in this direction. Indeed, this model is based on the provisioning of configurable computing resources in a distributed environment allowing for an on-demand resource allocation from a virtual unlimited resources and infrastructure functionality. Thus, with respect to the use of traditional cluster-based platform, Cloud Computing allows for easy scalability in a cost effective way since it eliminates unnecessary purchases, allowing one to pay only for the resources actually used, and does not require management and maintenance of the overall IT infrastructure.

As a consequence, the migration of SBST techniques to the Cloud leads to two main advantages for software companies:

1. Achieving a greater efficiency and scalability, thus reinforcing the cost-effectiveness of these testing approaches.
2. Allowing for the exploration of solution spaces larger than those considered by canonical sequential Search-Based techniques, by means of an easy-to-use parallelization mechanism.

In this chapter, we focus on the problem of test data generation and the use of Genetic Algorithms. We start by providing background on Genetic Algorithms and its application to software testing. Then, we describe three possible architectures for migrating Genetic Algorithms to the Cloud exploiting the MapReduce paradigm (Dean, 2004). Moreover, we provide a proof-of-concept, with some initial experimental results, based on Google's Cloud infrastructure, namely App Engine (Google, 2012). Some indication on future research directions and final remarks close the chapter.

BACKGROUND: GENETIC ALGORITHM AND ITS USE FOR TEST DATA GENERATION

Genetic Algorithms (GAs) are meta-heuristics that simulate the evolution of natural systems, emphasizing the principles of survival of the strongest to solve, or approximately solve, optimization problems. Thus, these algorithms create consecutive populations of individuals, considered as feasible solutions for a given problem, to search for a solution that provides a good approximation of the optimum for the problem under investigation. In the literature several studies have reported that this approach consistently outperforms traditional optimization methods for many classes of problems (Goldberg, 1989; Harman, 2001).

In the implementation of a GA, there are several key aspects that have to be considered for its application to any given optimization problem (Harman, 2001). A crucial role is played by the way a solution is represented for the given domain. In general, such a solution is encoded by a fixed length binary string, called chromosome (in analogy with the biological equivalent), that embeds values for the variables involved in the problem. Each chromosome is evaluated by means of a properly defined fitness function that gives an indication of its goodness in solving the problem. Clearly, the choice of a good function plays a central role in the definition of a suitable GA. Consequently, in general, the elementary process of each GA is the following:

1. A random initial population, i.e. a family of chromosomes, is generated.
2. A new population (i.e. a generation), intended as a set of new chromosomes, is created, starting from the previous one, by applying genetic operators (e.g., crossover, mutation) to a subset of properly chosen chromosomes, in order to explore other solutions in the search space.
3. The second step is repeated until either (1) the fitness of the best solution has converged or (2) a maximum number of generations has been reached. The chromosome with the best solution in the last generation is taken, giving the best approximation to the optimum for the problem under investigation.

Summarizing, in the application of GAs, the following issues have to be addressed (Harman, 2001):

- Defining the way a chromosome encodes a solution and choosing the number of considered chromosomes (i.e., the population size).
- Defining the fitness function to measure the goodness of a chromosome.
- Defining how to apply genetic operators to generate new offspring.
- Defining the halting criteria.

For test data generation, the search space consists in the set of the possible inputs to the program (Harman, 2001; Srivastava, 2009). Consequently, each chromosome represents a specific set of values for the involved parameters and has to be encoded in a way that allows for mutation and crossover operations. The goodness of each chromosome is measured as the conformance to a given adequacy criterion, defined by the tester, and depends on the test problem under investigation. As an example, in the case of white box testing, fitness functions based on structural testing measures can be exploited to get indications on the

goodness of chromosomes. The most employed code coverage measures are (Glenford, 2004):

- **Statement Coverage:** Measures the ratio of covered statements with respect to the total number of statements. A statement is covered if it is exercised at least once.
- **Decision (or Branch) Coverage:** Measures the ratio of covered decisions with respect to the total number of decisions. A decision is covered if it is exercised on the *true* and *false* outcomes, at least once.
- **Condition Coverage:** Measures the ratio of covered conditions with respect to the total number of conditions. A condition is covered if each of its decisions takes on all possible outcomes at least once.

A general schema related to the use of GAs as test data generators is shown in Figure 1. Once the tester has defined the specific GA identifying the above aspects (e.g., the evaluation criterion, encoded within a fitness function), the GA generates test data to exercise the SUT, leading to an evaluation of the fitness value. It is worth noting that for white box testing, this observation can be done by properly utilizing the code (i.e., the

Figure 1. A generic GA scheme for test data generation

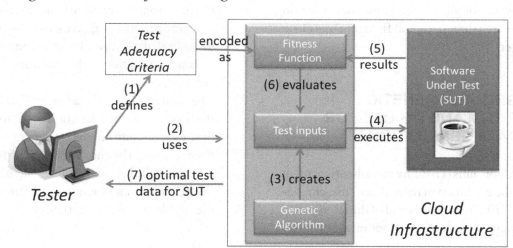

software execution must be traced), while for black box testing it is necessary to look at the obtained results. Once the evolutionary process of GA is terminated, the chromosome giving the best fitness value for the defined criterion is returned in output to the tester as the best set of test data.

MIGRATING GENETIC ALGORITHMS FOR SBST TO THE CLOUD

In this section we start by discussing how to parallelize GAs together with the main technical difficulties that must be faced. Then, we present different ways to exploit the Cloud Computing and the MapReduce model to achieve distributed GAs for software test data generation.

Parallelizing GAs for SBST

To date, SBST solutions have found limited application in industry (Bertolino, 2007). As in other fields of Search-Based Software Engineering, this is principally due to the fact that in general when applied to large problems, Search-Based approaches (including GA) may require too much computational efforts (Harman, 2007) and "many approaches that are attractive and elegant in the laboratory, turn out to be inapplicable in the field, because they lack scalability" (Harman, 2007).

In this scenario, parallelization may be a suitable way to improve SBST performance, both in terms of computational time and effectiveness in the exploration of the search space. Let us note that GAs are "naturally parallelizable" (Harman, 2007) since their population based characteristics allows to evaluate in a parallel way the fitness of each individual, with a minimal overhead.

When dealing with GAs applied in the field of SBST, the benefits of the parallelism can be twofold. From one hand, it can be used to compute in a concurrent fashion how much each chromosome exercises the SUT. On the other hand, it can be used to perform genetic operators and thus to generate the next set of test data. Furthermore, these two strategies can be combined, giving rise to the following three main grains of parallelization:

- Fitness evaluation level (i.e., global parallelization model)
- Population level (i.e., coarse-grained parallelization or island model)
- Individual level (i.e., fine-grained parallelization or grid model)

In the global parallelization model there are two main roles: a Master and some Slaves. The former is responsible to manage the population (i.e., apply evolutionary operators) and to assign the individuals to the slaves. The latter are in charge to evaluate the fitness for each individual. This model does not require any changes to the sequential GA, since the fitness computation for each individual is independent and thus can be achieved in parallel.

In the island model the initial population is split in several groups and on each of them, typically referred to as "island," the GA proceeds independently and periodically exchanges information among islands by "migrating" some individuals from one island to another. The main advantages of this model are that (1) different subpopulations can explore different parts of the search space, and (2) migrating individuals among islands enhances diversity of the chromosomes, thus reducing the probability to converge into a local optimum.

The grid model extends the island one by enhancing the selection pressure by means of migrations among groups of chromosomes. This is obtained by assigning each individual to a single node and by performing evolutionary operations that involve also some neighbors of a solution. The effect is an improvement of the diversity during the evolutions, further reducing the probability to converge into a local optimum, with the drawback of requiring higher network traffic, due to the frequent communications among the nodes. The consequence of these models is that to date the parallelization of GAs is straightforward from a conceptual point of view. However, setting up an actual implementation may be not so trivial due to some common development difficulties that a programmer must tackle in a distributed environment. Probably these limitations have slowed the use of parallel GAs in software testing. In fact, to the best of our knowledge, there are in the literature few attempts to exploit parallel GAs for SBST (Alba, 2008; Harman, 2011; Di Gironimo, 2012).

We can distinguish two main classes of problems in the development and use of parallel GAs:

1. The need to devote extensive efforts to manage and maintain the overall IT infrastructure.
2. The need to handle the communication and/or synchronization among different modules.

The use of Cloud Computing may be a means of addressing the first issue since the Cloud infrastructure lets an on-demand resource handling and allocation, relieving the developers from the management of the distributed IT infrastructure.

As for the second issue, the use of the MapReduce paradigm can be a solution, as it allows for disregarding of taking care the coordination and execution of parallel tasks.

In the next section, we provide a proposal to exploit GAs for SBST in a Cloud-based environment using the MapReduce model.

Cloud Computing Technologies

Cloud Computing has been defined as "[…] a model for enabling convenient, on-demand network access to a shared pool of configurable resource (e.g. networks, servers, storage, applications and services) that can be rapidly provisioned and released with minimal management effort or service provider interaction." (Mell, 2009). Outsourcing IT commodities to a Cloud Computing provider can bring many benefits for a business. Among them (and apart from economical aspects) there is a better availability of resources, due to

the high redundancy of computational power in the data centers and an excellent scalability. Moreover, the Cloud is usually based on a pay-per-use concept where additional computational resources can be allocated on demand. Also from an ecological point of view, the Cloud solution can bring many benefits, since with this paradigm, different enterprises share computing power as well as data storage, with a drastic improvement of energy efficiency.

Today there are many Cloud providers, offering different kinds of services, ranging from the Infrastructure-as-a-Service (IaaS) up to the Software-as-a-Service (SaaS) solutions (Mell, 2009). Some of them support the development of Cloud-based applications delivering a computing platform, such as Amazon Elastic MapReduce (Amazon, 2012), Google App Engine (Google, 2012), or Microsoft Azure (Microsoft, 2012). These typically include operating system, programming language execution environment, database, and web server so that developers can build and run their software solutions on a Cloud platform without managing the underlying hardware and software layers. Moreover, they do not have to allocate resources manually for satisfying application demand since the compute and storage resources can scale automatically. This allows developers to focus mainly on their application features, without taking care of extensive deployment and/or configuration effort, e.g. setting up a server or replacing a failed hardware component.

In the following we briefly describe Google App Engine (GAE from now on) since it is the platform we employed in our study. GAE enables developer to build web applications by means of a well-documented SDK available in Java, Python, and Go programming languages (Google, 2012). GAE is also responsible to handle tasks such as load balancing and fault tolerance; it provides to user's applications the same large-scale services that power Google's applications for data storage, caching and network access. The main components of GAE are: the runtime environment, which is responsible to handle multiple requests, the DataStore, which is in charge of storing the data into the Google's storage system, and the scalable services, which allow applications to run on one or multiple instances depending on the resources needed to successfully run the application. User can choose among three different classes of instances characterized by different memory and CPU limits and specific hourly billing rate, as reported in Table 1. Differently from other platforms, such as the Amazon's one, GAE offers all these functionality with some free (but limited) quotas.

To support programmers, GAE offers a plugin for the Eclipse IDE, providing some wizards and debug configurations for GAE projects, and a local environment emulating the Cloud, to ease the development and let users to quickly test and verify the application directly on their local machine.

All the applications execute within a "sandbox," with three main limitations:

1. The application can have access only to other computers on the Internet through the provided URL fetch and email services.
2. Applications cannot write to the file system and can read only files uploaded with the application code. To have data persistence the application must use the App Engine DataStore, MemCache, or other similar services.
3. Application code only runs in response to a web request, a queued task, or a scheduled task, and must return response data within 60 seconds in any case (Google, 2012).

Table 1. Instance classes provided by Google App Engine (GoogleDeveloper, 2012)

Class	Memory	CPU	Cost per Hour per Instance
F1	128MB	600MHz	$0.08
F2	256MB	1.2GHz	$0.16
F4	512MB	2.4GHz	$0.32

The MapReduce Model

The most straightforward solution to integrate GAs into the Cloud could employ the existing implementations of parallel GAs, usually based on the Message Passing Interface (MPI). However, MPI-based solutions are not supported by all the Cloud platforms (e.g., Microsoft Azure) and have many drawbacks, mainly due to the fact that they do not scale well on multiple clusters (Verma, 2009) and do not provide any mechanism to support fault tolerance. As a consequence, if a computation fails during execution, the whole program needs to be restarted. Moreover, as these solutions are not supposed to work in a Cloud-based environment, they are not able to exploit the benefits provided by the infrastructure, such as an on-demand resource usage allocation. On the other hand, several Cloud providers support the use of the MapReduce model, which is an elegant, flexible, and highly scalable paradigm proposed to enable users to develop large-scale distributed applications by parallelizing computations and resource usage (Dean, 2004). Moreover, the MapReduce implementations available in the Cloud exploit the underlying infrastructure that is in charge of managing load balancing, resource allocation, fault tolerance, job startup, etc. Thus, this model and the corresponding implementations can represent a viable solution to integrate GAs into the Cloud.

In the following, we report the main aspects of this paradigm and the main implementations supported in the Cloud.

MapReduce relies on the definition of only two distinct functions, namely *Map* and *Reduce* (Dean, 2004). These functions are combined together in a divide-and-conquer way, so that the former is responsible to handle the parallelization while the latter collects and merges the results.

It is worth noting that, even if these two functions represent the main core of the model, their implementations are strongly related to the particular problem at the hand. As a consequence, while the MapReduce model supplies the abstraction of the overall parallel computational infrastructure, each problem must be integrated into the model by implementing these two functions, namely by expressing its execution in terms of these two functions. A typical computation in the MapReduce model encompasses the following three steps:

1. The program splits the input data into a set of partitions which are identified by a unique *key*. This aspect is crucial since each single split constitutes the input for the next step and consequently determines how different Map function invocations are distributed across multiple machines.
2. When all the data has been collected and split, the program assigns each group and its corresponding key to a single Map task. Each Mapper is executed independently and produces a set of intermediate key/value pairs. The way these keys are created determines the distribution of the work among Reducers

on different machines since the MapReduce model automatically allocates a new Reducer for each unique key. Moreover, Mappers typically use re-execution as technique to support fault tolerance (Verma, 2009).

3. Once all the Mappers terminate, the program is notified and it gets in charge to invoke the Reduce tasks. Each Reducer is responsible to group together all the intermediate values associated to the same key and to compute the list of output results.

The overall computation of the MapReduce model, as presented in the seminal paper (Dean, 2004), is depicted in Figure 2.

There are some well-known implementations of MapReduce supported in the Cloud, such as the App Engine MapReduce (GoogleMR, 2012) and the Hadoop MapReduce (HadoopMR, 2012). App Engine MapReduce is an open-source library for building applications compliant to the MapReduce model for Google App Engine

Figure 2. The MapReduce overall computation (Dean, 2004)

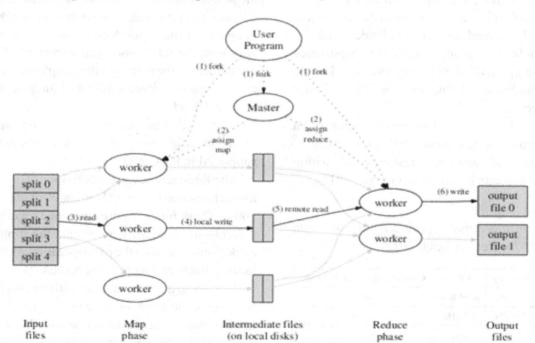

(GoogleMR, 2012). It makes available an implementation of the Mapper's functionality, while it is required to write the code for the Reducers. Moreover, it offers also an implementation of an InputReader and an OutputReader, two modules able to respectively read from and write to the DataStore provided by GAE. The Hadoop MapReduce is an open-source project of the Apache Software Foundation aiming at supporting developers in realizing applications that rapidly process vast amounts of data in parallel on large clusters of computing nodes. Its popularity is rapidly increasing due to its adoption by large companies such as IBM and Yahoo. With respect to App Engine MapReduce, Hadoop MapReduce provides both the Map and the Reduce modules, thus avoiding a developer to manage its own Reducer, and exploits a distributed file system, named Hadoop Distributed File System, to store data. It has been originally designed to work on Linux clusters, but it can now also run in the cloud thanks to services such as Amazon Elastic MapReduce (Amazon, 2012) and Windows Azure (Microsoft, 2011). Recently Microsoft has released to the research community an iterative MapReduce runtime, named Daytona (Daytona, 2011). It is designed to work on Windows Azure and provides a high-performance system for data analysis and machine learning algorithms. Similarly to App Engine MapReduce and Hadoop MapReduce, Daytona MapReduce uses Cloud storage services (i.e., Azure Blob Storage) for the dynamic data partitioning and Azure infrastructure services for robustness and dynamic scalability. In Table 2 we summarized the main characteristics of these MapReduce implementations supported in the Cloud.

Exploiting MapReduce and Cloud Infrastructure for SBST

In this section, we describe how to exploit MapReduce to support the parallelization of GAs for Search-Based Software Testing and its use in the Cloud. We propose three models which implements the levels of parallelization we described in the previous section (i.e., global, coarse-grained, and fine-grained). Let us note that in the following we refer to the App Engine-MapReduce since we employed it in our study (see next Section), but the proposal could be easily adapted to work also with other MapReduce implementations, such as Hadoop MapReduce.

The architecture for the global level of parallelization (i.e., parallelization of the fitness evaluation) using the MapReduce model is depicted

Table 2. Comparison among MapReduce implementations supported in the Cloud

	Google App Engine MapReduce	Apache Hadoop MapReduce	Daytona MapReduce
Data Handling	Google Data Store	Hadoop Distributed File System (HDFS)	Azure Blob Storage
Scheduling	Node/Rack Aware. Dynamic task scheduling through global queue	Data Locality. Rack aware. Dynamic task scheduling through global queue	Dynamic task scheduling through global queue
Failure Handling	Re-execution of failed tasks	Re-execution of failed tasks Duplicate execution of slow tasks	Re-execution of failed tasks Duplicate execution of slow tasks
Environment	Google App Engine	Linux Clusters Amazon Elastic MapReduce on EC2 Compatible with Windows Azure	Windows Azure Compute, Windows Azure Local Development Fabric
Intermediate Data Transfer	Http	File, Http	File, TCP

in Figure 3. The underlying idea is to delegate to each Mapper the burden of evaluating the fitness for each chromosome in parallel, while a single Reducer is responsible to collect the results and to perform the evolving operations, namely crossover and mutation, to generate the new offspring. In this architecture, we can highlight four main modules, i.e., the User Program, the Master, the Mappers and the Reducer, together with two other units, responsible to handle the I/O.

To give a deeper insight into the proposed architecture, in the following we describe the responsibility of each component depicted in Figure 3:

- The User Program is responsible to create an initial random population and to start the evolutionary process by invoking the InputReader. Moreover, it is also responsible to stop the process according to some termination criteria, such as population convergence or a max number of performed executions.

- The InputReader module is in charge to read the (possibly instrumented) source code of the SUT from the DataStore and to assign the chromosomes of the current generation to a bunch of Mappers. To parallelize the computation of the fitness function for each chromosome, we have to assign each of them to a different Mapper. This is achieved by generating a unique key for each chromosome, which will be calculated as a function of the triple <chromosome, current generation, specific unit of the SUT>. It is worth noting that we suggest considering also the unit, in this way the model supports the application of multiple instances of GA to different units composing the SUT.

- The Mapper is responsible to evaluate each received chromosome exercising the

Figure 3. The proposed architecture for the global parallelization approach

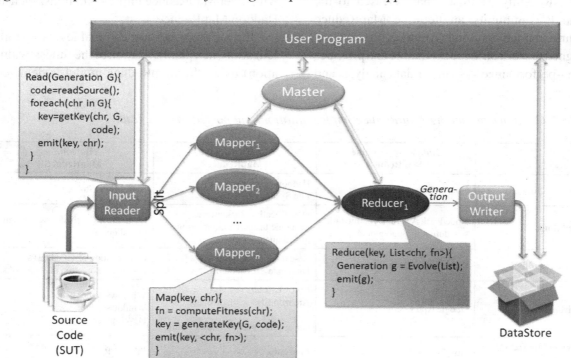

unit of the SUT with the corresponding test data and observing the software behavior to compute chromosome fitness value (e.g., branch coverage). Then, the Mapper generates an intermediate pair <key, value>, where the key is needed to properly assign the Reducers, while value is the pair <chromosome, fitness value>. By assigning the same key to all intermediate pairs we can realize a global parallelization model, this forces the model to use exactly one Reducer.

- The Reducer module is invoked once all the Mappers terminate their execution. Once collected all the pairs, it applies the selection on the entire population and then the evolution operators, to obtain a new offspring.

- At the end of each iteration, the OutputWriter saves the data relative to the new offspring into the DataStore.

- The *Master* module manages the overall computation together with the resource assignment. As the InputReader begins to emit the *<key, value>* pairs the Master module assigns chromosomes to Mapper. Similarly, when Mappers emit *intermediate <key, value>* pairs the Master module is responsible to collect them to properly assign the input to the Reducer module. Finally, once the Reduced outputs the new offspring, the Maste*r* module notifies the User Program to check according to the stopping criterion if the computation should be terminated or restarted by invoking the InputReader on the new offspring.

Let us observe that the above architecture allows us to obtain a parallelization only of the fitness evaluation. This is not a limitation, since in the considered domain, the computation of the fitness function is usually the most costly task (Michael, 2001) requiring to execute the target program and to evaluate the fitness for each new chromosome created by the genetic algorithm.

If a higher level of parallelization is required, this architecture can be extended to achieve a coarse-grained level (i.e., to parallelize also the execution of selection and genetic operators). In this case, as shown in Figure 4, some modules of the above architecture remain unchanged (i.e., User Program, Reducer, OutputWriter, and Master), while others have to be modified, i.e., InputReader and Mapper. In particular, we have to define a partition strategy able to assign each island of chromosomes to a different Reducer. This can be obtained by modifying the algorithm necessary to generate the keys in the InputReader. Now the key is calculated considering also the island that a chromosome belongs to. As for the Mapper, it has to emit a pair *<key, value>* where *value* is computed as in the previously described architecture, while *key* is now function also of the island containing the chromosome. As a result, each chromosome belonging to the same island, in the same generation and exercising the same code, will be fed to the same Reducer. Also in this architecture, the Reducers are responsible to apply selection and evolution operators for the new offspring, making it available to the OutputWriter. Finally, since the coarse-grained model strongly relies on the concept of migrating chromosomes among islands, this duty will be in charge of the Mapper module that randomly changes the island used in the computation of the key value, with the consequence that the involved chromosomes will be assigned to a different Reducer.

As final level of parallelization, a fine-grained model can be achieved with a slight variation in the last proposal. In this model, each chromosome is assigned to a single Mapper and then to a randomly selected Reducer. This can be obtained by acting on the way the Mapper module produces *key* values, which now are pseudo-randomly generated. It is worth noting that in the MapReduce model on the Cloud we have no knowledge on

Figure 4. The proposed architecture for the coarse-grained parallelization approach

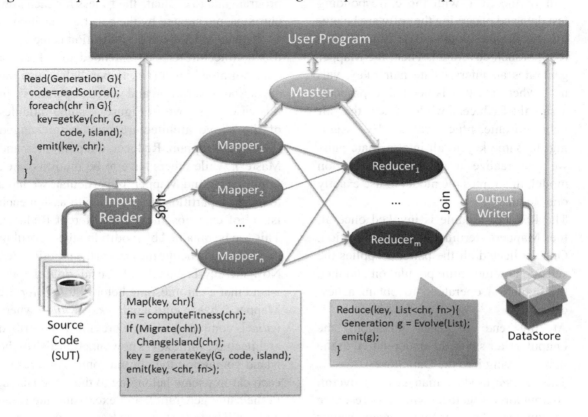

the actual node containing a chromosome, so the pseudo-random function is a way to implement the neighboring required by the fine-grained model.

PROOF OF CONCEPT

To provide a proof of concept, in the present section we describe how we parallelized an existing GA for test data generation (Michael, 2001) exploiting GAE MapReduce and the global parallelization model detailed in the previous section. To this aim, we carried out a preliminary analysis on the effectiveness of applying the proposed approach on two different target functions, by executing the parallel algorithm on a local server machine and on three different configurations of the Google's Cloud. The first function implements a simple numeric program already applied in other related works, while the second one provides a computational-intensive example, useful for a qualitative evaluation of the approach in terms of computational time and usage of resources.

In the following, we first recall the main aspects of the employed algorithm, then describe considered configurations and subjects, and finally discuss the obtained results.

The Employed Genetic Algorithm for Test Data Generation

The GA proposed by Michael et al. (Michael, 2001) is based on the Condition-Decision coverage so that for each condition in the code two requirements (true and false) must be taken at least by one input. Moreover, it follows the dynamic test data generation paradigm (Miller, 1976) using the data collected during the execution as feedback to determine which input tests satisfy the requirements (Michael, 2001). To this end, the algorithm exploits a coverage table to track the requirements to be reached and those which have been satisfied. More details about the Michael's algorithm can be found in (Michael, 2001). In the following we describe the main aspects of the parallel version we designed.

Starting from the first test requirement, an initial random population of n=100 chromosomes (each representing a test input) is generated. Then, the evolutionary process is started by invoking the InputReader, which splits the population in several crunches of data to be distributed among Mappers by the Master node. Each Mapper executes the instrumented code of the program under test to calculate the fitness value of the assigned chromosomes exploiting a fitness function based on the Korel function (Korel, 1990). Table 3 shows how the fitness is calculated for some typical conditions. A small fitness value indicates that the test input is close to satisfying the target

requirement. If the program's execution fails to reach the target, then the fitness function takes its worst possible value (i.e., MAXVALUE).

Once all Mappers terminate their execution, the Reducer starts the reproduction phase by applying on the received population traditional single point crossover and mutation operators. The crossover operator generates a new offspring from two parent chromosomes, selecting a random point of cut in the parents and swapping the corresponding test genes (i.e., a test input) with a rate of 0.5. As for the mutation operator, it replaces with probability 0.25 each gene in the chromosome with a new random test input. Let us note that if the test inputs are integer, these will be encoded in binary code by using the GrayCode before applying the genetic operators, otherwise if the input is real the standard binary encoding will be employed. Previous experimental results showed that the use of GrayCode allowed for finding suitable inputs more quickly (Michael, 2001). Once genetic operators are applied, the next generation is formed selecting the first n/2 best individuals, while the other chromosomes will be taken randomly from the offspring and parents.

At the end of this phase, data related to the new generation is saved through the OutputWriter into the DataStore, where it is retrieved by the Master module to check if the algorithm should be terminated or restarted by invoking the InputReader on the new offspring. The algorithm is stopped if it has found one chromosome that satisfies the test requirement or if it has performed a maximum number of generations (i.e., 30). In both cases, the next requirement to be satisfied is recovered from the coverage table and a new random population of n=100 chromosomes is generated to restart the search for an input that covers this requirement. This process continues until all requirements have been examined.

Table 3. Computation of the fitness function

Condition	Fitness Value
$x = y$	$\|x - y\|$
$x \mathrel{!=} y$	MAXVALUE if $x = y$
	0 otherwise
$x > y$	1/MAXVALUE if $x = y$
	$x - y$ if $x < y$
	0 otherwise
$x \geq y$	$x - y$ if $x < y$
	0 otherwise
$x < y$	1/MAXVALUE if $x = y$
	$y - x$ if $x > y$
	0 otherwise
$x \leq y$	$y - x$ if $x > y$
	0 otherwise
flag	MAXVALUE if flag is true
	0 otherwise

Subject

The assessment has been conducted considering two different functions, namely quad and compareSumAndProduct. Figure 5 reports the pseudocode of both programs.

Quad solves quadratic equations of the form $ax^2 + bx + c$. It takes three double input variables corresponding to the three different coefficients, namely a, b, and c, and derives the nature of the solutions for the corresponding equation depending on the relationship defined by the discriminant:

$$D = b^2 - 4ac.$$

CompareSumAndProduct takes three integer input variables, namely n, j, and k, and evaluates if the sum of the first n natural numbers is greater, equal, or less than the value corresponding to the product of other two parameters, namely $j*k$.

Experimental Setting

We executed the parallel GA both on a local server and in the Cloud. The configuration of the server is reported in Table 4. As for the Cloud, we employed three different configurations characterized by different resources, namely F1, F2, and F4, and reported in Table 5. Moreover, for each different configuration we employed 30 multiple shards, i.e., the total number of Mappers running concurrently.

Figure 5. Pseudocode of the employed functions, quad and compareSumAndProduct

```
public String quad(double a, double b, double c) {

    double discr, root1, root2;
    String result = "";

    // Solve the discriminant
    discr = (b * b) - (4 * a * c);

    // Determine number of roots
    // if discr > 0 equation has 2 real roots
    // if discr == 0 equation has a repeated real root
    // if discr < 0 equation has imaginary roots

    if (discr > 0) {
        result += "Equation has 2 roots";
        root1 = (-b + Math.sqrt(discr)) / (2 * a);
        root2 = (-b - Math.sqrt(discr)) / (2 * a);
        result += " First root = " + root1;
        result += " Second root = " + root2;
    }

    if (discr == 0) {
        result += "Equation has 1 root";
        root1 = -b / (2 * a);
        result += " Root = " + root1;
    }

    if (discr < 0)
        result += "Equation has imaginary roots";

    return result;
}
```

```
public String compareSums(Integer i, Integer j, Integer k) {
    String response = "";
    Integer sum = calculateSum(Math.abs(i));
    Integer product = k*j;

    if (sum > product)
        response = "sum > product";

    if (sum == product)
        response = "sum == product";

    if (sum < product)
        response = "sum < product";

    return response;
}

public Integer calculateSum(Integer n) {
    int res = 0;
    if (n <= 0)
        return res;
    res = 1;
    for (int i = 2; i <= n; i++)
        res = res + i;
    return res;
}
```

Table 4. Configuration of the employed local server

Hardware	
CPU	Intel Xeon E5645 2.4 GHz (6-core)
RAM	24 GB
Hard Disk	2 x HD SATA 300GB 10K rpm
Connectivity	2 x Gbit LAN on board
Software	
Operating System	Windows Server 2007
Java Virtual Machine	Java SE Runtime v.1.7.
Google App Engine	v. 1.6.1

Table 5. Google app engine configurations

Frontend Class	Memory Limit	CPU Limit	Cost per Hour per Instance (05/2012)
F1 (default)	128MB	600MHz	$0.08
F2	256MB	1.2GHz	$0.16
F4	512MB	2.4GHz	$0.32

Evaluation Criteria

The performance of the GA has been assessed in terms of execution time, measured using the system clock, and of condition coverage, given by the percentage of satisfied test requirements. It is worth noting that we executed ten runs for each configuration in order to cope with the inherent randomness of the search-based approaches, and reported the average results together with the standard deviation.

Results

Tables 6 and 7 contain the results obtained running the algorithm both on local server and in the Cloud with the functions quad and compareSumAndProduct, respectively.

As for the quad function, we can notice that the achieved coverage was almost the same for all the cases, but the local server was by far faster than all the considered configurations in the Cloud.

This is due to the fact that the activation of each instance in the Cloud requires some time, especially when using services such as the MemCache or DataStore that usually take many resources just to start-up, making the Cloud solution not convenient for applications requiring a limited amount of computational power. It is also worth noting that there is no significant difference in running times among the three different configurations provided by Google.

On the other hand, with the more computationally intensive compareSumAndProduct function, the benefits of the Cloud become more evident. Indeed, while using the server took approximately 81 minutes, in the Cloud the execution required only 36 minutes using F4. In this latter scenario, the differences among the three Cloud configurations become more relevant: F4 takes less than half the time of F1 to complete the execution. The conclusion we can draw is that the Cloud platform provided by GAE has an initial overhead to start the computation, but once everything is

Table 6. Results for quad

Configuration		Coverage		Time (minutes)	
		Mean	Std. Dev.	Mean	Std. Dev.
Server		75.00%	0.08	1'29"	0'04"
Cloud	F1	78.33%	0.08	2'55"	0'16"
	F2	71.67%	0.08	3'19"	0'34"
	F4	73.34%	0.08	3'08"	0'59"

Table 7. Results for compareSumAndProduct

Configuration		Coverage		Time (minutes)	
		Mean	Std. Dev.	Mean	Std. Dev.
Server		83.34%	0	81'25"	19'11"
Cloud	F1	83.34%	0	79'41"	13'54"
	F2	83.34%	0	45'54"	10'48"
	F4	83.34%	0	35'54"	8'43"

running, the benefits of the parallelization clearly outperform a local machine.

Consequently, Cloud solutions are particularly useful in presence of non-trivial and computational-intensive problems.

As for the required resources, in Table 8 we report values of the percentage usage of free available quotas, expressed in terms of DataStore Write and Read operations and of Task Queue API Calls. Since these results are only influenced by the different executions of the genetic algorithm, we report mean values and standard deviation for usage of quotas calculated on the thirty experimental trials performed (i.e., ten per each CPU configuration).

The quotas of Datastore usage immediately remark the computational-intensive nature of the compareSumAndProduct function. The amount of resources used by this function is by far higher than the one used by the quad function. Moreover, while Write and Read quotas are slightly the same for the quad function, compareSumAndProduct performs a lot of Read operations, thus requiring a lot of resources. This is due to the fact that GA performs a lot of iterations before reaching the final coverage.

Finally, the obtained results suggest the effectiveness of some optimizations we designed to limit the usage of DataStore resources. Indeed we exploited only the freely available ones, without requiring the activation of the billing system. Those optimizations are illustrated in the next section.

Lesson Learned on the Problems to Migrate GAs to the Cloud

Even if the migration of applications to the Cloud provides an easy-to-use solution to leverage the benefits of a scalable and distributed environment, it imposes a set of different constraints that have to be considered during the design and the implementation of algorithms. In general, these constraints may be classified in two distinct categories, namely software restrictions and infrastructure restrictions, respectively referred to limitations on software libraries and components running into the Cloud and to the specific features of the provided computational platform.

However, in practice, these limitations are different for each Cloud provider, such as Amazon or Google, and strongly depend on the specific kind of service offered, e.g., Platform-as-a-Service (PaaS) or Infrastructure-as-a-Service (IaaS).

In this section we describe some limitations and issues we faced for the migration of the considered GA to GAE, the Google PaaS Cloud solution, using the Java SDK. Moreover we report the details of some additional improvements made to the source code in order to leverage the benefits of the parallelization provided by the MapReduce model and to optimize the corresponding resource usage.

The first important software-related restriction to consider concerns the set of classes in the Java standard library (the Java runtime environment, or JRE) that can be accessed by applications running on GAE. The full white list of supported classes may be found in (GoogleJavaWhitelist, 2012).

Table 8. Resource usage

Function	DataStore Write Ops		DataStore Read Ops.		Task API Calls	
	Mean	Std. Dev.	Mean	Std. Dev.	Mean	Std. Dev.
quad	19.67%	15.75	18.37%	14.62	3.97%	3.44
compareSumAndProduct	28.93%	4.86	62.90%	12.89	6.63%	1.19

Most of these limitations are imposed for security reasons in order to limit potential vulnerabilities and malicious behaviors derived by manipulating the byte-code executed on the JVM running in the Google Cloud. As a consequence, this list does not include packages such as java. lang.reflection. This is an important restriction since this package is mostly used by many Java-based code instrumentation tools, such as JPF (JPF, 2012) or CodeCover (CodeCover, 2012), exploited by many test-input data generation systems to evaluate the coverage of the code. Thus it was not possible to use those tools to evaluate coverage and the proposed GA exploited an instrumentation strategy specifically suited for GAE. However such an implementation does not yet support an automatic code instrumentation technique, requiring that instrumentation probes are manually injected into the code. Other software restrictions concern limitations on spawning multiple threads and on writing to files. In fact, due to the distributed nature of the application, writing to local files is not supported and the storage of data is supported only through the distributed storage system provided by Google, i.e., the distributed datastore.

In addition there are some infrastructure-related features of the platform that are worth considering to properly adapt existing algorithms or to design new ones. Such limitations mainly concern the specific GAE protocols to control the executions and the data storage.

Process execution on GAE is controlled by Tasks: each process is associated to a single GAE task, and all the tasks are organized in different Task Queues. These queues are used to manage different load balancing configurations (e.g., setting the maximum number of tasks in each queue) and to control the level of parallelization among different tasks. For instance, in our study the execution of tasks relied on two different queues: a high rate queue, called genetic-task-queue, devoted to run parallel and multiple Map-tasks for the evaluation of the fitness function, and a lower rate one, the process-queue, performing one task at a time corresponding to a single step in the GA process (e.g., fitness evaluation, generation of new population, and so on) in order to control the correct execution of the overall workflow. However GAE imposes that the execution of each task cannot take more than 10 minutes, which is an important constraint to consider when designing the execution of tasks. Moreover, it is worth mentioning that GAE currently lacks of fault tolerance strategies for tasks: if an error occurs during the execution, it may potentially freeze the overall application, since it does not provide any execution recovery system or a mechanism to exclude faulty tasks from queues.

Another key aspect concerns issues related to the communication with the Google Datastore. These issues are very important for the design of an application running into the Cloud, since the distributed nature of the datastore introduces an intrinsic communication latency that may drastically worsen the performance if multiple and useless operations are executed. Reducing Datastore operations determines a faster execution of tasks and an optimized usage of resources.

To this aim, we designed several optimizations and realized a package of classes based on the Java JDO APIs (GoogleJDO, 2012), which constitutes a wrapper layer between our application and the underlying Google Storage APIs.

All of these optimizations for the Datastore are mainly devoted to reduce as much as possible the usage of the free limited quotas imposed by Google, especially write operations. We optimized the code of the MapReduce library to avoid the creation of Datastore indexes for different entities attributes, drastically reducing the consumption of the "Datastore Write operation quota" from the 34% to the 4%. Moreover, we also performed writing operations to a properly defined "batch writing process," i.e., a single write operation to save multiple entities at a time. Thus we avoided single write operations, reducing time and quotas necessary to save information into the datastore.

RELATED WORK

Parallel Genetic Algorithms Based on MapReduce

In the literature, we can find two proposals to use the MapReduce model to parallelize GAs (Gin, 2008) and (Verma, 2009). However, such proposals did not take into account the specific context of software testing. In (Gin, 2008) an extension of MapReduce, named MRPGA, has been proposed and motivated by the observation that a parallel GA cannot follow the two phases of MapReduce due to its iterative nature. The extension is based on a further phase for the global selection performed at the end of any iteration of parallel GAs. Moreover, a coordinator client is introduced to coordinate the executions of the parallel GA iterations. The proposed architecture consists of one Master node and multiple Mapper and Reducer nodes (Gin, 2008). The difference with the classical MapReduce is the introduction of a second reduce phase finalized to select the global optimum individuals. In order to simplify fault handling, the Master replicates the optimum individuals that the proposed extension of MapReduce has selected for each round of evolutionary operations. In case a node (e.g., a computer) resulted to be not available during the execution, the proposed algorithm just restarts the execution from the last round. This fault tolerance mechanism does not need a complex distributed file system for reliability purpose. The proposed extension of MapReduce for parallel GAs has been implemented using C# language on .NET platform and the developer runtime system has been evaluated in several student laboratories at the University of Melbourne. All the architectures we proposed in this work to parallelize GAs by means of MapReduce differ from the one of (Gin, 2008), none of them employ the additional reduction phase which is not necessary as suggested also by Verma et al. (Verma, 2009). Moreover, in their proposal a single coordinator affecting the scalability of their approach makes a huge

amount of work regarding mutation, crossover, and evaluation of the convergence criteria. To avoid this problem, in our first architecture we split these jobs among the master node (performing evaluation of the convergence criteria) and the reducer (performing mutation and crossover), while the other two architectures do not suffer of this problem as these operations are carried out in a parallel fashion.

(Verma, 2009) provided another approach for using MapReduce for parallel GAs and highlighted several concerns and limitations of the proposal described in (Gin, 2008). The main concern was about scalability of parallel GAs. The previous proposal does not scale above 32 nodes, due to the inherent serial organization imposed by the use of a single coordinator, which performs mutation, crossover, and evaluation of the convergence criteria. Furthermore, they highlighted that the extension proposed in (Gin, 2008) could easily be implemented in the traditional MapReduce model using a Combiner instead of the proposed local reduce, as shown in (Dean, 2008). Finally they pointed out that using the same value (i.e., 1) as keys produced by the mapper, the reducer and the local reducer, MRPGA does not employ any characteristics of MapReduce model (i.e., the grouping by keys and the shuffling). Differently, Verma et al. (Verma, 2009) exploited the traditional MapReduce model by implementing GA in Hadoop to solve the ONEMAX problem. They investigated scalability and convergence of the proposed GA and found that larger problems could be resolved by adding more computational resources without changing algorithm implementation. Our second architecture is similar to (Verma, 2009) since the authors followed a coarse-grained parallelization model performing a local survival selection on multiple reducers to speed-up the overall execution time. However as pointed out in (Verma, 2009) a local selection can led to a reduction in selection pressure affecting the time taken to converge. This together with the fact that in the domain we considered the computation of the fitness function is the most time consuming task (Michael, 2001) motivated us to investigate other architectures proposed in this work (i.e., GAs following global parallelization and grid parallelization models).

Parallel Genetic Algorithms for Automated Testing

In Di Gironimo (2012), a parallel Genetic Algorithm conceived for JUnit test suite generation and based on the global parallelization model proposed in this work has been realized. A preliminary evaluation of the proposed algorithm was carried out aiming to evaluate the speed-up with respect to the sequential execution. The obtained results highlighted that using the parallel genetic algorithm allowed for saving over the 50% of time. Differently from this work, the algorithm was conceived for test suite generation (and not for test data generation), realized exploiting Hadoop MapReduce, and its performance was assessed only on standard cluster.

Another approach to address parallelization of SBST has been recently proposed in Yoo (2011), where a parallel multi-objective Genetic Programming for test suite minimization was devised for exploiting the computational power of modern graphic cards. The obtained results showed that for their problem the speed-up achieved by using GPU was logarithmic correlated to the problem size (i.e., SUT and test suite size) and ranged from 1x to 25x with respect to the use of a single-threaded version of the same GP.

Migrating Software Testing to the Cloud

Recently high interest has been attracting the use of Cloud computing for addressing the significant computing resources and the lengthy execution times requested by software testing. In Tilley (2010) authors took into account the characteristics of an application under test and the types of

testing to decide if migrate software testing to the Cloud. A proposal for distributing the execution of test cases in the Cloud was presented in Oriol (2010) where the authors described a framework for the distributed execution of the York Extensible Testing Infrastructure (YETI), a language agnostic random testing tool (Oriol, 2010). They employed the MapReduce primitives. Before the execution, the needed files (i.e., the test cases and the employed testing tool) are uploaded to the distributed file system file to be later read by the Mapper nodes. Then, the Master node launches a Mapper for each test case and each Mapper reads its data and executes the corresponding test case. Finally, the Reducer collects the test case results from each Mapper and outputs them to a file on the DFS. The preliminary results reported in Oriol (2010) were promising, showing that exploiting the proposed framework on the Amazon Elastic Computing Cloud (Amazon, 2012) the performances of YETI improved reducing the testing time.

FUTURE RESEARCH DIRECTIONS

The migration of SBST approaches in the Cloud is still in its early phases, so several research directions can be prospected.

First of all, it is important to carry out an extensive empirical evaluation of the solutions we proposed. This is necessary to highlight on the field their strength and weakness, as well as to assess their actual scalability. Furthermore, it will be very interesting to investigate how and if other Search-Based techniques previously employed in SBST, such as the Tabu Search or the Hill Climbing, can be migrated to the Cloud. Once this migration will be implemented, it will be very interesting to compare these different meta-heuristics, both in terms of performances and effectiveness, for each specific testing problem and strategy. Moreover, in the solutions proposed in this chapter, we have only considered the problem of the test data generation. Other types of SBST may present specific issues, thus probably requiring other types of architectures.

Another interesting direction might be to assess the effort versus cost benefit trade-offs in using PaaS rather than an IaaS, which is typically less expensive than PaaS.

Finally, as a long-term research goal, SBST approaches can be integrated in a Validation-as-a-Service Cloud platform able to support companies in the entire software testing process.

CONCLUSION

In this chapter, we have proposed some solutions to migrate Genetic Algorithms to the Cloud, aiming at obtaining an automatic generation of test data. This migration is motivated by the need to achieve a greater efficiency and scalability of this Search-Based technique, thus possibly reinforcing its effectiveness thanks to the available computational power of the Cloud.

To simplify such a migration, we have suggested the use of the MapReduce paradigm, relieving programmers by the most of low level issues in managing a distributed computation. This is also motivated by the fact that MapReduce is natively supported by several Cloud infrastructures, such as Google, Amazon, and Microsoft. We have suggested several models implementing three different levels of parallelization (i.e., global, coarse-grained, and fine grained), with the aim to automatically generate test data and discussed issues and concerns about them. Finally we have provided a proof of concept, implementing the proposed solution taking advantages of the Google App Engine framework. Preliminary results show that, unless for toy examples, the Cloud can heavily outperform the performances of a local server.

REFERENCES

Alba, E., & Chicano, F. (2008). Observations in using parallel and sequential evolutionary algorithms for automatic software testing. *Computers & Operations Research, 35*(10), 3161–3183. doi:10.1016/j.cor.2007.01.016

Ali, S., Briand, L. C., Hemmati, H., & Panesar-Walawege, R. K. (2010). A systematic review of the application and empirical investigation of search-based test case generation. *IEEE Transactions on Software Engineering, 36*(6). doi:10.1109/TSE.2009.52

Amazon. (2012). *Amazon Elastic Compute Cloud.* Retrieved June 9th, 2012, from http://aws.amazon.com/ec2

Bertolino, A. (2007). Software testing research: Achievements, challenges, dreams. In *Proceedings of International Conference on Future of Software Engineering.*

Code Cover. (2012). Retrieved June 14th, 2012 from http://codecover.org/

De Millo, R. A., & Offutt, A. J. (1991). Constraint-based automatic test data generation. *IEEE Transactions on Software Engineering, 17*(9), 900–909. doi:10.1109/32.92910

Dean, J., & Ghemawat, S. (2004). MapReduce: Simplified data processing on large clusters. In *Proceedings of Sixth Symposium on Operating System Design and Implementation.*

Di Geronimo, L., Ferrucci, F., Murolo, A., & Sarro, F. (2012). A parallel genetic algorithm based on Hadoop MapReduce for the automatic generation of JUnit test suites. In *Proceedings of the 5th International Conference on Software Testing,* (pp. 785-793).

Glenford, J. M. (2004). *The art of software testing* (2nd ed.). Wiley.

Goldberg, D. E. (1989). *Genetic algorithms in search, optimization, and machine learning.* Addison-Wesley.

Google App Engine. (2012). *JDO APIs*. Retrieved June 14, 2012, from https://developers.google.com/App Engine/docs/java/datastore/jdo/

Google App Engine. (2012). *JRE Whitelist*. Retrieved June 14, 2012, from https://developers.google.com/App Engine/docs/java/jrewhitelist

Google App Engine. (2012). *MapReduce*. Retrieved June 9, 2012, from http://code.google.com/p/App Engine-mapreduce/

Google App Engine. (2012). Retrieved June 9, 2012, from http://code.google.com/App Engine

Google Developer App Engine. (2012). Retrieved June 12, 2012, from https://developers.google.com/App Engine/

Hadoop. (2012). *MapReduce*. Retrieved June 14, 2012, from http://hadoop.apache.org/mapreduce/

Harman, M. (2007). The current state and future of search-based software engineering. In *Proceedings of the Workshop on the Future of Software Engineering*, (pp. 342-357).

Harman, M., & Jones, B. F. (2001). Search based software engineering. *Information and Software Technology, 43*(14), 833–839. doi:10.1016/S0950-5849(01)00189-6

Java Path Finder. (2012). Revised June 14, 2012, from http://javapathfinder.sourceforge.net/

Korel, B. (1990). Automated software test data generation. *IEEE Transactions on Software Engineering, 16*(8), 870–879. doi:10.1109/32.57624

Lakhotia, K., McMinn, P., & Harman, M. (2009). Automated test data generation for coverage: Haven't we solved this problem yet? *Testing: Academic and Industrial Conference - Practice and Research Techniques*, (pp. 95–104).

McMinn, P. (2004). Search-based software test data generation: A survey. *Software Testing. Verification and Reliability, 14*(2), 105–156. doi:10.1002/stvr.294

Mell, P., & Grance, T. (2009, August 21). *NIST working definition of cloud computing* (Draft), Vol. 15.

Michael, C., McGraw, G., & Schatz, M. (2001). Generating software test data by evolution. *IEEE Transactions on Software Engineering, 12*, 1085–1110. doi:10.1109/32.988709

Microsoft. (2011). *Daytona project*. Retrieved June 9, 2012, from http://research.microsoft.com/en-us/projects/daytona/

Microsoft. (2012). *Azure platform*. Retrieved June 9, 2012, from http://www.microsoft.com/windowsazure/

Miller, W., & Spooner, D. (1976). Automatic generation of floating-point test data. *IEEE Transactions on Software Engineering, 2*(3), 223–226. doi:10.1109/TSE.1976.233818

Oriol, M., & Ullah, F. (2010). YETI on the cloud. In *Proceedings of the Third International Conference on Software Testing, Verification, and Validation Workshops*, (pp. 434-437).

Tilley, S. R., & Parveen, T. (2010). When to migrate software testing to the cloud? In *Proceedings of Third International Conference on Software Testing, Verification, and Validation Workshops*, (pp. 424-427).

Verma, A., Llorà, X., Goldberg, D. E., & Campbell, R. H. (2009). Scaling genetic algorithms using MapReduce. In *Proceedings of the 2009 Ninth International Conference on Intelligent Systems Design and Applications*, (pp. 13-18). Washington, DC: IEEE Computer Society.

Yoo, S., Harman, M., & Ur, S. (2011). Highly scalable multi objective test suite minimisation using graphics cards. In *Proceedings of the 3rd Symposium on Search Based Software Engineering*, (pp. 219-236).

ADDITIONAL READING

Binz, T., Leymann, F., & Schumm, D. (2011). CMotion: A framework for migration of applications into and between clouds. In *Proceedings of IEEE International Conference on Service-Oriented Computing and Applications (SOCA)*, 2011, (pp. 1-4).

Briand, L. C., Feng, J., & Labiche, Y. (2002). Using genetic algorithms and coupling measures to devise optimal integration test orders. *Proceedings of the 14th International Conference on Software Engineering and Knowledge Engineering*, (pp. 43–50).

Briand, L. C., Labiche, Y., & Shousha, M. (2005). Stress testing real-time systems with genetic algorithms. In Proceedings of *Genetic and Evolutionary Computation Conference*, (pp. 1021–1028).

Dean, J., & Ghemawat, S. (2008). MapReduce: Simplified data processing on large clusters. *Communications of the ACM, 51*, 107–113. doi:10.1145/1327452.1327492

Del Grosso, C., Antoniol, G., Merlo, E., & Galinier, P. (2008). Detecting buffer overflow via automatic test input data generation. *Computers & Operations Research, 35*(10). doi:10.1016/j.cor.2007.01.013

Foley, J. (2009, 23 June). The cloud's next big thing: Software testing. Information Week. Retrieved from www.informationweek.com/blog/229206200

Hajjat, M., Sun, X., Sung, Y.-W. E., Maltz, D., Rao, S., Sripanidkulchai, K., & Tawarmalani, M. (2010). Cloudward bound: Planning for beneficial migration of enterprise applications to the cloud. *SIGCOMM Computer Communication Review, 40*(4), 243–254.

Harman, M., & McMinn, P. (2010). A theoretical and empirical study of search-based testing: Local, global, and hybrid search. *IEEE Transactions on Software Engineering, 3*(2), 226–247. doi:10.1109/TSE.2009.71

Jia, Y., & Harman, M. (2011). An analysis and survey of the development of mutation testing. *IEEE Transactions on Software Engineering, 37*(5), 649–678. doi:10.1109/TSE.2010.62

Korel, B. (1992). Dynamic method for software test data generation. *Software Testing. Verification and Reliability, 2*(4), 203–213. doi:10.1002/stvr.4370020405

Korel, B. (1996). Automated test generation for programs with procedures. In *International Symposium on Software Testing and Analysis* (pp. 209–215).

Korel, B., & Al-Yami, A. M. (1996). Assertion-oriented automated test data generation. In *Proceedings of the 18th International Conference on Software Engineering*, (pp. 71-80).

Li, Z., Harman, M., & Hierons, R. (2007). Meta-heuristic search algorithms for regression test case prioritization. *IEEE Transactions on Software Engineering, 33*(4), 225–237. doi:10.1109/TSE.2007.38

Mansour, N., Bahsoon, R., & Baradhi, G. (2001). Empirical comparison of regression test selection algorithms. *Systems and Software, 57*(1), 79–90. doi:10.1016/S0164-1212(00)00119-9

Mylavarapu, V. K., & Inamdar, M. (2011). *Taking testing to the cloud.* Cognizant report. Retrieved June 9, 2012 from at http://www.cognizant.com/InsightsWhitepapers/Taking-Testing-to-the-Cloud.pdf

Pargas, R. P., Harrold, M. J., & Peck, R. R. (1999). Test-data generation using genetic algorithms. *The Journal of Software Testing. Verification and Reliability, 9*, 263–282. doi:10.1002/(SICI)1099-1689(199912)9:4<263::AID-STVR190>3.0.CO;2-Y

Prodan, R., Sperk, M., & Ostermann, S. (2012). Evaluating high-performance computing on Google app engine. *Software, 29*(2), 52–58. doi:10.1109/MS.2011.131

Riungu, L. M., Taipale, O., & Smolander, K. (2010). Software testing as an online service: Observations from practice. In *Proceedings of the 3rd International Software Testing, Verification, and Validation Workshop, IEEE CS,* (pp. 418–423).

Riungu-Kalliosaari, L., Taipale, O., & Smolander, K. (2012). Testing in the cloud: Exploring the practice. *Software, 29*(2), 46–51. doi:10.1109/MS.2011.132

Sanderson, D. (2009). *Programming Google app engine.* Sebastopol, CA: O'Reilly Media.

Severance, C. (2009). *Using Google app engine.* Sebastopol, CA: O'Reilly Media.

Sripanidkulchai, K., Sahu, S., Ruan, Y., Shaikh, A., & Dorai, C. (2010). Are clouds ready for large distributed applications? *Proceedings of SIGOPS Operation Systems Review, 44*(2), 18–23. doi:10.1145/1773912.1773918

Tonella, P. (2004). Evolutionary testing of classes. In *Proceedings of the International Symposium on Software Testing and Analysis.*

Tracey, N., Clark, J., Mander, K., & McDermid, J. (2000). Automated test data generation for exception conditions. *Software, Practice & Experience, 30*(1), 61–79. doi:10.1002/(SICI)1097-024X(200001)30:1<61::AID-SPE292>3.0.CO;2-9

Tran, V. T. K., Lee, K., Fekete, A., Liu, A., & Keung, J. (2011). Size estimation of cloud migration projects with cloud migration point (CMP). In *Proceedings of Empirical Software Engineering and Measurement* (pp. 265-274).

Wegener, J., Baresel, A., & Sthamer, H. (2001). Evolutionary test environment for automatic structural testing. *Information and Software Technology, 43*(14), 841–854. doi:10.1016/S0950-5849(01)00190-2

Yoo, S., & Harman, M. (2007). Pareto efficient multi-objective test case selection. In *Proceedings of International Symposium on Software Testing and Analysis,* (pp. 140-150).

Zhan, Y., & Clark, J. A. (2005). Search-based mutation testing for simulink models. In *Proceedings of Genetic and Evolutionary Computation Conference,* (pp. 1061–1068).

Chapter 7
Testing Web Services in the Cloud

Harry M. Sneed
Independent Consultant, Germany

ABSTRACT

Cloud Computing makes it possible for users to access a wide range of web services in the public domain and to embed these global services in their local applications. This promises to save a significant amount of individual development cost. The biggest obstacle to using this technology is the problem of trust. To gain trust in the services offered they have to be extensively tested, either by the user himself or by a trusted agent. This chapter deals with the testing of web services in the cloud. There are many similarities to testing web services in a local service-oriented architecture, but there are also significant differences. In a company specific SOA, testers can gain access to the source. This is not true of the cloud. There is no possibility of accessing the source. Therefore, testers must rely solely on the specification contained in the service level agreement – SLA – and the web service interface definition – WSDL or REST – to base their test upon. Testing in the cloud is strictly a black-box test. The goal of a cloud service test is also not to find errors but to assess the suitability of the service to the purpose of the user. It may be necessary to test several services in order to find that one best suited to the requirements of the user. To judge suitability it is necessary to define an ideal usage profile, including performance, security and other non-functional criteria, and to compare that with the actual profile of each potential service. For this both static and dynamic analysis methods must be applied. The chapter presents an automated approach to assessing cloud services and selecting that one most suitable to the user's application.

1. THE RATIONALE FOR USING WEB SERVICES IN THE CLOUD

Cloud computing, as defined by the U.S. National Institute of Standards and Technology allows users to lease data and processing capacity from a pool of interconnected computing systems, maintained by a provider and shared by others to the level required (Mell & Grance, 2011). Web services play an important role in the manifestation of cloud computing, particularly when it comes to a public cloud. They are made available on demand and can be used in any context the user may have. They are the elementary building blocks upon

DOI: 10.4018/978-1-4666-2536-5.ch007

which the users build their business processes. In view of the total cost of ownership, users are encouraged to use ready-made components to implement their applications rather than developing the components themselves, which is much too costly in the long run. The maintenance and evolution of the components, i.e. services, is left to the provider. The cloud service provider Ariba offers a wide range of uniform trading, ordering and supplying services to over 730.000 customers. Each service is maintained by a small team of approximately seven developers. If each customer were to maintain the service themselves with even only one person, that would amount to a cost of one person year per service to the user and 730.000 person years to the economy as a whole. Ariba can offer to maintain a service at a cost of one person day per annum and still make a significant profit. It may be added that the Ariba users are turning over no less than 319 billion dollars per year with their trading services (Hackel, 2012).

There is no way to beat this business model. Before beginning any new application or migrating an old one, a user organization should carefully consider using available cloud services from a qualified service provider. Any new or modernized IT-application should consist to a great extend out of ready-made services offered via the cloud, independently of whether it be a public or a private cloud. The way the services are composed can still be designed and implemented by the user himself with a business process modeling language. However the basic building blocks, i.e. the components and classes, should be taken from the cloud. The madness of every commercial user developing and maintaining his own basic software building blocks must be stopped. The fact that a user can select from among a wide range of services offered only strengthens this argument. If he is not satisfied with the price or the performance of a particular service, the user can replace it with the same service from another provider. He needs only to adapt the interface (Rinngu-Kalliosaari, Taiple, & Smolander, 2012).

2. OBSTACLES TO USING WEB SERVICES IN THE CLOUD

2.1 The Problem of Trust in Using Cloud Services

The biggest obstacle to using cloud services is that of trust. The economic rationale for using web services offered in the cloud is overwhelming, but how can users know if they can trust them. Most cloud researchers agree that there is definitely a trust problem. According to the CBDI Forum, the big issue is "will the service work every time when I need it?" That forum is concerned about the fact that too few potential users are thinking about the issues of testing and certification. It suggests that the testing and certification of web services in the cloud in not business as usual and that new approaches are needed to assure that those services can really be trusted (CBDI, 2010). In recent years a number of researchers have turned their attention to this problem and some are calling for a formal certification of public cloud services. Others, such as the author of this chapter, are calling for testing organizations to offer the testing of cloud services as a service. The goal of such a service is to offer quantitative evidence of whether a service can be trusted or not (Vossen, 2011).

2.2 The Problem of Finding the Most Suitable Cloud Service

The second biggest obstacle to the use of cloud services is the selection process itself. It requires a lot of technical knowledge and the appropriate tools to evaluate web services in the cloud. Not only do the services need to be tested, but they also need to be assessed against the service level agreement. Most of the run of the mill users have neither the know-how nor the tools to make such an evaluation. That is another reason for engaging an external agent to evaluate alternate services for a specific task and to make recommendations as to which service is best suited to the user needs. The testing agent should be able to rate services according to the criteria agreed upon by the user and documented in the service level agreement (Ojala & Tyrvainen, 2011). The result of the evaluation should be an assessment report on the strengths and weaknesses of each service investigated with an overall numeric rating.

2.3 The Problem of Integrating Global Web Services into Local Business Processes

Once a cloud service is found to be trustworthy and suitable to the task at hand there is yet another obstacle to be overcome. The selected service must be built into the business process it is intended to support and tested together with the other services supporting that process. This initial integration test of web services within the target process can become an expensive undertaking. Here again the user requires the proper testing knowledge and tools to accomplish this task (Shull, 2012). If these are not available, as will be the case with most IT-users, then it will be better for the user to engage a testing agent to make this integration test for him. Once the services are integrated it should be possible for the user to take over the tested processes and repeat the test himself whenever the process is altered or the services exchanged.

All of these obstacles require a specialized testing service in order to be overcome. This service provider should have a proven service testing process, testers with skills in testing web services and tools dedicated to the testing of such services. Provided these requirements are fulfilled the testing service will be well worth its money, especially considering the enormous savings to be made on the maintenance and evolution of the applications. Testing and certifying web services in the cloud is definitely a service which needs to be offered (Sneed, 2012).

3. THE NATURE OF WEB SERVICES IN THE CLOUD

A web service sends and receives messages via the internet. These messages are defined by a standard web service definition language (WSDL) which is common for both the clients of the service as well as for the services themselves. It is governed by an international standard so that any service anywhere in the worldwide web can be accessed provided the user has the appropriate access rights. Thus, in constructing a service-oriented application the user is not restricted to using only his own services, he may drawn on services from anywhere – from service suppliers, from open service libraries, from public clouds or even from a foreign private cloud to which he has access. Thus, a service-oriented architecture is actually a virtual container of diverse services which may be physically located anywhere. Their physical location is irrelevant. The important criteria, is that one can send requests to them and they will return a correct response within a given time (Srimivasan & Getov, 2011).

Using web services in the cloud has some additional constraints that do not apply to services in a local SOA or services taken from the open source community. There the users and testers of the services have access to the source code as well as to the design model, provided there is one. That allows the tester to make either a code-based or a model-based test. He can also measure his test coverage in terms of code branches executed or model elements traversed and he can trace the execution of his test cases through the code, i.e. through the model. With services taken from the cloud this is not the case. The tester will has neither access to the code nor to the design model behind the code. He also has no access to the data model. All he can access is the UDDI description, the service level agreement – SLA – and the web service interface definition – WSDL. That means he has to base his test solely upon these documents. Thus, the test of cloud services is truly a black-box test.

Besides having no access to any internal descriptions there are a few other factors which distinguish cloud web services from local web services. Since services in a public cloud are exposed to the general public, they are also more vulnerable to attack. They need to have particularly strict authorization and authentication features which have to be tested. Public services need to be much more adaptable than local dedicated services. That means they need a lot of initial parameters which control the switches to determine how the operations are executed. Thus, when the operations are tested they have to be tested for every potential parameter setting. On top of that cloud services are intended to work with different data sets. These are determined by the user at run time. So, not only must all operations be tested with all parameter sets, but also with all data sets. Test coverage is measured in terms of data states covered rather than code covered. Finally, cloud service testing has another focus. Rather than being focused on the removal of errors, it is focused on assessing the suitability of the service under test. All of this contributes to making cloud service testing a cost intensive and time consuming activity. Without appropriate automation, it cannot be done adequately (Xie et al., 2012).

3.1 The Service Concept in IT-Systems

In the past IT Systems have included the same functions and the same data in many of their component parts. A good example is that of dates and date-processing functions such as deriving the weekday from the date. Every programmer would store the data in his own favourite format and solve the date processing function in his own way. This lead to a pleritheration of date variables and date functions which in the case of the millennium change of the year 2000 cost users several million dollars. Each date format and each date function had to be converted individually.

The same applies to common business functions like calculating the value-added tax or calculating the interest on a loan. There is no reason for every application to have its own solution. A common solution would suffice for all. Many developers will claim that their data type and their algorithms are unique and customized to the task at hand, but in taking a closer look, one will discover that there can be a general solution which when given different parameters, will provide the desired results.

Already in the 1970's there was the concept of a common subroutine library. Different developers could take over these common subroutines for arithmetic, geometrical or mathematical functions and build them into their own system. They were then invoked with a list of parameters. Later such routines were put into classes together with their data. This led to the use of class libraries in object-oriented programming. Developers of new classes could inherit the readymade functions of standard base classes in their class libraries.

Today the standard subroutines and base classes are referred to as services and are accessible via a predefined interface. As opposed to the subroutines and base classes they need not be physically available. They are not linked to the client components which use them. They are invoked at run time. This gives them the advantage of loose coupling. They can be exchanged at any time and if they are, then the new version is immediately available to all clients. This characteristic is of particular importance to cloud computing. There is no need for rolling out new releases, the source of many errors. There is no need for remote hot fixes since there is only one copy of the system and there is no need of keeping local development teams, since everything is centralized. The total cost of ownership is significantly reduced (Tsai et al., 2008).

The cloud makes it possible to access such services from any place in the world at any time, thus overcoming the limitations of time and space. The service concept may not be new, but together with the worldwide web and cloud computing it has opened up a powerful new potential. The big question is whether users can take advantage of that potential (Carr, 2007).

3.2 Benefits of Using Web Services from the Cloud

To take advantage of the cloud, users must be able to select the proper services. That is not as simple as it may sound. Services offered must be assessed in accordance with the benefits they offer and the costs they occur. The benefits need to be quantifiable in terms of the costs they save. These costs should then be compared with the cost of using the cloud services. The most obvious benefits to the user are:

- The elimination of redundancy
- The reduction of maintenance and evolution costs
- The reduction of test costs
- The increase of reliability
- The independence from a particular platform (Narasimhan, & Nichols, 2011)

3.2.1 Eliminated Redundancy

By using a common standard version of a particular algorithm or data object type it is possible to reduce the size of the code significantly. There are not five different ways to calculate an insurance premium or to determine the day of the week but only one. There are also not ten versions of a salary scale but only one. These standard elementary operations are available to every client program regardless of the language. Since the web service is independent of the client programming language it may be used by components in any language.

The language need only be able to dock onto the web service interface (Canfora & DiPenta, 2008). This benefit is measurable in terms of code size. It should be possible to reduce the business application code to less than 50% of what it was.

3.2.2 Reduced Maintenance and Evolution Costs

The costs of maintaining and evolving their own customized systems are what is driving users into the cloud. Users simply have too much old code around. The costs of maintaining the code are proportional to the size, complexity and quality of that code. If the size of systems can be reduced by including foreign services then the maintenance costs will go down. For every common service used that is one less piece of software to deal with. Of course the complexity of the systems may go up as the number of dependencies on external services increases, but this is a small penalty to pay compared to the costs of maintaining the whole application system oneself. This benefit is measurable in terms of lower personal costs. It should be possible to reduce the IT staff by at least half (Becker, 2011).

3.2.3 Reduced Test Costs

It is known that testing makes up for 50 to 75% of total development cost (Chen, Tse, & Zhou, 2011). By reducing the number of variations of an algorithm, the effort for testing that algorithm will decrease proportionally. If there is a table lookup function which requires 8 test cases to test and this function is embedded in 10 different systems then that would require 80 test cases. By having only one copy of that function as a web service the number of test cases may go up from 8 to 16 but that is still much less than the 80 required to test all of the distributed copies. To this comes the fact that since there is only one single version of the service on a single platform. There is no need to have to reinstall it every time it changes. This benefit is measurable by the decrease in required test cases.

3.2.4 Increased Reliability

By having a single copy of a service on a single server there are fewer possibilities for configuration errors. Distributing a software product always bears the risk that the distributed versions are not synchronized. One of the greatest sources of errors in Java is non-matching interfaces among components. The one component may have been updated to have three parameters. The calling component may still only have two. Or, the components may not have identical views of a database because the current view is added to all components but one. Such inconsistencies can be avoided if there is only one copy of the current product on the server with one common interface definition to it. On top of that, web service interfaces with their well defined sets of inputs and outputs makes it possible to find errors more easily (Grassi, 2004). This benefit can be measured in terms of error removal costs. Since, as James Whittaker of Google points out, cloud services are being tested by all of their users, then all users share the burden of detecting errors and it is up to the service provider to correct them (Shull, 2012). This amounts to a tremendous savings.

3.2.5 Platform Independence

Another major advantage of using web services in the cloud is that they can be accessed from anywhere. The user is not tied to a particular platform. He can access them from a tablet computer just as well as he can access them from a mainframe. The web service interface has a virtual interface that can be accessed from any hardware platform and from any software environment. It does not matter on what platform the services are running. This adds up to total portability. If the user migrates from one platform to another, he still has access to the same services. There may be some performance differences but not in the functionality itself. The provider of the services can use any language and any database system he wants. How the services are implemented remains hidden from those who use them (Ardagna et al., 2011).

3.3 Fitting Cloud Services into the Enterprise Service Hierarchy

That brings up the next topic - the construction of a service hierarchy. Web services, also those offered in public and private clouds, are constructed to serve a number of different types of requests at different levels of granularity. At the lowest level a web service may be requested to return a currency rate or the day of a week, i.e. one or two calculated results. At the intermediate level a web service can be requested to prepare an invoice for a customer or to produce a report. Here we are speaking of a data object as the result. At the next, higher level a web service is requested to return a whole set of objects, for instance, all customers who have yet to pay their bills or all accounts which have a negative balance. Finally, at the highest level a web service may be requested to make an inventory or to process the request for a loan. In this case, the web service is at the application level (Smith & Lewis, 2007).

3.3.1 Establishing a Service Hierarchy

Since web services have so many levels of granularity, it is necessary to organize them in hierarchies. The services at one level use the services at the next lower level. At the top of the hierarchy are the applications like payroll and loan processing, or bill of materials and stock inventory. At the next lower level are the services which process object sets like database queries and master file updates. At the even lower level are the services which return single objects – a report or a table entry. At the lowest level there are services which return a single return value such as the amount due.

The consequence of these different levels of abstraction is a service tree in which the services at each level rely on other services below them. Whether the tree might become a network is a question of the architecture. For the sake of simplicity, it may be better to allow services to only invoke services at the next level below them. This way complexity can be controlled and there is no danger of recursion. In a network complexity increases and testing becomes more difficult and costly. Building hierarchies is the classical way of controlling complexity. A strict hierarchical structure is the first prerequisite to a stable service-oriented architecture (see Figure 1).

To make sure that this hierarchical principle is adhered to, the services should be named in terms of their hierarchical level so that is easy to control whether an invoked service is at a higher, a lower or at the same level as the invoking service. Only invocations of lower level services are allowed.

3.3.2 Specifying Required Granularity

In evaluating potential web services the granularity of the services should be taken into account. The evaluator must assess the services in accordance with their role in the service hierarchy. If they are at a high level, more effort must go into testing and rating them. A team of testers will be required. Lower level services can be tested and evaluated by one or two persons. The costs of testing cloud services depend very much on the width of their interfaces. Thus, test costs may range from a few person days to several person months. It all depends on the number of operations to be performed and the number of parameters for each operation. Any one service can contain any number of operations, i.e. functions. For instance it could create a table, insert entries into it, delete entries, change entries or look up a certain entry. The number of operations that a given service can perform is physically unlimited, but then the service becomes unwieldy and difficult to test. If this is the case, it should be split up into a main service and several sub-services with a separate WSDL interface to each sub-service. This is referred as service refactoring (Yau & Ho, 2011).

Figure 1. Web service hierarchy

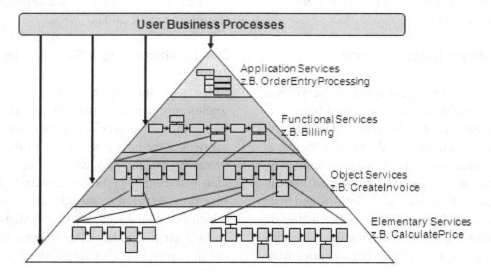

In addition, a web service should only have a limited number of parameters. The number of parameters, i.e. arguments, determines the width of the service interface. To remain testable there should be more than a maximum number of such arguments. This number should average out to no more than seven arguments per operation, whereby some arguments may be used by many operations. Here too the goal is to restrict complexity, by reducing the volume of data to be processed by any one service (Stylianou & Kumar, 2000).

3.3.3 Defining Service Size Limits

Finally, there is the size of the service interfaces. No single interface definition should exceed a given size, for instance no more than 500 statements. If the service is larger it should delegate functionality to lower level services. In the case of services at the application level, the service will only consist of decisions and delegations to the functional services. In the case of functional services, the service will again contain only decisions and calls to the object processing. Functional services are strictly control services. Processing is done at the level of the object and elementary services. The object services will process whole business objects such as customers and orders, whereas the calculation of individual data variables and the checking of specific business rules is delegated to elementary services. In the end an enterprise Service Architecture will consist of several hundred thousand elementary services, several thousands of object services, several hundreds of functional services and up to a hundred application services. A SOA is simply the mirror image of an enterprise and enterprises are known to be complex structures. The important thing is that a significant portion of the services required – more than 75% - should be taken from a pool of ready-made services provided in a public or private cloud.

It should not be surprising that it takes an enormous investment and many years to put together a set of web services capable of covering all essential user requirements. Rome was not built in a day, and neither will a SOA be built in a year. Experience has shown that it may take up to five years and several hundred person years to construct such a service hierarchy (Worms, 2010).

3.3.4 Testing the Service Hierarchy

It is one thing to test individual web services in regard to their suitability for the task at hand. It is another thing to integrate them into a service hierarchy. The recommended approach is to integrate and test them from the bottom-up. One should start with the elementary services and test them in conjunction with the object services. Once this is working, the object services should be tested together with the higher level functional services. Finally, all the functional services of an application, i.e. business process, are linked together and submitted to an end-to-end test. In testing each higher level, all subordinate levels are retested under differing conditions. This is the same testing approach as that suggested by Stan Siegel in his book on object-oriented testing (Siegel, S., 1996). (see Figure 2).

3.4 Using a Standard Platform (PaaS)

Cloud Services will normally be offered on a standard commercial platform. This should be in a secure, ripened and established framework. IBM, Google, Oracle and Microsoft, all offer such a platform. These platforms are themselves services which user can build on – platform as a service (PaaS). PaaS solutions offer a complete application development and hosting site as a cloud service.

Besides managing the underlying infrastructure and providing a metered-by-use cost model, PaaS also facilitates application development, testing, deployment and ongoing maintenance, thus freeing the application service provider from the burden of dealing with the infrastructure and allowing him to focus on the applications.

Figure 2. Testing the enterprise service hierarchy

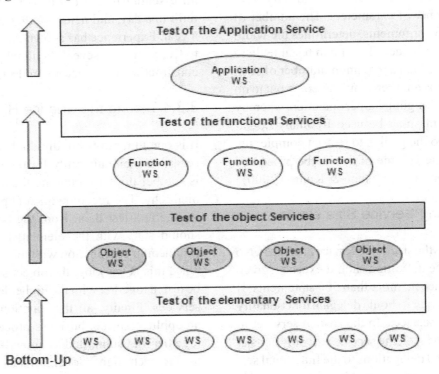

Even more important in this context is that he PaaS framework has been thoroughly tested by the other users so that the users can make some assumptions about the reliability and security of the environment their services are running in. Just as the cloud is the mainframe of the 21st century, the PaaS is the operating system of this century (Khalidi, 2011).

The problem here is that the platform becomes part of the application. It has to be tested together with the services it is carrying. Of course, the platform should have already been tested by many others before, but maybe not those features required by the services this user is using. So it has to be tested as well.

4. QUALITY REQUIREMENTS ON WEB SERVICES IN THE CLOUD

The fact that web services in the cloud are intended to be used in different ways by different users places high demands on their quality. They have to be highly reliable and efficient. Errors and performance bottle necks that could be tolerated in conventional systems can become catastrophic in a service-oriented architecture. For this reason, services must be thoroughly tested. Besides these external quality characteristics they should be maintainable, reusable and portable. The costs of maintaining a Service-oriented Architecture can get out of hand if the internal quality is not managed properly.

4.1 Quality Goals of a Service-Oriented System

The major quality goals of a service-oriented system are:

- Correctness
- Reliability
- Security
- Efficiency
- Reusability
- Portability
- Maintainability

In regard to correctness, a cloud service is expected to behave exactly as is stated in its specification. It should fulfill each specified function and deliver the specified results (ISO, 2009).

In regard to reliability a cloud service should perform its specified behavior without the slightest interruption. If it contains faults then these faults should occur rarely and their effects cushioned by the environment, i.e. the services should be robust. Faults should be captured and handled by fail soft procedures which allow the system to continue operation even if individual services are not functionally correctly.

In regard to security, cloud services should always have their inputs checked before processing them. Authentication and authorization procedures should ensure that no unauthorized persons can gain access to a service and that all links to the outer world are controlled. It may be even necessary to place web services within a security wrapper, which filters all incoming and outgoing messages. It goes without saying that any attempt to access user data via web services without adequate access rights should be thwarted.

In regard to efficiency, cloud services should be able to process their requests in the time allocated to them. There should never be any time-out problems. If any service turns out to be a performance bottleneck, it should be replaceable by another service with equivalent behavior. That implies that there should be backup services available (Menasce, Ruan, & Goma, 2007).

In regard to reusability, cloud services should be reusable within a different context. If the services adhere to a standard WSDL interface then they should be reusable provided they do not refer to submodules or base classes which are not web services. No accesses to software outside of the web service hierarchy can be allowed. All accesses to the common database should be in a separate access shell at the elementary level. This also applies to printing reports and writing export files. The business logic must be kept separated from the data access and file operations. As with other architectures, the service architecture should have frontend and backend services to communicate with the environment.

In regard to portability the services should be executable on different platforms. The best were if they were in a universal language like Java which runs on all platforms. But COBOL and C++ are acceptable since they can be compiled on most all machines. What should not be permitted is to have the services in a proprietary language which cannot be ported.

In regard to maintainability, the services should be coded in such a way that they can be readily corrected and changed. Of course, this may not be true of services extracted from legacy code, but one should work toward improving them through restructuring and refactoring measures.

Al in all, one can say that the quality requirements on cloud services are significantly higher than those placed on earlier systems and for this reason a much greater investment in quality assurance is needed. The costs of quality assurance should be at least double those of constructing a service based system (Calinescu et al., 2011).

4.2 Service Level Agreements for Cloud Services

To ensure the quality of cloud services purchased from a vendor or used on demand, the user of the service should negotiate a service level agreement – SLA. The SLA is necessary as a base of reference as to what the quality of the service – QoS - should be. Without it quality can be interpreted in any way. If a service breaks or returns a wrong result in every second transaction the vendor might claim that this is good enough. The user may have another opinion and a judge must decide who is right. Without a legally binding contract as to what quality is meant, the judge will in doubt support the accused, who is considered innocent until proven guilty. Without a service level or service quality agreement the provider of the service is always right (Keller & Ludwig, 2003). The quality assurance of web services in the cloud is particularly dependent on a well defined service agreement. A test is always a test against something and here it is a test against the SLA (see Figure 3).

Therefore, the formulation of a service level agreement must be taken very seriously. As a minimum the agreement should state what functions the service should perform, i.e., the invocable operations:

1. What results the service should return with their valid value domains.
2. The maximum tolerable error rate per 1000 transactions.
3. The minimum availability of the service in percentage of total operating time.
4. The minimum degree of security in terms of thwarted intrusions relative to all attempted intrusions.
5. The maximum tolerable response time for a request.
6. The maximum average response time for all requests.

In addition the agreement might include:

7. What percentage of false input arguments should be recognized and reported (integrity).
8. What security checks should be performed (security).
9. What degree of independence from the underlying database should be achieved (data independence).
10. The maximum number of sub services that can be invoked (coupling).
11. The maximum number of data attributes that can be used relative to the number of operations (cohesion).

Figure 3. Testing services against a SLA

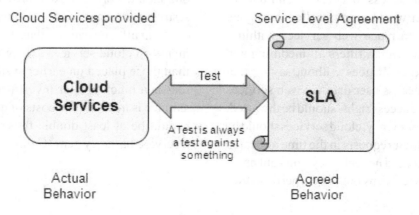

Cloud Services provided   Service Level Agreement

Cloud Services

Test

A Test is always a test against something

SLA

Actual Behavior   Agreed Behavior

12. The minimum degree of testing coverage to be achieved (coverage).
13. The minimum degree of compliance to the coding rules (conformance).
14. The minimum level of documentation.
15. The minimum level of the code quality index on a ratio scale of 0 to 1.

The important thing with all points made in a service level agreement, is that they are measurable. Either they are expressed as a number such a the response time in seconds and the errors per transaction, or they are a binary decision either yes or no, for instance is a result correct or not, is a function present or not? There should be no room left for interpretation. Interpretation as witnessed by the many court decisions on faulty software almost always ends in a decision in favor of the supplier, according to the traditional principle, when in doubt then in favor of the accused. The author of this chapter has served several times as an expert witness in court for accused software suppliers and never lost a case. There was always a doubt about what was required by a consumer since it was never explicitly stated in his contract. Users should know that they have the burden of proof. Without a well defined agreement, their claims regarding the quality of a service will always be disputed (Kienle & Vasilu, 2008). Figure 4 serves as a sample of how a service level agreement for a web service taken from the cloud might look like.

4.3 Certifying Cloud Services

The certification of a cloud service implies that it complies with both its functional and non-functional requirements. These requirements are expressed in the service level agreement. As in object-orientation classes are inherited, service level agreements may also be inherited. There may be a master agreement which is valid for all services within a given service hierarchy. This base

Figure 4. Sample service level agreement

Web Service Level Agreement	
RequirementType	**Degree of Fulfillment**
Functions:	Compute Day of Week Identify invalid Dates
Results:	DayofWeek (GermanWeekDays, FrenchWeekDays, ItalianWeekDays) DateValidity ('date is valid', 'date is invalid')
Arguments:	Date (TTMMYYYY) LanguageCode (1 = German, 2 = French, 3 = Italian) TextAdjustment (L = Left, R = Right)
MinimumCorrectness:	0,005 (errors per 1000 Requests)
MinimumAvailability:	96% (percent of total time)
MinimumSecurity:	90% (percent of attacks detected)
MedianResponseTime:	2 Sec. (from sending of request to receipt of response)
MaximumResponseTime:	4 Sec. (highest response time)
MinimumConformance:	85% (adherence to interface convention)
MinimumInternalQuality:	0,7 (measured internal quality index)

agreement can then be specialized for individual services to identify their exact operations, arguments and expected results. There may also be deviations within the non-functional requirements, i.e. the minimum level of achievement may be raised for a particular service or group of services, but it may not be lowered. This corresponds to Liskov's law of substitution, which can be applied here to certification. Lower level agreements may strengthen higher level ones, but they may never weaken them (Liskov & Guttag, 1988).

There are two ways of checking if a cloud service conforms to its service level agreement. One is by examining the cloud service interface definition. The other is by executing the service and observing its behavior. The first approach is referred to as static analysis, the second as dynamic analysis. Both are needed to certify the services (Sneed, 2008).

5. AN AUTOMATED PROCESS FOR TESTING CLOUD SERVICES

The test process foreseen here is intended to lead to an assessment of a potential service. It is not intended to remove errors contained in the service. That is the job of the provider. If errors are found it only serves to show that the service is unreliable. Judging the reliability and functionality of a web service is the goal of dynamic analysis. Assessing the performance of a service is the task of a performance analysis. If the performance criteria are not met, it shows that the service is not suitable for the usage planned. Other non-functional characteristics such as security, interoperability and adaptability of the service interface are objects of a static analysis. Thus, there are three parallel testing activities aimed at delivering the interested user a comprehensive report on the pros and cons of a required service. This chapter is focused on the static and dynamic analysis activities.

The service test team begins by analyzing the service level agreement and the service interface definition. The goal here is to assess the static quality of the service and to generate a set of test cases which can be used to dynamically analyze the service. This work involves operating the analysis tools and evaluating the results.

The next step is to dynamically analyze the target service, bombarding it with test cases and measuring the throughput time. All deviations from the expected behavior should be recorded and the response times compared with the required times. Here the work involves running the test tools and evaluating the test results. The result should be a quantified report on the suitability of the service for the user needs. It is then up to the user to decide whether to use the service or not. The process recommended here foresees 8 steps starting with the formulation of the service level agreement and proceeding from there to a final evaluation of the service under investigation (see Figure 5).

It may be that there are several alternative services. In this case the test team will repeat this cycle for each service and compare them in the end. In this way the user has a choice. It will cost more, but it may well be worth it to select between cloud service offers before deciding on a particular one.

In view of the time and cost constraints put on the evaluation of potential services it is imperative that the test activities be automated. As proposed at the beginning of the chapter users will be contracting test agents to assess one or more services for them. They expect for these services to be evaluated at a fixed price within a fixed period of time. The contracted test team must be able to analyze the service level agreement and the cloud service interface definitions within a week. Within another week it must be able to generate a set of test cases from the SLA and the WSDL. The dynamic analysis of the cloud service should

Figure 5. Cloud service evaluation process

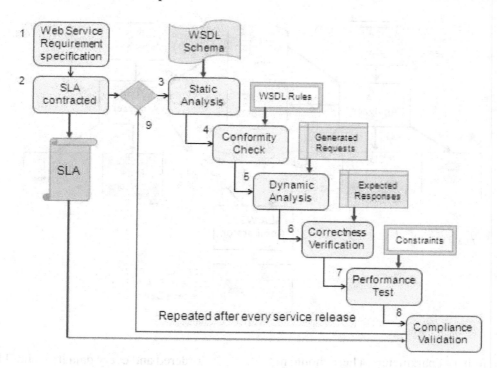

take no more than two weeks. After that a report is prepared and presented to the user. Considering that no more than two persons are involved the total costs of assessing a median sized cloud service should not exceed two person months.

6. STATIC ANALYSIS OF CLOUD SERVICE INTERFACES

Unfortunately, it will seldom be possible to gain access to the source code of a public web service, unless it is an open source product. Commercial services will remain a black box. But, the user does have the interface description and that can be analyzed as a proxy of the service behind it. It can be checked for rule conformance and it can be measured to assess the size, complexity and quality of the service as viewed from outside. There are a number of criteria points in the service level agreement which can be confirmed by static analysis, among them:

- What functions the service offers.
- What results the service provides.
- What exception handling measures are foreseen.
- What security functions are offered.
- What sub services can be invoked.
- What data is required for the operations.
- The degree of conformity to the rules for designing interfaces.
- What links exist between services.

These possibilities are examined here in this section (see Figure 6).

6.1 Rules for Cloud Service Interface Definitions in WSDL

There are many rules for constructing web service interfaces. Some of them have already been mentioned in connection with the quality requirements on cloud services. The interfaces should not be too wide, meaning they should not contain more than

Figure 6. Static analysis of WSDL interfaces

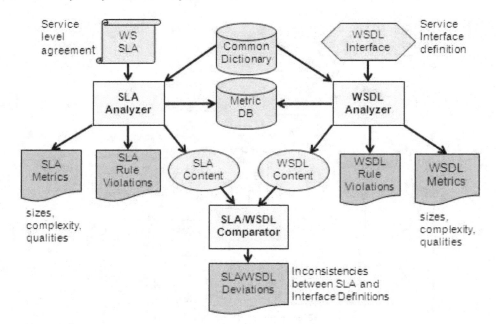

a limited number of parameters. There should not be multiple schemas used, as this would be similar to multiple inheritance and all data items should be qualified by their name space. This author has identified 10 rules which can be checked by a static analyzer tool:

1. The interface specification should conform to the latest standard, now WSDL-2.1 and contain only language elements prescribed by that standard.
2. Every data item should be qualified by a name space, but only prescribed name spaces should be used. The valid name spaces should be available in a name space table to be checked by the static analyzer.
3. The interface should include inline documentation to provide the semantic information, which unfortunately is missing in the original WSDL language. Schematron assertions are a good example of a language extension (ISO/IEC-19757, 2006). Every data group should correspond to a pattern in Schematron in which the rules for that group are lexically

ordered and every data item should have an assertion as to its domain. For every operation there should be a comment explaining what the operation does. Finally both the input arguments and the response results should have precise specifications, i.e. enumerations of possible values according to the validation rules. These values or value ranges should be subsets of the domains specified for the data elements. The comments can be expressed by the <doc> attribute, the assertions by the <assert> attribute.

4. The data type "any" should be avoided since this is equivalent to a typeless data variable. Using it would lead to problems in converting the data and to creating test data. Web service interfaces need be static in order to remain testable.
5. The basic XML data types like integer, double, character and string should never appear directly in the input and output messages, but instead be referred to indirectly by user types. The user type "amount" refers to the basic type "double."

6. The first normal form for data structures should be adhered to, which means there should never be more than one maxOccurs clause with a value greater than 1 in the same data structure, as that would imply a two dimensional array. The passing of complex arrays as parameters should be avoided since this requires the service to use multiple indexes and multiple indexes are a source of errors.

7. It may also be that certain data types such as "float" and "date" are not allowed for certain types of services. There may be even wrapped legacy services which prohibit binary data types altogether. This may be the case when old mainframe or AS400 software is wrapped. The static analyzer should check if only allowed data types are used in the interface specification.

8. Naming conventions are very important for a service-oriented architecture. The operations should be named so that it is indicated what is to be done – the verb – with what data – the object. The names of data should indicate their types and purpose. The data names in the underlying schema should be checked against a data dictionary.

9. The number of operations should be checked that they do not exceed a given limit – otherwise the interface will become overloaded. It is up to the user to set that limit. Just because a service offers 50 operations does not mean that all of them have to be defined in one interface definition.

10. The number of data elements in any one message should also be checked that it does not exceed a given limit. Too many parameters drive up complexity and increase the effort required for testing (Sneed, 2010).

There are many other features of a web service interface description which could be checked, for instance interfaces with too deep a data structure or interfaces with hidden dependencies. The goal should be to eliminate as many potential quality problems as possible via static analysis before testing even begins, since this is indisputably the cheapest form of error detection. Any problem detected by static analysis is money saved when it comes to dynamic analysis (see Figure 7).

6.2 Measuring WSDL Interfaces

Like other software artifacts, web service interfaces can be measured in terms of size, complexity and quality. These measurements are important in determining how much effort is required for testing the services. The wider an interface is, i.e. the greater the size, the more test cases are required to test the operations. The greater the complexity of the data structures, the harder it is to generate sufficient test data to cover them. The lower the quality of the interface, the greater the error probability and the more effort is required to maintain and evolve them. Thus all three dimensions of a cloud service should be measured:

- Quantity
- Complexity
- Quality

6.2.1 Measuring Cloud Service Size

The functional size of a cloud service can be derived indirectly thru the width of its interface. From the view point of the service user it is irrelevant how many lines of code or how many statements it contains. The user is only interested in that part which he uses and that part is expressed in the data and functions he uses, both of which are specified in the interface. Thus, the size of the interface corresponds to the portion of the service used. The metric for the size in data is the Data-Point. Data-points were first used in the 1980s to measure the size of systems based on their data model (Sneed, 1990). Data elements are weighted with 1, data keys or data relations with 2 and data objects or groups with 4 Data-

Figure 7. Sample WSDL deficiency report

```
                    WSDL Interface Deficiency Report

+--------------------------------------------------------------------+
|                  S O F T A N A L     A U D I T O R                  |
|                        I N T E R F A C E                           |
|              C O N F O R M A N C E     R E P O R T                  |
|    LANGUAGE: XSD                               DATE: 19.04.11       |
|    SOURCE: RSFWBMServiceTypes                  PAGE:        4       |
+--------+-----------------------------------------------------------+
| LINE   |   INTERFACE RULE VIOLATION / CODE DEFICIENCY              |
+--------+-----------------------------------------------------------+
| DEFI:  | Data Structure is too deeply nested                       |
|   512  | </GetTopicResponse>                                       |
|        |                                                           |
| DEFI:  | Any Data Type should not be used                          |
|   601  | <AccountType type = "any"/>                               |
|        |                                                           |
| PROB:  | Input arguments do not match specified Arguments          |
|   719  | <input message="tns:saveAccessRequest" />                 |
|        |                                                           |
| DEFI:  | Document has more than maximum allowed Structures         |
| DEFI:  | Document has more than maximum allowed Parameters         |
|   795  | RSFWBMService                                             |
|        |                                                           |
+--------+-----------------------------------------------------------+
|                                                                    |
|    Number of major Rule Violations    =        1                   |
|    Number of media Rule Violations    =       52                   |
|    Number of minor Rule Violations    =        3                   |
|    Total Number of Rule Violations    =       56                   |
|    Number of Interface Statements     =      736                   |
|                                                                    |
|    Rate of Rule Conformity            =    0.925                   |
+--------------------------------------------------------------------+
```

Points. Data-Points are counted by analyzing the data schemas used by the interface specification. In WSDL each elementary data type is one Data-Point, each complex data type is four and each data type with an id attribute is two Data-Points.

The metric for functional size is the Function-Point. Function-Points date back to the 1970s. In the function-models of those times it was easy to identify elementary processes with their inputs and outputs and their data stores. Inputs were weighted from 3-6, outputs from 4-7 and data stores from 7-15. As function models went out of fashion, it became more and more difficult to count function points. With the advent of web services it has again become convenient to count function-points. In the original IFPUG function point counting method there were besides data stores, also data imports and exports, which were weighted from 5 to 10 (IFPUG, 1999). Every service port can be considered to be an import/export. If it has a complexity above 0.6 it should have a weight of 10.

With a medium complexity between 0.4 and 0.6 it should be weighted 7. Otherwise it will weigh 5. In addition, every service port contains a number of functional operations. Each operation has in input and an output message. The input messages can be given a weight of 3 to 6 depending on the number of data groups they contain, whereas the output messages are weighted 4 to 7. Thus, it is rather easy to sum up the number of function points a web service interface has.

Provided the user has productivity data on the number of Data-Points and Function-Points produced per day, the size of a service in Data-Points and Function-Points is a good indicator not only of how much effort is required to develop the web service, but also how much effort is required to test it (see Figure 8).

Figure 8. Sample WSDL size metrics

```
                   WSDL Size Metrics
+-------------------------------------------------------------------+
I              Q U A N T I T Y    M E T R I C S                      I
+-------------------------------------------------------------------+
I          C O D E   Q U A N T I T Y    M E T R I C S               I
I  Number of Source Members analyzed    =======>        1           I
I  Number of Source Lines in all        =======>      205           I
I  Number of Genuine Code Lines         =======>      215           I
I    S T R U C T U R A L   Q U A N T I T Y   M E T R I C S          I
I  Number of Modules                    =======>        1           I
I  Number of Schemas                    =======>        2           I
I  Number of Classes  declared          =======>        6           I
I  Number of Classes  inherited         =======>        5           I
I  Number of Interfaces declared        =======>        1           I
I  Number of Object-Points              =======>      107           I
I          D A T A   Q U A N T I T Y    M E T R I C S               I
I  Number of Data Structures            =======>        6           I
I  Number of Data Constants declared    =======>        1           I
I  Number of Data Variables declared    =======>       81           I
I  Number of different Data Types used  =======>       10           I
I  Number of Data References            =======>      181           I
I  Number of Arguments / Input Variables =======>      19           I
I  Number of Results / Output Variables =======>       19           I
I  Number of Predicates / Conditional Data =======>     6           I
I  Number of Parameters / Function Arguments=======>  219           I
I  Number of Data-Points                =======>      117           I
I        P R O C E D U R A L   Q U A N T I T Y   M E T R I C S      I
I  Number of Statements                 =======>      201           I
I  Number of Input Operations           =======>       19           I
I  Number of Output Operations          =======>       19           I
I  Number of Exception Conditions       =======>        5           I
I  Number of Foreign Functions referenced =======>    100           I
I  Number of Nesting Levels (Maximum)   =======>        3           I
I  Number of Test Cases (Minimum)       =======>       43           I
I  Number of different Statement Types  =======>      101           I
I  Number of Assertions made            =======>       12           I
I  Number of Function-Points            =======>       89           I
+-------------------------------------------------------------------+
```

6.2.2 Measuring Cloud Service Complexity

The literature on software complexity identifies three types of software complexity:

- Lingual
- Structural
- Algorithmic

Lingual complexity depends on the number of different language element types contained in a text message relative to the number of elements used in all. Examples of lingual complexity metrics are Shannon's communication density measure (Shannon, 1949) and Halstead's code complexity measure (Halstead, 1977). WSDL has a number of syntactic element types such as:

- Basic data types
- User defined data types
- Elementary data types
- Data sequences
- Data selections
- Message parts
- Message types
- Port types
- Input messages
- Output messages
- Fault messages
- Operations
- Bindings
- Services
- SOAP packaging types

When analyzing a WSDL source it is necessary to count which of these types are used and how often they are used. The lingual complexity of a WS-interface is:

syntactic types used/total data defined

Of course the wider the interface is, the less will be the complexity as the same types are repeated many times. So there has to be an upper limit as to the number of occurrences that are counted.

Structural complexity is measured in terms of the number of relationships between entities of a structure. In measuring code the entities are the statements and the relationships the branches from one statement to another. This is what the McCabe metric measures (McCabe, 1976). In measuring interfaces the entities are the operations and their parameters which can be data elements and data groups. The more parameters there are relative to the number of operations, the higher the structural complexity.

This is considered to be horizontal complexity since it measures relationships between two different entity types at the same semantic level – operations and parameters. There are also hierarchical relationships between entities of the same general type, such as among the data items. One data group may contain other data groups and so on until one comes to the indivisible data elements. The deeper and wider the data hierarchy, the greater is the structural complexity, measurable in terms of the average width and depth of the data trees.

Operations cannot be subdivided so that excludes measuring functional structural complexity. Also, since the interface specification is strictly descriptive there is no algorithm complexity. Algorithm complexity can only be measured within the web service itself. So this leaves us with the structural complexity metric of a web service interface as being

(1 − (operations / parameters) *
(1 − (data groups / data elements))

6.2.3 Measuring Web Service Quality

The quality of a service definition can be interpreted in many ways. There is no one all encompassing view of quality. It is in the eyes of the beholder. If he happens to be a tester, then testability is for him the essence of quality. If he is responsible for maintenance, then maintainability is the key issue. If he is a system integrator then reusability and modularity are the most important features. Finally, if he is the business application developer, he is looking for usability and reliability. The service should fit well to his business process and work as is expected by him (see Figure 9).

By means of static analysis, it is not possible to determine whether a web service performs as it should or not. That is a matter for dynamic analysis. However, it is possible to partially judge such quality features as

- Usability
- Reusability
- Testability
- Modularity
- Maintainability (Stylianou & Kumar, 2000)

Usability in regards to cloud services is the degree to which the service can be adapted to the requirements of the user. In terms of the service interface, usability is equivalent to flexibility. Flexibility implies a highly granular hierarchy of data with only user defined data types. There should be no constant values assigned within the interface specification, only variable values are possible. To measure this requires counting all variable and user data types and comparing them with the total number of data types.

Usability = (user data types / all data types)*
(valuable data types / all data types) *
(data groups / data elements)

Figure 9. Sample WSDL metric report

WSDL Complexity & Quality Metrics

```
+-------------------------------------------------------------------+
|  S O F A U D I T   I N T E R F A C E   M E T R I C   R E P O R T  |
|                                                                   |
|  LANGUAGE: WSDL                                  DATE: 19.04.11    |
|  MODULE: Billing                                 PAGE:        2    |
+-------------------------------------------------------------------+
|            C O M P L E X I T Y        M E T R I C S               |
+-------------------------------------------------------------------+
|     INTERFACE DATA COMPLEXITY            =======>   0.750         |
|     INTERFACE RELATION COMPLEXITY        =======>   0.800         |
|     INTERFACE FORMAT COMPLEXITY          =======>   0.300         |
|     INTERFACE STRUCTURE COMPLEXITY       =======>   0.350         |
|     DATA FLOW COMPLEXITY                 =======>   0.800         |
|     LANGUAGE COMPLEXITY                   =======>   0.880         |
|                                                                   |
|     AVERAGE INTERFACE COMPLEXITY         =======>   0.646         |
+-------------------------------------------------------------------+
|            Q U A L I T Y        M E T R I C S                     |
+-------------------------------------------------------------------+
|     INTERFACE MODULARITY                 =======>   0.350         |
|     INTERFACE ADAPTABILITY               =======>   0.650         |
|     INTERFACE REUSABILITY                =======>   0.888         |
|     INTERFACE TESTABILITY                =======>   0.100         |
|     INTERFACE PORTABILITY                =======>   0.496         |
|     INTERFACE CONFORMITY                 =======>   0.957         |
|                                                                   |
|     AVERAGE  INTERFACE QUALITY           =======>   0.573         |
+-------------------------------------------------------------------+
```

Reusability is a question of independence from a particular environment. It the ease with which a piece of software can be taken out of its original environment and reused in another. The less dependent the software is on the other software around it, i.e., the fewer its external relationships, the higher its reusability. Dependencies in web service interfaces are the references to different schemas and different name spaces. The more different schemas and name spaces are referred to, the less is the reusability of that particular interface.

Reusability = 1 – (schemas + name spaces used) / data types used

Testability implies a minimum of test effort. Test effort is determined by the number of operations to be tested and the number of parameters they have. The least the individual operations and the less parameters they have, the greater the testability, because there will be less test cases required.

Testability = 1 – (operations + message parts)/ all data elements used

Modularity is interpreted in the literature on software design as being maximum cohesion and minimum coupling (Chidamer & Kemerer, 1994). High cohesion of a service interface can be measured in terms of the number of data types relative to the number of operations performed with them. The fewer data types there are relative to the number of operations, the higher the cohesion

Cohesion = operations / data types

Coupling can be seen as the interface fan-out, i.e. the number of operations invoked per port relative to all ports. That leads to the equation:

Coupling = 1 – (ports / operations)

Modularity as a whole is then the arithmetic mean of cohesion and coupling as follows:

Modularity = (cohesion + coupling) / 2

Maintainability is interpreted here as being adherence to the rules for specifying web interfaces. Of course the rules vary in their significance. There are rules with mayor significance, rules with minor significance and rules with medium significance. Violations of rules with a major significance are weighted by 2, violations of rules with a medium significance are weighted by 1 and violations of rules with a minor significance are weighted by 0,5. To measure the degree of maintainability the number of weighted rule violations is summed up to compare with the total number of checks made in all:

Maintainability = 1 – (weighted rule violations/ total rule checks)

6.3 Evaluating the Static Quality of Cloud Services via their Interfaces

The rules and metrics for evaluating a web service interface can all be checked automatically. The tool needs only to have access to the WSDL interface specification and to the data schemas which are referenced by it. Thus, it is possible to check and measure several interfaces within only minutes. However, this automated analysis is not enough. A human quality assessor must still read through the interface description to evaluate the overall quality. In particular, he must compare the logical content of the interface with the service level agreement. That entail checking if all of the functions specified in the service level agreement are also defined as operations in the web service interface, that all of the results to be delivered are defined the output messages and that all of the arguments to be used are defined in the input messages.

In the end, it is up to the quality assessor to confirm the consistency of the cloud service interface with the service level agreement. In addition to that he must judge whether the rules violated and the limits exceeded are serious enough to justify refusing the service. Much of what is referred to as software quality, such characteristics as functional completeness, reusability, portability and maintainability can and should be controlled statically. Others such as reliability, security and efficiency have to be controlled dynamically. Thus, static analysis is necessary but alone it is not enough (Sneed, 2005).

7. DYNAMIC ANALYSIS OF CLOUD SERVICES

Dynamic analysis entails using the service interface definition to test the cloud service. In production the cloud service would normally be used by a business process implemented with BPEL or Java Ajax or some other client language. However, when cloud services are being considered for use, the business processes for which they are intended may not yet be available. It follows, that a service-oriented architecture has to be constructed bottom-up. First the services are made available and then the processes are placed over top of them.

In assessing cloud services each and every service has to be tested individually. Since there can be hundreds of services involved in an enterprise SOA, their testing can require a tremendous effort, especially if it is done thoroughly. The only way to constrain that effort is by test automation. Other possible approaches such as risk-based testing or creative testing are only applicable when integrating the services or testing the architecture as a whole. The construction of a service-oriented architecture is much too complex and too critical to be tested in a random way (Zhu, 2006). It is like eating an elephant. It has to be tested systematically one piece at a time (see Figure 10).

Furthermore, since the user is not the owner of the services, the purpose of this test is to provide the user with a recommendation and not to uncover errors. Normally it would be the job of the testers to find and report errors. Here it is their job to find out if the cloud service is suitable to the purpose of the user. They must measure the degree to which it fulfills the user requirements as laid down in the SLA. Each and every service has to be carefully evaluated and approved, before the user begins to integrate them into his architecture (Dai et al., 2007). There are five basic steps to testing a web service taken from the cloud:

1. Deriving the test cases
2. Designing the test scenario
3. Generating the test data
4. Executing the tests
5. Evaluating the test results

7.1 Deriving Test Cases for a Cloud Service Test

The first step in testing cloud services is to derive the test cases for testing them. A test case

is defined here as the sending of a request and the receipt of the corresponding response, i.e. a single invocation of a single operation. There may, however, be cases in which a sequence of operations has to be invoked in order to come to a final result. The results of the single operations are only intermediate results. In this case we speak of a compound test case, i.e. one which contains several basic test cases.

7.1.1 Deriving Test Cases from the Web Service Specification

The problem remains as to where the test cases should be taken from. In their survey on testing web services, Bozkurt, Harman and Hassoun point out "all of the information a user receives about a web service is its specification as posted in the UDDI. In this situation specification-based testing becomes a natural choice. Test case generation for web services, as might be expected, is based

Figure 10. Dynamic analysis of Web services

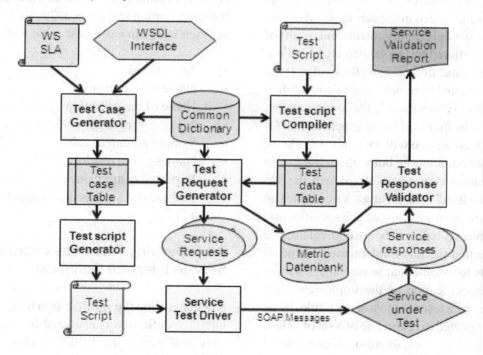

on the web service specifications. This applies to cloud services as well. The provided specifications should include abstract information on the available operations, their arguments and their results. Information taken from the specifications allows the generation of test cases with boundary value analysis, equivalence class testing or random testing using the XLM schema data type information." (Bozkurt, Harman, & Hassoun, 2007). There are then two sources from which test cases are derived:

1.   The service specification
2.   The service interface definition

In the service interface definition, the operations and their parameters are defined. There should be at least two test cases for every operation, one for a positive and one for a negative outcome. If the operation has an exception condition handling, i.e. a fault message, then there should also be a test case to trigger that exception (Dwyer et al., 1999).

The service specification should be either attached to or included in the service level agreement. There, not only the arguments and results of all functions offered by the service are specified, but also their value domains and their rules. If the service is expected to return a specific result like the local sales tax then the rule for computing that result should be included in the specification. Of course, the web service will have its own rule for making that computation, but without the rule in the specification it is not possible to verify the rule in the service itself. A test is always a comparison of two objects or two rules – the one specified and the one implemented. If they are equivalent, one can assume that the one implemented is true. If not, one has to assume that something is wrong, either the specification or the implementation. There has to be a test case to test each rule. If the service is expected to return one of a set of values like the days of the week, then those names should be listed out in an enumeration. If the returned

value is expected to be within a given range of values, then the upper and lower bounds of that range should be specified. And, if the web service should provide a certain text like a Spanish translation of an English sentence submitted as an argument, then that text has to be given in the specification as a sample of what translated texts should look like. Even if they are not exactly the same, the tester still has a reference to refer to (Tosic et al., 2003).

In an ideal world, the specification would be a mirror image of all that is provided by a particular service. In reality many potential results will be omitted, but at least the critical results should be well defined with their rules and value domains. The more exact the specification, the better the test will be.

There are now tools available for parsing natural language texts and deriving test cases from them. If the text is formatted, these tools work quite well. They identify the operations, the parameters and their expected values and automatically generated a test case for each function with each set of parameters and each rule specified in the specification text (Sneed, 2007). These cases are then stored in a test case table with the:

- Test case id
- Name of the service
- Name of the operation
- Names of the arguments
- Sample argument values
- Names of the results
- Expected result values
- Constraints, such as time limits (see Figure 11)

7.1.2 Deriving Test Cases from the Service Interface Definition

After analyzing the specification text, the WSDL interface definition is analyzed by another tool. This tool parses the WSDL syntax and picks out the operations and parameters. These are then compared against those extracted from the specification. If they do not match, then already a discrepancy is noted. If the WSDL interface definition contains operations, parameters or fault conditions not included in the specifications then additional test cases are created for them. In the end, the test case table is a union of test cases derived from the specification and test cased derived from the interface definitions. This automatically generated table can still be enhanced by the human tester, who adds additional test cases which may not be recognizable, neither in the specification nor in the interface definition. Such cases could be events in the environment such as a communication breakdown which are not foreseen in the specification (Sneed, 2008).

Assuming that the specification text is adequately formatted and the requirements are identifiable by keywords in context, and the web service interface definition is complete, it is possible to derive a much as 90% of the test cases automatically. The remaining 10% need to be inserted manually.

A method for specifying a validation script is the already mentioned Schematron XML validation language, which applies equally well to WSDL (ISO/IEC-19757, 2006). That language offers a formal framework consisting of patterns and phases with natural language assertions. A pattern is a set of logically ordered rules whereas a rule is an unordered set of assertions. The assertion is a statement of a constraint which is either fulfilled or not fulfilled. It relates actual values to expected values whereby the expected values have to be specified in some way. The assertions refer to the data elements defined in the patterns as depicted in Box 1.

The assertions can also be expressed formally in the web service specification as shown in the following sample (see Figure 12).

7.2 Designing the Service Test Scenario

The next step after the test cases have been collected is to design a service test scenario. In a web service specification just as in the web service interface definition, the operations, i.e. functions, can be specified and defined in any order. There is no prescribed sequence in which the operations

Figure 11. Web service test cases

Test Case	Test Purpose	Test Objects	Pre/Post Conditions
DayofWeek_TC01	Test for valid German day of week	GetWeekdayInput GetWeekdayOutput	Valid German Weekday
DayofWeek_TC02	Test for valid French day of week	GetWeekdayInput GetWeekdayOutput	Valid French Weekday
DayofWeek_TC03	Test for valid Italian day of week	GetWeekdayInput GetWeekdayOutput	Valid Italian Weekday
DayofWeek_TC04	Test for invalid English day of week	GetWeekdayInput GetWeekdayOutput Exception	Error Message Invalid Language
DayofWeek_TC05	Test for invalid German day of week	GetWeekdayInput GetWeekdayOutput	Error Message Invalid date
DayofWeek_TC06	Test for invalid French day of week	GetWeekdayInput GetWeekdayOutput	Error Message Invalid date
DayofWeek_TC07	Test for invalid Italian day of week	GetWeekdayInput GetWeekdayOutput	Error Message Invalid date

are to be performed. The order does not matter. So it is up to the tester to specify sequences of test cases. If he is testing a web service to manage customers, he must first insert the customer object before updating it and if he wants to update it, this must be done before deleting it. If he is testing a functional service such as billing, he must first collect charges, post prices and insert customer data before the operation create invoice can be invoked. So there are dependencies between test cases. From the viewpoint of a process, the order matters. It can also be that time constraints effect the order in which test cases are executed (Do et al., 2010).

The tester should draw an activity diagram to depict the temporal dependencies between operations. He may also design state transition diagrams to gain better insight into the sequence of the services. He is now into model-based testing. The idea is to model all possible temporal relationships between services and their states. Having done that, he can then proceed to insert these dependencies into the test case descriptions. This may also lead to additional test cases. There should be a column in the test case table, indicating for each test case, its predecessor or predecessors. If there happens to be more than one, another column is required to indicate the selection criteria. This is the trigger column. In this way a procedural view of the services emerges for testing purposes (Baker, 2008).

7.3 Generating Service Test Data

The third step involves generating the test data. This is equivalent to generating web service test scripts (Ofutt & Xu, 2004). A web service test script is generated from a test case table. It identifies the test case and the one or more operations to be invoked by that test case. For each operation the request and response assertions are defined. The request assertions assign the data values which are fed to the web service. They can be value ranges, value sets, value relations or explicit values. The response assertions assign the data values which are expected to come back from the web service. They can be ranges, value sets, value relations or explicit single values. The difference is that the request value will be checked against those values returned in the service response. The following excerpt from a test script depicts how such a data specification might look like (See Figure 13)

From the test script the final web service request is generated. This is done by creating a service interface framework from the WSDL schema and then filling in the values taken from the test script. The result is a complete service request which can be packed into a SOAP message and forwarded to the target service. The following WSDL request is taken from the schema description and the test script depicted in Figure 12 (See Figure 14).

7.4 Executing Web Services in the Cloud

To actually run the tests a test driver is required which feeds the web service requests to the web service in the cloud. This is done by placing the SOAP message containing the web request in packed form into a message queue. The message queue is processed by the service bus which takes

Box 1. Pattern for Schematron XML

```
<sch:pattern is-a="table" id="calendar">
    <sch:param name="table" value="calendar/year"/>
    <sch:param name="row" value="week"/>
    <sch:param name="entry" value="day"/>
</sch:pattern>
```

Figure 12. Web service test specification

```
file: Calender;
  if ( object = "DayofWeekRequest" );
    assert in.DAY = set (0 ! 1 ! 12 ! 30 ! 31);
    assert in.MONTH = set (1 ! 2 ! 6 ! 10 ! 11 ! 12 ! 13);
    assert in.YEAR = range (1960:2001);
    assert in.LANGUAGE = set (1 ! 2 ! 3 ! 0);
    assert in.ALIGNMENT = "L" ! "R";
  endObject;
  if ( object = "DayofWeekResponse");
    assert out.WEEKDAY = set ("Montag" ! "Dienstag" ! "Mittwoch" ! "Donnerstag" ! "Freitag" !
                              "Samstag" ! "Sonntag" ) if in.LANGAUGE = 1;
    assert out.WEEKDAY = set ("Lundi" ! "Marti" ! "Mercredi" ! "Jeudi" ! "Vendredi" !
                              "Samedi" ! "Dimanche" ) if in.LANGAUGE = 2;
    assert out.WEEKDAY = set ("Lunedi" ! "Martedi" ! "Mercoledi" ! "Geovedi" ! "Venerdi" !
                              "Sadato" ! "Domenica" ) if in.LANGAUGE = 3;
    assert out.WEEKDAY = "??????????" if in.LANGUAGE != 1 ! 2 ! 3,
                              if in.DAY < 0 ! In.DAY > 31,
                              if in MONTH < 0 ! In.DAY > 12;
  endObject;
```

the next message, loads the service provided it is not already loaded and invokes it. The target service processes the request, creates a response, and places it in the output queue to be forwarded back to the sender in a SOAP envelope. The sender – in this case the driver – is alerted that it has a message. The driver unpacks the SOAP envelope, takes the response text out and places it in a file of service responses to be verified (see Figure 15).

It is not necessary to process the responses immediately, unless the sending of the next request is dependent on the outcome of the last one. If a test request is intended to trigger an exception condition then the next test case will be intended to handle that condition. In this respect the test process is deterministic. The tester should be able to predict, before starting the test, in what sequence the services will be executed and what will be their final results. However, should something unexpected happen, then the test driver must

notice it and terminate the test. One must expect the unexpected. There has to be a mechanism in the test driver to detect situations like a timeout and to react accordingly.

7.5 Evaluating Cloud Service Test Results

Only after a test has been completed and shut down, it is possible to validate the responses. During the test the responses are accumulated in an output file. Afterwards they are read from that file and checked one at a time, if the values of the response types correspond to the values specified in the test script. It could be that they have to have an exact value like 42, or they have to lie within a range of values from 40 to 50, or they have to be one of a set of values like the colors "red," "white" and "blue." It depends on the tester how precisely he wants to specify the

Figure 13. Web service test script

```
service: DayofWeek
  if (testcase = „DayofWeek_TC01"); // German
    if ( operation = "GetWeekDay");
      if ( request = "GetWeekDayInput");
        assert in.P1-DATE = „12101977";
        assert in.P2-LANGUAGE = "1";
        assert in.P3-ALIGNMENT = "L";
      endRequest;
      if ( response = "GetWeekDayOutput");
        assert out.P4-DAYNAME = „Mittwoch";
      endResponse;
    endOperation;
  endCase;

  if (testcase = „DayofWeek_TC02");
    if ( operation = "GetWeekDay"); //French
      if ( request = "GetWeekDayInput");
        assert in.P1-DATE = „12101977";
        assert in.P2-LANGUAGE = "2";
        assert in.P3-ALIGNMENT = "L";
      endRequest;
      if ( response = "GetWeekdayOutput");
        assert out.P4-DAYNAME = "Mercredi";
      endResponse;
    endOperation;
  endCase;
```

```
if (testcase = „DayofWeek_TC03"); // Italian
  if ( operation = "GetWeekDay");
    if ( request = "GetWeekDayInput");
      assert in.P1-DATE = „12101977";
      assert in.P2-LANGUAGE = "3";
      assert in.P3-ALIGNMENT = "L";
    endRequest;
    if ( response = "GetWeekdayOutput");
      assert out.P4-DAYNAME = "Mercoldi";
    endResponse;
  endOperation;
endCase;

if (testcase = „DayofWeek_TC04"); //English
  if ( operation = "GetWeekDay");
    if ( request = "GetWeekDayInput");
      assert in.P1-DATE = „11312000";
      assert in.P2-LANGUAGE = "4";
      assert in.P3-ALIGNMENT = "R";
    endRequest;
    if ( response = "GetWeekdayOutput");
      assert out.P4-DAYNAME = "Unknown";
    endResponse;
  endOperation;
endCase;
end; // service DayofWeek
```

results. Any value which lies outside of the specified range or set of valid values, or which fails to match the result computed by the assertion, will be reported in a protocol of deviations as depicted below (see Figure 16).

It is left to the tester to judge if a reported deviation is really an error or not. The report contains all response values which do not match exactly to the values specified. Besides reporting non-matching responses, it also reports missing responses, i.e. responses which are expected but which never come. Any mismatch indicates a potential problem which the tester must note in his report to the user. If he is uncertain, he should refer to the specification and consult with the potential user. In any case, the tester should be in contact with the potential service users, since he is testing on their behalf and representing their interests. He needs to know how they intend to use the service and what they understand under

correct behavior. In particular, he must be able to interpret the results. If a result is a floating point number, he must be able to judge the degree of precision the user expects.

In evaluating the results of a cloud service test, the performance measurements must also be taken into account. A service monitoring tool will register when a service request is submitted and when the service response is returned. The time interval between these two points in time is the response time. The monitoring tool can identify the largest response time. It can also compute the average response time. Finally it can register how much time of the tool testing time a service is available. If these times exceed the time limits set in the service level agreements, an error is reported.

Another factor to be considered in evaluating the test results is the test coverage. Since the service itself is a black box, the tester has no way to

Figure 14. Web service test request

```
<XSDCOB:complexType type = "group" name = "P1"
 content = "eltOnly" model = "closed" level = "02"
 occurs = "ONEORMORE" minOccurs = "0001" maxOccurs = "0001">
 <XSDCOB:element type = „date" name = "P1-Date"
  content = "TextOnly" model = "closed" level = "03"
  occurs = "ONEORMORE" minOccurs = "0001" maxOccurs = "0001"/>
 </XSDCOB:complexType>

<XSDCOB:complexType type = "group" name = "P4"
  content = "eltOnly" model = "closed" level = "02"
  occurs = "ONEORMORE" minOccurs = "0001" maxOccurs = "0001">
  <XSDCOB:element type = „string" name = „P4-DayName"
   content = "TextOnly" model = "closed" level = "03"
   occurs = "ONEORMORE" minOccurs = "0001" maxOccurs = "0001"/>
  </XSDCOB:complexType>
</definitions>

<service name = "DayofWeek" >
 <operation name = "GetWeekDay" >
    <request name = „GetWeekDayinput" >
       <P1-Date xsi:type = "date"> 12101977 </P1-Date>
       <P2-Language xsi:type = „char">1</P2-Language>
       <P3-Alignment xsi:type = „char">L</P3-Alignment>
    </request>
    <response name = „GetWeekDayOutput" >
       <P4-DayName xsi:type = „string" >Mittwoch</P4-DayName>
    </response>
 </operation>
```

Schema

WSDL

Figure 15. Web service test execution

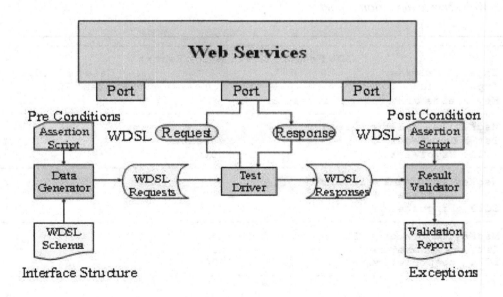

know how much of the code is covered. It would not matter anyway since every user of a common service will most likely only be using a subset of all possible paths through that service. Therefore coverage has to be measured from outside, that is by measuring the interface. 100% functional coverage means here that every operation with every fault handling operation has to be invoked at least one time. Data coverage implies that every specified input value has been submitted at least once in some test case. The goal is to test every specified operation with every specified input value. When this goal is reached and there are no further serious deviations reported, the test can be considered complete (Sneed, H. & Huang, S. 2006).

8. TOOLS FOR TESTING CLOUD SERVICES

In considering the tools for testing cloud services, one must distinguish between tools required and tools available.

8.1 Tools Required for Testing Web Services in the Cloud

The tools required for testing web services in the cloud can be divided into two categories:

1.   Static analyzers
2.   Dynamic analyzers (see Figure 17)

The static analyzers process text-either specification or source texts. The dynamic analyzers process the test scripts.

8.1.1 Specification Analyzer

The specification analyzer parses the service level agreement as well as the attached specification to:

*   Extract the specification-based test cases.
*   Check the completeness and consistency of the SLA.
*   Measure the size, complexity and quality of the web service specification document.

Figure 16. Web service deviation report

```
+------------------------------------------------------------------------+
|                   WSDL Response Validation Report                      |
| Object: Kalender                                    Date: 19.06.04 |
| Type  : XML                                         System: TEST    |
| Key Fields of Response (ist,soll)                                      |
+-----------------------------------------+------------------------------+
| MsgKey:DayofWeek = 12101977             |                              |
| Ist : DayofWeek                         | Mercoledi                    |
| SOll: DayofWeek                         | Mittwoch                     |
+-----------------------------------------+------------------------------+
| MsgKey:DayofWeek = 12101977             |                              |
| Ist : Language                          | 2                            |
| SOll: Language                          | 1                            |
+-----------------------------------------+------------------------------+
| MsgKey:DayofWeek = 12101977             |                              |
| Ist : responseTime                      | 1022                         |
| SOll: responseTime                      | 1000                         |
+-----------------------------------------+------------------------------+
```

8.1.2 Interface Analyzer

The interface analyzer parses the WSDL interface definition sources as well as their XML schemas to:

- Extract the database test cases.
- Check the conformity of the WSDL to the presented rules.
- Measure the size, complexity and quality of the WSDL interface.
- Generate test scripts.

The results are a table of functional test cases enhanced by the representative data values, a deficiency report, a metric report and a test script for every web service interface.

8.1.3 Test Data Generator

The web service test data generator compiles the test scripts and combines the test scripts and combines them with the structural information taken from the schemas to produce web service requests. The inputs are web service requests including their input data values and their expected result values.

8.1.4 Test Driver

The web service test driver dispatches the web service requests and collects the web service responses returned. It should also log which operations in which parts are executed and how often. From this information it should produce a functional test coverage report.

8.1.5 Test Result Validator

The web service test result validator reads the responses collected at test time and compares the response values with the expected values specified in the test script. Based on this comparison

Figure 17. Web service test tools

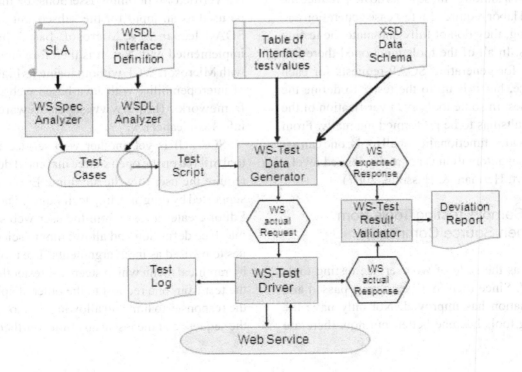

it reports all deviations of actual responses from expected responses. In addition, it should count the response values actually produced by the test and compare the count with the number response values specified. This gives the degree of data coverage. The results of the validator are:

- Deviation report
- Log of tested requests
- Data coverage report

8.2 Tools Available for Testing Web Services in the Cloud

In a survey from the year 2007 made by researchers at King's College London, the author refer to the gap between what is needed as tools for testing web services and what is offered on the commercial market. They point to the tools

Parasoft SOATest, SOAPSmar, HP's Service Test, and Oracle's Application Testing Suite are representative of what was available on the commercial market at that time. The authors claim that "even although these tools do help reduce the manual labor required for test case generation and reporting, they do not fully automate the testing process. In all of the tools mentioned there is a facility for generating SOAP requests for each test case, but it is up to the tester to define the test cases. In some tools even verification of the test results has to be performed manually. From the provided functionality of all tools, one can assume that automation is not at the desired level." (Bozkurt, Harman, & Hassoun, 2007)

8.2.1 Sample Testing Tools from the Open Source Community

Such was the state of web service testing tools in 2007. Since then four years have passed and the situation has improved. Not only have the existing tools become better, but now there are more of them to choose from, especially in the open service community. Representative of these tools is ASTRAR from Tsai and his associates. ASTRAR supports a form of n-version testing where multiple web services with similar business logic are tested together with the same test suite. Although the main goal of this cluster testing approach is to test multiple services at one time to reduce the cost of testing, it also achieves the purpose of establishing a test base line. The tool can be applied both to the testing of single services – unit testing – as well as to the testing of service clusters – integrated testing (Tsai et al., 2002).

Another tool of this type is SOA-Cleaner. It reads the web service interface definition (WSDL) and automatically generates a graphical user interface for composing a message to be sent to the web service in a native and intuitive way. The input arguments, http headers, attachments, etc. are edited through a generated graphical interface. The tool can be used to emulate a complete business process by defining sequential web service calls. The responses returned from the web services are verified by defining assertions, or they can be used as an input for the subsequent service. SOA-Cleaner is a Microsoft-based product implemented with.Net. It is therefore compliant with Microsoft WCF without losing its high level of interoperability with Java-based web service frameworks (http://www.supersareware.com/info/soa-cleaner).

SOAPUI is yet another web service testing tool offered on the open source market. It does not require the user to write anything. Every step is supported by drag and drop techniques. The Form Editor creates a form from the user web service interface definition and allows him to select values to be used as input arguments. The tool has a hierarchical menu which steers the tester through the test from one request to the other, displaying the responses to him and allowing him to change the sequence of the test at any time. Furthermore, the user is allowed to enter assertions during the test, so that the test scenario can be adjusted to changed conditions.

WebInject is another freeware tool for automated testing of web services. It can be used to test individual system components with HTTP interfaces as well as to create a suite of HTTP level automated functional, acceptance and regression tests. The test harness allows the tester to start a number of test cases at one time and to collect the results in report files for which the tool offers a real-time display of the web service results. In addition, WebInject can be used for monitoring web service performance.

As a test framework, WebInject can be used optionally as a standalone test engine or it can be bound together with other test frameworks or applications to be used as an extended test service. For this purpose it has an API interface which allows it to be called dynamically to dispatch web requests. The loading and defining of test cases is made via an XML-WSDL interface. The test cases are stored in XML files, using XML elements and attributes. From there they are passed to the WebInject engine for executing the service under test via a WSDL interface. This way the internal implementation is hidden from the non-technical user while the technical user has the possibility of customizing the open architecture to his specific testing needs. The test results are generated in HTML for viewing and in XML for interpretation by user specific display tools. The results include the pass/fail status, error messages and response times.

In monitoring the service level, WebInject collects and evaluates HTTP response times which are displayed on a monitor window at test time. When used together with a plotting utility like GnuPlot, a response time graph is generated and updated in real-time. This performance data can be used to verify that responses from the web application or web service under test are within the acceptable range to satisfy the SLA or Quality of Service agreement. In this respect, WebInject can be interpreted as being a plug-in tool for other web service testing tools while on the other hand it can be used alone as a standalone testing tool (http://webinject.org).

8.2.2 Sample Testing Tools from the Commercial Market

A good example of a commercial unit testing tool for web services is ParaSoft's SOAPTest. It is one of several commercial tools offered to test web services in a SOA environment. Although its name implies that its only purpose is to identify and diagnose problems in SOAP messages, SOAPTest really delivers comprehensive regression, unit and security testing for web services. The tool has two primary uses, but it functions as an automatic test generator in both cases.

- First, it creates static WSDL verification tests for the content of a Web service's WSDL document. The tests that SOAPTest builds check not only for proper WSDL syntax but also for correct WSDL semantics -- for example, it verifies the document's internal consistency.
- Second, SOAPtest reads the WSDL document's contents and creates unit tests for the Web service's methods. SOAPtest can also create its tests from the Web service's UDDI information, as well as from an HTTP traffic log file involving Web services.

Although these unit tests begin as simple, single calls into Web service methods, they don't stay that way. The tester can easily configure a test to execute repeatedly, drawing its succession of input parameters from a data table, a comma-delimited file, an Excel spreadsheet, or a database. If the tester requires instilling more intelligence into a particular test, he can augment the test's behavior with scripts written in Jython (Python written in Java), Java, or JavaScript.

This is SOAPtest's real power. Beginning with a small, simple set of static and dynamic tests automatically generated by a wizard (one of the new features of SOAPTest 4.0), you can extend, duplicate, and modify those tests to build -- Lego-style -- an increasingly powerful suite. Tests are executed in sequence; by properly ordering tests, one can simulate a lengthy session between Web client and Web service.

The tool's best feature is its seemingly instantaneous creation of tests, and the equally speedy way it iteratively extends and modifies those tests. SOAPTest allowed the tester to assemble my tests in such a way that what began as a collection of unit tests blossomed into an array of functional tests. And throughout this process, he never has to deal with the source code. With SOAPTest, subsequent tests can use data from preceding tests as their inputs, and that allows you to build a "mock" workflow of a user carrying out a complex series of transactions with the particular Web service. By incrementally layering tests on a suite's foundation, you produce a comprehensive project that -- taken as a whole -- ends up being greater than the sum of its parts (http://www2.parasoft.com/SoapTest).

A good example of a commercial integration testing tool for web services is the eValid tool from Software Research Associates. eValid is a GUI level testing tool. Rather than simulate the client to test the web service directly as is done in unit testing, eValid executes the client together with its underlying web services as is done in integration testing. The clients are most likely implemented with some Web2 technology such as JavaScript or AJAX. Of course they could also be implemented in BPEL. When implemented with JavaScript or AJAX eValid is a readable solution. It works with the events from the end-user's interactions within the Web application. eValid supports simple Web

as well as modern JavaScript-based applications. The eValid scripting engine is fully embedded within the browser, and behaves like a true browser client. It utilizes a unique, patented approach to object recognition and processing, which makes it an extremely flexible and extensible solution for testing AJAX and Web 2.0 applications. By moving the scripting engine into the browser in an updated and greatly simplified form, the eValid technology makes scripting much easier. GUI level recording, based on the browser's own DOM, also allows nontechnical users to participate in script creation. The user simply interacts with an application, and the powerful eValid recording engine captures every step in the form of a script. No coding or programming skills are required.

The recording mechanism in SR's eValid technology is fully interactive and is based on an IE-clone browser. When users interact with a web application, they can observe the script being developed on the screen. Every action is sensed automatically and creates a playback command, written in an easy-to-understand English-like language. Using a unique, patented approach to object recognition, the script automatically recognizes and inserts the names of web objects as they exist in the application. The eValid recording engine also automatically includes data that, at playback time, will allow the playback engine to take alternate equivalent automation steps, saving the tester time on script debugging and troubleshooting.

To enable the script to more accurately represent a real world production environment, the tester can enhance it with parameters, replacing static data values with variables, and replacing key URLs and other values with environment variable settings. To enable acceptable performance levels, he can add include commands that measures the amount of time it takes to perform a certain function. These timer commands can also be recorded from the eValid GUI. To check the accuracy of the transaction, the tester can add any number of verification steps. For example, he can select any visible text passage and eValid will accept that as the defined value that needs to be verified at playback time. Or one may want to validate that the amount of money that's been added to the account matches the number that one has asked to transfer, so the tester can specify the exact value that he expects at playback time.

To provide greater flexibility in testing a broad range of applications, there is provision for eValid to emulate a wide range of browser types including those used in mobile applications. This capability allows load testing runs to emulate thousands of browser users at one time using different browser types. In this way eValid can also test the use of hundreds of web services at one time. The web services are not visible to the tester since they are contained within the black box he is testing, but they are tested none the less and if they are faulty, this will result in either invalid results or an exception condition, both of which will be picked up by the eValid recorder. Here the web services are tested not individually but as parts of the whole, as links in a chain of functions. In this way their interactions with one another are tested, which is what integration testing is all about (Software Research, 2011).

9. AUTOMATION OF CLOUD SERVICE TESTING

The key to evaluating cloud services is automation. SOA systems and applications in the cloud are far too complex to be tested manually. Canfora and DiPenta have pointed out that the main problem in the testing of web services is the high cost of testing all potential usages (Canfora & DiPenta, 2006). This author has made a similar observation, in a project to wrap old COBOL programs for reuse as web services in a service-oriented archit4ecture several services could be wrapped per day, but it took at least two days to test such a service. The

old data submitted via the terminal maps was no longer usable. The new data to set up the web service requests had to be submitted manually to the test driver. Before that, hard copies of the old map images were made in order to replicate the old test cases. The responses were printed out to compare them manually with the content of the old output maps. Considering the fact that there were several hundred services to test, this was definitely not a solution (Sneed, 2009)

More has to be done to automate the testing of cloud services. The testing process described here is directed toward testing against a specification enforced by a Service Level Agreement. As was the case with the reuse of the old COBOL programs there are also situations in which the services must be tested against a previous system. For that, ways have to be found to transfer the test inputs to the previous system, for instance in the form of fixed formatted panels, over into WDSL-type requests. Then it should be possible to compare the values returned in the service responses with the values in the old output panels. Special tools need to be developed for making such a selective regression test (Ruth et al., 2007).

In summary, it can be concluded that the biggest obstacle to the wide scale use of cloud services is their testing. Testing of conventional IT systems was expensive enough, but there the system owner could impose restrictions on how the system could be used. With service based systems this is no longer the case. The many foreign services composing a SOA system can be used in any way and combined in any form. All potential usages and all potential linkages need to be tested before the services are even selected. To achieve this requires exponentially more test cases than if the usage is restricted to predefined use cases. Not only is the volume of the test greater, but the consequences of errors are greater than in conventional systems (Grundy et al., 2012). In a silo type system architecture each application is an island in itself. Problems that come up in a silo application only affect the users of that application. Problems that come up in cloud services affect all applications in which that service is used.

Ergo, cloud services have to be thoroughly tested and that requires time and effort. The positive side of public cloud services is that everyone who uses them is also testing them. That reduces the burden on the individual user, but still he must test to ensure that the services he selects suit to his purposes. The only way to reduce his time and effort is via automation. To achieve a high degree of test automation requires a significant investment up front. It is up to the testing community to make that investment to clear the way to service-oriented architectures and cloud computing.

REFERENCES

Ardagna, D. (2011). A service-based framework for flexible business processes. *IEEE Software Magazine, 28*(2), 61–67.

Baker, P., Schieferdecker, I., & Williams, C. (2008). *Model-driven testing – Using the UML testing profile*. Berlin, Germany: Springer Pub.

Becker, B. (2011). The cloud scenario is developing. *Computer Weekly, Special Issue on Cloud Guide*, 4-6.

Bozkurt, M., Harman, M., & Hassoun, Y. (2007). *Testing web services – A survey*. Technical report TR-10-01.

Calinescu, R. (2011). Dynamic QoS management and optimization in service-based systems. *IEEE Transactions on Software Engineering, 37*(3), 387. doi:10.1109/TSE.2010.92

Canfora, G., & DiPenta, M. (2006). Testing services and service-centric systems – Challenges and opportunities. *IT Professional, 8*, 10. doi:10.1109/MITP.2006.51

Canfora, G., & DiPenta, M. (2008). A framework for QoS-aware binding and rebinding of composite web services. *Journal of Systems and Software, 81*(10), 1754. doi:10.1016/j.jss.2007.12.792

Carr, N. (2007). *The big switch*. New York, NY: Harpers Books.

CBDI. (2011). *CBDI forum* (Online). Retrieved from http://CBDIForum.com

Chen, T. Y., Tse, T. H., & Zhou, Z. Q. (2011). Semi-proving – An integrated method for program proving, testing and debugging. *IEEE Transactions on Software Engineering, 37*(1), 109. doi:10.1109/TSE.2010.23

Chidamer, S., & Kemmerer, C. (1994). A metrics suite for object-oriented design. *IEEE Transactions on Software Engineering, 20*(6), 476. doi:10.1109/32.295895

Dai, G., Bai, X., & Wang, Y. (2007). Contract-based testing for web services. *IEEE COMPSAC 2007 Computer Software and Applications Conference*, Beijing, (p. 517).

Do, H., Mirarab, S., Tahvildari, L., & Rothermel, G. (2010). The effects of time constraints on test case prioritization. *IEEE Transactions on Software Engineering, 36*(5), 593. doi:10.1109/TSE.2010.58

Dwyer, M., Avrunin, G., & Corbett, J. (1999). Property specification patterns for finite state verification. *21st International Conference on Software Engineering*, (p. 411).

Grassi, V. (2004). Reliability prediction for service-oriented computing. *IEEE Workshop Architecting Dependable Systems*, 2004, (p. 279).

Grundy, J., Kaefer, G., Keong, J., & Liu, A. (2012, March). Software engineering for the cloud. *IEEE Software Magazine*, 26.

Hackel, P. (2012). SAP kauft Ariba for 4.4 billion dollars. *Computer Weekly, 22*, 8.

Halstead, M. (1977). *Elements of software science*. Amsterdam, The Netherlands: Elvesier, North-Holland.

IFPUG. (1999). *Function-point counting practices. Manual Release 4.1*. Westerville, OH: International Function-Point User Group.

ISO. (2009). *ISO20000- Standard for software system service management*. Geneva, Switzerland: International Standard Organisation.

ISO/IEC. (2006). *ISO/IEC-19757 document schema definition language – Part 3 Rule-based validation schematron*. Geneva, Switzerland: International Standard Organisation.

Keller, A., & Ludwig, H. (2003). The WSLA framework specifying and monitoring service level agreements for web services. *Journal of Network and Systems Management, 11*(1), 57. doi:10.1023/A:1022445108617

Khalidi, Y. (2011, March). Building a cloud computing platform for new possibilities. IEEE Computer Magazine, p. 29.

Kienle, H., & Vasiliu, C. (2008, October). *Evolution of legal statements on the web*. 10th Workshop on Web Systems Evolution, (p. 73). Bejing, China: IEEE Computer Society Press.

Liskov, B., & Guttag, J. (1988). *Abstraction and specification in program development*. New York, NY: MIT Press, McGraw-Hill Books.

Litoiu, M. (2010, September). *A performance engineering method for web services. 12th Symposium on Web Systems Evolution*, (p. 101). Temesvar, Hungary: IEEE Computer Society Press.

Martin, R. (2005). The test bus imperative - Architectures that support automated acceptance testing. *IEEE Software Magazine, 22*(4), 65.

McCabe, T. (1976). A complexity measure. *IEEE Transactions on Software Engineering, 2*(4), 308. doi:10.1109/TSE.1976.233837

Mell, P., & Grance, T. (2011, September). *The NIST definition of cloud computing*. US National Institute of Standards & Technology. Retrieved from http://csrc.nist.gov/publications/nistpubs/800-145/Sp800-145.pdf

Menasce, D., Ruan, H., & Gomaa, H. (2007). QoS management in service-oriented architectures. *Performance Evaluation, 64*(7), 646. doi:10.1016/j.peva.2006.10.001

Narasimhan, B., & Nichols, R. (2011, March). State of cloud applications and platforms – The cloud adapter's view. *IEEE Computer Magazine*, p. 24.

Ofutt, J., & Xu, W. (2004). Generating test cases for web services using data perturbation. *ACM SIGSOFT Software Engineering Notes, 29*(5), 1. doi:10.1145/1022494.1022529

Ojala, A., & Tyrvainen, P. (2011, July). Developing cloud business models. *IEEE Software Magazine, 22*(4), 42.

Riungu-Kalliosaari, L., Taipale, O., & Smolander, K. (2012, March). Testing in the cloud – Exploring the practice. *IEEE Software Magazine*, p. 46.

Ruth, M., et al. (2007, July). Towards automatic regression test selection for web services. *COMPSAC'07: Proceedings of the 31st Annual International Computer Software and Applications Conference*, Vol. 2, Bejing, (p. 729).

Shannon, C. (1949). A mathematical theory of communication. *The Bell System Technical Journal, 27*, 379.

Shull, F. (2012, March). A brave new world of testing – An interview with Google's James Whittaker. *IEEE Software Magazine*, p. 4.

Siegel, S. (1996). *Object-oriented software testing – A hierarchical approach* (p. 93). New York, NY: John Wiley & Sons.

Smith, D., & Lewis, G. (2007, March). *Standards for service-oriented systems.* Paper presented at the 11th European Conference on Software Maintenance and Reengineering (CSMR10), Amsterdam.

Sneed, H. (1990). The data-point estimation method. *Online - Zeitschrift für Datenverarbeitung, 5,* 48.

Sneed, H. (2005, March). Testing an egovernment website. *7th IEEE International Symposium on Web Site Evolution* (WSE2005), Budapest, (p. 3).

Sneed, H. (2007, October). *Testing against natural language requirements.* Paper presented at 7th Int. Conference on Software Quality (QSIC2007), Portland.

Sneed, H. (2008, April). Certification of web services. *2nd Workshop on SOA-Based Systems, CSMR2008,* Athens, 2008, (p. 336).

Sneed, H. (2008, Oct.). *Bridging the concept to implementation gap in software testing.* 8th International Conference on Software Quality (QSIC2008), Oxford.

Sneed, H. (2009). A pilot project for migrating COBOL code to web services. *International Journal of Software Tools Technology Transfer, 1*(2), 103.

Sneed, H. (2010, Sept.) Measuring web service interfaces. *Workshop on Website Evolution – WSE2010,* Temesvar, Romania, (p. 41).

Sneed, H. (2012, June). *Offering cloud service testing as a service.* Paper presented at Ignite Conference, SQS Ignite-Swiss, Geneva, 2012.

Sneed, H., & Huang, S. (2006). WSDLTest – A tool for testing web services. *Proceedings of WSE-2006,* Sept. 2006, (p. 14). Philadelphia, PA: IEEE Computer Society Press.

Software Research Associates. (2011a). Automated testing of modern Web Applications, *SRA Business White Paper.* SRA Inc., San Francisco

Software Research Associates. (2011b). *eValid business description* (white paper). San Francisco, CA: Author.

Software Research Associates. (2011c). *Automated testing of modern Web Applications,* (white paper). San Francisco, CA: Author.

Spanoudakis, G., & Zisman, A. (2010). Discovering services during service-based system design using UML. *IEEE Transactions on Software Engineering, 36*(3), 371. doi:10.1109/TSE.2009.88

Srinivasan, S., & Getov, V. (2011, March). Navigating the cloud computing landscape – Technologies, services and adapters. *IEEE Computer Magazine,* p. 22

Stylianou, A., & Kumar, R. (2000). An integrative framework for IS quality management. *Communications of the ACM, 43*(9), 99. doi:10.1145/348941.349009

Tosic, V., Pargurek, B., & Patel, K. (2003). WSQL – A language for the formal specification of classes of service for web services. In L. Zhang (Ed.), *International Conference of Web Services,* (p. 375).

Tsai, W. T., Paul, R., Song, W., & Cao, Z. (2002). Coyote: An XML-based framework for web services testing. *Proceedings of the 7th IEEE International Symposium on High Assurance Systems Engineering, HASE 2002,* October 25-26, 2002; Tokyo, Japan, (p. 173).

Tsai, W. T., Zhou, X., Chen, Y., & Ai, X. (2008, August). On testing and evaluating service-oriented software. *IEEE Computer Magazine,* p. 40.

Vossen, G. (2011). The great mistrust of small and middle-sized enterprises towards cloud computing. *Digital Zetschrift, 23*.

World Wide Web Consortium. (2002a). *Web service definition*. Retrieved from http://www.w3.org/tr/2002 wd-wsa-reqs-20021011

World Wide Web Consortium. (2002b). *Web service definition*. Retrieved from http://www.w3.org/tr/wsdl

World Wide Web Consortium. (2008) *Web service definition*. Retrieved from http://www.w3.org/tr/wsdl20

World Wide Web Consortium. (2011a). *SuperSareware*. Retrieved form http://www.supershareware.com/info/soa-cleaner

World Wide Web Consortium. (2011b). *Parasoft SoapTest*. Retrieved from http://www2.parasoft.com

World Wide Web Consortium. (2011c). *Web inject*. Retrieved from http://www.webinject.org

Worms, K. (2010). *Experience of a Swiss Bank in migrating to SOA*. Paper presented at 25th International Conference on Software Maintenance – ICSM2010, Temisoara, Romania.

Xie, T., Tillmann, N., Halleux, P., et al. (2012, March). Environmental modelling for automated cloud application testing. *IEEE Software Magazine*, p. 30.

Yau, S., & Ho, G. (2011, October). Software engineering meets services and cloud computing. *IEEE Computer Magazine*, p. 47.

Zhu, H. (2006). A framework for service-oriented testing of web services. Paper presented at *COMPSAC '06: Proceedings of the 30th Annual International Computer Software and Applications Conference*, Vol. 2, (pp. 145–150).

Chapter 8
Using Test Clouds to Enable Continuous Integration Testing of Distributed Real-Time and Embedded System Applications

James H. Hill
Indiana University-Purdue University Indianapolis, USA

Douglas C. Schmidt
Vanderbilt University, USA

ABSTRACT

It is critical to evaluate the quality-of-service (QoS) properties of enterprise distributed real-time and embedded (DRE) system early in their lifecycle—instead of waiting until system integration—to minimize the impact of rework needed to remedy QoS defects. Unfortunately, enterprise DRE system developers and testers often lack the necessary resources to support such testing efforts. This chapter discusses how test clouds (i.e., cloud-computing environments employed for testing) can provide the necessary testing resources. When combined with system execution modeling (SEM) tools, test clouds can provide the necessary toolsets to perform QoS testing earlier in the lifecycle. A case study of design and implementing resource management infrastructure from the domain of shipboard computing environments is used to show how SEM tools and test clouds can help identify defects in system QoS specifications and enforcement mechanisms before they become prohibitively expensive to fix.

DOI: 10.4018/978-1-4666-2536-5.ch008

INTRODUCTION

Current Trends and Challenges

Enterprise distributed real-time and embedded (DRE) systems, such as large-scale traffic management systems, supervisory control and data analysis (SCADA) systems, and shipboard computing environments, are becoming increasingly ubiquitous. As these systems grow in scale and complexity they are becoming ultra-large-scale cyber-physical systems (Institute, 2006), which exhibit the following characteristics:

- Requirements for simultaneously satisfying competing and conflicting QoS properties, such as low latency, high reliability, and fault tolerance, in addition to meeting their functional requirements.
- Heterogeneous in both their operating environment (*e.g.*, target architecture and hardware resources) and technologies (*e.g.*, programming language and middleware).
- Developed as monolithic, vertically integrated stovepipes, which are brittle, and hard to implement, maintain, and evolve.

These and other related characteristics not only increase enterprise DRE system complexity, but also complicate their development, certification, and sustainment, resulting in elongated lifecycles characterized by expensive project runs and missed delivery deadlines (Mann, 1996).

Due to increased complexity and size of enterprise DRE systems and their lifecycles, it is important to validate enterprise DRE system QoS properties early in their lifecycle, rather than waiting until system integration (*i.e.*, late in the lifecycle), when they are expensive and time-consuming to fix. System execution modeling (SEM) tools (Smith & Williams) are one method for enabling DRE system developers and testers to validate QoS properties during early phases of the lifecycle. In particular, SEM tools provide enterprise DRE system developers and testers with the following capabilities:

- Rapidly model behavior and workload of the distributed system being developed, independent of its programming language or target environment, *e.g.*, the underlying networks, operating system(s), and middleware platform(s).
- Synthesize a customized test system from models, including representative source code for the behavior and workload models and project/workspace files necessary to build the test system in its target environment.
- Execute the synthesized test system on a representative target environment testbed to produce realistic empirical results at scale.
- Analyze the test system's QoS in the context of domain-specific constraints, *e.g.* as scalability or end-to-end response time of synthesized test applications, to identify performance anti-patterns (Smith & Williams), which are common system design mistakes that degrade end-to-end QoS.

By using SEM tools to validate QoS properties throughout the lifecycle, DRE system testers can locate and resolve QoS bottlenecks in a timely and cost-effective manner.

Although SEM tools enable early validation of QoS properties, enterprise DRE system testers may lack resources needed to support testing efforts. For example, to support early integration testing of an enterprise DRE system, testers need hardware resources that may not be readily available until later in the lifecycle. Likewise, both software and hardware resources may change throughout the lifecycle. The number of test that must execute also often exceeds the operational capacity of resources available in-house for testing (Porter, Yilmaz, Memon, Schmidt, & and B. Natarajan,

2007). Enterprise DRE system testers therefore need improved methods to support early integration testing of enterprise DRE system applications.

Solution Approach → Use Test Clouds to Support Early Integration Testing

Cloud computing (Vouk, 2008) is an emerging computing paradigm where computing resources are managed by external service providers. End-users then provision (request) the cloud's resources as needed to support their computational goals. Although cloud computing has traditionally been used for enterprise workloads, such as office applications, web servers, and data processing, the availability of the computing resources can also be provisioned to support testing efforts (*i.e.*, test clouds). For example, enterprise DRE system testers can provision resources available in the cloud to evaluate applications using resources that is not readily available in-house. Using test clouds is hard, however, without the proper infrastructure and tool support.

For example, test clouds are typically designed to support general-purpose workloads, which imply that cloud resources are allocated without any knowledge of how they will be used. End-users (*e.g.*, enterprise DRE system testers) therefore need to manage provisioned resources, as follows:

- *Coordinate and synchronize testing efforts.* Different testing efforts require different methods. For example, when evaluating end-to-end response time, it is necessary to coordinate software running on many different machines for extended periods of time. It is also the responsibility of testers to supply the necessary framework to support such needs, if the test cloud does not provide it.
- *Gather data collected from many networked machines.* As a test is running, it

generates metrics that can be used to analyze its behavior, *e.g.*, worst cast end-to-end response time for the system at different execution times. Unless the test cloud provides such capabilities, end-users are responsible for providing the necessary framework to support these needs.

- *Correlate and analyze collected metrics.* After metrics have been collected from many different networked machines, they must be correctly correlated to undergo analysis. Failure to correlate metrics can result in either false positive or false negative results. Unless the test cloud provides such capabilities, end-users must do so themselves.

Completing the actions above can be a daunting task for enterprise DRE system developers and testers. Moreover, if not done correctly, each task must be repeated for each new enterprise DRE system that undergoes QoS testing within a test cloud. To simplify these tedious and error-prone tasks, this chapter shows by example how SEM tools can be extended to support test clouds, and overcome the challenges outlined above. In particular, this chapter describes how:

- An instrumentation and logging framework can autonomously collect data from networked machines and store them in a central location while tests are executing.
- A test management framework can coordinate and synchronize testing efforts that execute on many networked hosts in a test cloud.
- Combining test clouds with continuous integration environments (Fowler, 2006) enables integration testing that validates QoS properties in parallel with system development, with the goal of identifying and rectifying QoS-related defects during early phases of the lifecycle.

BACKGROUND

Before discussing the use of test clouds to evaluate enterprise DRE system QoS properties, we examine the current state of testing with respect to cloud computing environments. In particular, Testing as a Service (TaaS) (Yu, Zhang, Xiang, Su, Zhao, & Zhu, 2009) is an emerging paradigm where testing processes, such as test data generation, test execution, and test analysis, is provided as a service to end-users. This paradigm is in contrast to always (re)inventing the test infrastructure for different application domains. Moreover, it tries to alleviate testing overhead, such as having dedicated human and computing resources.

Many companies now provide TaaS, *e.g.*, searching for TaaS on the Web locates a company named Sogeti (www.sogeti.com) that provides TaaS using a test cloud. Their business model offers a pay-per-use software testing model where clients can perform both functional and performance testing on resources provisioned from their cloud. This model is similar to the Amazon EC2 (aws.amazon.com/ec2), which offers a pay-per-use model for computing resources. In the Sogeti model, however, the services are test services that can be accessed via a web portal.

Lu et al. (Yu, et al., 2010) explored the feasibility of TaaS by deploying unit testing web service over a cloud. Their feasibility study highlighted key concerns of deploying such a service, including (1) clustering requests (since many request and testing needs are different), (2) scheduling resources for testing (which is similar to traditional clustering scheduling problems), (3) monitoring testing resources and the test progress, and (4) managing processes in the test cloud.

MOTIVATIONAL CASE STUDY: THE RESOURCE ALLOCATION CONTROL ENGINE (RACE)

The Resource Allocation and Control Engine (RACE) (Shankaran, Schmidt, Chen, Koutsoukous, & Lu, 2007) is an open-source distributed resource manager system from the shipboard computing domain developed using the CIAO (Deng, Gill, Schmidt, & Wang, 2007) implementation of the Lightweight CORBA Component Model (CCM) (Lightweight CORBA Component Model RFP, 2002) over the past decade. RACE was developed as part of the DARPA ARMS program, which focused on total ship computing environments. RACE therefore deploys and manages Lightweight CCM application shipboard computing component assemblies (*i.e.*, called operational strings) based on resource availability/usage and QoS requirements of the managed operational strings. Figure 1 shows the architecture of RACE, which is composed of four components assemblies (Input Adapter, Plan Analyzer, Planner Manager, and Output Adapter) that collaborate to manage operational strings for the target domain.

RACE performs two types of deployment strategies—static and dynamic—for enterprise DRE systems. Static deployments are operational strings created offline by humans or automated planners. RACE uses the information specified in a static deployment plan to map each component to its associated target host during the deployment phase of a DRE system. A benefit of RACE's static deployment strategy is its low runtime overhead since deployment decisions are made offline; a drawback is its lack of flexibility since deployment decisions cannot adapt to changes (e.g., variations in resource availability due to failures or reprioritized tasks) at runtime.

Dynamic deployments, in contrast, are operational strings created online by humans or automated planners. In dynamic deployments, components are not given a target host. Instead, the initial deployment plan contains component

Figure 1. High-level overview of the RACE architecture

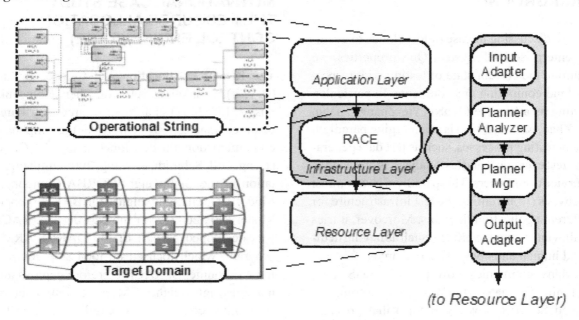

metadata (*e.g.*, connections, CPU utilization, and network bandwidth) that RACE uses to map components to associated target hosts during the runtime phase of a DRE system. A benefit of RACE's dynamic deployment strategy is its flexibility since deployment decisions can adapt to runtime changes; a drawback is its higher runtime overhead.

The initial implementation of RACE contained 26,644 lines of C++ code and ~30 components. Subsequent enhancements to RACE (after 50 source code check-ins to the repository) added 14,041 lines of code and 9 components, for a total of 40,685 lines of code and 39 components.

The RACE Baseline Scenario

Our case study focuses on RACE's baseline scenario. This scenario exercises RACE's ability to evaluate resource availability (*e.g.*, CPU utilization and network bandwidth) with respect to environmental changes (*e.g.*, node failure/recovery). Moreover, it evaluates RACE's ability to ensure lifetime of higher importance operational strings

deployed dynamically is greater than or equal to the lifetime of lesser importance operational strings deployed statically based on resource availability.

Since RACE performs complex distributed resource management services we wanted to evaluate its QoS properties as early as possible in the lifecycle to help overcome the serialized-phased development problem (Rittel & Webber, 1973), which is common in enterprise DRE systems. In the serialized-phasing problem, the system is developed in layers, where components in the upper (application) layer(s) are not developed until after (often long after) components in the lower (infrastructure) layer(s) are developed. Design flaws that affect QoS properties are thus often not discovered until system integration, when they are more costly and harder to fix. We wanted to know as early as possible if RACE could evaluate resource availability with respect to environmental changes to properly manage operational strings deployed dynamically versus those deployed statically.

Because RACE is considered infrastructure components, we needed application components to evaluate its baseline scenario successfully. Due to serialized-phasing development, applications would not exist for several months after development started. We therefore relied on CUTS (see Box 1) to provide the application-level components for evaluating RACE's baseline scenario.

Testing Concerns with RACE and DRE Systems

Although we used CUTS to emulate RACE's application-level components, we lacked the physical resources in-house to conduct the desired testing efforts. We therefore decided to use a cloud environment to evaluate RACE's baseline scenario. In particular, we leveraged a test cloud powered by Emulab software (Ricci, Alfred, & Lepreau, 2003) to support our testing efforts. We selected Emulab because it enabled us to provision both host and network resources to create network topologies that emulate production shipboard computing environments.

Emulab's capability enabled us to create realistic experiments based on realistic networking conditions. We therefore were not bound to a predefined network topology and configuration, which is seen with the emerging TaaS paradigms built atop a test cloud. This capability is particularly important when testing enterprise DRE systems in a cloud since these systems have many different network topologies and characteristics, such as bandwidth constraints, packet drop rates, and packet queuing schemes, because of the heterogeneity of their target execution environment. Unfortunately, emerging test clouds (outside of Emulab) often lack the necessary capabilities to support the characteristics of enterprise DRE systems, such as RACE.

Like many clouds, Emulab provides infrastructure support for managing its resources, but it does not provide readily available infrastructure that supports testing DRE systems. For example, there was no support to instrument RACE. Moreover, there was no support for *internally* managing

Box 1. The CUTS system execution modeling tool

CUTS (Hill, Edmondson, Gokhale, & Schmidt, 2010) is a system execution modeling (SEM) tool that enables enterprise DRE system developers and testers to performance system integration tests that valid QoS properties during early lifecycle phases, instead of waiting to perform this evaluation during system integration, which can be too late to resolve problems in a timely and cost-effective manner. Enterprise DRE system developers and testers use CUTS via the following steps:

1. Use domain-specific modeling languages (Ledeczi, et al., 2001) to model behavior and workload efficiently (Hill, Tambe, & Gokhale, Model-driven Engineering for Development-time QoS Validation of Component-based Software Systems, 2007).

2. Use code generation techniques (Hill & Gokhale, Using Generative Programming to Enhance Reuse in Visitor Pattern-based DSML Model Interpreters, 2007) to synthesize a complete test system from constructed models that conform to the target architecture (i.e., generate compo nents act like real components in terms of their exposed attributes and interfaces).

3. Use emulation techniques (Hill, Slaby, Baker, & Schmidt, 2006) to execute the synthesized system and validate its QoS properties in its target execution environment.

Enterprise DRE system developers and testers can also replace emulated portions of the system with its real counterpart as its development is completed, thereby allowing the testers to perform continuous system integration testing, i.e., the process of execution system integration test to validate QoS properties continuously throughout the lifecycle.

RACE's resources for testing purposes, such as taking nodes offline to exercise enterprise DRE system fault tolerance test scenarios. We were therefore responsible for developing the necessary infrastructure that allowed us to (1) coordinate and synchronize testing efforts, (2) gather data collected from many different nodes, and (3) execute many tests automatically.

Since we were developing RACE, we could have easily created handcrafted shell scripts designed for RACE to manage the testing process in Emulab, which is the traditional way of manage the test process of a DRE system in such environments. This approach, however, would not have been ideal since it would reduce the portability of our solution. Moreover, it would be hard for us to leverage Emulab's existing infrastructure (*e.g.*, configuration and dynamic resource management) that requires stateful and interactive processes.

The remainder of this chapter discusses how we extended the CUTS SEM tool to support the Emulab test cloud. The goal of this extension was to provide the underling infrastructure beyond what Emulab provides, so that testing enterprise DRE systems is not only simplified, but also automated.

COMBINING SYSTEM EXECUTION MODELING TOOLS AND CLOUD COMPUTING ENVIRONMENTS

This section discusses the extensions we added to the CUTS SEM tool to support evaluating RACE in the Emulab test cloud. In particular, we describe the infrastructure and logging infrastructure implemented to collect data for analyzing the RACE baseline scenario. We also present the extensions added to CUTS to support managing testing exercises in Emulab and show how we integrated the test management extensions and the logging/ instrumentation extensions to create a complete framework for executing many tests in the Emulab test cloud.

Instrumentation and Logging Infrastructure for Test Clouds

Enterprise DRE systems consist of many software components executing on many hosts that are connected via a network. When validating their QoS properties (*e.g.*, end-to-end response time, scalability, and throughput) it is necessary to collect data about system behavior in a realistic target environment. Such behaviors could be execution lifecycle events, the state of the system at different points in time, or data points needed to calculate the end-to-end response of an event.

Data (or metrics) in a distributed environment, such as a test cloud, is collected and analyzed either offline or online. In offline collection and analysis, data from each host is written to local persistent storage, *e.g.*, a file, while the system executes in the test cloud. After the system is shutdown, the collected data in local storage on each host is combined and analyzed. The advantage of this approach is that network traffic is minimized since collected data is not transmitted over the network until after the system is shutdown. The disadvantage is that collected data is not processed until the system is shutdown, which can pose a problem for enterprise DRE systems with long execution lifetimes, or when trying to monitor and analyze a system in real-time. More importantly, once a system has shutdown, its resources are released back into the cloud, so there is a potential risk that data stored on local storage can be lost if they are not removed completely.

In online collection and analysis, data is collected and transmitted via network to a central host. The advantage of this approach is that it allows metric analysis to occur on a host that has little or no impact on system performance. The disadvantage of online collection and analysis is that it is necessary to devise a strategy for efficiently collecting data and submitting it to a central location without negatively impacting the executing systems QoS, especially if the system generates heavy network traffic. Although online collection has it disadvantages, using online data collection a test cloud is more practical because it guarantees metrics are collected and archived periodically during execution (*i.e.*, before resources are given back to the cloud). Moreover, online data collection can facilitate real-time feedback.

Extending CUTS with Logging and Instrumentation Infrastructure

Instrumentation and logging infrastructure should not be (re-)implemented for each application undergoing testing in a test cloud. Moreover, it should not be a something that enterprise DRE system and developers must provide. Instead, it should be a service provided by the test cloud that enterprise DRE systems use to collect and archive metrics of interest. This way, developers and testers can focus on deciding what to collect and let the test cloud infrastructure determine the best method for collecting metrics from the enterprise DRE system under test.

Figure 2 shows how CUTS was extended with logging and instrumentation infrastructure to sup-

port the Emulab test cloud. As shown in this figure, each host provisioned in the test cloud executes a logging client. Likewise, the controller node for the provisioned assets executes a single logging server. The controller node for the provisioned assets is not the same as the controller node for the cloud because each experiment executing in a test cloud has a controller node that coordinates tasks on the different test nodes, as described in the section *Managing Enterprise DRE System Tests in the Cloud*.

The logging client is responsible for collecting data from individual software components executing on its host. As the logging client receives data from software components, it submits it to the logging server for storage and analysis. The logging client does not know the physical location (*i.e.*, IP address) of the logging server because it can change depending on what assets are provisioned by the test cloud for a given experiment. Instead, the logging client knows the test-specific hostname of the logging server and its listening port. Likewise, the coupling between the logging client and logging server can be further loosened by using a naming service to resolve the location

Figure 2. Overview of CUTS logging and instrumentation framework to support the Emulab test clouds

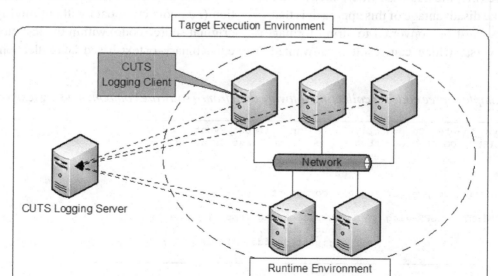

of the logging server (*i.e.*, request the logging server for a given test).

In contrast to the logging client resolving the logging server, the process that software components used to resolve the logging client is straightforward. Since software components submit metrics to logging clients executing on their host machine, the software components only need to know what port the logging client is listening. After a software component opens a connection to the logging client's port, it can submit data for collection and archiving.

On Data Formatting and Archiving

Since an enterprise DRE system is inherently distributed—and its metrics can range from structured to unstructured data and binary to text data—there are many way to store data. We therefore extended CUTS to support both a text and binary methods for archiving metrics. In the text method, metrics are archived in string format—similar to log files of an execution trace stored in a database.

Box 2 shows how CUTS collects text-based data from the Input Adapter component in RACE. The advantage of this approach is that data values can be viewed just by viewing the contents of the archive (*i.e.*, the database where metrics are stored). The disadvantage of this approach is that all metrics must be converted to string format, and vice versa, which can result in unwanted overhead—especially when collecting metrics from real-time software components.

In the binary method, data is stored in its raw binary representation. The advantage of this approach is that there is no extra overhead associated with packaging the data. The disadvantage of this approach is that special care is needed when packing and unpacking the data if the endianness, *i.e.*, the ordering of individually addressable sub-components within the representation of a larger data item (Wikipedia, 2012), of the host used for data analysis is different than the host where the data originated. Likewise, it is almost impossible to see the contents of the data just by viewing the archive since the data will be in non-textual format.

In our experience, the text-based format for collecting and storing metrics is easier to integrate into an existing application than the binary method when using intrusive data collection (*i.e.*, modifying the source code to collect metrics of interest). This simplicity occurs because the binary format method requires a special framework to manage packaging and unpackage the data, which can add unwanted complexity to the solution. In contrast, the text-based format can be achieved using simple string-formatting semantics, as shown in Box 2.

When performing non-intrusive data collection (*i.e.*, collecting data without modifying the original source code) within the test cloud, then either binary- or text-based data collection suffices

Box 2. Example source code for collecting software data from a software component using text formatting

```
void Input_Adapter_Component::handle_input (Input_Event * ev) {
 CUTS_CLIENT_LOGGER->log ("begin processing input %s at %d",
                         ev->input_name (),
                         ACE_OS::gettimeofday ().msec ());

 // make call to planner manager component

 CUTS_CLIENT_LOGGER->log ("ending processing input %s at %d",
                         ev->input_name (),
                         ACE_OS::gettimeofday ().msec ());
}
```

because the collection mechanisms are hidden from the client. For example, many enterprise DRE systems will use a logging framework for collecting text-based log messages. It is therefore possible to intercept those messages and pass them to the CUTS logging server—assuming the log messages contain metrics of interest.

Box 3 shows how CUTS can intercept log messages of the ACE logging framework (Schmidt, 1994), which is a C++ logging framework used by many enterprise DRE systems. The listing also shows how CUTS can intercept log message of the log4j logging framework (logging.apache. org), which is a Java framework used by many existing Java applications. As shown in this listing, the configuration files define what interceptors to load. When the CUTS interceptors are loaded into their respective framework, the interceptor receives log messages and forwards them to the CUTS Logging Server.

For the binary case, it is possible to use dynamic binary instrumentation tools to rewrite the binary program and inject instrumentation points into the program as it executes. Similar to the logging framework interceptor discussed above, the callback methods collect data of interest and forward it to the CUTS logging server.

Summary

Whether using text- or binary-based formatting, or intrusive vs. non-intrusive, when collecting metrics in a test cloud, the approach must seamlessly extract metrics from each host and store them in a central location. Failure to do so can result in metrics being lost after provisioned resources are released back to the test cloud. Since the Emulab test cloud does not provide such functionality out-of-the-box, we extended the CUTS SEM tool with a logging and instrumentation framework to support our testing efforts of RACE in the Emulab test cloud.

Box 3. Using interceptors to non-intrusively collect log messages in the log4j and ACE logging framework

```
Framework: log4j
Language: Java
How to integrate: Update log4j.properties (or similar file)
Illustrative example:

# define the loggers
log4j.rootCategory=ALL, C, A

# console appender
log4j.appender.A=org.apache.log4j.ConsoleAppender
log4j.appender.A.layout=org.apache.log4j.PatternLayout
log4j.appender.A.layout.ConversionPattern=%-4r [%t] %-5p %c %x - %m%n

# CUTS appender
log4j.appender.B=cuts.log4j.LoggingClientAppender
log4j.appender.B.LoggerClient=corbaloc:iiop:localhost:20000/LoggingClient

Framework: ACE Logging Facilities
Language: C++
How to integrate: Update svc.conf (or similar file)
Illustrative example:

dynamic CUTS_ACE_Log_Interceptor Service_Object * \
  CUTS_ACE_Log_Interceptor:_make_CUTS_ACE_Log_Interceptor() active \
  "--client=corbaloc:iiop:localhost:20000/LoggingClient"
```

Managing Enterprise DRE System Tests in the Cloud

Enterprise DRE system testing and execution environments, such as Emulab, consist of many nodes. Each node in the target environment executes many different processes that must support the overall goals of the execution environment. For example, nodes in the execution environment may host processes that (1) manage software components, (2) synchronize clocks with a central server, and (3) collect instrumentation data.

When dealing with many processes that must execute on a given node, a traditional testing approach is to create a script that launches all processes for that given node. For example, Bash scripts can be used to launch a set of processes in Unix environments. The advantage of such scripts is that they provide a lightweight and repeatable approach for ensuring that all process for a given node are launched in the correct order. Moreover, the scripts can be easily updated to either add or remove processes as needed.

Although scripts are sufficient when working in a distributed testing environment, this approach adds more complexity to the testing process in a test cloud. First, scripts do not easily support dynamic injection/removal of processes. It is assumed in the script used to configure the host before the test is executed. At that point, it is assumed that all processes injected/removed from the host are part of all the processes on that machine. Second, it is hard to switch between different execution environments where an execution environment is set of environment variables and a set of processes that are needed for a test to execute correctly in the test cloud.

Extending CUTS with Test Management Infrastructure

Due to the shortcomings of existing approaches for managing enterprise DRE system tests, which are used heavily in the Emulab test cloud, we extended CUTS with test management infrastructure. More specifically, we added the following entities to CUTS:

- **The CUTS Node Manager:** A daemon that manages processes executing on its respective node, similar to a traditional task manager. The difference between a traditional task manager and the CUTS Node Manager is that the CUTS Node Manager exposes an interface that is used by the Node Manager Client (explained next) to remotely spawn new processes on the node, or terminate existing processes executing on the node.

The CUTS Node Manager also provides mechanisms for remotely starting all process under its control without having to physically restart the machine in the test cloud. The CUTS Node Manager accomplishes this using a concept called *virtual environments,* which is a set of environment variables and processes that define a self-contained execution environment for testing purposes. Box 4 shows an example configuration for the CUTS Node Manager.

As shown in Box 4, there are two different virtual environments defined in the configuration where the main difference is the value of the variable named RACE_ROOT. The environment named RACE.HEAD is the active virtual environment when the CUTS Node Daemon is first launched. At runtime, however, it is possible to switch between the RACE.HEAD and RACE.Baseline virtual environments.

This runtime flexibility is beneficial when testing many configurations that require different execution environments, *e.g.,* different versions of RACE that have diverse software dependencies, because DRE system developers and testers do not have to *physically* reset (or restart) the machine to switch configurations. Moreover, DRE

Box 4. Example configuration for the CUTS Node Manager illustrating the use of virtual environments to manage different execution configurations

```xml
<?xml version="1.0" encoding="utf-8" standalone="no" ?>
<cuts:node>
 <environment id="RACE.HEAD" inherit="true" active="true">
 <!-- environment variables for this environment -->
 <variable name="NameService"
 value=">${TAO_ROOT}/orbsvcs/Naming_Service/Naming_Service" />
 <variable name="RACE_ROOT"
 value=">/opts/RACE" />

<startup>
 <!-- NamingService -->
 <process id="dance.naming.service">
 <executable>${NameService}</executable>
 <arguments>-m 0 -ORBEndpoint
 iiop://localhost:60003 -o ns.ior</arguments>
 </process>

<!-- DAnCE node manager -->
 <process id="dance.nodemanager.pingnode">
 <executable>${DANCE_ROOT}/bin/dance_node_manager</executable>
 <arguments>-ORBEndpoint iiop://localhost:30000
 -s ${DANCE_ROOT}/bin/dance_locality_manager
 -n PingNode=PingNode.ior -t 30
 --instance-nc corbaloc:rir:/NameService</arguments>
 <workingdirectory>../lib</workingdirectory>
 </process>

<!-- //... -->
 </startup>
 </environment>

<environment id="RACE.Baseline" inherit="true" active="false">
 <!-- environment variables for this environment -->
 <variable name="NameService"
 value=">${TAO_ROOT}/orbsvcs/Naming_Service/Naming_Service" />
 <variable name="RACE_ROOT"
 value=">/opts/RACE-baseline" />

<startup>
 <!-- NamingService -->
 <process id="dance.naming.service">
 <executable>${NameService}</executable>
 <arguments>-m 0 -ORBEndpoint
 iiop://localhost:60003 -o ns.ior</arguments>
 </process>

<!-- DAnCE node manager -->
 <process id="dance.nodemanager.node1">
 <executable>${DANCE_ROOT}/bin/dance_node_manager</executable>
 <arguments>-ORBEndpoint iiop://localhost:30000
 -s ${DANCE_ROOT}/bin/dance_locality_manager
 -n Node1=Node1.ior -t 30
 --instance-nc corbaloc:rir:/NameService</arguments>
 <workingdirectory>../lib</workingdirectory>
 </process>

<!-- //... -->
 </startup>
 </environment>
</cuts:node>
```

system developers and testers do not have to *manually* terminate existing process and execute a different script just to switch configurations. Instead, the CUTS Node Manager can manage all the processes for each execution environment, and can quickly swap between them.

- **The CUTS Node Manager Client:** An application that allows end-users to control a CUTS Node Manager remotely. The CUTS Node Manager Client therefore prevents end-users from having to manually log into each machine in the test cloud to modify its configuration. For example, enterprise DRE system developers and testers can remotely switch between different virtual environments, spawn new processes on remote host, or terminate an existing process on a remote host. The CUTS Node Manager Client is mainly used by the CUTS Test Manager (explained next) to inject behaviors into the execution environment at runtime. For example, the CUTS Test Manager can use to CUTS Node Manager Client to terminate a remote process hosting software components to evaluate the robustness of the system under testing during faults.
- **The CUTS Test Manager:** An application that executes for a user-specified amount

of time and manages the testing exercise of an enterprise DRE system in the test cloud. The CUTS Test Manager application achieves this by first, wrapping itself around the deployment tools for the system under test. For example, when evaluating the RACE baseline scenario, the CUTS Test Manager wraps itself around DAnCE (Deng, Balasubramanian, Otte, Schmidt, & Gokhale, 2005), which is a deployment and configuration engine for CORBA Component Model (CCM) applications. Box 5 highlights a portion of the CUTS Test Manager configuration that defines what tool to use to deploy the system under testing into the test cloud.

As shown in Box 5, the CUTS Test Manager uses the <startup> section to determine how to launch the system under test (*i.e.*, RACE in the example above). The <shutdown> section determines how to stop the current system under testing. Since the startup and shutdown sections are generic, the CUTS Test Manager can wrap any deployment tool. While the CUTS Test Manager is active (*i.e.*, the test is executing in the test cloud), the CUTS Test Manager can execute test actions. A test action is an operation that occurs independently of the system under test, but can have an effect on the system under test.

Box 5. Snippet of the CUTS Test Manager configuration illustrating the use of DAnCE to deploy RACE into the test cloud

```xml
<?xml version="1.0" encoding="utf-8" standalone="no" ?>
<cuts:test>
 <startup>
 <executable>${DANCE_ROOT}/bin/dance_plan_launcher</executable>
 <arguments>-x RACE.cdp -k file://EM.ior</arguments>
 </startup>

<shutdown>
 <executable>${DANCE_ROOT}/bin/dance_plan_launcher</executable>
 <arguments>-x RACE.cdp -k file://EM.ior -s</arguments>
 </shutdown>
 <!-- // remainder of test script -->
</cuts:test>
```

For example, the CUTS Test Manager can use the CUTS Node Manager Client to send a command to the CUTS Node Manager to terminate an existing process on the machine. Box 6 shows a snippet of the CUTS Test Manager configuration for sending commands to nodes throughout the test execution. As shown in this listing, the CUTS Test Manager sleeps for 30 seconds. After the sleep delay, it resets the CUTS Node Manager running on node1.isislab.vanderbilt.edu (i.e., forces all its managed processes to restart).

Summary

When evaluating an enterprise DRE system in a test cloud, such as Emulab, it is necessary for the test cloud to have infrastructure support for managing the complete testing operation. As discussed in this section, this support mainly involves having infrastructure manage processes executing on remote machines (*i.e.*, the CUTS Node Manager and CUTS Node Manager Client) and infrastructure for managing different test scenarios (*i.e.*, the CUTS Test Manager). Without such infrastructure in place, it is hard for enterprise DRE system testers to leverage a test cloud for their testing exercises because they will spend significant time and effort trying to manage many remote resources, which is an daunting task.

Coordinating Logging, Instrumentation, and Testing Management Infrastructure in the Test Cloud

The previous two sections discussed topics related to (1) logging and instrumentation infrastructure for collecting test data from an enterprise DRE system and (2) test management infrastructure that coordinate the testing effort across different nodes in the test cloud. The discussion in each section and resulting artifacts, however, are disjoint in that the logging and instrumentation infrastructure does not know about the test management infrastructure.

A disjoint solution has both its advantages and disadvantages. For example, one advantage of a disjoint solution is that the loose coupling between the two allows the use of either one without the other. For example, it is possible to use the CUTS Node Manager to manage virtual environments and processes without including the CUTS Test Manager. Likewise, it is possible to use the CUTS Test Manager to manage different test scenarios

Box 6. Snippet of the CUTS Test Manager configuration illustrating the use of test actions to alter the behavior to the test environment at runtime

```xml
<?xml version="1.0" encoding="utf-8" standalone="no" ?>
<cuts:test>
 <!-- // startup/shutdown commands removed from script -->

<actions>
 <action delay='30' waitforcompletion='true'>
 <executable>${CUTS_ROOT}/bin/cutsnode</executable>
 <arguments>-ORBInitRef
NodeManager=node1.isislab.vanderbilt.edu:50000/CUTS/NodeManager
--reset</arguments>
 </action>

<!-- // more test actions go here -->
 </actions>
</cuts:test>
```

without ever using the CUTS Logging Client and CUTS Logging Server.

One disadvantage of having a disjoint solution is that it is hard to ensure that data collected by the logging and instrumentation infrastructure is associated with the correct test. This association is not problematic if only one enterprise DRE system is instrumented for a given test. If there are multiple systems being instrumented that use the same logging infrastructure and want their data associated with different tests, however, then having a disjoint solution is not ideal. The problem is that there is no easy way to ensure the test data is associated with the correct test without introducing some form of compiling that associates data with a given test.

Integrating Logging and Test Management Infrastructure in CUTS

Since there is occasionally a need to associate collected data with a given test, we allow the CUTS Test Manger to support testing services. A testing service is an entity that adds domain-specific behavior based on the lifetime of the testing exercise. The main motivation for sup-porting testing services is that it is hard to know in advance all the needs of a testing exercise that must be associated with the testing lifecycle. For example, some testing exercises may need to associate data with a given test, and other testing exercises may not. Testing services will therefore support both needs and enhances the flexibility of CUTS extensions for testing enterprise DRE systems in test clouds.

Box 7 shows a portion of the CUTS Test Manager configuration that loads the CUTS Logging Server as a service (*i.e.*, logging in Box 7) into the CUTS Test Manager. It also loads a service that exposes an external endpoint (*i.e.*, daemon in Box 7) for remotely connecting to the CUTS Test Manager. By loading the CUTS Logging Server into the CUTS Test Manager, it has access to the CUTS Test Manger attributes, such as test id and test lifecycle events (*e.g.*, start, stop, and pause).

The CUTS Testing Service also exposes an interface that allows clients to query information about the current test, such as test id. When an enterprise DRE system is deployed into the test cloud, the loggers use the interface provided by the CUTS Test Manager to query for a new test id. The loggers then associate the returned test id

Box 7. Snippet of CUTS Test Manager configuration illustrating services to load into the test manager

```xml
<?xml version="1.0" encoding="utf-8" standalone="no" ?>
<cuts:test>
 <!-- // startup/shutdown commands and test actions removed -->
 <services>
 <service id="daemon">
 <location>CUTS_Testing_Server</location>
 <entryPoint>_make_CUTS_Testing_Server</entryPoint>
 <params>-ORBEndpoint iiop://localhost:50000</params>
 </service>

 <service id="logging">
 <location>CUTS_Testing_Log_Message_Listener</location>
 <entryPoint>_make_CUTS_Testing_Log_Message_Listener</entryPoint>
 <params>-ORBInitRef
LoggingServer=
corbaloc:iiop:localhost:20000/LoggingServer</params>
 </service>
 </services>
</cuts:test>
```

with the data that it submits to the CUTS Logging Client and CUTS Logging Server.

Summary

Although separating the logging and instrumentation infrastructure from the test management infrastructure has advantages, coupling the two is sometimes necessary, such as when testing infrastructure has information that the logging infrastructure requires to associate data with the correct test. Infrastructure for the test cloud should therefore support both use cases. Otherwise, it can be hard to associate data with a given test.

One concern not discussed in this section is when new software components are deployed during the middle of a test. If there is only one test executing, then the solution is straightforward (*i.e.*, request the id of the currently executing test). If t multiple tests are executing (*i.e.*, multiple test ids), however, it can be hard to determine what test the new components should be associated with. One solution to this problem is to pre-assign test ids before the system is deployed into the test cloud, so that when new components come online they know which test to associate its data. Otherwise, if test ids are auto-generated (as discussed above), some mechanism is needed to determine which groups of test ids belong to the same overarching test. This approach, however, can be hard if the testing exercise is dynamic (*i.e.*, has many software components that are deployed and destroyed throughout the testing lifecycle).

EXPERIMENTAL RESULTS: USING TEST CLOUDS TO EVALUATE THE RACE BASELINE SCENARIO

This section shows the design and results of experiments that applied the extended version of CUTS for the Emulab test cloud to evaluate the RACE's baseline scenario in the Emulab test cloud. These experiments evaluated the following hypotheses:

H1: CUTS allows developers to understand the behavior and performance of infrastructure-level software (such as RACE) within a test cloud (such as Emulab) before system integration.

H2: CUTS allows developers use test clouds to continuously evaluate QoS properties of infrastructure-level software throughout its lifecycle.

Experiment Design

To evaluate the two hypotheses in the context of the RACE baseline scenario, we constructed 10 operational strings using CUTS. Each string was composed of the same components and port connections, but had different importance values and resource requirements to reflect varying resource requirements and functional importance between operational strings that accomplish similar tasks, such as a primary and secondary tracking operation. Figure 3 shows a model for one of the baseline scenario's operational strings, which represents a single operational task in the shipboard computing environment composed of interconnected software components, based on the Platform Independent Component Modeling Language (PICML) (Gokhale, Balasubramanian and Balasubramanian), which is a domain-specific modeling language for modeling compositions, deployments, and configurations of Lightweight CCM applications. This model contains 15 interconnected components represented by the rounded boxes. This operational string was replicated 10 times to create the 10 operational strings in the baseline scenario.

The four components on the left side of the operational string in Figure 3 are sensor components that monitor environment activities, such

Figure 3. Graphical model of the replicated operational string for the baseline scenario

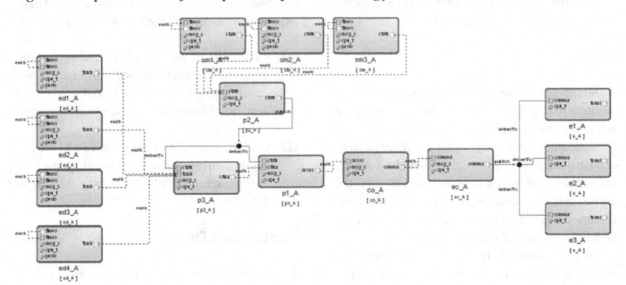

as tracking objects of importance using radar. The four components in the top-middle of Figure 3 are system observation components that monitor the state of the system. The four linear components in the bottom-center of Figure 3 are planner components that receive information from both the system observation and sensor components and analyze the data, *e.g.*, determine if the object(s) detected by the sensor components are of importance and how to (re)configure the system to react to the detected object(s). The planner components then send their analysis results to the three components on the right side of Figure 3, which are effector components that react as stated by the planner components, *e.g.*, start recording observed data.

To prepare RACE's baseline scenario for CUTS usage, we used PICML to construct the 10 operational strings described above. We then used the CUTS to generate Lightweight CCM compliant emulation code that represented each component in the operational string managed by RACE (see Figure 3) in the baseline scenario. We also used PICML to generate the operational strings' deployment and configuration descriptors for RACE.

The deployment of each operational string used the strategy specified in Table 1. The importance values assigned to each operational string reflects its mission-critical ranking with respect to other operational strings. We chose extreme importance values because RACE was in its initial stages of development and we wanted to ensure that it honored importance values when managing operational strings. These importance values can easily be changed to evaluate RACE's ability to handle operational strings with closely related importance values, though this use case was outside the scope of our experiments. Finally, we instrumented RACE's source code with logging

Table 1. The importance values of the baseline scenario operational strings

Operation String	Importance Value
A – H	90
I – J	2

messages so that the CUTS Logging Client and CUTS Logging Server can collect data about the test, such as time of operational string deployment/teardown or time of node failure recognition.

To run the experiments using CUTS, we create configuration scripts for the CUTS Test Manager that captured the serialized flow of each experiment. The configuration scripts contained commands that (1) signaled RACE to deploy/teardown operational strings, (2) sent commands to individual nodes to cause environmental changes, and (3) queried the logging database for test results. Finally, we created a custom graphical display that analyzed the log messages to show whether the lifetime of dynamic deployments exceed the lifetime of static deployments based on resource availability with respect to environmental changes.

Experiment Results

This section presents the results of experiments that validate hypotheses H1 and H2 in context of the RACE baseline scenario.

Using CUTS to Understand the Behavior and Performance of Infrastructure-Level Software when Testing in a Test Cloud

Hypothesis H1 conjectured that CUTS assists in understanding the behavior and performance of infrastructure-level software, such as RACE, using a test cloud well before system integration. Figure 4 shows an example result set for the RACE baseline scenario (*i.e.*, measuring the lifetime of operational strings deployed dynamically vs. operational strings deployed statically) where two hosts were taken offline to simulate a node failure. As shown in this figure, the two hosts were hosting individual components (*i.e.*, the rectangle objects in Figure 3) from the higher importance operational strings.

The graphs in Figure 4, which are specific to RACE, were generated from the log messages stored in the database via the CUTS Logging Client and CUTS Logging Server described in the previous section. The x-axis in both graphs is

Figure 4. Graphical analysis of static deployments (bottom) vs. dynamic deployments (top) using RACE

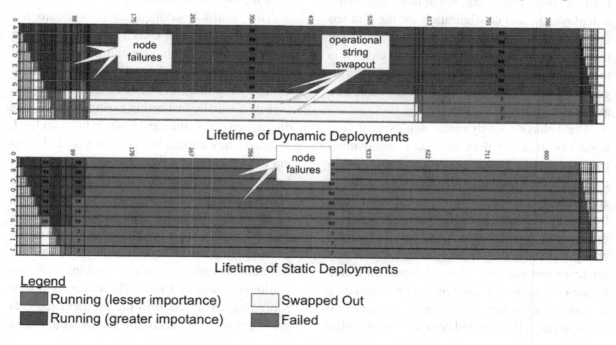

the timeline for the test in seconds and each horizontal bar represents the lifetime of an operational string, *i.e.*, operational string A-J.

The graph at the bottom of Figure 4 depicts RACE's behavior when deploying and managing human-generated static deployment of operational string A-J. The graph at the top of Figure 4 depicts RACE's behavior when deploying and managing RACE-generated dynamic deployment of operational string A-J. At approximately 100 and 130 seconds into the test run, the CUTS Test Manager shutdown two nodes hosting individual components from higher importance operational strings, which is highlighted by the "node failures" callout. This shutdown was accomplished by sending a kill command to the corresponding CUTS Node Manager.

As shown in the static deployment (bottom graph) of Figure 4, static deployments are not aware of the environmental changes. All operational strings on failed nodes (*i.e.*, operational string A-G) therefore remain in the failed state until they are redeployed manually. In this test run, however, we did not redeploy the operational strings hosted on the failed nodes because the random "think time" required to manually create a deployment and configuration for the 7 failed operational strings exceeded the duration of the test. This result signified that in some cases it is too hard to derive new deployments due to stringent resource requirements and scarce resource availability.

The behavior of dynamic deployment (top graph) is different than the static deployment (bottom graph) behavior. In particular, when the CUTS Test Manager kills the same nodes at approximately the same time (*i.e.*, section highlighted by the "node failure" callout), RACE's monitoring agents detect the environmental changes. RACE then quickly determines if any higher importance operational strings are affected by the environmental change, which in this case is lost of resources. Since the environmental failed negatively impacted components in higher importance operational strings, RACE attempts to find a way to redeploy them. In this example, RACE tears down the lower importance operational strings (*i.e.*, the section highlighted by the "operational string swap out") to regain their resources and redeploys the higher importance operational strings in their place (*e.g.*, the regions after the "node failure" regions).

The test run shown in Figure 4, however, does not recover the failed nodes to emulate the condition where the nodes cannot be recovered (*e.g.*, due to faulty hardware). This failure prevented RACE from redeploying the lower importance operational strings because there were not enough resources available. Moreover, RACE must ensure the lifetime of the higher importance operational strings is greater than lower importance operational strings. If the failed nodes were recovered, however, RACE would attempt to redeploy the lower importance operational strings. Figure 4 also shows the lifetime of higher importance operational strings was ~15% greater than lower importance operational string. This test case showed that RACE could improve the lifetime of operational strings deployed and managed dynamically versus statically.

The results described above validate hypothesis H1, *i.e.*, that CUTS enables developer to understand the behavior and performance of infrastructure-level software in Emulab. Without CUTS, we would have used *ad hoc* techniques, such as manually inspecting execution trace logs distributed across multiple hosts in the test cloud, to determine the exact behavior of RACE. By using CUTS, however, we collected the necessary log messages in a central location and used them to determine the exact behavior of RACE.

If we did not use CUTS to validate RACE within Emulab, we would have had to manually execute the different actions required to emulate different scenarios, such as deploying each operational strings and killing/\-recovering nodes. Moreover, each action in the scenario requires precise timing of execution, which would have been difficult and inefficient to do manually. Since CUTS uses an automated approach to testing via the CUTS Test Manager, it can simplify validating the QoS of enterprise DRE systems within a test cloud, such as Emulab. This result, however, is for a single experiment run. To fully determine if CUTS can simplify validating the QoS of enterprise DRE systems within test clouds, we need to run large numbers of tests, *i.e.*, validate hypothesis H2.

Using CUTS to Ensure Performance is within QoS Specification

Hypothesis H2 conjectured that CUTS would help developers use test clouds to ensure the QoS of infrastructure-level software is within its performance specifications throughout the development lifecycle. The results described above, however, represent a single test run of the baseline experiment. Although this result is promising, it does not show conclusively that CUTS can ensure RACE is within its QoS specifications as we develop and release revisions of RACE. We therefore integrated CUTS with the CruiseControl.NET (ccnet.thoughtworks.com), which is a continuous integration system (Fowler, 2006) we used to continuously execute variations of the experiment discussed above while we evolved RACE. Figure 5 highlights the maximum number of tests we captured from the baseline scenario after it

was executed approximately 427 times over a 2-week period.

The number of executions corresponds to the number of times a modification (such as a bug fix or an added feature to RACE) was detected in the source code repository at 30-minute intervals. The vertical bars in Figure 5 represent the factor of improvement of dynamic deployments vs. static deployments. The lower horizontal line was the acceptable measured improvement and the upper horizontal line was the target improvement (i.e., 10%).

The heights of the bars in this figure are low on the left side and high on the right side, which stem from the fact that the initial development stages of RACE had limited capability to handle dynamic (re-) configuration of operational strings. As RACE's implementation improved – and the modified code was committed to the RACE source code repository – CruiseControl.NET updated the testing environment with the latest version of RACE, and then executed the CUTS Test Manager. The CUTS Test Manager then executed a test scenario in the Emulab test cloud.

The circle portion in Figure 5 shows where we located an error in the specification because the measured improvements were not correlating correctly with what we were seeing in the graphs produced by the system execution traces (see Figure 4). At this point, we learned that the equation for measuring RACE's improvement

Figure 5. Overview analysis of continuously executing the RACE baseline scenario

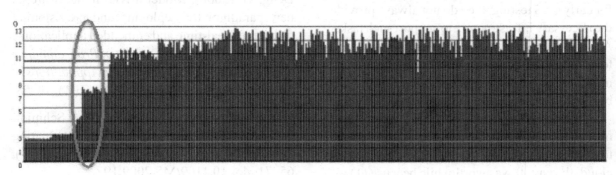

was incorrect due to a misunderstanding of the system's behavior and semantics in the target environment. After correcting the equation, we were able to meet the 10% target improvement.

The results in Figure 5 show how CUTS allowed developers to run test in Emulab and keep track of RACE's performance throughout its development. As the performance of RACE improved between source code modifications, the vertical bars increased in height. Likewise, as the performance of RACE decreased between source code modifications, the vertical bars decreased in height. Since each vertical bar corresponds to a single test run, if the performance of RACE changed between tests runs, developers and testers can simply view the graphical display for a single test run (see Figure 4) to further investigate RACE's behavior. These results therefore help validate hypothesis H2, *i.e.*, that CUTS helps developers ensure the QoS of infrastructure-level software is within its performance specifications throughout the development lifecycle. As modifications where checked into the source code repository, the CruiseControl.NET detected the modifications and automatically reran the CUTS tests for RACE.

CONCLUSION

This chapter presented an approach for using test clouds to evaluate QoS properties of enterprise DRE systems during early phases of their lifecycle. Although it is possible to use test clouds for early QoS testing, they do not always provide the necessary infrastructure to support such tasks. As shown throughout this chapter, we had to extend the CUTS SEM tool with logging and test management infrastructure to evaluate the RACE baseline scenario in the Emulab test cloud.

Although significant time and effort were needed to implement the necessary infrastructure to support our testing needs in the Emulab test cloud, the payoff was worthwhile because (1) we did not have to purchase the resources to meet our testing needs and (2) we were able to locate errors in RACE's specification and resolve them during its early stages of development. While these results do not prove definitively that test clouds are the solution to all testing problems, our experience with RACE indicate that test clouds have the potential to address key needs in the testing domain if the appropriate infrastructure is available to support the testing requirements.

The CUTS SEM tool presented in this chapter is freely available in open-source format for download from URL http://cuts.cs.iupui.edu.

REFERENCES

Deng, G., Balasubramanian, J., Otte, W., Schmidt, D. C., & Gokhale, A. (2005). DAnCE: A QoS-enabled component deployment and configuration engine. *3rd Working Conference on Component Deployment*, (pp. 67-82). Grenoble, France.

Deng, G., Gill, C., Schmidt, D. C., & Wang, N. (2007). QoS-enabled component middleware for distributed real-time and embedded systems. In Son, I. L. (Ed.), *Handbook of real-time and embedded systems*. CRC Press.

Fowler, M. (2006, May). *Continuous integration*. Retrieved from http://www.martinfowler.com/articles/ continuousIntegration.html

Gokhale, A., Balasubramanian, K., Balasubramanian, J., Krishna, A. S., Edwards, G. T., & Deng, G. (2008). Model driven middleware: A new paradigm for deploying and provisioning distributed real-time and embedded applications. *Journal of Science of Computer Programming: Special Issue on Foundations and Applications of Model Driven Architecture (MDA)*, *73*(1), 39–58.

Hill, J., Edmondson, J., Gokhale, A., & Schmidt, D. C. (2010). Tools for continuously evaluating distributed system qualities. *IEEE Software*, *27*(4), 65–71. doi:10.1109/MS.2009.197

Hill, J. H., & Gokhale, A. (2007). *Using generative programming to enhance reuse in visitor pattern-based DSML model interpreters. Institute for Software Integrated Systems*. Nashville, TN: Vanderbilt University.

Hill, J. H., Slaby, J., Baker, S., & Schmidt, D. C. (2006). *Applying system execution modeling tools to evaluate enterprise distributed real-time and embedded system QoS*. 12th International Conference on Embedded and Real-Time Computing Systems and Applications. IEEE.

Hill, J. H., Tambe, S., & Gokhale, A. (2007). Model-driven engineering for development-time QoS validation of component-based software systems. *14th International Conference and Workshop on the Engineering of Computer Based Systems* (pp. 307-316). Tucson, AZ: IEEE.

Ledeczi, A., Bakay, A., Maroti, M., Volgyesi, P., Nordstrom, G., & Sprinkle, J. (2001). Composing domain-specific design environments. *Computer, 34*(11), 44–51. doi:10.1109/2.963443

Mann, J. (1996). *The role of project escalation in explaining runaway information systems development projects: A field study*. Atlanta, GA: Georgia State University.

Object Management Group. (2002). *Lightweight CORBA component model RFP*. Object Management Group.

Porter, A., Yilmaz, C., Memon, A., Schmidt, D., & Natarajan, B. (2007). Skoll: A process and infrastructure for continuous quality assurance. *IEEE Transactions on Software Engineering, 33*(8), 510–525. doi:10.1109/TSE.2007.70719

Ricci, R., Alfred, C., & Lepreau, J. (2003). A solver for the network testbed mapping problem. *SIGCOMM Computer Communications Review, 33*(2), 30–44. doi:10.1145/956981.956988

Rittel, H., & Webber, M. (1973). Dilemmas in a general theory of planning. *Policy Sciences, 4*, 155–169. doi:10.1007/BF01405730

Schmidt, D. C. (1994). ACE: An object-oriented framework for developing distributed applications. *Proceedings of the 6th USENIX C++ Technical Conference*, USENIX Association.

Shankaran, N., Schmidt, D. C., Chen, Y., Koutsoukous, X., & Lu, C. (2007). *The design and performance of configurable component middleware for end-to-end adaptation of distributed real-time embedded systems*. 10th International Symposium on Object/Component/Service-oriented Real-time Distributed Computing. Santorini Island, Greece: IEEE.

Smith, C., & Williams, L. (2001). *Performance solutions: A practical guide to creating responsive, scalable software*. Boston, MA: Addison-Wesley Professional.

Software Engineering Institute. (2006). *Ultra-large-scale systems: Software challenge of the future*. Pittsburgh, PA: Carnegie Mellon University.

Vouk, M. A. (2008). Cloud computing — Issues, research and implementations. *30th International Conference on Information Technology Interfaces*, (pp. 31-40). Cavtat, Croatia.

Wikipedia. (2012, May 17). *Endianness*. Retrieved from http://en.wikipedia.org/wiki/Endianness

Yu, L., Tsai, W.-T., Chen, X., Liu, L., Zhao, Y., Tang, L., et al. (2010). Testing as a service over cloud. *International Symposium on Service Oriented System Engineering* (pp. 181-188). Nanjing, China: IEEE.

Yu, L., Zhang, L., Xiang, H., Su, Y., Zhao, W., & Zhu, J. (2009). A framework of testing as a service. *International Conference on Management and Service Science*, (pp. 1-4).

Chapter 9
Software Testing as a Service:
Perceptions from Practice

Leah Riungu-Kalliosaari
Lappeenranta University of Technology, Finland

Ossi Taipale
Lappeenranta University of Technology, Finland

Kari Smolander
Lappeenranta University of Technology, Finland

ABSTRACT

This chapter describes a qualitative study whose aim was to explore and understand the conditions that influence software testing as a service. Interviews were conducted with software professionals from 16 organizations. The study used qualitative grounded theory as its research method. The level of domain knowledge required by testers was an initial indication of whether testing could be delivered as a service. The benefits of software testing as a service included flexibility and cost effectiveness. Among top requirements were security and pricing. Cloud computing was envisaged as the delivery model for software testing as a service. Some potential research areas suggested were pricing models and handling of test data. There was an indication that the demand for software testing as a service was on the rise, albeit with mixed feelings. Organizations would have to make careful considerations before embarking on testing their systems and applications over the internet.

INTRODUCTION

In recent years, innovations towards service-oriented architecture (SOA) and software-as-a-service (SaaS) models have greatly affected the nature of software systems and organizations (Goth, 2008; Collard, 2009). This means that

software developers from different organizations are continuously surprised to find that their code is more inter-related than they would have initially anticipated (Young, et. al, 2009), so that their systems are able to work together easier than they would have done so in the past. At the same time, the goal of every software organization is to

DOI: 10.4018/978-1-4666-2536-5.ch009

produce high-quality software that is flexible and easy to use – as is the expectation of the modern world's technologically-savvy end user.

Initially, we drew the concept of software testing as a service from Turner et al. (2003) and Dubey and Wagie (2007). Turner et al (2003) envisaged the concept of software as a service (SaaS) into one that exists within a "demand-led software market in which businesses assemble and provide services when needed to address a particular requirement." As a result, SaaS distinguishes between the provider and user whereby, the software's functionality can be delivered as a set of combined services that are assembled during delivery time. Similarly, Dubey and Wagie (2007) described SaaS as a move from installing license-based software on local machines to using the software as an application service provided by a third party. This would grant the user freedom to choose and switch between vendors and reduce software maintenance efforts.

Our view of software testing as a service was aligned to the above mentioned early SaaS descriptions, such that software testing would be provided on-demand, by a third party and testing resources could be used without prior installation on local machines. For example, instead of acquiring hardware to set up a load testing environment, a user could make use of a third party's already existing testing environment, and access the resources via a communication channel, which in this case would be the internet. During the course of the study, we became aware of cloud computing as a delivery model that enables an application to be hosted by a provider and accessed by many users at the same time. Hence, it became imperative to contextualize the concept of software testing as a service within cloud computing.

Cloud computing is one model that is changing the way software is produced and consumed – mainly from the traditional desktop form to online software services. Popular models for delivering computing services in the cloud are software as a service (SaaS) – applications hosted in the cloud, and accessed by means of a web browser; platform as a service (PaaS) – programming and execution environments in the cloud through which users can run and access applications; and Infrastructure as a service (IaaS) – storage, processing and network capabilities for cloud users e.g. Amazon's EC2. Evidently, technologies are constantly evolving, and this implies that the methods, tools and concepts to test them must also change (Collard, 2009).

In this study, we wanted to gather views about software testing as a service from practitioners in the industry. Interviews were conducted with respondents from organizations that were either software testing providers or customers. The underlying research question was: "What conditions influence software testing as a service?" In addition, we also gathered important issues regarding software testing as a service so as to establish a direction for future research.

The chapter is organized as follows: The background section includes definitions, a literature review, a description of the research process and the grounded theory method used. The results section presents the analysis results including future research directions. Thereafter, we discuss the practical implications of the results followed by concluding remarks.

BACKGROUND

This section presents a literature review related to this chapter and the research process employed in the study.

Software testing as a service is defined as "a model of software testing used to test an application as a service provided to customers across the internet" (Aalst, 2009). It provides daily operation, maintenance and testing support through web-based browsers, testing frameworks and servers. This model supports a demand-led software testing market by enabling organizations to provide and acquire testing services whenever needed. It envisions an important contribution to the software industry owing to innovations such as Web services and cloud computing that provide new platforms for software testing. Another definition is as follows:

Testing-as-a-service (TaaS) is the ability to test local or cloud-delivered systems using testing software and services that are remotely hosted. It should be noted that while a cloud service requires testing unto itself, testing-as-a-service systems have the ability to test other cloud applications, web sites, and internal enterprise systems, and they do not require a hardware or software footprint within the enterprise. (Linthicum, 2010, p. 13)

Software testing as a service has several benefits: Testing customers do not have to incur major investments in installing and maintaining test environments (Aalst, 2009). This significantly lowers test costs while offering customers a flexible approach to acquiring testing services as the need arises, from anywhere around the globe. Secondly, software testing as a service opens up a wider market for both testing providers and customers (Turner, et. al, 2003). The testing provider attracts a larger base of customers while the customer gains access to international testing professionals. Thirdly, it has been claimed that software testing as a service can be delivered within a period of up to 10 working days (Sogeti, 2009). Consequently, this leads to shorter turn-around times, enabling the customers to achieve fast time to market. Furthermore, when dealing with testing infrastructure hosted on the internet, the web service APIs used can hide the complexity of using hosted testing infrastructure, hence encouraging developers and testers to use the infrastructure more frequently (Ciortea, 2009).

There are several commercial players and offerings addressing software testing as a service. To mention some examples, Unified Testpro from Software Development Technologies (sdtcorp.com) is a complete off-the-shelf key driven test and automation solution that can be used to test various technological areas (Sdtcorp, 2010). UTest provides software testing solutions to its customers through on-demand access to its community of professional testers i.e. crowdsourcing (Utest, 2009). Sogeti's recently launched testing solution called STaaS - Software Testing as a Service - is tailored to provide the clients with a flexible, easily obtainable cost-effective service (Sogeti, 2010). IBM offers its Infrastructure Optimization Services – IBM Smart Business Test Cloud that provides on-demand secure, dynamic and scalable virtual test server resources in a private test environment (IBM, 2010). Sauce onDemand is a software testing service based on Selenium that enables web applications to be tested across multiple browsers in the cloud (Saucelabs, 2010). Other software testing as service offerings are provided by Skytap, VM Logix, Zephyr and Cybernet-SlashSupport (Foley, 2009; Csscorp, 2010) with a projected growth of more providers in the future. We believe that this state of business will change drastically in the future when the market expands and also large corporations take their share of the business.

Currently, empirical research about testing as a service is scarce. We are aware that the Systems Testing Excellence Program (STEP) research team at the University of Memphis, Tennessee is following the information technology (IT) services paradigm that breaks down an IT unit into a set of valuable services such that the quality of an individual service can be quantified (Yang, et. al, 2009). Thus, it is working on a framework for measuring the quality of testing services so that issues such as software usability, user satisfaction, mapping onto business needs, information systems coherence, etc., are considered within the software testing context.

Robinson and Ragusa (2011) outline the business goals that should be considered in order to develop effective testing infrastructure in the cloud. The goals are cost effectiveness, simplicity, target representation, controllability, observability, predictability and reproducibility. They mention five ways in which the cloud may be used for testing, for example, testing in the cloud where a single cloud infrastructure provider hosts the software under test and the testing suite; and test-suite in the cloud in which the software testing in the cloud vendors host and control the test suite outside the domain of the system under test.

In another study, Jun & Meng (2011) highlighted two ways in which software testing can be performed in the cloud. One is by accessing the software testing services through the cloud software provider's webpage. The second one is by customers connecting to the software testing provider's virtual machines and using them to test. Some examples demonstrating how the cloud can be used for software testing are presented below.

Ganon and Zilberstein (2009) show an example of large-scale performance testing in the cloud where they tested a Network Management System (NMS) for a Voice over IP (VoIP) telephony switching system. Instead of running a simulator or using real elements, they preferred cloud-based testing because it was scalable and cost-effective. They report having achieved better software and spending very little to run the test.

Cloud9 is a cloud-based testing framework being developed at Ecole Polytechnique Federale de Lausanne (EPFL), Switzerland (Ciortea, et. al, 2009). It runs as a web service that enables parallel symbolic execution of computer clusters operating on public cloud infrastructures such as Amazon EC2 as well as on clusters running cloud software e.g. on Eucalyptus. Subsequently, Cloud9 is illustrated as suitable for automated software testing in the cloud – so that "developers can comprehensively test their code, end users can check the software they install, and consumers can choose among software products based on the products' measured reliability" (Candea, et. al, 2010). Another example of automated testing in the cloud is proposed by Yu et al (2010). They propose a cloud-based testing as a service platform that automatically clusters, schedules, monitors and manages the test tasks. It is also designed

to be elastic, so that it is able to cope with huge numbers of simultaneous requests.

D-cloud is a large-scale software testing environment that uses cloud computing technology i.e., Eucalyptus for cloud management and QEMU - an open source machine emulator - for virtualization (Hanawa, et. al, 2010). It can be used to test parallel and distributed processing of highly dependable systems. Other examples include autonomic self testing (AST) and testing support-as-a-service (TSaaS) that enhances self-testing applications (King and Ganti, 2010) and the York Extensible Testing Infrastructure (YETI) that randomly tests programs written in different programming languages (Oriol and Ullah, 2010). Additionally, the virtualized-aware automated testing service (VATS) executes tests and manages virtual infrastructure (Gaisbauer, et. al, 2008); and the remote network labs (RNL) allows its users to build test laboratories on an on-demand basis (Liu and Orban, 2010).

All of these implementations are cloud-based, demonstrating the fact that cloud computing is offering processing and virtualization capabilities that support testing. Cloud-based testing seems feasible and affordable, further encouraging its adoption in the industry as well as the research fraternity. An illustration is the test modeling using action words (TEMA) project at Tampere University of Technology, Finland which is working on turning its model-based testing methodology into a testing service on the web (Jääskeläinen, et. al, 2008).

Research Process

Software testing as a service is a relatively recent concept, in which little research exists. Hence, an exploratory, qualitative approach using grounded theory was deemed appropriate in order to better understand the issues related to software testing as a service. Qualitative methods can be used to explore substantive areas about which little is known or about which much is known to gain novel understandings (Strauss and Corbin, 1990). Seaman (1999) also recommends grounded theory as a valid choice for software engineering because it enables the identification of new theories and concepts. Furthermore, grounded theory, as elaborated by Strauss and Corbin (1990), means that the theory emerges from the data that has been gathered and analyzed. By so doing, we allow ourselves the opportunity to gain insight and sound understanding of the real dynamics being studied hence delivering a reliable direction and recommendations for future studies.

We used semi-structured (theme-based) questions during the interviews. We carried out two interview rounds for this study whose details are shown in Table 1. The first interview round focused on general aspects related to software testing as a service. In the second interview round, we incorporated aspects related to cloud computing as a delivery model for software testing services. The themes of both interviews are available at http://www2.it.lut.fi/project/MASTO/.

We interviewed respondents from sixteen different organizations. Six of the organizations participated in both interview rounds, five of which were represented by the same respondent. All except one of the interviews were face-to-face, conducted at the respondents' work locations. The exception was through email, because that particular respondent was widely on the move, and it was difficult to set a suitable time for a face-to-face interview. Theoretical sampling was used in selecting potential interview participants. Theoretical sampling, which selects themes and sources based on the needs of the emerging theoretical understanding, is particularly important when exploring new or uncharted areas because it enables the researcher to choose those avenues of sampling that bring about the greatest theoretical return (Strauss and Corbin, 1990). Snowball sampling was also used during the first interview round, whereby an interviewee recommended a representative from another organization as a suitable respondent.

Five organizations that were contacted declined to be interviewed during the first interview round. This was mainly because they did not think that software testing as a service fitted in with their existing testing practices. Three of these organizations participated in the second interview round. All three of them were interested in topics related to testing strategies, policies and plans, which are not in the scope of this study. However, one of these organizations was particularly interested in topics related to this study, e.g. cloud computing and SaaS. This was because it had had some of its small and medium-sized customers demanding for a SaaS-based version of the system the organization was providing. Hence, the organization was undertaking some considerations in planning how to meet that particular customer demand.

Table 2 gives information about the organizations and interviewees. The organizations listed as "customer" are those that said they would seek to acquire testing services from external vendors. On the other hand, those listed as "provider" are organizations that offered testing and quality

Table 1. Details of interview rounds

Interview Round	Duration	Type	Number of Interviews	Themes
1	October-November 2009	Semi structured	11 organizations	STaaS: Requirements, Applicable products and services, Effect on process model, Suitable verification and validation types
2	April-May 2010	Semi structured	11 organizations	Test policies, strategies and plans, Testing work, Software architecture, Delivery models, New software development concepts

Table 2. Details of organizations and interviewee roles

Organization	Business	Provider/Customer	Interviewee Role
1	Development of accounting software	Customer	Software manager
2	Information, logistics and mail communication	Customer	Quality and processes manager
3	Service development in banking	Customer	Program manager
4	Development of software for the energy market	Customer	Chief technology officer Mainline testing unit leader Tester
5	Development of systems for work time data collection	Customer	Project manager/test engineer
6	Testing services and consultancy	Provider	Testing and methodologies director
7	Performance testing services	Provider	Performance testing unit leader
8	Functional testing and test management	Provider	Functional testing unit leader
9	Testing and quality services	Provider	Vice president
10	Testing and quality services	Provider	Chief executive officer
11	Testing services	Provider	Testing manager Quality adviser
12	Customized automation provider	Provider	Manager Head of software development and hardware design
13	Web-based products and services	Provider	Head of software development
14	Building and construction software	Provider	Manager - Product development and product packages
15	Building and construction software	Provider	Unit manager – Documentation, testing and release
16	Naval software systems development	Provider	Manager - Software development and production

assurance services in addition to software and systems development for their customers.

We used the software tool Atlas.ti (2005) to perform the analysis and followed the coding procedures of Grounded Theory. These include: open coding, where concepts are classified according to their attributes and features; axial coding, where the identified attributes and features are used to establish relationships amongst concepts and selective coding, where the concepts are combined to build the theory (Strauss and Corbin, 1990). In this paper we report the classification of influencing conditions, which are mainly the results of axial coding.

RESULTS

The results of our analysis embody the main focus of this chapter. We identified the conditions that influence software testing as a service. They are classified as requirements, benefits, challenges and enabling conditions associated with software testing as a service. Subsequently, we present respondents views related to the suitability of cloud computing as the delivery channel for software testing as a service. Based on the respondents' views, we also outline a list of potential research issues and present it under future research directions.

Requirements

1. Domain Knowledge

Early in the research, it became evident that software testing as a service was not applicable for some application areas. Representatives from five organizations declined to participate in the first round of interviews citing reasons such as:

Most of our software is PLC [Programmable Logic Controller] software where the hardware is an essential part of the system just as the software. On the other hand our software/systems are so customer domain specific and a tester needs to be very familiar with the customer process, functional requirements and operational environment. From the viewpoint of UI [user interface] some parts of testing could be done as a service, but in our case UI is so tightly related to PLC software and it is also used for simulation testing (and in practice it is tested at the same time), so I don't see testing as a service as possible for UI either (Manager, org. 12).

The other four respondents came from organizations dealing with employee insurance business, emissions trading software and services, building and construction software products and software development for naval systems. They shared similar views, all emphasizing the need for testers to possess sufficient knowledge about the customer's business in order to efficiently test the applications. As a result, testing was an integral part of the whole software development cycle and it could not be outsourced to external parties.

Three of the above mentioned organizations participated in the second interview round. The building and construction organization was undertaking plans to provide a SaaS-based system as requested by its small and medium-sized companies, and was therefore looking into cloud computing.

I guess in our organization, cloud computing is something that a couple of guys have been researching, to see what it would mean for us, for example, on a technology level, yes. So we are trying to follow the trends (Unit manager, org. 15).

The organization dealing with naval systems was not particularly interested in cloud computing or SaaS. Despite the need for high level of domain knowledge, there was potential for delivering some kind of a SaaS-based service to its customers.

There's a small change in one application area, that we have this kind of SaaS, it's a reporting application that produces reports [at] real-time. It's possible that we offer the opportunity to sell that reporting application as a service, so that we host it (Unit manager, org. 16).

The third interviewee did not think cloud computing was suitable because the organization did not have systems requiring large amounts of data or virtual data storage.

2. Infrastructure

Different interviewees pointed out that cloud computing was going to be a driver for delivering software testing as a service. The interviewees seemed to agree that cloud computing presented a new approach to testing, both as an environment for testing and as a hosting platform for testing environments. Furthermore, a couple of the interviewees also perceived cloud computing as an appealing solution for systems requiring large amounts of computing power and virtual data storage:

Cloud computing will make software testing as a service more appealing and it will make software testing as a service easier to produce and, I see that as an enabler for software testing as a service (CEO, org. 10).

We took cloud computing as a lead for discussion during the second interview round and will present views about it later in this section.

3. Security

A software test as a service provider would be expected to assure customers that the information exchanged during a test process is safe. High levels of confidentiality were emphasized as being imperative so as to facilitate successful delivery of software testing as a service. While recognized as a vital requirement, security was also seen as a risk that would need to be addressed by all parties involved:

If for example there is tight integration with the software testing provider and the customer, then a security breach occurs at the software testing provider and that some hacker gains access to the software testing customer's systems. I see a big risk there, and it has to be addressed (Software manager, org. 1).

4. Pricing

Software test as service providers would be expected to provide transparent pricing models and service level agreements in order to attract customers:

... if the pricing models are transparent then it's very easy to see what the cost is so it's predictable (Quality and processes manager, org. 2).

Invoicing, e-invoicing, online bank transactions, paypal and credit cards were mentioned as ways to handle the payment process. However, the interviewees felt that the payment metrics were more important – what is a customer actually paying for? Is it for example effort, results, or test goal specifications? As mentioned by the chief technology officer of organization ten, "it doesn't make sense to pay for effort, at least it

doesn't make sense to pay for effort only but the pay should be somehow linked to the results." Another respondent had this to say:

I would say that the biggest obstacles[s] right now [are], pricing models, service descriptions and metrics that would cover the quality of service (Vice President, org. 9).

5. Communication

The interviewees maintained the view that effective, regular communication between the provider and the customer would be of high importance if at all software testing as a service was to be successful. Live meetings, video conferences, emails and telephones and instant reporting should be used for communication. At the same time, face-to-face meetings should not be underestimated especially at the beginning of a project. Formal software testing management system was also suggested as a way of harmonizing the communication.

Time zone differences are always a bit tricky. In the beginning of a project face-to-face meetings are important, but it's about getting used to another way of working because this is becoming the future, or presently also that you have global projects where people are in different places and then of course, any kind of live meetings, video-conferences are good alternatives, but, it cannot really beat face-to-face meetings (Functional testing unit leader, org. 8).

6. Testers' Skills

It was reported that software testers were going to have to develop a vast set of skills in order to keep up with the demands of software testing as a service. From both the provider and customer point of view, the successful execution of a test as a service process would depend on possession of technical and soft skills as outlined in Table 3.

Table 3. Skill set for testers

Skills
Adjusting to different working methods especially for global projects
Increased understanding of customer's business needs and requirements as well as the overall business environment
Communication, project management and other soft skills
Better technical skills (web technologes, testing environment setup and javascript among others)
Service mindset
Flexibility to learn and adapt to evolving technologies

Benefits

1. Reduced Costs

The interviewees were of the opinion that a well-planned software test as a service offering would help to cut down on costs. The service would be accessible on an on-demand basis. This would help to reduce the licensing and testing hardware costs as well as save on man-hours spent on setting up test environments.

Yes, I think costs can be reduced, for example license fees, you can have on-demand licensing, with that you can save quite a lot of money. You also don't have to invest in servers at your site, because somebody else is doing that for you. And, of course there's management. When you have less administration to do, of course that can also save time and money (Program manager, org. 3).

Well, at least the cost part, if you are able to make a well-working model, then the cost part could be reduced (CTO, org. 4).

2. Flexibility

Flexibility was viewed as a benefit that would offer customers the chance to start and/or stop testing whenever they wanted and only paying for the results. This would also create the possibility for one to make better cost estimates.

In general software as a service compared to traditional ways of delivering software is much more flexible of course, you can start now and stop after a month and you can, from a financial point of view, forecast your expenses more accurately (Software manager, org. 1).

Flexibility in resourcing, so that the supplier takes the risk of owning the resources or the network to deliver the service and you are only paying for the result, not for the effort. I think that's the most important thing (Quality and processes manager, org. 2).

According to the above respondent, an example of results would be finding "90 percent of the bugs" and an example of effort would be spending "one hundred hours in testing."

3. Access to Global Markets

Software testing as a service would internationalize software testing, presenting versatile opportunities both for the providers and customers. This would facilitate access to wider, global markets, hence a chance for the provider to serve a larger base of customers as well as for a customer to compare different providers.

Software testing as a service will just create more versatile opportunities, more options for serving the customers better, finding the best way to serve the customer in different situations and find the most economical and most feasible way of doing the testing (CEO, org. 10).

Furthermore, software testing as a service would support agile development methods by providing availability of continuous testing services. Therefore, shorter development cycles would be achieved leading to faster time to market of the software products.

...continuous service 24/7 for the international companies for example and shortening the lifecycle of the development process, I think in today's world, the big issue, is how you get time to market, to be shortened, so with continuous testing services, communication and iteration all the time, you could shorten the time to market (Software manager, org. 1).

Challenges

The test data used for testing determines the achieved test results. Sometimes, the original production data is necessary for testing so as to yield realistic and meaningful results. In such a case, the issue of the test data would have to be resolved. This was an issue particularly reported by testing service providers.

...I would say that the biggest challenge and at the same time the biggest requirement is connectivity to customers' development and testing environments and that's really, really hard (Vice President, org. 9).

...most of the time in a customer's agreement, for them to give some information out of their own office, they require first of all, non-disclosure agreements (NDAs) and then sometimes security assessments... the typical customer requirement is that they can give some information, some test data, but they cannot give, any sensitive test data out of their own premises... Sometimes, it's by law that they cannot give sensitive information.

So, there's a risk that testers are actually missing some information...So that's the risk that results in there (Testing and methodologies director, org. 6).

I don't know how easily the customer would give a copy of their production database, for example, to a third party. I don't know if that would be very easy or not (CTO, org. 4).

Software testing providers have to find ways of winning the trust of their customers. The providers need to have a positive reputation that can win their customers. One of the respondents had this to say:

Are customers willing to open up the interfaces giving enough data so that the testing could be helpful? ...in our accounting service, customers can make money transfers. I wonder, can customers trust us? But practically no one has really worried that anything bad would happen (Software manager, org. 1).

Additionally, software testing providers are faced with the challenge of having to invest in appropriate resources to facilitate availability of the software testing services at all times.

... a big risk, for the service providers, is in order to set up that [software testing] service, [they need to] develop this kind of investment (Testing manager, org. 11).

Other mentioned challenges were change management during the transition to adopting software testing as a service in an organization, lack of proper coordination especially for big projects, software testing provider falling short of promised service levels and legal issues in different countries. In addition, a customer may question the testing skills of the testers on the service provider's end. On the other hand, a provider may risk serving customers without having sufficient information about them.

Enabling Conditions

1. Standards

We investigated the effect of standards on software testing as a service. The general view was that standards e.g. Simple Object Access Protocol (SOAP) for e-business and 3GPP for the third generation mobile services (3G) were not an absolute necessity for the success of software testing as a service. Standards-based applications would only make the test service more predictable, easier and faster.

If we have a standard in use, and then we have, you know, a test library, related to that standard. Let's take for example the [user interface] UI requirements based on [a] certain standard, we would be then able to re-use some of the test library items for different kind of customers. So that would be easier and faster development cycle (Vice president, org. 9).

You know if I was to outsource testing and I was implementing something according to a standard then it would be a very well-defined thing to test (CTO, org. 4).

Telecommunications and web-based applications were also seen to be favorable for software test as service offerings. The adoption of software-as-a-service (SaaS) applications into business operations may drive the need for these applications to be tested in their host environment – the internet.

... at least with our customer from functional testing point of view, there are plans for the customers to take most of their applications online, which means that they want testing done on their software as a service ... and of course then that very much becomes not location specific (Functional testing unit leader, org. 8).

2. Verification and Validation Methods

Verification methods such as inspections, walkthroughs, technical reviews and tools like checklists were all deemed to be applicable as software test as a service offerings but not without shortcomings. One potential issue would be misunderstandings arising due to differences in perspectives regarding a specific verification method.

They can all be applied but of course the scope of how largely you can apply them is more limited if you are not onsite or if you don't have access to all the background information, but certainly they are all applicable (CEO, org. 10).

I think checklists are of course easy to use but if some walkthroughs or technical reviews are according to some standard or something like that, there comes differences in understanding. Because it's always humans using human-made program, it creates some misunderstanding. The word technical review could mean different things in different companies. I can't say if this is applicable just because it's a technical review, it has to depend on the programs and the companies using it and how they are using it. But always the checklist is one or zero, it's easy. That would be applicable (Performance testing unit leader, org. 7).

It was generally agreed that various validation methods could be tested as services, including usability, functional and system testing methods. Other suitable candidates were performance, load, compatibility and acceptance testing. However, there were certain exceptions as expressed below.

I don't think that recovery testing is so applicable, because, well, recovering from failures in for example hardware is hard to simulate (Project manager, org. 5).

... unit testing, I don't see how, if you don't have a piece of software running, you need a running platform to be connected with software testing provider (Software manager, org. 1).

I think usability testing, actually, maybe not applicable, because usability testing is something that we would test our interface, how our customers manage with it or something like that (Project manager, org. 5).

Cloud Computing

Cloud computing as the means for implementing software testing as a service was viewed with mixed reactions and attitudes. Most of the interviewees were aware of cloud computing.

1. Applicability

Cloud computing was deemed to enhance performance of certain services. It could be useful for organizations that experience peaks in their services, providing such organizations with the ability to scale up or down as per the demand.

But if I were a manager in some kind of, for example ticket service to concerts and stuff, I would absolutely buy software as a service from a cloud company, because their loads are so evenly distributed, so that if there's a normal day, they might get away with one server. But if Bon Jovi comes to Helsinki, then they have 100 000 users for one hour. And they want to have a good reputation that the system didn't crash when the big load came, so it would be really useful to buy computing power for one day, to get 100 machines now... (Software manager, org. 1).

With careful planning, cloud computing could also be used for performance testing of different applications, to benefit both small and large organizations.

Cloud computing is, at the moment, I would say, easy for those easy cases, and also for example, it is said that okay, cloud computing, you can test applications around the world. What about, network latencies, for example, if we have, load generators let's say in China and we test in US, so what? Should we generate and stack the whole traffic through the Internet because we generate the load to all the world. Of course not, but if we provide really great cloud computing, so then we should have load generators close to the servers. This is the main thing in the performance testing; load generators should be as close as possible to the server. So, can you really cover the whole world, or can you cover small areas and things like that? So, for a small amount of users, yeah, it's doable, but the big concept, for all our offices would be at the moment quite difficult for us because we are everywhere (Performance testing unit leader, org. 7).

Although most organizations had not adopted the use of cloud computing, some were looking further, or waiting to see how it would advance before considering using it.

And I guess in our level, there is a couple of guys researching what cloud computing would mean for us, so we are trying to follow the trends in that (Product development and product packages manager, org. 14).

Even with its desired applicability, cloud computing was expected to bring along issues that would in some way affect testing.

Cloud computing and SaaS, will create more complexity and they will actually create more needs for testing. So that will lengthen the projects. There should be more time spent on testing, because there's more complexity, which means more potential places for defects (Testing and methodologies director, org. 6).

It changes, or it may make some things more important, for instance as I think about performance testing and things like that, it makes them more important (Software development head, org. 13).

2. Data Governance

Different geographical regions have their own data regulations that govern how different data types are is managed and stored. Certain restrictions would limit how cloud computing would be adopted by some organizations, so that the region or country where the data is stored becomes a huge determining factor.

... In some areas we might, but we have legal restrictions on accounting and payroll data that we wouldn't be able to think about foreign cloud computing, for example Amazon or that sort of providers. We can't because the data has to be stored in Finland, and we have restrictions on that end (Software manager, org. 1).

...but most customers don't trust virtualization or cloud computing, I think because of data security. They need to keep all those databases in their own premises or actually, very often in hosted premises. But they want to create a relationship of trust, really, to some provider. I guess it will of course happen some time that one of those providers says that "OK, we are hosting your huge database, but it won't be in our vault here under this city, but it will be somewhere, and we don't say where". I'm sure this will happen and they will see what the customers will say. I don't know, I guess some people will say "OK, we don't care as long as you say that it will be secure". And people will say "OK, no matter what you say, it still needs to be in Finland under these rocks here, under the city, in these big vaults (Testing and methodologies director, org. 6).

Research Issues

It was also in our interest to elicit research issues on software testing as a service. We asked the interviewees to suggest issues they felt were important for research in future. Table 4 contains the suggested issues that have the potential to be researched in future. These issues are discussed in depth in another of our papers [24].

Table 4. Research issues

Application Issues
1. Business areas and applications suitable for online software testing
2. Providing a ready online performance testing package for any customer
3. Quality checks for applications that have been tested on the internet
4. Methods, tools and facilities for managing online software testing processes. Harmonizing test processes across multiple players
5. Online testing solutions for e-business applications
Management Issues
6. How to create a big enough available pool of testers
7. Effects of software testing as an online service on the customer's business and change management issues during the processes of adopting software testing as an online service.
Legal and Financial Issues
8. How to handle test data. Where does it come from? Who owns it? How is a system under test made accessible to the tester? What if signing of Non-Disclosure Agreements (NDAs) is required?
9. Pricing models and service descriptions for online software testing services

We classified the research issues into three groups; (1) application issues (2) management issues and (3) legal and financial issues. The first five research issues belong to application issues and they are concerned with different aspects associated with the nature of applications under test or in use for testing. The sixth and seventh research issues are classified under management issues. They deal with tasks that enable or support the success of software test as service offerings and require attention of managers. The legal and financial issues group incorporates the last two research issues. They relate to judicial and economic aspects that should be taken into consideration while undertaking software testing as a service. Table 5 summarizes the findings presented in this section.

Table 5. Summary of the results

Requirements	
Domain knowledge	Important especially for mission critical systems, is required throughout the development lifecycle, testing included. Difficult for such systems to be tested by external parties.
Infrastructure	Mainly includes cloud computing as a testing environment, and as a hosting platform for testing resources
Security	Data security across networks, confidentiality of customer data.
Pricing	Service level agreements, transparency
Communication	Meetings, video conferences, telephone calls, emails, formal software test management systems
Testers' skills	Testers would need to develop new and/or better skills, such as communication and global project management skills among others.
Benefits	
Reduced costs	No need to invest in testing servers, acquire testing resources as needed and pay only for what you use. Less license fees also help to reduce costs
Flexibility	A customer can obtain testing services only when needed, and pay only for what is used.
Access to global markets	Market base for both provider and customer becomes bigger
Challenges	
Test data management	Who owns data? Where is it stored?
Project and change management	How to manage multiple testing projects across different platforms, different customers, and/or even different providers.
Service level agreements	Customers should be assured of the reliability of the services
Enabling Conditions	
Standards	Applications and systems based on standards are easy to test. Testing parameters are predictable due to standards.
Verification and validation methods	Several of these methods can be tested, but the possibility to test them should be thoroughly considered and care should be taken to avoid misunderstandings.
Cloud Computing	
Applicability	Enables scaling up and down as per demand and enhances performance. May increase complexity hence increase need for testing.
Data governance	To be considered across various geographical regions
Research Issues	
Various	Listed in Table 4

PRACTICAL IMPLICATIONS

The objective of this study was to explore the conditions that influence software testing as a service. There is a growing awareness about software testing as a service and the industry seems to be ahead of academic research. The various demonstrations of testing in the cloud presented in the background section clearly show that there is an attempt by researchers and practitioners to implement software testing as a service. These are important in that they can contribute to the needs of the industry with solutions to relevant problems. In general, there seems to be more cloud implementations by the industry than by the research community. We advocate for collaborations between the industry and research, so that important issues can be addressed both scientifically and practically.

One way of collaborative interaction between research and the industry is the empirical perspective we have chosen to take. We also encourage other interested researchers to employ an empirical view so that there is a balanced approach to problem solving. Hence, there is a need for collaboration between the two in order to develop relevant directions of research for the needs of the industry.

As more and more software products shift from the traditional desktop form to becoming online services, we can expect software testing services to follow the same trend. Cloud computing is increasingly becoming the means through which online services are made available. Software testing within cloud computing may occur in three forms: the system under test is accessible online, testing infrastructure is hosted in the cloud, or testing of the cloud itself (Riungu, et. al. 2010).

We found that the requirement to possess the domain knowledge of some systems highly influenced the decision to consider software testing as a service. Organizations dealing with software requiring high level of domain knowledge, those dealing with mission critical systems and real-time data processing were reluctant in the idea of software testing as a service. For such organizations, a potential solution would be to have their testing infrastructure hosted as virtualization environments in private clouds. In doing so, they would maintain the control of their systems, while ensuring that testing is performed by their very own testers who have the required domain knowledge of the systems.

There are opportunities for software testing providers wanting to venture into delivering cloud-based testing services for SaaS and web-based applications. Such applications are deemed easy to test and are viable candidates for experiments and pilot projects.

Security was perceived to be an important requirement for software testing as a service. Just as with other services such as SaaS, a software test-as-a-service offering needs to be safe, bearing in mind the security of the test data and test results. The pricing of a software test-as-a-service offering should also be taken seriously. For example, Ciortea et al. (2009) describe a pricing model for their testing service whereby the users are charged according to their test goal specifications. Software testing providers have a challenge of developing transparent pricing models that truly reflect the worth of their work so as to sufficiently meet the customer expectations and enable the customer to predict costs.

While software testing as a service may offer cost cutting prospects for its customers, it may also pose the threat of customers losing control of the testing processes and resources. This would be risky for the customer in the event that the software testing provider failed to deliver the service. In addition, the customers may also lose internal software testing skills. On the other hand, due to the ability of web service APIs to conceal the complexity of the process they are running, it may result in shorter learning curves for software testing professionals (Ciortea et. al, 2009). On the overall, testing professionals would be expected to hone their skills so as to meet the demands of delivering software testing as a service.

The issue of test data needs to be resolved. It was reported that the success of some testing tasks depended on the actual customer or production data. Some rules and regulations prohibit the customers from supplying sensitive or production data to third parties. A solution to this problem may be the development of new models that would generate almost "identical" test data to facilitate productive testing results. Perhaps customers need to evaluate if their systems and platforms would by any reasonable amount be duplicated. If not, then it may mean that they would have little to worry about. With regard to problems related to differences in data governance across various geographical areas, a viable solution is to allow the customer to choose where they would like to have their data stored e.g. Amazon customers can choose between five different regions (Amazon, 2011).

The respondents' views about cloud computing were general in nature, and without in-depth experiences because most of the organizations interviewed were not using the cloud at the time of the interviews. However, between the two interview rounds, i.e. autumn 2009 and spring 2010, it could be seen that organizations were becoming more aware of cloud computing, or at least had heard about it. One unique case was that of an organization that had earlier not thought much of software testing as a service, to find itself considering delivering a SaaS-based system at the demand of its customers. This demonstrated that in some ways, the customer would have an impact on an organization's adoption or delivery of cloud-based services.

In order to understand the actual dynamics of testing in the cloud, we conducted a subsequent study comprising organizations that were already using the cloud (Riungu-Kalliosaari et. al, 2012). We studied the effects of testing in the cloud on actual testing work and on delivery and support

of testing services. The results suggest that testing in the cloud enables more efficient performance testing, shortens testing durations and generates more realistic test results. It also seems to enhance the delivery of testing services and provides access to a variety of testing tools and possibilities. When both development and testing are done in the cloud, it seems to improve interaction and communication between developers and testers.

Generally, the shift to the cloud will not only impact the delivery and consumption of software services and applications, it will also have an impact on testing. Telecommunications systems, web-based systems and those based on standards are all candidates for being tested over the internet. Various verification and validation methods were also viewed to be deliverable as software test-as-a-service offerings. Thus suggesting that software testing as a service is possible, if the challenges are addressed adequately. Testing professionals need to hone their skills so as to keep up with the new changes in technologies. On a higher level, organizations' test strategies will need to be aligned with the overall cloud strategies that might be in place.

The topic of this study is based on a rather new field of research. Practitioners seem to be aware of the changing information technology trends and some of them are gearing up for a future of cloud services. We believe that research in software testing as a service is related to SaaS research as recommended by Hertzen et al (2009). Other researchers are working on technical implementations of testing in the cloud as presented in the background section earlier. Parveen and Tilley (2010) have also given some guidelines on determining when it is safe to move to the cloud based on the type of testing to be done and depending on the application being tested. Empirical studies about testing as a service are scarce and we encourage other researchers to reflect on relevant research issues using an empirical approach. Hence, a balanced view could be achieved in understanding the dynamics of testing as a service.

CONCLUSION

In this chapter, we have presented our explorative study aimed at understanding the conditions that influence software testing as a service. Among influencing conditions were the requirements e.g. domain knowledge, infrastructure (including cloud computing) and pricing, as well as costs and flexibility among the benefits. Software testing as a service was deemed practical for web-based and telecommunications systems, as well as those based on standards. The problems associated with software testing as a service were found to include such things as data governance, testing providers' resource acquisition and change management among others. Generally, the results indicate that the trend towards software testing as a service is growing. The research areas suggested offer valuable starting points for future research.

The industry seems to be addressing cloud computing issues more than academic research is; and there is need for collaboration between the two in order to develop relevant findings. Technical implementations and empirical studies by researchers should be used to give a holistic view of software testing as a service, and to validate the results obtained. This study has presented empirical observations from 16 software organizations, most of whom were not implementing software testing as a service. We recommend future follow-up studies to involve organizations that would be using the cloud in some way so that more exhaustive observations can be made.

ACKNOWLEDGMENT

This study was supported by the ESPA-project (http://www.soberit.hut.fi/espa), funded by the Finnish Funding Agency for Technology and Innovation and by the companies mentioned in the project web site. It was also supported, in part, by SoSE – Doctoral Programme on Software and Systems Engineering (http://www.sose.oulu.fi/)

REFERENCES

Aalst, L. V. D. (2009). *Software testing as a service* (STaaS). Retrieved May 6, 2009, from http://www.tmap.net/Images/Paper%20STaaS_tcm8-47910.pdf

Amazon. (2011). *How is Amazon s3 data organized?* Retrieved April 14, 2011, from http://aws.amazon.com/s3/faqs/#How_is_Amazon_S3_data_organized.

ATLAS.ti. (2005). *The knowledge workbench.* Scientific Software Development.

Candea, G., Bufur, S., & Zamfir, C. (2010). Automated software testing as a service. *1st ACM Symposium on Cloud Computing,* (pp. 155-160).

Ciortea, L., Zamfir, C., Bucur, S., Chipounov, V., & Candea, G. (2009). *Cloud9: A software testing service.* 3rd SOSP Workshop on Large Distributed Systems and Middleware (LADIS), Big Sky, MT.

Collard, R. (2009). Performance innovations, testing implications. *Software Test & Performance Magazine, 6*(8), 19–20.

Csscorp. (2010). *Cloud based performance testing.* Retrieved February 5, 2010, from http://www.csscorp.com/product-lifecycle-services/cloud-based-performance-testing.php

Foley, J. (2009). *The cloud's next big thing: Software testing.* Retrieved September 14, 2009, from http://www.informationweek.com/cloud-computing/blog/archives/2009/06/the_clouds_next.html

Gaisbauer, S., Kirschnick, J., Edwards, N., & Roila, J. (2008). *VATS: Virtualized-aware automated test service*. 5th International Conference on Quantitative Evaluation of Systems.

Ganon, Z., & Zilberstein, I. E. (2009). Cloud-based performance testing of network management systems. *14th International Workshop on Computer Aided Modelling and Design of Communication Links and Networks*, (pp. 1-6).

Goth, G. (2008). "Googling" test practices? Web giant's culture encourages process improvement. *IEEE Software*, *25*(2), 92–94. doi:10.1109/MS.2008.28

Hanawa, T., Banzai, T., Koizumi, H., Kanbayashi, R., Imada, T., & Sato, M. (2010). Large-scale software testing environment using cloud computing technology for dependable parallel and distributed systems. *2nd International Workshop on Software Testing in the Cloud (STITC), 3rd IEEE International Conference on Software Testing, Verification and Validation (ICST)*, (pp. 428-433).

Hertzen, M. V., Laine, J., Kangasharju, S., Timonen, J., & Santala, M. (2009). Drive for future software leverage: The role, importance and future challenges of software competences in Finland. *Tekes Review, 262*.

IBM. (2010). *Infrastructure optimization services – IBM smart business test cloud*. Retrieved January 19, 2010, from http://www-935.ibm.com/services/us/index.wss/offering/midware/a1030965

Jääskeläinen, A., Katara, M., Kervinen, A., Heiskanen, H., Maunumaa, M., & Pääkkönen, T. (2008). Model-based testing service on the web. *20th IFIP TC 6/WG 6.1 International Conference on Testing of Software and Communicating Systems: 8th international Workshop, Lecture Notes in Computer Science, 5047*, (pp. 38-53).

Jun, W., & Meng, F. (2011). Software testing based on cloud computing. *2011 International Conference on Internet Computing and Information Services*, (pp. 176-178).

King, T. M., & Ganti, A. S. (2010). Migrating autonomic self-testing to the cloud. *2nd International Workshop on Software Testing in the Cloud (STITC), 3rd IEEE International Conference on Software Testing, Verification and Validation (ICST)*, (pp. 438-443).

Linthicum, D. S. (2010). *Cloud computing and SOA convergence in your enterprise: A step-by-step guide*. Upper Saddle River, NJ: Addison-Wesley.

Liu, H., & Orban, D. (2010). Remote network labs: An on-demand network cloud for configuration testing. *ACM SIGCOMM Computer Communication Review*, *40*(1), 93–101.

Oriol, M., & Ullah, F. (2010). YETI in the cloud. *2nd International Workshop on Software Testing in the cloud (STITC), 3rd IEEE International Conference on Software Testing, Verification and Validation (ICST)*, (pp. 434-437).

Parveen, T., & Tilley, S. (2010). When to migrate testing to the cloud. *2nd International Workshop on Software Testing in the cloud (STITC), 3rd IEEE International Conference on Software Testing, Verification and Validation (ICST)*, (pp. 424-427).

Riungu, L. M., Taipale, O., & Smolander, K. (2010). Research issues for software testing in the cloud. *2nd International Conference on Cloud Computing Technology and Science*, (pp. 557-564).

Riungu-Kalliosaari, L., Taipale, O., & Smolander, K. (2012). Testing in the cloud: Exploring the practice. *Special Issue on Software Engineering for the Cloud. IEEE Software*, 46–51. doi:10.1109/MS.2011.132

Robinson, P., & Ragusa, C. (2011). Taxonomy and requirements rationalization for infrastructure in cloud-based software testing. *IEEE Third International Conference on Cloud Computing Technology and Science,* (pp. 454-461).

Saucelabs. (2010). *Sauce OnDemand: Cloud testing service.* Retrieved January 27, 2010, from http://saucelabs.com/products/sauce-ondemand

SDTCorp. (2010). *Unified TestPro – Keyword driven automation and manual testing tool.* Retrieved January 25, 2010 from http://www.sdtcorp.com/utp_solution.html

Seaman, C. B. (1999). Qualitative methods in empirical studies of software engineering. *IEEE Transactions on Software Engineering, 25,* 557–572. doi:10.1109/32.799955

Sogeti. (2009). *STaaS - Software testing as a service.* Retrieved May 10, 2009, from http://www.sogeti.com/upload/Looking%20for%20Solutions/Documents/STaaS_leaflet%20v%20Feb%2009.pdf

Sogeti. (2010). *STaaS - Software testing as a service.* Retrieved January 25, 2010, from http://www.sogeti.com/looking-for-solutions/Services/Software-Control-Testing/STaaS-/

Strauss, A., & Corbin, J. (1990). *Basics of qualitative research: Grounded theory procedures and techniques.* Newbury Park, CA: SAGE Publications.

Turner, M., Budgen, D., & Brereton, P. (2003). Turning software into a service. *Computer, 36*(10), 38–44. doi:10.1109/MC.2003.1236470

Utest. (2009). *Case study: Community testing for agile-development web applications.* Retrieved May 10, 2009, from www.utest.com/download/uTestCaseStudyCommunityTestingForAgileDev.pdf

Yang, Y., Onita, C., Dhaliwal, J., & Zhang, X. (2009). TESTQUAL: Conceptualizing software testing as a service. *15th Americas Conference on Information Systems,* San Francisco, California, USA, paper 608.

Yu, L., Tsai, W. T., Chen, X., Liu, L., Zhao, Y., Tang, L., & Zhao, W. (2010). *Testing as a service over cloud.* 5th IEE International Symposium on Service Oriented System Engineering.

ADDITIONAL READING

Ananth, B. (2010). *Testing cloud and testing using cloud.* Retrieved 16 August, 2010, from http://www.sonatasoftware.com/export/sites/Sonata/sonata_en/innovation/resources/articles/pdfs/Cloud_Testing.pdf

AppLabs. (2007). *Testing the cloud.* Retrieved April 18, 2011, from http://www.qaguild.com/upload/app_whitepaper_testing_the_cloud_1v00.pdf

AppLabs. (2008). *Future of software testing.* Retrieved April 18, 2011, from http://www.applabs.com/ap-private/pdf-download/3263%3Fnid%3D569%2526Print%3Dpdf

AppLabs. (2009). *Approach to cloud testing.* Retrieved April 18, 2011, from http://www.applabs.com/html/download_Knowledgecenter.html/3238?nid=19

Dubey, A., & Wagle, D. (2007, May). Delivering software as a service. *The McKinsey Quarterly.* Retrieved April 20, 2011, from http://www.mckinsey.de/downloads/publikation/mck_on_bt/2007/mobt_12_Delivering_Software_as_a_Service.pdf

Durkee, D. (2010). Why cloud computing may never be free. *Communications of the ACM, 53*(5), 62–69. doi:10.1145/1735223.1735242

Eisenhardt, K. M. (1989). Building theories from case study research. *Academy of Management Review, 14*(4), 532–550.

Girmonsky, A. (2009). *Cloud-testing*. White Paper. Retrieved April 18, 2011, from http://www.cloud-intelligence.com/sites/www.cloud-intelligence.com/files/Cloud%20Testing%20White%20Paper_0.pdf

Gleeson, E. (2010). *Computing industry set for a shocking change*. Retrieved April 20, 2010, from http://www.moneyweek.com/investment-advice/computing-industry-set-for-a-shocking-change-43226.aspx

Gold, N., Mohan, A., Knight, C., & Munro, M. (2004). Understanding service-oriented software. *IEEE Software, 1*(2), 71–77. doi:10.1109/MS.2004.1270766

Haines, M. N., & Rotherberger, M. A. (2010). How a service-oriented architecture may change the software development process. *Communications of the ACM, 53*(8), 135–140. doi:10.1145/1787234.1787269

Louridas, P. (2010). Up in the air: Moving your applications to the cloud. *IEEE Software, 27*(4), 6–11. doi:10.1109/MS.2010.109

McFedries, P. (2008). The cloud is the computer. *IEEE Spectrum Online, Electronic Magazine*. Retrieved October 6, 2010, from http://www.spectrum.ieee.org/aug08/6490

Mylavarapu, V. K., & Inamdar, M. (2011). *Taking testing to the cloud*. Retrieved April 18, 2011, from http://www.cognizant.com/InsightsWhitepapers/Taking-Testing-to-the-Cloud.pdf

Spirent. (2010). *The ins and outs of cloud computing and its impact on the network*. Retrieved June 10, 2010, from http://www.spirent.com/White-Papers/Broadband/PAB/Cloud_Computing_WhitePaper.aspx

Torode, C. (2009). *Tapping the cloud as a software testing service*. Retrieved April 18, 2011, from http://searchcio-midmarket.techtarget.com/news/1356175/Tapping-the-cloud-as-a-software-testing-service

Utest. (2010). *What we test*. Retrieved June 9, 2010, from http://www.utest.com/what-we-test

Vaquero, L. M., Rodero-Merino, L., Caceres, J., & Lindner, M. (2009). A break in the clouds: Towards a cloud definition. *ACM SIGCOMM Computer Communications Review, 39*(1), 50–55. doi:10.1145/1496091.1496100

Weiss, A. (2007). Computing in the clouds. *netWorker, 11*(4), 16–25. doi:10.1145/1327512.1327513

KEY TERMS AND DEFINITIONS

Cloud Computing: A model for enabling convenient, on-demand network access to a shared pool of configurable computing resources (e.g. networks, servers, storage, application and services) that can be rapidly provisioned and released with minimal management effort or service provider interaction (Taken from the US National Institute of Standards and Technology (NIST) definition).

Online Service: Software applications and systems which are delivered mainly through the internet. This includes parts of the software development life cycle such as testing.

Software Testing: A process performed as part of the software development life cycle. It is done to ensure the validity and correctness of the software. Many definitions exist. One of them is: Testing is verification and validation (Kit, E., (1995). Software Testing in the Real World: Improving the Process).

Chapter 10
Using the Cloud for Testing NOT Adjunct to Development

W. Morven Gentleman
Computers for People, Canada

ABSTRACT

Software testing, whether performed by the software development organization itself or on behalf of the software development organization by an independent testing organization, is typically described in the literature as part of the development or maintenance process for the purpose of improving the quality of the software product (i.e. finding and removing defects). Nevertheless, interested parties other than the software development organization perform software testing for reasons other than finding and removing defects, and such testing can be facilitated when the software is available as a service in the cloud. Unfortunately, access to software only as a service in the cloud can inhibit certain kinds of testing. In this chapter, the author discusses who such other interested parties might be, what they intend to learn from software testing, and what some of the techniques are they might use.

WHAT IS SOFTWARE TESTING?

This chapter focuses on the opportunities that are created by testing of software that is offered as a service in the cloud. (Software testing could itself be offered as a service in the cloud, but this chapter does not address that.) Software testing is the empirical systematic scientific investigation of a specific existing software artifact. Most commonly, software testing is dynamic in that it involves execution of the software under test, although use of tools to perform static analysis of the software under test is also software testing. Dynamic testing enables examination of the behavior of the software artifact on one particular execution, with particular input in a particular environment. Software that can be available as a service in the cloud opens up the possibility of dynamic testing of that software by many different interested parties. Static testing enables the examination of the behavior in any possible execution, with any possible input in any possible environment. Unfortunately, the access enabled to most software provided as a service in the

DOI: 10.4018/978-1-4666-2536-5.ch010

cloud prevents such static testing. Persistent data for such software in many cases could be made part of the service-offering tool-accessible in the cloud without undue risk. Whether the manual inspection of a software artifact should also be considered software testing is more contentious. Are the results of manual inspection reproducible, systematic and scientific or merely anecdotal? For Software as a Service, what manual inspection might be plausible?

Software testing is primarily intended to reveal attributes and behavior of the software itself. Sometimes, however, what we need to explore is the behavior and reactions of people when they have to work with that software. We will elaborate on this later. When the software is accessed as a service in the cloud, the people being studied can be anywhere, and the observations can be made at any time, which can be enormously advantageous.

Since software testing is empirical, we need to consider what kind of experiments might be performed, what observations might be made, and how such observations might be analyzed, as well as how the results should be interpreted. Software as a Service in the cloud can affect these.

Risk-based testing is a unifying notion: all software testing can be viewed as risk reduction. A test must enable reduction of some risk for someone. Risks do not relate only to software developers. Other interested parties are often referred to as stakeholders. Unfortunately, many authors restrict the use of the term "stakeholder" to those with financial interest in the product, whereas many interested parties have interest that is not strictly financial, so for increased generality we will stick to the term "other interested parties". Different interested parties are concerned about different risks, and both the potential damage and the associated probability of occurrence differ for different interested parties even for a risk of the same event.

Defects represent a significant risk to software development organizations. If there are too many defects, or if there are defects that are too serious, the software development organization may not be able to ship the product. In a custom development contract, the client may not accept the product due to defects. For commercial software products, a reputation for buggy software can affect future sales even if the actual known defects are not that relevant. The developer may be liable for damages due to faults. And so on. However, for software development organizations the risk of defects is manageable, in that the developer can make investments to locate and repair defects.

Other interested parties, such as potential customers, are not in a position to repair defects nor are they motivated to do so. These parties are generally more interested in identifying, counting, and summarizing defects than in locating specific defects. That is, their interest is in the consequences of working with the software under test despite its defects. They may be interested in defect density, i.e. which aspects of the software seem to be associated with more bugs, and which aspects seem relatively bug free. Defect density may influence the use of aspects of the software. We shall explore who some of these interested parties may be, and what they hope to learn from testing the software. Note that when interested parties are not part of the development process, getting access to the software in order to learn about it is often a major challenge, which makes the software being available in the cloud as a service very appealing.

Software as a Service has the distinct advantage when performing testing that the testers do not need to have direct access to the source code or the executables of the software under test and do not need to install that software on their own execution platform. Unless the hardware execution platform is being co-developed, the software development organization normally installs the software on their own platforms as it is being produced; in the co-development situation standard practice is to use simulators. On the other hand, not having access to the software itself or to the execution platform (let alone to the source code for the software) restricts what can be tested and the kinds of software testing that other interested parties can perform. We need to examine testing techniques that work or don't work for Software as a Service. Traditional black-box testing (i.e. where test cases consist only of supplying input to the software in order to detect failures by observing and analyzing the results) is an obvious candidate technique that could work – we will show that there are more.

BACKGROUND

Traditional software testing (Myers, 1979) not only was merely an adjunct to software development; it was framed in the context of contract custom software development. It was intended to eliminate software defects, which were then regarded as any violation of the software specification. The contrapositive assertion is more revealing: unless the software under test conflicted with the software specification, and in particular if the specification was silent on an issue, then there was no defect, regardless of how extremely arcane the behavior or the attribute of the software was. This may have made sense at the time. However, the rise of the commercial software product industry (where the same product is sold to many different customers, with few if any playing any role whatsoever in developing the specification or even being aware of it (Kaner, 1996)) makes this a poor choice of context, quite unlike the consumer protection applied in other industries. More modern definitions of a bug are typically broader: a bug is something someone who matters does not like about the software, regardless of the specification. Such a modern definition raises the interesting issue of an oracle: how should one decide what one should expect of the software?

Three types of software testing have long gone beyond defect detection in that they are not normally framed as pass/fail criteria: 1) software performance testing, 2) software stress testing, and 3) software security testing. The purpose of software performance testing is normally to establish a quantitative model (a model usually parameterized by offered load and background activity) for predicting performance measures such as throughput, response time, or resource consumption. The purpose of stress testing is to establish that the system degrades gracefully when it is operated outside the operating environment normally anticipated. The purpose of security testing is to expose vulnerabilities whereby an attacker can exploit unauthorized access to compromise the confidentiality, integrity, authentication, availability, authorization and non-repudiation of information, or can hijack the software to perform unauthorized actions (Potter, 2004).

The software development organization may choose to engage in human-oriented software testing specific to the product under development. Usability testing (first used by Intuit (Taylor, 2003) p. 22) facilitates improvement in user satisfaction with the resulting software product. Globalization testing establishes whether the product is suitable for an international marketplace. Testing productivity improvements among developers can guide tool adoption for accomplishing this project. Testing quality and rate of work completion can provide guidance on staffing issues not only for developers, but also for customer support - such as maintenance groups, installers, help desk call centers, and so on. Such staffing guidance can suggest optimum team size in different categories as well as required skills. If necessary skills are not available the guidance can suggest training requirements. The availability of the product as a service in the cloud is not really necessary for any of this, but it could help the conduct of the testing for those research subjects who are physically remote.

BROADENED PERSPECTIVES

Other Interested Parties

Beyond the software development organization, other interested parties who could possibly use testing on Software as a Service include the following.

1. Potential Customers

Potential customers (business units more likely than individuals) choosing among alternate products and services are commonplace in today's competitive marketplace. Procurement decisions are influenced by many factors, such as price, customer service level, corporate stability, or availability of trained staff. A fit with the customer's culture and practices is particularly important. Depending on the scale, the adoption of a system, framework or even just an application can be a major long-term commitment, and software customers are prepared to make an investment in understanding the implications of a particular choice. Marketing blurbs and sales pitches rarely provide enough detail to make an informed decision, and moreover, they often cannot be taken at face value. Experience with the actual product is essential, and so pilot studies using that particular software artifact, as a service in the cloud, is an attractive option. Benchmarking has traditionally been important, but given the scalability of modern information technology solutions, capacity on a single specific platform is no longer such an overwhelming consideration. This is especially true because processing performance achievable on a "representative" workload through optimization by vendor's expert personnel is a poor predictor of typical operational experience. Nevertheless, throughput and response time indications are interesting. Failure rates and defect density might also be relevant. Difficulties found in restoration of service after an outage can be revealing. Workarounds can keep most individual defects

from being showstoppers. Moreover, within any category of software, such as ERP (Enterprise Resource Planning) systems, GIS (Geographic Information Systems), or even Email, the differences between nominally equivalent alternatives are so profound that only empirical evidence, such as that provided by usability testing based on the software customer's business processes, is helpful. Generic testing by the supplier is not sufficiently discerning to allow the potential customer to make a decision.

2. Configuration Selectors

Once a system is chosen, selecting a configuration is another valuable use by software customers (current or potential) for Software as a Service. When a particular software product is offered in the cloud as Software as a Service, the vendor typically has made all configuration choices, so a customer of that product has no option to explore choices. Virtual machine service offerings (Platform as a Service in the cloud), on the other hand, enable studies of the same software on different hardware configurations with respect to performance, reliability, and capacity, because software today is generally scalable across a range of hardware configurations and may even be platform independent. Sizing and capacity planning decisions still need to be made, and despite the noted obsolescence of benchmarking shootouts, performance testing on virtual machines in order to answer what-if questions can be insightful. More seriously, software today often has configurable (typically separately priced) functionality, and the customer has to choose which components to include (SAP ERP is one well known example, Blackboard Learn is another). Value to the customer can vary, as can design and implementation quality. Third-party alternatives to some components may have advantages over native ones. Again testing to support configuration decisions is mainly usability testing, with some attention to failure rates and defect density. In short, a product customer can make a rich investigation of configuration options if they can find a supplier in the cloud who chooses to offer virtual machines to support the range of configurations of the product.

3. Change Management Planners

Software customers (current and potential) need to test new features with their users in order to assess what training and change management activities will be required before general rollout – results obviously specific to their particular organization. Such pilot studies can be awkward and disruptive if imposed on their normal enterprise service. Conducting such pilots on decoupled Software as a Service systems is a possible option, but access to shared data and interoperation with other systems can mean that isolation of pilot studies is unrealistic.

4. Systems Integrators

Today few systems live in isolation. System integrators have the challenge to make a new system interoperate with the existing systems that it must mesh with. Generally the system integrators have had no involvement in implementing any of the systems that they must interface, nor were they involved in choosing the systems – they instead are merely responsible for creating the glue to hold these systems together. In bringing together systems of systems (Meier, 1998), it is not uncommon to find that the component subsystems were never designed to work with other systems, so that each system suffers from the "center of the universe" symptom and believes that any accommodation must be made by the others. More seriously, systems being combined may not be under the control of the client, and their autonomy and other responsibilities may not be submerged after integration. Systems Integration is easier now that many systems (perhaps even systems that are services in the cloud) are net-centric and use service-oriented architecture (SOA). Nev-

ertheless, documentation is often inadequate or obsolete, so the main need for testing is to examine what has gone wrong with attempted integration and to investigate how the integration can be improved. Particularly important is the recovery and restoration of a service after disruptions. Such experiments are most readily conducted if the services are accessed from the cloud.

5. Service Operators Engaging Fallback Capability

For many services provided through the cloud, it is expected that the service operator will provide a Service Level Agreement (SLA). Disruptions and outages often cannot be avoided, so meeting a SLA requires engaging fallback capability Unless the service provider is sufficiently large to be able to support their own internal fallback capacity, fallback involves establishing a relationship with a third party, perhaps even a competitor, to cover such contingencies. Practice drills, with testing to examine sensitive criteria, must be done regularly either to confirm that a current fallback arrangement continues to be satisfactory or to establish that a potential fallback arrangement will indeed be so. Such drills can take advantage of virtualization and scalability in the cloud.

6. Operational Issues for Current Customers

Current customers of a software product are primarily concerned about operational issues. Is the size of their current operational staff appropriate to run the service, or should it be increased or decreased? Have the operational issues for an upgrade been practiced enough that it is ready for prime time, or are there change management activities that need to be in place? Can growth or reduction in load be predicted well enough that adjustment can be planned in advance in order to avoid crisis? What about changes in usage patterns – can they be anticipated? Continuous monitoring and testing are essential to keep on top of such issues. Specific testing to address such questions is called operations testing. Employing services in the cloud to supplement corporate facilities can reduce the impact of pilot studies on mandated responsibilities.

7. Regulators

Regulators are a fact of life in many industries – corporate decisions and practices cannot be implemented until sanctioned by an independent official body (FAA, FCC, and FDA are but three well-known examples). Regulatory approval is typically based on on-going inspections and reviews, but most significantly by testing. It is vital for regulators to be seen to be independent, but regrettably in some industries, the agencies do not have access to staff or facilities, or even to the regulated products and services in order to perform their own testing. Instead, they must require the regulated organizations to perform and report on specified tests. Regulators typically are uncomfortable about this. Apart from suspicions of overt dishonesty by the regulated organizations, the mechanism is cumbersome and susceptible to missing occasional anomalies. If the software under test is made available as a service from the cloud, the regulators are in a better position to perform their testing themselves, or to contract third parties to do it for them.

8. Certifiers

Some software is widely used but is available in versions from many different suppliers. It has sufficient complexity that individual end-users are not likely to have the competence to test it for themselves and are not likely to make the effort to try to do so. They must take the software on faith, or accept certification by some authority. Tax preparation software is a perfect example. Some suppliers provide it online as a service, others sell it to be run on the user's own computer.

There is obviously risk to the users if the software malfunctions, but there is also risk to the tax collection agency – improperly prepared returns, or improperly submitted returns, could disrupt the agency's computerized filing process especially at peak filing dates. The Canada Revenue Agency (CRA) therefore maintains a web page of certified Netfile products (Certified Software, 2012), which it has certified as acceptable to use. The CRA has no role in development of these products, and may not even be able to run the software on its own computers. Certification by CRA involves testing which is much easier when the products are available as a service in the cloud.

9. Trainees

Trainees learning to work with a software product require not just documentation and theory to work from, but also access to the software itself, in order to gain a gut level, in-depth understanding of the product, especially its dynamic effects. Software testing is used to resolve ambiguity, observe transient and ephemeral effects, and appreciate internal implications of apparently innocuous effects that may be unintuitive. This exposure to the software in use can be done with Software as a Service in the cloud. The load generated by a single trainee is likely to be light, so Pay-per-use pricing is essential.

10. Instructors

Instructors intending to teach about a software product also require access to that product in order to develop familiarity that will allow them to choose what to emphasize, to prepare them to answer questions, and to help them avoid being blindsided by discrepancies between the documentation and the behavior of the actual software artifact. This kind of testing is largely exploratory black-box testing (Kaner et al, 2001; Whittaker 2002), with many of the questions of what next to investigate being driven by what has been seen so far. Defects are not likely to be of much interest, although anomalies might be. A serious challenge for instructors (as well as, to a lesser extent, for trainees and some of the other interested parties mentioned earlier) is that Software as a Service is not by itself enough: many software artifacts can only be understood and appreciated in the context of persistent data, often massive persistent data. Relational databases are but one form of persistent data; others include repositories of music, photographs, video, documents, blueprints, maps, scientific data, etc. The instructor is not likely to own such persistent data himself – Data as a Service is an essential complement to the Software as a Service.

11. Competitors

Competitors may seem unlikely candidates for a software developer to want to test his product. Standardization activities, however, can produce strange bedfellows. In these circumstances we have seen occasions where a software development organization has been keen to encourage competitors to become intimate with the development organization's product, and software testing is the best way to do this. For the standard a supplier may want to promote the features of his product version, the persistent data of his implementation as a representation for problem interchange, his user interface as the prototype for further enhancements and even his algorithms to characterize solution properties. To persuade competitors to support his proposals, it is key that he familiarizes them with his product, and the experience of testing it can be convincing. Exposure to that product through the controlled access of Software as a Service in the cloud would be a useful vehicle for buttressing standardization arguments. Of course competitors are likely to want to gather the competitive intelligence of better understanding of the products of others.

Outsider Testing of Software as a Service

Software as a Service can be provided in either of two forms. The service can be offered directly to an end-user at a browser (or other device, e.g., a smartphone). Online completion and filing of a personal income tax return is an example. The other form is a web service to be used directly in a service-oriented-architecture (SOA) by other software running on different computers attached to the Internet. GIS capabilities offered through the National Spatial Data Infrastructure and the Canadian Geospatial Data Infrastructure are examples.

Any conventional software testing tools and techniques can be used for testing Software as a Service by or on behalf of the software developer. The web site operator providing Software as a Service also has great flexibility in choosing software testing tools and techniques. One technique that has garnered lots of attention from researchers, web site operators, and testing companies is remote usability testing (Scholtz, 2001; Gardner, 2007). Another technique is to run the Software as a Service inside a virtual machine that can monitor for unauthorized external access that might expose a security violation.

For the interested parties discussed in the previous section - outsiders who are neither the software developers nor the operators of the Software as a Service web site used - testing options are more limited. They can only test by making service requests of the Software as a Service and analyzing the results. This is not unlike black-box testing, and indeed most black-box testing fits. Putting instrumentation and data logging into the browser from which the service request is made, or into the client program that makes the service requests, facilitates test automation. The biggest challenge is not the absence of a specification, nor the lack of source code. Rather it is restricted access to the machines on which the software is running. Of course, service requests and results need not be considered individually. The aggregate effect of many requests, or the effects on requests of background load, can provide additional information. For instance, a study (of which (Walters, 2002) was part) of operations in an email server revealed much aggregate behavior that can be learned without being able to instrument the code of the mail server itself.

Although the inaccessibility of source code to these interested parties makes much conventional structural testing (Jorgensen, 2007) impossible, software architecture is sometimes accessible to these interested parties, or can be plausibly conjectured. This means that architectural-based testing (Richardson, 1996) can sometimes be an option, especially with SOA, standard components and instrumented middleware. Conventional coverage measures are described in terms of source code structure, and so not available without source code, but alternative coverage measures can be expressed in terms of functionality and known or conjectured architecture.

Workaround testing is important to systems operators, systems integrators, end-users, and even the supplier's systems maintainers because all but the last are in no position to repair a known failure (indeed the underlying fault may not be known) and there is often time pressure to address the situation quickly before a fix can be found. For example, in Apple's iLife release 11, a bug had been noted in the iPhoto subsystem that when a sequence of images and tunes are exported as a Quicktime movie, the movie plays only the first tune, repeating it over and over as the sequence of images is presented. (This functionality had not failed in previous releases.) The user group found a workaround whereby if the sequence of images was exported from iPhoto as a silent Qucktime move, that silent movie then imported to a different subsystem, GarageBand, and the tunes added to the movie there at this point, then the combined images and sound exported to a Quicktime movie from GarageBand, the resulting movie played correctly.

Testing workarounds are different from most other defect testing, in that defect testing usually examines software with no known failures to discover whether there might be a hidden fault. Workaround testing, on the other hand, tests software with a known failure to investigate whether an alternate process for accomplishing the same desired result will avoid triggering the known failure. Without access to the source code, even finding potential workarounds is challenging, let alone confirming that a postulated workaround actually exercises an independent path. Standard black box testing techniques, such as boundary test cases, equivalence classes, or all-pairs test cases, focus on exploring the domain of a particular functionality regarded as a function. Workarounds, by comparison, typically focus on the various different functionalities offered by the software, to find out if they can be combined in some less obvious way in order to achieve the desired result when the documented way approach is known to fail.

Unfortunately, the lack of access to source code, design and specification mean that known techniques for searching for security vulnerabilities (Potter, 2004) are not open to the interested parties considered here. Black-box testing has a role in security testing, but suspicions of what to look for have to come from somewhere, perhaps bitter experience.

Conventional Black-Box Testing

Conventional black-box testing is a powerful and versatile context in which to choose tests, whether testing on behalf of the software development organization or on behalf of other interested parties. It can test functional and non-functional properties. Black-box testing facilitates many types of testing and many strategies for choosing test cases.

Error guessing is a practical approach for choosing test cases. Lists of common design and coding defects are available to suggest hints, but we are unaware of any with an associated corresponding statistical probability of risk. Moreover, what would be very useful (and is definitely not available) would be to have such risks weighted by developer, and by category of application.

In the belief that many defects occur at or near boundaries of a function's domain, boundary value analysis is frequently used to suggest test cases. A related belief is that defects at or near a function's domain boundary are readily recognized because the range of function values corresponding to the boundary of the domain has distinctive properties. Boundary value testing thus usually suggests testing values on the boundary together with nearby values both inside and outside the boundary. Although boundary value analysis can identify and locate defects, transitions between regions of the domain where different formulaic representations of required computation are used is exactly a situation where the software developer is likely to have thoroughly examined with unit testing, so it is less likely that integration testing, system testing, or the kind of outsider testing considered here will turn up anything new.

It is widely recognized that exhaustive testing is infeasible, so it is essential to reduce the number of necessary test cases. Equivalence partitioning is an effective way to do this: there is no need to run more than one test from a partition of the input domain for which what could possibly be learned from any two tests would be equivalent. The hitch is that except for trivial applications, identifying potential test cases that truly are equivalent is nontrivial. For example, how to know that rendering two different map images might not trigger different alarms?

Again, reducing the number of potential tests is essential in the common situation where there is more than a single input, perhaps a great many inputs. The effects of the different input items may well not be independent. One way to investigate at least pair-wise interactions is All Pairs testing. This can be done with other statistical advantages

by choosing test cases using the Orthogonal Array Testing Strategy (OATS).

Decision Table testing is a systematic way of organizing all the different situations that software must address. Each column represents a particular situation. Each row at the top of the table represents a condition by which the situations can be distinguished. Each row at the bottom of the table represents an action that must be taken in that situation. The display helps to avoid ambiguous situations, and helps to avoid situations being overlooked. The cells in the table suggest test cases and observations that should be made on those test cases.

Test cases should be created both for valid and for invalid input. Robustness testing checks that the violation of assumptions made in the software does not have catastrophic effect. (This might also provide insight into exception handling.) Confirmation that input is checked for consistency should be tested and, since input is often provided incrementally, that suggestions made for possible choices of input yet to be provided should be tested to show that they are consistent with input already entered. Volume tests check that the ability to handle large workloads has not been overlooked. Stress testing establishes that excessive loads lead only to graceful degradation rather than catastrophic failures.

When the software under test progresses through several discernable states, it can be useful to do navigation testing, state transition testing, and testing to enable cause-effect graphing.

Comparison testing of the behavior of the software under test relative to other similar software has direct relevance to the other interested parties as well as to the software development organization.

Availability to the software under test through Software as a Service is sufficient for all such conventional black-box testing.

Beyond Conventional Black-Box Testing

The definition we have given for black-box testing reflects the way it is often described in the literature and used in practice. We find this unnecessarily restrictive, especially for testing conducted by or on behalf of other interested parties instead of merely on behalf of the software development organization. The following discussion all relates to what can be learned without access to knowledge of the internal workings of the software under test.

Black-box testing is often described as equivalent to functional testing. Black-box testing is also often described as being equivalent to behavioral testing. This implies that the software must be run and do something so the dynamic properties can be observed. That may not even be necessary – static properties may suffice. As an example, consider testing a particular localization of globalized software. To the software vendor this is just one more localization instance, but to the operations staff of the product or service it can be essential. Just as localization is rarely done by the original software development organization (because doing so requires familiarity with the linguistic and cultural issues of that locale), testing of localization likewise can only be done by testers who are sensitive to the linguistic and cultural issues of that locale. Translation of text and dates is not good enough. Is a translated idiom still appropriate? Is an image that works for another localization still appropriate? Does a video clip convey the same connotation? Does multimedia translate and synchronize? Does a particular query make sense in the context of that locale? (Educational qualifications, street addresses, and even telephone number formats, for instance, differ between countries.) Might something be considered impolite or insensitive? Does page or screen layout still fit, or do overlaps occlude essential clues? What represents "good enough" localization will vary from one interested party to

another, and perhaps even for the same interested party from one situation to another.

This example also illustrates another unnecessary limitation of conventional black-box testing. Some testers, and many writers about testing, insist on expressing all tests in Pass/Fail terms, rather than with quantitative or qualitative assessment, even when these are more natural and more informative. It is possible to imagine that in a custom contractual development, the software development organization and the client might come to agree on some arbitrary acceptance value of a particular metric, but it is unlikely that a common value would be satisfactory to all interested parties. Load testing and performance testing illustrate this well. Load is often too complex to represent by a single variable, and performance too complex to represent by a single metric. For example, consider load or performance testing of an email client or email server. We might agree to measure performance by the time to read or send a message, but we need to remember that these depend on the length of the message and the background activity on the host computer. Moreover, with a modern HTML message, the times will depend on how elaborate the message is, and whether there are URLs of objects to be accessed and incorporated in the display. Attachments in various MIME formats will also have an effect. Statistical and exploratory data analysis techniques can be used to fit mathematical models with all these factors to experimental observations, then to determine how well these functional models fit and how accurately further observations can be predicted. Such experimentally-based predictive models are much more valuable to interested parties than pass/fail test results.

There is an unstated assumption behind much of conventional black-box testing that all the control variables (i.e. all the input) are under the tester's control, so that when the tester provides the same input the same results will be produced. For many software products this deterministic behavior is not the case. Software that monitors and reacts to online input, such as medical instrumentation or automation for stock market "buy and sell" orders, very often does not have provision for testers to instead provide this online input directly, and hence testing must be done with live real data. This typically means that test results may not be reproducible.

Another situation where results may not be reproducible is with human-oriented software testing. Consider usability testing. This is not GUI testing, i.e. confirming that the graphic widgets and controls function as intended. Anyone who thinks usability testing can be phrased in pass/fail terms has missed the point. Usability testing is a measurement-based (local or remote measurement) quantitative and qualitative study of individual interactive end-users, and how effectively they are able to use the software under test. It includes how hard it is for the end-user to learn how to use the software, but encompasses much more than that. How accessible is the software to users with disabilities (now legally required in some countries for some software (England, 1996))? Which displays prove to be confusing, and take excessive time to assimilate? Which actions prove to be unnecessarily tedious and error-prone? Will a layout choice cause confusion because it conflicts with analogous choices in other systems or in earlier versions of this one? Which actions are ambiguous and trigger reference to help-facilities? How many mouse clicks or keystrokes are required to accomplish a commonly used task? Is the count of page-turnings used to collect answers to questions excessive? Are the foci of attention too widely separated, as detected by eye-tracking? Which displays force the user to employ magnification? Which actions are aborted and repeated? Would alternate skins improve usability for certain classes of interactive end-users? Is there functionality that should be masked from certain classes of interactive users? Should mash-ups be used to integrate functionality from unrelated service offerings? In a contractual custom software development context, the customer might well use such detailed information to require design changes. In the commercial software product context, the other interested parties are more likely to use this information to make product choices, to anticipate erroneous input, to manage work assignments, to assess staffing levels, or to plan training.

Similar to usability testing, but at the organizational rather than the interactive end-user level, black-box testing can be used to assess whether a particular software product really is effective for that organization. Is all the required input data readily available in the specified format, how well do the provided options match the business practices of that organizational unit, how much effort will it take to make use of the results as produced by the software, how well does the scale of the software product correspond to the scale of activity of that business unit. Could pre-processing or post-processing improve the fit? What persistent data would be worth maintaining, what archiving should be performed for business and legal reasons? Conducting such what-if studies is much more intuitive if the software product can actually be used as Software as a Service. Potential roadblocks are better found by trial runs than by hypothetical reasoning. IS benchmarking is often carried out by comparing metrics for one organization with those of others performing similar functions.

Operation testing is another type of human oriented testing. This can be hard to test by black-box testing on Software as a Service because service providers often only choose to offer their service to end-users and go out of their way to hide operational considerations, thereby making it difficult to do Recovery testing (let alone Disaster Recovery testing), Install/Uninstall testing, Compatibility testing, Concurrency testing, Race Condition testing, or Reliability testing in response to an operational profile of concurrent requests). Some of these can be inferred from results of concurrent requests from multiple sources (Zhang,

2007), there is no reason black-box testing need be restricted to single tests conducted in isolation. Nevertheless Operations testing is more straightforward in the cloud if the service provider offers the software product through Software as a Service at more levels than just end-user.

Issues, Controversies, Problems

Today only large enterprises can afford to maintain an internal software development organization that is strong enough for a software "make or buy" decision as a realistic alternative. Few of these maintain an internal independent testing group strong enough to assure quality in internal software systems. Too often, testing is limited to unit testing conducted by developers. Hence adequate testing often means testing is outsourced to a specialized testing supplier. Companies in the software development industry itself are more likely to maintain their own independent internal testing group for their products, but even in this case it is commonplace to outsource to a specialized testing supplier. Smaller companies today mostly buy software products or buy Software as a Service from the cloud. Customers too often take software development organization testing at face value, or even worse ignore it, trusting that the developers will have done all that is needed. Although we are aware of customer organizations practicing software testing by other interested parties as described here, this is largely a nascent business opportunity yet to be followed up.

Solutions and Recommendations

As the commercial software product marketplace continues to grow, and as the service marketplace in the cloud continues to expand, testing will increasingly become an issue more for other interested parties than for a software development organization with its unique contractual customer. Built-in test facilities are commonplace for other products and have been used for decades to aid installation of software products. Built-in test could be provided to meet the needs of other interested parties. Software as a Service aimed as easing software testing by other interested parties could be another marketing come-on. Software vendors today often provide a free trial period to encourage adoption of their products. Service offerings of software products not just as Software as a Service and not just at the interactive end-user level will facilitate testing by other interested parties. Instrumentation built into browsers and middleware to support client/server and SOA will facilitate broader automation of testing by other interested parties. There will be a role for more courses on software testing than are available now - at universities, from commercial training organizations, and especially from online e-learning suppliers - for students to learn effective testing practices.

In the spirit of "let a hundred flowers bloom" and "more players in a marketplace validates for all the existence of such a market," marketers and designers of a new entrant into a competitive marketplace need to use competitive intelligence to develop an understanding of how to position their product. Part of collecting such competitive intelligence is the ability to test products already available.

CONCLUSION

Software testing has often been presented as the exclusive domain of the software development organization. There are other interested parties who want independent software testing directed at issues relevant to them, especially in competitive situations of commercial software products or Software as a Service offerings.

Software testing is often presented in the context of contract custom software development, where conformance to specification is the one and only issue. There are other contexts in which conformance to specification is irrelevant, because the concerns of stakeholders and other interested parties go beyond issues represented in the contractual specification.

Software testing is often presented as pass/fail activities intended to identify and locate defects. There are many circumstances in which quantitative and qualitative results are more informative, and where there are other objectives beyond defect detection.

Software testing is often presented as focused solely on features of the software itself. There is much software testing that is focused on the way people interact with the software under test.

Testing in the Cloud emphasizes that access for software testing to services and products through the cloud, even to partial and unfinished products can be of immense value to other interested parties and so ultimately to the software development organization itself.

Are Today's Cloud Services Up To It?

From the perspective of interested parties outside the development process, the benefits of using software as a service when it is available are convincing, and such testers will try to make do with whatever capabilities they are given. For them, whether today's cloud services are up to this kind of testing is not so much a question of capabilities and mechanisms as a question of current offerings on public and private clouds.

There are many definitions for cloud computing. (Vaquero et al, 2009). Commercial cloud offerings, from Amazon Web Services to Microsoft Live to Google Cloud Services to Apple iCloud to Rackspace Cloud Servers to Skytap Cloud and so forth are just as diverse. Some of these do not normally provide Software as a Service, but some do. The business model of many Service Providers seems to be that Software as a Service means providing a coherent suite of apps to an isolated end-user for his or her production use. (Indeed, Microsoft criticized its own Live Essentials for

the included apps not fitting together well enough. (Sinofsky, 2012)) This business model does support some testers for interested parties outside the development process examining some software products and answering some of the questions discussed above, but it has many mismatches with others. To start with, what we have discussed is testing arbitrary software products, and this model does not suggest a business case for service providers to provide arbitrary software products. Perhaps a more plausible business model would be for vendors of different software products to field them on the vendor's own private clouds as part of marketing and promotion campaigns. (However, this raises the workplace issue of interacting with multiple clouds). Vendor-supported private clouds could resolve another mismatch: testing usually involves relatively light usage, which with Pay-as-you-go pricing implies testing would be a limited revenue stream in the first business model, not warranting much specific investment to license and install alternate software products. Testing apps that involve massive customer-specific data likely raises issues of interacting clouds in order for the app to access the data, or for interacting apps to access each other. Another mismatch is that individual end-users want scalability and platform choice to be automatic and hidden, whereas non-development testing may deliberately involve controlled variation of these factors (meaning there might be a better match with providers of Infrastructure as a Service or Platform as a Service than with providers of Software as a Service). Yet another blatant mismatch is that some of the suggested investigations explicitly address issues for operations staff, who are deliberately hidden in the isolated end-user only business model. Moreover, operational testing may require cloud services going beyond isolated end-users to support interacting groups of users.

Consequently, although testing in the cloud may be technically possible and attractive, the business context needs to evolve for it to be a widespread practical reality. Cloud characteristics such as Resource Heterogeneity, Virtualization, Internet Centric, and User-Friendliness are largely immaterial to this.

REFERENCES

Canada Revenue Agency. (2012). *Certified software*. Retrieved May 31, 2012, from http://netfile. gc.ca/sftwr-eng.html

England, E., & Finney, A. (1996). *Managing multimedia*. Harlow, UK: Addison Wesley.

Gardner, J. (2007). Remote web site usability testing – Benefits over traditional methods. *International Journal of Public Information Systems*, *2*, 63–72.

Horgan, J. R., & Mathur, A. P. (1995). Software testing and reliability. In Lyu, M. R. (Ed.), *Handbook of software reliability engineering* (pp. 531–566). McGraw-Hill.

Jorgensen, P. (2007). *Software testing: A craftsman's approach* (3rd ed.). Boca Raton, FL: Auerbach Publications.

Kaner, C. (1996). What is a software defect? *Software Q&A, 3*(6). Retrieved April 2, 2011, from http://www.kaner.com/pdfs/defects4.pdf

Kaner, C., Bach, J., & Petticord, B. (2001). *Lessons learned in software testing: A context-driven approach*. New York, NY: Wiley Computer Publishing.

Meier, M. W. (1998). Architecting principles for systems-of-systems. *Systems Engineering, 1*(4), 287–384.

Myers, G. (1979). *The art of software testing*. John Wiley & Sons, Inc.

Potter, B., & McGraw, G. (2004). Software security testing. *IEEE Security and Privacy, 2*(5), 81–85. doi:10.1109/MSP.2004.84

Richardson, D. J., & Wolf, A. L. (1996). Testing at the architectural level. In *Proceedings of the Second International Software Architecture Workshop (ISAW-2)* (pp. 68-71). San Francisco, California.

Scholtz, J. (2001). Adaptation of traditional usability testing methods for remote testing. In *Proceedings of the 34th Annual Hawaii International Conference on System Sciences (HICSS-34)*, Volume 5.

Sinofsky, S. (2012, 2 May). *Cloud services for Windows 8 and Windows Phone: Windows Live, reimagined*. MSDN Blog. Retrieved May 31, 2012, from http://blogs.msdn.com/b/b8/archive/2012/05/02/cloud-services-for-windows-8-and-windows-phone-windows-live-reimagined. aspx

Taylor, S., Schroeder, K., & Doerr, J. (2003). *Inside Intuit: How the makers of Quicken beat Microsoft and revolutionized an entire industry*. Boston, MA: Harvard Business School Press.

Walters, L. O., & Kritzinger, P. S. (2002). *Email message interarrival time analysis*. Retrieved April 11, 2011, from http://pubs.cs.uct.ac.za/archive/00000107/01/mailTrace.pdf

Whittaker, J. A. (2002). *How to break software: A practical guide to testing*. Wiley. Vaquero, L. M., Rodero-Merino, L., Caceres, J., & Lindner, M. (2009). A break in the clouds: Towards a cloud definition. *Computer Communication Review, 39*(1).

Zhang, S., Ding, Z., Zong, Y., & Gu, N. (2007). Remote software testing system based on grid workflow. In *Proceedings of 11th International Conference on Computer Supported Software Work in Design (CSCWD 2007)* (pp. 577-581). Melbourne, Australia.

KEY TERMS AND DEFINITIONS

Black-Box Testing: Looking for defects in a software artifact without knowledge of its internal workings.

Cloud Computing: Use of a service through the network from some arbitrary service provider.

Failure: The inability of software to achieve its intended result.

Fault: An incorrect step, process, data definition or data value in a program.

Other Interested Parties: People who will be affected by a software product who may influence its use.

Software Testing: Objectives and techniques for investigating a software artifact.

Stakeholders: People with interest in a software project and influence to affect it. (Sometimes restricted to those whose interest is financial).

Usability Testing: Measurement-based investigation of effectiveness of human use of a software artifact.

Chapter 11
Concolic Test Generation and the Cloud:
Deployment and Verification Perspectives

Nikolai Kosmatov
CEA LIST, France

ABSTRACT

Software testing in the cloud can reduce the need for hardware and software resources and offer a flexible and efficient alternative to the traditional software testing process. A major obstacle to the wider use of testing in the cloud is related to security issues. This chapter focuses on test generation techniques that combine concrete and symbolic execution of the program under test. Their deployment in the cloud leads to complex technical and security issues that do not occur for other testing methods. This chapter describes recent online deployment of such a technique implemented by the PathCrawler test generation tool for C programs, where the author faced, studied, and solved many of these issues. Mixed concrete/ symbolic testing techniques not only constitute a challenging target for deployment in the cloud, but they also provide a promising way to improve the reliability of cloud environments. The author argues that these techniques can be efficiently used to help to create trustworthy cloud environments.

INTRODUCTION

Testing is nowadays the primary way to improve the reliability of software. Software testing accounts up to 50% of the total cost of software development. Automatic testing tools provide an efficient alternative to manual testing and reduce the cost of software testing. However, automatic testing requires considerable investments: purchase and installation of testing tools, additional computing resources to run these tools, employing or training competent validation engineers to maintain and operate them, etc. These resources are necessary only during the testing steps of software development, and their cost for the company outside this period can be avoided by sharing them between several projects and with other companies.

The paradigm of cloud computing brings obvious benefits for the software testing process.

DOI: 10.4018/978-1-4666-2536-5.ch011

The deployment of software testing services in the cloud makes them easily available for different companies and projects and allows their on-demand usage. The companies do not have to purchase and maintain powerful servers and testing tools all the time, but use them just when it is required.

On the other hand, for the providers of testing tools, this approach makes it easier to update and to support the tools and to provide flexible on-demand solutions to the clients. Various testing tasks, taking from several seconds up to several weeks, can be optimally scheduled in the cloud. Thus a testing service can be offered to a larger number of companies and becomes appropriate for testing software of almost any size.

Before testing in the cloud becomes widely accepted and used in industry, various technical, security and privacy protection issues must be resolved. In this chapter, we focus on test generation techniques combining concrete and symbolic execution, also known as concolic testing. Concolic testing is an advanced technique of structural unit testing, that is one of the most suitable kinds of testing for the cloud (Parveen & Tilley, 2010). We address two facets of concolic testing in the cloud: migrating concolic testing to the cloud and usefulness of concolic testing for the cloud. The deployment of concolic testing in the cloud raises particularly challenging technical and security problems that do not necessarily appear in other testing methods. Relevant to any version of concolic testing, the security and efficiency concerns become even more critical for a publicly available testing service in the cloud. While for a local deployment used by a restricted number of people, an intentionally malicious software is very unlikely to be submitted to the tool, a publicly available testing service runs a much greater risk. We have recently implemented and deployed an online version for such a technique where we faced, studied and solved many of these problems. We show how a concolic testing tool can be decomposed into safe and unsafe parts in order to preserve the efficiency of the method, and how the unsafe part can be secured. On the other hand, concolic testing provides an excellent means for improving the reliability of the cloud itself. We present the most recent results on verification of operating systems and cloud hypervisors and show the role of various concolic testing approaches for creating more reliable cloud environments.

We start by providing some background on testing in the cloud and migrating software testing to the cloud. Next, we give an overview of concolic testing tools and outline their main features. We describe the method of PathCrawler, a concolic testing tool for C programs. Some implementation issues, that are usually omitted, will be described here in detail in order to illustrate the particular problems that this technique raises for an implementation in the cloud. Next, we describe the problems we faced, and provide the solutions we found during the implementation of PathCrawler-online, a prototype of testing service in the cloud whose limited evaluation version is available at (Kosmatov, 2010b). This web service implements all basic features of an online test generation service: uploading a C program to be tested, customizing test parameters and an oracle, generating and executing test cases on the program under test, and providing to the user the generated test cases and test coverage statistics. Next, we present recent results on verification of operating systems and cloud hypervisors. We underline several successful applications of concolic testing illustrating how this testing technique can improve the reliability of cloud environments. We finish by pointing out future work directions and a conclusion.

TESTING IN THE CLOUD

Cloud computing is an emerging paradigm (Zhang, Cheng, & Boutaba, 2010). The term *cloud* became popular after Google's CEO Eric Schmidt used the word to describe the business model of providing services across the Internet in 2006. In mid-2009, the U.S. National Institute of Standards and Technology (NIST) gave the following definition of the concept (Mell & Grance, 2011): Cloud computing is a model for enabling convenient, on-demand network access to a shared pool of configurable computing resources (e.g., networks, servers, storage, applications, and services) that can be rapidly provisioned and released with minimal management effort or service provider interaction. The essential characteristics of a cloud include on-demand self-service, broad network access, resource pooling, rapid elasticity and measured service.

The key idea behind the term cloud computing is the following: computing services are delivered on demand from a remote location rather than residing on one's own desktop, laptop, mobile device, or even on an organization's server. Computing becomes location- and device-independent, in the sense that it does not matter where information is stored nor where computation/processing is taking place. Three service models of cloud computing were defined (Mell & Grance, 2011):

- In the Software as a Service (SaaS) model, the client uses the provider's applications running on a cloud infrastructure.
- Platform as a Service (PaaS) offers to the client the capability to create and deploy onto the cloud infrastructure applications created using programming languages, services and tools supported by the provider.
- Finally, in the Infrastructure as a Service (IaaS) model, the clients can provision processing, storage, networks, and other fundamental computing resources where they can deploy and run arbitrary software, which can include operating systems and applications.

The client does not manage or control the underlying cloud infrastructure, except limited user-specific application configuration settings and, for IaaS, limited control of some network-ing components (e.g., host firewalls). The NIST definition also describes four deployment models: private, community, public or hybrid cloud.

Cloud computing started to be used for testing around 2002. The research has focused on techniques for online testing, ranking, automated test case generation, monitoring, simulation, and policy data provenance (Yu et al., 2010). In Aalst (2010), Software Testing as a Service is defined as a model of software testing used to test an application as a service provided to customers across the Internet. It enables daily operation, maintenance and testing support through web-based browsers, testing frameworks and servers.

The major benefits of cloud-based testing include the following (see e.g. (Parveen & Tilley, 2010; Gao, Bai, & Tsai, 2011)):

- Provide an efficient way to obtain a virtual and scalable test environment over a cloud infrastructure.
- Share and leverage computing resources using the cloud.
- Support testing operations and obtain required computing resources at anytime.
- Share and reuse software testing tools.
- Use a utility model (*pay-as-you-go*) as a way to charge provided testing services.
- Enable large-scale test data and traffic simulation for system testing.

Candea, Bucur, and Zamfir (2010) argue that the Testing as a Service (TaaS) paradigm will have a significant impact on software engineering. It can be compared to the introduction of high level programming languages and compilers in the 1950s that eliminated most direct use of assembly language and improved the productivity-to-bugs ratio. Another important turning point in software development was the creation of faster hardware and compilers, providing quick feedback on syntax errors and low-level programming errors during the build process. These two events transformed the way programmers' write code:

less concern for the minor details and more time devoted to the higher level thought process. Like a modern compiler almost immediately reports *syntax* errors, TaaS can provide quick feedback on *semantic* correctness that will lead to higher software reliability in general. The authors also describe three forms of TaaS: $TaaS_D$ for developers to more thoroughly test their code, $TaaS_H$ for end users to check the software they install, and $TaaS_C$ certification services that enable consumers to choose among software products based on the products' measured reliability.

However, migrating to the cloud can be costly, and it is not always the best solution to all testing problems. (Parveen & Tilley, 2010) discuss when and how to migrate software testing to the cloud, and in particular, what kinds of programs and what kinds of testing are suitable for testing in the cloud. The characteristics of a program that make it feasible for its testing process to be migrated to the cloud include the following:

- Test cases are independent from one another (or their dependencies are easily identifiable).
- A self-contained and easily identifiable operational environment.
- Programmatically accessible interface that is suitable for automated testing.

Among the kinds of testing that could benefit from migrating to the cloud, the authors indicate unit testing, high-volume automated testing and performance testing.

(Riungu, Taipale, & Smolander, 2010b, 2010a) present a recent qualitative study on software testing as an online service from the practitioners' point of view. Based on several interviews with software testing providers and customers, the authors show that the demand for TaaS is on the rise. The underlying research question was: "What conditions influence software testing as an online service?" Based on the received responses, they discuss the requirements, benefits, challenges,

and some research issues from the perspectives of online business vendors and practitioners.

One recent example of testing in the cloud is D-Cloud (Banzai et al., 2010; Hanawa et al., 2010), a large-scale software testing environment for dependable distributed systems. It uses computing resource provided by the cloud to execute several test cases simultaneously, and thus to accelerate software testing process. D-Cloud takes advantage of virtual machine technology to provide a fault injection facility that allows hardware faults to be emulated according to the user's request. It also offers an advanced configuration utility that facilitates the system setup and the testing process.

The York Extensible Testing Infrastructure (YETI) is another example of testing in the cloud (Oriol & Ullah, 2010). YETI is an automated random testing tool for Java with the ability to test programs written in different programming languages. The stand-alone implementation of the tool suffered from two issues, low performances and security problems related to the execution of user-provided code. A new cloud implementation of YETI significantly improves the performances (by testing in parallel) and solves potential security issues (by executing Java classes on clean virtual machines).

(Ciortea, Zamfir, Bucur, Chipounov, & Candea, 2009) introduces Cloud9, a cloud-based testing service that promises to make high-quality testing fast, cheap, and practical. Based on the KLEE testing tool (Cadar, Dunbar, & Engler, 2008), Cloud9 enables parallel symbolic execution for computer clusters operating on public cloud infrastructures such as Amazon EC2 and clusters running cloud software like Eucalyptus. The authors show how to dynamically partition the complete testing task (i.e. the whole program execution tree) into smaller tasks (described as execution sub-trees) run in parallel. The authors currently prepare a public release of Cloud9, that is for the moment available only for identified users. Another facet of testing in the cloud, for testing of the cloud itself, is addressed in (T. M. King & Ganti, 2010).

Reliability and security of the cloud are widely recognized by practitioners and researchers as a vital requirement, both for testing in the cloud (Riungu et al., 2010b; Parveen & Tilley, 2010) and for cloud-based services in general (Zhang et al., 2010). This issue is the main concern of this chapter, that we will address from two points of view, for migrating software testing to the cloud and for testing of the cloud. We will focus on the promising testing techniques presented in the next section.

TEST GENERATION TECHNIQUES COMBINING CONCRETE AND SYMBOLIC EXECUTION

Among other novel testing techniques, various combinations of concrete and constraint-based symbolic execution (see e.g. (Kosmatov, 2010a)) were developed during the last decade. By concrete execution, we mean the usual execution of a program, for instance, of the compiled binary executable of a C program, where the program is run with a (concrete) input data. Symbolic execution was introduced in software testing in 1976 by L. A. Clarke (Clarke, 1976) and J. C. King (J. C. King, 1976) in order to reason about executions of a program without running it. The key idea behind it is to use symbolic values, instead of concrete ones, as input values, and to represent the values of program variables as symbolic expressions. As a result, the outputs computed by a program are expressed in terms of the symbolic inputs. Symbolic execution is often performed with help of constraints that represent particular conditions on symbolic input values under which program execution follows a particular path or, more generally, verifies some property at some program point. Test generation is performed by solving the corresponding constraints, using a decision procedure or constraint solver, and produces a set of test cases. A test case contains an input

data for the program under test, and may contain the expected result of its execution.

For example, take the following C program:

```
1    //returns minimum of X, Y
2    int min(int X, int Y){
3      if(X > Y)
4        return Y;
5      else
6        return X;
7    }
```

Line 4 is executed if and only if the inputs X and Y satisfy the constraint $X > Y$, and in this case the program returns Y. This is an example of symbolic reasoning. For the constraint $X > Y$, a constraint solver finds a solution that represents the input data of a test case, say, $X = 15$, $Y = 7$. The program can be (concretely) executed by this test case and will return 7, a concrete value.

Symbolic execution can also be used for program debugging, where it checks for runtime errors or assertion violations and generates test inputs that trigger those errors. We present constraint-based symbolic execution in detail in the next section.

Combined concrete/symbolic techniques, with various modifications, were successfully applied for implementation of several testing tools for white-box testing, that is, for the testing approach in which the implementation code is examined for designing tests. These techniques are often called dynamic symbolic execution, or concolic (CONCrete/symbOLIC) testing. The first concolic tools for C programs, PathCrawler (Williams, Marre, Mouy, & Roger, 2005) and DART (Godefroid, Klarlund, & Sen, 2005), perform symbolic execution while the program is executed on some concrete input values. DART uses concrete values and randomization to simplify the constraints when it cannot reason precisely. UIUC's CUTE (Sen, Marinov, & Agha, 2005) (for C) and jCUTE (for Java) extend DART to handle multi-threaded programs that manipulate dynamic data structures using pointer operations. CUTE represents and solves pointer constraints approximately. In multi-threaded programs, CUTE systematically generates both test inputs and thread schedules by combining concolic execution with dynamic partial order reduction.

Stanford's EXE (Cadar, Ganesh, Pawlowski, Dill, & Engler, 2006) is designed for testing complex software, including systems code, so it accurately builds bit-level constraints for C expressions, including those involving pointers, casting, unions, and bit-fields. It performs mixed concrete/symbolic execution where the concrete state is maintained as part of the normal execution state of the program. A new version of the EXE tool, KLEE (Cadar et al., 2008) stores a much larger number of concurrent states, employs a variety of constraint solving optimizations, and uses search heuristics to get high code coverage.

NASA's Symbolic (Java) PathFinder (Anand, Pasareanu, & Visser, 2007) analyzes both Java bytecode and statechart models, e.g., Simulink/ Stateflow, Standard UML, Rhapsody UML, etc., via automatic translation into bytecode. It handles mixed integer and real constraints, as well as complex mathematical constraints by means of solving heuristics.

Microsoft's PEX (Tillmann & Halleux, 2008) implements dynamic symbolic execution to generate test inputs for.NET code, supporting languages such as C#, VisualBasic, and F#. PEX uses concrete values to simplify constraints and treats almost all.NET instructions symbolically, including safe and unsafe code, as well as instructions that refer to the object oriented.NET type system, such as type tests and virtual method invocations. PEX supports primitive and (recursive) complex data types, for which it automatically computes a factory method that creates an instance of a complex data.

Another tool from Microsoft, SAGE (Godefroid, Levin, & Molnar, 2012) implements automated whitebox fuzzing, a modified concolic

technique for symbolically executing very long execution traces with billions of instructions, for symbolic execution at the x86 assembly level and for compact representation of path constraints.

UC Berkeley's CREST (Burnim & Sen, 2008) is an open-source extensible platform for building and experimenting with concolic search heuristics for selecting which paths to test for programs with far too many execution paths to exhaustively explore.

Unlike other concolic tools, PathCrawler aims for complete coverage of a certain class of programs rather than for incomplete coverage of any program. It runs the program under test on each test case in order to recover a trace of the execution path. However, in PathCrawler's case concrete execution is used merely for reasons of efficiency and to demonstrate that the test does indeed activate the intended execution path. PathCrawler does not approximate constraints for program instructions that it cannot treat since these results can only provide an incomplete model of the program's semantics.

In the next section, we present an advanced unit testing technique combining constraint-based symbolic execution and concrete execution of the program under test. This is essentially the technique implemented by the PathCrawler tool. We consider the *all-path test coverage criterion* which requires to generate a set of test cases such that every possible execution path of the program under test is executed by at least one test case. Since this criterion is very strong, weaker path-oriented criteria were proposed, requiring to cover only paths of limited length, or with limited number of loop iterations, etc. Test generation methods for these weaker criteria are obtained from the all-path test generation method by slight modifications that do not impact the main idea of the method and its deployment online.

PATHCRAWLER METHODOLOGY

Description of the PathCrawler Method

The PathCrawler tool is basically composed of three main modules that we call Analyzer, Path explorer and Solver. PathCrawler uses COLIBRI, an efficient constraint solver developed at CEA LIST and shared with two other testing tools: GATeL (Marre & Arnould, 2000) and OSMOSE (Bardin & Herrmann, 2008). COLIBRI provides a variety of types and constraints (including non-linear constraints), primitives for labelling procedures, support for floating point numbers and efficient constraint resolution (Leconte & Berstel, 2006; Gotlieb, Leconte, & Marre, 2010; Michel, 2002; Marre & Michel, 2010). Experiments in (Bardin, Herrmann, & Perroud, 2010) using SMT-LIB benchmarks show that COLIBRI can be competitive with powerful SMT solvers.

The PathCrawler method contains two main stages. The first stage is illustrated by Figure 1. The user provides the source code of the C program under test, in one or several files, denoted here for simplicity by f.c, and indicates the function to be tested.

Analyzer parses the program f.c, generates its instrumented version and translates its statements into an intermediate representation in constraints (see Figure 1). These constraints encode all the information on the control and data flow of the program (assignments, branches, loops, function calls, etc.) necessary for symbolic execution at the second stage. The instrumented version, denoted here by fi.c, contains the original source code of f.c enriched with path tracing instructions. The compilation of this instrumented version, performed here with gcc, provides an executable test harness that we call Launcher. Launcher runs the program under test with a given input and records the program path that was activated.

The user may also provide C code with an optional oracle, denoted here by o.c, that checks if the result of the program executed by a given test case is correct or not. When provided, the oracle is loaded into Launcher, and called after the execution of a test case to produce a verdict on the results.

Figure 2 illustrates the second stage where a depth-first exploration algorithm with constraint-based symbolic execution (in Path explorer) and a constraint solver are used to generate test cases. This stage uses the module Launcher and the intermediate program representation in constraints obtained at the first stage. In addition, the user defines a precondition, i.e. the conditions on the program's input for which the behavior is defined. Any generated test case must satisfy the precondition. For example, a typical precondition for a function computing a square root of *x* will

Figure 1. PathCrawler analyzer

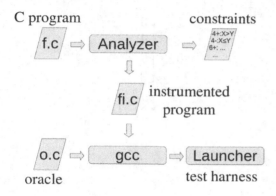

Figure 2. PathCrawler generator

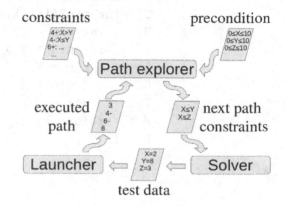

be $x \geq 0$ (unless we intentionally want to check the behavior for negative numbers). A precondition for dichotomic search of a given element in a given sorted array should specify that the input array is sorted and may restrict the intervals of values for the size and the elements of the array.

At this stage, three modules are used one after another in a loop: Path explorer, Solver and Launcher. In the beginning of each iteration, Path explorer determines the next (partial) program path to be covered, and sends the corresponding path constraints to Solver. Solver generates test data satisfying the constraints and sends it to Launcher. Launcher executes the program under test on the test data and sends the executed program path to Path explorer, which starts the next iteration.

When Solver fails to generate a test case (e.g. for an infeasible program path), the method skips the concrete execution step with Launcher and goes directly to Path explorer for a next path choice. When Path explorer has no more paths to cover, all paths are covered and test generation stops. In the first iteration, Path explorer starts with the empty partial path. In the following iterations, Path explorer explores remaining program paths in a depth-first search.

A Running Example

Let us illustrate the method on a running example. Consider the program min3 and its control flow graph (CFG) shown in Figure 3. The function min3 takes three integer parameters X, Y, Z, and returns the minimum among them. The logical variables X, Y, Z will denote the values of the input parameters. For simplicity, we restrict the domains of the parameters to [0, 10], so the precondition is defined by:

$$0 \leq X \leq 10, \; 0 \leq Y \leq 10, \; 0 \leq Z \leq 10$$

The CFG illustrates possible execution paths of the program. We denote an execution path by a sequence of line numbers of its statements, e.g. 3, 4−, 6+, 7, 8. A decision is denoted by the line number of the condition followed by a "+" if the condition is satisfied, and by a "−" otherwise.

The first stage of the method creates a constraint representation of the program and the module Launcher (cf Figure 1). Let us describe in more detail the test generation loop of the second stage illustrated by Figure 4. The first iteration starts with Path explorer that sends to Solver the path constraints for the empty path ε, i.e. just the precondition constraints, denoted by <precond>. In other words, it asks for any test data satisfying the

Figure 3. Function min3 returning the minimum of its three arguments, and its CFG

```
1    //returns minimum of X, Y, Z
2    int min3(int X, int Y, int Z){
3      int min = X;
4      if( min > Y )
5        min = Y;
6      if( min > Z )
7        min = Z;
8      return min;
9    }
```

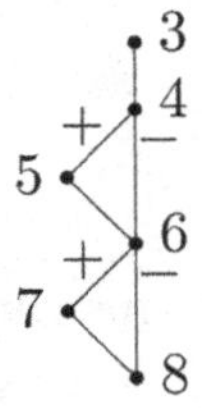

precondition. Solver generates Test 1, say, $X = 3$, $Y = 7$, $Z = 2$. Next, Test 1 is executed by Launcher and the executed path is sent to Path Explorer (see the right column boxes of Figure 4).

Path explorer finds, in a depth-first search, the next partial program path to be covered and symbolically executes it. Technically, it takes the previously explored path, negates the last not-yet-negated branch on this path and drops the statements that follow it.

In the second iteration, the last not-yet-negated decision in the path 3, 4+, 6+, 7, 8 is 6+, so the next partial path to be covered is 3, 4−, 6−. Path explorer maintains a representation of the program memory state at every moment of symbolic execution and uses it to produce a constraint solving problem (see the left column boxes of Figure 4) corresponding to the selected program path, so that any solution of this problem gives a test case exercising the desired path. The constraints are

expressed in terms of program inputs. Then Solver generates Test 2, and Launcher executes it on the instrumented version of the program under test to obtain the exercised path 3, 4−, 6−, 8.

Since the last not-yet-negated condition of this path is now 4−, in the third iteration Path explorer defines the next partial path to be covered as 3, 4+ and constructs the corresponding constraints. Next, Solver generates Test 3, which exercises the path 3, 4+, 5, 6−, 8.

The last not-yet-negated condition of this path being 6−, in the fourth iteration Path explorer asks to cover the partial path 3, 4+, 5, 6+. Notice that the constraint $Y > Z$ takes into account the current value of the variable min at the decision 6+ modified by the assignment line 5. Next, Test 4 is generated and executed.

Since all decisions of the executed path 3, 4+, 5, 6+, 7, 8 have been already negated, all possible paths have been explored and the test generation

Figure 4. Test generation for the function min3 of Figure 3

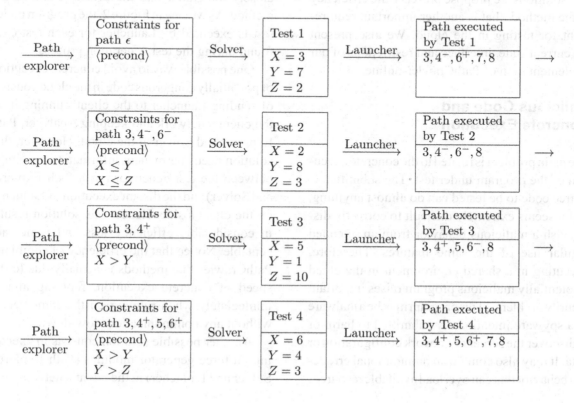

process stops. The four generated tests cover the four feasible program paths of the program in Figure 3.

DEPLOYMENT IN THE CLOUD: PROBLEMS AND SOLUTIONS

This section describes the problems we encountered during the online deployment of the PathCrawler test generation tool and the solutions we found and implemented. We discuss several important risks that should be taken into account while creating the architecture of a similar testing service in the cloud, or more generally, in PaaS clouds like Google App Engine (Google, 2012) where the code submitted by the user runs in the cloud. To some extent, these risks affect any deployment of concolic testing, from a local one to that in the cloud. However, the risks are all the greater for a publicly available web service given its larger accessibility for users all over the world. The solutions we propose preserve the efficiency of the method, that is another important requirement for testing in the cloud. We also present the current state, interface and restrictions of our implementation of PathCrawler-online.

Malicious Code and Concrete Execution

The main problem is related to the concrete execution of the program under test. The submitted C source code to be tested can do almost anything, and it seems extremely difficult to correctly distinguish a malicious behavior from an intended regular use of the same features. Therefore, executing in a shared environment in the cloud a potentially malicious program raises important security problems. This program may be a malware or a spyware intentionally submitted to harm or to discover the server or network configuration or data. It may also contain an unintentional erroneous behavior that can overload available resources

or destabilize the server, executed programs or other clients' sessions.

By definition of software testing, any testing approach requires execution of the program under test on the selected test data. However, test generation and test execution can often be separated and need not to be run in the same environment. For example, in model-based testing, test cases are derived from the model without any knowledge of the implementation's source code (see e.g. (Kosmatov, 2010a)). Therefore, the test generation step and the execution of the program on the generated tests can easily be separated: the test generation utility can be deployed in the cloud, while the test execution remains on the client's side or runs in a dedicated, highly secured environment. Similarly, in white-box testing approaches using symbolic execution only, concrete execution of the client's source code is not necessary at the test generation step.

The specificity of PathCrawler-like methods is that concrete execution of the client's code is closely integrated into the second stage of the method. As we saw in Figure 2, the program under test is executed by Launcher for each test case found during the test generation process.

One possible way to avoid concrete execution of potentially dangerous code in the cloud consists of sending Launcher to the client, running it on the client's network and keeping Analyzer, Path Explorer and Solver in the cloud. However, this solution needs permanent information exchange between the test generator (with Path Explorer and Solver) and the distant execution of Launcher on the client's side. Hence, this solution results in considerable efficiency loss and is not acceptable. Notice that the efficiency of combined PathCrawler-like methods is actually due to the speed of concrete execution, replying almost immediately when running on the same server without any communication slow-down.

Another possible solution consists in executing all three generator modules (Path Explorer, Solver and Launcher) in the client's network, but it essentially requires installation of the tool on the client's side, that obviously does not correspond to the objectives of a deployment in the cloud.

How to ensure secure execution of the client's code in the cloud without diminishing the performances of the method? The solution we used in our implementation proposes to split the complete method into two parts, secure and insecure ones, and to run the potentially insecure steps (including concrete execution of the client's code) in a virtual machine. In our presentation in the previous section we split the method into two stages that correspond exactly to this requirement. The first stage shown in Figure 1 analyzes and transforms the source code under test without executing it, so it can be considered secure. It is therefore more efficient to keep this part outside the virtual machine that isolates concrete execution. The second stage illustrated in Figure 2 executes the compiled instrumented version of the submitted program, so it runs the risk of malicious behavior. We isolate this stage in a separate virtual machine.

Particular Reliability and Security Risks

Isolating a potentially dangerous process in a virtual machine is nowadays a well-known paradigm that has been implemented in various trustworthy technical solutions. Many of them have reliable support and quite satisfactory performances. For security reasons we do not communicate on the particular virtualization mechanism we used in PathCrawler-online.

Let us present several particular risks that we studied to secure our implementation, and that must be kept in mind during any implementation of a similar testing service.

The submitted program may read, modify, or destroy files on the system. The virtual machine will protect from unauthorized access to the files outside, but a limited information exchange with outside files has to be allowed in some way in order to transfer into the virtual machine the files related to the desired test generation task and to extract the results. A typical error would be to allow broad access to files of the underlying machine such as to a disk containing other sensitive data or used by other processes. Indeed, the program under test can try to modify the accessible files, or read and encode the discovered data in test generation results. The privileges of the users executing the virtual machine and the program under test inside it must be carefully checked and restricted.

The submitted program may saturate disk space on the system. The program under test can fill up the disk producing a great amount of information, or provoke generation of huge test data files, that can result in lack-of-space problems in the system. Therefore, it will be dangerous to allow access even to a subdirectory of a disk containing sensitive data or used by other processes, since saturating this disk can lead to negative consequences. We think the best way to set up information exchange with the virtual machine is a separate, dedicated partition. At the same time, we periodically check the size of written files, including those with test generation results.

The submitted program may contain a fork bomb. This is a well-known denial-of-service attack that should be explicitly checked and excluded. A fork bomb is a program creating a large number of processes very quickly in order to saturate available system resources, for instance, like in

```
while(1) { fork(); }
```

that infinitely tries to copy itself into a new process. This risk can be easily prevented by setting a limit on the number of processes that one user may own, without completely forbidding the fork operation.

The submitted program may try to overload other available resources (processor, RAM, etc.). This risk is normally prevented by using the virtual machine, which should be allowed to use only limited resources. However, it is still worth testing.

The submitted program may maliciously send or receive data using the internet. This is definitely the risk the most difficult to prevent, since we can neither easily detect a malicious behavior on the Internet nor protect distant machines from such a behavior. In our implementation, we deactivate network access in the virtual machine and do not treat programs under test using Internet. In our opinion, the number and variety of various attacks using Internet today makes it improbable to provide a reliable public testing service in the cloud for software using Internet.

Security of testing in the cloud was also addressed in YETI (Oriol & Ullah, 2010), in which virtual machines are used to secure test execution. However, the problem of splitting the method into secure and insecure parts does not occur in YETI since it implements random testing, in which test generation and test execution steps are not so closely tied as in PathCrawler.

The issues described in this section are related to those encountered in commercial PaaS clouds where the user code is executed in the cloud. For example, Google App Engine (Google, 2012) also uses virtualization to secure execution, but its limitations are different from PathCrawler-online. C code is not allowed to be executed in Google App Engine, while PathCrawler is designed for testing C code. In Google App Engine, applications cannot write to the file system in any of the runtime environments, while PathCrawler-online allows read-write access to files inside the virtual machine, that is necessary e.g. to write test generation results. Google App Engine forbids creating sub-processes while PathCrawler-online allows a limited number of sub-processes to be opened by the program under test. Google App Engine also restricts access to and from the Internet, that is not allowed in PathCrawler-online.

Online Test Generation with PathCrawler

PathCrawler-online (Kosmatov, 2010b) provides a web service with all basic features of an online testing tool:

- Uploading a complete multi-file C project and an oracle.
- Generating default test parameters.
- Customizing test parameters, such as input variables, precondition, test generation strategy.
- Generating test cases in XML format.
- Executing them on the program under test in a secure environment.
- Generating C source code of ready-to-use test drivers that allow to execute the program under test on each test case on the client's testing environment.
- Providing to the user the test cases, test execution and coverage statistics on-the-fly in a web browser.

Figure 5 shows the initial page of the service where the user can select one of the available examples and start test generation. Another page allows the user to upload an archive with the user's C project. It is possible to use default precondition, testing strategy and oracle, or to customize them first. After the test generation, the user can see the summary of the test session, the list of all explored paths and the list of test cases. Figure 6 shows an example of generated test cases, some of which fail (the failure verdict appears in red). For each test case, a separate page shows the generated test data, the executed path, its predicate (also called *path condition*), concrete values of the output variables, their symbolic expression in terms of inputs, the oracle's verdict and the generated test driver.

This free evaluation version does not allow the user to identify himself, to save a test generation session, to continue it later, to use a makefile

Figure 5. PathCrawler-online home page

Figure 6. PathCrawler-online test generation results (test cases)

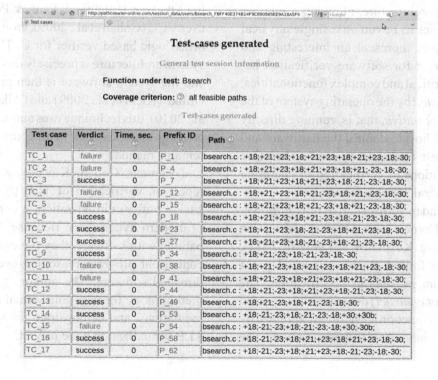

or customized compilation options and to download the generated test cases and statistics in XML format. Besides, the current version sets restrictive bounds for the number of explored paths, the number of generated test cases, test generation time and disk space for generated files that cannot be overpassed.

TOWARDS RELIABLE CLOUD ENVIRONMENTS

Cloud computing nowadays becomes pervasive in many domains. A substantial expansion of mobile devices will make it all the more popular in the future. As we mentioned before, reliability and security of cloud environments are currently major challenges for research and industry (Zhang et al., 2010).

In this section, we describe some of the most representative results of the past five years in this domain, and show the promising role that concolic testing based techniques can play for this goal. We focus on cloud hypervisors, that virtualize the underlying architecture, allowing a number of guest machines to be run on a single physical host. Hypervisors represent an interesting and challenging target for software verification because of their critical and complex functionalities. They can be *hosted* by the operating system of the physical host, or *native*, that is, running directly on the physical host to control the hardware and to manage guest operating systems. Therefore recent contributions to verification of operating systems in general are also relevant.

A recent trend in verification of operating systems and cloud hypervisors is formal verification (Loulergue, Gava, Kosmatov, & Lemerre, 2012), that includes a formal machine-checked proof that the program satisfies its specification. The specification (or *contract*) describes the expected behavior of each function and is often expressed by logical formulae associated to the source code. The

machine-checked mathematical proof guarantees that the code respects the contract.

A recent work (Klein et al., 2009) presented rigorous, formal verification for the OS microkernel seL4. The proof being complete, this work allows devices running seL4 to achieve the highest assurance level, such as the EAL7 evaluation level "formally verified design and tested" of the Common Criteria for Information Technology Security Evaluation (CCRA, 2012), a modern standard for software security evaluation. Another formal verification of a microkernel was described in (Alkassar, Paul, Starostin, & Tsyban, 2010). In both cases, the verification used interactive machine-checked proof with the theorem prover Isabelle/HOL (Nipkow, Paulson, & Wenzel, 2002). Although interactive theorem proving requires human intervention to construct and guide the proof, it has the benefit to serve a general range of properties and is not limited to specific properties treatable by more automated methods of verification such as static analysis or model checking.

The formal verification of a simple hypervisor in (Alkassar, Hillebrand, Paul, & Petrova, 2010) uses VCC (Cohen et al., 2009), an automatic first-order logic based verifier for C. The underlying system architecture is precisely modeled in VCC, and the system software is then proved correct. Unlike (Klein et al., 2009) and (Alkassar, Paul, et al., 2010), this technique uses automated theorem proving methods, but writing the specification remains manual.

(Alkassar, Cohen, Kovalev, & Paul, 2012) report on verification of TLB (translation lookaside buffer) virtualization, a core component of modern hypervisors. Because devices run in parallel with software, they typically necessitate concurrent program reasoning even for single-threaded software. The authors give a general methodology for verifying virtual device implementations, and demonstrate the verification of TLB virtualization code in VCC.

Does it mean that reliability of cloud environments will be formally verified in the very near future, excluding any risk of error or attack? Despite the spectacular progress in application of formal verification methods to the cloud, fully, formally verified cloud environments are unlikely to become the reality of cloud computing over the next years.

Indeed, formal verification still has important limitations. First of all, it is very costly. According to (Klein, 2010), the cost of the verification of the seL4 microkernel was around 25 person-years, and required highly qualified experts. seL4 contains only about 10,000 lines of C code, and verification cost is about $700 per line of code. Even if these techniques may optimistically scale up to 100,000s lines of code for appropriate code bases, realistic systems with millions of lines of code still seem out of reach for the near future.

Second, formal verification of a microkernel or a hypervisor remains valid only for a particular version being verified. Therefore, any evolution of the software can potentially alter the verified properties, and requires new verification.

Third, the verification is currently performed for the source code with several assumptions (Klein, 2010). It assumes that the C compiler and linker are correct. Although first certified compilers, whose correctness for some supported processors is formally established, have been developed (Leroy, 2009), they are not yet commonly used in industry. The verification in (Klein et al., 2009; Alkassar, Hillebrand, et al., 2010) assumes sequential execution, and its extension to a concurrent hypervisor seems very challenging. The verification also assumes correctness of hardware, cache-flushing instructions, and boot code. Some specific hardware failures, for instance provoked by overheating, or hardware details beneath the lowest verification level can still be attacked. Therefore, "you still need orthogonal methods to ensure that you are building the right system with the right requirements, and not the wrong system correctly" (Heiser, Murray, & Klein, 2012).

Among such orthogonal methods, structural software testing techniques based on concrete/symbolic execution are of great interest for testing of the cloud. They do not have the three aforementioned limitations. First, they are highly automated, so their cost is almost negligible compared to formal verification. Second, an updated version of software can be easily tested again without human intervention. Finally, testing in the realistic cloud environment takes into account all real-life environment details related to hardware, boot code, compiled code, etc. Moreover, concolic testing can efficiently benefit from a cloud infrastructure since it can be easily parallelized (Ciortea et al., 2009). Another strength of concolic testing is its capacity to achieve a high level of structural test coverage, that aims at activating by some tests all program statements, or all program branches, or all program paths (of limited length), etc. Structural coverage is required by many software evaluation standards, for example, the Common Criteria (CCRA, 2012), DO-178B (in the avionics domain), ECCS-E-ST-40C (space), ISO 26262 (automotive), EC/EN 61513 (nuclear), etc.

One of the most encouraging examples of concolic testing is reported in (Godefroid et al., 2012). Based on modified concolic testing, the SAGE tool has discovered many security-related bugs in many large Microsoft applications, notably during the development of Windows 7. Finding these bugs has saved Microsoft millions of dollars by avoiding security patches to more than one billion PCs. Since 2008, SAGE has been running 24/7 on approximately 100 machines automatically testing hundreds of applications in Microsoft security testing labs. SAGE is also able to test large applications, where it can find bugs resulting from problems across multiple components. (Godefroid & Molnar, 2010) argue that fuzz testing in the cloud will revolutionize security testing.

Another concolic tool, EXE (Cadar et al., 2006) discovered deep bugs and security vulnerabilities in a variety of complex code, ranging from library code to UNIX utilities, file systems, packet filters, and network tools. Its successor KLEE (Cadar et al., 2008) was applied to 452 applications (over 430K total lines of code) including GNU COREUTILS, containing roughly 80,000 lines of library code and 61,000 lines in the actual utilities, and the HiStar OS kernel. KLEE found 56 serious bugs, some of which had been missed for over 15 years.

As long as complete formal verification of realistic cloud environments remains impossible, software testing keeps its place for assuring their reliability and security. (Klein, 2010) proposes to design the whole system in such a way that its critical components are small and amenable to formal verification. Non critical components will be assumed to do anything they are allowed to subvert the system and will not be formally verified. The security of the system is then reduced to the security mechanisms of the kernel and the behavior of the critical components only. Concolic testing remains a promising technique for testing software components that cannot be formally verified in the real-life environment.

FUTURE WORK

Future work includes the development of a complete web service suitable for industrial software testing. We have already implemented the core of such a service in our current prototype PathCrawler-online, but systematic use in industrial software engineering requires additional routines, such as secure data transfer, client identification and account management, test session history, test results download, facilities for integration into the clients' test execution environment, deployment in a reliable cloud infrastructure, etc.

Concolic test generation techniques are also used as part of recent combined methods with other verification techniques, for instance, with partition refinement (Gulavani, Henzinger, Kannan, Nori, & Rajamani, 2006), or with value analysis and

program slicing (Chebaro, Kosmatov, Giorgetti, & Julliand, 2012). Future work also includes implementation of a web service for combined verification techniques such as the SANTE method (Chebaro et al., 2012) combining static analysis and PathCrawler-like test generation.

Applying concolic testing in complement to formal verification for verification of the cloud is another promising future work direction that will help to create reliable cloud environments.

CONCLUSION

Using cloud computing to make software testing services available online and to share them between different companies is an attractive perspective for modern software engineering. In this chapter we addressed security of testing in the cloud for concolic testing, an advanced structural testing technique proposed in the mid 2000s. We reported on PathCrawler-online, a recent implementation of a concolic testing web service. We showed why this kind of testing techniques is particularly challenging for deployment in the cloud. We examined the risks encountered when potentially malicious user code is run in the cloud, and showed how a concolic testing technique can be decomposed into secure and insecure parts and how the insecure part can be isolated using virtualization.

Our experience shows that these technical problems can be successfully resolved. Since its deployment in 2010, PathCrawler-online was used thousands of times. The initial objective of this limited evaluation version has been fully achieved. PathCrawler-online is appreciated by our academic and industrial partners as a convenient tool for discovering concolic test generation with PathCrawler, demonstrating its capabilities and teaching testing in several universities (Kosmatov, Williams, Botella, Roger, & Chebaro, 2012). Initially demonstrated at CSTVA 2011 (Kosmatov, Botella, Roger, & Williams, 2011), it is now frequently used for tutorials on structural unit testing at international events (TAP 2012, TAROT 2012, QSIC 2012, ASE 2012) where several dozens of participants simultaneously run test generation online.

This experience showed an increasing interest to automatic test generation and encouraged us to continue the development of automatic test generation tools and their online versions. Although concolic testing is still a young technique, it has an interesting potential for software verification, both for testing in the cloud and for testing of the cloud. The advantages of concolic testing include automation, easy replay for a new version of software, parallelization, low cost and the possibility to test a program in its real-life environment. Concolic testing can easily achieve high structural test coverage that is required by many modern software verification standards. Even if it cannot guarantee the absence of errors, its advantages make of concolic testing a promising complement to formal verification of cloud environments. We believe that concolic testing in the cloud will provide new reliable and cost-efficient solutions that will become the reality of software testing tomorrow.

ACKNOWLEDGMENT

The author would like to thank Bernard Botella, Fabrice Derepas, Matthieu Lemerre, Frédéric Loulergue, Bruno Marre, Benjamin Monate, Muriel Roger and Nicky Williams for their advice and useful discussions, as well as the editors and anonymous referees for lots of valuable remarks and suggestions.

REFERENCES

Alkassar, E., Cohen, E., Kovalev, M., & Paul, W. J. (2012, January). Verification of TLB virtualization implemented in C. In the *4th International Conference on Verified Software: Theories, Tools, Experiments* (VSTTE 2012) (pp. 209–224). Philadelphia, PA: Springer.

Alkassar, E., Hillebrand, M. A., Paul, W. J., & Petrova, E. (2010, August). Automated verification of a small hypervisor. In the *Third International Conference on Verified Software: Theories, Tools, Experiments* (VSTTE 2010) (pp. 40–54). Edinburgh, UK: Springer.

Alkassar, E., Paul, W., Starostin, A., & Tsyban, A. (2010, August). Pervasive verification of an OS microkernel. In the *Third International Conference on Verified Software: Theories, Tools, Experiments* (VSTTE 2010) (pp. 71–85). Edinburgh, UK: Springer.

Anand, S., Pasareanu, C. S., & Visser, W. (2007, March). JPF-SE: A symbolic execution extension to Java PathFinder. In the *13th International Conference on Tools and Algorithms for the Construction and Analysis of Systems* (TACAS 2007) (pp. 134–138). Braga, Portugal: Springer.

Banzai, T., Koizumi, H., Kanbayashi, R., Imada, T., Hanawa, T., & Sato, M. (2010, May). D-cloud: Design of a software testing environment for reliable distributed systems using cloud computing technology. In the *10th IEEE/ACM International Conference on Cluster, Cloud and Grid Computing* (CCGrid 2010) (pp. 631–636). Melbourne, Australia: IEEE Computer Society.

Bardin, S., & Herrmann, P. (2008, April). Structural testing of executables. In the *First IEEE International Conference on Software Testing, Verification, and Validation* (ICST'08) (pp. 22–31). Lillehammer, Norway: IEEE Computer Society.

Bardin, S., Herrmann, P., & Perroud, F. (2010, March). An alternative to SAT-based approaches for bit-vectors. In the *16th International Conference on Tools and Algorithms for the Construction and Analysis of Systems* (TACAS 2010) (pp. 84–98). Paphos, Cyprus: Springer.

Burnim, J., & Sen, K. (2008, September). Heuristics for scalable dynamic test generation. In the *23rd IEEE/ACM International Conference on Automated Software Engineering* (ASE 2008) (pp. 443–446). L'Aquila, Italy: IEEE.

Cadar, C., Dunbar, D., & Engler, D. R. (2008, December). KLEE: Unassisted and automatic generation of high-coverage tests for complex systems programs. In the *8th USENIX Symposium on Operating Systems Design and Implementation* (OSDI 2008) (pp. 209–224). San Diego, CA: USENIX Association.

Cadar, C., Ganesh, V., Pawlowski, P. M., Dill, D. L., & Engler, D. R. (2006, November). EXE: Automatically generating inputs of death. In the *13th ACM Conference on Computer and Communications Security* (CCS'06) (pp. 322–335). Alexandria, VA: ACM Press.

Candea, G., Bucur, S., & Zamfir, C. (2010, June). Automated software testing as a service. In the *First ACM Symposium on Cloud Computing* (SoCC 2010) (pp. 155–160). Indianapolis, IN: ACM Press.

CCRA. (2012). *The common criteria for information technology security evaluation*. Retrieved from http://www.commoncriteriaportal.org

Chebaro, O., Kosmatov, N., Giorgetti, A., & Julliand, J. (2012, March). Program slicing enhances a verification technique combining static and dynamic analysis. In the *27th Annual ACM Symposium on Applied Computing* (SAC 2012) (pp. 1284–1291). Riva del Garda, Italy: ACM Press.

Ciortea, L., Zamfir, C., Bucur, S., Chipounov, V., & Candea, G. (2009). Cloud9: a software testing service. *Operating Systems Review, 43*(4), 5–10. doi:10.1145/1713254.1713257

Clarke, L. A. (1976). A system to generate test data and symbolically execute programs. *IEEE Transactions on Software Engineering, 2*(3), 215–222. doi:10.1109/TSE.1976.233817

Cohen, E., Dahlweid, M., Hillebrand, M. A., Leinenbach, D., Moskal, M., Santen, T., et al. (2009, August). VCC: A practical system for verifying concurrent C. In the *22nd International Conference on Theorem Proving in Higher Order Logics* (TPHOLs 2009) (pp. 23–42). Munich, Germany: Springer.

Gao, J., Bai, X., & Tsai, W.-T. (2011). Cloud testing - Issues, challenges, needs and practice. *Software Engineering: An International Journal, 1*(1), 9–23.

Godefroid, P., Klarlund, N., & Sen, K. (2005, June). DART: Directed automated random testing. In the *ACM SIGPLAN 2005 Conference on Programming Language Design and Implementation* (PLDI'05) (pp. 213–223). Chicago, IL: ACM Press.

Godefroid, P., Levin, M. Y., & Molnar, D. A. (2012). SAGE: Whitebox fuzzing for security testing. *Communications of the ACM, 55*(3), 40–44. doi:10.1145/2093548.2093564

Godefroid, P., & Molnar, D. (2010, March). *Fuzzing in the cloud* (Position Statement) (Tech. Rep. No. MSR-TR-2010-29). Redmond, WA: Microsoft Research. Retrieved from http://research.microsoft.com/apps/pubs/?id=121494

Google. (2012). *Google app engine documentation*. Retrieved from https://developers.google.com/appengine/

Gotlieb, A., Leconte, M., & Marre, B. (2010, September). *Constraint solving on modular integers.* In the CP 2010 Workshop on Constraint Modelling and Reformulation (ModRef 2010). St Andrews, UK: Springer.

Gulavani, B. S., Henzinger, T. A., Kannan, Y., Nori, A. V., & Rajamani, S. K. (2006, November). SYNERGY: A new algorithm for property checking. In the *14th ACM SIGSOFT International Symposium on Foundations of Software Engineering* (FSE 2005) (pp. 117–127). Portland, OR: ACM Press.

Hanawa, T., Banzai, T., Koizumi, H., Kanbayashi, R., Imada, T., & Sato, M. (2010, April). Large-scale software testing environment using cloud computing technology for dependable parallel and distributed systems. In the *Third International Conference on Software Testing, Verification and Validation Workshops* (ICSTW 2010) (pp. 428–433). Paris, France: IEEE Computer Society.

Heiser, G., Murray, T. C., & Klein, G. (2012). It's time for trustworthy systems. *IEEE Security & Privacy, 10*(2), 67–70. doi:10.1109/MSP.2012.41

King, J. C. (1976). Symbolic execution and program testing. *Communications of the ACM, 19*(7), 385–394. doi:10.1145/360248.360252

King, T. M., & Ganti, A. S. (2010, April). Migrating autonomic self-testing to the cloud. In the *Third International Conference on Software Testing, Verification and Validation Workshops* (ICSTW 2010) (pp. 438–443). Paris, France: IEEE Computer Society.

Klein, G. (2010, November). From a verified kernel towards verified systems. In the *8th Asian Symposium on Programming Languages and Systems* (APLAS 2010) (pp. 21–33). Shanghai, China: Springer.

Klein, G., Elphinstone, K., Heiser, G., Andronick, J., Cock, D., Derrin, P., et al. (2009, October). seL4: formal verification of an OS kernel. In the *ACM SIGOPS 22nd Symposium on Operating Systems Principles* (SOSP 2009) (pp. 207–220). Big Sky, MT: ACM Press.

Kosmatov, N. (2010a). Constraint-based techniques for software testing. In Meziane, F., & Vandera, S. (Eds.), *Artificial intelligence applications for improved software engineering development: New prospects.* Hershey, PA: IGI Global.

Kosmatov, N. (2010b). *Online version of the PathCrawler test generation tool.* Retrieved from http://pathcrawler-online.com/

Kosmatov, N., Botella, B., Roger, M., & Williams, N. (2011, March). Online test generation with PathCrawler: Tool demo (Best tool demo award.). In the *3rd Workshop on Constraints in Software Testing, Verification, and Analysis* (CSTVA 2011) (pp. 316–317). Berlin, Germany: IEEE Computer Society.

Kosmatov, N., Williams, N., Botella, B., Roger, M., & Chebaro, O. (2012, May). A lesson on structural testing with pathcrawler-online.com. In the *6th International Conference on Tests and Proofs* (TAP 2012) (pp. 169–175). Prague, Czech Republic: Springer.

Leconte, M., & Berstel, B. (2006, September). *Extending a CP solver with congruences as domains for software verification.* In the CP 2006 Workshop on Constraints in Software Testing, Verification and Analysis (CSTVA 2006). Nantes, France: Springer.

Leroy, X. (2009). Formal verification of a realistic compiler. *Communications of the ACM, 52*(7), 107–115. doi:10.1145/1538788.1538814

Loulergue, F., Gava, F., Kosmatov, N., & Lemerre, M. (2012, July). (To appear). *Towards verified cloud computing environments*. In the 2012 International Conference on High Performance Computing and Simulation (HPCS 2012). Madrid, Spain: IEEE. *Computers & Society*.

Marre, B., & Arnould, A. (2000, September). Test sequences generation from Lustre descriptions: GATeL. In the *15th IEEE International Conference on Automated Software Engineering* (ASE'00) (pp. 229–237). Grenoble, France: IEEE Computer Society.

Marre, B., & Michel, C. (2010). Improving the floating point addition and subtraction constraints. In the *16th International Conference on Principles and Practice of Constraint Programming (CP 2010) (Vol. LNCS 6308*, (pp. 360–367). St. Andrews, UK: Springer.

Mell, P., & Grance, T. (2011, September). *The NIST definition of cloud computing* (NIST Special Publication No. 800-145). Gaithersburg, MD: The National Institute of Standards and Technology (NIST).

Michel, C. (2002, January). Exact projection functions for floating point number constraints. In the 7th International Symposium on Artificial Intelligence and Mathematics (AIMA 2002). Fort Lauderdale, Florida, USA.

Nipkow, T., Paulson, L. C., & Wenzel, M. (2002). *Isabelle/HOL—A proof assistant for higher-order logic (Vol. 2283)*. Springer.

Oriol, M., & Ullah, F. (2010, April). Yeti on the cloud. In the *Third International Conference on Software Testing, Verification and Validation Workshops* (ICSTW 2010) (pp. 434–437). Paris, France: IEEE Computer Society.

Parveen, T., & Tilley, S. R. (2010, April). When to migrate software testing to the cloud? In the *Third International Conference on Software Testing, Verification and Validation Workshops* (ICSTW 2010) (pp. 424–427). Paris, France: IEEE Computer Society.

Riungu, L. M., Taipale, O., & Smolander, K. (2010a, December). Research issues for software testing in the cloud. In the *Second International Conference on Cloud Computing* (CloudCom 2010) (pp. 557–564). Indianapolis, IN: IEEE.

Riungu, L. M., Taipale, O., & Smolander, K. (2010b, April). Software testing as an online service: Observations from practice. In the *Third International Conference on Software Testing, Verification and Validation Workshops* (ICSTW 2010) (pp. 418–423). Paris, France: IEEE Computer Society.

Sen, K., Marinov, D., & Agha, G. (2005, September). CUTE: A concolic unit testing engine for C. In the *5th Joint Meeting of the European Software Engineering Conference and ACM SIGSOFT Symposium on the Foundations of Software Engineering* (ESEC/FSE 2005) (pp. 263–272). Lisbon, Portugal: ACM Press.

Tillmann, N., & de Halleux, J. (2008, April). White box test generation for. NET. In the *2nd International Conference on Tests and Proofs* (TAP 2008) (pp. 133–153). Prato, Italy: Springer.

van der Aalst, L. (2010). *Software testing as a service* (STaaS) (Tech. Rep.). Vianen, The Netherlands: Sogeti. Retrieved from http://www.leovanderaalst.nl/Software Testing as a Service - STaaS.pdf

Williams, N., Marre, B., Mouy, P., & Roger, M. (2005, April). PathCrawler: Automatic generation of path tests by combining static and dynamic analysis. In the *5th European Dependable Computing Conference* (EDCC 2005) (pp. 281–292). Budapest, Hungary: Springer.

Yu, L., Tsai, W.-T., Chen, X., Liu, L., Zhao, Y., Tang, L., et al. (2010, June). Testing as a service over cloud. In the *Fifth IEEE International Symposium on Service-Oriented System Engineering (SOSE 2010)* (pp. 181–188). Nanjing, China: IEEE Computer Society.

Zhang, Q., Cheng, L., & Boutaba, R. (2010). Cloud computing: State-of-the-art and research challenges. *Journal of Internet Services and Applications*, *1*(1), 7–18. doi:10.1007/s13174-010-0007-6

Chapter 12
Leveraging the Cloud for Large–Scale Software Testing – A Case Study:
Google Chrome on Amazon

Anjan Pakhira
University of Newcastle upon Tyne, UK

Peter Andras
University of Newcastle upon Tyne, UK

ABSTRACT

Testing is a critical phase in the software life-cycle. While small-scale component-wise testing is done routinely as part of development and maintenance of large-scale software, the system level testing of the whole software is much more problematic due to low level of coverage of potential usage scenarios by test cases and high costs associated with wide-scale testing of large software. Here, the authors investigate the use of cloud computing to facilitate the testing of large-scale software. They discuss the aspects of cloud-based testing and provide an example application of this. They describe the testing of the functional importance of methods of classes in the Google Chrome software. The methods that we test are predicted to be functionally important with respect to a functionality of the software. The authors use network analysis applied to dynamic analysis data generated by the software to make these predictions. They check the validity of these predictions by mutation testing of a large number of mutated variants of the Google Chrome. The chapter provides details of how to set up the testing process on the cloud and discusses relevant technical issues.

DOI: 10.4018/978-1-4666-2536-5.ch012

INTRODUCTION

Large-scale software (Goth, 2008) usually integrates a very large number of components developed over many years, possibly by different companies or different units of large software companies. This makes understanding testing and maintenance of such software systems naturally very difficult with plenty of opportunities for leaving unnoticed integration bugs (i.e. pieces of software code that induce undesired behaviors of the software) in the software (Dadzie, 2005; Meyer, 2008; NIST & RTI, 2002; Porter, Siy, Toman, & Votta, 1997; Wolverton, 1974).

Such software is likely to contain millions of lines of code, written by many software developers, and tested in various contexts at component level. While the syntactic, semantic and general logical correctness of components can be assumed to large extent, the system-scale testing of such software is usually patchy due to the quick combinatorial explosion of the space of possible test cases and the high costs associated with detailed testing. Time constraints driven by commercial objectives also act against the realization of the ideal wide-scale testing of the software.

Cloud computing (Armbrust et al., 2009; Buyya, Shin, & Venugopal, 2008) has been introduced recently as very large scale remote computing service based on virtualization technology (Barham et al., 2003; Nanda & Chiueh, 2005). The computing cloud offers the possibility of running large number of virtual computers in parallel in a flexible manner, such that computing resources come on-line as they are needed and when they are not needed the overall resource set scales back automatically. Cloud computing provides flexible storage and processing resources that are accessible remotely through a relatively easy to use interface. Commercial cloud services currently provided by Amazon, Rackspace, Microsoft and Google amongst others; offer considerable flexibility in terms operating systems and other software that are available for use on the virtual machines. These services are currently offered at a low unit price for usage, which makes it attractive to use cloud instead of investing in captive infrastructure of similar capability.

The advent of cloud services in the form of platform-as-a-service (PaaS) like Amazon's EC2 and S3, makes it possible for these platforms to be fashioned for a variety of uses (computational, storage or both). Predominant amongst these is relatively cheap commercial shared scalable web-hosting, where it is possible to scale the number of web servers as required. This flexibility and scalability of use has led to some exploratory research on how cloud resources may be leveraged for software testing (Candea, Bucur, & Zamfir, 2010; Joglekar, 2009).

In theory it may be argued that by virtue of operational flexibility, and ability of the user to scale resource allocation and usage on demand, the cloud can benefit some types of software testing. Wide scale software testing requiring substantial compute and storage resources and where the testing process can be managed (automated) through a workflow needing minimal human intervention is representative of type of testing that may benefit from the use of the cloud. Such testing is generally not practicable on typical desktop computers, due to limitation of resource scalability and consequently time and cost limitations.

In this case study we present the use of cloud computing to support wide-scale testing of large software systems. The objective of our experiment (that forms the context of this case study) is to explore the notion that complex network analysis of software dynamic analysis data may be used to detect functionally important elements of object oriented software systems. The reported work is part of a series of experiments based on the premise that software systems can be viewed as complex networks, and software engineering may therefore benefit from analysis based on that viewpoint. The ultimate aim of these experiments is to verify applicability of network analysis methods to analyze software engineering data, so that these methods may be adopted for software analysis to support software testing.

Our approach to verification is based on black box testing, with a form of fault seeding evaluation and evaluation through a mutation scoring (Abran, Moore, Bourque, & Dupuis, 2004). In this experiment network analysis is applied to predict functional importance of methods of classes in Google Chrome web browser. Efficient and cost effective verification of these predictions required the use of cloud for generating Google Chrome mutants.

A method is considered functionally important with respect to a functionality of the software if a syntactically and semantically correct alteration of the method has a significant impact on the delivery of the respective functionality by the software system (e.g. the software crashes or some critical operation cannot be executed correctly). We describe in detail how to organize the workflow on the Amazon cloud that delivers several hundred parallel tests of the Google Chrome in a relatively short time and requiring relatively limited individual human effort.

The objectives of the chapter are as follows: (1) the description of a practical example of wide-scale testing on the cloud of a large software system; (2) the general discussion and description of the cloud-based testing of large-scale software grounded in the example case that we describe.

The rest of the chapter is structured as follows. First we review the relevant literature. Next we introduce briefly our approach to the concept of functional importance. Then we describe how we use network analysis to predict functional importance of methods – this leads to the need of large volume testing of complex software. Following this we focus on the details of organizing and executing large-scale testing on the cloud. Then we discuss key issues and formulate recommendations about testing on the cloud. Finally the chapter is closed by the conclusions and future work section.

BACKGROUND

The guide to the Software Engineering Body of Knowledge (SWEBOK) (Abran, et al., 2004) defines software testing as "an activity performed for evaluating product quality, and for improving it, by identifying defects and problems [...] Software testing consists of the dynamic verification of the behavior of a program on a finite set of test cases, suitably selected from the usually infinite executions domain, against the expected behavior." We follow the systems approach according to the SWEBOK and we use the terms software and software system interchangeably. The complexity and cost of software testing continually pushes research towards finding novel methods to improve the coverage and relevance of testing. A general issue in the context of testing large-scale software is the prioritization of testing (Elbaum, Malishevsky, & Rothermel, 2002; Rothermel, Untch, Chengyun, & Harrold, 2001) and the related automation of generation of test cases (Avritzer & Weyuker, 1995).

The relevance of testing depends on the relevance of the tested usage scenario in the context of real use of the software. An approach that aims to help in these respects is the use of dynamic analysis to support program comprehension (Cornelissen, Zaidman, van Deursen, Moonen, & Koschke, 2009) and through this the better prioritization of test cases. Various approaches combine the examination of dynamic analysis data with visualization techniques and search techniques to highlight conceptually important aspects of the program (Cornelissen, Zaidman, Holten, &.all, 2008; Lienhard, Ducasse, & Gırba, 2009). Others use various metrics and text mining methods for example to determine important classes in the software (Tahvildar & Kontogiannis, 2004; Zaidman & Demeyer, 2008).

Features of software are defined as user observable behaviors of the software, while software concepts are parts of the software code that implement as a logical unit a behavior of the software (both user observable behaviors and behaviors that the user cannot directly observe) (Chen & Rajlich, 2000; Rajlich & Wilde, 2002). Understanding software features and concepts underpin the understanding of what the software does to deliver its functionalities and this can be used to make test case prioritization more efficient. The automated and semi-automated detection of software code parts corresponding to features and software concepts has received intensive attention in the last decades (Bohnet & Döllner, 2006; Chen & Rajlich, 2000; Poshyvanyk, Gueheneuc, Marcus, Antoniol, & Rajlich, 2007; Rajlich & Wilde, 2002). For example, algorithms have been suggested for the detection of code segments responsible for features (in particular unwanted features or bugs) on the basis of text analysis of developer comments associated with parts of the software (e.g. methods of classes) (Poshyvanyk, et al., 2007) or on the basis of combination of dynamic analysis data and visualization techniques (Bohnet & Döllner, 2006). Software usage scenarios can be seen as a structured collection of delivery of software features and the analysis of the run-time behavior of the software during usage scenarios to some extent overlaps with the search for the parts of the software code responsible for the relevant software features.

In object-oriented software, intra- and inter-object level messages are exchanged at runtime. This exchange of messages at the object level can be represented as a network composed of nodes and links. A node being an object (instance of class), and links being method calls, this may be referred to as object collaboration graphing (Wirfs-Brock, Wilkerson, & Wiener, 1990). It has been shown that the collaboration graph of object oriented software can be analyzed in meaningful manner as a complex networks (Myers, 2003; Potanin, Noble, Frean, & Biddle, 2005). Complex network analysis (Albert & Barabási, 2002) of a system is based on the assumption of the strong correlation between the functional integrity of the system represented by the network and structural integ-

rity of the network representation of the system (Barabási & Bonabeau, 2003). Complex network analysis includes a range of heuristic techniques that are considered relevant in appropriate contexts for the determination of network components that are critically important for the delivery of the functionality of the system represented by the network (Albert & Barabási, 2002).

The concept of functional importance (Barabási & Bonabeau, 2003; Jeong, Tombor, Albert, & al., 2000) is established in the context of the analysis of complex biological and social systems. For example, well-defined and relatively small areas of the cortex in the brain are functionally important for the generation and understanding of human speech (i.e. the Broca and the Wernicke areas of the cortex (Kandel, Schwartz, & Jessell, 2000)). Similarly, a relatively small group of actors may play a functionally important role in maintaining successful teams of actors that can deliver highly successful movies (i.e. see the analysis of the network of movie actors (Barabási & Bonabeau, 2003). In the context of software engineering similar concepts have emerged as well. For example, (Zhang & Jacobsen, 2007) list four characteristics of important software elements (e.g. classes or methods) in the context of aspect mining: popularity (frequent usage), transitive popularity (connected by usage to popular elements), significance (connected by usage to a large number of distinct elements), and transitive significance (connected by usage to significant elements). (Poshyvanyk, et al., 2007) use information retrieval methods to identify methods that are important from the perspective of fixing reported bugs of complex software systems. The ability to predict such functionally important parts of a software system can facilitate the improving of the efficiency of software testing. In general test prioritization (Elbaum, et al., 2002; Rothermel, et al., 2001) can be also seen as the identification of the functionally most important parts of the software onto which testing should focus.

Cloud computing services do not currently have a defined standard, primarily because it is still evolving. The ideas behind cloud computing can be traced back to Grid computing. Grid computing developed out of research on meta-computing (Terekhov, 2003), high performance computing (Severance & Dowd, 1998) and high throughput computing (Chaudhry, Caprioli, Yip, & Tremblay, 2005). The motivation was to provide secure, reliable resource sharing to support computational science. The concept of Grid presented by Foster and Kesselman (Foster & Kesselman, 2003), and subsequent development of Globus Middleware (Globus.org), can together be considered as *de-facto* standard for the Grid. National research initiatives led to development of Grid service, notable examples include the National Grid Service (NGS) (UKeScience) in UK and TeraGrid (NSF) in USA amongst others. The research on Grid infrastructure setup and the use of Grid Computing had a wide focus, which included work on facilitating usability of the infrastructure. This aspect focused on security and access. An interface similar to Web Service was proposed, named Grid Service, however it proved complicated and access was predominantly based on use of secure shell (SSH), or a web interface embedded with SSH console. Grid software infrastructure is predominantly based on Unix/ Linux, and did not use virtualization. Major Grid services use Globus based software infrastructure, which aids interoperability, and resource sharing, however to the user the Grid resources present a set configuration. Grid operations are mostly sponsored by research funding, and operation is non-commercial in nature.

Cloud computing is primarily enterprise driven, and services are offered on commercial basis. Cloud infrastructure and services differ widely, and there is no explicit support for interoperability. Cloud resources are highly flexible in comparison to Grid resources, enabling users to adopt the base infrastructure for a wide range of computing end use, by virtue of use of virtualiza-tion (Barham, et al., 2003; S. Nanda & T.Chiueh, 2005). The user interface to most cloud services is web service based, and interactive access is possible using platform specific access technology, like SSH on Linux/Unix platform or remote desktop on Windows platform. Figure 1 presents a schematic diagram of the cloud infrastructure setup. In addition the figure shows how the various parts may be composed to provide the cloud service. EC2 and S3 are Amazon specific terms, used for illustration only. The aim is to be vendor agnostic; however for illustration purpose some Amazon cloud service names have been used. Cloud service providers; currently maintain large facilities housing computers that can be used for computation and storage. These facilities are usually provisioned with fast communication network, and computers that provide frontend and backend software based services. These services may be web services based interface facilitating user's interaction with the services. These services may deal with account setup, management and using cloud based resources. Amazon, Microsoft, Google, Rackspace, Salesforce are some commercial cloud service providers. Cloud services use the utility model (Pagden, 2003a, 2003b) of charging for use of the services. In this model users pay for resources used, and there is no standing charge.

The current interest in cloud computing infrastructure, platforms, services and applications, is partly driven by marketing hype, and partly genuine interest that this technology innovation may help address issues in large scale computing, particularly that of access to resource on demand. In software testing the oft quoted statistic is that software testing is resource intensive and can account for between 40-70 percent of the cost of software through its life cycle. Most of this cost is incurred in the post construction, production use, and maintenance phases. The main issues are how much to test (test sufficiency), what and where to direct testing resource (test prioritization) to achieve maximum reliability and consequently achieve high assurance. The latter question

Figure 1. Conceptual diagram to demonstrate how a cloud service may be setup, with computational and storage resource

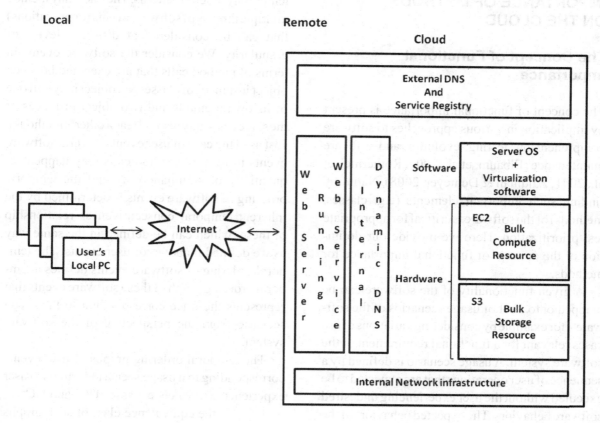

forms the central theme of program comprehension research.

The issue of resource is determined by decisions on test sufficiency and test prioritization factors, in addition to test objectives, and need for test environments fidelity to target use environment. In some cases the test resource is also determined by how the software is operated, i.e. whether it is primarily graphical user interface (GUI) driven, command line driven with or without scripting or both.

Most standard software testing today whether its purpose is system integration, regression testing based on a set of unit tests, or performance testing, rely on predetermined workflows that affords a degree of automation to the test process.

In most cases testing infrastructure is captive in nature, with significant degree of control over how it is managed and operated. Early research on software testing in the cloud (Riungu et al., 2010) has explored some of these issues. (Riungu, et al., 2010) also discusses research viewpoint on what considerations may form the basis on which a decision may be formed to migrate testing to cloud. (Riungu, et al., 2010) also presents some issues that deal with testing as a service (TaaS), many of these services are built on top of Amazon cloud platform, and target small and medium enterprise involved application testing. These services facilitate migration of existing testing process that use captive infrastructure to use cloud infrastructure for example (Green Hat).

TESTING THE FUNCTIONAL IMPORTANCE OF METHODS ON THE CLOUD

The Concept of Functional Importance

The concept of functional importance is present by implication in various approaches to software comprehension, testing, evolution and software maintenance (Elbaum, et al., 2002; Rothermel, et al., 2001; Zaidman & Demeyer, 2008). Naturally finding such important elements (e.g. classes, methods) of the software is critical for appropriate test prioritization. Here we provide our definition of the concept of functional importance for methods.

A given functionality of the software can be mapped onto a set of usage scenarios of the software – for example by considering variations of use cases relevant for a functional requirement of the software system. A usage scenario is defined by a sequence of user operations that are expected to be executed without the user experiencing undesired software behaviors. The expected behaviors of the software are set by the requirements specification of the software system. From the user's perspective the usage scenario can be represented as a set of user events, including both user perceptions and actions, which are arranged in temporally ordered patterns. Note that several user events may happen fully or partly simultaneously such that they may start and end at same time or at different times. The user events E1 and E2 are temporally consecutive if an event E1 has to terminate before the start of another event E2, and there is no intervening interval during which these two events overlap. The temporal consecutiveness of user events defines a temporal ordering graph over the set of user events corresponding to a usage scenario. An example of temporal ordering graph representation of a partial usage scenario is shown in Figure 2.

From the perspective of the software system the usage scenario is represented by a trace that is a set of software events that are arranged in temporally ordered patterns. The trace may include multiple threads of software events (or operations) that can be considered at different levels of granularity. We consider the software events in terms of method calls that are executed between object instances of classes (an object may call one of its own methods and two object instances of the same class may also call each other's methods). Just as in the case of user events, several software events in form of method calls may happen sequentially or simultaneously and the temporal ordering of software events is determined by the inherent temporal consecutiveness relationship of these, which can be defined in the same way as we defined it above for user events. The temporal ordering of software events defines a temporal ordering graph of these software events that represents the trace corresponding to the usage scenario from the perspective of the software system.

The temporal ordering graphs of user events corresponding to a usage scenario forms two user experience equivalence classes UC^+ and UC^-.

UC^+ – is the equivalence class of such graphs that correspond to the appropriate execution of the scenario that fits with the desired behavior of the software from the user's perspective; and UC^- – is the equivalence class of all other such graphs that correspond to inappropriate execution of the usage scenario that include undesired behavior of the software (e.g. experiencing a crash or inability to execute a required operation).

The desired behavior of the software may include some unexpected behavior of the software if these unexpected behaviors do not affect the expected functionality of the software (e.g. a slight change in the color shade of the background of the menu bar may be unexpected but may not affect the expected functionality of the software, because it is functionally unimportant). The undesired behavior of the software always includes some unexpected behavior that the software should not do if it conforms to the specification of the

Figure 2. Temporal ordering graph representation of a partial usage scenario from the perspective of the user. User events indicated by dashed surround are user perceptions, while the user events indicated by continuous surround are user actions. Temporal consecutiveness of user events is indicated by arrows.

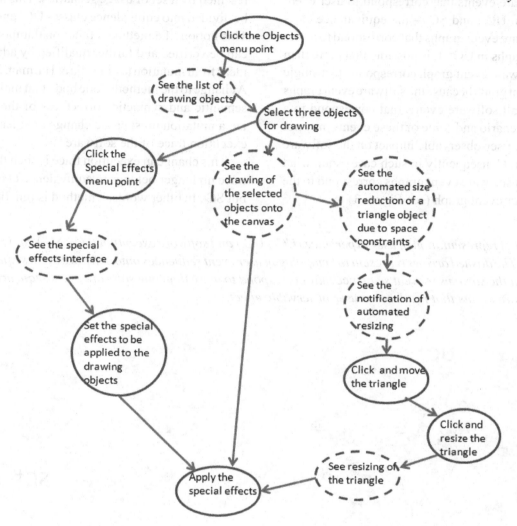

user requirements. We should also note that the desired behavior of the software may depend to some extent on the user as well and on the strictness of the definition of what is desired behavior and what is not desired behavior. For example, changing the background color of a panel from light blue to light red may be regarded as acceptable and within the limits of desired behavior by one user while the same may be regarded as undesirable by another user. The desirable behavior is defined as the expected behavior according to the requirements specifications – this defines the UC$^+$ equivalence class. To construct an approximation of the UC$^-$ equivalence class we may consider all kinds of possible undesired disturbances of the user experience – of course, possibly some of these will have no corresponding software execution trace.

The UC$^+$ and UC$^-$ equivalence classes induce a matching equivalence class structure over the possible temporal ordering graphs of software events that correspond to the considered usage scenario: SC⁺ – the equivalence class of such graphs of software events that correspond to user event graphs in UC⁺; and SC⁻ – the equivalence class of software event graphs that correspond to a user event graphs in UC⁻. It is possible that more than one software event graph corresponds to a single user event graph because the software event graphs include all software events that correspond to a usage scenario and some of these events may not have any user-observable impact on the software behavior. Consequently in such cases somewhat different software event graphs correspond to the same user event graph (see Figure 3).

A method is defined as functionally important with respect to functionality of the software represented by a set of usage scenarios. This set can be divided into equivalence classes UC⁺ and UC⁻. This notion of a method's functional importance can be verified and further qualified by adopting ideas from mutation testing (Jia & Harman, 2006). A change to the methods code body that maintains semantic and syntactic correctness of the code, i.e. a mutation must cause change to at least one execution trace of the software.

This change in execution trace is such that the trace no longer belongs to equivalence class SC⁺ but SC⁻. In other words, a method is functionally

Figure 3. A representation of user experience (UC⁺, UC⁻) and software execution (SC⁺, SC⁻) equivalence classes. The dashed arrows represent the mapping of user event sequences onto software event sequences. Note that the same user event sequence may correspond to more than one software event sequences due to software events that produce no user observable effect.

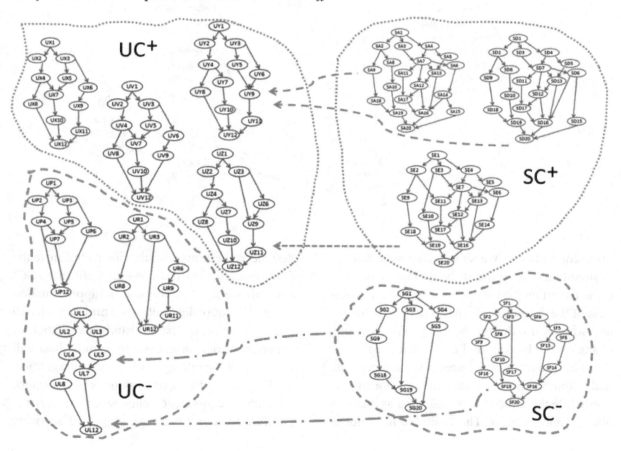

important if a syntactically and semantically correct change of the code of the method causes the software to produce some undesired behavior.

The above definition allows any kind of syntactically and semantically correct changes to the code of the method. The range and kind of changes of the method's code that cause the above described effect determine the extent of functional importance of the method. Constraining the possible changes to the code allows approximation of the functional importance of methods.

A simple and rough approximation of functional importance of a method can be determined by considering the simplest generic and major alteration of the method, which is its replacement by a syntactically and semantically correct empty stub that satisfies the interface requirements of the method (i.e. input and output variables have the appropriate types and are initialized appropriately, when this is required). The method is functionally important in this approximate sense with respect to a certain functionality of the software if the impact of replacing the method with a satisfactory empty stub moves at least one of the software event graphs corresponding to the delivery of the functionality from SC^+ to SC^-. In the rest of the chapter we use this approximation of functional importance of methods.

Network Analysis for Prediction of Functional Importance of Methods

We consider the use of network analysis to provide a prediction of the functional importance of methods. The key assumption of network analysis of complex natural and artificial systems is that the structural integrity of the network representation of the system correlates well with the functional integrity of the system represented by the network (Barabási & Bonabeau, 2003; Jeong, et al., 2000). This means that if nodes or edges (or groups of these) can be found in the network such that their removal significantly changes the structural integrity measures of the network, then

it is expected that the corresponding real-life components or interactions of the system represented by the network are also similarly important for the functional integrity of the system.

Network analysis methods aim to predict the structural importance of network elements (nodes, edges, arcs) and their groups (Barabási & Bonabeau, 2003). For example, calculating the number of edges that a node is part of (connectedness of the node) or the number of shortest paths between other nodes that contain a given node (betweenness of the node) can be used to find structurally important nodes corresponding to functionally important components of the system represented by the network (Myers, 2003). Partitioning the network into optimal clusters of nodes or edges, according to some appropriate optimality criteria, can reveal parts of the real system that functionally belong together (Barabási & Bonabeau, 2003; Jeong, et al., 2000). The applicability of these methods in general depends on the nature of the distribution of the connectedness of the network nodes. If this distribution is such that the likelihood of finding nodes with high number of connections is significantly larger than the likelihood of finding such nodes in a random graph with uniform probability of having connections between any two nodes (i.e. this is also called an exponential random graph) then the usually used network analysis methods are likely to lead to the identification of structurally highly important network components (Albert & Barabási, 2002; Barabási & Bonabeau, 2003).

Large-scale software systems are systems of many interacting components and, accordingly, can be represented as networks (Myers, 2003). In particular, in the case of object oriented software, the network can be considered as having nodes corresponding to classes or objects and edges or arcs corresponding to method or function calls. Alternatively, a network representation of the software system may contain nodes representing functions and arcs representing calls of functions from inside of another function (note that there are also other possibilities for the network representation of a software system). It has been shows that network analysis methods can be applied to network representation of software systems in meaningful manner (Baxter et al., 2006; Wang, Wang, Yang, Zhang, & Ye, 2009). For our analysis here we chose to represent classes as nodes and method calls as arcs, including the frequency of method calls as the weight of the arc representing the method call.

Dynamic analysis data about software is collected using appropriate instrumentation (Ball, 1999; Cornelissen, et al., 2008; Pakhira & Andras, 2010) while running the software in a usage scenario derived from the requirements specification. Dynamic analysis provides information about the execution of the software based on trace of the instantiated objects of classes and actual function and method calls between these objects. This data characterizes the execution of usage scenarios. The collected data describes caller – callee class relations, specifying the methods or functions of the callee class that are called and possibly also the method of the caller class from which the call is originated. The usage scenario specific runtime behavior is represented as a network with nodes corresponding to classes and arcs corresponding to method calls. The nodes and arcs are labeled accordingly with names of classes and methods.

Thus, the network representation of this data (e.g. having classes represented as nodes and method and function calls as edges or arcs) allows the use of network analysis methods to investigate the software system. Accepting the key assumption of network analysis means that the analysis of the network representing the dynamic analysis data generated by the software allows, at least in principle, to search for edges that correspond to functionally important methods. Network analysis of the dynamic analysis data is expected to predict the functional importance of methods used in the software system.

Google Chrome

Google Chrome web browser is popular open source software. Google Chrome has an active development community, and provides access to development documentation and source. It uses multiple software components, written in more than one language (including C++), is object oriented in design, and the software body has more than a million lines of code and thousands of classes and methods. This apart it is available to build and run on most popular operating systems. Size and inherent complexity of the software, makes it an ideal choice of software to use in our research.

The version of Google Chrome used for this test is 72930. Basic static analysis based on number of lines of code (LOC) was done using UNIX tool SLOCCount (Wheeler). Total physical source lines of code (SLOC) was found to be 8,942,123, spread over 480 Microsoft Visual studio projects. Google Chrome incorporates many advanced and novel features, like support for HTML5, native client execution, and a highly optimized java script engine and compiler called V8. The design objectives behind this browser are motivated by need to implement better program abstraction within web browser application for improved performance (Reis & Gribble, 2009). The choice of Google Chrome in this experiment is not based on comparative evaluation of comparable browser applications. We think every application is likely to display unique signature from complex network analysis. In context of these series of experiments Google Chrome is just another professionally designed object oriented software, that is open source, and available on a wide variety of platform providing a degree of flexibility in preparation of experiment environment.

The use of Google Chrome was found to be challenging, because of the custom build system it uses. Generate your projects (GYP) scripts that are used to build this complex application, are not easy to modify for experimental purposes, such as static instrumentation based on compiler features.

We used a tool (modified Slimtune (Roy)) based on Microsoft Visual Studio profiler to dynamically instrument Google Chrome to collect program execution trace data. The dynamic analysis data was represented as a graph with nodes representing the classes and arcs representing the method calls between classes. A representation of the Google Chrome network is shown in Figure 4.

A critical feature of the system that is required for the expectation of successful application of network analysis methods is that the network representation of the system should have a scale-free structure (Barabási & Bonabeau, 2003). This characteristic of the network can be tested by considering the distribution of the node connectedness values of the network. If this distribution follows a power law (i.e. the probability of finding a node with 'a' connections is $p(x=a)=c \cdot a^{\gamma}$, where 'c' is a constant, and γ is the exponent of the power law) then the network is likely to have a scale-free structure. Alternatively, a more robust test is to check whether the corresponding cumulative distribution follows the equation

$p(x=a)=c \cdot a^{1-\gamma}$ (Clauset, Shalizi, & Newman, 2009). In such networks the likelihood of finding highly connected nodes is much higher than in random networks where the likelihood of connections between any two nodes is the same. This means that highly connected nodes play a particularly important role in the structural integrity of these networks. Using appropriate algorithms (Rubinov & Sporns, 2010) to search for such nodes and other related network components (e.g. edges that are frequently part of the shortest paths between nodes) can identify the key structurally important components of the networks.

We found that the cumulative node connectivity distribution of the Google Chrome network representation follows a power law with the equation

$$p\left(x \geq a\right) = e^{3.2433} \cdot a^{1-1.466}$$

This means that we may expect that network analysis can reveal methods that are functionally important within the system represented by the network as shown in Figure 5.

Predicting and Verifying Functional Importance of Methods

We chose four usage scenarios for the analysis of the software system. The four usage scenarios were designed such that they include a variety of the software features in the corresponding functionalities of the analyzed software (details of the scenarios are available on request form the authors). The functionalities represented by the selected usage scenarios were constructed such that they are likely to match with usage scenarios corresponding to functional requirements of the considered software systems. The Google Chrome usage scenarios included various aspects of Internet browsing, including saving contents, opening multiple tabs, closing tabs, searching in the displayed web page contents and other operations that exercised the browser's adver-

Figure 4. Network representation of the Google Chrome on the basis of dynamic analysis data (node and edge labels – i.e. class and method names – are omitted)

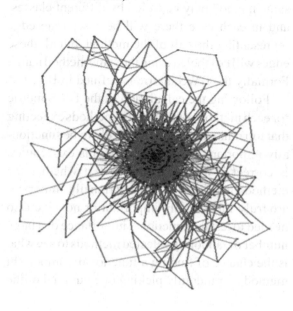

Figure 5. Cumulative node connectedness distribution of the network representation of dynamic analysis data generated by the execution of the Google Chrome, the linear relationship between the log (Connectedness), and log (CumFreq) indicates that the distribution follows a power law

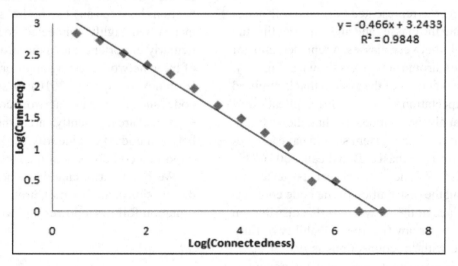

tised capabilities using applications supported by Google, like generating and viewing music videos using HTML5. For all considered usage scenarios we found between 500 – 800 classes and between 5000 – 8000 distinct methods that were used while running the usage scenario.

Use of Network Analysis to Predict Functional Importance

We used the betweenness score (BWS) network importance metric to predict functionally important methods in the Google Chrome. Since this network analysis method aims to determine arcs that connect relatively separated components of the network it is expected that these arcs are important for the structural integrity of the network. Consequently, following our expectation that network analysis is likely to determine functionally important components of the system represented by the network, we expect that the methods corresponding to these arcs will be functionally important in the software system with respect to the functionality of the software to which the network representation of the dynamic analysis data corresponds.

The BWS score of an edge in the network is given by the number of shortest paths between any two nodes of the network that contain the given edge. The BWS metric of a method is the maximum of the BWS metric values of all edges representing the method – note that a method may be represented by more than one edges since the same method may be called by different classes, and in each case there will be a separate edge representing the call of the method, but all these edges will be labeled using the same method name. Formally the BWS metric is defined in Box 1.

Following the calculation of the BWS metric for each method we ranked the methods expecting that top ranked methods are likely to be functionally important. To confirm that this expectation is correct it was necessary to test whether the methods predicted to be functionally important are truly functionally important or not. We also needed to test the functional importance of a large number of randomly selected methods to see what is the chance of finding a functionally important method by randomly picking one hundred of the

Box 1. BWS metric

$$BWS(m) = \max_{s} \begin{vmatrix} \left\{ e_1, ..., e_k \right\} \middle| e \in \left\{ e_1, ..., e_k \right\} \\ \sum_{i=1}^{k} \frac{1}{f(e_i)} \leq \sum_{j=1}^{k'} \frac{1}{f(e'_j)'} \\ \forall \left\{ e'_1, ..., e'_{k'} \right\} : \\ \left| nodes(e_1) \cap nodes(e'_1) \right| \geq 1, \\ \left| nodes(e_k) \cap nodes(e'_{k'}) \right| \geq 1, \\ \left| nodes(e_i) \cap nodes(e'_{i+1}) \right| = 1, \\ \left| nodes(e'_j) \cap nodes(e'_{j+1}) \right| = 1, \\ i = 1, ..., k; \; j = 1, ..., k' \end{vmatrix}$$

where *nodes(e)* is the set of the two nodes that are connected by the edge *e*.

methods of the software from the list of methods identified by the dynamic analysis of the software during the execution of a given usage scenario.

Verification of Predictions

To check the functional importance of methods predicted to be functionally important we altered the code of the software by replacing the chosen methods by a satisfactory empty stub as we described this above. The methods that we considered were replaced by the appropriate empty method one-by-one, and only one such method was replaced at each time. The expected behavior of the software was defined implicitly by defining in a strict sense the behavior that is undesired such as crashing of the software and inability to execute the strictly defined operations included in the usage scenario.

To evaluate the impact of the replacing of each method with the corresponding empty stub, the modified code was run with the same usage scenario that led to the prediction of the method as functionally important. Since we defined the user expectation in a strict manner that does not allow subjective interpretation of the user experience we used a single user (a computer science graduate

student) to evaluate the modified variants of the software for each usage scenario. The user experiences were grouped in two equivalence classes UC+ and UC− as we described above.

The Results of the Verification

To check whether the prediction of being functionally important works better than chance, we considered a random selection of 100 methods from methods of the Google Chrome software system that were used in the considered usage scenarios. We evaluated each of these to determine the likelihood of finding a functionally important method by randomly picking one. For Google Chrome, we found that 50% of randomly picked method qualifies as functionally important (in the approximate sense as we stated above) for the relevant usage scenario. In comparison, we found that the most highly ranked methods according to the network analysis metric are significantly more likely to be functionally important than 50% (see Figure 6). For each top-k (k between 1 to 20) set of predicted functionally important methods the graph shows the average percentage of methods that are shown experimentally to be functionally important (continuous line). The dashed lines show

Figure 6. The accuracy of the predictions of functional importance based on the BWS network analysis metric

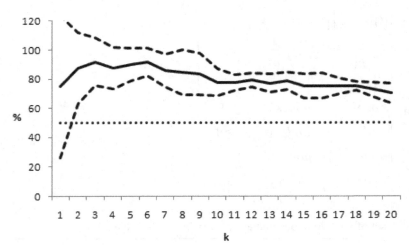

the 95% confidence bounds around the average value and the dotted line shows the expected percentage of functionally important method among a randomly chosen set of methods (50%). Note that the upper confidence bound reaches above 100%; this is just in order to be consistent about the numerical calculation of the bound value, the actual percentage value naturally cannot be above 100%.

The process of verification of result of mutation is extremely time intensive, specifically in the case of Google Chrome due to the reasons highlighted in preceding discussion. The mutation build alone took considerable time (over 4 hours on a high specification machine with 8GB RAM). We found that the process can be trivially parallelized or task farmed, to improve efficiency of the complete testing process, leading us to use the Amazon cloud to run simultaneously around many virtual machines to check the impact of the code alteration of the selected methods.

Setting up Testing on the Cloud

Figure 7 presents a schematic diagram of the cloud experiment that we performed. The experiment of validating predictions of functionally impor-

tant methods of Google Chrome consists of six distinct phases. The experiment commences with data generation of execution trace for multiple usage scenarios. Data analysis of these trace using network analysis provide us with a set of predictions of functionally important methods, for each scenario trace data, analyzed. In the absence of an oracle against which predictions can be validated, the approach used is to apply mutation testing technique. In this approach, we decided to test the top 60 predictions of all the lists of predictions, generated, In addition a baseline was generated by choosing to do mutation testing on the top 100 distinct methods of a separate list. This list was generated by random selection from the superset of all methods exercised in the execution domain. Total number of mutant tests generated by following this process was 820, leading to use of the cloud.

The Amazon Cloud provides separate web service based interfaces to manage S3 storage and EC2 compute resources. The basic operations that can be performed on S3 are uploading and downloading of data to and from a user's PC. S3 is location abstracted. This enables pervasive access to data on S3 from outside and within the Cloud, using a uniform interface. The basic operations

Figure 7. Schematic diagram of the experiment to test functional importance of Google Chrome

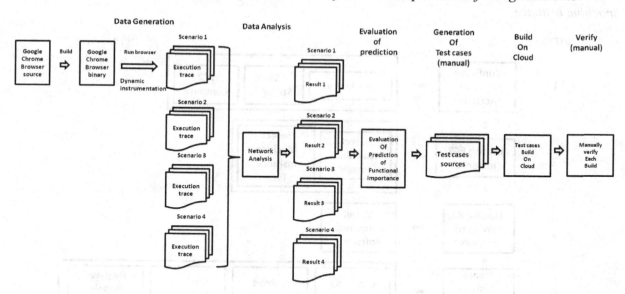

that can be performed on EC2 are, starting and stopping an instance. In addition it also provides advanced facility to create, attach and release additional disk space. Amazon provides a set of command line and web based user tools to enable users to use the web service based interface with ease. Many of these tools have been developed using the open source model, which are free to use. Some user tools are made available on a commercial basis for a payment, however this particularly applies to machine images provided by resellers so it was not a consideration in our case. An Amazon Machine Image (AMI) is a bundle of operating system and other software provided as a bundle that can be run on a cloud instance. Machine images are preconfigured for specific architecture or machine type. Amazon provides a wide selection of machine images, for use as part of its service. Using Amazon's machine images do not incur additional charges. Commercial vendors who provide Cloud service by using Amazon's infrastructure also provide machine images, however there may be a charge involved to use these. Individual users can use Amazon's machine images, and configure and create custom machine images, at no additional cost, apart from license related cost. License related cost typically arise when using commercial off the shelf software (COTS) like Windows OS, or software available for windows. In the case of most Linux distributions, this is not a cause for concern.

Amazon client tools are available for Firefox web browser. This tool is Elasticfox (AmazonEC2) which is available as a plug-in. Elasticfox provides an easy to use intuitive browser based graphical user interface. This interface enables users to browse, select and launch a machine image, as a cloud instance. For the sake of brevity it is assumed that user has an appropriately configured Amazon account, to launch an instance. In Figure 8, Step 2, Launch EC2 instance, is composed of two constituent tasks, first selection of machine image and second selection of machine type. A large selection of machine images is available. Two basic types of image exist depending on software configuration of the image. One is base or vanilla and the other is an image which may include an operating system along with some application software.

Figure 8. Schematic diagram to illustrate the steps involved in the process of preparation of an Amazon machine instance

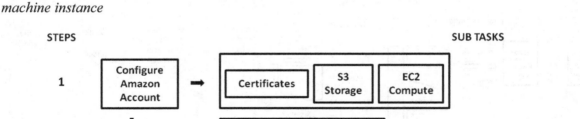

Amazon provides a wide selection of machine types, classified on the basis of number of processors, main memory i.e. RAM and underlying architecture 32/64 bit maximum storage is an additional feature. Machine image and machine type both have associated availability zones. It is recommended that users launch a machine image with care so that there is no zone conflict. An instance can be launched in any availability zone; however conflicts arise, if Elastic Block Storage (EBS) is used in conjunction with an instance. EBS is storage that is independent of instance, and can be mounted to an instance on request. EBS provisioning is availability zone specific, so conflicts arise if user tries to mount an EBS volume of one availability zone on an instance in a different availability zone. Snapshots of EBS can be taken, and persisted on S3, to enable reuse.

Command line tool: Amazon also makes available a relatively easy to use collection of command line tools called EC2ApiTools (EC2ApiTools & AmazonEC2). In contrast to the web browser based interface, the command line tool may ap-

pear comparatively less easy to use. Command line tools can be used to script repetitive tasks or complex workflow to facilitate automated use of cloud resources. The use of these tools depends on use case: in our case we found scripting our analysis workflow led to efficient use of resources. Cloud instance does not negate the need to prepare a software test platform with the same attention that one would give in case of test on local resource.

In our experiment of testing Google Chrome web browser, we prepared the test platform using Ubuntu 10.04.1 workstation AMI suitable for x86_64 bit architecture. The process of machine image preparation is well documented (Amazon Cloud AMI), and figure 8, provides an illustration of the procedure. One needs to be aware that most Linux machine images, come preconfigured to enable SSH based interactive use. X11 forwarding is however tricky, as most machine images are of headless type, i.e. Desktop software elements are not installed by default. In case of windows however access is possible using Microsoft's Remote Desktop Protocol. In our experience Windows support on Amazon is limited by license terms and conditions. This has meant limited user flexibility, which can seriously impede purpose. In our case, in view of these limitations, we restricted ourselves to using Linux on the cloud.

Simultaneous Testing of Hundreds of Google Chrome Instances

From Figure 7 it is apparent that in our experiment, the process of validating predictions, involves manual generation of mutants. Mutants are Google Chrome builds with modified source. The modification of source involved replacing the method body with stubs such that the stub methods do not break Chrome build dependencies. Mutation testing may follow various strategies of generating mutants. Our aim is not to introduce source code level semantic changes to simulate defects, but to alter the alter control flow path, by removing a potentially functionally important component of the control flow path responsible for functionalities exercised during the usage scenario. The possible coarse outcome cases are:

- On exercising the same scenario the system functional delivery is fulfilled with no significant user experience impairment.
- On exercising the same scenario the system functional delivery is not fulfilled with significant impairment of user experience (i.e. the software crashes or does not work as the user expects it to work).

In the case of Google Chrome the build of each test case may take between 1-4 hours depending on the build machines' processor and memory provision, in our case on a 64 bit Dual –Core dual processor Zeon MP SMP workstation with 8 GB of memory the build took around 4 hours. The projection to complete 820 builds on the local machine is 137 days working round the clock. Each build produces about 15 GB of data which would mean storage requirement of 25 hard disks

of 500 GB capacity. These figures make local build for this scale of testing impractical. In contrast a on an m2.xlarge (Amazon EC2) instance on Amazon each build took roughly 1.5hour. In such a resource and time intensive test scenario, use of cloud based testing is an obvious choice.

Moving from a local machine to the cloud requires consideration of various factors, keeping in mind that in the utility model, usage is charged under various heads, including use of network, apart from machine and storage usage. The need is to consider using a workflow automating the process of data and process management. Data management involves, transferring data to and from cloud storage. Process management involves launch and termination management, apart from executing the test process. Various tasks are intertwined and time ordered, and this orchestration of tasks needs to be managed efficiently. Quite often workflow engines are used for tasks orchestration. Workflow service usually resides on an intermediate computational infrastructure, and depending on requirement one may use solutions that already exist.

In our experiment, requirements and time constraints meant use of a custom scheme. In this scheme we used a bash script to manage the test workflow on the cloud. In Figure 9 the main tasks are numbered in the order of operation, and they represent a set of calls to Amazon S3 and EC2 commands provided by S3Cmd (AmazonS3) and EC2ApiTool (EC2ApiTools & AmazonEC2). The following script is an example script used to launch a build instance. The main sections of this script are commented for ease of use.

We found that the decision to test in the cloud is not trivial, due to evolution of the service, resulting in some solutions and accompanying documentation being stale. This has motivated us to present the scripts developed as part of this experiment (see Box 2), and we hope that they will provide a guiding beacon on tackling the mechanistic elements of using the cloud as a testing platform.

Figure 9. Schematic diagram of the cloud-based testing workflow that was used to test Google Chrome on the cloud

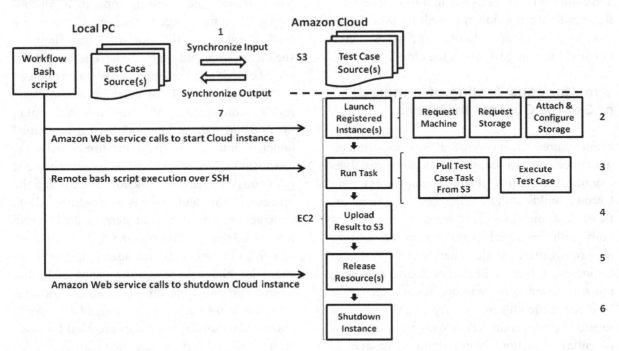

The script in Box 2 manages the complete workflow for one build. In order to launch multiple Amazon instances simultaneously to build different mutants we used the command script in Box 3. This script allows launching each build instance using a separate terminal, and has distinct process identifier.

On the build server instance a script resides, this script deals with initializing additional dynamic file system, and copying mutant build source from S3 storage, launching Google Chrome build, and finally copying the build output to S3 storage. The sample script in Box 4 is an example of what was used in our experiment.

The three scripts that we presented here, all three deal with managing the workflow, which broadly consists of launching a Cloud instance, managing the actual test process, and managing data. Scripts runTest.sh and runBuild.sh deal with the actual workflow and form the core of work flow implementation. Script LaunchMultipleT-

ests.sh is a client side script, to deal with the finer issue of ensuring that each test workflow execution has unique process identifier, while this script does not contribute to the core workflow it makes managing the process easier.

DISCUSSION AND RECOMMENDATIONS

The experiment setup and process discussed in the preceding sections, is specific to a particular application, i.e. Google Chrome. The main issues that confront users for testing on the cloud are:

- How much of the test workflow can benefit from use of the cloud?
- How can we setup, and manage a platform that closely replicates the local development or reference platform?

Box 2. Scripts developed

```
Script: runTest.sh
#!/bin/bash

clear
echo "runTest.sh called with cmd argument $1"

#$1=name of test

#set env

#Constants
ami_id="ami-900xxxxx"
key="id_rsa-esc_key"
group="default"
zonestr="us-east-1d"
itype="m2.xlarge"
dtype="/dev/sdh"
group="default"
size=25
#vars for files
vl="vol_log"
il="inst_log"
vf=$HOME/vlm-$BASHPID


echo "CREATING VOLUME"
#create volume
ec2-create-volume --size $size --availability-zone $zonestr >$vf
vol_id=`less $vf | grep VOLUME | cut -f2`
echo $vol_id >>$vl
echo "VOLUME ID: "$vol_id
ec2-create-tags $vol_id --tag "tag"
sleep 100
ec2-describe-volumes $vol_id >$vf
stat=`less $vf |grep VOLUME | cut -f6`
echo "VOLUME" $stat
echo "LAUNCHING INSTANCE"

#launch instance
ec2-run-instances $ami_id -k $key -z $zonestr -t $itype -g $group >$vf
inst_id=`less $vf | grep INSTANCE | cut -f2`
echo $inst_id >>$il
echo "INSTANCE ID:" $inst_id
ec2-create-tags $ami_id $inst_id --tag "tag"
public_url=`less $vf | grep INSTANCE | cut -f4`
sleep 200
ec2-describe-instances $inst_id >$vf
stat2=` less $vf | grep INSTANCE | cut -f6 `
public_url=`less $vf | grep INSTANCE | cut -f4`
echo "INSTANCE"$stat2
echo "ATTACHING VOLUME TO INSTANCE"
sleep 100
#attach volume to instance
ec2-attach-volume $vol_id -i $inst_id -d $dtype
sleep 50
ec2-describe-volumes $vol_id >$vf
stat3=`less $vf | grep ATTACHMENT | cut -f5`
echo "INSTANCE<->VOLUME" $stat3
if [ $stat3 != "attached" ];
```

continued on following page

Box 2. Continued

```
then
echo "Error:Failure to attach volume-trying again."
sleep 20
ec2-attach-volume $vol_id -i $inst_id -d $dtype
sleep 20
ec2-describe-volumes $vol_id >$vf
stat3=`less $vf | grep ATTACHMENT | cut -f5`
echo "INSTANCE<->VOLUME" $stat3
else
echo "volume attached"
fi


#synchronize change localsystem directory to s3://chromesrc

echo "Uploading local changes to S3"
`s3cmd sync $HOME/Chromium/tests/$1.tgz s3://chromesrc`
#`s3cmd sync $HOME/Chromium/chromium.r72930.tgz s3://chromesrc`
#try get instance url again
ec2-describe-instances $inst_id >$vf
public_url=`less $vf | grep INSTANCE | cut -f4`
echo $public_url
#sync s3 changed_source.tar.gz and instance chrome.tar.gz

#launch sync s3 changed_source.tar.gz and instance chrome.tar.gz runBuild.sh
if [ $public_url == "" ];
then
echo "Error:Failure to get instance url"
goto cleanup
else
echo "instance url retrieved"
fi


# Launch remote build through SSH

echo "connecting to " $public_url "to run build"
terminal="ssh -i .ec2/id_rsa-esc_key ubuntu@$public_url \"/home/ubuntu/runBuild.sh $1\""
echo "using command "$terminal
eval $terminal
echo "REMOTE BUILD DONE"
#launch cleanup.sh

#s3 sync out to localhost

`s3cmd sync s3://ChromeOuts/$1.tar.gz /home/a9911584/Chromium/outs/`
cleanup:
echo "CLEANUP"
sleep 100
echo "DETACHING VOLUME"
ec2-detach-volume $vol_id -i $inst_id -d $dtype -f
sleep 100
echo "TERMINATING INSTANCE"
ec2-terminate-instances $inst_id
echo "DELETING VOLUME"
sleep 100
ec2-delete-volume $vol_id
echo "PROCESS COMPLETE"
```

Box 3. Command script to launch multiple instances

```
Script: LaunchMultipleTests.sh
#!/bin/bash
#1
gnome-terminal -e " $HOME/runTest.sh testTag1"
....
#n
gnome-terminal -e " $HOME/runTest.sh testTagn"
```

- How can we efficiently manage input and output data?
- How can we efficiently utilize the resource to reduce overall cost of usage?

In the context of our experiment, the requirement is to build, multiple manually prepared mutants of Google Chrome based on our prediction. The build process is automated and does not require interactive human intervention, and can be batch processed.

The data collection platform in our workflow was Microsoft Windows 7 Professional 64 bit. The user driven test scenarios were generated by using data a Google Chrome Windows browser application.

Our natural choice of platform for building mutants would have been Microsoft Windows 7 Professional 64 bit. However we found Amazon or Microsoft Azure services did not offer Microsoft Windows 7 Professional 64 bit as a choice. In our experiment, only function calls within Google Chrome are considered, which in theory means the application can be built on another platform, based on assumption of that non system level higher level method calls are common for all platforms. From the analysis point of view this introduces a threat to validity, however so far as the use of use cloud is concerned the process is valid. In our experiment the cloud instances that we used are based on the Ubuntu 10.04.1 64 bit platform.

In our experiment, involving the build of 820 mutants, we implemented a scheme to manage all the data so that each one of the input and output data can be isolated. This was done in the first instance by using an unambiguous naming scheme. This naming scheme handling was then automated in the workflow script. A careful scan of the data was done for all the scenarios to ensure that no duplicate mutant was prepared. Large number of common elements occurs across predictions, in all this cases only one mutant was prepared, and analysis table referred to the instance for which mutant was generated. In this way 820 builds were reduced to 186. This is approximately 75% reduction in initial estimation of costs. The total data input data across all builds is approximately 100 Gigabytes (GB) and output consisting of only the built executable and supporting libraries is 52 Gigabytes (GB).

Total computation time used as per Amazon is 561 hours approximately which is 25% reduction over 744 hours it would have taken to run the same test on the local workstation, These figures fail to point to the fact that 561 hours is actually clocked in a 7 days of test runs, and includes some repeats. 744 hours on a local workstation would have taken 31 days with building process running 24 hours a day. The compressed input data of 0.5 GB at build time expands to about 15GB each, which would require about 2.7 Terabytes (TB) of storage. The approximate total charge for use of the Amazon Cloud for this experiment is $1000.00. This includes the use of data transfer, use of S3 storage, and m2.xlarge EC2 instances. The cost advantage of using the cloud is amply clear, in addition to time efficiency related saving. If cost and time saving are the main factors that influence the use of cloud based testing, in our

Box 4. Script on build server

```
Script: runBuild.sh
#get and set credentials

echo "Setting Environment"
s3cmd sync s3://anjanchrome/.ec2 .
export EC2_PRIVATE_KEY="$HOME"/.ec2/pk-***.pem
export EC2_CERT="$HOME"/.ec2/cert-***.pem
#set depot tools path
#s3cmd sync s3://chromesrc/chromium.r72930.tgz /home/ubuntu/Chromium
s3cmd sync s3://chromesrc/$1.tgz /home/ubuntu/Chromium
export PATH=$PATH:$HOME/Chromium/depot_tools
export CHROME_SRC=$HOME/Chromium/$1.tgz

#initialize and mount volume
echo " Preparing volume"
sudo mkfs -t ext3 /dev/sdh
sudo mkdir /mnt/vol2
sudo mount /dev/sdh /mnt/vol2
sudo chmod 777 /mnt/vol2/
cd /mnt/vol2

#untar Chromium set paths
echo "Preparing Chrome source"

tar -zxvf $CHROME_SRC

export CHROMIUM_HOME=/mnt/vol2/home/chrome-svn/tarball/chromium/src
#build Chromium
cd $CHROMIUM_HOME
export GYP_DEFINES="target_arch=x64"

echo "Starting build"

$CHROMIUM_HOME/build/gyp_chromium -f make -D library=shared_library
make out/Debug/chrome -j6

#tar compress out file and upload to s3 bucket

echo "argument " $1
var=$CHROMIUM_HOME/$1.tar.gz
echo $var
echo "TAR.GZ of out file named"

echo "Compressing Out directory"

tar czfv $var out/ --exclude="*.o"

echo "Transferring out file"

s3cmd sync $var s3://ChromeOuts
echo "Output file transfer complete"
```

view, it certainly presents a clear advantage over captive storage and computational infrastructure. These may not however be the main influencing factors; in our view the main factors are flexibility of configuration and the use of a test platform.

Amazon Cloud services are well documented, and their use is facilitated by access to a large number of tools, which we found easy to use. In our view inexperienced users may find some of the more advanced interactive access based use of the cloud difficult due to the x.509 certificate based security infrastructure. In this respect Amazon's security mechanism is significantly more user friendly than similar mechanism used on Grid infrastructures. This not withstanding it is still not transparent to the user, and on occasion can present difficulties that may require advanced level of knowledge to troubleshoot.

The main drawback we noticed in use of the Amazon Cloud is the inflexible licensing structure that limits the choice of platform and software. This is our experience of trying to use Windows on Amazon EC2. In the case of Linux users there is a wide range of choice of platforms and software.

The workflow scheme presented in this case study is one of the many possible schemes. Software solutions exist to script workflows, or one can develop custom solutions, like the one provided in this study. Large scale testing of software is likely to involve large volume of data transfer and storage. It may also involve a need to build large number of mutants in batch mode. In our view some form of workflow management need to be implemented to efficiently use Cloud services for Software testing.

The bash scripts workflows used for this experiment were deliberately kept simple, without use of flow controls like loops. Time delays have been used to ensure robust operation, one of the reasons is that bash scripts can be quite challenging to get correct. The second reason was that response to some web service calls was found to be unreliable, and parsing the text of response was a problem. Introducing time delays instead of trying to perfect a script, resolved most of the teething issues around use of bash script. In our view a test rig if create using similar structure would benefit from use of Python or similar scripting languages, which are easier to use. The scripts in themselves are broadly generic, and can be mapped to any test that has similar requirements. One can however

create more flexible and user friendly solutions using this scheme.

The case study presented in this chapter, presents one way of leveraging cloud services for large scale testing. In our view the main considerations that will determine efficacy of cloud as a testing platform are:

- Flexibility of software environment, leading to ability to configure environment exactly as required.
- Support software infrastructure, like workflow engines etc.
- Cost of usage.
- Guaranteed isolation of test processes, where performance study is being done.

We found that in its present form the cloud is viable option for large scale software testing, but the initial setup may require significant effort to deal with teething issues. The broad areas that our technique focused on are, data management, and process management automation, by using a workflow implemented in a script. The technique is broadly generic, and can be applied to similar test requirements, on similar cloud services.

The main consideration should however be, need based, we have demonstrated that this use cased needed use of cloud, but only for a one part of the test workflow. In our case it the tests were not performance sensitive, it was a build of mutants, we can envisage other tests where performance is paramount. On the cloud there is no way to ensure 1:1 contention of computation resource, so performance tests may be prone to spurious results. In the future cost of cloud usage may change, making testing more expensive than the figures presented here. At the present time, in our view the technique followed in doing cloud based testing provided us with significant cost benefit, over using a similar captive resource.

CONCLUSION AND FUTURE RESEARCH DIRECTIONS

In this case study, the cloud has been leveraged as tool, to perform large scale software testing of the Google Chrome. The context for the testing on the cloud is provided in our case by the need to test the predictions of functional importance of methods, which were obtained by applying network analysis to dynamic analysis data of the Google Chrome. In order to show that the predictions are better than chance we needed to perform hundreds of tests of the software system. Since the Google Chrome is large and complex software compiling and testing mutated variants of it takes long time for each variant. The use of the cloud for simultaneous parallel build of multiple mutated software variants made the execution of the large-scale testing feasible.

Our experience shows that the cloud-based testing of the Google Chrome works efficiently on the Amazon Cloud. This approach to testing saves large amount of time and cost. Thanks to the relatively easy-to-use interface of the Amazon Cloud it is relatively straightforward the development of the workflow management scripts that guide the running of many (hundreds) tests in parallel and also manage the flow of the data generated by the tests.

The large-scale testing experiment that we executed also highlighted key issues related to the practical organization and execution of cloud-based testing. In particular, the licensing issues of required software may limit the usability of the cloud – and we had to use Linux-based cloud environments to circumvent these issues. The appropriate managing of the workflow is critically important – and we provide in this chapter detailed examples of workflow managing scripts that we used successfully.

In general we found that the cloud offers a viable environment for large-scale testing. This is due primarily to its flexibility and scalability

to fit the task at hand in a highly cost effective manner. It is also important that the Cloud interface provides appropriate ways to administer the workflow and the data flow related to the testing.

Our future work in the context of cloud-based testing is driven by our interest in elaboration of measurement and prediction of functional importance of methods and their patterns in the context of large-scale software systems. This requires further automation of generation of test cases and also the management of large-scale distributed testing of mutated variants of the software system by teams of testers. Developing methods for these, including the development of workflow and data flow management tools for setting up such large-scale testing experiments is very important for the establishing of cloud-based testing in academic and industrial context.

A related important issue is the possibility of development of cloud-based services that support the running of large-scale testing on the cloud. In the experiment described in this chapter we used generic Cloud services to manage the workflow and data flow of our testing experiment. However if specific testing tools become available on the cloud to support such testing that could facilitate the take up of cloud-based testing by the industry. We intend to extend our research in this direction as well in the sense of packaging our workflow and data flow management toolkits as cloud services that could be incorporated into the service packages provided by cloud operators.

Finally, a further aspect of future directions of cloud-based testing that is important is the support for multi-version software testing and the provision of related bug and update reporting and data management services. At the moment such services are not provided by the cloud, but merging cloud services with other services that deliver such functionality appears to be the natural step forward. Of course such integration of services will need significant research and development effort. We expect that when such support services will be made available by cloud providers the take-up of cloud-based testing by the industry will expand rapidly.

REFERENCES

Abran, A., Moore, J. W., Bourque, P., & Dupuis, R. (Eds.). (2004). *Guide to the software engineering body of knowledge* (3rd ed.).

Albert, R., & Barabási, A.-L. (2002). Statistical mechanics of complex networks. *Reviews of Modern Physics*, *74*, 48–94. doi:10.1103/RevModPhys.74.47

Amazon Cloud, A. M. I. (2008). *Creating and Preparing AMIs*. Retrieved from http://docs.amazonwebservices.com/AWSEC2/2008-02-01/DeveloperGuide/index.html?CreatingAndBundlingAMIs.html

Amazon EC2. (n.d.). *Instance types*. Retrieved from http://aws.amazon.com/ec2/instance-types/

Amazon S3. (n.d.). *S3cmd*. Retrieved from http://s3tools.org/s3cmd

Amazon EC2. (n.d.). *Elasticfox*. Retrieved from http://aws.amazon.com/developertools/609?_encoding=UTF8&jiveRedirect=1

Armbrust, M., Fox, A., Griffith, R., Joseph, A. D., Katz, R. H., & Konwinski, A. (2009). *Above the clouds: A Berkeley view of cloud computing*. University of California at Berkeley.

Avritzer, A., & Weyuker, E. J. (1995). The automatic generation of load test suites and the assessment of the resulting software. *IEEE Transactions on Software Engineering*, *21*(9), 705–716. doi:10.1109/32.464549

Ball, T. (1999). *The concept of dynamic analysis*. Paper presented at the ESEC/FSE.

Barabási, A.-L., & Bonabeau, E. (2003). Scale-free networks. *Scientific American*, *288*, 50–59. doi:10.1038/scientificamerican0503-60

Barham, P., Dragovic, B., Fraser, K., Hand, S., Harris, T., Ho, A., et al. (2003). *Xen and the art of virtualization*. Paper presented at the SOSP.

Baxter, G., Frean, M., Noble, J., Rickerby, M., Smith, H., Visser, M., et al. (2006). *Understanding the shape of Java software*. Paper presented at the OOPSLA.

Bohnet, J., & Döllner, J. (2006). *Visual exploration of function call graphs for feature location in complex software systems*. Paper presented at the 2006 ACM Symposium on Software Visualization.

Buyya, R., Shin, Y. C., & Venugopal, S. (2008, 25-27 September). *Market-oriented cloud computing: Vision, hype, and reality for delivering it services as computing utilities*. Paper presented at the HPCC.

Candea, G., Bucur, S., & Zamfir, C. (2010). *Automated software testing as a service*. Paper presented at the SoCC.

Chaudhry, S., Caprioli, P., Yip, S., & Tremblay, M. (2005). High-performance throughput computing. *Micro*, *25*, 32–45.

Chen, K., & Rajlich, V. (2000). *Case study of feature location using dependence graph*. Paper presented at the IWPC/ICPC.

Clauset, A., Shalizi, C. R., & Newman, M. E. J. (2009). Power-law distributions in empirical data. *SIAM Review*, *51*(4), 661–703. doi:10.1137/070710111

Cornelissen, B., Zaidman, A., & Holten, D., &. all, e. (2008). Execution trace analysis through massive sequence and circular bundle views. *Journal of Systems and Software*, *81*, 2252–2268. doi:10.1016/j.jss.2008.02.068

Cornelissen, B., Zaidman, A., van Deursen, A., Moonen, L., & Koschke, R. (2009). A systematic survey of program comprehension through dynamic analysis. *IEEE Transactions on Software Engineering, 35*(5), 684–702. doi:10.1109/TSE.2009.28

Dadzie, J. (2005). Understanding software patching. *ACM Queue, 3*(1542-7730), 24-30.

EC2ApiTools. (2006). *EC2ApiTools, & AmazonEC2*. Retrieved from http://docs.amazonwebservices.com/AmazonEC2/gsg/2006-06-26/

Elbaum, S., Malishevsky, A. G., & Rothermel, G. (2002). Test case prioritization: A family of empirical studies. *IEEE Transactions on Software Engineering, 28*(2), 159–182. doi:10.1109/32.988497

Foster, I., & Kesselman, C. (2003). *The grid 2: Blueprint for a new computing infrastructure*. Morgan Kaufmann Publishers Inc.

Globus.org. *Globus*. (n.d.). Retrieved from http://www.globus.org/

Goth, G. (2008). Ultralarge systems: Redefining software engineering? *Software, 25*(3), 91–94. doi:10.1109/MS.2008.82

GreenHat.com. *Green Hat*. (n.d.). Retrieved from http://www.greenhat.com/

Jeong, H., Tombor, B., & Albert, R. (2000). The large-scale organization of metabolic networks. *Nature, 407*, 651–654. doi:10.1038/35036627

Jia, Y., & Harman, M. (2006). *An analysis and survey of the development of mutation testing*. King's College London. doi:10.1109/TSE.2010.62

Joglekar, S. (2009). *A foray into cloud-based software testing*. Paper presented at the STeP-IN SUMMIT 2009, Bangalore, India.

Kandel, E. R., Schwartz, J. H., & Jessell, T. M. (2000). *Principles of neural science* (4th ed.). New York, NY: McGraw-Hill.

Lienhard, A., Ducasse, S., & Gırba, T. (2009). Taking an object-centric view on dynamic information with object flow analysis. *Computer Languages, Systems & Structures, 35*, 63–79. doi:10.1016/j.cl.2008.05.006

Meyer, B. (2008). Seven Principles of Software Testing. *IEEE Transactions on Computers, 41*(8), 99–101.

Myers, C. R. (2003). Software systems as complex networks: Structure, function, and evolvability of software collaboration graphs. *Physical Review E: Statistical, Nonlinear, and Soft Matter Physics, 68*.

Nanda, S., & Chiueh, T. (2005). *A survey on virtualization technologies*. SUNY at Stony Brook.

NIST & RTI. (2002). *The economic impacts of inadequate infrastructure for software testing*. (No. RTI Project Number 7007.011): National Institute of Standards and Technology.

NSF. (n.d.). *TeraGrid*. Retrieved from https://www.teragrid.org/

Pagden, E. (2003a). *The IT utility model—Part I*. Sun Professional Services.

Pagden, E. (2003b). *The IT utility model—Part II*. Sun Professional Services.

Pakhira, A., & Andras, P. (2010). *Can we use network analysis methods to discover functionally important method calls in software systems by considering dynamic analysis data?* Paper presented at the PCODA, Beverley, MA.

Porter, A. A., Siy, H. P., Toman, C. A., & Votta, L. G. (1997). An experiment to assess the cost-benefits of code inspections in large scale software development. *IEEE Transactions on Software Engineering, 23*(6), 329–346. doi:10.1109/32.601071

Poshyvanyk, D., Gueheneuc, Y. G., Marcus, A., Antoniol, G., & Rajlich, V. (2007). Feature location using probabilistic ranking of methods based on execution scenarios and information retrieval. *IEEE Transactions on Software Engineering, 33*(6), 420–432. doi:10.1109/TSE.2007.1016

Potanin, A., Noble, J., Frean, M., & Biddle, R. (2005). Scale-free geometry in OO programs. *Communications of the ACM, 48*(5), 99–103. doi:10.1145/1060710.1060716

Rajlich, V., & Wilde, N. (2002). *The role of concepts in program comprehension.* Paper presented at the IWPC/ICPC.

Reis, C., & Gribble, S. D. (2009). *Isolating web programs in modern browser architectures.* Paper presented at the Eurosys 2009.

Riungu, L. M., Taipale, O., Smolander, K., Hanawa, T., Banzai, T., Koizumi, H., et al. (2010). *Software testing in the cloud.* Paper presented at the 2nd International Workshop on Software Testing in the Cloud Co-located with the 3rd IEEE International Conference on Software Testing, Verification, and Validation (ICST 2010).

Rothermel, G., Untch, R. H., Chengyun, C., & Harrold, M. J. (2001). Prioritizing test cases for regression testing. *IEEE Transactions on Software Engineering, 27*(10), 929–948. doi:10.1109/32.962562

Roy, P. (n.d.). *Slimtune.* Retrieved from http://code.google.com/p/slimtune/

Rubinov, M., & Sporns, O. (2010). Complex network measures of brain connectivity: Uses and interpretations. *NeuroImage, 52*(3), 1059–1069. doi:10.1016/j.neuroimage.2009.10.003

Severance, C., & Dowd, K. (1998). *High performance computing* (2nd ed.). O'Reilly Media.

Tahvildar, L., & Kontogiannis, K. (2004). Improving design quality using meta-pattern transformations: A metric-based approach: Research Articles. *Journal of Software Maintenance Evolution, 16*(4-5), 331–361. doi:10.1002/smr.299

Terekhov, I. (2003). Meta-computing at D0. *Nuclear Instruments & Methods in Physics Research. Section A, Accelerators, Spectrometers, Detectors and Associated Equipment, 502*(2-3), 402–406. doi:10.1016/S0168-9002(03)00452-2

UKeScience. (n.d.). *National Grid Service (NGS).* Retrieved from http://www.ngs.ac.uk/

Wang, L., Wang, Z., Yang, C., Zhang, L., & Ye, Q. (2009). *Linux kernels as complex networks: A novel method to study evolution.* Paper presented at the ICSM.

Wheeler, D. (n.d.). *SLOCCount.* Retrieved from http://www.dwheeler.com/sloccount/

Wirfs-Brock, R., Wilkerson, B., & Wiener, L. (1990). *Designing object-oriented software.* Prentice-Hall, Inc.

Wolverton, R. W. (1974). The cost of developing large-scale software. *IEEE Transactions on Computers, C-23*(6), 615–636. doi:10.1109/T-C.1974.224002

Zaidman, A., & Demeyer, S. (2008). Automatic identification of key classes in a software system using web mining techniques. *Journal of Software Maintenance and Evolution, 20*(6), 387–417. doi:10.1002/smr.370

Zhang, C., & Jacobsen, H.-A. (2007). *Efficiently mining crosscutting concerns through random walks.* Paper presented at the 6th International Conference on Aspect-Oriented Software Development.

Chapter 13
Threatening the Cloud:
Securing Services and Data by Continuous, Model–Driven Negative Security Testing

Philipp Zech
University of Innsbruck, Austria

Philipp Kalb
University of Innsbruck, Austria

Michael Felderer
University of Innsbruck, Austria

Ruth Breu
University of Innsbruck, Austria

ABSTRACT

Today's increasing trend towards outsourcing IT landscapes and business processes into the Cloud is a double-edged sword. On the one side, companies can save time and money; however, on the other side, moving possible sensitive data and business processes into the Cloud demands for a high degree of information security. In the course of this chapter, the authors give an overview of a Cloud's various vulnerabilities, how to address them properly, and last but not least, a model-driven approach to evaluate the state of security of a Cloud environment by means of negative testing. Besides, the authors incorporate the idea of living models to allow tracking and incorporating of changes in the Cloud environment and react properly and, more important, in time on evolving security requirements throughout the complete Cloud Life Cycle.

DOI: 10.4018/978-1-4666-2536-5.ch013

INTRODUCTION

Since the early beginnings of software development, testing has always been an important part of assuring the proper and required behavior of a system. However, still nowadays testing is often the one phase during the Software Development Lifecycle (SDLC) which is mostly performed very poorly and by far does not cover the complete software product by incorporating all its requirements, especially when it comes to security testing of a software system. This is mainly motivated by the fact, that often only positive requirements are used, yet the idea of incorporating negative requirements, describing a successful abuse of the system, is neglected. However, the usage of such negative requirements should be motivated strongly, as besides the positive requirements, negative requirements also describe part of the possible behavior of a system, which demands to be examined with the intention to detect and mitigate it.

Considering today's advancements in the area of software development, it is quite obvious that software security has to be ascribed an important status. This is mainly motivated by the growing complexity and usage of software systems in high security sensitive domains, i.e., eHealth. Talking about contemporary advancements in software development, especially one paradigm of salient relevance protrudes, namely Cloud Computing. Being mostly used as a buzzword in the early 2000s, Cloud Computing nowadays has grown to a quite mature technology that has gained lots of acceptance, especially in the corporate IT world. This growing acceptance mainly is because of a Cloud's great opportunities in the area of IT outsourcing, allowing small and mid-sized business to save vast amounts of time and money. The key factor for this success of outsourcing lies in a cloud's elasticity. This concept of dynamically distributing resources through virtualization and intelligent hardware management allows companies to successfully move complete IT landscapes

and business processes into the Cloud, by in the end only being accounted for the computing time they actually consumed, thereby eradicating wasted idle times.

However, as it is quite often with newly approaching technologies and computing paradigms, despite its opportunities, a Cloud also has to deal with various drawbacks in terms of information security. Despite the classical vulnerabilities, inherent in the employed technologies, a Cloud introduces various security risks, specifically inherent in the idea of Cloud computing (Siemens, 2010) (CloudSecurityAlliance, 2011). One of the major security concerns coming along with the idea of Cloud Computing is data protection. Inside a Cloud loads of users are doing their computations side by side, often using sensitive data. Hence, a Cloud has to assure that user data is protected vigorously to avoid accidental or malicious leakage. Another important issue, besides proper data protection, is the possible risk of a Cloud environment to degenerate into a hacker's playground. Compromising such an environment with all its computational resources and power allows a hacker to launch rogue attacks against institutions of any kind. Yet, this by far is not the complete story of a vulnerable Cloud, there are a lot of other considerations to be taken into account, i.e., protecting running applications and prevent loss of reputation or financial resources, yet it already indicates the relevance of proper security assurance. Additionally, by considering the security of a Cloud, one has to think differently as opposed to a stand-alone application. In contradiction to the classical SDLC the actual lifecycle of a Cloud differs seriously. Whereas in the classical SDLC security is mainly examined during the testing phase, in the Cloud Lifecycle (CLC), security is an evolving requirement, which needs to be taken into account throughout the whole uptime of the Cloud. Changing or new deployments of applications, newly virtualized instances of different platforms, all these alterations actually change the current configuration of the

Cloud and demand for reevaluating the security of the Cloud environment, as the performed changes often introduce new flaws.

Based on the above observations, we introduce a novel, two-tracked model-driven approach for the risk-based security testing of Cloud systems to improve Cloud environment security. On the one side, to examine the service interface, put another way, the attack surface of a Cloud, a risk analysis is performed on the system model of the Cloud Under Test (CUT). This risk analysis yields a tailored risk model, used to generate a dedicated misuse case model, describing possible malicious activities to abuse the Cloud. Subsequently, this misuse case model is used to generate executable test cases by employing an own code generator. On the other side, to assure proper data protection in the Cloud, we employ XACML (OASIS, 2008) policies. These policies are used to derive the set of consumer specific privacy rules (S1). This set further-on is reduced in accordance with the Cloud Data Management Interface (CDMI) (SNIA, 2011) in a way that the resulting rule set covers the complete operation specification of the CDMI (S2). Finally, this reduced rule set is mutated (S3) to be employed during mutation testing against the Cloud Storage System to assure that the concrete CDMI implementation is in accordance to consumer tailored data privacy policies. The needed test code again is generated by an own test code generator. We utilize the Living Models approach (Breu, 2010) which results in changing CUT models and hence, allows incorporating security as an evolving requirement throughout the complete CLC. The application of risk analysis is motivated by the fact that, in theory, there is an infinite number of tests to be performed to assure security. Thus, to foster efficient testing, the resulting ranked risks aid as a starting point for the testing process. We justify the use of a model-driven approach by the circumstance, that often design flaws are the cause for possible risks in a software system (Verdon & McGraw, 2004) hence, performing risk analysis on the design

level results in more secure software. Reducing the actual effort spent for data protection testing to CDMI conformance testing in terms of XACML policies, is motivated by the fact, that by securing the service interface of the Cloud, classical data-related attacks like SQL or XPATH injection are already considered, as they count to the group of attacks, commonly performed on service centric systems. As a modeling language UML (OMG, 2007) has been chosen as it is a common, industry-wide accepted standard.

The remainder of this chapter is structured as follows. In the next section we give an overview of existing related work and present the relevant background knowledge, fostering the understanding of our approach. A Secure Cloud presents our novel approach to improve and assure the overall security of Cloud environments by means of negative testing. Before we conclude our chapter we discuss possible future research directions and ideas coming along with our current work.

BACKGROUND

In this chapter we, beneath giving relevant background information, position our research idea in respect to related work and provide background information. The presented background on relevant technologies by far is not complete, yet it suffices to foster understanding of our approach.

Positioning in Respect to Related Work

Currently, most of the research focusing on software testing in the Cloud is actually concentrated on how to harness the power of the Cloud to be used as a testing environment (Yu et al., 2010), (Oriol & Ullah, 2010). Hereby, the idea is to provide Cloud consumers with the ability to test their own software using resources and services of the Cloud. However, all those approaches actually neglect to take into consideration testing of the

Cloud and its various aspects, especially security, as proposed in (Riungu et al., 2010).

Generally it can be distinguished between two types of security testing (Potter & McGraw, 2004), i.e. security requirements testing and risk-based security testing. Security requirements testing validates the correct implementation of positive security requirements by applying classical testing techniques (Michael & Radosevich, 2005). Risk-based security testing focuses on negative requirements, so called misuse cases, depicting malicious activities, likely performed by an attacker (Michael & Radosevich, 2005).

To the best of our knowledge, up to now there exists no testing approach, addressing security, especially risk-based security testing of Cloud environments. (Felderer et al., 2010) propose an approach to testing security requirements of SCS based on the Telling TestStories framework. However, their approach is based on positive security requirements and does not incorporate negative requirements, derived from risk analysis. The work presented in (King & Ganti, 2010) follows the idea of providing Test Support as a Service (TSaaS) to Cloud consumers for enhanced application testing. Nevertheless, as their approach attempts testing from inside the Cloud environment, it is not applicable for security testing, also focusing on the examination of risks posed from outside the Cloud. Another noteworthy approach to Cloud infrastructure testing is proposed in (Rings et al.) focusing on Cloud interoperability testing. Yet, this approach does not take security aspects of any kind into consideration at all.

Searching concurrent literature concerning data protection testing is a very devastating task. Although the testing community is aware of the fact, that data should be incorporated in testing, however, most of the time, testers focus on how to optimize their tests using tailored data and not on how to examine whether the tested software treats data in the intended way. What comes closest to the idea of data protection testing is

the idea of policy testing. Talking about policy testing, there are two approaches deserved to be mentioned at this point. In a first one, LeTraon et al. (Le Traon et al., 2007) reuse functional test cases for testing security policies, however, their approach only focuses on policies as a whole, and does not specifically focus on data to be protected. The other approach, proposed by Martin et al. (Martin et al., 2006) is based on the idea of policy coverage testing. Again, this approach, like the work presented by LeTraon et al. (Le Traon et al., 2007), does no focus on data in particular, but also on policies as a whole.

Model versioning is already a huge research area which produced several systems but every systems focus is different than the change-driven approach used in this chapter, i.e., UNICASE (Helming & Koegel, 2010) focuses on model-driven software engineering and comes with a tool to version models in a central repository. CDO (Eclipse, 2011a) is a repository to share Eclipse EMF models among various stakeholders focused on resource optimization during collaboration. We found no scientific or open source system supporting model versioning with state machines. The tools most similar to our approach are Doors (IBM, 2011) and in-Step (microTool, 2010). Doors supports the management of requirements in a central repository, focused on traceability through the life cycle. Notifications on changes and possible impacts are also announced as features. in-Step is a tool for process driven project management in the area of system and software development.

The Cloud in a Nutshell

Although this book is solely intended to discuss the topic of software testing with respect to the Cloud, we nevertheless take the liberty to give a very brief definition of the Cloud. In doing so, we refer to the National Institute of Standards and Technology's (NIST) definition of the Cloud (Mell & Grance, 2009), motivated by the fact, that this definition actually gives the most complete view of the Cloud model and takes into consideration most the aspects of the different views and definitions which exist aside of the NIST's one.

According to the NIST, the Cloud model is defined by its five essential characteristics, the three service layers, and its four different deployment models. Hereby, the five characteristics are:

1. **On-Demand Self-Service:** Automatic provisioning of resources without human interaction with a service provider.
2. **Broad Network Access:** Ubiquitous access through standardized mechanisms to the offered capabilities.
3. **Resource Pooling:** Dynamic and flexible assignment of physical and virtual resources to serve multiple consumers based on a multi-tenant model.
4. **Rapid Elasticity:** Allows to rapidly and elastically assigning resource as needed by consumers.
5. **Measured Service:** Realizes a transparent and service type specific billing system to reduce consumer's costs.

The service model, as motivated by the NIST, currently is divided into three different layers, according to the following list:

1. **Software-as-a-Service (SaaS):** Allows a Cloud consumer to access the providers offered applications through web-based services.
2. **Platform-as-a-Service (PaaS):** Allows a Cloud consumer to deploy his/her own applications onto the Cloud, by being provided with various different virtualized platforms and runtimes.
3. **Infrastructure-as-a-Service (IaaS):** Allows a Cloud consumer to hire infrastructural resources like processing time or storage devices to run arbitrary software or store his data.

Finally, what completes this brief discussion of the Cloud model as motivated by the NIST, are the four different deployment models, as listed below:

1. **Private:** A Cloud residing in-house and only used by consumers located in-house.
2. **Public:** A Cloud offered by a third party and access by a broad variety of users.
3. **Community:** A Cloud provided by various third parties, offering services to a community sharing similar needs.
4. **Hybrid:** A mixed deployment consisting of two or all three of the above mentioned deployment models.

Yet, as already mentioned above, this is only one of the many Cloud definitions currently in use, yet it gives the most complete view of the idea of a Cloud. Another, worth mentionable model of a Cloud is the Cloud Cube Model as defined by the Jericho Group (Jericho, 2011), which rather focuses on enabling secure collaboration in terms of the Cloud. However, as this chapter is not intended to discuss the variety of Cloud Computing models and its realization in detail, the interested reader is advised to take a look at the Additional Reading Section at the very end of this chapter.

Background on Testing

Testing is the evaluation of software by observing its execution (Ammann & Offutt, 2008). The executed system is called System Under Test (SUT) or more specifically Cloud Under Test (CUT) if a Cloud system is tested. Software testing consists of the dynamic verification of the behavior of a program on a finite set of test cases, suitably selected from the usually infinite executions domain, against the expected behavior (Bourque & Dupuis, 2004). In a test case, the actual and intended behavior of a SUT is compared with each other, which then results in a verdict. Generally, verdicts can be either of pass (behaviors conform), fail (behaviors don't conform), and inconclusive (not known whether behaviors conform) (ISO/IEC, 1994). A test oracle is a mechanism for determining the verdict. Testing comprises several activities.

According to the level of detail, we can distinguish unit testing which is applied to the smallest unit of program code, module testing which tests the conformance of distinct components of a system, and system testing which is applied to a complete system. System testing in our respect is based on the system requirements. We therefore do not consider acceptance testing as separate testing category because acceptance testing is requirements testing from the customers perspective and an extension of system testing focusing on usability requirements (Bertolino & Marchetti, 2005).

According to the characteristics, we can distinguish functional testing which examines whether a system is a correct refinement of its design or specification and various types of non-functional testing like performance testing, usability testing or security testing. Security testing is testing of security requirements like availability, confidentiality or integrity.

In principle, any form of software testing can be seen as model-based. The tester always forms a mental model of the system under test before engaging in activities such as test case design (Binder, 1999). The term model-based testing (MBT) is applicable when these mental models are documented and subsequently used to generate tests, to execute tests or to evaluate their results (Hartmann et al., 2005). There are many definitions of MBT (Roßner et al., 2010) but each contains at least one of the two aspects modeling of tests and generation of tests from models. Model-based testing raises the abstraction level of test design, supports the early validation of the quality of tests, and facilitates test automation. The topic of model-based testing is well-covered in the literature (see (Broy et al., 2005) for an overview) and many tools are already on the market supporting model-based approaches

(Goetz et al., 2009). According to (Zander et al., 2005) we define model-driven testing as testing-based model-driven architecture (MDA) (OMG, 2003). Model-driven testing therefore comprises the derivation of executable test code from test models and can be considered as a specific type of model-based testing.

Breaking Software Security

Considering the task of software testing from a very rudimentary point of view reveals that under the bottom line, testing has no other intention than trying to break the software. However, this idea of breaking is often misunderstood in a way, that most of the time, testing teams focus on the requirements and try to verify them by testing, instead of choosing the other way round and try to effectively disprove them. Hence, the software actually only will be broken, if occasionally some misbehavior is detected. This is especially crucial when it comes to security testing. Only relying on specified requirements and trying to assure that the software only implements what was specified by far does not suffice. Considering the simple example of a login form with the imposed requirement of only allowing user with valid credentials to login. Yet, this definitely assures a certain degree of security, as it prohibits users to login with wrong credentials. However, such a requirement for example does no incorporate the case, where a malicious user logs into the system by i.e., either by bypassing the validation process or crafting input in a way, that the validation process erroneously grants the login.

This quite simple, yet illustrative example shows that during testing, especially security testing of software systems, it does not suffice to only incorporate the positive requirements, specifying what is allowed in terms of the behavior of the software. Also the often neglected negative requirements are an inevitable part of the test requirements to be considered during testing. In doing so, it allows changing the testing process fundamentally in a way, that testers not anymore try to assure the proper behavior of the software by assuring a certain degree of security, but instead testers follow the anticipation of a malicious user, which is, that the system in fact is not secure in any aspect. Seeing a software system from such a perspective allows incorporating concealed, negative test requirements totally neglected otherwise.

Keeping the above in mind, software security testers are equipped with a powerful idea of how to examine, whether the tested systems are actually secure not only in accordance with the customer's requirements but also in terms of common attacks, modern software systems are exposed to on a daily basis. Another reason, why concurrent systems need to be tested exhaustively is their increasing complexity due to their distributed deployment and tight interconnectivity. Today's degree of complexity inherent in software systems is a fertile ground for possibly exploitable security flaws. In the following we give a brief overview on the most common types of attacks (yet, this overview by far is not complete, however it gives an overview on those techniques, involved in most attacks).

- **Crafted Input:** Amongst the most common types of attacks to software systems. This is mainly due to their ease of feasibility. In performing such an attack, a malicious user concentrates on any kind of system interface, allowing interaction with the user, whether intended or not. By inspecting this so-called attack surface a malicious user feeds the system with manually crafted, malicious input and tries to observe abnormal behavior of the system, thereby unveiling the chance for a possible exploit. In the following we discuss the most common types of input based attacks:
  - **Path Traversal:** May be performed on any type of system where a user has the chance to access remote files. The idea hereby is to manipulate the input string, depicting the remote file-

name, in a way, to allow a malicious user to access system specific files containing probable sensitive data, i.e., user account credentials. This kind of path traversal attacks can as well be performed on web URLs in a way that the URL string is manipulated to get direct access to files, residing on the remote server.
  - **Buffer Overflows:** By far the most annoying but therefore also most studied attacks known to the IT world. Since 1988 (Seeley, 1988), when the first well-explained buffer overflow had been performed, software system again and again have been exploited by using this powerful attack technique. In doing so, a malicious user crafts input in a way, that the memory of a running process is overwritten, with the goal, that the value of the return address is finally overwritten with the address of the memory location, where the own exploit code relies. However, thanks to advancements in the area of programming languages, nowadays buffer overflows are mostly a thing of the past as concepts like *sandboxing* and *runtime checking* strictly prohibit overwriting memory and leaving the assigned execution context.
  - **Format Strings:** Although being very powerful and able to easily exploit software systems, format string attacks have not been detected earlier than in 1990 (Miller et al., 1990). In contradiction to buffer overflows, where a malicious user tries to overwrite memory contents until a memory location, allowing execution of the exploit, is reached, format string attacks attempt to directly write the exploit code to specified locations in

memory. In doing so, attackers can easily gain control over complete processes.

○ **Code Injections:** Injection-based attacks may also be counted to crafted input attacks, yet they are not always that obvious to perform like simple crafted input attacks. This is basically motivated by the fact that they often are tailored onto dedicated technologies like XML, SQL or XPATH. The idea hereby is to manipulate input, in this case also complete data structures, destined to be processed by special parsers, to be crafted in a way that those parser misbehave or crash. The hereby used crafted input employs special *escape characters* of the dedicated languages, triggering the parsers to misbehave or fail in their execution.

- **Cross Site-Scripting (XSS):** Performed with the main intention to snatch user specific data by placing malicious HTML or script code into the web page, loaded into the victim's browser. Residing inside the browser's process, malicious code will be executed, as it is being trusted, hence allowing an attacker to steal session information or user specific cookie data. Such attacks may be used to infest multiple web pages and user collect data to be sent to third parties for further usage.

- **Denial of Service (DoS):** Besides buffer overflows, DoS attacks also belong to the most common and well-studied kinds of attack types. The idea of such attacks is, as the name already indicates, to denial a service, located on a remote server, to be executed, i.e., accessing a web page or invoking a web service. In performing such an attack, a malicious user does nothing but simply overload the remote system for that it becomes unresponsive. This kind of attack especially is interesting in terms of Cloud computing, not only because a Cloud could literally be broken by doing so. What makes a Cloud that interesting in terms of Denial of Service attacks is the idea of compromising a complete Cloud environment and misusing its computational power to perform invasive *virtually* Distributed Denial of Service (DDoS) attacks against any kind of institution.

As already mentioned above, this discussion on attacks by far is not complete, as it would go beyond the scope of this book. Anyhow, the interested reader is advised to take a look at the Additional Reading Section, where we provide a list of books, giving a broad discussion on the topics of breaking software and security testing.

Data Privacy Testing

As already mentioned above, when positioning our work in respect to related work, the topic of data privacy testing up to now has not received a lot of attention in the software testing world. Hence, we use this section to expose and motivate our own idea of data privacy testing.

As the name already indicates, the idea of data privacy testing in terms of software testing is to assure, that the tested software system treats data as actually stated in according policies, used in the software system. Put another way, the data management component of the software has to be implemented in accordance with the CIA paradigm (Confidentiality, Integrity, and Authorization). Besides, for that the idea of data privacy testing also is in accordance with the new Cloud storage paradigm, newly evolving data management requirements, concerning data removal and de-duplication also need to be incorporated and considered, as otherwise, new flaws are going to be introduced into the concept of Cloud storage.

The usage of policies at this point is quite obviously, they offer a clean and standardized way to specify who is allowed to do what in terms of data access and manipulation. However, if policy testing ever is to be performed as part of the testing phase during the SDLC, testers generally on one side, only evaluate whether policies are properly specified, or, on the other side, examine whether the underlying Policy Decision Points (PDP) evaluate and enforce the policies properly. Unfortunately, from our point of view this does not really suffice, as using this approach one can actually only state, whether policies are properly formulated or the underlying PDPs enforce them as intended. What we miss in terms of such an approach for data privacy testing in the context of policies, is the possibility to assure that also the underlying system conforms to the policies and also to the various obligations, coming along with the policies. Hence, what we also describe in the following is an idea of how to incorporate policies in a way, that we can derive data specific privacy rules from them, which in turn are used to assure the a system's conformance in terms of data privacy rules, derived from policies.

Change-Driven Development: Living Models

The idea of Change-Driven Development is a central part of the Living Models paradigm developed by R. Breu (Breu, 2010). The living model paradigm focuses on model-based management, design and operation of dynamically evolving systems. Summarizing the Ten Principles for Living Models (Breu, 2010) one can identify several important and innovative concepts.

- **Stakeholder Centric Modeling Environments:** A Living Models environment is focused on stakeholders and their views on the systems. This means that views can abstract concepts for stakeholders and hide lower levels which are not interesting for them. As a result the modeling environ-

ments of stakeholders do not have to be homogeneous.

- **Close Coupling of Models and Code:** A model must reflect the running system to allow expedient model analysis. Therefore models and code need a close coupling. This implies that changes on a model are adapted in the associated code and vice versa. Tight coupling means in this case that model and code are in consistent states and that there is tool support to connect models and code. As an additional result of close coupling, code and configurations can be generated from models. Test cases can be derived from a requirement mode (Felderer, Breu et al., 2009).

- **Common System View:** To allow a cooperation of all stakeholders and to support a continuous quality management process, a common system view is a mandatory requirement. As a basis for tool support and to describe the common system view precise, a System Meta Model is introduced. It contains meta-model elements and their relationship. The meta- model builds a backbone for tool support and the change management process.

- **Persistence:** To allow reactions to changes and evolution, models need to be persistent and versioned. As a result models can be described as a sequence of versions. Since the System Meta Model and the System Model may change versioning needs to be supported for both. Since development of models may result in different solutions, branching of development trees must be considered.

- **Model Element States:** Each model element can have a state that reflects certain aspects in its life cycle.

- **Change-Driven Process:** The software development process in a Living Models environment is driven by change events, the state of the model elements and their inter-relationships with other model elements.

- **Change and Change Propagation:** In the context of Living Models any change is perceived as an event which triggers consecutive steps of actions. Three types of events are defined.
  - **Timer Event:** This is an event that is triggered periodically.
  - **Model Element Change:** A model element was changed, added or deleted.
  - **Action Event:** An event that was triggered by a stakeholder.

Under the bottom line Living models is a paradigm that fosters change driven model-engineering by reacting on changes of models. The state of a model element is handled by attached state machines which allow a fine granular reaction on model changes and event chains. Close coupling between models and code guarantees that the actual system and the abstract model are always up to date.

A SECURE CLOUD

In this section we present our approach of how to test whether a Cloud computing environment is secure in terms of information security or not. Besides, prior to describing our idea, we give an overview on the vulnerable Cloud, and lay down the various aspects of security to be considered in the Cloud context.

Vulnerable Cloud

Talking about vulnerabilities in the context of Cloud computing, we can roughly categorize them into the four categories below:

- Network-related vulnerabilities
- Data-related vulnerabilities
- Implementation- and service-related vulnerabilities
- Technology-related vulnerabilities

In the following we discuss those various categories in more detail.

Network-related vulnerabilities. As the name already indicates, network-related vulnerabilities are located in the networking layer of the Cloud computing environment. These may be unsecure ports or flaws intrinsic to used protocols. Yet, at this point we have to differ between low-level networking protocols like TCP or UDP, and high-level application layer protocols, like HTTP or SIP. Hence, if talking about protocol specific vulnerabilities, we motivate to distinguish between such low and high-level protocols, as we count vulnerabilities, coming along with high-level protocols to the category of implementation- and service-related vulnerabilities. For the broad range of network-related vulnerabilities there already exists a vast amount of tools, like penetration testing tools or port scanners, to detect and mitigate them consecutively.

Data-related vulnerabilities. Although this category might seem to be a little redundant to the network- and implementation- and service-related vulnerabilities, from our point of view, it has a right to exist. This is mainly motivated by the fact, that in a Cloud computing environment, data needs to be treated differently as compared to a stand-alone application. Especially if considering a Cloud storage system, data plays the central role, hence if performing a vulnerability analysis, it should be done with the main focus relying on data and not the application itself. Thence, this category comprises all kinds of vulnerabilities in the context of data management capabilities which may, but must not, violate the CIA principle (i.e., final deletion of data from the Cloud environment can lead to a vulnerability, if for example, the storage device is not completely formatted but instead only *flagged* as being *empty*; yet, such a flaw does not violate the CIA principle).

Implementation- and service-related vulnerabilities. The broadest range of possible vulnerabilities, confronting a Cloud computing environment, is assigned to this category. The root causes of vulnerabilities counted to this category mainly are insecure coding practices. However, as already mentioned earlier, also vulnerabilities related to high-level, application layer protocols are assigned to this category as they also lead to unwanted behavior of the applications. Beneath, we also count any kind of service-related vulnerability to this category, motivated by the fact, that most often these are not vulnerabilities intrinsic to the used service technology itself, but to its very different usage in the underlying implementation.

Technology-related vulnerabilities. The last category of vulnerabilities a Cloud is affected with are technology-related vulnerabilities. This is due to the fact of the amount of already-existing technologies, i.e., virtualization, incorporated in state-of-the-art Cloud offerings. Again, this category is slightly redundant to the implementation- and service-related vulnerabilities, yet, we again believe that it has a right to exist, i.e., taking into consideration XML, one has the choice between SAX and DOM. Yet, DOM is prone to DoS attacks, as it loads the complete (maliciously crafted) XML file into memory, whereas SAX is not affected by such kind of vulnerabilities, as only the needed elements of the XML file are loaded. Hence, a complete crash of the application is not possible, as it would be the case with DOM. Considering this example, it is quite obvious that based on the parser technology, a flaw is possible, and not based on its concrete implementation, as it would be the case with SAX.

In the following we are going to present our idea of how to examine whether a Cloud is affected by any kind of vulnerability. However, our approach only focuses on data- and implementation- and service-related vulnerabilities. This is justified by the circumstance, that for network-related attacks, already lots of tools exist to be used to examine a system and, in the case of technology-related vulnerabilities we assume that the provider of specific technology already has performed exhaustive security testing.

Securing the Cloud

After outlining the various types of vulnerabilities, this section is intended to present our idea on how to test a Cloud's security, based on models. As already mentioned in the introduction, we use a two-way approach to examine, both, environmental security of the Cloud system and data privacy of the underlying Cloud storage system, implementing the CDMI interface. Hence, at first we present how we intend to test a Cloud's security and secondly how we address the problem of assuring proper data privacy in a Cloud Computing environment. However, prior to describing our ideas in detail, we first discuss the primary CUT system model, as it represents the fundamental basis of our approach.

The CUT System Model

As the CUT system model acts as the main input for our approach, we discuss it in more detail in the following to foster understanding of our idea.

Figure 1 depicts the meta-model for the CUT system model as used by our approach. As can be seen, the root element of the model is the model itself. The model itself contains five different packages, namely *SaaSPackage, PaaSPackage, DaaSPackage, IaaSPackage,* and *PolicyPackage,* respectively.

Taking a closer look at the *PolicyPackage,* one can see that this package may only contain policies, written in XACML, but nothing else. The information contained inside this package is vital for data privacy testing.

The other group of packages, contained in the CUT system model are all related to the different service layers, offered by a Cloud, put another way, each different layer gets assigned its own package, to depict the offered services. Each of

Figure 1. CUT system model meta-model

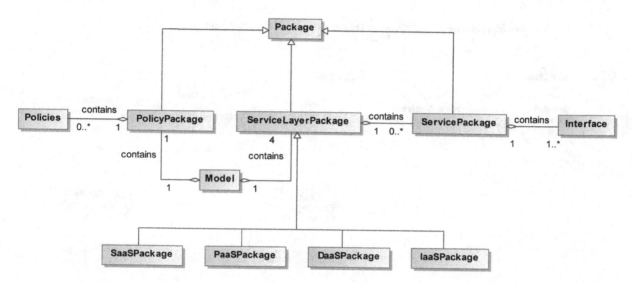

these packages may again contain an unlimited number of packages, encapsulating the interfaces, describing the offered capabilities. These packages contain the necessary information, relevant for the risk-based testing of the Cloud environment.

The reason for why we chose to give our CUT system model this underlying structure is motivated by the circumstance, that by doing so we can react on changes in the Cloud environment very fine granularly. To put it another way, if only very small changes are made in one single interface, or at least only one offered capability is modified, we can react on such small changes in a way, that we actually only need to retest the modified interfaces, and not the complete Cloud environment *en bloc*.

Threatening the Cloud

In this section we introduce our methodology on how to address the problem of efficiently and effectively test the software security of a Cloud computing environment. As already mentioned earlier, this only constitutes one part of our whole idea, the second part, focusing on invading data privacy is presented in the subsequent section.

Figure 2 depicts the idea of our approach on how to address to problem of securing the Cloud service layers, and hence also the applications running behind, inside the Cloud. In doing so, our basic assumption is to investigate the complete attack surface, provided by the Cloud in terms of services. This is due to the fact, that besides low level networking attacks, which we neglect, as we assume that the network infrastructure is secure, attacks tailored on the service infrastructure are the only other possible way to break into the Cloud to abuse running applications, stored data or the Cloud's resource capabilities itself. Put it another way, the underlying idea of our methodology is to view the Cloud from an attacker's point of view, thus without any knowledge of the internals, trying to break into the Cloud by misusing the offered services.

Basically this part of our approach consists out of four main activities, namely *Risk Analysis, Misuse Case Model Generation, Offline Fuzzing* and *Code Generation*, respectively. As already

Figure 2. Risk-based security testing methodology for the cloud

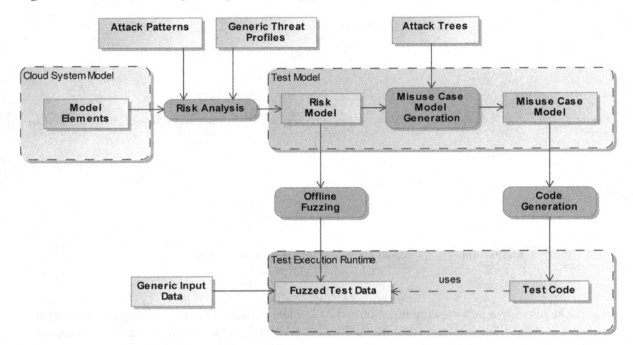

mentioned earlier, the CUT system model is the only input employed by this methodology, yielding as a result executable test code in terms of attacks and according test data, retrieved from an offline fuzzer.

In the following, each of these four activities, its required inputs and the yielded outcome are discussed in more detail

Risk Analysis

As a first step, we apply an automated risk analysis onto the CUT system model. As already described in Section The CUT System Model, this very model describes the complete set of offered services using notions of UML class diagrams and interfaces. During the risk analysis, we map different attack patterns on the system model, to identify possible spots, an attacker may use for his malicious activities. Hereby, an attack pattern defines the way on how to perform a particular attack in a formalized way, using notions of OCL.

Besides the attack patterns, the risk analysis also employs a generic threat profile, allowing to be instantiated to profile a real, possible threat to the Cloud system. By using those three artifacts, viz. the CUT system model, the attack patterns, and the generic threat profile, our automated risk analysis is capable of identifying possible intrusion points in the Cloud, and allows generating a dedicated risk model, picturing the various risks, the Cloud environment is possibly exposed to. The generated risk model contains graphical description of possible risk the Cloud is exposed to using notions of UML. The description itself contains classical risk related values like probability of occurrence, the possible impact and for sure, the threat level, calculated from the former two values. Besides those classical values, the risk is also associated with a tailored threat profile, describing the parameters of the attack, namely the affected asset, the intrusion point, the kind of vulnerability to be exploited and the final outcome of the attack.

Misuse Case Model Generation

The second, most crucial step is the successful generation of the misuse case model. Again, this is a fully automated task, employing a Model-To-Model (M2M) transformation from the risk model into the misuse case model. The underlying idea of the model transformation is to employ the generated risk model in combination with attack trees (Schneier, 1999). The concept of an attack tree is to provide a graphical, formalized way to describe the anatomy of an attack, i.e., the various steps necessary to be performed in timely order. The mapping from an attack tree onto an identified risk is possible due to the fact, that each risk is associated the final outcome of the performed attack in the dedicated threat profile. Besides, each attack tree has as a root node the final, intended outcome of the attack, i.e., Denial of Service. Hence, by taking the root node of an attack tree it is possible to assign a specific attack to a risk. This in fact is crucial, as this is how we generate graphical representations of attacks to be performed onto the CUT. Put it another way, this mapping enables us to identify possible security test cases. After the generation of the misuse case model has finished, we receive as an output, as already mentioned a few times earlier, a dedicated misuse case model triggered on the CUT. This misuse case model again employs notions of UML, however, at this point we employ UML activity diagrams to graphically represent a test case, in other words, the activities necessary to break the system.

Offline Fuzzing

The basic idea of fuzz testing is to provide the input interface of a software system with incomplete, malformed or unexpected inputs to detect possible misbehavior, which further could be exploited. Hence, it is quite obvious, that fuzz testing very well fits into the area of software security testing, as basically, an attacker does nothing else than providing a software with such input to observe misbehavior, exposing a possible, exploitable flaw. The reason why we chose a fuzzer to search for test data is due to the fact that other approaches in search based test data generation (McMinn, 2004) generally rely on an optimality criteria, used to examine, whether data fits for a test case or not. However, as we know nothing more than just the signature of the service operations (in fact, the same as an attacker knows), defining such an optimality criteria is an impossible task. Thence, using a fuzzer to generate test data is quite obvious, as based on a protocol specification, the fuzzer simply mutates possible (predefined) input data to trigger misbehavior. As our approach heavily employs UML notations, luckily we can provide such a protocol specification in terms of the misuse case model, as it contains all the possible assets (service operation signatures).

The reason why we only perform offline fuzzing instead of online fuzzing, i.e., also perform the test with the fuzzing tool, is due to various reasons. One of the most important are cost factors, coming along with frequent invocations of services. Also, as we intend to integrate our methodology in the already existing Telling TestStories framework, we do not need any functionality concerning test execution and evaluation, as this very framework already provides these features in a very powerful way. Hence, we employ a fuzzer for the offline search for test data, based on the risk model and a fixed set of predefined, generic input data, unaware of the specific CUT.

Code Generation

As one of the last steps, prior to execution of the test cases, their formalized representation needs to be transformed into executable code. In doing so, a Model-to-Text (M2T) transformation is employed onto the misuse case model to generate executable test cases (currently only Java is supported). For this purpose, the already existing M2T test code generator of the Telling TestStories framework (Felderer, Fiedler et al., 2009), which has already been employed in (Felderer et al., 2010) to generated security test cases, is reused and adapted as necessary. The mechanics of this generator are quite straight-forward, based on the distinct activities contained in the misuse case, various predefined code templates are expanded and dynamically adapted to meet the test case specific requirements.

After this discussion of how we intend to find security test cases in the context of a Cloud's service offerings, in the following we are going to describe how we address the problem of data privacy testing.

Invading Data Privacy

This section introduces the second part of our approach, dealing with the problem of data privacy testing. The underlying idea we attempt to follow with our approach is not to test the correctness of the policies nor the correct implementation of a Policy Enforcement Point (PEP) or Policy Decision Point (PDP). What we attempt to test,

is whether the underlying implementation of the DaaS service offering, following the guidelines of the Cloud Data Management Interface, is implemented in a way that it conforms to the policies. Put it another way, we do not want to know whether the PEP or PDP do their proper job, we want to know whether the system itself is flawless in following the policy rules in terms of data management. The policies itself are specified using XACML and contained in the Cloud system model. We use XACML due to two reasons, on the one side it currently represents and industry-wide accepted standard in the context of Role-Based Access Control and Policy Management. On the other side, we use XACML, as a policy written in XACML from our point of view also can be considered as a model, as it is built upon a clearly defined meta model in terms of an XML schema file.

Figure 3 depicts our approach in terms of data privacy testing. Again, it consists of four automated activities, namely Rules Extraction, Covering Rule Set Calculation, Rules Mutation and Code Generation, respectively. Again, the

Figure 3. Data privacy testing methodology for the cloud

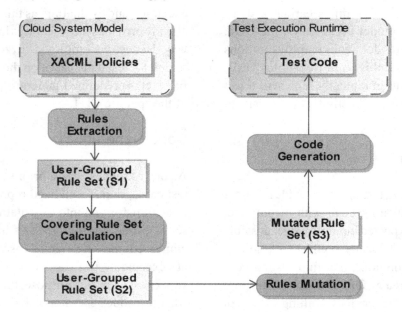

CUT system model is the only input required by our approach. Based on the policies contained in the *Policies* package, we calculate a final rule set S3, which we employ to generate test cases for data privacy testing in the context of the Cloud Data Management Interface.

In the following, besides giving a sketch of the Cloud Data Management Interface, each of these four activities, its required inputs and the outcome are discussed in detail.

Cloud Data Management Interface

The Cloud Data Management Interface (CDMI) (SNIA, 2011) is a novel attempt by the Storage Network Industry Association (SNIA) to standardize the idea of Data-as-a-Service (DaaS – currently ignored by the NIST) by means of providing a generic service interface, declaring common operations for data management capabilities (i.e. data object creation or deletion). Besides, the CDMI also defines a hierarchical object model in terms of container and data objects, allowing efficiently storing, managing and retrieving data from the Cloud. In doing so, the SNIA attempts future Cloud providers to use their standardized interface when offering DaaS capabilities. However, also current Cloud providers already can use this interface, as it allows to be implemented on top and mapped onto their own, proprietary implementation of DaaS.

Yet, providing a further discussion of the CDMI and the topic of Cloud storage at this point would go beyond the scope of this chapter, hence we skip it and move on by discussing our approach.

Rules Extraction

In this first activity, out of the XACML policies, contained in the CUT system model, the various rules are extracted. Besides specifying the condition, a rule also contains a target, on which to be evaluated, the effect if the condition evaluates to true, and finally, advices and obligations to

which the environment may, or as in the latter, has to conform after the granted action has been performed. In doing so we calculate a first set of rules, further on referred as *S1*, relevant for testing the implementation of the CDMI in terms of data privacy. This rules are thus of special interest, as they later on can be employed to calculate a reduced set of rules, covering the complete CDMI interface specification in terms of implementation requirements. Additionally, in all conscience, we can ignore the target elements of the policy files during extraction, as the rule itself also contains a target element, stating on which decision request the rule has to be evaluated on. The extraction itself is quite straight-forward, a simple XML parser searching for the relevant elements inside the policy files.

Covering Rule Set Calculation

After extracting the various rules from the XACML policies by calculating the set S1, in this second activity a crucial calculation, coming down in the quality and coverage of the resulting test cases, takes place. Based on the set S1 and the CDMI, we calculate a reduced set *S2*, containing exactly that set of rules, covering all common operations, declared by the CDMI specification. The calculation of this covering set therefore is possible, as the rule itself, as already mentioned earlier, contains a target element. This target element is used to define which decision request the associated rule has to be evaluated on to grant or deny an action. By now formalizing the CDMI in terms of XML, we can use an XML based mapping algorithm to extract the set of rules from S1, covering the service specification by matching the target of a rule with the corresponding CDMI operation. Yet, the finally calculated, reduced set S2 may not be complete in terms of covering the whole CMDI common operation declaration, however, if this case occurs, we provide dummy rules, allowing to complete the set in terms of coverage. Although these rules may be quite generic and simple, they provide a first chance of achieving full coverage of the implementation during testing, and detect flaws, otherwise overseen.

Rules Mutation

We employ mutation of the rules due to two main reasons. At a first glance, the set S2 has full coverage, however, only in terms of the CDMI. Yet, by performing slight mutation on the rules and hence changing them, we attempt to reach coverage of the policy language itself and provide a more diverse set of rules for generating test cases. Furthermore, by performing mutations on the rules, the above mentioned dummy rules also get more diverse and hence, more sophisticated in terms of testing. The mutation of the rules itself is currently based on a simple mutation operator implemented by a simple *coin-flip*. If the flip evaluates to true, a rule element will be mutated, otherwise not. The mutation itself focuses on the various elements, contained inside a rule and performs slight changes on them, i.e., change condition parameters or exchange targets. After this mutation we get a final set *S3* containing mutated rules based on the contents of S2, yet providing also coverage in terms of the policy language. This set further on is used to finally generate test cases for data privacy testing.

Code Generation

In the case of data privacy testing, test code generation is not that straight-forward. Again, we use a template based approach, however, in this case based on the CDMI. Put it another way, this means, that we provide generic, execution-ready templates of requests to a CDMI, yet to be filled with the relevant parameters, all derivable from the rules contained in set S3. The selection of the proper template to be used for evaluating a rule is based on the target contained in the rule itself. The specified decision request is used to identify the request template to be instantiated for testing.

The template itself, as already mentioned above, remains to be filled with the relevant parameters. After filling up the template with the request and user data, we finally get an executable test case, ready to be executed against the CUT. The different types of test data to support are automatically generated into the test code by means of mechanics to create directories, files or archives. The reason why we draw back on such simple data for testing is simply motivated by the fact, that the contents of the data to be secured is irrelevant, as long as the data itself is secure. Hence, we can easily support test data generation within our generated test cases.

Test Execution and Evaluation

The execution of tests in the context of our approach is performed by a dedicated test engine as implemented in the course of the Telling TestStories framework. In the case of testing a services security, the basic mechanism of this test engine simply is to load test cases and their according data files and execute them similar to the Fitnesse (Mugridge & Cunningham, 2005) testing framework. The various columns in the test table represent parameters and expected outcomes whereas the amount of lines defines how often to execute the test case. This basic mechanism of execution also applies for data privacy testing, however, as already mentioned above, in this case no data files are needed, as the amount of test cases already varies broadly due to mutated rules, and additionally, test data is generated in test cases inline.

What remains the same for both types of execution of test is the idea that we perform negative testing. Put it another way, this means that a passing test case actually shows some flaw in the Cloud environment and hence indicates that the system fails in terms of security. In contrast, if a test case fails, we know that the system passed in terms of security. We consider a test case to be successful (pass) if it either ends without throwing any exception or granting access or by actively triggering an exception, thrown by the Cloud system. This is motivated by the fact that an exception prints down lines of code, revealing information about the internals of a software system. This information may be misused by an attacker as it probably contains exactly that piece of information, the attacker needs, to succeed with his exploit. Hence, for a test case to fail and the system to pass, the system must provide both, some mitigation for a possible exploit and conform to the privacy rules contained in policies in terms of its implementation. In doing so, the system also must not throw any exceptions but instead provide well-founded error messages or codes.

The rules how to evaluate a specific test case are defined inside an assertion, unique for every test case. This special construct states what actually needed to have happened to be able to determine whether a test case has succeeded or failed. The concept of assertions as used in our approach is very powerful. Based on the implementation of the Telling TestStories framework, we allow defining very powerful assertions, specifying constraints over both functional requirements like contents of object structures, but also non-functional requirements like policy rules. After each test run, the test case specific assertion is evaluated to determine whether the system is secure or not. Based on all the outcomes of the single test runs, in the end we can determine the overall security of the Cloud environment and feed this information back into the model.

Continuous Security Assurance

During the life time of a software system it is always under change. This is caused by adaption to changing software requirements or evolution by extensions such as plug-ins. Changing hardware may also cause a change in the software system. Due to all of these reasons the CUT system model described in Section The CUT System Model is not static through the life cycle of an application but is subject to various changes, therefore some new challenges arise: First of all it can become important for a company to show that the software system fulfilled certain security requirements in a specific version, i.e., if a hacking attack occurred and the security engineer has to proof some properties to an insurance company. Another important challenge is to restart the testing procedure after every change of the software system automatically for continuous security assurance and evaluate the results which can then be used to notify developers and security engineers about the current state of the system. If the system changes it must be tested again to make sure it is still secure and the changed parts did not cause new exploits. To solve those new challenges we propose a change driven model versioning system which is explained in this chapter. We start by introducing concepts for change driven model versioning and a methodology to add security assurance to the model versioning process. To show the technical feasibility of continuous security assurance we use the MoVE framework (Breu et al., 2010).

State-Aware System Models

The CUT system model is the main input for our Cloud testing methodology. This model contains a description of all service layers as packages together with sub-packages which contain a description of service interfaces and their implementation. It can be seen as a fingerprint of the current software system and is therefore the central model for our continuous security assurance approach. Every time the software system changes, this model is changed too and reflects the systems current status. Due to this, we version this model to get a history of all system versions. Versioning a model means to commit and manage it with a versioning system such as Subversion (Apache, 2011b). Due to the importance of versioning in software engineering, a lot of different approaches exist. In the end of this chapter we explain shortly how the MoVE framework handles this task.

To overcome this problem our approach introduces state machines for *ServiceLayerPackages* and *ServicesPackages* of the CUT-model respectively each package is extended by a state property. In general each package has three different states:

- **Changed:** The package is new or was changed from the last to the current version.
- **Insecure:** The package is not secure or not tested at all.
- **Secure:** The package was tested and is secure.

Every package starts with the state *Changed*. It means that no tests were executed for this package or that it was changed and the results of the previous tests are not valid anymore. This state is automatically set if a service interface in one of the packages, or a policy in case of the *PolicyPackage,* changed from the last version of the CUT-model to the current version. A package with the state *Changed* must be tested. After the tests were executed, the state machine changes the package's state to *Insecure* or *Secure*. This change is automatically done by the state machine, in more detail by executing a state machine transition. A state machine transition changes a state depending on a certain condition. Since the conditions are different for *ServiceLayerPackages* and *ServicePackages* we define two different state machines. The conditions for each transition can be formulated in OCL but due to OCLs complex and difficult

syntax we only give an informal description of each state transition. Both state machines have the same states as mentions above and each state has an empty transition to the *Changed* state, to denote that an element is new.

Transitions for state machines of *ServiceLayerPackages* (see Figure 4):

- **A (from *Changed* to *Secure*):** This transition is allowed if all *ServicesPackages* contained in the current *ServiceLayer Package* have their state set to *Secure*.
- **B (from *Changed* to *Insecure*):** If at least one sub-*ServicePackage* is not in state *Secure* this transition must be executed.

We implemented an additional feature for state machines, which we call state machine action. An action allows a state machine to trigger the execution of a different state machines transition, i.e., a *ServicePackage's* state machine can trigger the execution of a transition of its parent *ServiceLayerPackage*. The idea of this feature is to support dependencies of state machines and make execution easier. In the case of our CUT-model, we know that the states of *ServiceLayerPackages* only change if child packages of type *ServicePackage* change, therefore we do not need to execute *ServiceLayerPackages* state machines separately but we can trigger them with actions of ServicePackage state machines.

Figure 4. State machines for ServiceLayerPackage and ServicePackage

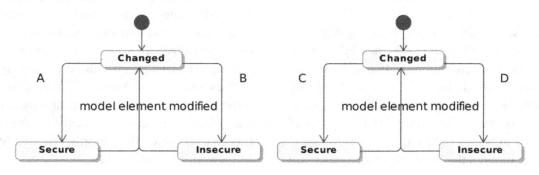

Transitions for state machines of *ServicePackages* are:

- **C (from *Changed* to *Secure*):** The transition from *Changed* to *Secure* has the condition that all Risks that have assets, related to some service interfaces of the current package, did not pass a single test that was generated by the related misusecases. This transition also triggers the execution of the parent *ServiceLayerPackage*'s state machine.
- **D (from *Changed* to *Insecure*):** The opposite of transition C, at least one misuse case test passed. As well as C, this transition triggers its parent packages state machine execution.

The general workflow for model versioning with security aware state machines can be described in 6 steps:

1. The software system was changed therefore a new CUT system model is generated.
2. This model is committed to the model versioning system.
3. Changes from the last version to the current version are calculated and analyzed. The state property is set to *Changed* if a sub-element is *new* or was *changed*.
4. Calculate changed risk model and start the testing procedure with the updated risk model.
5. Execute the state machine of each package with state *Changed* to find a possible transition to *Secure* or *Insecure*-state. The state property is changed in this step.
6. Return information about state changes to the user who committed the new version of the service model.

System Architecture

To come back to the initial challenge for continuous security assurance namely model versioning, we show the architecture of our implementation of a change-driven model versioning system. That is a model versioning system that supports state machines as explained in this chapter. While model versioning is already implemented in various systems, using a change-driven approach is new. This system described in this section is called MoVE (Model Versioning and Evolution) and is an infrastructure for living models.

Figure 5 shows the slightly simplified architecture of MoVE. The architecture of MoVE is twofold: it consists of client-side and server-side components. To provide typical features of a standard Version Control System (VCS) and a stable and well tested communication protocol, subversion is used as a core component on the client- and server-side.

On the client-side we developed several adapters which are integrated as plug-ins into modeling tools. The MoVE Client provides an interface for all communication actions between client-side and server-side and wraps protocol calls to provide a simple interface for adapters. The intend of this architecture is that models can be shared between several developers and different modeling tools without using a complicated system but only tools integrated in the familiar modeling environment.

On the server-side MoVE consists of two core components:

- A subversion server as a basic VCS
- The MoVE Server with pluggable components to cover non-standard VCS features

Subversion has support for a simple event management. Events, such as the creation of a new revision or the modification of an unversioned property, trigger the execution of scripts called hooks. After the set-up of SVN these scripts are

Figure 5. Architecture of MoVE

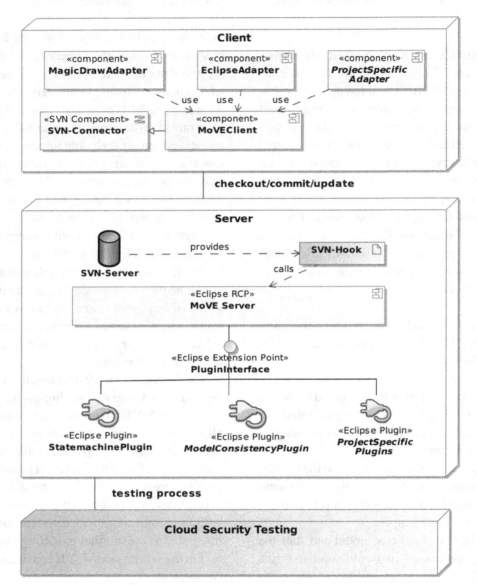

only empty templates. MoVE overwrites the hooks with scripts that start the MoVE-Server.

The MoVEServer is the core component of MoVE. It loads the changed models from the SVN-Server and provides a runtime environment for plug-ins. The MoVEServer is also responsible to handle communication with the MoVEClient, it does not alter models but propagates this task to plug-ins and coordinates the appropriate feed-

back for the client. The MoVEServer component provides a mechanism to collect messages from plug-ins and send them to the MoVEClient, i.e., state changes are transmitted with this mechanism.

Plug-ins contain the actual project specific functionality. The set of plug-ins can be different for every project. To cover the needs of the continuous security assurance process for change propagation and change handling we implemented a state machine controller. The basic conception of our state machine implementation is to associate state machines to a state attribute of the context element. At the current stage each model element can have one associated state machine and therefore one property called State. The State property stores the current state of the state machine. State machines are defined with the W3C language SCXML. SCXML stands for State Chart XML and is a markup language to describe complex state machines. Apache provides a SCXML framework for state machines execution called Apache Commons SCXML (Apache, 2011a) which was used in our implementation. To model guards and invariants for state transitions and states we use OCL.

The process of executing a state machine starts with the analysis of the changes between the current version of the corresponding model and the previous version. This is done with a plug-in called *ChangePropagationPlugin*, which analyses the changes and assigns the state *Changed* to packages if child elements changed. Afterwards the state machine plug-in is executed for all changed packages which means that the testing process is executed. After the execution the possible state machines transitions are triggered, also considering Actions.

In summary we use SVN for basic versioning and communication and enhance it by plugins. One of the plug-ins is a state machine plug-in that uses SCXML to describe state machines such as the two we suggested in this chapter. The state machine plug-in is able to start the testing process and delivers results via the communication method provided by MoVE. Everything is integrated into modeling environment such as MagicDraw (NoMagic, 2011) or Eclipse (Eclipse, 2011b).

FUTURE RESEARCH DIRECTIONS

Based on our current work we have identified three different areas of future research. First, we want to integrate the concept of an intelligent system in the test generation process. By doing so, we attempt to use outcomes of test runs and feed them back into the various model transformation, code generation and fuzzing processes, to enhance test cases. Doing so allows us to improve the generated misuse cases, the mutated rules, as well as the generated test data. This is mainly due to the fact, as by using historical information about former test runs, the various processes could be enhanced with reasoning capabilities to try to generate more sophisticated and effective test cases. Also, such an incorporation of knowledge could be used to not only employ information about former test runs, but to actually reuse knowledge of former, real-world incidents and generate even more intelligent and adaptable test cases.

Another area of interest in the context of testing a Cloud is to incorporate the concept of virtualization testing into our approach. Currently we have neglected this topic completely, mainly due to the fact of modeling incapabilities. However, considering UML deployment diagrams in combination with UML profiles would allow developing a methodology to test isolation, i.e., data privacy, in virtualized environments.

Finally, we intend to make our approach of data privacy testing more generic in terms of the used policy language. Currently we rely on XACML, both to avoid the additional burden of reinventing a new language and also as XACML is an industry- and academia-wide accepted standard. However, in developing an own policy language, we could especially focus on Cloud peculiarities. Another idea would be to enable a user to define on mutation operators used during data privacy testing to allow triggering test cases onto different functionalities of the CDMI.

CONCLUSION

In the course of this chapter we discussed an important topic coming along with the paradigm of Cloud computing, namely information security and its various aspects. Not only is it necessary to secure the Cloud itself, but also the data that remains inside the Cloud to prevent abuse. In doing so we identified the main areas of concern in the context of Cloud-related vulnerabilities, viz. network-related, implementation- and service-related, data-related and technology-related vulnerabilities, respectively. Besides, we not only identified those four areas of major concern, but we also presented an idea of how to address the problem of assuring information security in a Cloud computing environment. By doing so we presented a twofold approach, employing risk analysis and policy mutation techniques to generate test cases, to assure the environmental security of the Cloud itself. Additionally, we incorporated the idea of living models to allow reacting in time on changes in the Cloud's environmental configuration to reevaluate the environmental security.

ACKNOWLEDGMENT

This research was partially funded by the research projects MATE (FWF P17380), and QE LaB – Living Models for Open Systems (FFG 822740).

REFERENCES

Ammann, P., & Offutt, J. (2008). *Introduction to software testing*. Cambridge, UK. doi:10.1017/CBO9780511809163

Apache. (2011a). *Commons SCXML*. Retrieved April 21, 2011, from http://commons.apache.org/scxml/

Apache. (2011b). *Subversion*. Retrieved April 21, 2011, from http://subversion.apache.org

Bertolino, A., & Marchetti, E. (2005). A brief essay on software testing. In Thayer, R. H., & Christensen, M. J. (Eds.), *Software engineering, the development process*. Wiley-IEEE Computer Society Press.

Binder, R. (1999). *Testing object-oriented systems: Models, patterns, and tools*. Addison-Wesley Professional.

Bourque, P., & Dupuis, R. (2004). *Software engineering body of knowledge (SWEBOK)*. IEEE Computer Society.

Breu, M., et al. (2010). *Living on the MoVE: Towards an architecture for a living models infrastructure*.

Breu, R. (2010). *Ten principles for living models - A manifesto of change-driven software engineering*. Paper presented at CISIS 2010, The Fourth International Conference on Complex, Intelligent and Software Intensive Systems.

Broy, M. (2005). *Model-based testing of reactive systems. LNCS 3472*. Berlin, Germany: Springer. doi:10.1007/b137241

CloudSecurityAlliance. (2011). *Top threats to cloud computing*.

Eclipse. (2011a). *The CDO model repository*.

Eclipse. (2011b). *Eclipse*. Retrieved April 30, 2011, from http://www.eclipse.org/

Felderer, M., et al. (2009a). Concepts for model-based requirements testing of service oriented systems. *Proceedings of the IASTED International Conference* (Vol. 642, p. 18).

Felderer, M., et al. (2009b). *Towards adaptive test code generation for service oriented systems*. Paper presented at the Ninth International Conference on Quality Software (QSIC 2009).

Felderer, M., et al. (2010). *Security testing by telling TestStories*.

Goetz, H., et al. (2009). *iX Studie Modellbasiertes Testen.*

Hartmann, J., et al. (2005). A UML-based approach to system testing. *Proceedings of the 4th International Conference on The United Modeling Language, Modeling Languages, Concepts, and Tools* (Vol. 1).

Helming, J., & Koegel, M. (2010). *Managing iterations with UNICASE.*

IBM. (2011). Rational DOORS. Retrieved April 21, 2011, from www.ibm.com/software/awdtools/doors/ISO/IEC. (1994). *Information technology - Open systems interconnection - Conformance testing methodology and framework.*

Jericho. (2011). *Cloud cube model o.*

King, T. M., & Ganti, A. S. (2010). *Migrating autonomic self-testing to the cloud.*

Le Traon, Y., et al. (2007). *Testing security policies: Going beyond functional testing.*

Martin, E., et al. (2006). Defining and measuring policy coverage in testing access control policies. *Proceedings of the 8th International Conference on Information and Communications Security,* (pp. 139-158).

McMinn, P. (2004). Search based software test data generation: A survey. *Software Testing. Verification and Reliability, 14*(2), 105–156. doi:10.1002/stvr.294

Mell, P., & Grance, T. (2009). The NIST definition of Cloud computing. *National Institute of Standards and Technology, 53*(6).

Michael, C. C., & Radosevich, W. (2005). Risk-based and functional security testing. *Build Security In.* microTool. (2010). *in-Step.* Retrieved April 21, 2011, from http://www.microtool.de/instep/en/

Miller, B. P. (1990). An empirical study of the reliability of UNIX utilities. *Communications of the ACM, 33*(12), 32–44. doi:10.1145/96267.96279

Mugridge, R., & Cunningham, W. (2005). *Fit for developing software: Framework for integrated tests.*

NoMagic. (2011). *MagicDraw.* Retrieved April 21, 2011, from http://www.magicdraw.com/

OASIS. (2008). *eXtensible access control markup language* (XACML). Retrieved April 21, 2011, from http://www.oasis-open.org/committees/tc_home.php?wg_abbrev=xacml

OMG. (2003). *MDA guide version 1.0.1.*

OMG. (2007). *OMG unified modeling language (OMG UML): Superstructure,* V2.1.2.

Oriol, M., & Ullah, F. (2010). *YETI on the cloud.*

Potter, B., & McGraw, G. (2004). Software security testing. *Security & Privacy, 2*(5), 81–85. doi:10.1109/MSP.2004.84

Rings, T., et al. (2010). On the standardization of a testing framework for application deployment on grid and cloud infrastructures. *Proceedings of the 2010 Second International Conference on Advances in system Testing and Validation Lifecycle,* (pp. 99-107). Washington, DC: IEEE Computer Society.

Riungu, L. M., et al. (2010). *Research issues for software testing in the cloud.*

Roßner, T. (2010). *Basiswissen modellbasierter Test.* Dpunkt-Verlag.

Schneier, B. (1999). Attack trees. *Dr. Dobb's Journal, 24*(12), 21–29.

Seeley, D. (1988). *A tour of the worm.* Department of Computer Science, University of Utah.

Siemens. (2010). *Towards a cloud-specific risk analysis framework.*

SNIA. (2011). *Cloud data management interface.*

Verdon, D., & McGraw, G. (2004). Risk analysis in software design. *Security & Privacy, 2*(4), 79–84. doi:10.1109/MSP.2004.55

Yu, L., et al. (2010). *Testing as a service over cloud.*

Zander, J., et al. (2005). *From U2TP models to executable tests with TTCN-3 - An approach to model-driven testing.*

ADDITIONAL READING

Beydeda, S., Book, M., & Gruhn, V. (2005). *Model-driven software development.* Springer. doi:10.1007/3-540-28554-7

Chris, W., Lucas, N., Dino Dai, Z., & Elfriede, D. (2006). *The Art of software security testing: Identifying Software security flaws.* Addison-Wesley Professional.

Clark, T., & Warmer, J. B. (2002). *Object modeling with the OCL: The rationale behind the object constraint language.* Springer.

CSA. (2009). *Security guidance for critical areas in cloud computing.* CSA.

CSA. (2010). *Top threats to cloud computing.* CSA.

ENISA. (2009). *Cloud computing risk assessment.* ENISA.

Ferdinand, W., Ruedi, S., Thomas, W., & Peter, W. (2006). *Modeling software with finite state machines.* Auerbach Publications.

Hafner, M., & Breu, R. (2008). *Security engineering for service-oriented architectures.*

Hoglund, G., & McGraw, G. (2004). *Exploiting software: How to break code.* Pearson Higher Education.

Jürjens, J. (2005). *Secure systems development with UML.* Springer Verlag.

Krutz, R. L., & Vines, R. D. (2010). *Cloud security: A comprehensive guide to secure cloud computing.* Wiley.

Takanen, A., DeMott, J., & Miller, C. (2008). *Fuzzing for software security testing and quality assurance.* Artech House Publishers.

Van der Linden, M. A. (2007). *Testing code security.* Auerbach Publications. doi:10.1201/9781420013795

Whittaker, J. A. (2003). *How to break software.* Addison-Wesley.

KEY TERMS AND DEFINITIONS

Change-Driven: A software engineering process that is driven by change events, the state of the model elements and their interrelationships with other model elements.

Cloud Lifecycle (CLC): The lifecycle of a Cloud, spanning over its whole uptime and incorporating all changes in configuration, i.e., deployments, virtualized instances and the like.

Cloud Under Test (CUT): The Cloud Computing environment undergoing the testing process.

Model-Driven Testing: A testing approach employing the idea of incorporating models to derive test cases, executable against a System Under Test (SUT).

Model-To-Model Transformation: The process of transforming a source model into a destination model-based on transformation rules.

Model-To-Text Transformation: The process of generating source code out of a graphical model, usually based on predefined templates.

Security Testing: The process of assuring that a software system adheres to non-functional security requirements and protects data as expected.

Chapter 14
Testing of Future Internet Applications Running in the Cloud

Tanja Vos
Universidad Politécnica de Valencia, Spain

Mark Harman
University College London, UK

Paolo Tonella
Fondazione Bruno Kessler, Italy

Wishnu Prasetya
University of Utrecht, The Netherlands

Joachim Wegener
Berner & Mattner, Germany

Shmuel Ur
Bristol University, UK

ABSTRACT

The cloud will be populated by software applications that consist of advanced, dynamic, and largely autonomic interactions among services, end-user applications, content, and media. The complexity of the technologies involved in the cloud makes testing extremely challenging and demands novel approaches and major advancements in the field. This chapter describes the main challenges associated with the testing of applications running in the cloud. The authors present a research agenda that has been defined in order to address the testing challenges. The goal of the agenda is to investigate the technologies for the development of an automated testing environment, which can monitor the applications under test and can react dynamically to the observed changes. Realization of this environment involves substantial research in areas such as search based testing, model inference, oracle learning, and anomaly detection.

INTRODUCTION

The Future Internet (FI) will be a complex interconnection of services, applications, content and media running in the cloud. It will offer a rich user experience, extending and improving current hyperlink-based navigation. Key technologies contributing to the development of FI services and applications include a rich, complex, dynamic and stateful client. This client interacts asynchronously with the server, where applications are organized as services and run in the cloud, taking advantage

DOI: 10.4018/978-1-4666-2536-5.ch014

of dynamic service discovery, replacement and composition. Adaptivity and autonomy improve the user experience, by dynamically changing both the client and the server side, through capabilities such as self-configuration and self-healing. As a consequence, FI applications will exhibit emergent behavior which makes them hard to predict.

Our society will become increasingly dependent on services built on top of this complex and emerging Future Internet. Critical activities such as public utilities, social services, government, learning, finance, business, but also entertainment will depend on the underlying software and services. As a consequence, the applications running on top of the Future Internet will have to meet high quality and dependability demands. Not only the functional quality aspect is important, but non-functional aspects like performance, security, and privacy will become increasingly more important. All these make verification and validation for quality assurance of FI applications extremely important. In this chapter, we discuss how to address the FI testing challenges, by describing the features of an integrated environment for continuous evolutionary automated testing, which can monitor the FI application under test and adapt to the dynamic changes observed. FI testing will require continuous post-release testing since the application under test does not remain fixed after its release. Services and components could be dynamically added or even programmed by customers and the intended use could change significantly. Therefore, testing should be done continuously after deployment to the customer, either in vitro or in vivo. The testing environment we describe integrates, adapts and automates techniques for continuous FI testing (e.g. dynamic model inference, log-based diagnosis, oracle learning, classification trees and combinatorial testing, concurrent testing, regression testing). To make it possible for the above mentioned techniques to deal with the huge search space associated with FI testing, evolutionary search based testing will be used. Search-based algorithms will be used to

guide the solution of identified problems so as to optimize properly defined objective functions. In this way, we can address the ultimate challenge of FI applications: testing unexpected behavior that may originate from the dynamism, autonomy and self-adaptation involved.

BACKGROUND

FI testing demands for major advancements in several areas of software testing. We discuss the state of the art in each of these areas separately, in the following.

Beyond the State of the Art of Search Based Techniques

The current state of the art in search based techniques is described in (Harman, 2007; Harman & Afshin, 2010). The area of testing is the most prominent software engineering domain for the application of search techniques. Search based testing techniques have been applied to various real world complex systems (e.g., embedded systems) (Vos et al., 2010; Baars et al., 2010) to deal with automated test case generation for structural (white-box) as well as functional (black-box) testing. Also the testing of various non-functional properties have been investigated (Afzal et al., 2009). While these testing targets remain relevant for FI applications as well, the continuous, autonomous testing framework that we envision introduces new opportunities for search based exploration of the solution space. Correspondingly, novel fitness function definitions and search algorithms will be required.

Innovative approaches to genetic programming applied to testing may also contribute to FI testing. So far, genetic programming has received limited attention in testing. It has been successfully used to conduct unit testing of object oriented code, by providing a simple and effective mechanism to bring the object under test to a proper internal state (Tonella, 2004). We think genetic programming can be pushed beyond such simple applications, by considering it as a powerful technique to co-evolve the testing engine together with the self-modifying, adaptive FI application under test.

Beyond the State of the Art of Web Testing

The vast, existing literature (Ricca & Tonella, 2001; Elbaum et al., 2005; Sampath et al., 2007) on Web testing is focused on client-server applications which implement a strictly serialized model of interaction, based on *form submission–server response* sequences. Testing of Ajax and rich client Web applications has been considered only recently (Mesbah & van Deursen, 2009; Marchetto et al., 2008). To address FI testing, such results should be extended in the direction of increasing the level of automation and of supporting continuous, unattended test generation and execution. These extensions require research in the area of automated model and invariant inference, anomaly detection and input data generation. If these involve monitoring or logging production runs, the introduced overhead may be significant; so ultimately the issue of performance also needs to be addressed.

Beyond the State of the Art of Model Inference

FI testing requires major advancements of the state of the art for model inference. Existing techniques (Lorenzoli et al., 2008; Dallmeier et al., 2006) rely either on algorithms for regular language learning or on predefined, hardcoded abstraction functions. The former techniques produce a state model which is hardly interpretable by humans. In fact, while event sequences are meaningful, states do not necessarily correspond to an internal state of the FI application. Since we want to provide meaningful feedback to testers, this approach is not attractive. The other option is applicable to

the dynamic, adaptive context of the FI only if mechanisms are developed to learn the abstraction function dynamically and to adapt it in order to balance its level of over and under generalization. This requires major advancements in the field.

Beyond the State of the Art of Log Based Diagnosis and Oracle Learning

In order to carry out FI testing in continuous mode, as proposed above, logs will play an important role, since they provide the raw feedback mechanism for the whole FI testing cycle. There has been substantial work in the use of logs for testing (Andrews & Zhang, 2000; Ducasse et al., 2006; Rozinat & van der Aalst, 2007; Barringer et al., 2010), in particular for observing errors from logs. Also logs are the basis of automating Exploratory Testing as described by Douglas Hoffman in (Graham&Fewster, 2012). We need to extend this by maximizing what we can learn from logs. E.g. we want to be able to infer atypical/suspicious executions (we call this *diagnosis*), because they may indicate that further testing on certain parts of the program is required. We also want to infer likely oracles. Furthermore, we need to extend current log-based oracle inference techniques (Lorenzoli et al., 2008; Hangal & Lam, 2002), which rely on invariant inference a-la Daikon (Ernst et al., 2007), to also support temporal properties (e.g. LTL). Such properties are appropriate for the finite state models, which are used for modeling internet applications (Marchetto et al, 2008). All those extensions will require much more information to be put in the logs. Current logging tools cannot scale up to that need. So, we also need a new logging technique, that maximizes information while keeping the time and space overhead acceptable. Indeed, logs can also be used to monitor security properties (Sridhar & Hamlen, 2010). But logs themselves can also be abused (e.g. when an unauthorized 3rd party manages to acquire them – this may happen). The risk will increase as we put more information into it. Therefore the issue of security and privacy must also be addressed.

Beyond the State of the Art of Coverage Testing

FI applications are (ultra-)large systems. For such a system current coverage criteria are not meaningful and require substantial extensions (Adler et al., 2009). One difficulty is that when an application is tested on its own, its code is expected to be fully utilized, while not all the capabilities of a solution composed by off-the-shelf components are used, or can be used. Consequently, when 50% method coverage is measured, it is not clear whether we have performed a really good test that covered all the relevant functionality or there is still is a lot of relevant functionality left to be tested. In order for coverage to be useful we need a methodology for severely limiting the false reporting, and for filtering out the code which is not relevant to the solution.

Beyond the State of the Art of Concurrency Testing

State of the art techniques for concurrency testing are focused on single applications that exhibit some degree of internal parallelism and distribution (Křena et al., 2009). We need solutions to the FI context, where applications are not self-contained and act more as service composers and integrators than as simple functionality providers. Such integration is characterized by a class of concurrency which is harder to treat and control than in traditional concurrency testing. Substantial enhancements are required to approaches based on explicit, direct control of timings and scheduling, since the integration itself is comprised of multiple concurrently executing parts and therefore must be augmented with capabilities of altering the ongoing communications as well as the distribution over multiple machines of the different

components. Novel mechanisms for debugging and novel record-replay functionalities are also needed to support testers trying to identify the causes of bugs. Artificial load creation is another way to exercise an FI integrator application in a way that increases the chances of revealing faults.

Beyond the State of the Art of Combinatorial Testing

Combinatorial testing using classification trees is a test case generation technique widely used in industry (Kruse & Luniak, 2010). For FI technologies, the number of classes in a classification tree could become very large, resulting in a tremendous amount of possible test cases. To address FI testing, more research is needed to increase the level of automation and support for continuous, dynamic generation of classification trees and fault-sensitive test case generation. These extensions require research in the area of new combinatorial techniques for test case generation, e.g. the inclusion of statistical information like operational profiles of internet applications to generate a representative set of test cases, the application of evolutionary search techniques to search for the optimal test suites, and the combination of classification trees with oracle learning to automate expected values prediction.

Beyond the State of the Art of Empirical Evaluation

In order to assess the testing techniques developed, evaluative research must involve realistic FI systems and realistic subjects. It should be done with thoroughness to ensure that any benefits identified during the evaluation study are clearly derived from the testing technique studied. It should be done in such a way that different studies can be compared. This type of research is time-consuming, expensive and difficult. However, they are fundamental since claims made by analytical advocacy are insupportable (Fenton et al., 1994).

What is needed (Hesari et al., 2010) is a general methodology evaluation framework that will simplify the evaluation procedure and make the results more accurate and reliable.

CHALLENGES

FI applications will be characterized by an extremely high level of dynamism. Most decisions, normally made at design time, are deferred to execution time, when the application can take advantage of monitoring (self-observation, as well as data collection from the environment and logging of the interactions) to adapt itself to a changed usage context. The realization of this vision involves a number of technologies, including: observational reflection and monitoring; dynamic discovery and composition of services; hot component loading and update; structural reflection, to support self-adaptation and modification; asynchronous communication; high configurability and context awareness; composability into large-scale systems of systems.

While offering major improvements over the currently available Web experience, such features pose several challenges to testing, summarized in Table 1.

Self modification, Autonomic behavior (CH1, CH2). The first challenge (CH1) is due to the self-modifiability of FI applications. Such a feature affects both the client side (e.g., by means of Web 2.0 technologies such as Ajax (Asynchronous JavaScript and XML)) and the server side (e.g., when a new service is discovered or a service being used is replaced with a better one). In this context, the target of testing becomes a moving target. It is not possible to know in advance which components are going to be actually used at run time, which means that the object of testing is only partially known before releasing the system. Moreover, the interface offered to the user is also self-modifying, such that a fixed input template becomes inadequate. Client side modifications must be taken into account and modeled properly for adequate testing. Re-execution with the same input but in a different context (e.g., different service availability) may result in completely different behaviors, because of alternative compositions chosen at run time. Self modification is often coupled with autonomic behavior (CH2), where the driving force for adaptation is the

Table 1. Main testing challenges for FI applications

	Challenge (CH)	Description
1	Self modification	Rich clients have increased capability to dynamically adapt the structure of the Web pages; server-side services are replaced and recomposed dynamically based on Service Level Agreements (SLA), taking advantage of services newly discovered in the cloud; components are dynamically loaded.
2	Autonomic behavior	FI applications are highly autonomous; their correct behavior cannot be specified precisely at design-time.
3	Low observability	FI applications are composed of an increasing number of 3rd-party components and services running in the cloud, accessed as a black box, which are hard to test.
4	Asynchronous interactions	FI applications are highly asynchronous and hence hard to test. Each client submits multiple requests asynchronously; multiple clients run in parallel; server-side computation is distributed over the cloud and concurrent.
5	Time and load dependent behavior	For FI applications, factors like timing and load conditions make it hard to reproduce errors during debugging.
6	Huge feature configuration space	FI applications are highly customizable and self-configuring, and contain a huge number of configurable features, such as user-, context-, and environment-dependent parameters.
7	Ultra-large scale	FI applications are often systems of systems running in the cloud; traditional testing adequacy criteria cannot be applied, since even in good testing situations low coverage will be achieved.

feedback control loop. Systems which implement such a loop exhibit a variety of different behaviors, triggered by different execution conditions. Designers of these systems delegate as many decisions as possible to the system itself, which is self-regulating in response to the sensed environment and conditions. This means that the specifications of the system, traditionally used as an oracle for the test cases, are quite weak and underdefined. The actual behavior may change autonomously, provided some high level goals are achieved. In such a context, the notions of faulty execution and bug become shaky, especially if the system is supposed to autonomously react to faults in its components.

Low observability (CH3). Services are hardly available in the form of source code. Even worse, often they cannot even be invoked for testing purposes only, since every invocation is charged as a service usage and produces irreversible changes in the persistent state of the system. This means that most assumptions traditionally made during testing about the possibility to observe executions and executed elements of the system often do not hold or hold only under partial or restricted conditions. While it may be reasonable to assume that in the future some level of Service Oriented Architecture (SOA) test governance, which ensures service executability for testing purposes (under proper restrictions and conditions), will be granted, white box access remains problematic. Testing techniques should be re-shaped to take into account the decreased level of observability typical of applications running in the cloud.

Asynchronous interactions, Time and load dependent behavior (CH4, CH5). High user responsiveness, load balancing and distribution of services are among the main factors that favor asynchronous over synchronous communication for FI applications. However, along with the related benefits of asynchronous communication come increased difficulties during the testing phase. In fact, a system composed of a number of components that interact asynchronously with each other may exhibit different behavior depending on the interleaving between and inside components. Typically, the number of possible interleavings is exponentially proportional to the length of the communication, making exhaustive testing impractical. It should be noted (CH4) that with FI applications the sources of asynchronous messages tend to proliferate due to at least four factors: (1) rich, Web 2.0 clients interact with the server asynchronously; (2) the server is often a collection of (geographically distributed) nodes that collaborate to balance the load; (3) multiple services provided by multiple sites are involved; (4) multiple users execute concurrently the same service.

Another consequence of the asynchronous interactions and distributed computation that characterize FI applications is that time and load could affect the system behavior (CH5). The same interaction sequence, with the exact same interleaving, may lead to different behaviors if delays are arbitrarily increased or reduced, due to their effects on time-outs, decisions and quality of service in general. Moreover, variable load conditions may also trigger different distributions of the computation across nodes, exposing bugs only under very special load balancing conditions. Creating interesting time-dependent and load-dependent behavior, and then capturing and replaying it, is a challenge for testing and debugging FI applications, due to their intrinsic nature of highly de-coupled, distributed, self-configuring and asynchronous systems.

Huge feature configuration space (CH6). One of the promises of FI applications is an extreme, multi-dimensional degree of customizability and self-configurability. FI applications recognize the user, including profile, typical behavior and history, but also the execution environment and conditions. They can sense the quality of service delivered by the other services contributing to the service composition. They can react to the discovery of new services or the appearance of new or updated components. All these dimensions define multiple configuration parameters that are dynamically adjusted to properly fit the user and the running conditions. While this results in an improved user experience of the service and in a higher quality of the delivered service, such a huge space of possible configurations is problematic for testing. In fact, testing should ensure that no fault will appear under specific combinations of configurations, triggered by particular user profile and run time conditions. However, exhaustive exploration of all possible combinations is intractable and traditional combinatorial testing approaches (pair-wise or T-way testing) are probably also inadequate, due to the extreme level of (runtime) configurability achieved when all dimensions of adaptations are considered as potential variation points.

Ultra-large scale (CH7). FI applications are supposed to be recursively composable. Legacy systems can be exposed as services and can be incorporated into FI applications, which in turn may be visible as services and may be integrated into larger compositions, possibly including other (ultra) large software systems. This feature opens the door to the so-called ultra-large scale software systems (or systems of systems). For such systems, current coverage testing levels and adequacy criteria are impractical and inapplicable. Coverage can be extremely low, but still sufficient to ensure high dependability. Regression testing cannot take into account any arbitrary change occurring in the system and change impact analysis is hardly achievable with such systems. Novel adequacy criteria are needed.

RESEARCH AGENDA

The testing challenges enumerated in Table 1 can be addressed by developing tools and techniques for continuous evolutionary automated testing, which can monitor the FI application and adapt themselves to the dynamic changes observed. FI testing will be continuous post-release testing since the application under test does not remain fixed after its release. Services and components could be dynamically added by customers and the intended use could change. Therefore, testing has to be performed continuously after deployment to the customer.

The underlying technology we devise for FI testing, that will make it possible for the above mentioned techniques to cope with FI testing challenges like dynamism, self-adaptation and partial observability, will be based on evolutionary search based testing. The impossibility of anticipating all possible behaviors of FI applications suggests a prominent role for evolutionary testing techniques, because this relies on very few assumptions about the underlying problem it is attempting to solve. In addition, stochastic optimization and search techniques are adaptive and, therefore, able to modify their behavior when faced with new unforeseen situations. These two properties – their freedom from limiting assumptions and their inherent adaptiveness – make evolutionary testing approaches ideal for handling FI applications testing, with their dynamic, self-adapting, autonomous and unpredictable behavior.

To achieve this overall aim, a number of research objectives that directly map to the identified challenges should be investigated in the future. A summary of such research objectives is in Table 2. Below we describe the approaches and techniques that can be followed to conduct research and achieve practical results in each of these areas.

Continuous, automated testing (OBJ1). Today's traditional testing usually ends with the release of a planned product version. All testware (test cases as well as the underlying behavioral model) are constructed and executed before delivering the software. These testwares are fixed, because the System Under Test (SUT) has a fixed set of features and functionalities since its behav-

Table 2. Research objectives in FI testing

	Objective (OBJ)	Description
1	Continuous, automated testing approach	Since the range of behaviors is not known in advance, testing will be done continuously. Feedback from post-release executions will be used to co-evolve the test cases for the self-adaptive FI application. Humans alone cannot achieve the desired levels of dependability, so automation is required.
2	Evolutionary, search based testing approach	To cope with dynamism, self-adaptation and partial observability that characterize FI applications, search based software testing will be used. Evolutionary algorithms themselves exhibit dynamic and adaptive behavior and, as such, are ideally suited to the nature of the problem. Moreover, evolutionary algorithms have proved to be very efficient for solving general undecidable problems and provide a robust framework.
3	Dynamic model inference	Self-adapting applications with low observability demand dynamic analysis; models will be inferred continuously rather than being fixed upfront.
4	Model based test case derivation	Behavioral models inferred from monitored executions will be the basis for automated test case generation. Paths in the model associated with semantic interactions will be regarded as interesting execution sequences. Test case generation will proceed fully unattended, including the generation of input data and the verification of feasibility for the test adequacy criteria of choice.
5	Log-based diagnosis and oracle learning	Since correct behaviour cannot be fixed upfront, executions will be analysed to identify atypical ones, indicating likely faults or potential vulnerabilities.
6	Dynamic classification tree generation	The huge configuration space will be dealt with by testing combinatorially, using dynamically and continuously generated classification trees.
7	Test for concurrency bugs	A mechanism to control and record factors like communication noise, delays, message timings, load conditions, etc., in a concurrent, cloud centric setup will be developed.
8	Testing the unexpected	Due to the high dynamism, it is impossible to define the expected interactions upfront. Genetic programming can be used to simulate unpredicted, odd, or even malicious interactions.
9	Coverage and regression testing	Novel coverage and regression testing criteria and analytical methods will be defined for ultra-large scale FI applications running in the cloud, for which the standard criteria and analysis techniques are not applicable since they do not scale, and do not work for system composed of off the shelf components.
10	General methodological evaluation framework for FI testing	Large scale case studies will be performed using realistic systems and software testing practitioners. The studies will be executed using an instantiation and/or refinement of the general methodological evaluation framework to fit specific software testing techniques and tools and evaluation situations.

ior is determined before its release. If the released product needs to be updated because of changed user requirements or severe bugs that need to be repaired, a new development cycle will start and regression testing needs to be done in order to ensure that the previous functionalities still work with the new changes. The fixed testwares, designed during post-release testing, need to be adapted manually in order to cope with the changed requirements, functionalities, user interfaces and/or work-flows of the system. See Figure 1 for a graphical representation of traditional testing.

Future Internet Testing will require continuous post-release testing since the SUT does not remain fixed after its release. The test cases defined before releasing the system may become inadequate with respect to the executing system, because the latter is subjected to self-modifications (CH1), context and environment dependent autonomous behaviors (CH2), as well as user defined customization and dynamic re-configuration (CH6). Services and components could be dynamically added and even programmed by customers and the intended use could change significantly. Therefore, testing has to be performed continuously after deployment to the customer. The necessity of testing sessions has to be detected automatically. Therefore, testing sessions need to

Figure 1. Traditional testing versus FI testing

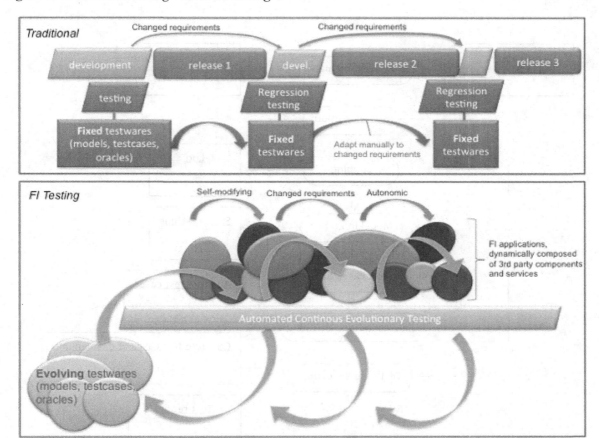

be triggered by behaviors and configurations monitored at execution time and testwares need to evolve and adapt accordingly. For example, adequate test cases have to be generated on demand, behavior models have to be extracted on the basis of dynamic analysis or using search based state exploration. Consequently, advanced FI testing tools have to be aware of the current state of the SUT supporting dynamic runtime classification of applications and online test case generation and execution. A typical workflow of how this could work is in Figure 2. Things to take into account are that testing tools will need a small footprint to avoid disturbance of ongoing services. Moreover, the instrumentation required to implement continuous testing may introduce additional security and privacy threats. These could

be addresses by applying state of the art techniques for data anonymization and security testing, as well as by ensuring maximum non interference of the instrumentation with the core application logics. The latter is required also to protect the application from failure during continuous testing. See Box 1.

Evolutionary, search based testing approach (OBJ2). FI testing will take advantage of evolutionary, search based, testing. Search based software testing provides a robust framework for testing, which can be adopted even in the presence of the dynamism (CH1), self-adaptation (CH2) and partial observability (CH3) that characterize FI applications. The key ingredients required by search based algorithms are (Harman, 2007): (1) an objective function that measures the degree to

Figure 2. Workflow for continuous testing

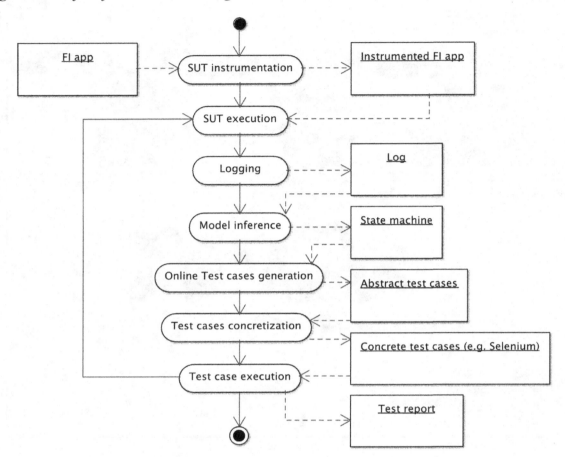

Box 1. Research direction

Research will be directed towards an approach to FI testing that goes beyond the release stage, continuing unattended when the system is in production. Continuous FI testing assumes availability of feedback information about the operational system, obtained through monitoring. Analysis of such information allows for example:
• *Refinement of the FI application model used for testing.*   • *Co-evolution of the test case generator, which self-adapts to the self-modifying SUT (tracking the moving target).*   • *Generation, execution and verification of the outcome of new test cases.*
In order for this approach to work in practice, most (if not all) steps will be automated, since the continuous testing activity tends to become unmanageable without proper tool support.

which the current solution (test case, test suite, etc.) achieves the testing goal (e.g., coverage, semantic interactions, concurrency problems, etc.); (2) operators that modify the current solution, producing new candidate solutions to be evaluated in the next iterations of the algorithm. The search-based algorithms will then be used to guide the execution of the various testing tasks by optimizing the defined fitness functions. Box 2 explains the research concentration.

Dynamic model inference (OBJ3). Model-based testing is extremely effective with applications whose behavior is strongly dependent upon the internal or the persistent state. We expect FI applications to be stateful and highly dependent on state information about themselves, the environment, the context and the user. Hence, model-based testing seems appropriate for them. However, it is hard to conceive a-priori a model that holds in every possible execution environment, for every user configuration and under any arbitrary time and load constraint. In fact, FI applications are self-modifying (CH1), decide autonomously to change their behavior (CH2), are highly configurable (CH6) and self-adapt to optimize the computational resources (CH5). As a consequence, testing models used with FI applications should be continuously updated and refined, in accordance with a continuous testing approach (see OBJ2). Moreover, it can be difficult to obtain FI testing models from static code analysis since the source code might not be available (CH3) to testers or, if available, it is subject to modifications (CH1) at run time. These include client side changes of the Document Object Model (DOM) structure, accessible via reflection, server-side service composition (e.g., triggered by poor performance of available services or newly discovered services), end-user programming, dynamic component loading and hot updates. In such a context, dynamic analysis seems more promising. Despite intrinsically under-approximating the possible behaviors of the software, dynamic analysis does not suffer from the presence of reflection or dynamic component loading, which are severe limitations for static approaches. See Box 3.

Model based test case derivation (OBJ4). Once an FI testing model has been dynamically obtained, it will be used for automated test case generation. This is a prerequisite for the realization of the continuous testing approach envisioned in OBJ2. With automated test case generation, we can continue to exercise an FI application even after it is put into production, hence addressing testing challenges that are hardly reproducible in the testing lab before delivery (e.g. CH1, CH2, CH4, CH5, CH6). Box 4 explains an important research objective.

Not all paths in the model inferred for an FI application are equally interesting. Paths that involve independent actions are subsumed by test cases exercising the individual actions in isolation. On the contrary, paths that involve long sequences of actions that trigger cause-effect chains are extremely interesting and potentially more likely to reveal faults (Arcuri, 2010). Hence, it is more important to test long concatenations of actions that interact with each other, in order to increase the confidence on the correctness of behavior

Box 2. Research specification

> *Research will concentrate on defining objectives that precisely and unambiguously describe those aspects that need to be optimized to adapt different existing testing techniques to continuous FI testing (e.g. model-based testing, combinatorial testing, log based diagnosis, oracle learning, concurrency testing and regression testing). Initial ideas on how this can be done, will be described in the corresponding objectives.*

Box 3. Dynamic analysis framework

> *Research will aim at the development of a dynamic analysis framework for the automated inference of FI testing models. The models can then be used for automated test case generation, in order to address the challenges of self-modification (CH1) and autonomic behavior (CH2). The inferred models will be also used as a surrogate for 3rd party components and services, when these are not available for testing (CH3). Dynamic analysis for model inference coupled with continuous testing provides a mechanism to test self-modifying systems with minimal human intervention. The under-approximation, intrinsic of dynamic analysis, will be mitigated by resorting to search based techniques, which will be oriented toward maximizing the level of state exploration achieved by the inferred model.*

Box 4. Automation

> *A research objective that is fundamental for continuous FI testing is the reduction of the need for human intervention and the automation of test case generation. Search based testing will play an important role both for test sequence derivation and for input data generation.*

during complex interactions with the user. The search based algorithms that could be used for the selection of an interesting sequence of actions will aim at optimizing a fitness function that takes into account the length, complexity and level of semantic interactions involved in a sequence of states and transitions associated with a path in the inferred models.

However, selection of an interesting sequence of actions does not yet provide a full test case. In fact, in order to be executable against the FI application, proper input data must be supplied. In some cases, the path is infeasible, i.e., no input data exist that allow the given path to be traversed (e.g., because the path involves mutually exclusive conditions that are never simultaneously satisfied). Static techniques for input data generation and feasibility check are severely limited by the extreme dynamism of FI applications. Self-modification (CH1), autonomic behavior (CH2) and low observability (CH3) make most available static techniques (such as model checking, symbolic execution, linear programming) inapplicable as standalone approaches. To solve

this problem, search based testing could be used with an objective function targeting the traversal of an interesting and promising path in the model inferred for the FI application. Failure in input data generation by the search based algorithm is used as an approximate surrogate of an infeasibility check (we obtain a check of likely infeasibility, of course, not a formal proof of infeasibility in general).

Log-based diagnosis and oracle learning (OBJ5). A fundamental consequence of the highly dynamic nature of FI applications (CH1, CH2, CH6) is that it is very hard to obtain a reasonably complete upfront prediction of the range of their behavior, which is why we should resort to continuous testing (OBJ2). Continuous testing relies on feedback obtained by monitoring production runs, so that it can adapt its goals and refine the models it uses. With log-based diagnosis we let production runs to co-generate logs, which are then analyzed. The goal is to collect atypical runs. They indicate newly found vulnerabilities in the target application, and thus set new goals for continuous testing. The collected runs themselves are valuable as the base for generating new test cases to expose the suggested vulnerabilities.

An oracle is used for determining whether a test case has passed or failed. It functions by comparing the output(s) of the SUT, for a given test case input, to the outputs that the oracle defines. In current practice, oracles are derived from specifications. However, high dynamism implies that detailed specifications cannot be drawn upfront. Hence, the oracles to be used for testing will be weak and under-defined. We propose therefore to complement them with oracles learned from logs. Of course, learned oracles cannot be equivalent to hand-crafted, precise oracles. However, failing them can be considered as atypical. Whether such an atypicality is actually a fault cannot be determined automatically and one must eventually resort to human judgment. Still, if the number of false positives produced by the diagnosis module is low compared to the true positives, the human effort required is kept small, while the expected benefits are enormous, especially when no alternative oracle exists. Box 5 explains another research effort.

Dynamic classification tree generation (OBJ6). The number of properties and features that can be configured or adapted for an FI application is expected to be huge (CH6). Moreover,

they may change dynamically due to run time adaptations triggered by the execution context and environment (CH1, CH2). As a consequence, testing the relevant combinations of configurations must be also done dynamically, in the post-delivery phase, as an integral part of the proposed continuous, automated testing approach (OBJ2). See Box 6.

Test for concurrency bugs (OBJ7). Concurrency will be a major problem when testing FI applications. Concurrency arises from multiple sources, such as asynchronous requests from (multiple) clients, distributed server side computation, etc. (see CH4). The objective of FI testing for concurrent bugs is to reveal the conditions under which those concurrent bugs manifest and to reproduce the same conditions during testing and debugging. However, concurrent bugs depend on properties of the execution that are hard to capture and replay in existing, general purpose testing environments, such as the interleaving of threads and processes, the relative and absolute timing, the load conditions (see CH5). Existing techniques (Edelstein et al., 2003) should be extended to find bugs resulting from the interaction between large components. See Box 7.

Testing the unexpected (OBJ8). One of the most distinctive features of FI applications is the

Box 5. Scalable diagnosis

> *Research efforts will concentrate on the development of scalable diagnosis and oracle learning approaches for FI applications, balancing their strength (ability to report true positives) with the level of spurious findings (false positives).*

Box 6. Classification trees

> *Classification trees (Grochtmann, M. & Grimm, 1993) will be trained to partition the relevant configuration space into equivalence classes, based on the application's behaviors and states observed at run time, during monitored executions. This allows us to apply combinatorial testing techniques even in the presence of extreme dynamism and self-modifications. Search techniques could be used to find a minimal set of test cases fulfilling the "combination requirements" introduced by the tester.*

Box 7. Concurrency bug testing

> *A concurrency testing and debugging environment for FI applications will be researched and developed that specifically supports easy manipulation and reproduction of the conditions under which concurrency bugs appear. Combined with search based test case generation, this approach has the potential to make a major contribution to a fully automated, continuous search for intricate and complex concurrent bugs. We aim to investigate proper fitness functions that can guide the search towards revealing instances of typical concurrency problems in FI applications.*

high degree of dynamism and change that they exhibit at run time (CH1, CH2), which makes them a moving target for testing. Research activities will investigate the most extreme cases of dynamism, where the FI application is allowed to reconfigure itself, its components and its interactions with other systems and services almost completely. In such a context, the testing strategy should co-evolve and adapt itself, as soon as modifications of the FI applications are monitored at run time. One approach to achieve co-evolution of the test case generation strategy is by means of genetic programming. Test cases are the result of running a program, which can modify itself through reflection, resort to newly discovered external services, or update or integrate new components. In other words, the testing engine behaves as a self-modifying, autonomous system, which is evolved in parallel with the SUT by means of genetic programming. See Box 8.

Coverage and regression testing (OBJ9). Since FI applications are intrinsically integrators of services, components, (legacy) systems and other FI applications, their size can be really huge (see CH7). Further, the FI application is expected to use only part of the functionality of each component and service it is composed of. As a consequence, coverage and regression testing percentage are expected to provide poor indications about the adequacy of the testing performed. In fact, we expect only a small part of the system to be covered by the (regression) test cases. However, poor coverage does not necessarily mean inadequate testing, in this context, as most of the code is likely to be generic component code, not relevant to the current solution. See Box 9.

Box 8. Testing the unexpected

> *Research efforts will seek to innovate and develop imaginative new approaches to search based optimization of FI testing using genetic programming and co-evolutionary optimization. Of course, testing a system that co-evolves with a self-adaptive SUT is extremely visionary and far reaching.*

Box 9. Coding and qualifying

> *In order to get a qualitative interpretation of coverage that goes beyond the quantification of the coverage percentage, we will take advantage of linguistic, informal information associated with code elements (such as function names, comments, etc. (Adler et al., 2009)). The final objective is to qualify coverage in terms of high level, human understandable functionalities that are covered or yet to be covered. With this information available, qualitative and informed decisions can be made about coverage targets and regression testing.*

General methodological evaluation framework for FI testing (OBJ10). Evaluative research for FI testing techniques and tools must involve realistic systems and realistic subjects. It should be done thoroughly and in such a way that different evaluations can be compared. Most existing work present organizational frameworks that describe what a case study should consist of. To present, no methodological framework exists that can be instantiated to easily design studies to evaluate different FI testing techniques, and that facilitates the creation of a repository of comparable evaluations. See Box 10.

CONCLUSION

We believe that the challenges involved in testing FI applications running in the cloud can be addressed by resorting to a combination of advanced testing technologies (i.e. dynamic model inference, model-based test case derivation, combinatorial testing, concurrent testing, regression testing, etc.) adapted to ensure a level of automation that enables testing in a continuous mode. Those applications are expected to be complex and can adaptively and dynamically change themselves. We propose to deal with this by observing their live behavior over long periods of time, in order to detect that such changes have taken place. Observed behaviors are to be classified as normal or anomalous, and will be used to automatically trigger additional testing. In this way we expect to be able to maintain high testing coverage.

Test oracle is another key element in ensuring the strength of testing. Manually maintaining oracles (in quantity and strength) of FI cloud applications is going to be very expensive. Hence, methods for automated learning of oracles from the observations would have a big potential to reduce the cost of their testing.

The flexibility of the search based testing approach makes it highly potential to be used as the unifying base for us in addressing the FI testing challenges. We expect that traditional fitness functions, used to guide test case generation, can be adapted to the features of FI applications and can be used to track their continuous evolution and autonomous modifications over time. Furthermore, genetic programming is an appealing option to co-evolve test suites themselves to make them adapt to an evolving FI application.

ACKNOWLEDGEMENT

This work has been partially funded by the European Union FP7 project FITTEST (grant agreement n. 257574). We also thank these people for their useful assistance: Jurriaan Hage, Alexander Elyasov.

Box 10. Developing the framework

> *There is a need for a methodological framework for defining empirical studies for evaluating FI testing techniques. Once the framework exists, a body of evidence will be created by the whole testing community that consists of instantiations of the framework that evaluate FI testing techniques and tools through case studies that involve real systems and users.*

REFERENCES

Adler, Y., Farchi, E., Klausner, M., Pelleg, D., Raz, O., Shochat, M., et al. (2009). Advanced code coverage analysis using substring holes. In *Proceedings of the Eighteenth International Symposium on Software Testing and Analysis (ISSTA '09)*, (pp. 37-46). New York, NY: ACM.

Afzal, W., Torkar, R., & Feldt, R. (2009). A systematic review of search- based testing for non-functional system properties. *Information and Software Technology, 51*(6), 957–976. doi:10.1016/j.infsof.2008.12.005

Andrews, J. H., & Zhang, Y. (2000). Broad-spectrum studies of log file analysis. In *Proceedings of the International Conference on Software Engineering* (pp. 105-114).

Arcuri, A. (2010). Longer is better: On the role of test sequence length in software testing. In *Proceedings of the International Conference on Software Testing* (pp. 469-478).

Baars, A., Vos, T., & Dimitrov, D. (2010). Using evolutionary testing to find test scenarios for hard to reproduce faults. *IEEE International Conference on Software Testing Verification and Validation Workshop*, (pp. 173-181).

Barringer, H., Groce, A., Havelund, K., & Smith, M. (2010). Formal analysis of log files. *AIAA Journal of Aerospace Computing, Information and Communications, 7*(11).

Dallmeier, V., Lindig, C., Wasylkowski, A., & Zeller, A. (2006). Mining object behavior with ADABU. In *Proceedings of the ICSE Workshop on Dynamic Analysis*.

Ducasse, S., Girba, T., & Wuyts, R. (2006). *Object-oriented legacy system trace-based logic testing*. IEEE Computer Society.

Edelstein, O., Farchi, E., Goldin, E., Nir, Y., Ratsaby, G., & Ur, S. (2003). Framework for testing multi-threaded Java programs. *Concurrency and Computation, 15*(3-5), 485–499. doi:10.1002/cpe.654

Elbaum, S. G., Rothermel, G., Karre, S., & Fisher, M. II. (2005). Leveraging user-session data to support web application testing. *IEEE Transactions on Software Engineering, 31*(3), 187–202. doi:10.1109/TSE.2005.36

Ernst, M., Perkins, J., Guo, P., McCamant, S., Pacheco, C., Tschantz, M., & Xiao, C. (2007). The Daikon system for dynamic detection of likely invariants. *Science of Computer Programming, 69*(1-3), 35–45. doi:10.1016/j.scico.2007.01.015

Fenton, N., Pfleeger, S. L., & Glass, R. L. (1994). Science and substance: A challenge to software engineers. *IEEE Software*, (July/August): 86–95. doi:10.1109/52.300094

Graham, D., & Fewster, M. (2012). *Experiences of test automation: Case studies of software test automation*. Addison-Wesley Professional.

Grochtmann, M., & Grimm, K. (1993). Classification trees for partition testing. *Software Testing. Verification and Reliability, 3*(2), 63–82. doi:10.1002/stvr.4370030203

Hangal, S., & Lam, M. S. (2002). Tracking down software bugs using automatic anomaly detection. In *Proceedings of the International Conference on Software Engineering*.

Harman, M. (2007). The current state and future of SBSE. In *Proceedings of Foundations of Software Engineering* (pp. 342-357).

Harman, M., & Mansouri, A. (2010). Search based software engineering: Introduction to the special issue. *IEEE Transactions on Software Engineering, 36*(6), 737–741. doi:10.1109/TSE.2010.106

Hesari, S., Mashayekhi, H., & Ramsin, R. (2010). Towards a general framework for evaluating software development methodologies. *COMPSAC, 2010*, 208–217.

Krena, B., Letko, Z., Nir-Buchbinder, Y., Tzoref-Brill, R., Ur, S., & Vojnar, T. (2009). A concurrency testing tool and its plug-ins for dynamic analysis and runtime healing. In *Runtime Verification, Lecture Notes in Computer Science 5779/2009*, (pp. 101-114).

Kruse, P., & Luniak, M. (2010). Automated test case generation using classification trees. In *Proceedings of STAREAST- Software Testing Conference, Analysis & Review*.

Lorenzoli, D., Mariani, L., & Pezzè, M. (2008). Automatic generation of software behavioral models. In *Proceedings of the International Conference on Software Testing* (pp. 501-510).

Marchetto, A., Tonella, P., & Ricca, F. (2008). State-based testing of Ajax web applications. In *Proceedings of the International Conference on Software Testing* (pp. 121-130).

Mesbah, A., & van Deursen, A. (2009). Invariant-based automatic testing of AJAX user interfaces. In *Proceedings of the International Conference on Software Engineering* (pp. 210-220).

Ricca, F., & Tonella, P. (2001). Analysis and testing of web applications. In *Proceedings of the International Conference on Software Engineering* (pp. 25-34).

Rozinat, A., & van der Aalst, W. M. P. (2007). Conformance checking of processes based on monitoring real behavior. *Information Systems, 33*(1), 64–95. doi:10.1016/j.is.2007.07.001

Sampath, S., Sprenkle, S., Gibson, E., Pollock, L. L., & Greenwald, A. S. (2007). Applying concept analysis to user-session-based testing of web applications. *IEEE Transactions on Software Engineering, 33*(10), 643–658. doi:10.1109/TSE.2007.70723

Sridhar, M., & Hamlen, K. (2010). ActionScript in-lined reference monitoring in Prolog. *Proceedings of the 12th International Conference on Practical Aspects of Declarative Languages*, (pp. 149–151). Springer.

Tonella, P. (2004). Evolutionary testing of classes. In *Proceedings of the International Symposium on Software Testing and Analysis* (pp. 119-128).

Vos, T., Baars, A., Lindlar, F., Kruse, P., Windisch, A., & Wegener, J. (2010). Industrial scaled automated structural testing with the evolutionary testing tool. In *Proceedings of the 2010 Third International Conference on Software Testing, Verification and Validation* (ICST '10), (pp. 175-184). Washington, DC: IEEE Computer Society.

Chapter 15
Towards Improving the Testability of Cloud Application Services

Tariq M. King
North Dakota State University, USA

Annaji S. Ganti
North Dakota State University, USA & Microsoft Corporation, USA

David Froslie
Microsoft Corporation, USA

ABSTRACT

In cloud computing, applications are hosted, deployed, and delivered as services over the Internet. New cloud application services can be developed by tailoring existing ones, while hiding the complexity of the underlying implementation. Cloud applications may be able to adapt to changes in their environment, which should be secure and reliable. The infrastructure on which cloud applications are built is characterized by power, storage, and virtualization. But how does all of this affect the ability to adequately test cloud applications? This chapter investigates the testability of cloud application services. It focuses on the specific problem of reduced controllability and observability of software services hosted in the cloud, and proposes a novel solution referred to as Test Support as-a-Service (TSaaS). A prototype of TSaaS is also presented, and is used to discuss the feasibility, challenges, and benefits of the approach.

INTRODUCTION

Cloud application services use computing resources to deliver Software-as-a-Service (SaaS) over the Internet (Armbrust, 2009). Like conventional applications, SaaS is designed to help a user perform a task, but is hosted and deployed in a cloud computing environment. A provider hosts the application service and the user's data in the cloud, allowing them to be accessed from any location via the World Wide Web. From a software construction perspective, one advantage of such

DOI: 10.4018/978-1-4666-2536-5.ch015

a model is that new application services can be built by tailoring existing ones, while hiding the complexity of the underlying implementation (Greiler, 2009). The cloud provides ubiquitous access to several reusable software services, thereby facilitating rapid application development.

Although much work is being done to model and build cloud application services, there is significantly less research devoted to testing them (Chan, 2009; Rimal 2009). For the software tester, the use of remotely-hosted services within an application represents a significant challenge. When testing an application that uses another service over the Internet, controllability and observability over the remotely-hosted service is generally limited due to security and privacy concerns (King, 2010). As a result, testability is reduced since developers may not be able to stimulate the service with certain inputs, nor check whether actual test results match the expected results. (Beizer, 1990; Binder, 1994). Since testing continues to be the primary means of validation used in the software development industry, it is important to study the impact of emerging paradigms such as cloud computing on software testability.

In this chapter we investigate the testability of cloud application services. As a preliminary step to our investigation, we analyze the characteristics of cloud computing that can make the resulting applications easier, or more difficult to test than non-cloud applications. Analyzing these characteristics provides a means for identifying the major challenges associated with testing cloud applications, and investigating ways in which the cloud infrastructure itself can be harnessed to mitigate those challenges. To narrow the scope of the chapter, we tackle the specific research problem of reduced testability of cloud application services due to remoteness and information hiding. Recommendations are made for improving the testability of cloud application services through the description of a novel approach, referred to as Test Support-as-Service (TSaaS). TSaaS leverages the automated tests and infrastructure, which were used to validate a service during development, for the provision of a set of test support operations to aid remote collaborators who are extending the service.

The major objectives of this chapter are to: (1) identify and analyze the key factors that influence the testability of cloud applications, (2) outline a development methodology for TSaaS and define the major architectural components of its implementation, (3) describe the lessons learned from developing the first prototype of TSaaS, and (4) discuss the viability and future directions of approaches to testing cloud application services.

BACKGROUND

Cloud computing is the use of computer technology to provide services over the Internet (Armbrust, 2009). Software-as-a-Service (SaaS) refers to applications that are designed to help users perform a task. Examples of SaaS include Google Docs, Salesforce, and Paypal. The concepts of Platform-as-a-Service (PaaS) and Infrastructure-as-a-Service (IaaS) are similar to that of SaaS. However, instead of application services, PaaS and IaaS deliver software development platforms and hardware infrastructures, respectively. An example of PaaS is Windows Azure (Microsoft, 2011), while the Elastic Compute Cloud (Amazon, 2011) is an implementation of IaaS. Hardware virtualization may be used in the cloud to create abstract computing resources from more powerful physical resources (Barham, 2003; Page, 2008). In a virtualization system, the component responsible for managing virtual resources is called a hypervisor.

Software testing involves applying a set of inputs to a piece of software, and comparing the actual results of program execution against the expected results (Beizer, 1990). In other words, testing provides a means of validating whether or not the software is operating as intended. A software system is said to be testable if it facilitates the execution of test cases to check whether or not some predefined criteria have been satisfied (IEEE, 1990). In practice, test automation is done at the scripting-level, where test cases are stored in an automated test script. The script is then passed to a class or utility program that applies them to the system under test (Mosley, 2002). Interplay between software testing and cloud computing can be divided into the following categories, as described by Tilley (2010): Testing in the Cloud – leveraging the cloud for concurrent test execution or testing in a virtual computing environment; Testing of the Cloud – validating applications that are hosted and deployed in the cloud; and Testing to the Cloud – migrating the testing process, and other assets to the cloud. The primary content of this book chapter has been positioned under the category Software Testing of the Cloud.

Some researchers have begun to tackle issues related to software testing of the cloud. Chan (2009) uses graph theory to represent the computations of cloud applications and define model-based criteria to support testing them. Part of the model describes interactions among cloud computations, and defines the notion of inconsistency detection between nodes. These definitions and testing criteria help to formalize the problems associated with cloud integration. Zech (2011) proposes a model-driven approach to address security testing of cloud applications. The approach uses risk analysis to derive a set of misuse cases, which are then used to generate tests that attack the application environment. Although the content of this chapter does not address security testing, it is a critical aspect of testing cloud applications and should be considered at an early stage of development. Greiler (2009) describes challenges for runtime integration and testing for service-oriented architectures (SOA). Due to the close relationship between SOA and cloud computing, many of the factors they describe have motivated the research in this chapter. However, since this chapter focuses on cloud computing, we also investigate how web

and virtualization technologies can be harnessed to tackle the problem of testing software services deployed in the cloud.

HEADING TOWARDS A TESTABLE CLOUD

The research in this chapter investigates the testability of cloud application services. As a preliminary step to our investigation, we analyze the characteristics of cloud computing that can make the resulting applications easier, or more difficult to test than non-cloud applications. Analyzing these characteristics provides a means of identifying the major challenges associated with testing cloud applications, and investigating ways in which the cloud infrastructure itself can help to mitigate those challenges.

Research Questions

In order to guide our investigation, the following three research questions were formulated:

Question 1: How does the cloud computing paradigm affect the testability of applications which are either built or deployed in a cloud environment? This question seeks to reveal factors associated with cloud computing that can make the resulting software applications easier or more difficult to test.

Question 2: How can the test artifacts and tools used to validate cloud application services during development be harnessed to improve the overall testability of the cloud? This question investigates ways in which existing test suites, tools, and scaffolding for a cloud application service can be leveraged to provide remote developers with support for testing applications that use the service.

Question 3: How can web-based techniques and virtualization technologies be employed to improve the testability of cloud applications? This question aims to discover ways in which the cloud infrastructure itself can be used to enhance the process of testing cloud applications.

Inquiry into the first research question has provided the primary motivation for this work, which is discussed in the next section. Investigation into the second and third research questions has led to the formulation of an approach that seeks to improve the testability of cloud applications.

On the Testability of Cloud Application Services

The topic of software testability has been well-studied in the literature, with authors presenting general factors that can influence the testability of software systems (Bach, 2003; Binder, 1994). These general factors include considerations such as controllability, observability, documentation, implementation characteristics, built-in test capabilities, test suites, and testing tools. In this section, we describe specific characteristics of cloud applications that can have a negative or positive impact on their testability. For clarity and understanding, our cloud-specific testability factors are explained in the context of the general factors that influence testability.

Several characteristics of the cloud computing paradigm have a negative impact on the testability of cloud application services. These include:

- **Information Hiding and Remoteness:** The cloud computing paradigm facilitates ubiquitous access to computing resources as services over the Internet. However, this dependency on the Internet means that cloud services are typically hosted remotely, rather than locally in a controlled environment. Controllability and observability of a remotely-hosted service are limited to what has been exposed via its public interface, which may be highly restricted due to

security and privacy concerns. Information hiding due to the use of remote services makes it difficult for developers to setup and verify specific test scenarios for cloud applications.

Ownership of different components in the application is shared among different stakeholders, and therefore testing requires the coordination of these stakeholders. A common solution to testing under such circumstances is to develop a mock version of the component, which simulates the behavior of the actual component, for the purpose of testing. However, this also poses significant challenges due to lack of knowledge of the remote host's implementation. Even with the required implementation knowledge, creating accurate stubs may still prove difficult due to the high complexity of the host's underlying infrastructure.

- **Complexity and Statefulness:** Cloud applications are hosted on intrinsically complex and distributed infrastructures, with multiple layers extending from the underlying network to the top-level client interface. Testing must check the behavior of each layer, the interactions among multiple layers, and various functional and non-functional aspects of the fully integrated system in different deployment configurations (Frye, 2008). The distributed nature of the cloud computing architecture means that applications must be tested for synchronization faults, which can arise due to variation in the order in which concurrent events occur.

Although service-oriented architecture tools have been aiming for the composition of stateless services into applications, the reality is that many existing services are stateful (Troger 2007). Cloud application services tend to represent complex, real-world behaviors. Such real-world services typically assume functional understanding between the client and server, and involve the creation of a joint session between the two entities during interactions (Greiler, 2009). In other words, the result of service invocation does not only depend on the input parameters, but also on the current state of the session. The ability to apply state-based validation techniques may therefore be necessary to adequately test cloud application services. However, this is difficult since high security requirements typically leads to the production version of a service having significantly less control and observation points than its development version.

- **Autonomy and Adaptiveness:** Services in a cloud application can change independently of each other. A common reason for changing an individual service is for the purpose of software maintenance, and includes: fixing bugs in the service, adapting the service to a new environment, and extending the service to meet the changing needs of clients (Sommerville, 2001). Regression testing should be performed on changed services to check whether modifications have introduced new errors into previously tested components (Beizer, 1990). In addition, any cloud applications that use the changed service (directly or indirectly) should also be retested to check for cascading failures.

The trend towards autonomic and adaptive computing means that the future generation of software systems is expected to be capable of self-management (Kephart, 2003). As such researchers have proposed that clouds should be adaptive (Rimal, 2009), continually seeking to detect and adjust themselves to environmental changes. Examples include automatic updating of a service via download and installation of security patches; dynamic replacement of a failed service with a logically equivalent alternative; and automatic

integration of clouds to seek additional resources to achieve better performance. Adaptation in the cloud presents a significant challenge with respect to software testing. A self-configuring cloud application may be able to dynamically add, remove, and replace services in response to external conditions. In order to safeguard against system failures such structural and behavioral changes to the application must be validated at runtime (Costa, 2010; King, 2007). However, the high availability and performance requirements of the cloud means that runtime testing of cloud services should be sufficiently transparent (King, 2009). In other words, any degradation of the performance characteristics due to runtime testing should be negligible, or within acceptable limits. In addition to self-configuration, other autonomic properties such as self-optimization, self-healing, and self-protection must also be tested.

- **Dependability and Performance:** Cloud computing must address high dependability criteria such as security, availability, robustness, reliability, and fault tolerance. Since information is communicated over the Internet, security testing of the cloud is critical to make sure data confidentiality and integrity are maintained. Furthermore, there tends to be a general lack of trust about the information used to advertise and describe cloud services, which makes the task of designing tests for applications that integrate these services even more difficult. High availability requirements means that there is little downtime for maintenance changes to cloud services, and testing the resulting changes after they have been implemented. Testing for service robustness, reliability, and fault tolerance are also important to ensure correct and continuous operation of cloud applications. Load and stress tests should also be developed to check system performance criteria such as response time, memory usage and throughput. This requires testing tools to simulate users and workloads, as well as instrumentation tools to profile the services during the validation process. If the autonomic property of self-optimization has been incorporated into a service, testing must verify that the appropriate set of corrective actions is taken whenever the service is not operating within acceptable performance limits. This includes generating test data in the form of user loads to simulate each stress condition that could occur, and checking that the system correctly identifies the condition and handles it appropriately. For autonomic dependability properties such as self-healing and self-protection, similar tests must be generated to check the ability of the system to diagnose failures, repair faults, and ensure resources are secure in the presence of threats.

- **Paradigm Infancy:** At the time of writing, cloud computing remains an emerging paradigm with its tools and technologies still in the infancy stage. Although there is a plethora of testing tools for conventional applications, the level of test support and tooling for cloud applications is inadequate. Furthermore, many conventional testing tools were not designed to meet the validation requirements of concurrent, distributed, networked environments such as those characterized by cloud computing. This general lack of automated testing tool support for cloud applications greatly reduces their testability. We classify this factor is a temporary one, and expect that it is likely to become less of an issue in the near future.

Analyzing the list of negative factors provides insight into the challenges of testing cloud application services. Understanding such challenges is a fundamental step towards formulating effective solutions for software testing of the cloud.

On the other hand, not all aspects of the cloud applications are a hindrance to testability. Indeed the environment in which cloud applications are deployed provides an infrastructure well-suited for software testing. This infrastructure has been the primary motivation for software testing in the cloud, and its characteristics represent positive factors that impact cloud application testability. These include:

- **Computational Power and Storage:** Cloud environments typically provide an abundance of computing power and cheap storage, while software testing tends to consume such resources in large amounts. This complementary relationship has led to a model of software testing in which testing activities are performed in the cloud, as an on-demand service for customers. Testing in a cloud environment is easier because it provides the high processing capabilities necessary for concurrent test case execution, instrumentation, analysis, and logging.

- **Virtualization:** Cloud computing providers are increasingly using virtualization techniques to deliver software, platform, and infrastructure as services over the Internet. Major benefits of employing virtualization in the software testing activity include convenience, and cost savings through the use of fewer physical machines (Page, 2008). In addition, virtualization makes it easier to setup, execute and teardown a variety of test scenarios that use multiple resources and/or resource configurations. The ability to save and load virtual machine snapshots may also result in time and space savings during test execution, and allow testers to reproduce bugs quickly and easily.

Testing the Cloud, in the Cloud

The remainder of this chapter investigates ways in which automated integration testing mechanisms can be rapidly realized for cloud application services. In this section, we provide an overview of an approach that uses web technologies and hypervisor-based virtualization to mitigate the challenges associated with reduced cloud application testability. The idea is to use the cloud infrastructure itself to enhance the process of testing cloud applications.

Figure 1 provides an overview of the research problem being addressed, and outlines our recommended solution. As shown in Figure 1, cloud computing involves multiple providers such as A and B who are delivering Software-as-a-Service (SaaS) over the Internet. These providers typically deploy SaaS in a production environment, where it can be consumed by clients using various computing devices (e.g., personal computers, cellular phones, and tablets), or by other cloud providers to create and deliver custom applications. For example, provider C in Figure 1 can develop a new cloud application based on the services of A and B, by including calls to those services

within the application. However, recall that such a development model reduces the controllability and observability of the application. Also note that even if C's application is not cloud-based, the problem still exists.

To address the aforementioned problem, we propose to reuse existing test automation for the cloud services deployed by A and B, to create a set of test support services for providers such as C. The idea is that, prior to deployment in the production environment, providers such as A and B would have validated their respective service(s) to check for accurate functionality, interoperability, performance and other quality attributes. Due to the inherent drawbacks of manual testing, these providers are likely to have used automated software testing techniques during validation. If so, each provider would have a pre-configured local test environment, test scripts, and scaffolding to facilitate automatically executing test cases on the development builds of their services. These automated tests and infrastructure can therefore be used to rapidly realize test support operations for the service being hosted, and expose them "as-a-service" for providers who are building applications that extend that service. For example,

Figure 1. Cloud providers A and B expose test support as-a-service to provider C

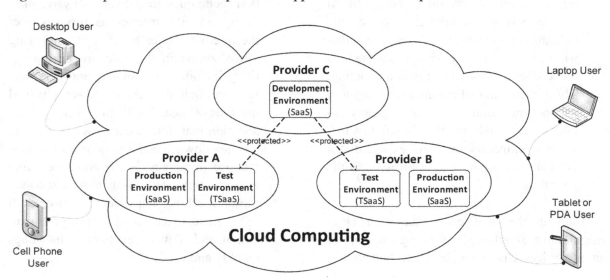

as shown in Figure 1, Providers A and B expose Test Support as-a-Service (TSaaS) to Provider C.

In order to avoid unnecessary security risks when applying the approach, we propose that TSaaS be delivered via a protected interface that is only accessible to trusted cloud providers, referred to as partners in this chapter. Cloud testability is improved by allowing partners to observe and control the private members of a test-enabled version of the service. Privacy of the data accessible via TSaaS is not a concern because only non-confidential test data is made available. Furthermore, using a separate copy of the service, within a controlled test environment, does not interrupt the regular operations of the service hosted in production. This ensures that the proposed approach is applicable to cloud application services that have high availability requirements.

An obvious concern of the proposed approach as it has been described thus far is scalability. Ideally, the test environment would need to be powerful enough to facilitate the concurrent execution of requests for testing services from multiple partners, each having a separate handle to a copy of the service and its hardware and software environment. This would certainly lead to increased production costs due to the need to develop, purchase, setup, and manage additional hardware and software resources. Therefore, in order to reduce the overhead associated with setting up, operating, and maintaining separate test environments and service copies for each partners, we have incorporated runtime virtualization techniques into the control flow of TSaaS.

Building Test Support as-a-Service

In this section we describe a development method that can be followed to implement the proposed testing approach. Figure 2 shows the major process steps involved in TSaaS development, as well as the artifacts that are input to, and output from each step.

The steps of the TSaaS development method, as relates to Figure 2, are summarized as follows:

1. *Build test automation for Software-as-a-Service.* Our description begins with a cloud provider who is developing an application

Figure 2. Development method for building test support as-a-service

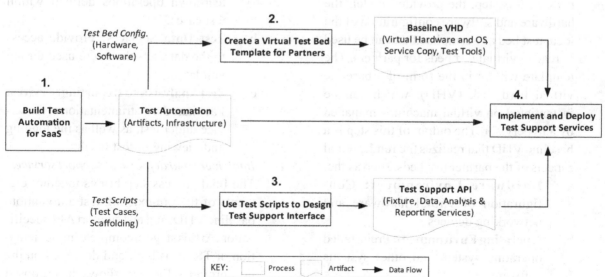

service in isolation (i.e., no inter-provider service dependencies), and is building the test automation for that service. Note that this step will most likely be performed whether or not the provider opts to offer TSaaS. However, it serves as a good starting point for the discussion because both the design and degree of test automation will impact TSaaS development. In general, the higher the quality of the test automation design, and the greater the level of test automation achieved, the easier it will be to implement TSaaS on the host provider. A reasonable effort should therefore be made during this process step to design good test cases, and invest in appropriate tooling for building successful test automation. The output of this process step includes:

a. **Test Automation Artifacts:** Test scripts containing a finite set of test cases and the scaffolding to support test execution.

b. **Test Automation Infrastructure**: A local test bed consisting of all the hardware and software components required to validate the service under test.

2. *Create a virtual test bed template for partners.* In this step, the provider models the hardware and software configuration of the local test bed as a template that can be used to realize virtual test beds for partners. The template will be in the form of a baseline virtual hard disk (VHD), which can be instantiated on virtual machines managed by a hypervisor. The output of this step is a baseline VHD that realizes the fundamental aspects of the partner test beds, such as the:

a. **Hardware Environment:** Configuration of virtual hardware and networking devices.

b. **Operating Environment:** Preinstalled operating system and other systems software.

c. **Service Copy:** A copy of the cloud application service under test, including any dependencies such as software libraries, web servers, database management software.

d. **Test Support Tools:** Frameworks and other support tools to facilitate the automated testing process.

3. *Use test scripts to design the test support interface.* Test scripts provide a wealth of information on the artifacts that were developed during test automation. A test script for a service consists of a set of encoded test cases for checking its functional and non-functional properties, along with the scaffolding necessary to set up and execute those tests. In this step, test scripts are decomposed with the goal of identifying reusable test-related functions to aid the design, and implementation of the test support interface for partners.

The output of this step is an application programming interface (API), which defines the signatures of the test support functions to be implemented. Categories of the services to be specified during this step include

a. **Test Fixture Services:** Model the setup procedures, inputs, assertions, and teardown operations defined within test cases.

b. **Test Data Services:** Provide access to the data sets that were used during validation.

c. **Test Analysis and Reporting Services:** Facilitate the instrumentation of the service under test, as well as the logging and viewing of test results.

4. *Implement and deploy test support services.* The final process step brings together elements of the pre-existing test automation, baseline VHD, and test support API specification. At this stage, a complete implementation of TSaaS is built and deployed on the host provider. Figure 3 shows the proposed

Figure 3. Architectural diagram for test support as-a-service

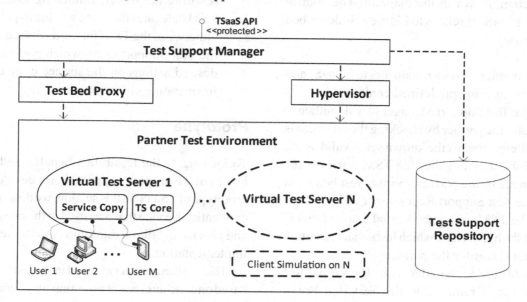

architecture of TSaaS, which includes the following components (starting from the top):

a. **Test Support Manager:** A controller component that coordinates underlying components to deliver the test support services defined in the TSaaS API. This component is also responsible for authenticating partners, and enforcing authorization policies.

b. **Hypervisor:** A virtual machine monitor for creating, managing and destroying the virtual test servers where TSaaS requests will be realized.

c. **Test Bed Proxy:** A component that interfaces between the Test Support Manager and the virtual test servers when handling user requests. This component allows the virtual test servers to remain anonymous for security purposes, and facilitates logging usage statistics.

d. **Partner Test Environment:** A hardware and software platform for hosting the virtual test servers that are being

managed through the hypervisor, and accessed by partners via the test bed proxy.

e. **Test Support Core:** A service implementation of automated testing functions for the service under test, which do not require the use of virtualization.

f. **Test Support Repository:** A data store containing artifacts that are used and generated by TSaaS, including VHD images, snapshots, data sets, test results, server logs, configuration files, etc.

Control Flow

Under TSaaS, partner requests for test support can range from simple actions such as invoking the service under test using specified inputs, to more complex actions like simulating clients and user loads via virtualization. Figure 4 presents an activity diagram that describes how the architectural components of TSaaS collaborate to realize test support requests. Horizontal swimlanes have been used to denote which components perform each action shown in the diagram. The control flow of TSaaS, as relates to Figure 4, is described as follows:

1. A partner provider connects to TSaaS, and logs in using predefined credentials.
2. The Test Support Manager (TSM) authenticates the partner by checking the credentials entered against the known set of valid users.
3. If the user is valid, the TSM retrieves the image of the partner's virtual test bed from the Test Support Repository (TSR).
4. The TSM passes the virtual test bed image to the hypervisor, which instantiates a virtual test server for the partner.
5. A handle to the address of the virtual test server is returned to the Test Bed Proxy (TBP), which updates its list of server-user connections.
6. The TBP notifies the TSM that the new virtual test server is ready for use, and the TSM starts accepting test support requests from the user.
7. If a test support request requires hypervisor-based virtualization (e.g., loading a snapshot,

resetting the server, simulating loads), the TSM delegates the request to the hypervisor.
8. Otherwise, the TSM forwards the request to the Test Support Core, which performs the desired actions on the service copy and/or its operating environment.

Prototype

To investigate the feasibility, benefits and challenges of the proposed approach, we developed a prototype of TSaaS. In this section, we describe the application service that was used in the prototype, and provide details on our setup environment and implementation.

The application service used in the prototype is based on consumer credit reporting functionalities. Credit Reporting Service (CRS) is characterized by the following features:

- **Payment History:** Determines if there are any negative items associated with a consumer's payment record.
- **Debt:** Computes the total amount and type of debt owed by a consumer.

Figure 4. Activity diagram showing the control flow of test support as-a-service

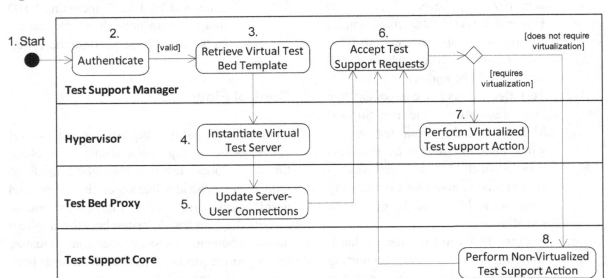

- **Age:** Calculates the age of a consumer's oldest credit account, and the average age of all accounts in his/her credit report.
- **Diversity:** Establishes whether or not the consumer has multiple account types.
- **Inquiries:** Checks for recent inquiries on a consumer's credit report.

Note that the central role of services such as CRS when making financial decisions can result in lending agencies building their own applications around them. For example, a bank may use CRS in an initial step of the business process for an online loan service; or a new credit reporting provider may develop a custom version of CRS by overriding part of its functionality. Extensions and derivatives of CRS may in turn be used as the basis for developing other services.

A survey performed as part of our preliminary investigation (King, 2010) led us to select Microsoft Windows Server 2008 R2 as the operating environment for the prototype. The primary reason for choosing this platform is that it uses the same tools and technologies upon which Microsoft Windows Azure is built (Microsoft, 2011). These include hypervisor-based server virtualization technology through the Hyper-V server role, and support for runtime virtualization via calls to the Hyper-V Windows Management Instrumentation (WMI) APIs. Using these tools and technologies allowed TSaaS development to begin immediately in a local environment, with the goal of building an implementation that could be easily migrated to the Windows Azure cloud computing platform.

Using Visual Studio 2010, we developed CRS as a Windows Communication Foundation (WCF) service so that it could be deployed in the Windows Azure web role. The following operations, corresponding to a subset of the aforementioned CRS features, were implemented as WCF web methods: *CalcHistory, CalcDebt, CalcAvgCreditAge,* and *CalcInquiries*. Access to a representative set of consumer credit report information was achieved through the use of a SQL Server 2008 R2 database.

CRS interacts with the database using the .NET 4.0 entity frameworks. A trivial algorithm was implemented to compute the credit score based on weighted percentages of the consumer's payment history (35%), debt utilization (30%), age (15%), diversity (10%), and inquiries (10%). WCF diagnostic tracing capabilities were enabled on the service to facilitate logging runtime calls, warnings, exceptions, and other events. A total of 28 automated tests for CRS were developed using the unit testing framework which is integrated into Visual Studio. To allow the automated tests to be customizable and extensible for delivering TSaaS, we applied an XML-based test specification technique to parameterize data values used in the test fixture. Figure 5 provides a snippet of the test case specification XML (.tsx) of CRS.

As shown in Figure 5, the test case specification XML is divided into the three tagged sections *ClassInitialize, TestCase,* and *ClassCleanup,* representing the test setup, procedure, and teardown aspects of the automated test fixture respectively. For example, each *TestCase* element consists of tagged subsections defining the pa-

Figure 5. Snippet of test case specification XML used in the TSaaS prototype

```xml
<?xml version="1.0" ?>

<Tests>

  <ClassInitialize>
    <DB>TestDBConnection</DB>
  </ClassInitialize>

  <TestCase Name="CalculateDebtTest">
    <Inputs>
        <SSN>123-45-678</SSN>
    </Inputs>
    <ExpectedOutputs>
        <Value>1024.50</Value>
    </ExpectedOutputs>
  </TestCase>

  <ClassCleanup />

</Tests>
```

rameterized inputs and expected output values of the test. Using the Linq-to-XML framework, the specified test structure is loaded into a TestCase object as part of the test initialization process. A helper method then retrieves the specific test input and expected output values, and creates the instance of the test case. This process is repeated until a complete set of tests for CRS has been built, and then packaged into a dynamic-link library called *CRSTests.dll*. Automated tests were stored in the *CRSTests.dll* assembly, which can be run programmatically using the command line tool MSTest. Test execution produces a test results XML (.trx) log file indicating whether each test passed or failed, along with any error messages associated with test case failures.

The CRS service was instrumented for code coverage through the use of a configuration file named *Local.testsettings*. This configuration file and *CRSTests.dll* can be passed as arguments to the MSTest tool at runtime to execute the test cases with code coverage enabled. The parameterized test fixture implementation, consisting of the *CRSTests.dll*, test specification XML, and MSTest

tool, was reused to develop a set of fundamental test support operations for CRS. These test support operations were themselves encapsulated and deployed as a WCF service. Table 1 lists the operations that were implemented within this core test support service, and describes their purpose. The operations are divided into the categories: (1) Test Specification and Execution, (2) Test Configuration, and (3) Test Reporting.

Hypervisor-based server virtualization was achieved via the Hyper-V role of Windows Server 2008 R2. We prepared a virtual hard disk (VHD) image of the CRS test environment, which allowed virtual test beds for partner providers to be instantiated on-demand. The VHD specified a uniform hardware configuration for each virtual test server, and was loaded with all of the software components necessary for replicating a controlled test environment for CRS. Figure 6 provides an overview of the software configuration of the VHD image used for the virtual test servers. As shown in Figure 6, the image consisted of the following software components: (1) Windows Server 2008 R2 with the.NET 4.0 runtime in-

Table 1. Summary of operations in the test support core of the TSaaS prototype

Operation	Description
Test Specification and Execution	
UpdateTestSpec	Facilitates editing and overwriting the set of test cases contained in the test specification XML.
RunTests(in TestName)	Executes a specific test case, whose name is denoted by the input parameter *TestName*, in the test specification.
RunAllTests	Executes all test cases defined in the test specification.
RunAllTestsWithCoverage	Executes all test cases defined in the test specification with code coverage enabled.
Test Configuration	
UpdateTestConfig	Facilitates editing and overwriting a server-side settings file that is used to configure the test harness (*Local.testsettings*).
UpdateServiceConfig	Facilitates editing and overwriting a server-side settings file that is used to configure the service under test (*Web.config*).
ResetWebServer	Performs a reset action on the Web server to use updated configuration settings, or to reinitialize the server after failures.
Test Reporting	
GetLatestTestResults	Facilitates retrieving the test results XML produced from the most recent test run performed on the service under test.

Figure 6. Software configuration of the VHD used for the virtual test servers

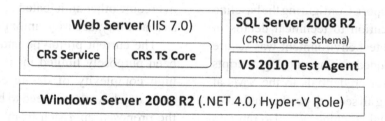

stalled; (2) SQL Server 2008 R2 with the CRS data schema applied; (3) Internet Information Services 7.0 Web Server with CRS and the TS Core Service hosted; and (4) Visual Studio 2010 Test Agent, which includes the MSTest tool. Our implementation of the test support manager (TSM) invoked the Hyper-V Windows Management Instrumentation (WMI) APIs to create, configure, and destroy the virtual test servers at runtime. The broker design pattern was used to structure the TSaaS components, and allow the TSM to call the methods exposed by the test support core on the respective virtual test servers.

Discussion

One of the main reasons for developing the prototype was to investigate the feasibility of the proposed approach, and discover practical issues surrounding its implementation and usage. In this section we elaborate on our practical experiences when developing and applying TSaaS, including the major successes and challenges identified during the project. An evaluation plan for further investigation into the research problem is also discussed.

The TSaaS prototype provided us with a framework within which we could build and adequately test extensions and derivatives of the remotely-hosted service. As proof-of-concept we developed and performed integration testing on a banking loan service that incorporates CRS in its business process, and a customized version of CRS that overrides part of its functionality. The

prototype facilitated quick and easy access to a cross section of automated testing operations, preexisting test data, and a controlled test environment for CRS during integration. In addition, having access to server-side logging and trace information through TSaaS was extremely useful for testing and debugging.

Successful implementation of the prototype suggests that the approach and research ideas presented in this paper are feasible. Our prototype implementation addresses a simplified view of the research problem, and validates several of the components defined in the TSaaS architectural model. A major factor that contributed to the success of the project was the use of the XML-based test case specification technique, which allowed us to decouple the test case definitions from the test fixture implementation for direct reuse in the TSaaS prototype. Another contributing factor was having built-in virtualization support via the Hyper-V role of Windows Server 2008 R2, and the Hyper-V WMI APIs. This made it possible for us to expose remote procedures for instantiating and destroying virtual test servers, and configuring their virtual hardware resources.

A number of technical challenges were experienced during prototype development, most of which surrounded the need to integrate multiple tools and technologies. Implementing TSaaS required a good combination of programming experience, test automation skills, virtualization expertise, and access to proper frameworks and tools to support the approach and development process. However, at this time of writing cloud computing is an emerging technological model, with limited tool support. Configuring the baseline VHD required attention to technical details in order to ensure the test environment was secure and stable. This included writing auto-login scripts that provide the user credentials to the VMs at startup, and applying all security patches and other updates to the virtual machine. We also ran into the issue where it was possible for a VM to restart if automatic updates were enabled, and therefore had to adjust this setting to prevent test support sessions from being interrupted unexpectedly.

Our investigation also revealed the need for practical ways to keep the VHDs up-to-date with the latest versions of the service, its environmental configuration, and test support tools. To avoid inconsistencies due to human error, such maintenance should be automated through VM tools and update scripts. The relatively large size of VHDs also means that manipulating these images, and re-deploying them to the cloud environment, may also present a significant challenge during maintenance. Recommendations for tackling these issues include the development of an automated process to update the VHDs whenever there is a new release or build of the service under test. In addition, instead of maintaining separate VHDs for each service configuration, multiple snapshots of the same VHD could be used to reduce the storage overhead.

A grand challenge to be addressed is the provision of standardized testing interfaces for building test support implementations for cloud infrastructures. Our goal with TSaaS is to stimulate research that leads to standard definitions of the interfaces and contracts for partner authentication, hypervisor, server diagnostics, test execution and test management services. The level of standardization of a cloud testing service could then be measured by how well they implement the various TSaaS interfaces. This type of research direction is necessary for the successful adoption of the approach, and can provide benefits to the general movement towards software testing as an online service. Standardization could also help to overcome other anticipated challenges including as scalability, security, among others.

The current prototype and investigation has been purposely limited in scope to manage the high complexity of the research problem. As such, much work still need to be done to evaluate the proposed approach to integration testing of cloud-based applications. In particular, conducting experiments on a cloud computing platform is necessary to reveal the essential difficulties associated with the research problem. With this objective in mind we have carefully designed the prototype in a way that streamlines the process of moving it to the cloud. The Windows Server 2008 R2 image developed for the prototype is directly supported by Windows Azure through its VM role. The VM role provides a high degree of control over the server instances, and facilitates many of the goals required for the proposed approach to be successful in practice (i.e., scalability, in-place upgrades, integration with other service components, and load-balanced traffic).

We have identified that the following steps are necessary for migration to the Windows Azure cloud platform: (1) install the Windows Azure SDK and its prerequisites on the development environment; (2) use the Windows Azure SDK to configure the baseline VHD and then upload it to a Windows Azure storage drive in the cloud, and (3) move the SQL Server 2008 R2 database to SQL Azure. With the prototype hosted and deployed in Windows Azure, we plan to conduct a series of controlled experiments to determine the effectiveness of the proposed approach. The experiments will seek to: (1) provide evidence that TSaaS can be used to overcome challenges associated with cloud application testability, and (2) demonstrate the benefits of harnessing virtualization technologies in the cloud for testing cloud application services. Lastly, we plan to investigate the industrial applicability of TSaaS, and compare it to approaches such as test-isolation and testing in production.

FUTURE RESEARCH DIRECTIONS

There continues to be a growing trend toward providing *everything-as-a-service* in the cloud. The development of software-as-a-service represents a grand challenge for software testing researchers and practitioners. However, at this time of writing, the majority of research on software testing in the cloud is concentrated on providing testing as an online service. Although testing in the cloud is appropriate for several types of software applications, the current state-of-the-art is not effective for validating cloud applications themselves since there is little to no test collaboration among service providers.

The approach presented in this chapter represents a research direction in which the cloud infrastructures, and test automation tooling, controlled by each stakeholder are used to provide test support as an online service for partner providers. This type of collaborative testing model better matches the software development and operation models of cloud computing, but is challenging because of the need to set up, manage, and synchronize distributed testing processes. However, as more and more application services are deployed in the cloud, these types of testing approaches will become vital to the success of the paradigm. Our hope is that by investigating Test Support as-a-Service (TSaaS) at this early stage, we can stimulate research that leads to the design and development of software testing tools and techniques that fit the needs of the cloud computing paradigm.

TSaaS serves as a first step towards our futuristic vision of self-testing clouds (King, 2010). We envision cloud application services that not only have the ability to self-adapt to continually changing environmental conditions, but can also test themselves to ensure that software adaptations do not introduce faults into the system at runtime. Instead of automated testing in the cloud, there would be an evolution to Autonomic Self-Testing. Cloud application testing would be characterized by autonomic test managers that continually moni-

tor distributed services for runtime changes, and validate those changes via TSaaS in a virtualized environment. Furthermore, most or all of these cloud testing activities would be performed with little or no human intervention. While this is a grand vision, there is indeed a view of cloud computing as a natural progression of autonomic and grid computing. Therefore, there is potential for software testing research in these closely related fields to be cross-pollinated and combined when investigating software testing of the cloud.

CONCLUSION

This chapter investigated the testability of cloud application services, and made recommendations for addressing some of the associated issues. The negative testability factors identified for cloud computing are an indication of the grand testing challenges to come as we move to the cloud. From a research perspective, all of the challenges associated with runtime testing of adaptive and distributed systems should be considered. These include, but are not limited to, the need for: automatic test case generation; dynamic test planning and optimization; and test synchronization and safety techniques. From a practical standpoint, a new wave of development and testing tools need to be created to support cloud computing.

While the positive factors of cloud testability can help to offset the negative ones, our prototype experience revealed that these also present some difficulties. The use of runtime virtualization for testing implies that developers and test engineers would need to be well-versed in the tools and techniques used to manage virtual resources. Furthermore, testing in a virtualized environment raises the question of whether or not one can rely on the test results. After all, one of the key advantages of testing is that it provides information about the behavior of a system in its actual environment. To guarantee that the results obtained from testing in a virtualized environment are reliable, one would need to prove the virtualization to be consistent with the actual environment. Nonetheless, it appears that the software industry is rapidly heading towards the cloud, and so we must continue to rethink the ways in which software testing is done on this emerging computational model.

ACKNOWLEDGMENT

The authors would like to thank the participants of the 2010 Workshop on Software Testing in the Cloud, and the 2011 Microsoft Fargo Engineering Day Excellence Expo for their valuable feedback on this work. Annaji would also like to express his gratitude to the Microsoft tuition reimbursement program that supports his graduate studies. Any opinions, findings, conclusions, or recommendations expressed in this material are those of the authors, and do not necessarily reflect the views of the Microsoft Corporation.

REFERENCES

Amazon. (2011). *Amazon web services: Amazon elastic compute cloud.* Retrieved April 22, 2011, from http://aws.amazon.com/ec2/

Armbrust, M., Fox, A., Griffith, R., Joseph, A. D., Katz, R. H., Konwinski, A., et al. (2009). *Above the clouds: A Berkeley view of cloud computing.* Technical report UCB/EECS-2009-28. EECS Department, University of California, Berkeley.

Bach, J. (2003). *Heuristics of software testability.* Retrieved April 22, 2011, from http://www.satisfice.com/tools/testable.pdf

Barham, P., Dragovic, B., Fraser, K., Hand, S., Harris, T., Ho, A., et al. (2003). Xen and the art of virtualization. In *ACM Symposium on Operating Systems Principles* (pp. 164–177). New York, NY.

Beizer, B. (1990). *Software testing techniques* (2nd ed.). New York, NY: Van Nostrand Reinhold Co.

Binder, R. V. (1994). Design for testability in object-oriented systems. *Communications of the ACM, 37*(9), 87–101. doi:10.1145/182987.184077

Chan, W. K., Mei, L., & Zhang, Z. (2009). *Modeling and testing of cloud applications.* In IEEE Asia-Pacific Services Computing Conference. Los Alamitos, CA, USA.

Costa, A. D., Nunes, C., Silva, V. T., Fonseca, B., & Lucena, C. J. P. (2010). JAAF+T: A framework to implement self-adaptive agents that apply self-test. In *International Symposium on Applied Computing (SAC'10)*, (pp. 928-935). New York, NY: ACM.

Frye, C. (2008). *Cloud computing creates software testing challenges.* Retrieved April 22, 2011, from http://searchcloudcomputing.techtarget.com/news/1355198/cloud-computing-creates-software-testing-challenges

Greiler, M., Gross, H. G., & Nasr, K. A. (2009). Runtime integration and testing for highly dynamic service oriented ICT solutions - An industry challenges report. In *Testing: Academic and Industrial Conference on Practice and Research Techniques* (pp. 51–55).

IEEE. (1990). *IEEE Std 610.12-1990: IEEE standard glossary of software engineering terminology.* New York, NY: IEEE Software Engineering Standards Committee.

Kephart, J., & Chess, D. (2003). The vision of autonomic computing. *Computer, 36*(1), 41–52. doi:10.1109/MC.2003.1160055

King, T. M. (2009). *A self-testing approach for autonomic software.* Doctoral dissertation. Florida International University, Miami, FL.

King, T. M., & Ganti, A. S. (2010). Migrating autonomic self-testing to the cloud. In *3rd International Conference on Software Testing, Verification, and Validation Workshops*, (pp. 438-442). Paris, France.

King, T. M., Ramirez, A. E., Cruz, R., & Clarke, P. J. (2007). An integrated self-testing framework for autonomic computing systems. *Journal of Computers*, *2*(9), 37–49. doi:10.4304/jcp.2.9.37-49

Microsoft. (2011). *Windows Azure: Microsoft's Cloud services platform*. Retrieved April 22, 2011, from http://www.microsoft.com/windowsazure/windowsazure/

Mosley, D. J., & Posey, B. A. (2002). *Just enough software test automation*. Upper Saddle River, NJ: Prentice Hall PTR.

Page, A., & Johnston, K. (2008). *How we test software at Microsoft*. Microsoft Press.

Rimal, B. P., Choi, E., & Lumb, I. (2009). A taxonomy and survey of cloud computing systems. In *International Joint Conference on Networked Computing, Advanced Information Management & Services, and Digital Content Multimedia Technology and its Applications*, Washington, DC, USA (pp.44-51).

Sommerville, I. (2001). *Software engineering* (6th ed.). Boston, MA: Addison-Wesley Longman Publishing Co., Inc.

Tilley, S. (2010). Distinct facets of the Software Testing in the Cloud 2010 workshop. *Proceedings of the 2nd International Workshop on Software Testing in the Cloud*, (p. 1). Retrieved April 17, 2010, from http://www.stitc.org/2010/proceedings/index.html

Troger, P., Meyer, H., Melzer, I., & Flehmig, M. (2007). Dynamic provisioning and monitoring of stateful services. *Proceedings of the 3rd International Conference on Web Information Systems and Technology (WEBIST '07)*, (pp. 434-438). Barcelona, Spain.

Zech, P. (2011). Risk-based security testing in cloud computing environments. *Proceedings of the 4th International Conference on Software Testing, Verification and Validation (ICST 2011)*, (pp. 411-414). Berlin, Germany.

Chapter 16
D-Cloud:
Software Testing Environment for Dependable Distributed Systems Using Cloud Computing Technology

Toshihiro Hanawa
University of Tsukuba, Japan

Mitsuhisa Sato
University of Tsukuba, Japan

ABSTRACT

Various information systems are widely used in the information society era, and the demand for highly dependable system is increasing year after year. However, software testing for such a system becomes more difficult due to the enlargement and the complexity of the system. In particular, it is often difficult to test parallel and distributed systems in the real world after deployment, although reliable systems, such as high-availability servers, are parallel and distributed systems. To solve these problems, the authors propose a software testing environment for dependable parallel and distributed system using the cloud computing technology, named D-Cloud. D-Cloud consists of the cloud management software as the role of the resource management, and a lot of virtual machine monitors with fault injection facility in order to simulate hardware faults. In addition, D-Cloud introduces the scenario manager, and it makes a number of different tests perform automatically. Currently, D-Cloud is realized by the use of Eucalyptus as the cloud management software. Furthermore, the authors introduce FaultVM based on QEMU as the virtualization software, and D-Cloud frontend that interprets test scenario, constructs test environment, and dispatches commands. D-Cloud enables automating the system configuration and the test procedure as well as performing a number of test cases simultaneously and emulating hardware faults flexibly. This chapter presents the concept and design of D-Cloud, and describes how to specify the system configuration and the test scenario. Furthermore, the preliminary test example as the software testing using D-Cloud is presented. As the result, the authors show that D-Cloud allows easy setup of the environment, and to test the software testing for the distributed system.

DOI: 10.4018/978-1-4666-2536-5.ch016

INTRODUCTION

According to the formulation of advanced information society, various information systems are widely used. Since such systems are closely related to daily life, they must employ highly dependable facilities to avoid undesirable behavior caused by the underlying bugs and interference from the external environment. In order to certificate the dependability of such systems, these systems should be tested sufficiently. However, as recent information system becomes larger and more complicated, software testing for such a system becomes more difficult. In order to check whether components work correctly or not, tremendous test cases are needed for various input patterns, and environment to execute a great number of tests immediately should be provided.

Although highly dependable systems such as high-availability servers especially likely to form parallel and distributed systems, the testing of large-scale parallel and distributed system is troublesome job in the real world after deployment. When a failure occurs in such complex systems, the reproducibility of the failure in the actual system is so poor that the detection of the defective part has been a serious problem.

On the other hand, a highly dependable system should be equipped with the combination of multiple functions of fault tolerance against hardware faults. Even though testing fault tolerant facilities should be done under hardware fault conditions or anomaly loads, it is too difficult to destroy a specific part of actual hardware or to concentrate an unrealistic overload in a hardware device.

To solve these problems, we proposed a software testing environment for reliable distributed systems using cloud computing technology, named "D-Cloud" (Hanawa, 2010, Banzai, 2010). In this chapter, we present the concept and design D-Cloud, discuss the description of the system configuration and the test scenario, and demonstrate the preliminary test example using D-Cloud.

After that, we explain related works, then we explain the concept of D-Cloud. Next, we describe the design of D-Cloud as a software testing environment, and the test configuration and test scenario is denoted. In addition, preliminary test examples using D-Cloud are demonstrated. Finally, we conclude our study and discuss future works.

RELATED WORK

A number of fault injection techniques in program tests have been proposed. DOCTOR (Han, 1995) is a software fault injector, which supports memory faults, CPU faults, and communication faults. However, software fault injection in the DOCTOR requires modification of the source codes to be tested. Xception (Carreira, 1998) uses the kernel module to inject the fault, and the tester sets the hardware breakpoint to the specified address. When the process reaches the breakpoint, the fault is injected into the register or memory as an incorrect value.

On the other hand, BOND (Baldini, 2000) uses a special agent to intercept the system call of Windows NT 4.0 OS. The agent hooks the system call from the target application and returns an incorrect value to the application. Although this scheme does not require any modification of either the OS or the target application, the fault can only be injected to a location that can be accessed through the software, such as the register and memory. Moreover, this scheme cannot be applied to test the OS.

FAUmachine (Potyra, 2007) performs a software test using virtual machines for the fault injection mechanism. However, since FAUmachine does not provide an automated test environment, the tester must configure the test environment manually.

Meanwhile, large-scale software testing has been studied. GridUnit (Duarte, 2006) executes software tests automatically on the grid referred to as OurGrid (Andrade, 2003) by distributing the execution of JUnit test suites with minimum user intervention. GridUnit is naturally limited to the execution of JUnit test code by Java. When test nodes are crashed and stopped in GridUnit, they cannot execute remaining program tests. ETICS (Begin, 2007) also provides automated test environments for grid and distributed software on a grid computing platform using Condor as a workload management system. However, since ETICS handles test on the service level and does not provide the virtual machine, ETICS cannot test dependability on the kernel layer. Open Solaris Test Farm (Walker, 2008) uses a cloud computing environment, and enables to create and execute VM instances for program tests through a web portal. However, since the functions that a test can use on Open Solaris Test Farm are limited, the tester cannot configure flexible test environments. Cloud9 (Ciortea, 2010) is proposed as a cloud computing facility for software testing, and performs parallel symbolic execution based on the source code. However, Cloud9 cannot test the system as-is.

CONCEPT OF D-CLOUD

In this section, we describe the concept of D-Cloud including the background of this research. As mentioned in Introduction section, in the large scale system such as the distributed system since each test consumes the actual execution time depending on the software size and complexity, the only way for speedup of software testing process is that a lot of tests should be performed in massively parallel. In order to manage massive computing resources, we introduce the cloud computing infrastructure to the software testing.

Meanwhile, fault tolerance is one of important capabilities so that the system can tolerate hardware failures and anomaly behaviors. In order to realize fault tolerance, the redundant configuration must be used. Parallel and distributed systems can provide the solution by the redundant resources because of multiprocessor and multiple nodes. However, in this case, the software testing has several serious problems. First, since each process runs in parallel independently, the behavior of the software may become nondeterministic on the actual hardware. It means that it is too difficult to reproduce the same failure after a failure occurred on such a system. Toward this problem, virtual machine technology helps the reproducibility by adding the management mechanism for the time synchronization. Second, in the case of a large-scale distributed system, to build the test environment becomes complicated job. In order to test such a system, usually the preliminary test with restriction is done in the small-scale system, then, the comprehensive test under the full-scale environment is conducted. However, it may stretch the time and raise the cost for the system test unless the test system almost similar to the target environment is prepared. On this point, the cloud services based on IaaS (Infrastructure as a Service) also provide an answer. They permit the use of a huge number of computing nodes, and the emulation of the entire system without modification of the source codes using a virtual machine on each node.

Furthermore, although testing of fault tolerant facilities is important in the highly dependable system, it is too difficult to make the specific hardware fault conditions or to generate anomaly loads in the real world. The solution of this problem is to use virtual machine technology to provide the fault injection facility, and it can emulate hardware faults of several devices within the virtual machine according to the request from the tester.

Based on above discussions, D-Cloud aims for the realization of the software testing environment as follows:

1.   By the use of computing resource provided by the cloud computing system, a number of

test case can be performed simultaneously; thus software testing can be accelerated.

2. By the description of the system configuration and test scenario, a series of complex test procedure can be automated.

3. Hardware fault and anomaly state can be emulated flexibly as many times as needed.

4. The target parallel and distributed system can be built onto the cloud computing system, and the execution of the system on the cloud helps the detection of the timing bug and the reproduction of the failure.

D-CLOUD SOFTWARE TESTING ENVIRONMENT

Toward the goal described in the previous section, we have been developing D-Cloud for software testing environment. D-Cloud consists of multiple virtual machine nodes, which execute guest operating systems with fault injection, a controller node, which controls all of the guest operating systems, and a frontend, which manages the hardware and software configurations and the test scenarios.

Fault Injection in a Virtual Machine

D-Cloud uses a virtual machine to execute system tests. The virtualized hardware device can simulate failures on the guest OS, and fault injection using virtual machines allows system tests to be executed without changing the program. Using the virtual machine, D-Cloud can test software running not only in the userland layer but also in the kernel layer. When software bugs on the kernel layer are detected during a system test, the OS may hang-up naturally due to a kernel panic. When the system runs on real machines, it is difficult to obtain helpful information for the bug fix in this case, because the user cannot manipulate the OS under the kernel panic. However, when using a virtual machine, a bug in the OS running on the virtual machine does not affect the host OS running

on a physical machine. Therefore, the tester can continue system tests, and the tester can collect information for debugging even if the guest OS crashes. Furthermore, the snapshot of the previous states in the guest OS permits the operation to return until the desired state repeatedly.

Management of Computing Resources

For developing dependable systems, it is important that system tests must be executed for as many cases as possible in order to find and fix as many bugs as possible. In addition, in order to execute many tests, large amount of resources must be managed efficiently and flexibly. In D-Cloud, resources are managed by a cloud computing system. For example, a number of systems that require high reliability and dependability consist of multiple nodes linked by a network. In this case, D-Cloud can test such distributed systems using several guest operating systems.

Automating System Configuration and Testing

D-Cloud automates the system setup process of the tested system and the test-process, including the fault injection, based on a scenario written by a tester. When the tester writes a number of configurations of system test environments in a scenario description file, D-Cloud sets up appropriate test environments and executes appropriate tests automatically. Therefore, D-Cloud enables the behavior of dependability functions on the system to be tested exhaustively and enables system tests to be executed quickly.

DESIGN OF D-CLOUD

D-Cloud uses QEMU as virtualization software with expansion for the fault injection facility and Eucalyptus as cloud management software, which is an open-source implementation having the same API as AmazonEC2 (Nurmi, 2009). Figure 1 shows an overview of D-Cloud. D-Cloud consists of the following components:

1. **QEMU Nodes:** Available with the fault injection facility.
2. **Controller Node:** Manages the QEMU nodes using Eucalyptus.
3. **D-Cloud Frontend:** Issues test and fault injection commands and transfers input/output data with QEMU nodes.

Virtual Machine with Fault Injection Facility

In D-Cloud, we have been implementing FaultVM (Banzai, 2010) based on QEMU as the virtualization software by adding the fault injection facility. The advantages of using QEMU are described below.

- QEMU is an open-source software. This allows the modification to the emulation codes of the device for adding the fault injection facility, and the improvement for the reproducibility by adding the management of time synchronization.
- QEMU can support various processor architectures. Especially, emulators for several embedded processors, such as ARM and SH processor architectures, are already available.
- QEMU can emulate a number of hardware devices. Thus, QEMU may treat several hardware faults in the guest OS.

We added the fault injection functions to QEMU in order to emulate the hardware faults on a virtual machine, referred to as FaultVM. Table 1 lists the types of fault injection. Here, we implement the fault injection mechanism in the emulator function of QEMU for the hard disk

Figure 1. Structure of D-Cloud

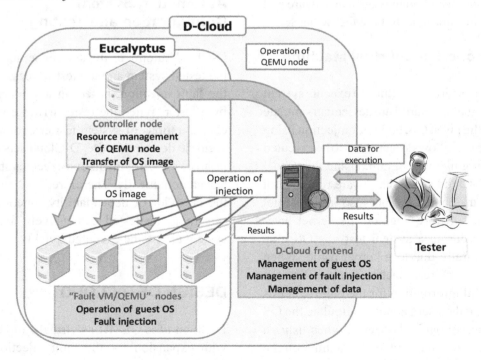

Table 1. Types of fault injection

Device	Fault	Value
Hard Disk	Error of specified sector	badblock
	Specified sector is read-only	Readonly
	Error detection by ECC	ecc
	Received data contains error	corrupt
	Response of disk becomes slow	slow
Network	1 bit error of packet	1bit
	2 bit error of packet	2bit
	Error detection by CRC	crc
	Packet loss	loss
	NIC is not responding	nic
Memory	Bit error	bit
	Byte at specified address contains error	byte

controller, the network controller, and the memory as target devices.

Management of Computing Resources Using Eucalyptus

In order to execute many tests simultaneously, large amount of resources must be managed efficiently and flexibly. Therefore, we introduced a cloud management system for managing the resource of the testing environment. In this case, customization and improvement are required for the management software, such as the network management and VM image management, and open-source software is strongly needed. Eucalyptus (Nurmi, 2009) is a cloud computing infrastructure that manages machine resources flexibly using a virtual machine, and widely used since it is an open-source implementation having the same API as AmazonEC2 (Varia, 2008). Thus, we used Eucalyptus as a prototype implementation of D-Cloud. The roles of Eucalyptus in D-Cloud are shown as follows:

- Management of various guest OS images on the controller node.
- Transfer of the specified guest OS images from the controller node to appropriate QEMU nodes.
- Beginning and completion of guest operating systems on QEMU nodes.

By these features, the tester does not need to be aware of the allocation for computing resources provided by D-Cloud.

Automated System Configuration and Testing

D-Cloud automates the system setup and the test process, including the fault injection, based on a scenario written by a tester. "D-Cloud frontend" manages guest operating systems, configures system test environments, transfers various data from the tester to guest operating systems for the execution of testing, and collects testing results from guest operating systems. D-Cloud frontend performs the following functions:

- Reception of a test scenario, a test program, input data, and a script including execution commands from a tester.
- Interpretation of the test scenario written in XML.
- Transfer of the test program, the input data, and the script to the guest operating system.
- Issue of the request for the startup of a guest operating system to the Eucalyptus controller node.
- Issue of the fault injection command for the target guest operating system to the appropriate virtual machine.
- Collection of the output data, logs, and snapshots from the guest operating system.

DESCRIPTION OF SYSTEM CONFIGURATION AND TEST SCENARIO

As described above, D-Cloud performs preparation and test according to a scenario written in XML. By providing multiple scenario files, various target systems can be tested simultaneously. Furthermore, since the cloud controller manages the computing resources appropriately, the tester can submit the test items one after another regardless of available computing resources. Testing scenario statement consists of four parts as follows.

- **machineDefinition:** Descriptions for the hardware configuration.
- **systemDefinition:** Descriptions for the software environment.
- **injectionDefinition:** Definitions of faults for injection.
- **testDescription:** Procedures of the entire test.

Configuration for the Hardware Environment

The description of the hardware configuration is given by the "machineDefinition" element. Table 2 lists the contents of the "machineDefinition" element. All hardware components used in the test must be defined by each "machine" element.

The "machine" element must include five elements, "name," "cpu," "mem," "nic," and "id." The "name" is referred in the "systemDefinition" element as the "machinename" described in the following sub-section. The "cpu" and "nic" indicate the number of CPUs and NICs, respectively, and "mem" represents the allocation size of the main memory. The "id" element designates the identifier for the system image to be used. Eucalyptus provides each system image with a unique identifier registered in the cloud system, and the identifier is also used in D-Cloud.

Setting for the Software Environment

The description of the software environment is given by the "systemDefinition" element containing elements shown in Table 3. The entire software environment used in the test must be defined by each "system" element. The "system" element must include two elements, "name" and "host." The "name" is referred in the "testDescription" element. Moreover, the "host" element contains three elements, "host- name," "machinename," and "config." The "hostname" determines the name of the host, and the "machine name" is selected from the "name" of "machine" within the "machineDefinition" element. The "config" designates a file containing the various kinds of parameters.

Table 2. "machineDefinition" element

Element Name	Meaning
machine	Delimiter for definition of the hardware environment
name	Name definition of the hardware environment
cpu	Number of CPUs
mem	Size of memory
nic	Number of NICs
id	ID of the system image

Table 3. "systemDefinition" element

Element Name	Meaning
system	Delimiter for definition of the software environment
name	Name of the software environment
host	Delimiter of the testing host
hostname	Name of the host
machinename	Name of the used machine element
config	Designation of the configuration file

Definition of Fault Injection

The definition of fault injection items is given in the "injectionDefinition" element containing elements shown in Table 4. It may have multiple "injection" elements, each of which has a "name" element and multiple "fault" elements. The "injection" element is assigned to each fault injection event. The "name" is referred in the "testDescription" element. The "fault" element must include four elements, "location," "target," "kind," and "time." The "location" and "target" specify the target device type and device name to inject a fault, respectively. The "kind" indicates the selection of fault injection elements listed in Table 1 as discussed in the previous section. The "time" represents the duration of fault injection.

Description for the Automatic Test Procedures

The execution of the test is described in the "testDescription" element using the contents shown in Table 5. The "run" element is used for the independent test descriptions, and multiple "run" elements may exist in a "testDescription" element. The "name" element defines the name of the system test to be performed. The output file containing test result is created with the file name based on the content of "name" element.

Table 4. "injectionDefinition" element

Element Name	Meaning
injection	Delimiter for definition of the fault injection
name	Name of the fault injection
fault	Delimiter for configuration of the injection
location	Designation of device type
target	Designation of target device
kind	Type of fault
time	Duration of the fault event

Table 5. "testDescription" element

Element Name	Meaning
run	Delimiter for definition of the test scenario
name	Name of the test scenario
systemname	Name of the used "systemDefinition" element
halt	Ending time of the test
script	Delimiter for definition of the execution script
on	Execution host
putFile	File transmitted to the guest OS
exec	Designation of the script file including the execution commands
inject	Execution of the fault injection

The "systemname" indicates the name in the "systemDefinition" element. The "halt" element with "when" attribute decides the finish time of the entire of the target system test. The "script" element includes four elements, "on," "putFile," "exec," and "inject" for each needed host. The "on" specifies the host name defined in the "systemDefinition" element. The "putFile" and "exec" specify the file name for the transfer to the host and the execute command, respectively. The "inject" is selected from the name defined in the "injectionDefinition" element. The "inject" element also has "when" attribute, which specifies the start time of the fault incidence.

D-Cloud Operation

D-Cloud configures four components as four services:

- **Portal:** D-Cloud provides a web portal to the tester. This web portal displays available OS images and provides the environment for data transfer.
- **Configure Test Environment:** D-Cloud configures the test environment using the "machineDefinition" element and the "systemDefinition" element.

- **Job Execution:** D-Cloud executes a program test according to a given scenario using the "testDescription" element and the "injectionDefinition" element.
- **Data Management:** D-Cloud transfers test data given by the tester to appropriate nodes. Moreover, D-Cloud transfers logs and snapshots such as memory snapshot from test nodes to the tester after testing.

D-Cloud executes a test scenario as follows.

1. A tester describes a test scenario, configuration files, and scripts.
2. The tester uploads the test scenario, the configuration files, the script, and the files to D-Cloud frontend. If the tester wants to use OS images customized by the testers, the tester uploads these images to D-Cloud frontend.
3. D-Cloud frontend issues instructions for setting up the guest operating systems for test to the Eucalyptus controller. If a tester has their own guest OS images, D-Cloud frontend transfers the OS images to the Eucalyptus controller. Otherwise, the tester must select a preconfigured OS image provided by Eucalyptus as a guest OS image to be transferred.
4. The Eucalyptus controller selects an available FaultVM node to boot the guest operating systems and to transfer the OS images to the selected FaultVM nodes.
5. OS images are booted on the selected QEMU nodes.
6. D-Cloud frontend transfers the files used in the tests in order to be executed on each guest OS. Each guest OS then configures a test environment.
7. According to the test scenario, system tests and fault injection are executed and snapshots are taken.

8. After the system tests, each guest OS transfers the output data, logs, and snapshots to D-Cloud frontend.
9. The tester then downloads the output data, snapshots, and logs obtained through system testing.

TEST EXAMPLE USING D-CLOUD

We preliminarily evaluate D-Cloud by testing the dependable system using two real examples:

1. Highly available server system (HA server system)
2. RI2N (Redundant Interconnection with Inexpensive Network) (Miura 2009)

Example of HA Server System

Figure 2 shows an example of an HA server system as a distributed system. In the HA server system, HTTP requests from the client are normally forwarded to two back-end servers ("ws0" and "ws1") by a load balancer using Linux Virtual server "lv0" in a round-robin manner. In addition, if "lv0" is accidentally halted in an abnormal state, rather than "lv0," the reserved node "lv1" starts load balancing services. In this distributed system test, each configuration for all of hosts is written. Guest OSes then start up according to the number of description of host elements. In the example shown in Figure 2, "lv0" and "lv1" start up as loadbalancers, which are configured according to a hardware environmental element called "LVS" and a software configuration file called "lvconfig." Next, "ws0" and "ws1" start up as web servers and are also configured in the same manner as "lv[0-1]." On the other hand, the "client" is booted as a client node, which issues HTTP requests. The "client" nodes are omitted in Figure 2, they are also configured according to another different hardware environmental element.

Figure 2. Example scenario and configuration of the HA server

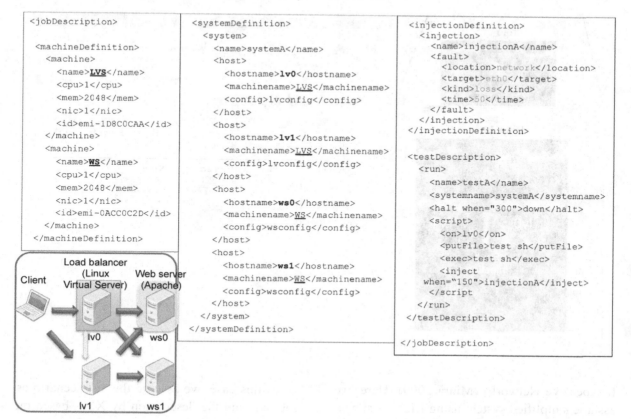

```
<jobDescription>

  <machineDefinition>
    <machine>
      <name>LVS</name>
      <cpu>1</cpu>
      <mem>2048</mem>
      <nic>1</nic>
      <id>emi-1D8C0CAA</id>
    </machine>
    <machine>
      <name>WS</name>
      <cpu>1</cpu>
      <mem>2048</mem>
      <nic>1</nic>
      <id>emi-0ACC0C2D</id>
    </machine>
  </machineDefinition>
```

```
<systemDefinition>
  <system>
    <name>systemA</name>
    <host>
      <hostname>lv0</hostname>
      <machinename>LVS</machinename>
      <config>lvconfig</config>
    </host>
    <host>
      <hostname>lv1</hostname>
      <machinename>LVS</machinename>
      <config>lvconfig</config>
    </host>
    <host>
      <hostname>ws0</hostname>
      <machinename>WS</machinename>
      <config>wsconfig</config>
    </host>
    <host>
      <hostname>ws1</hostname>
      <machinename>WS</machinename>
      <config>wsconfig</config>
    </host>
  </system>
</systemDefinition>
```

```
<injectionDefinition>
  <injection>
    <name>injectionA</name>
    <fault>
      <location>network</location>
      <target>eth0</target>
      <kind>loss</kind>
      <time>50</time>
    </fault>
  </injection>
</injectionDefinition>

<testDescription>
  <run>
    <name>testA</name>
    <systemname>systemA</systemname>
    <halt when="300">down</halt>
    <script>
      <on>lv0</on>
      <putFile>test sh</putFile>
      <exec>test sh</exec>
      <inject
when="150">injectionA</inject>
    </script>
  </run>
</testDescription>

</jobDescription>
```

Client — Load balancer (Linux Virtual Server) — Web server (Apache)

lv0   ws0
lv1   ws1

In this case, the fault injection is designated as "injectionA." It is executed into the network device "eth0" as packet loss for 50 seconds. Then, the name of the test is "testA," and the test output obtained by the tester is designated as "testA". In the test environment designated as "systemA," the guest OS named "node0" uses "files" as inputs for the system test. The system test is then executed according to contents of "script" element, which defines a series of test procedures. During the system test, the injection defined as "injectionA" is executed 150 seconds after booting and becoming ready, and system is then halted 300 seconds after the boot.

Figure 3 shows the current web portal UI for the management of D-Cloud, and test results of HA server system. Figure 3 demonstrates the part of the web interface for the management of test scenarios in D-Cloud, and it shows that several test scenarios (nic2.xml, and so on) are running simultaneously on D-Cloud.

In addition, test results of HA server system are indicated. Horizontal axis shows time, vertical axis shows HTTP responses per second. In this result, when the fault is injected to eth0 on lv0, that is, packet loss occurs, response falls transiently. However, soon HTTP response recovers to the same level as in the original condition due to fail-over by lv1.

Example of RI2N System

We have proposed and developed a fault tolerant and high-performance interconnection network based on the multi-link of Gigabit Ethernet (GbE) named RI2N (Redundant Interconnection with

Figure 3. Current management web portal UI of D-Cloud and test results

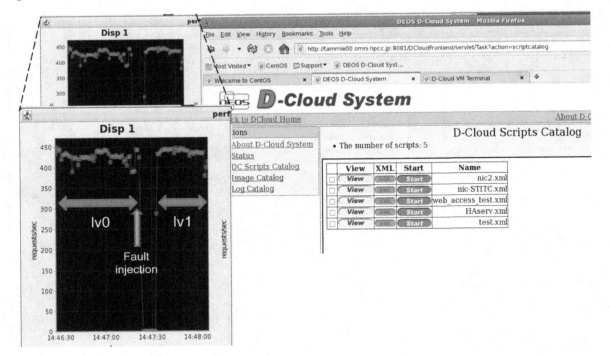

Inexpensive Network) (Miura 2009). Here, we assume simplified system using RI2N as shown in Figure 4. In this figure, Client1 is connected with server1 by two Ethernet links, net0 and net1. In this case, net0 and net1 form the RI2N logical link. Net2 is also available as the Ethernet link for issuing the command from D-Cloud frontend to each node and the collection of measurement results to D-Cloud frontend.

In this case, we assume the test scenario as follows, and the description by XML based on this scenario is denoted as shown in Figure 5:

1. Client1 performs burst data transfer to server1 using RI2N continuously. In this case, throughput is expected to be twice as high as a single link.

2. After 200 seconds from the power-on, the network interface "eth0" of client1 is down

Figure 4. Simplified system example using RI2N

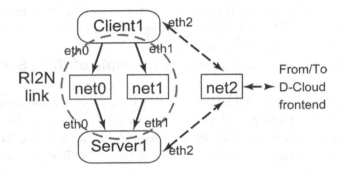

during 60 seconds. RI2N link will be down immediately, however, throughput should recover to the level of the single link after a few seconds.

3. After that, "eth0" interface on client1 is alive again. RI2N will detect the link recovery, and throughput should recover to the same level as in the beginning condition.

4. Finally, the system is halted 300 seconds after the power-on.

It is notable that step 2 can be expressed as the fault injection of the packet loss against eth0 of client1.

Figure 6 indicates the results obtained by the above scenario. Red arrow indicates the duration of the fault injection (60 sec.). In this result, when the fault is injected to eth0 of client1, throughput falls transiently, and soon throughput recovers to lower level than before. After eth0 is alive again, with a few seconds of delay, the throughput recovers to the same level as that in the original condition. The absolute values of the throughput are incorrect in current D-Cloud. It is because each packet transfer is performed via real network while the behaviors of client1 and server1 are emulated within each virtual machine. Even though we can confirm that the fault tolerant and recovery detection capability of RI2N work correctly by relative tendency of the results.

Figure 5. Example Test Scenario for RI2N by XML

```xml
<jobDescription>
  <machineDefinition>
    <machine>
      <name>server</name>
      <cpu>1</cpu> <mem>512</mem> <nic>3</nic>
      <id>emi-1D8C0CAA</id>
    </machine>
    <machine>
      <name>client</name>
      <cpu>1</cpu> <mem>512</mem> <nic>3</nic>
      <id>emi-0ACC0C2D</id>
    </machine>
  </machineDefinition>

  <systemDefinition>
  <system>
    <name>systemA</name>
    <host>
      <hostname>server1</hostname>
      <machinename>server</machinename>
      <config>serv.conf</config>
    </host>
    <host>
      <hostname>client1</hostname>
      <machinename>client</machinename>
      <config>client.conf</config>
    </host>
  </system>
  </systemDefinition>
```

```xml
<injectionDefinition>
  <injection>
    <name>injectionA</name>
    <fault>
      <location>network</location>
      <target>eth0</target>
      <kind>loss</kind>
      <time>60</time>
    </fault>
  </injection>
</injectionDefinition>

<testDescription>
  <run>
    <name>testA</name>
    <systemname>systemA</systemname>
    <halt when="300">down</halt>
    <script>
      <on>client1</on>
      <putFile>test.sh</putFile>
      <exec>test.sh</exec>
      <inject when="200">injectionA</inject>
    </script>
  </run>
</testDescription>
</jobDescription>
```

Figure 6. Test results of RI2N obtained by D-Cloud

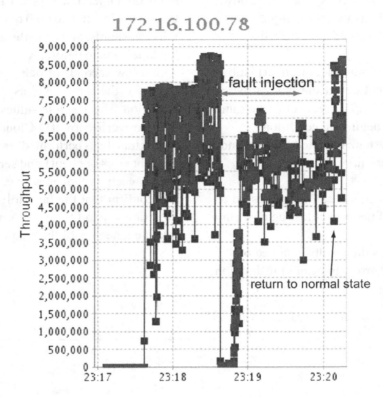

FUTURE RESEARCH DIRECTIONS

FaultVM Integrated with the Device Model Simulator in SpecC

As shown in the previous section, FaultVM demonstrates that the fault injection facility can work correctly. However, FaultVM can only perform tests using a device prepared in QEMU.

In embedded systems, in particular, newly designed and proprietary devices are often used. In order to simulate such devices in FaultVM, the simulation codes for the device must be written in C as virtual hardware within the hardware abstraction layer of QEMU. Moreover, the fault injection facility must also be attached to the simulator. With the design of each new device, implementing the simulator and fault injector by modifying QEMU is very inefficient, and a sophisticated method of customizing FaultVM is strongly needed.

In order to customize FaultVM flexibly, we adopted the SpecC language, known as a System Description Language, to describe hardware devices (Gajski, 2000), and proposed the device fault emulator using the virtual machine integrated with the SpecC device model, namely, FaultVM-SpecC (Hanawa, 2010b). FaultVM-SpecC can be obtained by the integration of FaultVM and the simulator described in SpecC.

We confirmed the feasibility of FaultVM-SpecC through a simple example of control flow and a typical device model in the SpecC language. FaultVM-SpecC also makes flexible the definition and injection of faults without the need to modify the original QEMU source codes. This facility permits D-Cloud to test distributed systems with customized devices. We are developing the operation flow using FaultVM-SpecC in order to integrate to the D-Cloud system.

Integration with DS-Bench

We proposed DS-Bench (Ishikawa, 2009) as a dependability benchmarking framework for a dependable operating system. A dependability benchmark is a technique to evaluate the dependability of a system. It characterizes the dependability of a system component or a whole system, either qualitatively or quantitatively (Kanoun, 2008). A conceptual framework for a dependability benchmark was developed under the DBench project (Kanoun, 2004) from late 1990 to early 2000. The DBench project developed several application-specific benchmark environments and reported them. However, DBench did not provide a software stack to support the framework based on the available information, and did not consider the runtime software environment needed to enable developers to execute the dependability benchmark in a systematic way throughout the system life cycle. Thus, measurement tools that did not share any common evaluation environment were individually developed. Unlike DBench, we have been focusing on usability and re-usability of the dependability benchmark.

DS-Bench provides evidence by testing and evaluating the system quantitatively under anomaly situations such as hardware faults, software bugs, human errors, and overloads, which are enumerated during the development. D-Cloud is so useful as the virtual platform for DS-Bench since anomaly loads can be generated automatically from the request given by the scenario file using D-Cloud. Therefore, D-Cloud helps incremental benchmark improvement, and DS-Bench with D-Cloud leads to the improvement of dependability in the target system.

Currently, DS-Bench Toolset has been developed and it includes D-Case Editor, DS-Bench, and D-Cloud. D-Case Editor is an assurance case editor. It makes a tool chain with DS-Bench and D-Cloud, and exploits the test results as evidences of the dependability of the system. DS-Bench manages dependability benchmarking tools and anomaly loads according to benchmarking scenarios. D-Cloud is a test environment for performing rapid system tests controlled by DS-Bench. It combines both a cluster of real machines for performance-accurate benchmarks and a cloud computing environment as a group of virtual machines for exhaustive function testing with a fault-injection facility. DS-Bench Toolset enables to test systems satisfactorily and to explain the dependability of the systems to the stakeholders. An example of a use case of DS-Bench Toolset using a simple web server system is demonstrated, and it showed how DS-Bench Toolset has provided evidence of the dependability of the system (Fujita, 2012).

CONCLUSION

In this chapter, we presented the concept and design of the software testing environment using the cloud computing technology, named D-Cloud. D-Cloud permits the automatic configuration, testing with fault injection along the description of the testing scenario. The features of D-Cloud are listed as follows.

- D-Cloud enables testing of fault-tolerant functions with respect to hardware failures that occur in a physical machine using the fault injection facility implemented in the virtual machine layer.
- The computing resources can be managed flexibly. If resources are available, then test cases can be executed quickly by simultaneously using the resources.
- D-Cloud automates testing using descriptions of the system configuration and the test scenario to execute tests on cloud computing systems.

We have been developing D-Cloud using Eucalyptus as a cloud management software and QEMU as virtualization software. The preliminary test examples using D-Cloud were denoted, and the results demonstrated that D-Cloud allows to set up the environment easily, and to perform the software test for the distributed system. The prototype D-Cloud can inject a number of faults into a HDD, NIC, or memory on a VM and can automatically execute a system test using a scenario file. At present, D-Cloud can obtain the testing results including the virtual console logs and the syslog outputs by the running processes and operating system in FaultVM/QEMU on each node.

ACKNOWLEDGMENT

This study is supported in part by Core Research of Evolutional Science & Technology (CREST) program of Japan Science and Technology Agency (JST), entitled "Computation Platform for Power-aware and Reliable Embedded Parallel Processing System" in the research area of "Dependable Embedded Operating System for Practical Use."

The authors appreciate the contributions of Mr. Takayuki Banzai and Mr. Hitoshi Koizumi.

REFERENCES

Andrade, N., Cirne, W., Brasileiro, F., & Roisenberg, P. (2003). OurGrid: An approach to easily assemble grids with equitable resource sharing. *9th International Workshop on Job Scheduling Strategies for Parallel Processing, Lecture Notes in Computer Science, vol. 2862* (pp. 61–86). Springer Verlag.

Baldini, A., Benso, A., Chiusano, S., & Prinetto, P. (2000). `BOND': An interposition agents based fault injector for Windows NT. *International Symposium on Defect and Fault-Tolerance in VLSI Systems (DFT '00)* (p. 387). IEEE.

Banzai, T., Koizumi, H., Kanbayashi, R., Imada, T., Kimura, H., Hanawa, T., & Sato, M. (2010). D-Cloud: Design of a software testing environment for reliable distributed systems using cloud computing technology. *2nd International Symposium on Cloud Computing (Cloud 2010) in conjunction with CCGrid2010* (pp. 631-636). IEEE.

Begin, M. E., Sancho, G. D., Meglio, A. D., Ferro, E., Ronchieri, E., Selmi, M., & Zurek, M. (2007). Lecture Notes in Computer Science: *Vol. 4401. Build, configuration, integration and testing tools for large software projects: ETICS. Rapid Integration of Software Engineering Techniques* (pp. 81–97). Springer Verlag.

Carreira, J., Madeira, H., & Silva, J. G. (1998). Xception: A technique for the experimental evaluation of dependability in modern computers. *IEEE Transactions on Software Engineering, 24,* 125–136. doi:10.1109/32.666826

Ciortea, L., Zamfir, C., Bucur, S., Chipounov, V., & Candea, G. (2010). Cloud9: A software testing service. *ACM SIGOPS Operating Systems Review, 43*(4), 5–10. doi:10.1145/1713254.1713257

Duarte, A., Cirne, W., Brasileiro, F., & Machado, P. (2006). GridUnit: Software testing on the grid. *28th International Conference on Software Engineering (ICSE '06)* (pp. 779–782). Association for Computing Machinery.

Fujita, H., Matsuno, Y., Hanawa, T., Sato, M., Kato, S., & Ishikawa, Y. (2012). DS-Bench toolset: Tools for dependability benchmarking with simulation and assurance. *42nd IEEE/IFIP International Conference on Dependable Systems and Networks (DSN 2012)* (8 pages, to be published). IEEE.

Gajski, D. D., Zhu, J., Dömer, R., Gerstlauer, A., & Zhao, S. (2000). *SpecC: Specification language and methodology.* Springer Verlag. doi:10.1007/978-1-4615-4515-6

Han, S., Shin, K., & Rosenberg, H. (1995). DOCTOR: An integrated software fault injection environment for distributed real-time systems. *International Computer Performance and Dependability Symposium (IPDS '95)* (p. 0204). IEEE.

Hanawa, T., Banzai, T., Koizumi, H., Kanbayashi, R., Imada, T., & Sato, M. (2010). Large-scale software testing environment using cloud computing technology for dependable parallel and distributed systems. *2nd International Workshop on Software Testing in the Cloud (STITC 2010), co-located with the 3rd IEEE International Conference on Software Testing, Verification, and Validation (ICST 2010)* (pp. 428-433). IEEE.

Hanawa, T., Koizumi, H., Banzai, T., Sato, M., Miura, S., Ishii, T., & Takamizawa, H. (2010). Customizing virtual machine with fault injector by integrating with SpecC device model for a software testing environment D-Cloud. *2010 Pacific Rim International Symposium on Dependable Computing.* (pp. 47-54). IEEE.

Ishikawa, Y., Fujita, H., Maeda, T., Matsuda, M., Sugaya, M., & Sato, M. … Tokuda, H. (2009). Towards an open dependable operating system. *12th International Symposium on Object/Component/Service-Oriented Real-Time Distributed Computing* (pp. 20–27). IEEE.

Kanoun, K., Madeira, H., Crouzet, Y., Cin, M. D., Moreira, F., & Garcia, J. R. (2004). *DBench dependability benchmarks.* Retrieved May 1, 2011, from http://www.laas.fr/DBench/Final/DBench-complete-report.pdf

Kanoun, K., & Spainhower, L. (Eds.). (2008). *Dependability benchmarking for computer systems.* Wiley. doi:10.1002/9780470370506

Miura, S., Hanawa, T., Yonemoto, T., Boku, T., & Sato, M. (2009). RI2N/DRV: Multi-link Ethernet for high-bandwidth and fault-tolerant network on PC clusters. *The 9th Workshop on Communication Architecture for Clusters (CAC) in IPDPS* (pp. 1–8). IEEE Computer Society.

Nurmi, D., Wolski, R., Grzegorczyk, C., Obertelli, G., Soman, S., Youseff, L., & Zagorodnov, D. (2009). The Eucalyptus open-source cloud-computing system. *9th IEEE/ACM International Symposium on Cluster Computing and the Grid (CCGrid '09)* (pp. 124-131). IEEE Computer Society.

Potyra, S., Sieh, V., & Cin, M. D. (2007). Evaluating fault-tolerant system designs using FAUmachine. *Workshop on Engineering Fault Tolerant Systems (EFTS '07)* (p. 9). Association for Computing Machinery.

Varia, J. (2008). Cloud architectures. *AWS Cloud Computing Whitepapers.* Retrieved May 1, 2011, from http://aws.amazon.com/jp/whitepapers/

Walker, J. (2008). *Open Solaris test farm.* Retrieved May 1, 2011, from http://hub.opensolaris.org/bin/download/Community+Group+testing/files/opensolaristesting.pdf

Chapter 17
Cloud Scalability Measurement and Testing

Xiaoying Bai
Tsinghua University, China

Jerry Gao
San Jose State University, USA

Wei-Tek Tsai
Tsinghua University, China & Arizona State University, USA

ABSTRACT

Cloud computing introduces a new paradigm for software deployment, hosting, and service renting. Based on the XaaS architecture, a large number of users may share computing resources, platform services, and application software in a multi-tenancy approach. To ensure service availability, the system needs to support an advanced level of massive scalability so that it can provide necessary resources on demand following the pay-per-use pricing model. This chapter analyzes the unique requirements of cloud performance and scalability, compared with traditional distributed systems. Measurements are proposed with performance indicators, meters, and metrics identified from different perspectives. To support scalability testing in a dynamic environment, an agent-based testing framework is proposed to facilitate adaptive load generation and simulation using a two-layer control architecture.

1. INTRODUCTION

Cloud computing proposes a new architecture for multi-layered resource sharing, such as infra-structure-as-a-service (IaaS), storage-as-a-service (SaaS), data-as-as-service (DaaS), platform-as-a-service (PaaS), and software-as-a-service (SaaS) (Rimal, et al., 2009). Resources can be dynami-cally allocated based on usage demands following negotiated Service Level Agreement (SLA) in a pay-per-use business model to achieve cost-effective performance and resource utilization. Cloud-based infrastructure has a big impact on software engineering methods. It shifts the focus of software development from product-oriented programming to service-oriented reuse, composi-

DOI: 10.4018/978-1-4666-2536-5.ch017

tion, and online renting. It has a great potential to enhance the scalability, portability, reusability, flexibility, and fault-tolerance capabilities of software systems, taking the advantage of the new infrastructure architecture.

However, cloud-based infrastructure also introduces new risks to software systems. Software is remote deployed in a virtualized runtime environment, using rented hardware/software resources, and hosted in a third-party infrastructure. The quality and performance of the software highly depend on its runtime environment. For example, Amazon provides a huge cloud infrastructure EC2 (Elastic Compute Cloud) and web-hosting system AWS (Amazon Web Services) based on EC2 (Amazon). It promises to keep customers' sites up and running 99.95% of the year, which only allows for 4.4 hours of downtime. Unfortunately, an unexpected crash happens in April, 2011 due to operation mistakes during network reconfiguration (News, 2011). More than 70 organizations are affected including FourSquare, the New York Times, and Reddit, which pay to use AWS to run their websites on EC2. Due to the accident, the performance of these websites are greatly decreased, and some sites were even down for dozens of hours.

Scalability is one of the important quality concerns of cloud performance (Bondi, 2000; Chen&Sun, 2006; Duboc, et al., 2006; Gao, et al., 2011). Resources in the cloud allocated elastically to support application executions following a usage-based approach. Built upon the conventional concepts of distributed resource management, cloud computing presents new scalability features. Stakeholders in a cloud-based system have different performance concerns from their individual perspectives including infrastructure providers, software service providers, and end users. From the infrastructure providers' perspective, resource utilization is important. That is, it can timely release sources so that the system can re-allocate to other applications and customers.

From the service providers' perspective, it needs to balance between system performance and cost of resource reservation. If resources are reserved more than needed, they have to pay for wasteful resources. If resources are reserved less than needed, they cannot guarantee service availability and response time.

To address the issue, the chapter proposes new analytic techniques for cloud scalability measurement using Radar Chart Model. Performance indicators and meters are analyzed from three perspectives including resource allocation and utilization, system load and system performance. Scalability are measured by taking multiple variables into consideration.

Due to the uncertainties and dynamic nature of cloud infrastructure, continuous testing is necessary to gather data and evaluate system performance (Bai, et al., 2007; Chen, 2006; Gao, et al., 2011; Li, et al., 2010; Liu, 2009; Molyneaux, 2009; Steen, et al., 1998). In counter to the challenges of software testing under uncertainties, new testing capabilities are necessary including:

- **Adaptive Testing:** The ability to sense changes in target software systems and environment, and to adjust test accordingly.
- **Dynamic Testing:** The ability to re-configure and re-compose tests, and to produce, on-demand, new test data, test cases, test plans and test deployment.
- **Collaborative Testing:** The ability to coordinate test executions that are distributed dispersed.

The research proposes an agent-based testing framework to facilitate performance testing of software system built upon the cloud platforms (Bai, et al., 2006; Bai, et al., 2011; Tsai, et al., 2003; Tsai, et al., 2004). Agents are designed with necessary test knowledge, test goal and action plan. Performance testing is defined as a control problem to select the workload and test cases in order to achieve the goal of performance anomaly detection. Test agents are classified into two categories: test coordinator and test runners. Test runners are distributed located on host computers to exercise test cases on target systems. Test coordinator accepts test requests and coordinates test runners to achieve test objectives. A two-level control architecture is built: at the TR (Test Runner) level, agents decide the workload of concurrent requests; while at the TC (Test Coordinator) level, agents select test cases of different complexity levels. Agents communicate and collaborate with each other to share knowledge and test plan.

The rest of the chapter is organized as follows. Section 2 presents the background of motivating problems and testing needs. Section 3 introduces cloud performance measurements including resource meters and performance meter based on radar chart analysis model. It then introduces the metrics for cloud scalability analysis. Section 4 introduces the design of agent-based framework for cloud performance testing. Finally, section 5 concludes the chapter.

2. BACKGROUND

2.1 Cloud Scalability

As shown in Table 1, software hosted in a cloud environment differs from that in an in-house environment. The in-house environment is usually fully controlled by software operations or test organizations with dedicated hardware and software resources. In the cloud-based hosting, infrastructure resources, like CPU, disk and memory, are provided as rented services. Software deployed in the cloud share resources from resource pools. New techniques are introduced to support cloud-based massive scale resource sharing, such as virtualization and multi-tenancy. Different mechanisms can be incorporated for dynamic resource allocation following a usage-based approach. The purpose is to achieve a balance between the renting cost and resource utilization. A SLA (Service Level Agreement) is set up between infrastructure provider and its customers who rent resources for their application execution. With agreed service quality, the cloud automatically scales up to allocate more resources when the load increases, and scales down to reclaim unused resources when the load

Table 1. Comparison of software in cloud and in-house environment (Bai, et al., 2011)

	In-House Hosting	**Cloud Hosting**
Architecture	Centralized, limited parallel and fault tolerance	Build-in distributed parallel computing, high fault-tolerance
Configuration	Small number of options, limited scale, offline reconfiguration	Large number of options, online reconfiguration and dynamic scale
Resource Allocation	Stable dedicated resources, limited upper bound	Unlimited resource pools, dynamic allocation based on real-time usage
Resource Sharing	Limited sharing	Inherent multi-tenancy architecture, large scale resource sharing
Runtime Environment	Dedicated environment, in-house control	Virtualized computing services, unpredictable environment, low controllability
Scalability	Offline scale up / scale down	Online massive scalability with unlimited resource pool, dynamic scale up/down in response to usage

decreases. It can also change resource configurations in response to SLA changes or the needs of failure recovery. The process is mostly carried out online following pre-defined policies, which the users usually have very limited control over.

The resource sharing model introduces risks to application performance (Li, et al., 2010). For example, even an application is allocated with promised hardware, its performance cannot be guaranteed. Hosted in a virtualized instance, the application performance is affected by many factors such as Virtual Machine (VM) configurations, management policies, hypervisor scheduling algorithms, and fault recovery strategies. Some issues exist in conventional distributed systems. However, the complexity and scale of the issues in the cloud environment increase substantially. For example, Salesforce is one of leading platforms for cloud based web applications. It provides on-demand Customer Relationship Management (CRM) solutions. A report (Salesforce, 2011) shows that by September 11, 2011, about 12,557 websites using Salesforce. Among them, 1,466 websites within the top million most visited sites on the Internet.

2.2 Scalability Measurement

For conventional distributed and parallel computing, scalability is used to evaluate the ability that a system can accommodate growing amounts of work (Brataas & Hughes, 2004; Grama, et al., 1993; Hill, 1990; Jogalekar & Woodside, 2000; Kumar & Gupta, 1994; Lyon, 1995; Sun & Ni, 1993). With increased resources, the system is expected to increase its capacity in a linear (ideally) manner. For a distributed system, the efficiency of resource management and control is key to system scalability. To avoid considerable performance decline, the system needs a timely response to system load increases. It allocates enough resources to the computing nodes so that their computing capabilities can be enhanced in

short time. Resource management can be implemented in a centralized or a distributed manner. In a centralized manner, the core scheduler accepts and processes all requests for resource allocation. In a distributed manner, each node accepts requests individually; they communicate and negotiate with each other to allocate and reclaim resources. In general, there are two approaches to achieve scalability:

- **Scaling Up:** To replace with better and faster hardware. For example, it can migrate the applications to more powerful machine, with faster processors and more memory.
- **Scaling Out:** Leverages the economics of using more commodity hardware equipments to distribute load across multiple facilities.

Hill first proposed to use *speedup* and *efficiency* to measure system scalability (Hill, 1990). Given a problem of size *x*, *speedup(n,x)* is defined as the ratio between execution time on 1 processor *time(1,x)* and the time on *n* processors *time(n,x)*; while *efficiency(n,x)* is defined as the *speedup* divided by the number of processors. Ideally, a system is said to be scalable if *efficiency(n,x)* = 1 for all algorithms, number of processors and problem size.

$$speedup(n, x) = \frac{time(1, x)}{time(n, x)}$$

$$efficiency(n, x) = \frac{speedup(n, x)}{n} = \frac{time(1, x) / n}{time(n, x)}$$

Many discussions arose around the two conditions of scalability definition, that is, the number of processors and the size of problem, in the late 1980s for parallel computing. Various metrics have been proposed in the last 20 years to evaluate system scalability for architecture of heterogeneous processors or changing problem size. Bondi (2000) analyzed different categories of scalability and their impacts on performance, including load scalability, space scalability, space-time scalability, and structural scalability.

- **Load Scalability:** The ability of a system to function gracefully at light, moderate, or heavy loads while making good use of available resources.
- **Space Scalability:** The ability of a system to have its memory requirements increase at most sublinearly with the number of objects it supports.
- **Space-Time Scalability:** The ability that a system will not be impaired in performance as the number of objects it encompasses increases.
- **Structural Scalability:** The ability of a system to expand without major modifications to its architecture.

For cloud platforms, virtual instances are created to host and run applications. It usually allows for dynamic allocation of instances and computing resources following a usage-based approach. Scaling can be implemented either in an opaque or transparent manner. In an opaque mechanism, cloud providers like AWS require users to explicitly declare scaling policy. While in a transparent mechanism, scaling is achieved without users' intervention. Scalability can be measured at a various levels (Gao, et al., 2011), such as:

- **Application Level:** An individual application (or instance) is evaluated and validated in a private (or public) cloud for its system performance and scalability.
- **On Cloud Level:** Multiple application instances and cloud-based applications in a private (or public) cloud are evaluated and validated for performance and scalability.

- **Over Cloud Level:** Applications over a hybrid cloud infrastructure are evaluated for end-to-end system performance and scalability.

Since cloud-based system performance evaluation and scalability analysis requires powerful simulation solutions and environments to support large-sale data simulation and generation. This drives some research interest in VM-based simulation. Jamal et al. (2009) discuss and analyze virtual machine (VM) scalability on multi-core systems in terms of CPU, memory, and network I/O-intensive workloads. The paper demonstrates that VMs on the state-of-the-art multi-core processors based systems scale well as multiple threads on native SMP kernel for CPU and memory intensive workloads.

Binning, et al. (2009), identified following novel features of cloud storage systems compared with transactional database systems:

- **Elasticity to Changing Conditions:** Conventional systems are mostly used in a managed environment using a fixed configuration. Cloud enables dynamic resources allocation and de-allocation so that the systems can be adapted to load fluctuations on the fly.
- **Tradeoffs Between Consistency and Availability:** It is impossible for cloud storage systems to provide availability and strong consistency together in the presence of network failures. Most cloud providers thus offer only weaker forms of consistency for the sake of availability.
- **Pricing Problem:** Cloud aims to provide economy of scale. However, the promise of unlimited scalability is difficult to achieve. Given various pricing plan and granularity by different providers, such as infrastructure services and platform services, it leads to different overall cost.

Existing benchmarks like TPC-benchmarks are mostly built for transactional database systems. The metrics and architecture of them are not suitable for cloud systems. Binnig et al. (2009) hence suggested a new benchmark system specific for cloud scalability, pay-per-use and fault-tolerance testing and evaluation. The benchmark uses e-commerce scenario and defines web interactions as benchmark drivers. Particularly, following four new metrics are defined for cloud storage system evaluation.

1. **Scalability:** Cloud services are expected to scale linearly with a constant cost per web interaction. The paper suggests measures the deviations of response time to the perfect linear scale by using correlation coefficient R^2 or by determining the parameters of a power function of the form $f(x)=x^b$.

2. **Cost:** The economy of cloud performance is measured as $/WIPS$, where *WIPS* is for web interactions per second used by conventional TPC-W benchmark. In addition, it also measures standard deviation of the cost during the scaling.

3. **Peaks:** This is to measure how well a cloud can adapt to peak loads, including scale-up to reach peak loads and scale-down after peak loads. The adaptability is defined as the ratio between *WIPS in RT* (real-time) and *Issued WIPS*.

4. **Fault Tolerance:** Cloud infrastructure are usually based on huge number of commodity hardware. Hardware failures are common to the infrastructure services. Hence, the metric is introduce to analyze cloud self-healing capabilities. Given failures in a period of time, the recoverability is also defined as the ratio between *WIPS in RT* (real-time) and *Issued WIPS*.

Li et al. (2010) proposed CloudCmp to facilitate systematic comparison of performance and cost across different cloud providers. It focuses on the end-to-end system performance that customers perceive, and measures cloud performance from various dimensions including elastic computing, persistent storage, and networking services. For elastic computing, it defines three metrics including benchmark finishing time which measures the resources (such like CPU, memory, and disk I/O) required to complete benchmark tasks, cost which measures the monetary cost to complete each benchmark task, and scaling latency which measures the latency for creating new instances based on different elastic mechanisms. For persistent storage, three metrics are identified including operation response time, time to consistency, and cost per operation. For intra-cloud network, it uses path capacity, represented by TCP throughput, and latency as metrics. For wide-area network, it uses optimal wide-area network latency.

2.3 Cloud Scalability Testing

Scalability testing is necessary to quantitatively validate system performance. It simulates fluctuations in system scalable parameters such as resources and loads, observes system behavior and measures them using quantitative metrics such as the maximum number of users and the volume of transactions the software under test can support.

Cloud presents new scalability features and techniques. In traditional software lifecycle, testing is usually a stage in the whole process, which is performed offline by test engineers before product delivery. As cloud-based software presents unique lifecycle model and quality issues, new testing capabilities are necessary to meet the needs of cloud testing such as continuous online testing and massive scalability testing. We identify the following features required by cloud testing (Bai, et al., 2011):

- **Multi-Layer Testing:** Faults may exist at various cloud components including hardware, network, virtualization management, storage system, etc. As a large-scale distributed system, cloud is also built with complex fault-tolerant and failure recovery mechanisms. It is hard to localize fault in case an application fails. For thorough analysis, testing needs to be performed on each component at each layers. Each layer requires different testing focuses and techniques.

- **SLA-Based Testing:** For conventional software, testing is based on source code or software specifications which describe expected software behavior using natural language or formal models. For software deployed on the cloud, source code are usually unavailable. Instead, SLA is negotiated between software and infrastructure provider, including functionalities and QoS properties. SLA thus provides the basis for test design, execution, and evaluation. As SLA is encoded in machine-interpretable standard protocols, test cases can be automated generated from the SLA, and test results can be validated against the SLA.

- **Large Scale Simulation:** Testing needs to simulate various inputs and scenarios. As an open platform, cloud allows for quite flexibly access and operation. The number of possible usage scenarios is huge. The load is high and there are sometimes unexpected large fluctuations. For example, Tao Bao (2011) is a big e-commerce system in China. It has more than 300 million registered customers with about RMB 300 billion per year. It sold about 47,000 products per minute on average in year 2010. Taking an example of its order statistics in a week, at the peak of the week, it has over 3500 orders a day; while at the low, it's only about 100. In this example, each order is on average contributed by 318 page browses from 201 customers. To test the functionality and performance of such complex systems, large-scale simulation is needed. Actually, it needs to simulate not

only the usage of the system, but also the changes in the environment such as the infrastructure configurations.

- **On-Demand Test Environment:** Testing needs to be triggered online whenever a change occurs in the cloud including the application, runtime environment, and infrastructure system. An environment is helpful for test assets sharing, automatic test generation/ selection/execution, results collection and analysis.

In addition, there are a few papers discussing solutions and tools to support the evaluation of application performance and scalability in cloud environments. For example, Chen et al. (2006) propose their scalability testing and analysis system (STAS) and present its implementation with isospeed-e scalability metric. STAS provides the facility to conduct automated isospeed-e scalability measure and analysis. It reduces the burden for users to evaluate the performance of algorithms and systems. Yigitbasi et al. (2009) report a framework, known as C-Meter, which is used to generate and submit test workloads to computing clouds. They presented their experiments using EC2 cloud technology and analyzed the performance results in terms of response time, waiting time in queue, bounded slowdown with a threshold of 1 second and job execution time. Wickremasinghe et al. (2010) present CloudAnalyst, which is a tool to simulate large-scale Cloud applications with the purpose of studying the behavior of such applications under various deployment configurations. CloudAnalyst helps developers with insights about how to distribute applications among Cloud infrastructures, the value-added services (such as the optimization of application performance), and the providers using its Service Brokers.

Cloud storage system is characterized by highly parallelism and non-determinism. As part of the research and implementation of the Cloudy2 distributed database system, Moreno (2010) proposes a new distributed testing architecture for simulating parallel jobs. This framework contains two types of nodes - Master and Slave. Master is unique identified, which is responsible for distribution, synchronization and management of all slave nodes. Master is started with a given test. It waits for enough slaves to connect to it, then sends every slave corresponding tasks. During the execution, the master controls the execution sequence of slaves to guarantee that all tasks in a step start at the same time. The slaves run testing tasks and store test results locally, including nodes' states collected by daemon thread at each node. At the end of the test, master recollects every slave's results, analyzes and then generates statistics and graphs for analyzing test execution. A workload description is organized at three layers: task, step and test. A task is an atomic job in a test, which gives a clear set of instruction to execute, containing configurations about loads, actions, and limits. Each step is a collection of tasks, which are performed in parallel with a group of slaves. A test is a well-defined sequence of steps. In this way, this framework can simulate a variety of workload scenarios.

3. CLOUD SCALABILITY MEASUREMENT

Conventional monitoring tools (such as CloudWatch in Amazon EC2 (Amazon)) collect the performance data in terms of computing resource usage and response time. It is lack of effective analysis of these performance parameters and to compare performance behavior between different cloud systems. To address the needs of cloud scalability analysis, we propose a set of metrics for measuring system resources allocation and utilization, system performance and capacities. A radar chart model is used to graphically represent and analyze the multivariate data of performance indicators (Gao, et al., 2011).

3.1 Performance Indicators

As analyzed in (Liu, 2009), there are numerous factors contributing to system performance and scalability, covering all the layers of a system including hardware, system software, application software and their configurations.

Many researchers have discussed the issues, models, metrics, and tools for evaluating system performance and scalability in a distributed and parallel environment. Performance indicators in general can be classified into three categories, as listed below:

1. **Resource Utilization Indicators:** This group of indicators identifies how computing hardware/software resources are allocated and used to accommodate applications' needs, including CPU, disk, memory, network, and other system resources.
2. **Workload Indicators:** This group of indicators identifies the load of system usage in terms of concurrent users, requests and connectivity traffic loads.
3. **Application Performance Indicators:** This group indicates the observed system performance in terms of response time, reliability, availability, etc.

Various metrics can be defined for quantifying the indicators for system performance analysis. For example, Table 2 lists the metrics logged for Performance Tests in Windows Environment.

VWware also defines similar measurements for hypervisor resource monitoring, including CPU, Disk, Memory, Network, System and ClusterService. About 170 metrics are defined in details. For example, the metrics defined for CPU include average, maximum, minimum usage percentage, and the summation of different CPU status such as used, idle, extra, ready, wait, and guaranteed.

For cloud scalability, two groups of indicators are considered for validating applications in the

Table 2. Performance counters for Windows

Performance Object	Performance Counters
Processor	% Processor Time
System	Processor Queue Length
Process	Private Bytes, Thread Count, Virtual Bytes, Working Set
Memory	Available MBytes, Page Reads/sec, Page Write/sec
Physical disk or logical disk	%Idle time; Avg. Disk Read Queue Length; Avg. Disk Write Queue Length; Avg. Disk Bytes/Read; Avg. Disk Bytes/Write; Avg. Disk sec/Read; Avg. Disk sec/Write; Disk Read Bytes/sec; Disk Write Bytes/sec; Disk Bytes/sec; Disk Reads/sec; Disk Writes/sec
Network interface	Bytes Received/sec; Bytes Sent/sec; Bytes Total/sec

Table 3. Sample of performance indicators

Categories	Selected Indicators
Resource Utilization	CPU, Memory, Cache, Disk storage, Network traffic (e.g. network-in and network-out)
Performance	Process speed, system-user-response time, task speed, transaction speed, latency
	Reliability, availability, throughput, and scalability

clouds. Table 3 lists a sample of selected set of indicators.

3.2 Performance Meters Using Radar Chart

We can use radar chart to analyze performance indicators from various perspectives. Indicators are categorized into different groups such as resource, system performance, and system capacity. A group of quantified indicators are uniformed measured and presented on a radar chart. Runtime data are collected by monitoring mechanism to form the observations of system status.

3.2.1 Radar Chart Model

A radar chart is a widely used tool for analyzing multiple quantitative variables in the form of a two-dimensional chart. Starting from the same point, it consists of a sequence of equi-angular spokes. Each spoke represents a variable. The value of the variable is marked on its corresponding spoke in the chart, representing by the length from the central point to the data point, which is proportional to the maximum length of the spoke. A line is drawn connecting all the data values for each spoke, which gives a star-like appearance. A radar chart typically contains many stars on each page with each star representing one observation. Figure 1 gives an example of radar chart. The radar chart contains equi-angular six spokes, representing six variables $\{v_i \mid i = 1, 6\}$. Two starts, p_1 in blue and p_2 in red, represent two observations. They can be compared from six dimensions identified by the six variables.

Observations can be evaluated and compared in two ways. One way is to compare parameters one by one, and the other way is to compare comprehensively using the enclosed area as an indicator. The area of the observation can be calculated as follows where n is number of variables.

$$Area = 0.5 \times \sin(2\pi \,/\, n) \times \sum_{i=1}^{n} p_i \times p_{i+1}$$

Figure 1. Radar chart example

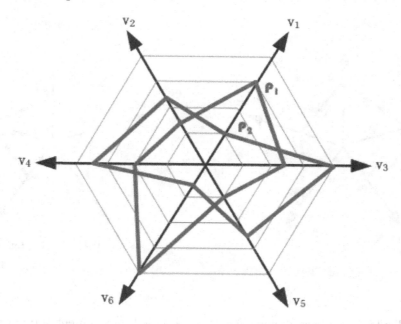

3.2.2 Resource Allocation and Utilization Meters

Given a service S in a cloud, Resource Allocation Meter, denoted as *CRAM(t)*, represents the total amount of resource allocations for S at the evaluating time t. Shown in the radar chart, each spoke represents a source performance indicator including Storage, Memory, CPU, Cache, and Network traffic. Resource allocations are quantified measured and marked on each spoke of indicators. Once the parameters at different spokes are normalized, the total resources allocated to S at time t are computed as the total area of its corresponding irregular polygon in the chart. Figure 2(a) shows an example of the radar chart where five indicators are identified, and the blue polygon represents an observation of the system performance.

Given a service S in a cloud, Resource Utilization Meter, denoted as *CRUM(t)*, represents the percentage of actual used computing resources with respect to allocated resources for S at the evaluating time t. Shown in the radar chart, each spoke represents a source performance indicator as for *CRAM(t)*. The usages of each type of resource are monitored at runtime and marked dynamically on the spokes of the graph. Similar to *CRAM(t)*, *CRUM(t)*, the total resources used by S at time t, can be viewed and computed as the area of corresponding irregular polygon enclosed in the chart. Figure 2(b) shows corresponding map of resource utilizations for the example in Figure 2(a).

3.2.3 System Load Meter

The system needs to handle various loads including (1) User access load, referring to the number of concurrent users who access the system in a given time unit; (2) Communication traffic load, referring to the amount of incoming and outgoing communication messages and transactions in a given time unit; (3) Data storage access load, referring to the number of database transactions and storage size. We use System Load Meter denoted as *SLM(t)* represents the load of service S in a cloud at time t. Radar chart model can be used

Figure 2. Resource allocation and utilization meters using radar chart model

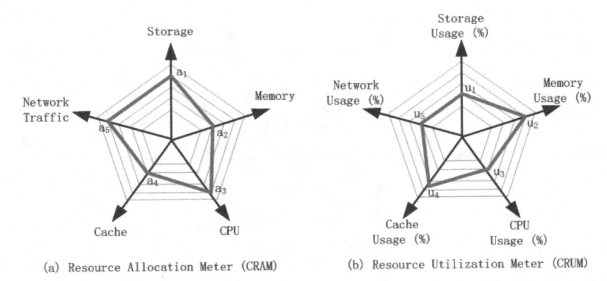

(a) Resource Allocation Meter (CRAM)　(b) Resource Utilization Meter (CRUM)

to analyze system load from the three dimensions, as shown in Figure 3.

3.2.4 System Performance Meter

Given a service S in a cloud, System Performance Meter, denoted as *SPM(t)*, evaluates its runtime behavior at time t against its QoS and SLA requirements. In general, users care more about external observable service properties such as availability and reliability. However, due to the dynamics of

the cloud environment, service performance may be affected by many uncertainties. For example, resources may be allocated following a usage-based approach. For an abrupt large fluctuation of requests, resource scheduler may have certain delay in response, resulting in temporarily performance degradation. *SPM(t)* shows how well a service S satisfies its performance expectations for any observation at time t. Similar to others, Figure 4 shows an example of SPM radar graph.

3.3 Scalability Measurement

As Bondi discussed (2000), "Scalability is the capability to increase resource to yield a linear (ideally) increases in service capacity. The key characteristic of a scalable application is that additional load only requires additional resources rather than extensive modification of the application itself." Customers who deploy their applications in the cloud usually have following concerns of cloud and system scalabilities:

Figure 3. System load meters

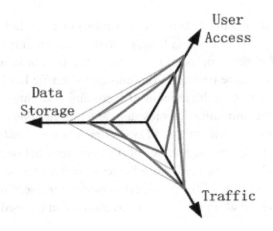

- How well does the cloud handle various load given different resource utilizations?

Figure 4. System load meters

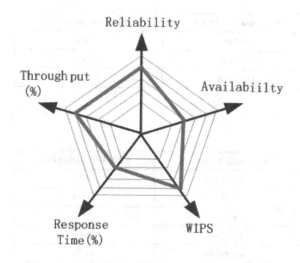

- How well does the infrastructure provider allocate (reclaim) resources timely when load increases (decreases)?
- How well does the application perform in terms of performance metrics for given system capacity?

Based on the meters above, we define a set of metrics for scalability analysis. Given a time period $[t_1, t_2]$, the scalability is defined as the change of system status from t_1 to t_2, where system status is calculated by the indicators and/or meters of system load, performance, and resource utilization. That is:

$$Scale_{pv}(t_1, t_2) =$$

$$\frac{\left(\dfrac{PSM_{pv}(t_2)}{SPM_{pv}(t_i)} * \prod_{i=1}^{m} \dfrac{SLM_{lv_i}(t_2)}{SLM_{lv_i}(t_1)} \right)}{\left(\prod_{j=1}^{n} \dfrac{CRAM_{uv_j}(t_2) * CRUM_{uv_j}(t_2)}{CRAM_{uv_j}(t_1) * CRUM_{uv_j}(t_1)} \right)}$$

Here, pv, lv_j and uv_k refer to a particular variable of performance meters, load meters and re-source meters respectively; while m, n are the number of variables in each category.

Following is an example of cloud scalability measurement. The experiments are exercised using Cloudstone performance testing tool (Sobel, 2008). Cloudstone is an open source project from the RADLad at UC Berkeley. It aims to address the performance characteristics of new system architectures and to compare across various development stacks. A benchmark toolkit is built using Olio (2011) and Faban (2011). Olio is an open source web application of social-event calendar system. Faban is a Markov-based workload generator, and automation tool to execute Olio following different workload patterns on various platforms. The experiment is carried on Amazon EC2 platform using EC2 infrastructure service. EC2 supports different size of VM instances, as shown in Table 4.

We run Cloudstone on different types of EC2 instances, and collect data from following perspectives:

1. System load, in terms of the number of concurrent users.
2. Olio response time of different operations, including HomePage, TagSearch, and EventDetail.
3. Resource utilization, including CPU utilization and memory utilization.

Table 5 and Table 6 show some of the experiment results.

Table 4. Example EC2 instances

VM Instance	Compute Units	Memory	Storage
Small	1	1.7 GB	160 GB
Medium	2	3.75 GB	410 GB
High-CPU Medium	5	1.7 GB	350 GB

Table 5. EC2 performance experiments 1

EC2 Instance Type	System Load (# Users)	Response Time* (s)	CPU Utilization (%)
Small	100	0.190488	62.65
Medium	100	0.071138	37.73
High-CPU Medium	100	0.052415	14.99

Table 6. EC2 performance experiments 2

	EC2 Instance Type	System Load (# Users)	Response Time* (s)	CPU Utilization (%)
L1	High-CPU Medium	100	0.052415	14.99
L2	High-CPU Medium	150	0.045789	21.28
L3	High-CPU Medium	200	0.052415	28.13
L4	High-CPU Medium	250	0.05769	36.00
L5	High-CPU Medium	300	0.098648	44.70

Example 1: We keep the workload the same, while migrating the system from one instance to another.

Response time RT is calculated by geometric average of the response time of different Olio operations rt_{op} as follows:

$$RT = \sqrt[n]{\prod_{i=1}^{n} rt_i} = \sqrt[3]{rt_{HomePage} \times rt_{TagSearch} \times rt_{EventDetail}}$$

1. When migrated from small to medium, the system scalability, with respect to system load, response time, and CPU usage, is

$$\frac{\left(\dfrac{100}{100} \times \dfrac{0.071138}{0.190488}\right)}{\left(\dfrac{2 \times 37.73\%}{1 \times 62.65\%}\right)} = 0.3$$

2. When migrated from medium to high-CPU medium, the scalability is

$$\frac{\left(\dfrac{100}{100} \times \dfrac{0.052415}{0.071138}\right)}{\left(\dfrac{5 \times 14.99\%}{2 \times 37.73\%}\right)} = 0.7$$

Example 2: We change the workload in the system VM instance. The experiment results are shown in Table 6.

Response time RT is calculated by geometric average of the response time of different Olio operations rt_{op} as follows:

$$RT = \sqrt[n]{\prod_{i=1}^{n} rt_i} = \sqrt[3]{rt_{HomePage} \times rt_{TagSearch} \times rt_{EventDetail}}$$

We then calculate the performance changes from one workload to another as follows:

$$S(L1, L2) = \frac{\left(\dfrac{150}{100} \times \dfrac{0.045789}{0.052415}\right)}{\left(\dfrac{350 \times 21.28\%}{350 \times 14.99\%}\right)} = 0.92$$

$$S(L2, L3) = \frac{\left(\frac{200}{150} \times \frac{0.052415}{0.045789}\right)}{\left(\frac{350 \times 28.13\%}{350 \times 21.28\%}\right)} = 1.15$$

$$S(L3, L4) = \frac{\left(\frac{250}{200} \times \frac{0.05769}{0.052415}\right)}{\left(\frac{350 \times 36\%}{350 \times 28.13\%}\right)} = 1.07$$

$$S(L4, L5) = \frac{\left(\frac{300}{250} \times \frac{0.098648}{0.05769}\right)}{\left(\frac{350 \times 44.7\%}{350 \times 36\%}\right)} = 1.65$$

$$S = \sqrt[4]{S(L1, L2) \times S(L2, L3) \times S(L3, L4) \times S(L4, L5)} = 1.17$$

4. AN AGENT-BASED TESTING FRAMEWORK

Workload generation and simulation are critical issues for performance and scalability testing. However, due to the open and dynamic nature of cloud platform, it is hard to simulate diversified system usage scenarios and system workload which may fluctuate dramatically. In our previous research, a MAST (Multi-Agent-based Service Testing) framework was proposed to facilitate service testing using intelligent agent technologies (Bai, et al., 2006; Bai, et al., 2011). Agents are characterized by persistence, autonomy, social ability and reactivity (Rao, 2000; Wooldridge & Jennings, 1995). Groups of agents can interact and collaborate with each other to form a multi-agent system (MAS). MAST examines agent-based modeling and simulation techniques to accommodate dynamic changes in the system under

test. In the rest of this chapter, we introduce the design of intelligent model of MAST test agents, and a two-level adaptive control architecture of load simulation for performance testing.

4.1 An Example of Adaptive Load Generation

SPECWeb is a widely used benchmark for web server performance testing, developed by the Standard Performance Evaluation Corporation (SPEC). It measures web server performance by simulating concurrent user sessions and representative usage scenarios. Web Server Performance is measured by the number of bytes received, the response time, and the QoS criteria such as Time_Good, Time_Tolerable, or Time_Fail. Take the Support package as an example the load for performance testing is generated by following parameters.

1. **Number of Simultaneous Sessions:** The sessions are allocated to a group of distributed clients identified URI. The number of sessions to run on each client can be individually defined or evenly distributed.

2. **Mix of Operations:** Each session emulates a sequence of web operations including "home," "search," "catalog," "product," "fileCatalog,", "file," and "download." SPECWeb uses Markov Chain to model the transition probability between operations. Table 7 shows a typical load profile of page mix percentage.

3. **Number of File Directories for Download:** Support allows for scalable file set configuration, by which the number of total file directories is a function of the requested number of simultaneous connections, as calculated below. Users can configure different parameters for the base number of directories BaseNumDirs, and directory scaling factor DirScaling:

TotalBaseDirs = BaseNumDirs
+ (Simultaneous_Sessions*DirScaling)

4. **File Size:** The size of download data is decided by the number of files under each directory and the size of each file. For example, for SPECWeb09 Support, each directory consists of 16 file downloads grouped into 6 categories of difference file size, and the size of files in each category stepwise increases.

5. **File Access Frequencies:** Support uses Zipf distribution to simulate the probability to access each directory. Table 8 shows an example of file size and the distribution of access frequencies.

Benchmarks like SPECWeb are used for performance evaluation and comparison across heterogeneous system implementations. A design objective for benchmark load generation is fairness so that system can be comparable with each other. When they are applied to product testing, it usually needs to simulate extreme scenarios to detect software performance issues for further optimization and improvements. In this case, load parameters have to be adjusted. In SPECWeb, the parameters are defined using configuration files such as SPECWeb_Support.config and support_downloads_props.rc. They are defined offline, based on testers' assumptions and experiences. The method is acceptable for performance evaluation of SUT in a relative stable environment. But for performance testing in general, it is hard to estimate exactly the applications' performance and load parameters. During system testing, it needs continuous try and test, to examine system behavior under various conditions. For example, the performance of different operations, operation mixes and data sizes. Based on the observed performance results, load parameters are changed accordingly in subsequent tests. The manual process of tray and test is both time and effort consuming.

We hence propose adaptive load generation to change load parameters at runtime for automatic performance testing. The objective is to analyze system behavior under various load fluctuations, considering different factors that may impact system performance. Each factor is represented by a load parameter. Mechanisms are defined to adjust the parameters to change load online based on previous testing results.

Table 7. SPECWEb support: Workload page mix percentage

Support	Home	Search	Catalog	Product	File Catalog	File	Download
Mix %	8.11%	12.61%	11.71%	24.78%	22.52%	13.51%	6.76%

Table 8. Example of SPECWeb file size and access frequency

SPECWeb						
Directory	0	1	2	3	4	5
File size (Mb)	0.1-0.5	0.6-0.9	1-2.5	4-5.5	10	38
# Files	5	3	4	2	1	1
Stepping increment (Mb)	0.1	0.13	0.5	1.4	N/A	N/A
Target Mix	13.66%	12.61%	28.4%	22.32%	12.5%	10.5%

Given a SUT, suppose the factor that affect system performance are identified by a set of parameters

$$P = \{p^i \mid i = 1, 2, \ldots, n\}$$

We use load profile, LPF_t to denote the setting of load parameters at time t. That is:

$$LPF_t = \langle p_t^1, p_t^2, p_t^3, \ldots, p_t^n, \rangle$$

where p_t^i denotes the value of parameter p^i at time t. Performance testing is driven by a sequence of load profiles, as follows:

$$PerfTest = \{LPF_{t_1}, LPF_{t_2}, \ldots, LPF_{t_m}\}$$

Adaptive load generation is the process to derive the value of a load parameter based on its previous value and testing results, that is:

$$p_{t_{i+1}}^j = f(p_{t_i}^j)$$

Taking the SPECWeb example, it defines QoS (Quality of Service) requirements for each workload in terms of *Time_Good* and *Time_Tolerable* (*Time_Tolerable*>*Time_Good*). For each page, 95% of the page requests are expected to be returned within *Time_Good* and 99% of the requests within *Time_Tolerable*. To test system's compliant to the QoS requirements and extreme load tolerance, it may progressively increase or decrease load following general rules such as follows:

- To increase the number of sessions of T times, in case of over 99% requests are within *Time_Good*. That is:

$$NumSession_{t+1} = T * NumSession_t$$

- To decrease the number of session of T' times, in case over 5% requests are outside *Time_Tolerable*. That is:

$$NumSession_{t+1} = \frac{1}{T'} * NumSession_t$$

4.2 Test Agent Design

Figure 5 shows the architecture of test agents design. Test agents are classified into two categories: test coordinator and test runners. Test coordinator analyzes test requirements, generates test plans including execution schedule and deployment configuration, creates test runners, and allocates test cases to test runners. Test runners accept test cases, carry test cases to target host computers, and exercise test cases on the services under test (SUT). MAST coordinates test agents to flexibly allocate tasks, schedule test plans, and adjust test workloads.

4.2.1 Intelligent Agent Preliminary

Intelligent agents are autonomous software entities that are capable of sensing the environment, re-configuring in response, introspective behavior and learning from history (Ferber, 1999; Rao, 2000; Wooldridge&Jennings, 1995). According to the definition of Wooldridge and Jennings, an agent can behave on its own without external control, and it is able to interact with other agents through certain language. Agents can react to the external environment or carry out a series of goal-directed behaviors.

Many research works have been devoted to the architecture of agent-based systems from various perspectives. An intentional system is always applied to describe agents that behave based on knowledge and goals with intelligence. For example, BDI is a typical model of agents with mental attributes, which represents the information, motivational, and deliberative states of the

Figure 5. Test agent model and architecture

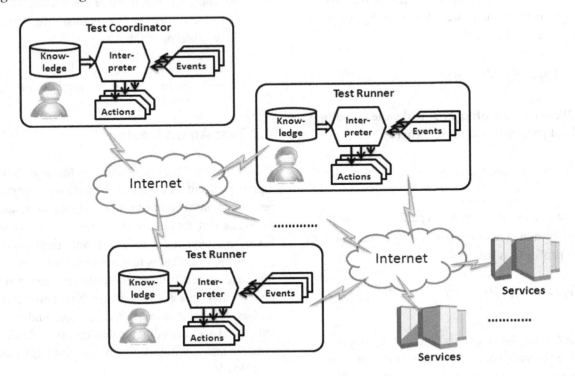

agents. In general, a BDI agent can be defined formally as follows:

Definition 1: A BDI agent is defined to be a tuple:

$$A := \{B, D, I, E, \Phi\}$$

where B is the set of agent's beliefs, which represents the agent's knowledge about external environment and internal agent society. D is the set of goals the agent aims to accomplish. I is the intention set which contains courses of actions an agent is to carry out. E represents the possible events and messages that an agent will receive or send out. Φ is the interpreter that determines agent's lifetime actions based on the four elements defined above.

Rao and Georgeff propose a dynamic data structure to represent agents' beliefs, desires and intentions, with an input query of events, to allow for dynamic updates of the model. The abstract architecture can be described as follows:

```
BDI-interpreter
Initialize-state();
LOOP
  Options:= option-generator(event-
queue);
  Selected-options:=
deliberate(options);
  Update-intentions(selected-op-
tions);
  Execute();
  Get-new-external-events();
  Drop-successful-attitudes();
  Drop-impossible-attitudes();
ENDLOOP
```

Different logic frameworks can be used for reasoning agents' intentions. A first-order logic framework represents beliefs and goals using first-order logic, where a list of intentions are generated during the reasoning process. A decision-tree framework models agent's states as decision/terminal nodes in the tree, where reasoning is the process of decision tree transformations.

Basic BDI model focuses on individual agents' intelligence. It can be extended to enable collective intelligence, that is, the social ability of multi-agents. Collective mental attributes are derived from the combination of individual mental attributes using two mechanisms: social commitments and joint intentions. In a group of collaborating agents, an agent's intentions can be taken as individual commitments to the society, and one's commitments as the intentions for others. To achieve collective intelligence, many architecture are designed such as interaction-based, and BDI extension with communications.

4.2.2 Generic Test Agent

The generic model of test agent is a customized BDI model, taking test-related intelligence into considerations (Ma, et al., 2010). BDI is a typical model of agents with mental attributes, which represents the information, motivational, and deliberative states of the agents. Basic BDI model focuses on individual agents' intelligence. It can be extended to enable collective intelligence, that is, the social ability of multi-agents.

An agent of either type is defined by a 4-tuple as follows:

$$TestAgent := \{K, E, A, \Phi\}$$

where

- $K := \{k_i\}$ is the set of knowledge. Test knowledge represents the necessary information for guiding a testing process, such

as test cases, test objectives, the status of target services and test agents in the society.

- $E := \{e_i\}$ is the set of events that agents receive. An event represents a message of information exchange or a trigger of state changes. Events capture changes in the target system and environment to trigger the adaptation of agent's behavior and test plans.
- $A := \{a_i\}$ is the set of agent actions. Actions are the predefined activities of agents to change test at runtime.
- $\Phi := K \times E \rightarrow A$ is the interpreter that derives an agent's action sequences based on its knowledge and triggering events.

4.2.3 Test Coordinator Design

Coordinator's knowledge is defined by a 4-tuple as follows:

$$K := \{Services, TestCases, Runner, Tasks\}$$

where

- *Services* represent the set of services to be tested.
- *TestCases* is the set of test cases to be assigned to test runner agents.
- $Runners := \{r_i\}$ represent the set of test runner agents under the coordinator's supervision. During testing process, the coordinator tracks runners' status (e.g. active, idle, etc.), controls test execution (e.g. start, stop, etc.), and adjusts task assignments. A runner r_i is defined by its unique identifier and real-time status, as *<ID, state, task>*.
- $Tasks := \{t_i\}$ defines the set of test tasks to be exercised by test runners. A task t_i is decided by a 3-tuple *<sID, tcID, result>*,

where *sID* represents target service to test, *tID* the test case to execute, and *result* the test results. *result* are recorded by pairs of properties and values, as $< p_i^{result}, v_i^{result} >$. For example, the result of performance testing can be represented as

$$\{< response\_time, 10ns >, < throughput, 10MB >\}$$

Three types of triggering events are considered for test coordinators:

1. **Test Tasks Changed:** During testing and re-testing process, there are many cases that test tasks change. For examples, test cases change due to changes in software functionalities or design; test objectives change to meet different validation purposes like performance, robustness and reliability; test resources change such as increased or decreased number of host computers for simulating distributed environment. In case test tasks change, coordinator needs to adjust test plans and runners' configurations.

2. **Runner Agents' Status Changed:** Once migrate to host computers carrying allocated test cases, runners complete their tasks autonomously. Coordinator tracks runners' status, such as their availability, load and testing results, and dynamic adjust task allocations among runners when necessary.

3. **Test Results Collected:** Collaborative runners and coordinators exchange test results information following pre-defined mechanisms. Coordinator synchronizes data from different runners and adjust test strategies.

Table 9 shows some basic events defined for the Coordinator agents. The events that are raised by Coordinator actions are identified as Internal events; while those triggered by Runners are identified as External events. Coordinator controls testing process in an event-driven approach.

Accordingly, three types of coordination actions are defined (see Table 10), including:

1. **Test Tasks Selection:** Coordinator plans test tasks including test data, test cases, test objectives, and etc. Test tasks are organized hierarchically as a task decomposition tree.

2. **Runner Agents Selection:** Coordinator may select agents of different status based on testing needs. For examples, it may create new runner agents or select an idle one for new tasks, or select a working one for adjusted assignments.

3. **Task Allocation:** Coordinator allocates the planned tasks to selected runner agents as necessary.

Table 9. Example coordinator events

Events	Description	Source
TEST_PARSED_OK	Test cases are successfully parsed and ready for creating tasks	Internal
TEST_PARSED_ERROR	Parsing fails	Internal
GENERATE_RUNNER_COMPLETE	Runners are successfully created	Internal
START_TEST	Testing starts	External
RUNNER_OK	The runner is ready	External
RUNNER_NOT_AVAILABLE	The runner is unavailable	External
RUNNER_REQUEST_TASK	A runner raises a request for new task assignment	External
RUNNER_SEND_RESULT	A runner submits testing results	External
RUNNER_UPDATE	A runner updates its state	External

Table 10. Example coordinator actions

Action	Description
GenerateRunner	To create test runners.
DeployRunner	To deploy test runners to host computers.
SelectRunner	To select available test runners to execute specific tasks.
ParseTestScenario	To parse test scenarios.
SelectTestCase	To select test cases for test runners.
AllocateTestTask	To allocate test tasks to test runners.

4.2.4 Test Runner Design

Runners' knowledge is defined by a 3-tuple as follows:

$$K := \{Hosts, Task, Configuration\}$$

where

- *Hosts* is the list of host computers that the runner agents are deployed at, represented by *<URL,resources>*. It tracks available computing resources of each host computer at runtime, such as memory, disk, CPU, and etc, represented by property-value pairs as $< p_i^{host}, v_i^{host} >$. The knowledge is shared by all runner agents. A runner can decide on-the-fly the host that it may be deployed to, in order to get enough resources for carrying out its tasks.
- *Task* is the shared knowledge between runners and coordinators. That is, the runner agent accepts tasks from coordinator about target services and test cases, while it returns test results to the coordinator.
- *Configuration* traces the runner's configuration during its execution history, such as concurrency and load. For example, a runner may migrate to host H1 for load testing with 50 simulated concurrent requests.

When load increases, it migrates to H2 which has more computing resources.

Three types of events are identified as triggers to runners' actions:

1. **Hosts Changed:** It identifies the changes in host computer availability or available computing resources. Computers may be added to, or removed from, test environment. As test progresses, available computing resources also change. Runners need to find the most proper host computers to provide necessary resources.
2. **Task Changed:** The coordinator may change task allocation. For example, it may allocate runners with a new set of test cases for different testing purposes. In this case, a runner needs to change its task with the new set of test cases.
3. **Test Results Changed:** Runner makes decisions of local test case selection and test configuration. Based on previous test results, runner can change its local testing strategies to accomplish its test objectives.

Table 11 lists some basic events defined for Runners. The runner reacts to events coming from its execution environment including the Coordinator and its host computer.

Runners are designed with three types of actions (see Table 12), as follows:

1. **Test Collaboration:** A Runner agent shares knowledge with other runners. Collaboration actions are designed for exchanging information between agents, for example, to exchange tasks, test results, and agent status with each other.
2. **Decision Making:** Runners make flexible local selections of the host, test cases, load, etc, in reaction to changes in test results and test objectives.

Table 11. Example runner events

Events	Description	Source
TASK_ARRIVAL	New tasks are allocated to the runner	External
MIGRATION	Runner is migrated to a new host	External/Internal
TASK_FINISH	Test task accomplished	Internal
RESOURCE_ERROR	Computing resource exceptions	External
HOST_ERROR	Host computer exceptions	External

3. **Test Execution:** Runners carry out activities like exercising test cases, migration, and results collection.

4.3 Performance Testing Architecture

The generic agent design is applied to performance testing with specially designed domain knowledge, events, and rules. Performance testing helps to analyze system behavior under different usage scenarios and workloads. For example, it tests the system's upper limit of capacity and bottlenecks under extreme load. The selection of scenarios and workloads is critical for effective performance analysis. It is always a try-and-test manual process to adjust test selection until the upper bound is detected. With the agent approach, coordinator and runners autonomously adjust test plans based on previous test results.

To separate concerns, a two-layer adaptive control architecture is designed, where a coordinator is responsible for selecting test cases of different complexity levels; and a runner decides the load of concurrencies. Taking the SPECWeb load generation as an example, the complexity of a test case is decided by two factors: operation mix and download size. In general, each operation mix represents a typical usage scenario. Web applications may have various usage patterns such as browse only, heavy search, or heavy download. Test cases are categorized into different classes of usage patterns. They are further ranked within each category based on their simulated load. When allocate tasks to runners, the coordinator decides

Table 12. Example runner actions

Action	Description
AcceptTask	To accept a task
ReturnResult	To return task to coordinator
SyncState	To synchronize with coordinator and other agents
Migrate	To migrate to a host computer
ExecuteTask	To execute a task
CollectResult	To collect test results
SelectHost	To select a host computer
RequireTestTask	To request a task
ConfigTest	To set test configurations

on the parameters like test case operation profiles and the directories to download files. The runners share their joint intentions of QoS goals (e.g. response time and throughput) and test objectives (e.g. extreme testing and load testing). They decide individually the number of simultaneous sessions and synchronized periodically with the server of testing results.

Figure 6 shows the architecture design and general process of agent-based performance testing. Test Coordinator records the allocation of test cases to Runners and test results in terms of QoS satisfaction from each runner in time sequence. Each test cases may contain multiple operations. Test Runner records the performance of each operation under different load settings. Coordinator and Runner maintains individually their rule base to direct load adaptations. The general process is composed of three phases:

1. **Initialization Phase:** The Coordinator initiates a test task, selects test cases and allocates them to test runners.

2. **Iterative Adaptation Phase:** Coordinator and Runner make local decisions to adjust load based on previous test results.

3. **Collaboration Phase:** Coordinator and Runners exchange information. The Coordinator sends command to Runners to reset their tasks. Runners periodically submit test results to the Coordinator for synthesizing results.

The generic process is as follows:

1. The coordinator initiates a test task.
2. The coordinator decides the complexity level of test cases.
3. The coordinator selects corresponding test cases and allocates to test runners.
4. The runner decides the number of concurrencies for test cases of certain complexity level.
5. The runner tests the target software and collects performance results.
6. Repeat 2-5 to find how software performs in reaction to various workloads in general, and to find its performance upper bound in particular.

Figure 6. The two-layer control architecture of performance testing

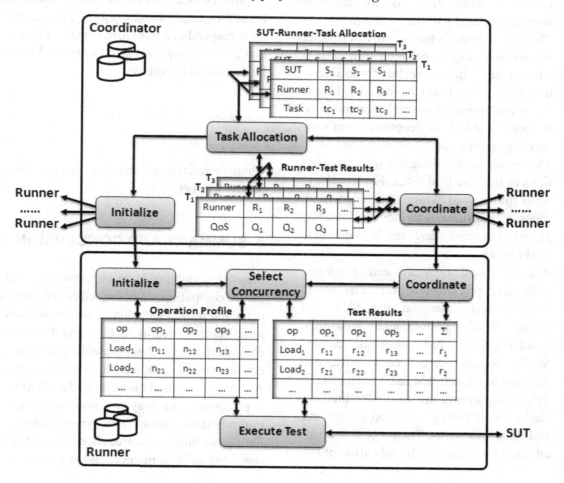

To support the process, specific events, actions and rules are defined for test coordinator and test runner:

- The coordinator categorizes test cases into various complexity levels of range [*cMin,cMax*] where *cMin* stands for simplest and *cMax* for most complicated test case. A state variable *cCur* records current selected complexity level.

- The coordinator is designed with three actions to find the complexity level: *FindComplexity(x,y)* is to find a complexity level within the range [*x,y*]; *IncreaseComplexity(c)* is to increase complexity level *c* by 1; and *DecreaseComplexity(c)* is to decrease complexity level *c* by 1.

- The runner controls the quantity of parallel executions, ranging between [*lMin,lMax*] where *l* marks the parameters for load control, *lMin* is the lower bound and *lMax* is the upper bound of runner's concurrency. A state variable *lCur* denotes current concurrency setting.

- The runner is also designed with three actions to find the load level: *FindLoad(x,y)* is to find a load within the range [*x,y*]; *IncreaseLoad(lCur)* is to increase load *l* by 1; and *DecreaseLoad(lCur)* is to decrease load *l* by 1.

- Actions *FindComplexity* and *FindLoad* both have precedent action Tests which exercise test cases on the SUT and gather SUT's performance indicators. *FindComplexity* has successor actions *SetCur* to set current complexity, and *Allocate* to allocate test cases to runners.

- Triggering events are also identified including start testing, overload exceptions, and light load status. The process is divided into two phases: 1) Initialization phase.

The coordinator first searches for the maximum test case complexity to cause overload exceptions. In this phase, runners do not set their concurrency loads; 2) Iterative adaptation phase. The runner adjusts its load setting to find the software's performance extremes. Whenever an overload occurs but the runner's load is decreased to its minimum, the runner sends a decrease-request to the coordinator to decrease test case complexity level. On the other hand, when the load is increased to runner's maximum, it sends an increase-request to the coordinator. It progressively finds load for any complexity level.

In this way, the overall workload is defined by a list of 2-tuples, <*complexity,load*>, each complexity is mapped to a workload *w* using a formula *f*, that is *w=f(complexity)*, the total workload can be calculated as follows:

$$workload = \sum_{i=cMin}^{cMax} f(c_i) \times l_i$$

where *f* represents a formula which maps a complexity to workload.

5. SUMMARY AND CONCLUSION

Massive scalability is an important demand for cloud computing. Without effective measurement and testing techniques, we cannot turn the promises into a reality. The chapter discusses the characteristics of cloud scalability compared to conventional distributed and parallel computing. An analysis method based on Radar Chart model is proposed to view system runtime status from multiple dimensions. Three types of meters are defined including resource allocation and utilization, system performance, and system capacity.

Based on the meters defined, cloud scalability are measure from three perspectives including capacity scalability, load scalability and system performance scalability.

Testing is one of the key method to evaluate system scalability against the defined metrics. To address the dynamic problem of cloud performance testing, an agent-based framework is proposed with a two-level adaptive control architecture. Taking the advantages of agent autonomous and collaborative capabilities, the agent-based testing framework can simulate scalable workload, which are dynamic adjusted in response to observed system performance. The chapter introduces the basic design of agent intelligent model and its applications to performance testing.

Cloud scalability is affected by my factors that interact with each other. The scaling policies usually reflect the tradeoffs among resource utilization, system performance, and cost. Hence, new scalability measurements are necessary to take considerations of multi-dimensional performance concerns and their impacts on each other. To test cloud scalability with complex indicators and large scales, it needs a scalable testing framework as well so that it can simulate diversified usage scenarios and validate system performance under various scenarios.

REFERENCES

Amazon. (n.d.). *Amazon web service*. Retrieved from http://aws.amazon.com/

Bai, X., Chen, B., Ma, B., & Gong, Y. (2011). Design of intelligent agent for collaborative testing of service-based systems. *International Workshop on Automation of Software Test* (pp. 22-28).

Bai, X., Dai, G., Xu, D., & Tsai, W.-T. (2006). A multi-agent based framework for collaborative testing on web services. *International Workshop on Collaborative Computing, Integration, and Assurance* (pp. 205-210).

Bai, X., Li, M., Chen, B., Gao, J., & Tsai, W. T. (2011). A survey of cloud testing tools. *International Symposium on Service Oriented System Engineering* (pp. 1-12).

Bai, X., Wang, Y., Dai, G., Tsai, W.-T., & Chen, Y. (2007). A framework for contract-based collaborative verification and validation of web services. *International Conference on Component-Based Software Engineering* (pp. 258-273).

Binnig, C., Kossmann, D., Kraska, T., & Loesing, S. (2009). How is the weather tomorrow? Towards a benchmark for the cloud. *International Workshop on Testing Database Systems* (pp. 9:1–9:6).

Bondi, A. B. (2000). Characteristics of scalability and their impact on performance. *International Workshop on Software and Performance* (pp. 195-203). ACM Press.

Brataas, G., & Hughes, P. (2004). Exploring architectural scalability. *International Workshop on Software and Performance* (pp. 125-129). ACM Press.

Chen, Y., & Sun, X. (2006). STAS: A scalability testing and analysis system. *IEEE International Conference on Cluster Computing* (pp. 1-10).

Duboc, L., Rosenblum, D. S., & Wicks, T. (2006). A framework for modelling and analysis of software systems scalability. *International Conference on Software Engineering* (pp. 949-952). ACM Press.

Faban Harness and Benchmark Framework. (2011). Retrieved from http://java.net/projects/faban/

Ferber, J. (1999). *Multi-agent systems: An introduction to distributed artificial intelligence*. Addison-Wesley Professional.

Gao, J., Bai, X., & Tsai, W. T. (2011). Cloud testing – Issues, challenges, needs and practice. *Software Engineering: An International Journal*, *1*(1), 9–23.

Gao, J., Pattabhiraman, P., Bai, X., & Tsai, W. T. (2011). SaaS performance and scalability evaluation in cloud. *International Symposium on Service Oriented System Engineering* (pp.61-71).

Garber, L. (2011). News briefs. *Computer, 44*(6), 18–20. doi:10.1109/MC.2011.185

Grama, A. Y., Gupta, A., & Kumar, V. (1993). Isoefficiency: Measuring the scalability of parallel algorithms and architectures. *IEEE Parallel and Distributed Technology, 1*(3), 12–21. doi:10.1109/88.242438

Hill, M. D. (1990). What is scalability? *SIGARCH Computer Architecture News, 18*(4), 18–21. doi:10.1145/121973.121975

Jamal, M. H., Qadeer, A., Mahmood, W., Waheed, A., & Ding, J. J. (2009). Virtual machine scalability on multi-core processors based servers for cloud computing workloads. *International Conference on Networking, Architecture, and Storage* (pp. 90-97).

Jogalekar, P., & Woodside, M. (2000). Evaluating the scalability of distributed systems. *IEEE Transactions on Parallel and Distributed Systems, 11*(6), 589–603. doi:10.1109/71.862209

Kumar, V., & Gupta, A. (1994). Analyzing the scalability of parallel algorithms and architectures: A survey. *Journal of Parallel and Distributed Computing, 22*(3), 379–391. doi:10.1006/jpdc.1994.1099

Li, A., Yang, X., Kandula, S., & Zhang, M. (2010). CloudCmp: Comparing public cloud providers. *Internet Measurement Conference* (pp. 1-14).

Liu, H. H. (2009). *Software performance and scalability*. New Jersey: John Wiley & Sons, Inc. doi:10.1002/9780470465394

Lyon, G., Kacker, R., & Linz, A. (1995). A scalability test for parallel code. *Software, Practice & Experience, 25*(12), 1299–1314. doi:10.1002/spe.4380251202

Ma, B., Chen, B., Bai, X., & Huang, J. (2010). Design of BDI agent for adaptive performance testing of web services. *International Conference on Quality Software* (pp. 435–440).

Molyneaux, I. (2009). *The art of application performance testing*. Sebastopol, CA: O'Reilly Media, Inc.

Moreno, J. (2010). *A testing framework for cloud storage systems*. Master thesis, Swiss Federal Institute of Technology Zurich.

Olio. (2011). Retrieved from http://incubator.apache.org/olio/

Rao, A. S., & Georgeff, M. P. (2000). BDI agents: From theory to practice. *International Conference on Multi-Agent Systems* (pp. 312–319).

Rimal, B. P., Eunmi, C., & Lumb, I. (2009). A taxonomy and survey of cloud computing systems. *International Joint Conference on INC, IMS and IDC* (pp. 44-51).

Salesforce Usage Trends. (2011). Retrieved from http://trends.builtwith.com/analytics/Salesforce

Sobel, W., Subramanyam, S., Sucharitakul, A., Nguyen, J., Wong, H., & Patil, S. … Patterson, D. (2008). CloudStone: Multi-platform, multi-language benchmark and measurement tools for Web 2.0. *Proceedings of the 1st International Workshop on Cloud Computing and its Applications*.

Steen, M. V. Van der zijden, S., & Sips, H. J. (1998). Software engineering for scalable distributed applications. *International Computer Software and Applications Conference* (pp. 285-292).

Sun, X. H., & Ni, L. M. (1993). Scalable problems and memory-bounded speedup. *Journal of Parallel and Distributed Computing, 19*(1), 27–37. doi:10.1006/jpdc.1993.1087

Taobao. (2011). Retrieved from http://www.taobao.com/

Tsai, W. T., Chen, Y., Paul, R., Liao, N., & Huang, H. (2004). Cooperative and group testing in verification of dynamic composite web services. *Workshop on Quality Assurance and Testing of Web-Based Applications* (pp. 170–173).

Tsai, W. T., Paul, R., Yu, L., Saimi, A., & Cao, Z. (2003). Scenario-based web service testing with distributed agents. *IEICE Transaction on Information and System. E (Norwalk, Conn.)*, *86-D*(10), 2130–2144.

Wickremasinghe, B., Calheiros, R. N., & Buyya, R. (2010). CloudAnalyst: A CloudSim-based visual modeller for analysing cloud computing environments and applications. *International Conference on Advanced Information Networking and Applications* (pp. 446-452).

Wooldridge, M., & Jennings, N. R. (1995). Intelligent agents: Theory and practice. *The Knowledge Engineering Review, 10*(2), 115–152. doi:10.1017/S0269888900008122

Yigitbasi, N., Iosup, A., Epema, D., & Ostermann, S. (2009). C-Meter: A framework for performance analysis for computing clouds. *IEEE/ACM International Symposium on Cluster Computing and the Grid* (pp. 472-477).

Chapter 18
Building a Cloud–Based Mobile Application Testbed

Hamilton Turner
Virginia Polytechnic Institute, USA

Jules White
Virginia Polytechnic Institute, USA

Jeff Reed
Virginia Polytechnic Institute, USA

José Galindo
Virginia Polytechnic Institute, USA

Adam Porter
University of Maryland, USA

Madhav Marathe
Virginia Polytechnic Institute, USA

Anil Vullikanti
Virginia Polytechnic Institute, USA

Aniruddha Gokhale
Vanderbilt University, USA

ABSTRACT

A proliferation of mobile smartphone platforms, including Android devices, has triggered a rise in mobile application development for a diverse set of situations. Testing of these smartphone applications can be exceptionally difficult, due to the challenges of orchestrating production-scale quantities of smartphones such as difficulty in managing thousands of sensory inputs to each individual smartphone device. This work presents the Android Tactical Application Assessment and Knowledge (ATAACK) Cloud, which utilizes a cloud computing environment to allow smartphone-based security, sensing, and social networking researchers to rapidly use model-based tools to provision experiments with a combination of 1,000+ emulated smartphone instances and tens of actual devices. The ATAACK Cloud provides a large-scale smartphone application research testbed.

DOI: 10.4018/978-1-4666-2536-5.ch018

INTRODUCTION

Emerging Trends and Challenges for Mobile and Social Computing Researchers

A growing trend in computing systems is the use of smartphone computing platforms, such as Google Android, the iPhone, and Windows Phone 7, as the basis of distributed mobile and social applications. This trend towards the use of smartphone platforms has been driven, in part, by their fast proliferation. For example, in the 3Q of 2010, Apple shipped approximately 2 million PCs and the largest market share holder, HP, shipped 4.59 million (Chou, O'Donnell, & Shrirer, 2010). During that same quarter, Apple shipped over almost 13.5 million iOS devices and other manufacturers shipped 20.5 million Android devices (Tudor & Pettey, 2010). Both smartphone computing platforms sold 3 to 4 times as many devices as the leading PC manufacturer.

A diverse set of research communities has begun intensive exploration into the ramifications of the ubiquitous computing environment created by the pervasiveness of smartphones. For example, researchers are investigating the intersections of mobile computing and social networks using a variety of techniques (N Eagle & Pentland, 2005; Kempe, Kleinberg, & Tardos, 2003; Miluzzo et al., 2008). Security researchers are looking at the ramifications of emerging malware threats to mobile computing platforms (H. Kim, Smith, & Shin, 2008; Lawton, 2008; Leavitt, 2005). Other investigators have focused on mechanisms to monitor the physical world using mobile crowdsourcing (Alt, Shirazi, Schmidt, Kramer, & Nawaz, 2010; Nathan Eagle, 2009; T. Yan, Marzilli, Holmes, Ganesan, & Corner, 2009), citizen scientists (Aoki et al., 2008; Burke et al., 2006), and opportunistic sensing (A T Campbell, Eisenman, & Lane, 2008; Mohan, Padmanabhan, & Ramjee, 2008; Tong, Zhao, & Adireddy, 2003).

Although there are a large number of research communities that are investigating smartphone-based computing paradigms, researchers are limited in the scale and accuracy of the systems that they can build, emulate, and test (Ahmed Alazzawe, Alazzawe, Wijesekera, & Dantu, 2009; Chintapatla, Goulart, & Magnussen, 2010; Heo, Terada, Toyama, Kurumatani, & Chen, 2010; Rensfelt, Hermans, Gunningberg, & Larzon, 2010). Static distributed computing testbeds, such as Emulab, exist to provide a mechanism for testing various network protocols, middleware and other predefined static features (Burtsev, Radhakrishnan, Hibler, & Lepreau, 2009; Casanova, 2002; Hibler et al., 2008; K. H. Kim, 1989; Matos & Grasser, 2010; Zhang, Freschl, & Schopf, 2003). Mobile computing environments, however, are subject to additional constraints that make using static computing environments to simulate mobile computing environments inaccurate. Static distributed computing testbeds are not effective for simulating mobile device interactions for the following reasons:

- *Device location and context can significantly impact application behavior.* Performance is affected by the current physical position of mobile devices in the network. Existing distributed experimentation platforms are focused on emulating or providing static resources, such as blade servers. Context, however, has a major impact on mobile devices and software. Mobile computing experimentation environments must be able to account for changes in context to provide realistic results.
- *Social networks dynamically change the interaction of applications.* In most existing distributed testbeds, communication patterns are fairly static and do not dynamically change based on an underlying social network. The communication be-

tween mobile devices is heavily influenced by the user's social network and behavior, which co-evolves with the communication network. Events occurring in either the social network or trigger secondary events to occur in both the original network and in other communication channels. Building and simulating these dynamic realistic social networks for experimentation is challenging.

- *Wireless protocols and approaches have a large influence on performance.* Real-world mobile devices are constantly dealing with changing signal conditions, lost packets, and other communication challenges. It is difficult to accurately simulate and predict how a given set of wireless protocols and communication technologies will impact mobile application performance.

- *Network failures can often lead to unexpected issues.* Network failures, especially the loss of nodes (including losses due to natural or man-made disasters) can lead to unforeseen consequences that are only revealed for large-scale experimentation. Understanding the failure modes and potential responses to the failure modes can help in retuning the network to adjust to losses infrastructure.

Solution Approach: The Android ATAACK Cloud

To facilitate the rapid development, refinement, and validation of smartphone-based security, sensing, and social networking research, we are developing the Android Tactical Application Assessment and Cloud Knowledge (ATAACK). The goal of the ATAACK Cloud is to provide a cloud computing environment that allows smartphone-based security, sensing, and social networking researchers to rapidly use model-based tools to provision experiments with a combination of 1,000+

emulated smartphone instances and tens of actual devices. The cloud will allow researchers to access a large-scale mobile research testbed that provides a novel combination of scale, realism from real-world device integration, software-defined radio nodes, and social/mobility network modeling and control. The emulation capabilities are based on the Android mobile device emulator, which provides a virtualized mobile device instance that runs the actual Android kernel, middleware, and software applications.

The ATAACK Cloud is a project that has been funded by the Air Force Research Laboratories and is a joint collaboration between Virginia Tech, the University of Maryland, and Vanderbilt University. This chapter describes prior work in the area of large-scale testing, the gaps in applying these existing techniques to large-scale mobile application testing, and the architecture of the cloud-based mobile application testing platform that we are developing.

A key attribute of the ATAACK Cloud will be its combined cyber and physical emulation capability will allow a wide range of researchers to precisely measure smartphone system phenomena at scale on a variety of middleware and hardware versions. A key component of the ATAACK Cloud is a hybrid experimentation environment that allows integrating real smartphone devices and software-defined radio protocols with emulated smartphone instances that receive environmental inputs, such as GPS coordinates and accelerometer values. This environment will allow researchers to validate key theoretical models and ideas, such as mathematical models predicting the spread of malware based on social network topology, with a combination of the scale provided by a 1,000 or more emulated devices and the real-world accuracy obtained from integrating actual device software and hardware.

When the ATAACK Cloud is completed, it will provide the following contributions to mobile computing research and simulation:

- Fast model-driven multi-application experimentation provisioning capabilities that will allow developers to analyze research ideas and theoretical models of mobile computing paradigms early in the investigation process.
- Hybrid experimentation with real and emulated devices that will simultaneously provide experimentation accuracy and scale.
- Pluggable social and mobility network simulation models that can adapt application interactions on-the-fly.
- An integrated software-defined radio testbed that will allow experiments to incorporate next-generation wireless communication techniques.

MOTIVATING MALWARE EXAMPLE

Increasing numbers of smart phones, lack of awareness regarding securing them, and access to personal and proprietary information, has resulted in the recent surge of mobile malware—viruses, worms, spam and other malicious software—that targets these devices (Havlin, 2009; Piercy, 2004; Steve, 2004; Töyssy & Helenius, 2006; Wilson & York, 2011). Traditional social-engineering techniques such as email and file-sharing, as well as vectors unique to mobile devices such as Bluetooth, Short Messaging Service (SMS) and Multimedia Messaging Service (MMS) are used by these malware (Bose & Shin, 2006; Dagon, Martin, & Starner, 2004; Mulliner & Vigna, 2006; Su et al., 2006; Wang, Gonzalez, Hidalgo, & Barabasi, 2009). By March 2008, F-Secure had counted 401 different types of mobile malware in the wild, and McAfee had counted 457 (Lawton, 2008). A recent survey by (Credant Technologies, 2009) shows poor smart phone security attitudes among mobile phone users. While 12% of those surveyed stored bank account details, 5% stored credit card information on mobile phones, and 1% even stored their pin and passwords.

A key challenge is in understanding how malware spreads and differing mechanisms of attack. Ideally, researchers should be able to setup a large-scale experiment where they release customized malware onto a large set of controlled mobile devices and track its spread and actions (Cai, Machiraju, & Chen, 2009; Enck, Ongtang, & McDaniel, 2009; Laurendeau & Barbeau, 2006; Provos & Holz, 2007). In order to understand how the malware affects the network of mobile devices, researchers need to be able to track its spread across a set of mobile devices at realistic scale and extrapolate key properties (Liu, Yan, Zhang, & Chen, 2009; A Shabtai et al., 2010). For example, researchers must be able to:

- Understand what communication protocols are utilized by the malware, packet inspection approaches that could detect it, and the resource usage ramifications of 1,000s of infected devices. Simple experiments using a few dozen to a few hundred device instances may not utilize communication protocols, applications, and middleware sufficiently to reveal important patterns.
- Ensure the fidelity of their validating experiments with respect to real mobile usage environments. Often, the assumptions about system behavior that are made in emulated or simulated environments do not hold true for real systems. For example, developers may make assumptions about the latency of device communication links and how these links influence the possibility of malware denial-of-service attacks. In low signal strength environments, such as urban environments, unexpected influences, such as interference from buildings, may create different resource utilization and denial-of-service capabilities than expected.

- Evaluate how new wireless communication and next-generation networking protocols will be impacted and can be attacked by malware. As new types of wireless communication protocols and standards are researched and developed, researchers must be able to determine how they will be impacted by different modes of attack. In order to answer these questions, researchers must be able to not only conduct large-scale malware experiments but also to experiment with how differing wireless and networking protocols impact spread, discoverability, and resource utilization.

Without a cloud infrastructure to emulate 1,000 or more malware infected mobile smartphones producing and consuming data, designers cannot determine how the malware will impact network resources, such as response time and throughput, or how well detection techniques perform. Emulation alone, however, does not provide sufficient accuracy for a firm understanding of malware affects and attack vectors (Fitzek & Reichert, 2007; Fritsch, Ritter, & Schiller, 2006). Experimentation and capture of data from real devices is needed to ensure experiment fidelity with real user environments. Therefore, designers need the ability to create experiments that can emulate 1,000s of handheld devices to achieve realistic scale and simultaneously integrate real smartphones to ensure experiment accuracy.

Since malware typically makes heavy use of communication infrastructure, developers need the ability to determine the impact that malware will have on next generation communication protocols, such as 4G, and the protocol implementations in mobile devices, applications, and middleware. Creating experiments that integrate new wireless protocols is not easy, however, due to the lack of testbeds that provide support for a combination of emulation, real handheld devices, and configurable wireless infrastructure, such as software-defined radios. Existing testbeds typically support only

one of these capabilities. This lack of testbeds with support for all of these capabilities forces researchers to wait until systems are fielded to determine how malware and other security threats will affect them.

OVERVIEW OF CURRENT LARGE-SCALE TESTING TECHNOLOGIES

Researching large-scale smartphone-based systems for security, social networking, mobile sensing, and other disciplines is a particularly vexing challenge due to the complexity of building realistic large-scale experiments (Hu, Zuo, Kaabouch, & Chen, 2010; Oberheide, Veeraraghavan, Cooke, Flinn, & Jahanian, 2008; Asaf Shabtai & Elovici, 2010; B. Zheng, Xiong, Zhang, & Lin, 2006). As shown in Figure 1, existing approaches for validating systems fail to simultaneously provide four key capabilities needed to validate large-scale smartphone-based systems:

Challenge 1: *Lack of scalable approaches for orchestrating realistic usage and interactions of multiple heterogeneous smartphone applications in a simulated environment.* Existing test systems for mobile applications are not designed to orchestrate, instrument, and analyze the interaction of multiple smartphone applications on hundreds or thousands of phones. Application unit and regression testing is possible, but these systems are designed to demonstrate the correctness of build and unit testing processes and to provide limited information on application behavior only in an isolated environment. In order to validate complex properties of mobile social networking, malware propagation, and other topics, developers need tools that allow them to rapidly model, provision, and execute experiments that involve the realistic coordination of multiple applications on a large set

Figure 1. Solution architecture

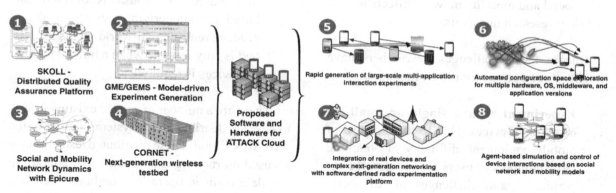

of smartphones. Manual methods for building experiments that incorporate multiple applications and hundreds or thousands of nodes do not scale.

Challenge 2: *Inability to create hybrid validation experiments that combine both large-scale smartphone emulation and real smartphone hardware and users.* Many cloud computing testbeds exist for emulating hundreds or thousands of OS instances. A key capability that these platforms lack is a facility for building experiments that combine emulated smartphone instances with real smartphone and wireless sensor network hardware (Cheng, Wong, Yang, & Lu, 2007; Frederick & Lal, 2007). This lack of an integration facility for including real-world hardware prevents smartphone and wireless researchers from understanding the effects of data from real usage patterns, such as driving through varying cellular coverage areas and hardware. Often, data streams and inputs from real- world hardware uncover design flaws in theoretical models that are difficult to find with purely simulation or emulation-based experiments. Conversely, experimentation solely with real hardware makes achieving the large-scale needed to accurately understand group dynamics and unveil emergent properties infeasible for routine testing.

Challenge 3: *Complexity of verifying and validating applications on multiple software/hardware platforms and versions.* Smartphones do not provide developers with a single unified target platform for development (Oliver, 2009, 2010; A.-D. Schmidt et al., 2009; Teng & Helps, 2010). Applications need to be tested on multiple versions of both the Android OS, supporting applications, and underlying hardware. There are significant variations in version/platform capabilities. This platform variability makes correct configuration of experiment applications, middleware, and emulated hardware challenging. Modeling and automation techniques are needed that can help developers to rapidly derive and test correct experiment configurations of smartphone middleware and applications.

Challenge 4: *Lack of methods for dynamically altering communication and interaction patterns based on social, proximity, and other network models.* Mobile device communication is tightly bound to the social network of the user and the other devices that are within range of the device (e.g. Bluetooth, WiFi). As the device moves through the world, the nearby devices that it interacts with change over time. Moreover, change in the user's social network can dynamically change the dominant communication endpoints. Developers need ways of determining how these social and mobility network effects impact key research questions.

Due to these challenges, researchers have roughly three options for experimentation:

- **Experiment with a single or small set of actual devices.** Due to the expense of mobile equipment, difficulty of obtaining large numbers of users for coordinated experiments, and challenges of real-world experiment setup, the number of physical devices that can be used to experiment is limited. This is particularly problematic since mobile computing environments traditionally involve large numbers of interacting devices.
- **Simulate a large-scale mobile system without actually executing real mobile software applications.** Simulation allows developers to test theories regarding social networks and human interaction without requiring the purchase, setup and coordination of physical devices. Unfortunately, the ability to capture real-world data using simulations alone is limited. Certain mobile computing characteristics, such as the impact of device software design and location based connectivity cannot be determined without tapping into a physical device. Many mobile computing problems, such as virus propagation between mobile devices, require real-world information that cannot be determined without accessing a physical device.
- **Execute real mobile application software on a small number of mobile device emulators.** Mobile platform emulators, such as the Google Android Emulator, allow researchers to accurately analyze how software will behave from a functional perspective on real hardware (Matos & Grasser, 2010). However, constructing experiments that orchestrate the interactions

of hundreds or thousands of emulators based on an underlying social network and produce realistic real-world inputs for context is only feasible when a limited number of devices is required.

There are a number of related existing efforts to develop distributed test systems similar to the ATAACK Cloud. These distributed testbeds have focused on running experiments that attempt to simulate realistic operating conditions across a series of networked computing nodes. Although these prior test platforms appear similar at first glance, they are not ideally suited for understanding large-scale mobile computing scenarios. Below, we discuss the suitability of each of these prior efforts and how the challenges of understanding mobile malware manifest in each system.

Network Emulation Testbeds

Many different testbeds have been developed to conduct research in networking and distributed computing. In particular, we provide a brief overview of Emulab (www.emulab.net), PlanetLab (www.planet-lab.org/) and GENI (www.geni.net/).

The Emulab testbed was originally developed at University of Utah and funded by the National Science Foundation (NSF) as an experimental platform to conduct research in advanced networking concepts, which is open to the scientific community. Users are required to create Emulab accounts and be part of official projects that are added upon requests by principal investigators. Users use the Emulab API to reserve resources in the testbed, set up the desired networking topology, define the operating systems and protocol stacks running on the reserved nodes, as well as configure the bandwidths, delays characteristics and loss rates of the communication links. The Emulab model has proven to be a significant success and several clones of Emulab have been developed. Despite its significant impact in evaluating new ideas, Emulab is based entirely on emulation, and moreover, highly accurate emulation of complex wireless protocols and mobile environments remains hard.

PlanetLab is another capability available to researchers to conduct research in networking and distributed computing, particularly, peer-to-peer computing and distributed storage. In contrast to Emulab, which has all its resources at one location, the PlanetLab requires institutions wishing to use the PlanetLab to also contribute both the computing and communication resources. At last count, PlanetLab had 1,120 nodes distributed across 510 sites worldwide. Users wishing to use PlanetLab resources require a user account, and use the API to request a slice. A slice is an abstraction of resources that is assigned to users to conduct experiments. PlanetLab has primarily been used as a vehicle to experiment with network overlays and multimedia streaming applications on a wired, wide area network. It is therefore hard to effectively use PlanetLab for experimentation with pervasive mobile devices, such as smartphones.

The Global Environment for Network Innovations (GENI) is a project also sponsored by NSF to conduct research on the next generation Internet architecture. The motivation behind setting up this capability was to foster new ideas in the design and implementation of the next generation of the Internet architecture. It was observed that retrofitting existing protocol stacks with new capabilities that are needed to keep pace with user demands was becoming infeasible. Hence a complete redesign of the internet was deemed necessary, which led to the formation of a testbed that can be used to test new ideas that are not possible to test with existing networks and testbeds. GENI is primarily interested in testing ideas for future networking technologies. Our aim is to experiment with both wireless communication technologies and large-scale malware infestations, which is outside the scope of GENI's focus on networking.

Simulation Environments

A number of mathematical and simulation-based approaches have been proposed to study epidemiological problems in wireless networks (Rhodes & Nekovee, 2008). Analytical models such as the one presented by (G. Yan & Eidenbenz, 2006) and (Mickens & Noble, 2007) can be used to predict worm spread. Simulations such as the ones presented by (Su et al., 2006; G. Yan & Eidenbenz, 2006; G. Yan et al., 2007) can also be used. Analytical models based on mathematical epidemiology provide a natural way to study large systems and have a number of desirable features, such as, closed form expressions for important epidemic quantities, e.g. total number of infected devices. Nevertheless, these models make a number of crucial assumptions (e.g. complete mixing, low resolution malware models) that do not hold in the real world. Detailed simulations that build on well-known network simulators such as NS-2 (Information Sciences Institute, n.d.) or Qualnet (Scalable Network Technologies, n.d.) provide a natural alternative. These simulators allow for a quick and easy implementation and evaluation of the worm, and have been used in a number of recent studies. Researchers can create different network topologies and observe the growth of an infection with these simulators. (G. Yan et al., 2007) use random networks with random mobility models and (Su et al., 2006) use traces from real Bluetooth activity at locations for the study. Recent research has considered real data from a mobile phone network to construct mobility and calling patterns to discover social networks and study the malware propagation. The granularity of the mobility is at the level of cell towers and within each tower's area they consider a uniform distribution of devices and construct the network based on Bluetooth range.

THE ATAACK CLOUD'S MOBILE APPLICATION TESTING ARCHITECTURE

Proper experimentation with malware, social networking applications, crowdsourcing, and next-generation communication protocols requires ensuring that real-world usage, resource availability, and communication behavior matches research assumptions. For example, predicting the exact impact of a malware denial of service attack emanating from devices in an urban environment is difficult due to complex wireless protocol, social network, and mobility dynamics. Researchers need insight into how next-generation wireless protocols, mobility models, and social networks will impact their theories, techniques, algorithms, and other research products.

A primary challenge of real-world experimentation is that it is difficult to achieve the scale needed to understand the ramifications of large-scale deployments. For example, it is extremely time-consuming and costly to configure and provision experiments involving thousands of human volunteers and mobile devices. Moreover, the complexity of creating large-scale real-world experiments limits their use, robbing researchers of critical information needed to make the best research analyses.

Simultaneously obtaining both scale and physical-world accuracy in experimentation is difficult. Experiments based on cloud emulation can rapidly achieve the scale needed to validate application and middleware behavior in large-scale deployments, but cannot accurately predict real-world phenomena. Real-world experimentation produces precise measurements of physical phenomena but is difficult to scale.

The ATAACK Cloud is being built to leverage both cloud-based Android emulation to build experiments with 1,000 or more mobile devices, and the Virginia Tech Cognitive Radio Network Testbed (CORNET) to realize experimental validation using data from a real-world wireless/cellular testbed. The ATAACK Cloud experiments will be able to achieve a scale of 1,000+ smartphone instances, will simultaneously incorporate smaller numbers of real Android handsets connected to a configurable cellular testbed, and will tap into data from a pre-existing software-defined radio infrastructure. The use of a hybrid emulated/real-world experimentation infrastructure will facilitate both large-scale and accurate real-world empirical validation. Finally, the ATAACK Cloud will use the EpiCure modeling environment to provide agent-based models and control mechanisms for dynamically adapting the social and proximity networks influencing communication across devices. EpiCure will allow experiments to leverage pluggable models for controlling mobility and social networking to provide critical insight into how these dynamics affect research hypotheses.

While prior approaches to testing mobile device software are generally limited to tens of application instances, this section outlines the ATAACK Cloud's approach to enabling hundreds or thousands of application instances to be executed and orchestrated at one time. By enabling flexible large-scale emulation, this system creates the ability to test applications at multiple levels. For example, a vertical test of the server-side components of a mobile application can be constructed by emulating thousands of devices and coordinating their interactions with the server, while a client-side test can consist of executing an Android application on hundreds of different software versions to ensure the software is reliable on each version.

Testing Architecture Overview

The ATAACK Cloud's testing system will be created in a number of stages, with each stage adding functionality onto the previous. We have a completed a testbed for running thousands of highly-configurable Android emulators simultaneously, and will showcase the architecture and experimental results of the work in this section.

We have yet to finish connecting emulators together to allow large-scale simulation, but the end of this section outlines our architectural analysis for these improvements. See Figure 2 and Figure 3 for illustrations of ATAACK's overview and architecture.

The ATAACK Cloud's testing system logically consists of a large number of Android emulators distributed across multiple servers. Each

emulator is composed of a set of disk images and a set of hardware options, where each image specifies an important subset of a complete Android system and each option defines a hardware emulation possibility. For example, the 'boot.img' image file contains the Linux kernel that will be utilized underneath the Android OS, and the 'D-Pad' binary option specifies if the device contains a d-pad style input. By providing different system

Figure 2. ATAACK overview

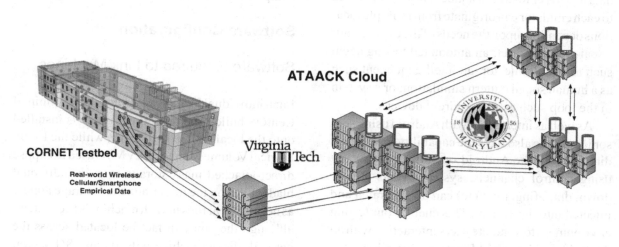

Figure 3. ATAACK architecture

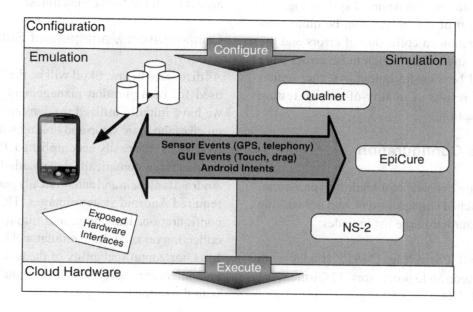

images and hardware configurations, our architecture will be capable of emulating multiple variants of a complete Android system. As each of these emulators is analogous to a complete Android mobile device (e.g. smartphone) we can install end-user software, such as proprietary applications, for testing purposes.

In addition to specifying software on an emulator-by-emulator basis, the ATAACK Cloud architecture will allow researchers to interface with the Android emulator and provide distinct sensor data to each emulator instance. The data provided to each emulator can originate from multiple locations depending upon the needs of the experiment: a real-world dataset; an automated testing agent such as a fault injector; an intelligent agent such as a human social pattern simulation; or a system in the loop such as real Android devices.

As well as interfacing with Android using sensor inputs, we also have the capability to interface directly with the Android operating system. By using control channels, system events (finger down, drag, finger up, etc) can be generated and injected into the system. This enables our testing environment to simulate users interacting with an Android application. Moreover, this allows our system to log metrics such as application response time by monitoring the Android system log.

The output of our system can be quite flexible. For example, a collection of errors and the versions of Android on which those errors were found could be a useful output. Another option may be the results of quality-of-service testing on an application.

Hardware Configuration

The hardware consists of a blade server system, a direct-attached storage system, and networking hardware. Our hardware list includes:

1. 34xDell PowerEdge M610 Blades with Intel Xeon 5645 processors, 12 Gb memory, 160Gb HD

2. 1xJetStor SAS 716S with 3TB storage
3. 4x1Gb Ethernet Switch

Additionally, we will be upgrading the memory on each blade from 12Gb to 36Gb. This configuration has a total of 68 processors, and 6 Intel Hyper-Threading enabled cores per processor, resulting in a total of 816 hardware threads (68*6*2). Each blade enclosure can hold 16 blades and has a 20-port 1Gb Ethernet switch attached to it. There is an additional 1Gb switch that's used to link all components together.

Software Configuration

Software Required to Link Machines

Each individual blade server runs a basic minimal CentOS build. The operating system is installed onto the local 160Gb hard drive, while the Linux Logical Volume Manager (LVM) is used to expose direct-attached mass storage to each individual blade. Files on the direct-attached storage appear as normal local files in each machine's file system, although they may in fact be located across the network. Each machine will run an SSH server, and one 'master' machine will be allowed SSH access to all the 'slave' machines.

Configuration Management Software

As discussed below, Skoll will be the technology used for configuration management. However, we have initially utilized the Jenkins system, as much of the basic setup and linking with Android toolchains was easily accomplished. Our current architecture automatically downloads the required Android toolchain and automatically generates and required Android system images. This provides configuration, launching, and output viewing / collection on an android emulator. This setup allows horizontal scalability of the testbed – slave computers can easily be launched and integrated with the testbed.

Architecture Testing Results

This section shows current results on the capabilities of our testbed. We highlight the two primary current challenges our work has overcome, which together allow simultaneous execution of thousands of valid Android emulator configurations.

Simultaneous Emulator Execution

A critical performance metric for any testbed is the number of tests it can operate in a given timeframe. In our work, this is realized through the number of Android emulators that can be executed simultaneously on a single slave machine. Initial versions of the Android toolset allow a single computer to execute up to sixteen Android emulators at a single time. Via emulator code modifications, we have removed the built-in limitation of sixteen and can launch as many emulators as the host computer can support. While it is difficult to formalize this to an algorithm for emulators per machine, our current hardware is capable of sustaining 32 Android emulators with ease, with the bottleneck being CPU utilization

rather than memory capacity. Across huge variability (Android version, emulator input/output options, etc), we have seen an emulator takes around 250MB +/- 50 MB, and the average CPU utilization of each emulator is typically 10% +/- 5% in steady-state operation. While horizontal scalability e.g. adding more computers, is the primary method for scaling of this architecture, increasing vertical scalability is critical to long term success. One critical component of vertical scalability is the CPU load. As shown in Figure 4, each emulator has a boot-up load spike and a steady-state load.

This boot-up spike can be an issue when the hosting machine is running near capacity, and therefore we use the snapshot feature of the emulator to avoid this spike for frequently used emulator images. Snapshot allows us to boot each emulator once, save an image of the current emulator process, and then re-load that emulator to its previous state. As shown in Figure 5, this feature greatly reduces the start-up CPU load spike, as well as reduces the startup time from ~60 seconds on average to ~5 seconds.

Figure 4. CPU load

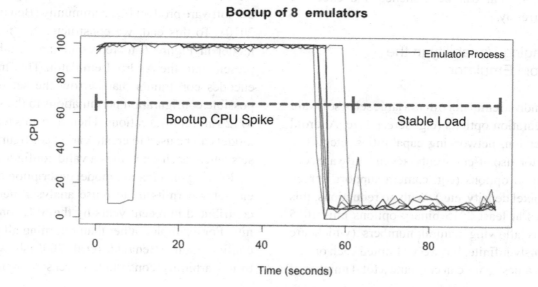

Figure 5. Bootup of 16 emulators with snapshot

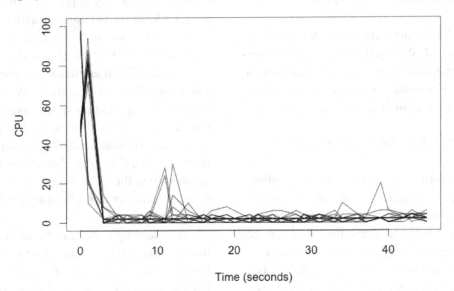

As shown in Figure 4 and Figure 5, each emulator is quite processor-intensive, as each process is executing the Android OS and an emulated ARM processor. This prompts us to consider alternative emulators in the future, such as the recently released Android-x86 version of the Android emulator. Our current version of the testbed can support up to 32 emulators per machine, and with 32 machines this results in 1024 emulators that can be launched and executed concurrently.

Managing Variability in the Android Emulator

The Android emulator offers a large set of software configuration options (e.g. screen size, Android OS version, networking capabilities, etc.). The emulator also offers twenty-seven hardware configuration options (e.g. camera support, screen size, pixel density, etc.). With no reductions, this enables at least 2^{15} binary options plus 10^5 options allowing natural numbers (which are obviously infinite, but we've limited each option to 10 values so we can compute a total number of permutations) plus the 14 different SDK versions, resulting in 4.58752 E15 emulator configuration permutations. However, not every permutation in that set of features will be needed for testing. For example, it is unlikely to desire testing of a WVGA screen with less than 120dpi, as no production devices feature such a configuration.

To effectively manage the set of possible configurations that the Android emulator offers, we decided to reuse existing knowledge from the software product line community (Benavides 2010). To this end, we constructed the feature model in Figure 6 to represent the variability present into the Android emulator. This model encodes constraints that narrow the set of all possible configuration permutations to the set of 5712 valid configurations. Therefore, this feature model can be used to create varied configuration sets where each set item is a valid configuration.

Relying on a feature model description of the emulator permits us to reuse analysis methods contributed in recent years by the SPL community. For example, rather than returning all valid configurations, (Benavides et al., 2005) show how to use arbitrary constraints to reason about the

Figure 6. Feature model

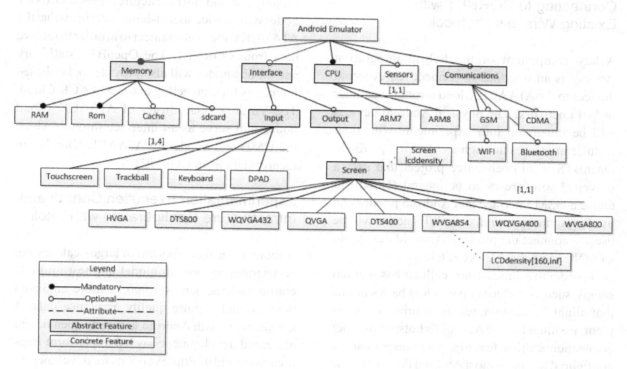

feature model, such as locating every valid configuration that matches the constraint "contains GPS, and has more than one input method." Another example of relevant SPL community knowledge is the CURE algorithm, which helps a user detect and repair non-valid configurations (White et al., 2010).

Architecture Improvements

This section outlines the future plans we have for the current ATAACK testbed infrastructure.

Hybrid Experimentation Infrastructure Built on CORNET

The ATAACK Cloud is being connected to Virginia Tech's Cognitive Radio Network Testbed (CORNET) to enable experiments that combine real Android devices, wireless software-defined radio experiments in CORNET, and 1,000 or

more emulated Android instances. Researchers will be able to provision experiments that produce accurate real-world data from the use of actual Android handsets in an urban environment, including in-building usage.

While providing high-accuracy, researchers will be able to also use the ATAACK Cloud to achieve the scale needed for large-scale research validation through emulating the effect that a 1,000 or more smartphone users has on mobile malware, social networking, and crowdsourcing scenarios. Since Android emulation and emulation of other large networking topologies will require server resources, we are developing additional Android emulation testbeds at the Virginia Tech and Maryland campuses. Finally, researchers will have the ability to test how integrating next-generation wireless networking protocols affect research scenarios by configuring large-scale software-defined radio experiments in CORNET.

Building a Cloud-Based Mobile Application Testbed

Connecting to CORNET with Existing Wireless Protocols

A key component of the hybrid integration strategy is an interface to connect real Android devices to the ATAACK Cloud through a cellular or WiFi network. The physical Android devices will be integrated into experiments with their cellular interfaces through the use of OpenBTS. OpenBTS is an opensource project that uses a universal software radio peripheral (USRP) to create a GSM interface that Android phones can use for communication. OpenBTS nodes will be used to connect the physical Android devices to CORNET and the ATAACK Cloud.

In order to mimic ad-hoc cellular base station setups, such as coffee shop wireless base stations that might be encountered in an urban environment, we intend to use Android's hotspot Internet connection sharing features. The hotspot can be configured to run on most Android devices to use the device's radio to serve as a WiFi access point for other handsets. The ad-hoc hotspot connection sharing pipes incoming/outgoing communication from the WiFi interface to the device's CDMA 3G data connection.

Researchers will be able to setup custom cellular environments that leverage a combination of fixed CORNET-based OpenBTS nodes and ad-hoc Droid-based movable WiFi access points. Allowing for a configurable set of cellular base-stations in indoor and outdoor environments will allow mobile malware, crowdsourcing, and social networking scenarios to be tested under a variety of network conditions, ranging from reduced indoor signal to unreliable ad-hoc base station scenarios. This level of configurability and scenario realism is not possible with existing mobile device testing platforms.

As shown in Figure 3, in order to connect CORNET and OpenBTS to the ATAACK Cloud, we are piping data from the CORNET back-end processing nodes to the ATAACK Cloud rack-mounted cloud infrastructure. The CORNET nodes will provide socket-based interfaces that the ATAACK Cloud can connect to in order to receive data from CORNET. The OpenBTS stationary and ad-hoc nodes will also provide socket-based interfaces for connecting to the ATAACK Cloud. The Virginia Tech cluster of ATAACK Cloud nodes will serve as an interface through which the UMD and Vanderbilt ATAACK Clouds can receive data from CORNET.

Experimentation Execution Control and Infrastructure Configuration with Skoll

Another critical component of large-scale testing is determining how to model and test multiple configurations, across 1,000 or more emulated devices, and capture quality assurance data. A known issue with Android is that its open nature and rapid development has led to platform fragmentation and multiple versions for developers to assess. At this scale of experimentation, manual approaches to launching and running experiments on multiple versions, as well as collecting data, are infeasible.

Skoll(A. Memon et al., 2004; Adam Porter, Yilmaz, Memon, Schmidt, & Natarajan, 2007), which is a distributed quality assurance system developed at the University of Maryland, will be used to automate the process of provisioning experiments across a 1,000 or more emulated and real devices in multiple applications. This automation will alleviate researchers from the burden of attempting to manually craft methods for deploying experiments across a 1,000 or more smartphone emulator instances and tens of physical devices. The Skoll automation intelligence will also aid in the selection and scheduling of experiments based on relevance to experimental hypotheses and volume of expected information gain.

Another critical attribute of Skoll that will enable researchers to verify and validate complex smartphone applications is its configuration space modeling. Skoll's configuration space modeling languages will capture variation points in Android middleware platforms, physical devices, and application configuration parameters. Skoll's code generators will be used to transform these models of variability into concrete experimentation configuration definitions that can validate applications on a large set of target software/hardware infrastructure setups.

Finally, Skoll will provide the results collection backbone needed to enable researchers to collect and quantify experiment results. Without a large-scale quality assurance infrastructure to harvest performance, exception, and other data from the emulators, it would be difficult for researchers to ensure that all needed data was obtained and accurately analyzed. Moreover, the reporting infrastructure of Skoll will allow developers to ascertain the accuracy of research predictions across a variety of usage, deployment, and scale configurations.

Controlling Social and Mobility Network Dynamics with EpiCure

Over the last few years at Virginia Tech, we have developed EpiCure—an individual-based, scalable HPC modeling environment to study malware propagation over realistic mobile networks. It runs extremely fast for realistic instances that involve: (*i*) large time-varying networks consisting of millions of heterogeneous individuals with time varying interaction neighborhoods, (*ii*) dynamic interactions between the malware propagation, device behavior, and the exogenous interventions, and (*iii*) large number of replicated runs necessary for statistically sound estimates about the stochastic malware evolution. It is designed specifically to work on commodity cluster architectures. We also have developed a framework to generate synthetic mobile social networks and realistic device networks – proximity and communication networks – from activity-based

mobility models and statistics on communication patterns for a synthetic population, which can be used with EpiCure.

EpiCure allows us to study mobile malware and especially the study of mobile malware that spread through proximity Bluetooth networks and cellular infrastructure – using short messaging service (SMS) or multimedia messaging service (MMS). It uses a "network-based-approach" which employs detailed representations of the underlying communication networks and parameterized models of within-host behavior and between-host interaction of the malware.

We are mapping EpiCure onto the ATAACK Cloud. The networked based representation approach used in EpiCure allows us to map these computations in a natural way on the emulation platform. Note that, apriori it is not clear how one could use ns-2 or aggregate approaches to do this mapping. In this case, EpiCure primarily provides models of device activity and mobility. The combination of EpiCure and the emulations of individual radios requires several extensions: (i) the current emulation platform is for individual radios that are static, as the radios move around based on the EpiCure mobility model, the middleware will work with dynamic connectivity of these devices – this poses well known challenges for mapping these computations on the cloud, especially as they pertain to load balancing and synchronization, (ii) malware specification will need to be implemented on individual radios and requires further work on understanding application abstractions.

We are combining EpiCure with the ATAACK Cloud to study a larger emulation+ simulation system. This will increase the scope of the network researchers can study. There are multiple reasons for representing a larger system. First, it is an open research question as to the appropriate system size one needs to consider to understand the dynamics of the malware spread – our recent work shows that small systems can sometimes have qualitatively different behavior than larger systems. The combined platform will allow us to develop models that span urban scale networks. Second, it allows us to study the device level abstractions within a larger context. Specifically, certain devices will be emulated while others will run an abstracted malware model. In earlier work we have calibrated and then validated abstract models using ns-2 as a benchmark. Use of the ATAACK Cloud will allow us to substantially extend environments within which we can calibrate our abstractions. An important technical problem that will need to be addressed here is to reconcile the simulation clock and the real time clock. This is a classic issue when developing such systems and a number of proposed solutions exist in the literature for the general problem at hand. We will investigate how these solutions can be adapted to our setting.

We are planning to use the ATAACK to study fundamental problems in malware epidemics; namely how can you detect the spread of malware, evaluation of existing interventions and their limitations, design of potentially new viruses that can spread more stealthily and can be used by security experts to understand the vulnerabilities in the existing mobile phones and novel interventions for controlling the spread especially in the emerging environment where peer-to-peer and ad-hoc communications are increasing leading to hybrid networks.

CONCLUSION

We have presented a method for developing, refining, and validating smartphone-based applications by emulating 1000+ heterogeneous Android devices and tens of actual devices. By enabling rapid provisioning and providing sensor inputs for each emulated Android device, we have enabled a diverse array of testing options. Moreover, direct access to the Android operating system allows us to monitor quality of service parameters such as screen rendering time and drive each emulator using a sequence of user-events, such as a sequence of button press operations. By building this framework on a scalable cloud architecture we are capable of scaling up to more resource-consuming scenarios.

REFERENCES

Alazzawe, A., Wijesekera, D., & Dantu, R. (2009). A testbed for mobile social computing. *2009 5th International Conference on Testbeds and Research Infrastructures for the Development of Networks Communities and Workshops*, (pp. 1-6). IEEE. doi:10.1109/TRIDENTCOM.2009.4976250

Alt, F., Shirazi, A. S., Schmidt, A., Kramer, U., & Nawaz, Z. (2010). Location-based crowdsourcing: Extending crowdsourcing to the real world. *Proceedings of the 6th Nordic Conference on Human-Computer Interaction: Extending Boundaries*, (pp. 13-2)2. ACM. Retrieved from http://portal.acm.org/citation.cfm?id=1868921

Aoki, P. M., Honicky, R. J., Mainwaring, A., Myers, C., Paulos, E., Subramanian, S., & Woodruff, A. (2008). Common sense: Mobile environmental sensing platforms to support community action and citizen science. *Adjunct Proceedings of the Tenth International Conference on Ubiquitous Computing*, (pp. 59-60). Retrieved from http://www.paulaoki.com/papers/ubicomp08-demo.pdf

Benavides, D., Segura, S., & Ruiz-Cortés, A. (2010). Automated analysis of feature models 20 years later: A literature review. *Information Systems*, *35*(6). doi:10.1016/j.is.2010.01.001

Benavides, D., Trinidad, P., & Ruiz-Cortés, A. (2005). Automated reasoning on feature models. *Advanced Information Systems Engineering, Lecture Notes in Computer Science, 3520*, (pp. 381-390). Retrieved from http://www.springerlink.com/content/qh6yvx3y6pxet8ex/

Bose, A., & Shin, K. G. (2006). On mobile viruses exploiting messaging and Bluetooth services. *Securecomm and Workshops, 2006*, 1–10. doi:10.1109/SECCOMW.2006.359562

Burke, J., Estrin, D., Hansen, M., Parker, A., Ramanathan, N., Reddy, S., & Srivastava, M. B. (2006). Participatory sensing. *IEEE Internet Computing, 14*(1), 12-42. Citeseer. doi:10.1109/MIC.2010.12

Burtsev, A., Radhakrishnan, P., Hibler, M., & Lepreau, J. (2009). Transparent checkpoints of closed distributed systems in emulab. *Proceedings of the Fourth ACM European Conference on Computer Systems EuroSys 09*, (p. 173). ACM Press. doi:10.1145/1519065.1519084

Cai, L., Machiraju, S., & Chen, H. (2009). Defending against sensor-sniffing ATAACKs on mobile phones. *Proceedings of the 1st ACM Workshop on Networking, Systems, and Applications for Mobile Handhelds* (pp. 31-36). New York, NY: ACM. doi:http://doi.acm.org/10.1145/1592606.1592614

Campbell, A. T., Eisenman, S. B., & Lane, N. D. (2008). The rise of people-centric sensing. *IEEE Internet Computing, 12*(4). Retrieved from http://www.computer.org/portal/web/csdl/doi/10.1109/MIC.2008.90 doi:10.1109/MIC.2008.90

Casanova, H. (2002). Distributed computing research issues in grid computing. *ACM SIGACT News, 33*(3), 50-70. ACM. doi:10.1145/582475.582486

Cheng, J., Wong, S. H. Y., Yang, H., & Lu, S. (2007). SmartSiren: Virus detection and alert for smartphones. *Proceedings of the 5th International Conference on Mobile Systems Applications and Services* (pp. 258-271). ACM. Retrieved from https://www.usenix.org/events/mobisys07/full_papers/p258.pdf

Chintapatla, B., Goulart, A., & Magnussen, W. (2010). Testbed experiments on the location to service translation (LoST) protocol for mobile users. *2010 7th IEEE Consumer Communications and Networking Conference*, (pp. 1-5). IEEE. doi:10.1109/CCNC.2010.5421603

Chou, J., O'Donnell, B., & Shrirer, M. (2010). Global PC market maintains double-digit growth in third quarter despite weak results in some segments, according to IDC. *International Data Corporation*. Retrieved from http://www.businesswire.com/news/home/20101013007002/en/Global-PC-Market-Maintains-Double-Digit-Growth-Quarter

Credant Technologies. (2009). Survey demonstrates poor smartphone security attitude amongst users. *Credant Technologies*. Retrieved from http://www.prosecurityzone.com/News/It_security/Mobile_computing_security/Survey_demonstrates_poor_smartphone_security_attitude_amongst_users_8942.asp#axzz1jxol1VYk

Dagon, D., Martin, T., & Starner, T. (2004). Mobile phones as computing devices: The viruses are coming! *Pervasive Computing, 3*(4), 11–15. doi:10.1109/MPRV.2004.21

Eagle, N. (2009). txteagle: Mobile crowdsourcing. In N. Aykin (Ed.), *International Conference on Internationalization Design and Global Development* (Vol. 5623, pp. 447-456-456). Berlin, Germany: Springer. doi:10.1007/978-3-642-02767-3

Eagle, N., & Pentland, A. (2005). Social serendipity: Mobilizing social software. *IEEE Pervasive Computing / IEEE Computer Society [and] IEEE Communications Society*, *4*(2), 28–34. doi:10.1109/MPRV.2005.37

Enck, W., Ongtang, M., & McDaniel, P. (2009). On lightweight mobile phone application certification. *Proceedings of the 16th ACM Conference on Computer and Communications Security* (pp. 235-245). New York, NY: ACM. doi:http://doi.acm.org/10.1145/1653662.1653691

Fitzek, F. H. P., & Reichert, F. (2007). *Mobile phone programming and its application to wireless networking*. Springer. Retrieved from http://books.google.com/books?id=s_OnKP3VAQ4C

Frederick, G. R., & Lal, R. (2007). Testing a mobile web site. *Beginning smartphone web development* (pp. 259-272).

Fritsch, T., Ritter, H., & Schiller, J. (2006). User case study and network evolution in the mobile phone sector (a study on current mobile phone applications). *Proceedings of the 2006 ACM SIGCHI International Conference on Advances in Computer Entertainment Technology*. New York, NY: ACM. doi:http://doi.acm.org/10.1145/1178823.1178836

Havlin, S. (2009). Phone infections. *Quantum*, *324*, 1023–1024. doi:doi:10.1126/science.1174658

Heo, J., Terada, K., Toyama, M., Kurumatani, S., & Chen, E. Y. (2010). User demand prediction from application usage pattern in virtual smartphone. *2010 IEEE Second International Conference on Cloud Computing Technology and Science*, (pp. 449-455). IEEE. doi:10.1109/CloudCom.2010.52

Hibler, M., Ricci, R., Stoller, L., Duerig, J., Guruprasad, S., Stack, T., et al. (2008). Large-scale virtualization in the emulab network testbed. *Proceedings of the 2008 USENIX Annual Technical Conference*, (pp. 113-128). USENIX Association. Retrieved from http://portal.acm.org/citation.cfm?id=1404023

Hu, W.-C., Zuo, Y., Kaabouch, N., & Chen, L. (2010). An optimization neural network for smartphone data protection. *2010 IEEE International Conference on Electro/Information Technology (EIT)*, (pp. 1-6).

Information Sciences Institute. (n.d.). *Network Simulator (NS-2)*. Retrieved from http://www.isi.edu/nsnam/ns/

Kempe, D., Kleinberg, J., & Tardos, É. (2003). Maximizing the spread of influence through a social network. *Proceedings of the Ninth ACM SIGKDD International Conference on Knowledge Discovery and Data Mining KDD 03*, (p. 137). ACM Press. doi:10.1145/956755.956769

Kim, H., Smith, J., & Shin, K. G. (2008). Detecting energy-greedy anomalies and mobile malware variants. *Proceedings of the 6th International Conference on Mobile Systems, Applications, and Services*, (pp. 239-252). ACM Press. doi:10.1145/1378600.1378627

Kim, K. H. (1989). An approach to experimental evaluation of real-time fault-tolerant distributed computing schemes. *IEEE Transactions on Software Engineering*, *15*(6), 715–725. doi:10.1109/32.24725

Laurendeau, C., & Barbeau, M. (2006). Threats to security in DSRC/WAVE. In T. Kunz & S. S. Ravi (Eds.), *Lecture Notes in Computer Science, 4104*, (pp. 266–279). Springer. Retrieved from http://www.springerlink.com/index/2328535l2q76hgt4.pdf

Lawton, G. (2008). Is it finally time to worry about mobile malware? *Computer, 41*(5), 12–14. doi:10.1109/MC.2008.159

Leavitt, N. (2005). Mobile phones: The next frontier for hackers? *Computer, 38*(4), 20–23. doi:10.1109/MC.2005.134

Liu, L., Yan, G., Zhang, X., & Chen, S. (2009). VirusMeter: Preventing your cellphone from spies. *Proceedings of the 12th International Symposium on Recent Advances in Intrusion Detection* (pp. 244-264). Berlin, Germany: Springer-Verlag. doi:http://dx.doi.org/10.1007/978-3-642-04342-0_13

Matos, V., & Grasser, R. (2010). Building applications for the Android OS mobile platform: A primer and course materials. *Journal of Computing Sciences in Colleges, 26*(1), 23–29. Retrieved from http://portal.acm.org/citation.cfm?id=1858449.1858455

Memon, A., Porter, A., Yilmaz, C., Nagarajan, A., Schmidt, D., & Natarajan, B. (2004). Skoll: Distributed continuous quality assurance. *Proceedings 26th International Conference on Software Engineering*, (pp. 459-468). IEEE Computer Society. doi:10.1109/ICSE.2004.1317468

Mickens, J. W., & Noble, B. D. (2007). Analytical models for epidemics in mobile networks. *Third IEEE International Conference on Wireless and Mobile Computing Networking and Communications WiMob 2007*, (WiMob), (p. 77). IEEE. doi:10.1109/WIMOB.2007.4390871

Miluzzo, E., Lane, N. D., Fodor, K., Peterson, R., Lu, H., Musolesi, M., et al. (2008). Sensing meets mobile social networks: the design, implementation and evaluation of the CenceMe application. *Conference on Embedded Networked Sensor Systems* (Vol. 10, pp. 337-350). ACM Press. doi:10.1145/1460412.1460445

Mohan, P., Padmanabhan, V. N., & Ramjee, R. (2008). Nericell: Rich monitoring of road and traffic conditions using mobile smartphones. *Proceedings of the 6th ACM Conference on Embedded Network Sensor Systems SenSys 08* (p. 323). ACM Press. doi:10.1145/1460412.1460444

Mulliner, C., & Vigna, G. (2006). Vulnerability analysis of MMS user agents. *22nd Annual Computer Security Applications Conference, ACSAC 06* (pp. 77-88).

Oberheide, J., Veeraraghavan, K., Cooke, E., Flinn, J., & Jahanian, F. (2008). Virtualized in-cloud security services for mobile devices. *Proceedings of the First Workshop on Virtualization in Mobile Computing*, (pp. 31-35). ACM. doi:10.1145/1622103.1629656

Oliver, E. (2009). A survey of platforms for mobile networks research. *ACM SIGMOBILE Mobile Computing and Communications Review, 12*(4), 56. doi:10.1145/1508285.1508292

Oliver, E. (2010). The challenges in large-scale smartphone user studies. *Proceedings of the 2nd ACM International Workshop on Hot Topics in Planet-Scale Measurement*, (pp. 1-5). ACM Press. doi:10.1145/1834616.1834623

Piercy, M. (2004). Embedded devices next on the virus target list. *Electronics Systems and Software, 2*(6), 42–43. doi:10.1049/ess:20040612

Porter, A., Yilmaz, C., Memon, A. M., Schmidt, D. C., & Natarajan, B. (2007). Skoll: A process and infrastructure for distributed continuous quality assurance. *IEEE Transactions on Software Engineering, 33*(8), 510-525. IEEE Computer Society. doi:10.1109/TSE.2007.70719

Provos, N., & Holz, T. (2007). *Virtual honeypots: From botnet tracking to intrusion detection* (1st ed.). Addison-Wesley Professional.

Rensfelt, O., Hermans, F., Gunningberg, P., & Larzon, L. (2010). Repeatable experiments with mobile nodes in a relocatable WSN testbed. *6th IEEE International Conference on Distributed Computing in Sensor Systems Workshops (DCOSSW), 2010* (pp. 1-6).

Rhodes, C. J., & Nekovee, M. (2008). The opportunistic transmission of wireless worms between mobile devices. *Physica A: Statistical Mechanics and its Applications, 387*(27), 6837-6844. Elsevier B.V. Retrieved from http://arxiv.org/abs/0802.2685

Scalable Network Technologies. (n.d.). *Qualnet.* Retrieved from http://www.scalable-networks.com/

Schmidt, A.-D., Schmidt, H.-G., Batyuk, L., Clausen, J. H., Camtepe, S. A., Albayrak, S., & Yildizli, C. (2009). Smartphone malware evolution revisited: Android next target? *2009 4th International Conference on Malicious and Unwanted Software MALWARE,* (pp. 1-7). IEEE. doi:10.1109/MALWARE.2009.5403026

Shabtai, A., & Elovici, Y. (2010). Applying behavioral detection on Android-based devices. *Mobile Wireless Middleware Operating Systems and Applications,* (pp. 235–249). Springer. Retrieved from http://www.springerlink.com/index/G404U422T1008740.pdf

Shabtai, A., Fledel, Y., Kanonov, U., Elovici, Y., Dolev, S., & Glezer, C. (2010). Google Android: A comprehensive security assessment. *Security & Privacy, 8*(2), 35–44. doi:10.1109/MSP.2010.2

Steve, G. (2004). Threats looming beyond the perimeter. *Infosecurity Today, 1*(6), 12-14. Retrieved from http://www.sciencedirect.com/science/article/pii/S1742684704001296

Su, J., Chan, K. K. W., Miklas, A. G., Po, K., Akhavan, A., Saroiu, S., et al. (2006). A preliminary investigation of worm infections in a Bluetooth environment. *Proceedings of the 4th ACM Workshop on Recurring Malcode WORM 06,* (p. 9). ACM Press. doi:10.1145/1179542.1179545

Teng, C.-C., & Helps, R. (2010). Mobile application development: Essential new directions for IT. *2010 Seventh International Conference on Information Technology New Generations,* (pp. 471-475). IEEE. doi:10.1109/ITNG.2010.249

Tong, L., Zhao, Q., & Adireddy, S. (2003). *Sensor networks with mobile agents. IEEE Military Communications Conference 2003 MILCOM 2003* (*Vol. 1,* pp. 688–693). IEEE. doi:10.1109/MILCOM.2003.1290187

Töyssy, S., & Helenius, M. (2006). About malicious software in smartphones. *Journal in Computer Virology, 2*(2), 109-119. Paris, France: Springer. doi:doi:10.1007/s11416-006-0022-0

Tudor, B., & Pettey, C. (2010). *Gartner says worldwide mobile phone sales grew 35 percent in third quarter 2010; Smartphone sales increased 96 percent.* Retrieved from http://www.gartner.com/it/page.jsp?id=1466313

Wang, P., Gonzalez, M., Hidalgo, C. A., & Barabasi, A. L. (2009). Understanding the spreading patterns of mobile phone viruses. *Science, 324*(5930), 1071–1076. Retrieved from http://arxiv.org/abs/0906.4567 doi:10.1126/science.1167053

White, J., Benavides, D., Schmidt, D. C., Trinidad, P., Dougherty, B., & Ruiz-Cortes, A. (2010). Automated diagnosis of feature model configurations. *Journal of Systems and Software, 83*(7), 1094–1107. http://www.sciencedirect.com/science/article/pii/S016412121000049X doi:10.1016/j.jss.2010.02.017

Wilson, A., & York, M. (2011). Perceived or real risks using smartphones. *ABIS 2011 Referenced Proceedings* (pp. 79-81).

Yan, G., Cuellar, L., Eidenbenz, S., Flores, H. D., Hengartner, N., & Vu, V. (2007). Bluetooth worm propagation: Mobility pattern matters! *Proceedings of the 2nd ACM Symposium on Information, Computer, and Communications Security*, (pp. 32-44). Retrieved from http://portal.acm.org/citation.cfm?id=1229294

Yan, G., & Eidenbenz, S. (2006). Bluetooth worms: Models, dynamics, and defense implications. *2006 22nd Annual Computer Security Applications Conference ACSAC06*, (pp. 245-256). IEEE. doi:10.1109/ACSAC.2006.18

Yan, T., Marzilli, M., Holmes, R., Ganesan, D., & Corner, M. (2009). mCrowd: a platform for mobile crowdsourcing. *Conference on Embedded Networked Sensor Systems* (pp. 347-348). ACM. doi:10.1145/1644038.1644094

Zhang, X., Freschl, J., & Schopf, J. M. (2003). A performance study of monitoring and information services for distributed systems. *Proceedings 12th IEEE International Symposium on High Performance Distributed Computing 2003*, (p. 12). IEEE Computer Society. Retrieved from http://arxiv.org/abs/cs/0304015

Zheng, B., Xiong, Y., Zhang, Q., & Lin, C. (2006). The spread of epidemics on smartphones. In Xiao, Y., Shen, X., & Du, D. (Eds.), *Wireless/mobile network security*. Springer.

Chapter 19
Testing in the Cloud:
Balancing the Value and Risks of Cloud Computing

Randall W. Rice
Rice Consulting Services, USA

ABSTRACT

Cloud-based applications offer great value and benefits to businesses and other application consumers. However, unlike traditional in-house developed systems or commercial-off-the-shelf (COTS) applications, the customer has little or no control over when and how functionality may change. The cloud consumer also has little or no control over how the data controlled by the application is processed, stored, and secured. This chapter explores how the testing of cloud applications is fundamentally different from other contexts where the customer has a greater degree of control. The limitations of risk mitigation are discussed as well as cloud computing models that may also reduce the cloud consumer's risk.

INTRODUCTION

The balance to be achieved in cloud computing is between the value of cloud-based applications and the cost of mitigating cloud computing risks such as functional correctness, fitness for use, performance and security. If the risks outweigh the value, then cloud computing is hard to justify and may not be the right course for an organization.

However, if cloud computing risks can be identified and mitigated to an acceptable level, then the discussion changes from "*Should* we adopt the cloud as a computing model?" to "*How should* we adopt the cloud as a computing model?"

The good news is that testing, based on the risks of cloud computing, can help mitigate these risks if appropriate actions are taken based on the tests and the risks. Testing can help mitigate cloud computing risks, evaluate the levels of these risks for your particular situation and help determine the extent to which the risks may impact you.

Before you can plan the right risk-based tests, however, it is necessary to understand the uniqueness and risks of cloud computing. Then, your tests can be aligned with the risks and deliver the information you and your management need to make informed implementation decisions going forward.

DOI: 10.4018/978-1-4666-2536-5.ch019

The key to aligning testing with the risks in your specific context is to develop a solid cloud-based test strategy. This article also outlines how to create a cloud testing strategy that reflects your implementation.

The New Landscape

The idea of global distributed computing is not new, but the widespread adoption of that computing model using the cloud is new. At first glance, cloud computing might appear as just another way to perform tasks on the web. However, there are many differences between cloud computing and the web sites and web applications we have built and tested in the past. Below are listed some of the key differences in cloud computing from other computing models. These attributes are referenced from the NIST report, *The NIST Definition of Cloud Computing, Special Publication 800-145.*

- **Measured and Metered Usage:** In the cloud you pay for what you use in terms of storage, bandwidth and other resources. This has an impact in terms of performance. Need more response time or more bandwidth? You can get what you need on demand. The issue is whether or not you are getting the service you are paying for, and are being charged the right amount for the service.

  In traditional computing models, the normal practice is to acquire the best estimate of resources such as CPU speed, disk space, and so forth. Resources are then increased as needed. In the traditional view it often takes extended time to acquire and provision additional resources.

- **On-Demand Self-Service:** Web sites of the past often required help from the site administrator to configure new features and services. In the cloud, much of that control is given to the user to provision resources as needed with little or no advance notice to the cloud provider.

- **Ubiquitous Network Access:** The cloud computing model has opened many ways to access applications, data, other devices and users. For example, the ability of mobile devices to provide rich data and applications is largely due to the capabilities provided in the cloud. The availability of Internet access may be a problem for some people, which is an area of risk that must be considered when deploying cloud-based applications. However, the vision of being able to access applications anywhere and at any time is becoming closer to reality with the cloud computing model.

- **Resource Pooling:** Not only do you only pay for what you use, but you can share resources with others to help bear the costs of the infrastructure. This has risks related to how other resources may be consuming the pooled resources. Like living in an apartment building, the actions of each tenant can impact the other tenants of the apartment building.

- **Rapid Elasticity:** A classic challenge for managing computing environments is to know how much processing capacity is needed. In the cloud, you can buy what you need when you need it. This is an attractive option when you need extra processing capacity immediately. You also don't have to buy more resources than you actually consume.

These are the differences and the main benefits seen in cloud computing, but there are risks and tradeoffs that must be addressed.

The Cloud is Everywhere?

The common marketing perception seen in cloud-based services is that because the Internet is accessible in so many places and in so many ways, you can access cloud-based services just about anywhere.

As a frequent traveler, both domestically and abroad, I can attest that the cloud is not yet truly ubiquitous. In fact, one doesn't have to travel any further than to rural areas of the U.S. to find the limitations of the cloud. Efforts are being made to establish wide area broadband service, but there are regulatory and technology hurdles that remain to be overcome.

Another example of limited cloud availability is in cities where one would think Internet access is prevalent and affordable, but isn't. Rome is one of my favorite cities, but good luck in finding a Wi-Fi hotspot, even in some of the better hotels. If you are fortunate enough to find Internet access, the quality of connection and speed may not be enough to effectively access cloud services.

International travelers also experience the challenge of the cost of mobile data access. The most recent cost I saw was $19 per megabyte of data in Europe. At that rate, international mobile computing over 3G and 4G connections gets expensive in a hurry. This issue can be resolved using SIM cards purchased in the region of travel, but it does require some effort. Plus, this is only a possible solution for wireless devices such as phones and wireless-enabled pads. This solution does not help in getting Wi-Fi access in limited areas.

The impact of all this is if your organization is offering products and services in the cloud, large segments of potential customers or users may be left out. Companies that transition services to the cloud need to consider where their market lives. So, it is good to provide options for those people that may not have high-speed web access.

One of the bright areas in cloud testing is the ability to use cloud-based test tools to access cloud applications from points of presence around the world, but from a single point of control. This helps greatly to measure performance and overall user experience on a frequent basis for cloud applications and mobile applications.

As an example, a major travel web site in the United States has a variety of brands in several other countries, such as the UK and Canada. The site's servers are located around the world at various data centers and because of the shared nature of searching for flights, hotels, and so forth, the traffic from one country brand may access the servers in another country.

To test the performance impact of this architecture, a cloud-based testing tool as described above is used to test end-user performance and experience in real time by doing flight searches and other common user actions. No special test environment is needed and this kind of test helps mitigate the risk of poor performance as seen from a variety of global locations.

BUSINESS STAKEHOLDERS

In traditional enterprise systems, business stakeholders such as sales and accounting have had responsibility to define needs and give acceptance to system delivery. However, one of the chronic problems in testing is getting people from the business side of the organization interested and involved in testing.

Cloud computing introduces new risks to the business which require business direction and expertise to identify, accept and mitigate. If the business doesn't accept this responsibility, the IT group alone can't make the decisions needed for a sound adoption of cloud applications, infrastructure and platforms.

The risks and test activities described in this chapter are opportunities for the business to play a key role in how the business will either benefit or suffer from cloud computing.

Key Risk Areas

There is a lot to like about the cloud, but like any technology we also need to consider the risks along with the benefits. One of the major determinants of risk is the cloud model in use such as public clouds, private clouds or hybrid clouds. This section examines each area of risk, giving consideration to these three cloud models.

In these risk areas, one might assume that Service Level Agreements (SLAs) offer adequate protection. Indeed, SLAs are needed and are helpful. However, SLAs are often one-sided toward the vendor and offer no protection against loss of business or loss of funds.

Loss of Control

In traditional systems and hosted web applications, the IT customer[1] often has some degree of control over changes to the application, the data stored and processed by the application and when releases are applied.

In public clouds a lot of control is ceded to the cloud vendor. The IT customer little or no physical control over data, control of software releases, or control of hardware. An example risk is when a functional change is made to a cloud-based application (Software as a Service), which causes the end-customer or user to experience problems. As an IT customer, you may know nothing in advance about the change until your users or customers start to report problems. Even more troubling is that you have no control over when the problems will be fixed.

In private clouds, there is more control but also more responsibility of the applications, data and other resources. It is possible to lose the cost savings of a public cloud, but sometimes the cost is justified if the need for control is high.

The hybrid cloud is a way to balance some of the cost and risk. For example, high-risk and high-control applications can be hosted in your own cloud with public clouds to leverage services that are not as critical.

Security

While you may be able to control access rights, the cloud provider is still holding the keys to the hardware and network. This is quite a challenge because some security attacks are accomplished through the hardware layer, even down to the chipsets.

Example Risk 1: A denial of service attack is launched against your cloud provider, which causes your services to be stopped.

Example Risk 2: Someone working for the cloud provider takes home a hard drive filled with private information for dozens of companies.

A private cloud may offer more control, but it also entails more responsibility on your part as the owner of the application. For example, if you store credit card information, you have PCI compliance to achieve. This can be a costly and involved effort.

A public cloud offers rights management, but no direct control of the security infrastructure. However, many people use cloud services to handle data and tasks they do not want to secure themselves. In a public cloud, the cloud provider has security responsibility but a security lapse still reflects badly on the business using the cloud services.

A hybrid cloud offers the options of securing and controlling key data and tasks in a private cloud, while handling lower risk data and tasks in a public cloud.

Functional Correctness

The risk in functional correctness is that changes made by a cloud provider may contain defects that are a total surprise to the cloud consumer.

Not only are the defects a surprise, but so also may be the changes that cause them.

Ideally, the IT customer knows in advance when changes will occur, but in reality the cloud provider may make a change at any time, for any reason.

In a private cloud, the IT customer is in complete control of the application environment and knows when changes will occur. However, this does not mean the changes or new features will work correctly. In addition, this does not mean that the organization's end-users and customers will know when changes occur. In a private cloud, functional correctness is under the control of the organization and is measured by testing.

In a public cloud, the cloud consumer is at the mercy of the cloud provider in terms of functional correctness. When functions fail to work correctly, the cloud consumer can only hope the cloud provider makes the needed changes quickly.

In a hybrid cloud, some of the risk may be offset by non-critical functionality being provided by a public cloud provider. However, the core issue of software quality remains the ultimate responsibility of the business using the cloud services to fulfill the needs of its customers.

Fitness for Use

While cloud-based applications may offer configuration options, it is still important to understand and assess fitness for use in the cloud consumer's business. Fitness for use can be seen in technical terms, such as accommodating needed browsers and platforms, as well as process terms, such as supporting needed tasks.

Private clouds give the ability to modify applications to meet specific needs, unless the application is a hosted package that cannot be modified or configured.

Public clouds may give the ability to perform limited configuration, but often it is an "as is" proposition. The application's usability is often apparent through testing, but you don't get a chance to substantially change it. In fact, the cloud provider may make changes that customers feel make usability worse.

Hybrid clouds give the ability to perhaps modify some applications hosted on a private cloud and use other applications as they are from a public cloud provider.

Performance

Performance is perhaps the largest and most unpredictable risk of all. In the globally distributed computing model of the cloud, performance can suffer just due to network fluctuations.

The choice of cloud model only shifts the location of the services. It doesn't take away the risk entirely.

For example, in a private cloud, the cloud owner can control the environmental resources (networks, servers, data, and so forth) and application changes, but the need remains for performance testing at levels that exceed expected usage. Performance monitoring is also still the responsibility of the cloud owner.

In a public cloud, the cloud consumer can test performance levels, but the risk of doing so is that others using the public cloud would be negatively impacted. Typically, public cloud consumers monitor application performance and take the risk of slower performance at times.

Hybrid clouds can help segment performance risks by locating critical applications on a private cloud and lesser critical applications on a public cloud. However, this only isolates part of the source of performance problems – the unpredictable outages encountered by others. Regardless of where the application is located, poor performance is still a risk.

Usability

As applications are becoming more intuitive, usability seems to be getting better across the board – cloud and otherwise. However, it is a mistake to assume that an application will be easy to use. For example, web meeting software is often cloud-based. There is a lot of functionality contained in a typically small control panel. It always amazes me at how much practice I need to learn a new web meeting system. Of course, reading instructions would help also.

When it comes to usability, the cloud model might only come into play when an application undergoes a major re-design, for the worse. In this case, the pubic cloud offers no recourse.

The Testing Challenge

The risks described above are general risks in cloud computing. Any organization considering a cloud computing solution needs to assess their level of risk in each of the areas such as performance, security, usability and so forth. Testing is one way the risks can be measured and mitigated.

However, there are some specific cloud-based testing risks that also deserve our attention.

Lack of a Basis for Testing (Requirements, SLAs, Etc.)

A long-standing complaint among testers is that of inadequate user requirements. This is across the board, in all technologies, in all development approaches, including agile. In cloud computing the need for a defined basis for testing is even more pronounced.

For Software as a Service (SaaS), the requirements should describe what is needed in terms of functionality, performance, usability and other attributes. From the customer perspective, much like requirements for Commercial off-the-shelf (COTS) applications, SaaS requirements describe what is being purchased, not built.

For Infrastructure as a Service (IaaS), requirements describe what is needed in terms of technical infrastructure such as platform configurations, storage, availability and so forth.

It is common that if requirements do exist, they are at a general level of detail and probably lack specific conditions for testing. However, customer requirements, especially as expressed in SLAs, can be the starting point for test design. Requirements express what is important to the customer.

Lack of Control (Releases, Data, Performance)

For the cloud customer desiring to test cloud-based applications such as SaaS, the lack of control over the application has a major impact on test scheduling, knowledge of what has changed in the application (or what can be tested in the initial evaluation), and the knowledge of what constitutes correct behavior. These are not necessarily new problems for testers, but lack of control can rise to new levels of impact in cloud computing because of the level and unpredictability of change.

For example, a company decides to adopt a cloud-based solution for video conferencing. A complete evaluation is performed with a pilot group of people and everything looks great. The company starts to use the application for weekly status meetings, training events and customer sales meetings.

One Monday morning, just before a customer sales meeting, the salesperson notices the user interface looks different. The salesperson tries to share their computer desktop in preparation for the meeting and learns that the "share desktop" function doesn't work. The get an "unknown error" message when trying to share their screen in the application. This is a big problem since the meeting starts in ten minutes!

As it turns out, the cloud application provider implemented some major changes over the weekend with no notice to the customers. One of the changes depends on a component found in the most recent version of Java. Without that component, screen sharing will not work.

In the case of this example, the salesperson was not able to diagnose and resolve the problem before the meeting, so it had to be rescheduled with the customer. This caused the company to look bad and placed their sale in jeopardy.

This problem also caused the cloud provider to look bad in how they handled the implementation of the new release of the application and is causing the customer to reconsider their selection.

In this example, only continuous testing would have found the problem on the user side. This is an unacceptable solution due to the amount of work required for that level of testing. As a customer, if I must continually test something, I will rethink my purchase.

The better solution is for the cloud application provider to give better notification to the customers, to provide a choice to customers to upgrade their application version, and to test the end-user "presenter" experience in using the new version. This is a good example of how the cloud provider has much responsibility in the testing process, but also how proactive support can impact user experience in a positive way.

Automation Challenges

Test automation as defined by unattended repeatable testing is an elusive goal for many testers. Test automation is a challenge even when the tester has a lot of control and knowledge of the application. In the cloud, applications can be highly dynamic, which can render test automation inoperable after some functional changes.

Decisions must be made around whether it makes sense to automate something that is likely to change soon, since the Return on Investment (ROI) is seen in the repeatability of the tests. Test automation based on application programming interfaces (APIs) is one way to reduce the impact of changes. However, APIs can also change, which may require changes to automation testware.

Awareness of the Need for Testing

Too often, management in cloud consumer companies has the idea that cloud computing removes the concern of testing. The mindset is that since the cloud application provider should be doing the testing, why should the cloud consumer be concerned with it?

While the cloud vendor does have testing responsibility, the cloud consumer also has testing responsibility from the acceptance perspective. The acceptance or organizational concerns are that the acquired cloud applications will work correctly with other applications that the organization use, and the cloud applications support the desired business needs.

Awareness of the Uniqueness of Cloud Testing

Some degree of cloud testing, such as for business process tests, can be performed manually from an external functional perspective. The differences of test cloud-based applications are often found in the things not immediately seen. It is the architectural view that reveals services, messaging, and other items that must be tested.

Since cloud applications and infrastructure is often built on Service-oriented Architectures (SOA), tools are needed to reach and evaluate the services and messages. This "headless testing" is seen in other contexts, but is pronounced in SOA and the cloud.

It is important to remember that cloud computing is a delivery model, not an architectural style. The impact of this distinction is that cloud applications, services, platforms, and infrastructure may need to be tested in very specific ways depending on architecture. For example, some services may be accessed with Web Services Description Language (WSDL) using Simple Object Access Protocol (SOAP), while other services may be accessed with Representational State Transfer (REST) services.

The Mobile Impact

Take all the challenges listed above and think about testing them on possibly over twelve thousand device configurations, worldwide, in different languages, on different wireless provider networks, with only a fraction of the functionality available to the user. That is mobile testing in a nutshell.

Thankfully, there are cloud-based test tools that can help to some extent in testing the compatibility across many platforms, but simulation versus actual device usage can yield differences in test outcomes.

There is Hope

With all of these risks and challenges, it may sound like cloud technology and the testing of the cloud computing model is futile. But, there are some solution strategies than can help perform cloud testing as a key way to measure the balance of cloud computing risks and benefits. This section explores how to mitigate some of cloud risks using testing.

Understanding the Risks is the First Step

In some cases, understanding risks may prevent you from doing something, such as swimming in shark-infested waters, placing money in risky investments, or playing golf during a lightning storm.

In other cases, understanding the risks involved in an endeavor may actually build your confidence by knowing the hazards and how to avoid them. That is the intent of this chapter – to realize the potential rewards as well as the risks, so you can make informed decisions that can be validated by testing them.

Once you understand the risks that you need to take seriously, you can then determine which cloud computing model is most appropriate for your situation – a private cloud, public cloud or hybrid cloud. Also, you will know how to balance your own applications with those offered as SaaS, and whether IaaS makes sense for you.

Understanding the risks also helps to shape your testing efforts and priorities. For example:

- What is the overall purpose of testing?
- Which types of tests will be needed?
- Who will design the tests?
- Who will perform the tests?
- What will be used as the basis of test design and evaluation?
- When will testing be performed?
- How will testing be performed – manually or automated?
- Which tools would be helpful?
- Which tools will be required?
- Where will testing be performed?

Many of these questions get answered in a test strategy. A test strategy outlines the big picture of the test, which is basically a description of "what" the test should accomplish. The specific methods, schedules, teams, and scope are described in a test plan that describes "how" the test is to be accomplished.

All too often, people focus on the "how" of cloud testing before the "what." For example, people want to know how to use the tools for cloud testing before they know which tests will be accomplished with the tools. This "tool first" approach is risky because a particular test tool may constrain your test options. You may find that a particular tool doesn't support your testing needs until it is too late – after the tool purchase.

DEFINING YOUR CLOUD TESTING STRATEGY

A cloud test strategy is a concise and general document. It doesn't take many hours to create a test strategy. In fact, a great early project activity is to brainstorm a test strategy.

The test strategy can also serve multiple purposes – guide testing direction, keep the project team focused on the test implications of cloud computing and to make sure the right test is designed. For example, you may design a test focused on finding defects when the greater need is to assess fitness for use. This is a risk not confined to cloud testing, but is worth remembering. The impact of designing and performing the wrong test is often not seen until the results are presented to stakeholders, which is far too late to discover the mistake.

However, it is a stretch to say that the test strategy helps to ensure the right test is performed because there have been too many well-planned tests that were never executed as such. Below are considerations for major test strategy topics.

What is the Overall Purpose of Testing?

There can be many objectives for testing something. In some cases, the goal of testing is to find as many defects as possible. In other cases, testing might be needed to certify if an application conforms to standards, or to determine if the application meets specific business needs. The key point is that you understand *your* purpose for testing, in *your* context. In this case, the context is cloud computing with differences seen in whether you are the cloud provider or the cloud customer.

The mission of your organization also drives your context. For example, a financial organization has different concerns than a hospital or a governmental organization.

In testing cloud-based applications, if you try to find all the defects you will miss the larger and more important objective of knowing if the application truly meets your workflow and business needs. In testing workflow support, you will likely find defects, which will help assess the overall quality of the application. The difference is that finding defects is not the main objective, but a secondary one.

Which Types of Tests Will Be Needed?

Perhaps another way to understand the types of tests needed is to ask, "What are the risks?" Test types, such as performance tests and security tests are directly related to risks, since their purpose is to perform tests that measure levels of risk as seen in non-functional behavior. You may also think of these as attributes to be realized.

The context of cloud computing can have many facets, such as:

*   How secure is the application?
*   How reliable is the application and infrastructure?
*   How usable is the application and does it meet the specific needs of the organization?

All of these test objectives relate to cloud computing risks and are expressed in test cases and test scenarios.

The great challenge in any testing is that we can't test even all the functionality of an application, let alone all the attributes of the application. This means we have to pick the test targets carefully, which involves selecting the most important attributes, such as correctness, performance, security and so on.

Considering that each of these types of testing can require special people, tools and skills implies that we can only address the truly critical risks, given most organizations' time and resource constraints.

This is a sobering reality since major problems and liability can be realized from any risk – even those risks we don't identify in advance. One way to address this balancing act is to test all attributes to some degree, realizing that those attributes receiving less testing may need contingency planning in case problems do occur.

For example, you may choose to focus on testing security and performance quite heavily, while testing usability to a much lesser extent.

Who Will Design the Tests?

The key word here is "design." Test design involves a thoughtful approach to testing that analyzes a situation (application, business process, service, or other entity to be tested) and devises effective tests. Test design is a fundamentally different skill set from test performance, test automation and other testing tasks, which implies there should be people dedicated specifically to that task.

Test design responsibilities should extend across the organization to reflect the perspectives of developers, testers, users, customers and any other stakeholder group. Although many people may contribute ideas and conditions to test design, it is good practice for a trained and experienced test designer to format and implement the tests. Otherwise, there will be inconsistency in the tests, both in quality and formatting.

Although some people may not want to accept the task of test design, the need for it still exists. For example, if a developer doesn't want to design structural tests of a service due to lack or time or lack of interest, code-based tests are still needed. Likewise, if the business stakeholders reject the idea of at least supplying input to test design, then the workflow tests will probably lack important scenarios to be tested.

Who Will Perform the Tests?

In some organizations, the test designers may also perform the tests. In other cases, these may be the responsibility of separate groups. Ideally, test performance will extend across the organization and will also be embraced by business units.

There is also the division of tests performed by the cloud provider and the cloud customer. The cloud provider has the responsibility of performing many types and levels of testing for the purpose of offering a solid product. The cloud customer has the responsibility of performing tests for the purpose of mitigating the risks to the enterprise and its customers.

In a cloud testing strategy, the people performing testing may just be indicated by role, not necessarily by name. The specific test assignments can be made later as the team structure emerges.

What Will Be Used as the Basis of Test Design and Evaluation?

This is where testing gets really challenging, especially if you are testing SaaS applications where the functionality may not be defined by documentation, but rather discovered by using the application to perform business tasks.

In private cloud development where your organization may be the creator of the applications, there is the possibility of basing tests on user requirements, use cases, and other forms of specifications. In public clouds and SaaS, you may be on your own to define what is acceptable when evaluating test results. In fact, a good basis of evaluation for cloud applications is how they work with your workflow processes and specific needs, regardless of what is specified in any documentation.

When Will Testing Be Performed?

SaaS applications don't have the same kind of project life cycle as in-house developed applications. So, testing may be more of an event than a process. However, in-house developed applications hosted in a private cloud may resemble any other development and test lifecycle.

SaaS testing may resemble an evaluation more than a full test, depending on your testing goals. The idea is that the application has already been developed, so testing is typically a high-level process view as opposed to the low-level detailed view. So, in theory, this is like a "big bang", blackbox test in many ways.

In the SaaS context, testing can performed at any time you are ready to perform an evaluation. The main determination of test readiness will be resource availability and co-ordination with related activities such as the evaluation of other related applications.

How Will Testing Be Performed: Manually or Automated?

Test automation is an attractive proposition, but SaaS applications are highly subject to change. Change and UI-based test automation don't go well together. Therefore, there may not be enough repetition of the test to achieve a positive return on investment.

Consider, for example, the user interface automation of some basic functions in a cloud-based accounting application. I use this example because this is where many people start in test automation.

Assume that you create a set of one hundred automated tests in one week. You could have performed those tests manually in about five hours or less.

A few weeks later, you learn that the application provider has applied a new release of the application. In some cases, you get the option of when to apply the new version, but in any event, you now wish to perform a regression test.

If the appearance and functionality of the application is largely unchanged, then your automated tests will be fine. However, if the vendor decides to make even some cosmetic changes, your automation may be rendered useless.

There are some automation strategies that can help deal with such situations, such as automating the messaging and non-UI aspects of the application. This does take the UI issues away, but there can still be impact due to unexpected structural changes.

Another option is to create automation using object recognition as opposed to co-ordinate positioning or image comparison. The good news is that many test automation tools have been adopting this approach for last few years.

Test automation decisions are difficult ones and go beyond the scope of this chapter. However, the key point in the test strategy is to at least understand to what extent you will employ test automation versus manual testing, and which test automation approaches will be most applicable.

Which Tools Would Be Helpful?

Not every test tool is a test automation tool, so there may be other tools such as test design tools, issue tracking tools and so forth. You may already have some tools in place and being used, but it is good to know which ones are helpful for cloud testing.

For example, cloud monitoring tools can help balance the performance risk. We know there are many factors that contribute to poor performance, such as network outages, code inefficiencies, data base inefficiencies, and so forth. Combine those factors with the challenge of creating a performance test environment and the need for something more than performance testing can be seen. Monitoring is a way to keep a virtual set of eyes on real-time application and infrastructure performance from many points of access.

Which Tools Will Be Required?

Some tools will be absolutely required. For example, if you plan on performance testing, then a performance test tool is needed for accuracy and the ability to test high levels of load. Another example is if you want to test services that have no user interface, a service test tool is needed to supply input to messages and verify results from services.

You may not be able to identify a specific tool or vendor, but you should have a general idea of your tool needs and requirements.

Where Will Testing Be Performed?

This is useful to define when testing is performed by people in various locations. You will likely be testing in a cloud-hosted test environment, so the physical location is important for organizational and control purposes rather than technical reasons.

For performance tests, the point of access is very important to consider. With cloud-based performance test tools, it is easy to distribute tests virtually across locations around the world.

STANDARDS ARE YOUR FRIEND

Although standards have the reputation for being constraining and generally a pain to follow, the intent of standards is to be a positive thing. They provide guidance in how to do things, plus you don't have to reinvent your own methods.

Standards are not necessarily meant to be prescriptive. They may not tell you exactly how to do something, just what should be addressed and to what extent. Standards are also meant to be tailored to meet specific needs. Tailoring requires thoughtful application, but is needed to apply standards intelligently.

Certainly there are issues with standards. They may be written in ambiguous ways on purpose, may be in conflict with other standards and get outdated.

For cloud testing, standards such as OWASP (The Open Web Application Security Project) for security testing (www.owasp.org) are very helpful in getting a grip on web services security vulnerabilities and how to test for them.

Standards from the World Wide Web Consortium (W3C) at www.w3.org cover a broad range of topics from web architecture to security. The WS- standards help testers to understand *what* to test, however, they do not focus specifically on testing techniques.

OASIS (Organization for the Advancement of Structured Information Standards) promotes and produces international standards for security, cloud computing, SOA, web services and other areas. OASIS has active initiatives for cloud computing standards.

Like the W3C standards, the OASIS standards don't directly impact test activities, but are still helpful in understanding what are being proposed as standards in cloud computing. The key here is "proposed," since there are no police for standards, therefore they will not be followed by everyone. However, they do indicate good practice as defined by consensus from a broad group of practitioners.

WS-I is the Web Services Interoperability Organization, which promotes standard practices for web service interoperability. Interoperability is a key attribute needed for cloud applications and is achieved through good design and implementation, not testing. Most of the WS-I focus is on web services, and since cloud applications often make use of web services, there is a useful help in these standards when it comes to testing interoperability.

TOOLS: GETTING BETTER ALL THE TIME

One of the bright areas of cloud testing is the availability and quality of tools for tasks such as testing web services, mobile applications and performance. In the past, it seemed that tools often lagged the demands of the technology. However, in cloud computing, some vendors have actually been out front of the technology in their offerings.

In fact, the cloud itself offers great support for test environments, which have also been traditional areas of challenge. Now, with cloud-based virtual environments, the problem isn't so much getting the right environment but managing the many possible environments.

Cloud-based tools eliminate the need for physical seat licensing of tools. This can be an attractive option for large test teams distributed geographically.

Earlier in this chapter, examples were presented of how cloud-based test tools can provide great advantage in the performance testing of mobile devices and cloud-based applications from many points of access around the world, but controlled from a single point of control. This is a form of testing never before possible, all because of the distributed nature of the cloud.

SUMMARY

The value of cloud computing must be balanced with a careful consideration of the risks. Testing is a classic way to help mitigate risks, but takes a much different and challenging perspective in cloud computing. The business stakeholders must play a key role in how to deal with cloud computing risks. Ultimately, the business or larger organization has responsibility of the services offered to its customers.

Understanding the risks and having a corresponding testing strategy is key to getting the business value from cloud computing. This is not just a job for testing. The entire organization should have a voice in how the risks will be mitigated and

should understand their role in effective testing of cloud-based applications and platforms.

REFERENCES

Mell, P., & Grance, T. (2011). *The NIST definition of cloud computing. (Special Publication 800-145), National Institute of Standards and Technology*. NIST.

ENDNOTES

[1] The term "IT customer" is used to describe the IT department in an organization that is the customer of a cloud vendor. This is as compared to the end-customer who uses cloud services as provided by a business whether provided by a cloud vendor or by the business.

Compilation of References

Aalst, L. V. D. (2009). *Software testing as a service* (STaaS). Retrieved May 6, 2009, from http://www.tmap.net/Images/Paper%20STaaS_tcm8-47910.pdf

Abd-El-Hafiz, S., & Basili, V. (1996). A knowledge-based approach to the analysis of loops. *IEEE Transactions on Software Engineering*, 22(5), 339–360. doi:10.1109/32.502226

Abran, A., Moore, J. W., Bourque, P., & Dupuis, R. (Eds.). (2004). *Guide to the software engineering body of knowledge* (3rd ed.).

Adler, Y., Farchi, E., Klausner, M., Pelleg, D., Raz, O., Shochat, M., et al. (2009). Advanced code coverage analysis using substring holes. In *Proceedings of the Eighteenth International Symposium on Software Testing and Analysis* (ISSTA '09), (pp. 37-46). New York, NY: ACM.

Afzal, W., Torkar, R., & Feldt, R. (2009). A systematic review of search- based testing for non-functional system properties. *Information and Software Technology*, 51(6), 957–976. doi:10.1016/j.infsof.2008.12.005

Alazzawe, A., Wijesekera, D., & Dantu, R. (2009). A testbed for mobile social computing. *2009 5th International Conference on Testbeds and Research Infrastructures for the Development of Networks Communities and Workshops*, (pp. 1-6). IEEE. doi:10.1109/TRIDENT-COM.2009.4976250

Alba, E., & Chicano, F. (2008). Observations in using parallel and sequential evolutionary algorithms for automatic software testing. *Computers & Operations Research*, 35(10), 3161–3183. doi:10.1016/j.cor.2007.01.016

Albert, R., & Barabási, A.-L. (2002). Statistical mechanics of complex networks. *Reviews of Modern Physics*, 74, 48–94. doi:10.1103/RevModPhys.74.47

Ali, S., Briand, L. C., Hemmati, H., & Panesar-Walawege, R. K. (2010). A systematic review of the application and empirical investigation of search-based test case generation. *IEEE Transactions on Software Engineering*, 36(6). doi:10.1109/TSE.2009.52

Alkassar, E., Cohen, E., Kovalev, M., & Paul, W. J. (2012, January). Verification of TLB virtualization implemented in C. In the *4th International Conference on Verified Software: Theories, Tools, Experiments* (VSTTE 2012) (pp. 209–224). Philadelphia, PA: Springer.

Alkassar, E., Hillebrand, M. A., Paul, W. J., & Petrova, E. (2010, August). Automated verification of a small hypervisor. In the *Third International Conference on Verified Software: Theories, Tools, Experiments* (VSTTE 2010) (pp. 40–54). Edinburgh, UK: Springer.

Alkassar, E., Paul, W., Starostin, A., & Tsyban, A. (2010, August). Pervasive verification of an OS microkernel. In the *Third International Conference on Verified Software: Theories, Tools, Experiments* (VSTTE 2010) (pp. 71–85). Edinburgh, UK: Springer.

Alt, F., Shirazi, A. S., Schmidt, A., Kramer, U., & Nawaz, Z. (2010). Location-based crowdsourcing: Extending crowdsourcing to the real world. *Proceedings of the 6th Nordic Conference on Human-Computer Interaction: Extending Boundaries*, (pp. 13-2)2. ACM. Retrieved from http://portal.acm.org/citation.cfm?id=1868921

Amazon Cloud, A. M. I. (2008). *Creating and Preparing AMIs*. Retrieved from http://docs.amazonwebservices.com/AWSEC2/2008-02-01/DeveloperGuide/index.html?CreatingAndBundlingAMIs.html

Amazon EC2. (n.d.). *Instance types*. Retrieved from http://aws.amazon.com/ec2/instance-types/

Amazon Web Services. (2012). *Amazon elastic compute cloud* (Amazon EC2). Retrieved from http://aws.amazon.com/ec2/

Amazon. (2011). *Amazon web services: Amazon elastic compute cloud.* Retrieved April 22, 2011, from http://aws.amazon.com/ec2/

Amazon. (2011). *How is Amazon s3 data organized?* Retrieved April 14, 2011, from http://aws.amazon.com/s3/faqs/#How_is_Amazon_S3_data_organized.

Amazon. (2012). *Amazon Elastic Compute Cloud.* Retrieved June 9th, 2012, from http://aws.amazon.com/ec2

Amazon. (2012). *Elastic MapReduce.* Retrieved from http://aws.amazon.com/elasticmapreduce/

Amazon. (n.d.). *Amazon web service.* Retrieved from http://aws.amazon.com/

AmazonEC2. (n.d.). *Elasticfox.* Retrieved from http://aws.amazon.com/developertools/609?_encoding=UTF8&jiveRedirect=1

AmazonS3. (n.d.). *S3cmd.* Retrieved from http://s3tools.org/s3cmd

Ammann, P., & Offutt, J. (2008). *Introduction to software testing.* Cambridge, UK. doi:10.1017/CBO9780511809163

Anand, S., Pasareanu, C. S., & Visser, W. (2007, March). JPF-SE: A symbolic execution extension to Java PathFinder. In the *13th International Conference on Tools and Algorithms for the Construction and Analysis of Systems* (TACAS 2007) (pp. 134–138). Braga, Portugal: Springer.

Anderson, J. Q., & Rainee, L. (2010, June). *The future of cloud computing.* Pew Research Center Publications. Retrieved June 26, 2011, from http://pewresearch.org/pubs/1623/future-cloud-computing-technology-experts

Andrade, N., Cirne, W., Brasileiro, F., & Roisenberg, P. (2003). OurGrid: An approach to easily assemble grids with equitable resource sharing. *9th International Workshop on Job Scheduling Strategies for Parallel Processing, Lecture Notes in Computer Science, vol. 2862* (pp. 61–86). Springer Verlag.

Andrews, J. H., & Zhang, Y. (2000). Broad-spectrum studies of log file analysis. In *Proceedings of the International Conference on Software Engineering* (pp. 105-114).

Aoki, P. M., Honicky, R. J., Mainwaring, A., Myers, C., Paulos, E., Subramanian, S., & Woodruff, A. (2008). Common sense: Mobile environmental sensing platforms to support community action and citizen science. *Adjunct Proceedings of the Tenth International Conference on Ubiquitous Computing,* (pp. 59-60). Retrieved from http://www.paulaoki.com/papers/ubicomp08-demo.pdf

Apache Software Foundation. (2010). Retrieved from http://www.apache.org/

Apache. (2010). *Ant.* Retrieved from http://ant.apache.org/

Apache. (2010). *Hadoop.* Retrieved from http://hadoop.apache.org/ Apache. (2011). *Commons SCXML.* Retrieved April 21, 2011, from http://commons.apache.org/scxml/

Apache. (2011). *Subversion.* Retrieved April 21, 2011, from http://subversion.apache.org

Arcuri, A. (2010). Longer is better: On the role of test sequence length in software testing. In *Proceedings of the International Conference on Software Testing* (pp. 469-478).

Ardagna, D. (2011). A service-based framework for flexible business processes. *IEEE Software Magazine, 28*(2), 61–67.

Armbrust, M., Fox, A., Griffith, R., Joseph, A. D., Katz, R. H., Konwinski, A., et al. (2009). *Above the clouds: A Berkeley view of cloud computing.* Technical report UCB/EECS-2009-28. EECS Department, University of California, Berkeley.

Armbrust, M., Fox, A., Griffith, R., Joseph, A., Katz, R., & Konwinski, A. ... Stoica, I. (2009, February). *Above the clouds: A Berkeley view of cloud computing.* University of California, Berkeley. Retrieved April 23, 2011, from http://www.eecs.berkeley.edu/Pubs/TechRpts/2009/EECS-2009-28.pdf

Assembla, L. L. C. (2011). *Assembla.* Retrieved April 27, 2011, from http://www.assembla.com

ATLAS.ti. (2005). *The knowledge workbench.* Scientific Software Development.

Avritzer, A., & Weyuker, E. J. (1995). The automatic generation of load test suites and the assessment of the resulting software. *IEEE Transactions on Software Engineering, 21*(9), 705–716. doi:10.1109/32.464549

Baars, A., Vos, T., & Dimitrov, D. (2010). Using evolutionary testing to find test scenarios for hard to reproduce faults. *IEEE International Conference on Software Testing Verification and Validation Workshop,* (pp. 173-181).

Bach, J. (2003). *Heuristics of software testability.* Retrieved April 22, 2011, from http://www.satisfice. com/tools/testable.pdf

Bai, X., Chen, B., Ma, B., & Gong, Y. (2011). Design of intelligent agent for collaborative testing of service-based systems. *International Workshop on Automation of Software Test* (pp. 22-28).

Bai, X., Dai, G., Xu, D., & Tsai, W.-T. (2006). A multi-agent based framework for collaborative testing on web services. *International Workshop on Collaborative Computing, Integration, and Assurance* (pp. 205-210).

Bai, X., Li, M., Chen, B., Gao, J., & Tsai, W. T. (2011). A survey of cloud testing tools. *International Symposium on Service Oriented System Engineering* (pp. 1-12).

Bai, X., Wang, Y., Dai, G., Tsai, W.-T., & Chen, Y. (2007). A framework for contract-based collaborative verification and validation of web services. *International Conference on Component-Based Software Engineering* (pp. 258-273).

Baker, P., Schieferdecker, I., & Williams, C. (2008). *Model-driven testing – Using the UML testing profile.* Berlin, Germany: Springer Pub.

Baldini, A., Benso, A., Chiusano, S., & Prinetto, P. (2000). 'BOND': An interposition agents based fault injector for Windows NT. *International Symposium on Defect and Fault-Tolerance in VLSI Systems (DFT '00)* (p. 387). IEEE.

Ball, T. (1999). *The concept of dynamic analysis.* Paper presented at the ESEC/FSE.

Banzai, T., Koizumi, H., Kanbayashi, R., Imada, T., Kimura, H., Hanawa, T., & Sato, M. (2010). D-Cloud: Design of a software testing environment for reliable distributed systems using cloud computing technology. *2nd International Symposium on Cloud Computing (Cloud 2010) in conjunction with CCGrid2010* (pp. 631-636). IEEE.

Barabási, A.-L., & Bonabeau, E. (2003). Scale-free networks. *Scientific American, 288,* 50–59. doi:10.1038/scientificamerican0503-60

Bardin, S., & Herrmann, P. (2008, April). Structural testing of executables. In the *First IEEE International Conference on Software Testing, Verification, and Validation* (ICST'08) (pp. 22–31). Lillehammer, Norway: IEEE Computer Society.

Bardin, S., Herrmann, P., & Perroud, F. (2010, March). An alternative to SAT-based approaches for bit-vectors. In the *16th International Conference on Tools and Algorithms for the Construction and Analysis of Systems* (TACAS 2010) (pp. 84–98). Paphos, Cyprus: Springer.

Barham, P., Dragovic, B., Fraser, K., Hand, S., Harris, T., Ho, A., et al. (2003). Xen and the art of virtualization. In *ACM Symposium on Operating Systems Principles* (pp. 164–177). New York, NY.

Barringer, H., Groce, A., Havelund, K., & Smith, M. (2010). Formal analysis of log files. *AIAA Journal of Aerospace Computing, Information and Communications, 7*(11).

Basarke, C., Berger, C., Homeier, K., & Rumpe, B. (2007). Design and quality assurance of intelligent vehicle functions in the "virtual vehicle.". In *Proceedings of the 11 (vol. 9).* Automobiltechnische konferenz –virtual vehicle creation.

Basarke, C., Berger, C., & Rumpe, B. (2007). Software & systems engineering process and tools for the development of autonomous driving intelligence. *Journal of Aerospace Computing, Information, and Communication, 4*(12), 1158–1174. doi:10.2514/1.33453

Baxter, G., Frean, M., Noble, J., Rickerby, M., Smith, H., Visser, M., et al. (2006). *Understanding the shape of Java software.* Paper presented at the OOPSLA.

Becker, B. (2011). The cloud scenario is developing. *Computer Weekly, Special Issue on Cloud Guide*, 4-6.

Beck, K. (1999). *Extreme programming explained: Embrace change*. Addison-Wesley Professional.

Begin, M. E., Sancho, G. D., Meglio, A. D., Ferro, E., Ronchieri, E., Selmi, M., & Zurek, M. (2007). Lecture Notes in Computer Science: *Vol. 4401. Build, configuration, integration and testing tools for large software projects: ETICS. Rapid Integration of Software Engineering Techniques* (pp. 81–97). Springer Verlag.

Beizer, B. (1990). *Software testing techniques* (2nd ed.). New York, NY: Van Nostrand Reinhold Co.

Bellay, B., & Gall, H. (1997). A comparison of four reverse engineering tools. In I. Baxter & A. Quilici (Eds.), *Working Conference on Reverse Engineering* (pp. 2-11). Los Alamitos, CA: IEEE Computer Society Press.

Benavides, D., Trinidad, P., & Ruiz-Cortés, A. (2005). Automated reasoning on feature models. *Advanced Information Systems Engineering, Lecture Notes in Computer Science, 3520*, (pp. 381-390). Retrieved from http://www.springerlink.com/content/qh6yvx3y6pxet8ex/

Benavides, D., Segura, S., & Ruiz-Cortés, A. (2010). Automated analysis of feature models 20 years later: A literature review. *Information Systems, 35*(6). doi:10.1016/j.is.2010.01.001

Bennett, K. (1995). Legacy systems: Coping with success. *IEEE Software, 12*(1), 19–23. doi:10.1109/52.363157

Bennioff, M. (2009). *Behind the cloud: The untold story of how Salesforce.com went from idea to billion-dollar company and revolutionized an industry*. Jossey-Bass.

Berger. C., & Rumpe, B. (2012). Autonomous driving – 5 years after the urban challenge: the anticipatory vehicle as a cyber-physical system. In *Proceedings of the INFORMATIK 2012*.

Berger, C. (2010). *Automating acceptance tests for sensor- and actuator-based systems on the example of autonomous vehicles. Aachener Informatik-Berichte* (*Vol. 6*). Aachen, Germany: Shaker Verlag.

Berger, C., & Rumpe, B. (2010). Supporting agile change management by scenario-based regression simulation. *IEEE Transactions on Intelligent Transportation Systems, 11*(2), 504–509. doi:10.1109/TITS.2010.2044571

Berger, C., & Rumpe, B. (2012). Engineering autonomous driving software. In Rouff, C., & Hinchey, M. (Eds.), *Experience From The Darpa Urban Challenge* (pp. 243–271). London, UK: Springer-Verlag. doi:10.1007/978-0-85729-772-3_10

Bertolino, A. (2007). Software testing research: Achievements, challenges, dreams. In *Proceedings of International Conference on Future of Software Engineering*.

Bertolino, A., & Marchetti, E. (2005). A brief essay on software testing. In Thayer, R. H., & Christensen, M. J. (Eds.), *Software engineering, the development process*. Wiley-IEEE Computer Society Press.

Bieberstein, N., et al. (2005). *Service-oriented architecture (SOA) compass: Business value, planning, and enterprise roadmap*. IBM Press, 2005.

Biermeyer. J. O., Templeton, T. R., Berger, c., Gonzalez, H., Naikal, N., Rumpe, B., & Sastry, S. (2010). Rapid integration and calibration of new sensors using the berkeley aachen robotics toolkit (bart). In *Proceedings of the 11. Braunschweiger Symposiums "Automatisierungssysteme, Assistenzsysteme und eingebettete Systeme für Transportmittel"*.

Binder, R. (1999). *Testing object-oriented systems: Models, patterns, and tools*. Addison-Wesley Professional.

Binder, R. V. (1994). Design for testability in object-oriented systems. *Communications of the ACM, 37*(9), 87–101. doi:10.1145/182987.184077

Binnig, C., Kossmann, D., Kraska, T., & Loesing, S. (2009). How is the weather tomorrow? Towards a benchmark for the cloud. *International Workshop on Testing Database Systems* (pp. 9:1–9:6).

Black, J., Melachrinoudis, E., & Kaeli, D. (2004). Bi-criteria models for all-uses test suite reduction. In *International Conference on Software Engineering* (pp. 106-115). Washington, DC: IEEE Computer Society.

Boehm, B. (1988, May). A spiral model of software development and enhancement. *Computer, 21*(5). doi:10.1109/2.59

Bohnet, J., & Döllner, J. (2006). *Visual exploration of function call graphs for feature location in complex software systems*. Paper presented at the 2006 ACM Symposium on Software Visualization.

Bolton, J. (2004, June). *Development of Homeland Security Presidential Directive (HSPD) - 7*. The Executive Office of the President. Retrieved April 13, 2011, from http://www.whitehouse.gov/sites/default/files/omb/assets/omb/memoranda/fy04/m-04-15.pdf

Bondi, A. B. (2000). Characteristics of scalability and their impact on performance. *International Workshop on Software and Performance* (pp. 195-203). ACM Press.

Bose, A., & Shin, K. G. (2006). On mobile viruses exploiting messaging and Bluetooth services. *Securecomm and Workshops, 2006,* 1–10. doi:10.1109/SECCOMW.2006.359562

Bourque, P., & Dupuis, R. (2004). *Software engineering body of knowledge (SWEBOK)*. IEEE Computer Society.

Bozkurt, M., Harman, M., & Hassoun, Y. (2007). *Testing web services – A survey*. Technical report TR-10-01.

Bradski, G., & Kaehler, A. (2008). *Learning Opencv*. Sebastopol, CA: O'Reilly Media.

Brataas, G., & Hughes, P. (2004). Exploring architectural scalability. *International Workshop on Software and Performance* (pp. 125-129). ACM Press.

Breu, M., et al. (2010). *Living on the MoVE: Towards an architecture for a living models infrastructure.*

Breu, R. (2010). *Ten principles for living models - A manifesto of change-driven software engineering*. Paper presented at CISIS 2010, The Fourth International Conference on Complex, Intelligent and Software Intensive Systems.

Broekman, B., & Notenboom, E. (2003). *Testing Embedded Software*. Upper Saddle River, NJ: Addison-Wesley.

Brown, A. W. (2005). *Large-scale component-based development*. Prentice-Hall.

Broy, M. (2005). *Model-based testing of reactive systems. LNCS 3472*. Berlin, Germany: Springer. doi:10.1007/b137241

Burke, J., Estrin, D., Hansen, M., Parker, A., Ramanathan, N., Reddy, S., & Srivastava, M. B. (2006). Participatory sensing. *IEEE Internet Computing, 14*(1), 12-42. Citeseer. doi:10.1109/MIC.2010.12

Burnim, J., & Sen, K. (2008, September). Heuristics for scalable dynamic test generation. In the *23rd IEEE/ACM International Conference on Automated Software Engineering* (ASE 2008) (pp. 443–446). L'Aquila, Italy: IEEE.

Burtsev, A., Radhakrishnan, P., Hibler, M., & Lepreau, J. (2009). Transparent checkpoints of closed distributed systems in emulab. *Proceedings of the Fourth ACM European Conference on Computer Systems EuroSys 09,* (p. 173). ACM Press. doi:10.1145/1519065.1519084

Buyya, R., Shin, Y. C., & Venugopal, S. (2008, 25-27 September). *Market-oriented cloud computing: Vision, hype, and reality for delivering it services as computing utilities*. Paper presented at the HPCC.

Cadar, C., Dunbar, D., & Engler, D. R. (2008, December). KLEE: Unassisted and automatic generation of high-coverage tests for complex systems programs. In the *8th USENIX Symposium on Operating Systems Design and Implementation* (OSDI 2008) (pp. 209–224). San Diego, CA: USENIX Association.

Cadar, C., Ganesh, V., Pawlowski, P. M., Dill, D. L., & Engler, D. R. (2006, November). EXE: Automatically generating inputs of death. In the *13th ACM Conference on Computer and Communications Security* (CCS'06) (pp. 322–335). Alexandria, VA: ACM Press.

Cai, L., Machiraju, S., & Chen, H. (2009). Defending against sensor-sniffing ATAACKs on mobile phones. *Proceedings of the 1st ACM Workshop on Networking, Systems, and Applications for Mobile Handhelds* (pp. 31-36). New York, NY: ACM. doi: http://doi.acm.org/10.1145/1592606.1592614

Calinescu, R. (2011). Dynamic QoS management and optimization in service-based systems. *IEEE Transactions on Software Engineering, 37*(3), 387. doi:10.1109/TSE.2010.92

Campbell, A. T., Eisenman, S. B., & Lane, N. D. (2008). The rise of people-centric sensing. *IEEE Internet Computing, 12*(4). Retrieved from http://www.computer.org/portal/web/csdl/doi/10.1109/MIC.2008.90doi:10.1109/MIC.2008.90

Canada Revenue Agency. (2012). *Certified software.* Retrieved May 31, 2012, from http://netfile.gc.ca/sftwr-eng.html

Candea, G., Bucur, S., & Zamfir, C. (2010). Automated software testing as a service. *ACM Symposium on Cloud Computing* (pp. 155-160). New York, NY: ACM.

Canfora, G., & DiPenta, M. (2006). Testing services and service-centric systems – Challenges and opportunities. *IT Professional, 8,* 10. doi:10.1109/MITP.2006.51

Canfora, G., & DiPenta, M. (2008). A framework for QoS-aware binding and rebinding of composite web services. *Journal of Systems and Software, 81*(10), 1754. doi:10.1016/j.jss.2007.12.792

Carreira, J., Madeira, H., & Silva, J. G. (1998). Xception: A technique for the experimental evaluation of dependability in modern computers. *IEEE Transactions on Software Engineering, 24,* 125–136. doi:10.1109/32.666826

Carr, N. (2007). *The big switch.* New York, NY: Harpers Books.

Casanova, H. (2002). Distributed computing research issues in grid computing. *ACM SIGACT News, 33*(3), 50-70. ACM. doi:10.1145/582475.582486

Catteddu, D., & Hogben, G. (2009A, November). *Cloud computing: Information assurance framework.* The European Network and Information Security Agency. Retrieved April 23, 2011, from http://www.usccu.us/documents/US-CCU%20Cyber-Security%20Check%20List%202007.pdf

Catteddu, D., & Hogben, G. (2009B, November). *Cloud computing risk assessment.* The European Network and Information Security Agency. Retrieved April 23, 2011, from http://www.enisa.europa.eu/act/rm/files/deliverables/cloud-computing-risk-assessment

CBDI. (2011). *CBDI forum* (Online). Retrieved from http://CBDIForum.com

CCRA. (2012). *The common criteria for information technology security evaluation.* Retrieved from http://www.commoncriteriaportal.org

Chan, W. K., Mei, L., & Zhang, Z. (2009). *Modeling and testing of cloud applications.* In IEEE Asia-Pacific Services Computing Conference. Los Alamitos, CA, USA.

Chaudhry, S., Caprioli, P., Yip, S., & Tremblay, M. (2005). High-performance throughput computing. *Micro, 25,* 32–45.

Chebaro, O., Kosmatov, N., Giorgetti, A., & Julliand, J. (2012, March). Program slicing enhances a verification technique combining static and dynamic analysis. In the *27th Annual ACM Symposium on Applied Computing* (SAC 2012) (pp. 1284–1291). Riva del Garda, Italy: ACM Press.

Chen, K., & Rajlich, V. (2000). *Case study of feature location using dependence graph.* Paper presented at the IWPC/ICPC.

Chen, Y., & Sun, X. (2006). STAS: A scalability testing and analysis system. *IEEE International Conference on Cluster Computing* (pp. 1-10).

Cheng, J., Wong, S. H. Y., Yang, H., & Lu, S. (2007). SmartSiren: Virus detection and alert for smartphones. *Proceedings of the 5th International Conference on Mobile Systems Applications and Services* (pp. 258-271). ACM. Retrieved from https://www.usenix.org/events/mobisys07/full_papers/p258.pdf

Chen, T. Y., Tse, T. H., & Zhou, Z. Q. (2011). Semi-proving – An integrated method for program proving, testing and debugging. *IEEE Transactions on Software Engineering, 37*(1), 109. doi:10.1109/TSE.2010.23

Chidamer, S., & Kemmerer, C. (1994). A metrics suite for object-oriented design. *IEEE Transactions on Software Engineering, 20*(6), 476. doi:10.1109/32.295895

Chikofsky, E. J., & Cross, J. H. II. (1990). Reverse engineering and design recovery: A taxonomy. *IEEE Software, 7*(1), 13–17. doi:10.1109/52.43044

Chintapatla, B., Goulart, A., & Magnussen, W. (2010). Testbed experiments on the location to service translation (LoST) protocol for mobile users. *2010 7th IEEE Consumer Communications and Networking Conference,* (pp. 1-5). IEEE. doi:10.1109/CCNC.2010.5421603

Chou, J., O'Donnell, B., & Shrirer, M. (2010). Global PC market maintains double-digit growth in third quarter despite weak results in some segments, according to IDC. *International Data Corporation.* Retrieved from http://www.businesswire.com/news/home/20101013007002/en/Global-PC-Market-Maintains-Double-Digit-Growth-Quarter

Christie, A. M. (1999). *Simulation: An enabling technology in software engineering* (pp. 25–30). Crosstalk-The Journal Of Defense Software Engineering.

Ciortea, L., Zamfir, C., Bucur, S., Chipounov, V., & Candea, G. (2009). *Cloud9: A software testing service.* 3rd SOSP Workshop on Large Distributed Systems and Middleware (LADIS), Big Sky, MT.

Ciortea, L., Zamfir, C., Bucur, S., Chipounov, V., & Candea, G. (2009). Cloud9: a software testing service. *Operating Systems Review, 43*(4), 5–10. doi:10.1145/1713254.1713257

Ciortea, L., Zamfir, C., Bucur, S., Chipounov, V., & Candea, G. (2010). Cloud9: A software testing service. *ACM SIGOPS Operating Systems Review, 43*(4), 5–10. doi:10.1145/1713254.1713257

Clarke, L. A. (1976). A system to generate test data and symbolically execute programs. *IEEE Transactions on Software Engineering, 2*(3), 215–222. doi:10.1109/TSE.1976.233817

Clauset, A., Shalizi, C. R., & Newman, M. E. J. (2009). Power-law distributions in empirical data. *SIAM Review, 51*(4), 661–703. doi:10.1137/070710111

Clements, P., & Northrop, L. (2001). *Software product lines: Patterns and practices* (3rd ed.). Addison Wesley.

Cloud Security Alliance. (2009, December). *Security guidance for critical areas of focus in cloud computing* V2.1. Cloud Security Alliance. Retrieved April 23, 2011, from http://www.cloudsecurityalliance.org/csaguide.pdf

Cloud Security Alliance. (2010, March). *Top threats to cloud computing* V 1.0. Cloud Security Alliance. Retrieved April 23, 2011, from https://cloudsecurityalliance.org/topthreats/csathreats.v1.0.pdf

CloudSecurityAlliance. (2011). *Top threats to cloud computing.*

CMU. (2010, November). *CMMi for development,* Version 1.3. (CMU/SEI-2010-TR-033, November 2010).

Code Cover. (2012). Retrieved June 14th, 2012 from http://codecover.org/

Cohen, E., Dahlweid, M., Hillebrand, M. A., Leinenbach, D., Moskal, M., Santen, T., et al. (2009, August). VCC: A practical system for verifying concurrent C. In the *22nd International Conference on Theorem Proving in Higher Order Logics* (TPHOLs 2009) (pp. 23–42). Munich, Germany: Springer.

Collard, R. (2009). Performance innovations, testing implications. *Software Test & Performance Magazine, 6*(8), 19–20.

Collins-Sussman, B., Fitzpatrick, B. W., & Pilato, C. M. (2004). *Version control with subversion.* Sebastopol, CA: O'Reilly Media.

Copeland, P. (2010). Google's innovation factory: Testing, culture, and infrastructure. In *3rd IEEE International Conference on Software Testing, Verification, and Validation* (pp.11-14). Los Alamitos, CA: IEEE CS Press. doi:10.1109/ICST.2010.65

Cornelissen, B., Zaidman, A., & Holten, D., &. all, e. (2008). Execution trace analysis through massive sequence and circular bundle views. *Journal of Systems and Software, 81,* 2252–2268. doi:10.1016/j.jss.2008.02.068

Cornelissen, B., Zaidman, A., & van Deursen, A. (2011). A controlled experiment for program comprehension through trace visualization. *IEEE Transactions on Software Engineering, 37*(3), 341–355. doi:10.1109/TSE.2010.47

Cornelissen, B., Zaidman, A., van Deursen, A., Moonen, L., & Koschke, R. (2009). A systematic survey of program comprehension through dynamic analysis. *IEEE Transactions on Software Engineering, 35*(5), 684–702. doi:10.1109/TSE.2009.28

Costa, A. D., Nunes, C., Silva, V. T., Fonseca, B., & Lucena, C. J. P. (2010). JAAF+T: A framework to implement self-adaptive agents that apply self-test. In *International Symposium on Applied Computing (SAC' 10),* (pp. 928-935). New York, NY: ACM.

Credant Technologies. (2009). Survey demonstrates poor smartphone security attitude amongst users. *Credant Technologies.* Retrieved from http://www.prosecurity-zone.com/News/It_security/Mobile_computing_security/Survey_demonstrates_poor_smartphone_security_attitude_amongst_users_8942.asp#axzz1jxol1VYk

CruiseControl. (2011). *Cruisecontrol.* Retrieved April 27, 2011, from http://cruisecontrol.sourceforge.net

Csscorp. (2010). *Cloud based performance testing.* Retrieved February 5, 2010, from http://www.csscorp.com/product-lifecycle-services/cloud-based-performance-testing.php

Dadzie, J. (2005). Understanding software patching. *ACM Queue, 3*(1542-7730), 24-30.

Dagon, D., Martin, T., & Starner, T. (2004). Mobile phones as computing devices: The viruses are coming! *Pervasive Computing, 3*(4), 11–15. doi:10.1109/MPRV.2004.21

Dai, G., Bai, X., & Wang, Y. (2007). Contract-based testing for web services. *IEEE COMPSAC 2007 Computer Software and Applications Conference*, Beijing, (p. 517).

Dallmeier, V., Lindig, C., Wasylkowski, A., & Zeller, A. (2006). Mining object behavior with ADABU. In *Proceedings of the ICSE Workshop on Dynamic Analysis.*

De Millo, R. A., & Offutt, A. J. (1991). Constraint-based automatic test data generation. *IEEE Transactions on Software Engineering, 17*(9), 900–909. doi:10.1109/32.92910

Dean, J., & Ghemawat, S. (2004). MapReduce: Simplified data processing on large clusters. In *Proceedings of Sixth Symposium on Operating System Design and Implementation.*

Deng, G., Balasubramanian, J., Otte, W., Schmidt, D. C., & Gokhale, A. (2005). DAnCE: A QoS-enabled component deployment and configuration engine. *3rd Working Conference on Component Deployment*, (pp. 67-82). Grenoble, France.

Deng, G., Gill, C., Schmidt, D. C., & Wang, N. (2007). QoS-enabled component middleware for distributed real-time and embedded systems. In Son, I. L. (Ed.), *Handbook of real-time and embedded systems*. CRC Press.

Di Geronimo, L., Ferrucci, F., Murolo, A., & Sarro, F. (2012). A parallel genetic algorithm based on Hadoop MapReduce for the automatic generation of JUnit test suites. In *Proceedings of the 5th International Conference on Software Testing*, (pp. 785-793).

Do, H., Mirarab, S., Tahvildari, L., & Rothermel, G. (2010). The effects of time constraints on test case prioritization. *IEEE Transactions on Software Engineering, 36*(5), 593. doi:10.1109/TSE.2010.58

Duarte, A., Cirne, W., Brasileiro, F., & Machado, P. (2006). GridUnit: Software testing on the grid. *28th International Conference on Software Engineering (ICSE '06)* (pp. 779–782). Association for Computing Machinery.

Duboc, L., Rosenblum, D. S., & Wicks, T. (2006). A framework for modelling and analysis of software systems scalability. *International Conference on Software Engineering* (pp. 949-952). ACM Press.

Ducasse, S., Girba, T., & Wuyts, R. (2006). *Object-oriented legacy system trace-based logic testing.* IEEE Computer Society.

Dwyer, M., Avrunin, G., & Corbett, J. (1999). Property specification patterns for finite state verification. *21st International Conference on Software Engineering*, (p. 411).

Eagle, N. (2009). txteagle: Mobile crowdsourcing. In N. Aykin (Ed.), *International Conference on Internationalization Design and Global Development* (Vol. 5623, pp. 447-456-456). Berlin, Germany: Springer. doi:10.1007/978-3-642-02767-3

Eagle, N., & Pentland, A. (2005). Social serendipity: Mobilizing social software. *IEEE Pervasive Computing/IEEE Computer Society [and] IEEE Communications Society, 4*(2), 28–34. doi:10.1109/MPRV.2005.37

EC2ApiTools. (2006). *EC2ApiTools, & AmazonEC2.* Retrieved from http://docs.amazonwebservices.com/-AmazonEC2/gsg/2006-06-26/

Eclipse. (2011). *The CDO model repository.*

Eclipse. (2011). *Eclipse.* Retrieved April 30, 2011, from http://www.eclipse.org/

EclipseSource. (2011). *Yoxos Ondemand.* Retrieved April 27, 2011, from http://ondemand.yoxos.com/geteclipse/start

Edelstein, O., Farchi, E., Goldin, E., Nir, Y., Ratsaby, G., & Ur, S. (2003). Framework for testing multi-threaded Java programs. *Concurrency and Computation, 15*(3-5), 485–499. doi:10.1002/cpe.654

Edwards, S. H. (2001). A framework for practical, automated black-box testing of component-based software. *Software Testing, Verification, and Reliability, 11*(2), 97–111. doi:10.1002/stvr.224

Elbaum, S. G., Rothermel, G., Karre, S., & Fisher, M. II. (2005). Leveraging user-session data to support web application testing. *IEEE Transactions on Software Engineering, 31*(3), 187–202. doi:10.1109/TSE.2005.36

Elbaum, S., Malishevsky, A. G., & Rothermel, G. (2002). Test case prioritization: A family of empirical studies. *IEEE Transactions on Software Engineering, 28*(2), 159–182. doi:10.1109/32.988497

Enck, W., Ongtang, M., & McDaniel, P. (2009). On lightweight mobile phone application certification. *Proceedings of the 16th ACM Conference on Computer and Communications Security* (pp. 235-245). New York, NY: ACM. doi:http://doi.acm.org/10.1145/1653662.1653691

England, E., & Finney, A. (1996). *Managing multimedia.* Harlow, UK: Addison Wesley.

Ernst, M., Perkins, J., Guo, P., McCamant, S., Pacheco, C., Tschantz, M., & Xiao, C. (2007). The Daikon system for dynamic detection of likely invariants. *Science of Computer Programming, 69*(1-3), 35–45. doi:10.1016/j.scico.2007.01.015

Faban Harness and Benchmark Framework. (2011). Retrieved from http://java.net/projects/faban/

Felderer, M., et al. (2009). Concepts for model-based requirements testing of service oriented systems. *Proceedings of the IASTED International Conference* (Vol. 642, p. 18).

Felderer, M., et al. (2009). *Towards adaptive test code generation for service oriented systems.* Paper presented at the Ninth International Conference on Quality Software (QSIC 2009).

Felderer, M., et al. (2010). *Security testing by telling TestStories.*

Fenton, N., Pfleeger, S. L., & Glass, R. L. (1994). Science and substance: A challenge to software engineers. *IEEE Software,* (July/August): 86–95. doi:10.1109/52.300094

Ferber, J. (1999). *Multi-agent systems: An introduction to distributed artificial intelligence.* Addison-Wesley Professional.

Fitzek, F. H. P., & Reichert, F. (2007). *Mobile phone programming and its application to wireless networking.* Springer. Retrieved from http://books.google.com/books?id=s_OnKP3VAQ4C

Foley, J. (2009). *The cloud's next big thing: Software testing.* Retrieved September 14, 2009, from http://www.informationweek.com/cloud-computing/blog/archives/2009/06/the_clouds_next.html

Foster, I., & Kesselman, C. (2003). *The grid 2: Blueprint for a new computing infrastructure.* Morgan Kaufmann Publishers Inc.

Fowler, M. (2006, May). *Continuous integration.* Retrieved from http://www.martinfowler.com/articles/continuousIntegration.html

Fowler, M. (2010). *Xunit.* Retrieved from http://www.martinfowler.com/bliki/Xunit.html

Frankel, D. S. (Eds.). (2004). *The MDA journal: Model driven architecture straight from the masters.* Meghan Kiffer Press.

Fredendall, L., & Hill, E. (2000). *Basics of supply chain management.* CRC Press. doi:10.1201/9781420025767

Frederick, G. R., & Lal, R. (2007). Testing a mobile web site. *Beginning smartphone web development* (pp. 259-272).

Fritsch, T., Ritter, H., & Schiller, J. (2006). User case study and network evolution in the mobile phone sector (a study on current mobile phone applications). *Proceedings of the 2006 ACM SIGCHI International Conference on Advances in Computer Entertainment Technology.* New York, NY: ACM. doi:http://doi.acm.org/10.1145/1178823.1178836

Frye, C. (2008). *Cloud computing creates software testing challenges.* Retrieved April 22, 2011, from http://searchcloudcomputing.techtarget.com/news/1355198/cloud-computing-creates-software-testing-challenges

Fujita, H., Matsuno, Y., Hanawa, T., Sato, M., Kato, S., & Ishikawa, Y. (2012). DS-Bench toolset: Tools for dependability benchmarking with simulation and assurance. *42nd IEEE/IFIP International Conference on Dependable Systems and Networks (DSN 2012)* (8 pages, to be published). IEEE.

Gaisbauer, S., Kirschnick, J., Edwards, N., & Roila, J. (2008). *VATS: Virtualized-aware automated test service.* 5th International Conference on Quantitative Evaluation of Systems.

Gajski, D. D., Zhu, J., Dömer, R., Gerstlauer, A., & Zhao, S. (2000). *SpecC: Specification language and methodology.* Springer Verlag. doi:10.1007/978-1-4615-4515-6

Gamma, E., Helm, R., Johnson, R., & Vlissides, J. (1994). *Design Patterns: Elements Of Reusable Object-Oriented Software.* Upper Saddle River, NJ: Addison-Wesley.

Gannod, G., & Cheng, B. (1999). A framework for classifying and comparing software reverse engineering and design recovery techniques. In F. Balmas, M. Blaha, & S. Rugaber (Eds.), *Working Conference on Reverse Engineering* (pp. 77-88). Los Alamitos, CA: IEEE Computer Society Press.

Gannod, G., & Cheng. (1996). Strongest postcondition semantics as the formal basis for reverse engineering. *The Journal of Automated Software Engineering, 3*(1-2), 1–27.

Ganon, Z., & Zilberstein, I. E. (2009). Cloud-based performance testing of network management systems. *14th International Workshop on Computer Aided Modelling and Design of Communication Links and Networks,* (pp. 1-6).

Gao, J., Pattabhiraman, P., Bai, X., & Tsai, W. T. (2011). SaaS performance and scalability evaluation in cloud. *International Symposium on Service Oriented System Engineering* (pp.61-71).

Gao, J., Bai, X., & Tsai, W.-T. (2011). Cloud testing - Issues, challenges, needs and practice. *Software Engineering: An International Journal, 1*(1), 9–23.

Garber, L. (2011). News briefs. *Computer, 44*(6), 18–20. doi:10.1109/MC.2011.185

Gardner, J. (2007). Remote web site usability testing – Benefits over traditional methods. *International Journal of Public Information Systems, 2*, 63–72.

Gerkey, B., Vaughan, R. T., & Howard, A. (2003). The Player/Stage Project: Tools for multi-robot and distributed sensor systems. In *Proceedings Of The 11th International Conference On Advanced Robotics* (pp. 317–323).

Geunes, J., & Pardalos, P. (2010). *Supply chain optimization.* Springer Verlag.

Gietelink, O., Ploeg, J., Schutter, B. D., & Verhaegen, M. (2004). Testing advanced driver assistance systems for fault management with the VEHIL test facility. In *Proceedings Of The 7th International Symposium On Advanced Vehicle Control* (AVEC'04) (pp. 579 – 584).

GIT. (2012). *Git Source Code Management.* Retrieved May 17, 2012, from http://git-scm.com

Glenford, J. M. (2004). *The art of software testing* (2nd ed.). Wiley.

Globus.org. *Globus.* (n.d.). Retrieved from http://www.globus.org/

Godefroid, P., & Molnar, D. (2010, March). *Fuzzing in the cloud* (Position Statement) (Tech. Rep. No. MSR-TR-2010-29). Redmond, WA: Microsoft Research. Retrieved from http://research.microsoft.com/apps/pubs/?id=121494

Godefroid, P., Klarlund, N., & Sen, K. (2005, June). DART: Directed automated random testing. In the *ACM SIGPLAN 2005 Conference on Programming Language Design and Implementation* (PLDI'05) (pp. 213–223). Chicago, IL: ACM Press.

Godefroid, P., Levin, M. Y., & Molnar, D. A. (2012). SAGE: Whitebox fuzzing for security testing. *Communications of the ACM, 55*(3), 40–44. doi:10.1145/2093548.2093564

Goethe, M. (2008). *Collaborative application lifecycle management with IBM rational products.* IBM Redbook.

Goetz, H., et al. (2009). *iX Studie Modellbasiertes Testen.*

Gokhale, A., Balasubramanian, K., Balasubramanian, J., Krishna, A. S., Edwards, G. T., & Deng, G. (2008). Model driven middleware: A new paradigm for deploying and provisioning distributed real-time and embedded applications. *Journal of Science of Computer Programming: Special Issue on Foundations and Applications of Model Driven Architecture (MDA), 73*(1), 39–58.

Goldberg, D. E. (1989). *Genetic algorithms in search, optimization, and machine learning*. Addison-Wesley.

Google App Engine. (2012). *JDO APIs*. Retrieved June 14, 2012, from https://developers.google.com/App Engine/docs/java/datastore/jdo/

Google App Engine. (2012). *JRE Whitelist*. Retrieved June 14, 2012, from https://developers.google.com/App Engine/docs/java/jrewhitelist

Google App Engine. (2012). *MapReduce*. Retrieved June 9, 2012, from http://code.google.com/p/App Engine-mapreduce/

Google App Engine. (2012). Retrieved June 9, 2012, from http://code.google.com/App Engine

Google Developer App Engine. (2012). Retrieved June 12, 2012, from https://developers.google.com/App Engine/

Google. (2012). *Google app engine documentation*. Retrieved from https://developers.google.com/appengine/

Goth, G. (2008). "Googling" test practices? Web giant's culture encourages process improvement. *IEEE Software*, *25*(2), 92–94. doi:10.1109/MS.2008.28

Goth, G. (2008). Ultralarge systems: Redefining software engineering? *Software*, *25*(3), 91–94. doi:10.1109/MS.2008.82

Gotlieb, A., Leconte, M., & Marre, B. (2010, September). *Constraint solving on modular integers*. In the CP 2010 Workshop on Constraint Modelling and Reformulation (ModRef 2010). St Andrews, UK: Springer.

Government Accounting Office. (2010, May). *Federal guidance needed to address control issues with implementing cloud computing*. Government Accounting Office. Retrieved April 23, 2011, from http://www.gao.gov/new.items/d10513.pdf

Graham, D., & Fewster, M. (2012). *Experiences of test automation: Case studies of software test automation*. Addison-Wesley Professional.

Grama, A. Y., Gupta, A., & Kumar, V. (1993). Isoefficiency: Measuring the scalability of parallel algorithms and architectures. *IEEE Parallel and Distributed Technology*, *1*(3), 12–21. doi:10.1109/88.242438

Grassi, V. (2004). Reliability prediction for service-oriented computing. *IEEE Workshop Architecting Dependable Systems*, 2004, (p. 279).

Graves, T., Harrold, M., Kim, Y., Porter, A., & Rothermel, G. (2001). An empirical study of regression test selection techniques. *ACM Transactions on Software Engineering and Methodology*, *10*(2), 184–208. doi:10.1145/367008.367020

Greenfield, J. (2004). *Software factories: Assembling applications with patterns, models, frameworks, and tools*. Wiley Press.

GreenHat.com. *Green Hat*. (n.d.). Retrieved from http://www.greenhat.com/

Greiler, M., Gross, H. G., & Nasr, K. A. (2009). Runtime integration and testing for highly dynamic service oriented ICT solutions - An industry challenges report. In *Testing: Academic and Industrial Conference on Practice and Research Techniques* (pp. 51–55).

Grochtmann, M., & Grimm, K. (1993). Classification trees for partition testing. *Software Testing. Verification and Reliability*, *3*(2), 63–82. doi:10.1002/stvr.4370030203

Gruber, T. (2009). Ontology. In Liu, L., & Özsu, M. T. (Eds.), *Encyclopedia of database systems*. New York, NY: Springer-Verlag.

Grundy, J., Kaefer, G., Keong, J., & Liu, A. (2012, March). Software engineering for the cloud. *IEEE Software Magazine*, 26.

Gulavani, B. S., Henzinger, T. A., Kannan, Y., Nori, A. V., & Rajamani, S. K. (2006, November). SYNERGY: A new algorithm for property checking. In the *14th ACM SIGSOFT International Symposium on Foundations of Software Engineering* (FSE 2005) (pp. 117–127). Portland, OR: ACM Press.

Hackel, P. (2012). SAP kauft Ariba for 4.4 billion dollars. *Computer Weekly*, *22*, 8.

Hadoop Wiki. (2009). *How many maps and reduces*. Retrieved from http://wiki.apache.org/hadoop/HowManyMapsAndReduces

Hadoop. (2012). *MapReduce*. Retrieved June 14, 2012, from http://hadoop.apache.org/mapreduce/

Halstead, M. (1977). *Elements of software science.* Amsterdam, The Netherlands: Elvesier, North-Holland.

Han, S., Shin, K., & Rosenberg, H. (1995). DOCTOR: An integrated software fault injection environment for distributed real-time systems. *International Computer Performance and Dependability Symposium (IPDS '95)* (p. 0204). IEEE.

Hanawa, T., Banzai, T., Koizumi, H., Kanbayashi, R., Imada, T., & Sato, M. (2010). Large-scale software testing environment using cloud computing technology for dependable parallel and distributed systems. *2nd International Workshop on Software Testing in the Cloud (STITC 2010), co-located with the 3rd IEEE International Conference on Software Testing, Verification, and Validation (ICST 2010)* (pp. 428-433). IEEE.

Hanawa, T., Koizumi, H., Banzai, T., Sato, M., Miura, S., Ishii, T., & Takamizawa, H. (2010). Customizing virtual machine with fault injector by integrating with SpecC device model for a software testing environment D-Cloud. *2010 Pacific Rim International Symposium on Dependable Computing.* (pp. 47-54). IEEE.

Hangal, S., & Lam, M. S. (2002). Tracking down software bugs using automatic anomaly detection. In *Proceedings of the International Conference on Software Engineering.*

Hanna, S. (2009, December). A security analysis of Cloud Computing. *Cloud Computing Journal.* Retrieved April 24, 2011, from http://cloudcomputing.sys-con.com/node/1203943

Harman, M. (2007). The current state and future of SBSE. In *Proceedings of Foundations of Software Engineering* (pp. 342-357).

Harman, M., & Jones, B. F. (2001). Search based software engineering. *Information and Software Technology, 43*(14), 833–839. doi:10.1016/S0950-5849(01)00189-6

Harman, M., & Mansouri, A. (2010). Search based software engineering: Introduction to the special issue. *IEEE Transactions on Software Engineering, 36*(6), 737–741. doi:10.1109/TSE.2010.106

Harmon, P. (2007). *Business process change,* 2nd ed. OMG Press, Morgan Kaufman.

Harrold, M., Gupta, R., & Soffa, M. (1993). A methodology for controlling the size of a test suite. *ACM Transactions on Software Engineering and Methodology, 2*(3), 270–285. doi:10.1145/152388.152391

Hartmann, J., et al. (2005). A UML-based approach to system testing. *Proceedings of the 4th International Conference on The United Modeling Language, Modeling Languages, Concepts, and Tools* (Vol. 1).

Havlin, S. (2009). Phone infections. *Quantum, 324,* 1023–1024. doi:doi:10.1126/science.1174658

Heiser, G., Murray, T. C., & Klein, G. (2012). It's time for trustworthy systems. *IEEE Security & Privacy, 10*(2), 67–70. doi:10.1109/MSP.2012.41

Helming, J., & Koegel, M. (2010). *Managing iterations with UNICASE.*

Heo, J., Terada, K., Toyama, M., Kurumatani, S., & Chen, E. Y. (2010). User demand prediction from application usage pattern in virtual smartphone. *2010 IEEE Second International Conference on Cloud Computing Technology and Science,* (pp. 449-455). IEEE. doi:10.1109/CloudCom.2010.52

Hertzen, M. V., Laine, J., Kangasharju, S., Timonen, J., & Santala, M. (2009). Drive for future software leverage: The role, importance and future challenges of software competences in Finland. *Tekes Review, 262.*

Hesari, S., Mashayekhi, H., & Ramsin, R. (2010). Towards a general framework for evaluating software development methodologies. *COMPSAC, 2010,* 208–217.

Hibler, M., Ricci, R., Stoller, L., Duerig, J., Guruprasad, S., Stack, T., et al. (2008). Large-scale virtualization in the emulab network testbed. *Proceedings of the 2008 USENIX Annual Technical Conference,* (pp. 113-128). USENIX Association. Retrieved from http://portal.acm.org/citation.cfm?id=1404023

Hill, J. H., Slaby, J., Baker, S., & Schmidt, D. C. (2006). *Applying system execution modeling tools to evaluate enterprise distributed real-time and embedded system QoS.* 12th International Conference on Embedded and Real-Time Computing Systems and Applications. IEEE.

Hill, J. H., Tambe, S., & Gokhale, A. (2007). Model-driven engineering for development-time QoS validation of component-based software systems. *14th International Conference and Workshop on the Engineering of Computer Based Systems* (pp. 307-316). Tucson, AZ: IEEE.

Hill, J. H., & Gokhale, A. (2007). *Using generative programming to enhance reuse in visitor pattern-based DSML model interpreters. Institute for Software Integrated Systems*. Nashville, TN: Vanderbilt University.

Hill, J., Edmondson, J., Gokhale, A., & Schmidt, D. C. (2010). Tools for continuously evaluating distributed system qualities. *IEEE Software, 27*(4), 65–71. doi:10.1109/MS.2009.197

Hill, M. D. (1990). What is scalability? *SIGARCH Computer Architecture News, 18*(4), 18–21. doi:10.1145/121973.121975

Hofmann, P., & Woods, D. (2010). Cloud computing: The limits of public clouds for business applications. *IEEE Internet Computing, 14*(6), 90–93. doi:10.1109/MIC.2010.136

Homeland Security. (2004, August). *Homeland Security Presidential Directive (HSPD)-12*. The US Department of Homeland Security. Retrieved April 13, 2011, from http://www.dhs.gov/xabout/laws/gc_1217616624097.shtm

Horgan, J. R., & Mathur, A. P. (1995). Software testing and reliability. In Lyu, M. R. (Ed.), *Handbook of software reliability engineering* (pp. 531–566). McGraw-Hill.

Hotle, H., & Landry, S. (2009). *Application delivery and support organizational archetypes: The software factory*. (Gartner Research Report G00167531, May 2009).

Hu, W.-C., Zuo, Y., Kaabouch, N., & Chen, L. (2010). An optimization neural network for smartphone data protection. *2010 IEEE International Conference on Electro/Information Technology (EIT)*, (pp. 1-6).

Humphrey, W. (1991). Software process improvement at Hughes Aircraft. *IEEE Software, 8*(4). doi:10.1109/52.300031

Hunter, R., & Thayer, R. (Eds.). (2001). *Software process improvement*. Wiley-IEEE Computer Society Press.

IBM. (2009, August). *Application assembly optimization: A new approach to global delivery*. IBM White paper.

IBM. (2009, September). *Give your software factory a health check: Best practices for executing with reduced risk and cost for real results*. IBM White paper.

IBM. (2010). *Infrastructure optimization services – IBM smart business test cloud*. Retrieved January 19, 2010, from http://www-935.ibm.com/services/us/index.wss/offering/midware/a1030965

IBM. (2011). Rational DOORS. Retrieved April 21, 2011, from www.ibm.com/software/awdtools/doors/

ISO/IEC. (1994). *Information technology - Open systems interconnection - Conformance testing methodology and framework*.

IEEE. (1990). *IEEE Std 610.12-1990: IEEE standard glossary of software engineering terminology*. New York, NY: IEEE Software Engineering Standards Committee.

IFPUG. (1999). *Function-point counting practices. Manual Release 4.1*. Westerville, OH: International Function-Point User Group.

Information Sciences Institute. (n.d.). *Network Simulator (NS-2)*. Retrieved from http://www.isi.edu/nsnam/ns/

IPG GmbH. (2011). *Carmaker 3.0*. Retrieved April 27, 2011, from http://www.ipg.de/CarMaker.609.0.html

Ishikawa, Y., Fujita, H., Maeda, T., Matsuda, M., Sugaya, M., & Sato, M. … Tokuda, H. (2009). Towards an open dependable operating system. *12th International Symposium on Object/Component/Service-Oriented Real-Time Distributed Computing* (pp. 20–27). IEEE.

ISO 17799. (n.d.). *What is ISO 17799?* ISO 17799 Information and Resource Portal. Retrieved April 13, 2011, from http://17799.denialinfo.com/whatisiso17799.htm

ISO. (2009). *ISO20000- Standard for software system service management*. Geneva, Switzerland: International Standard Organisation.

ISO/IEC. (2006). *ISO/IEC-19757 document schema definition language – Part 3 Rule-based validation schematron*. Geneva, Switzerland: International Standard Organisation.

Jääskeläinen, A., Katara, M., Kervinen, A., Heiskanen, H., Maunumaa, M., & Pääkkönen, T. (2008). Model-based testing service on the web. *20th IFIP TC 6/WG 6.1 International Conference on Testing of Software and Communicating Systems: 8th international Workshop, Lecture Notes in Computer Science, 5047,* (pp. 38-53).

Jamal, M. H., Qadeer, A., Mahmood, W., Waheed, A., & Ding, J. J. (2009). Virtual machine scalability on multi-core processors based servers for cloud computing workloads. *International Conference on Networking, Architecture, and Storage* (pp. 90-97).

Jansen, W., & Grance, T. (2011, January). *Guidelines on security and privacy in public cloud computing* (800-144). National Institute of Standards and Technology. Retrieved April 24, 2011, from http://csrc.nist.gov/publications/nistpubs/800-144/SP800-144.pdf

Java Path Finder. (2012). Revised June 14, 2012, from http://javapathfinder.sourceforge.net/

Jeong, H., Tombor, B., & Albert, R. (2000). The large-scale organization of metabolic networks. *Nature, 407,* 651–654. doi:10.1038/35036627

Jericho. (2011). *Cloud cube model o.*

Jewett, E. (2009). *Robotics Developer Studio 2008r2. Technical Report.* Microsoft Corp.

Jia, Y., & Harman, M. (2006). *An analysis and survey of the development of mutation testing.* King's College London. doi:10.1109/TSE.2010.62

Jogalekar, P., & Woodside, M. (2000). Evaluating the scalability of distributed systems. *IEEE Transactions on Parallel and Distributed Systems, 11*(6), 589–603. doi:10.1109/71.862209

Joglekar, S. (2009). *A foray into cloud-based software testing.* Paper presented at the STeP-IN SUMMIT 2009, Bangalore, India.

Joint Task Force. (2004, May). *Guide for the security certification and accreditation of federal information systems* (800-37). National Institute of Science and Technology. Retrieved April 23, 2011, from http://csrc.nist.gov/publications/nistpubs/800-37-rev1/sp800-37-rev1-final.pdf

Joint Task Force. (2009, August). *Guide for assessing security controls publication 800-53A Rev 3.* National Institute of Standards and Technology. Retrieved April 24, 2011, from http://csrc.nist.gov/publications/nistpubs/800-53-Rev3/sp800-53-rev3-final.pdf

Jorgensen, P. (2007). *Software testing: A craftsman's approach* (3rd ed.). Boca Raton, FL: Auerbach Publications.

Jun, W., & Meng, F. (2011). Software testing based on cloud computing. *2011 International Conference on Internet Computing and Information Services,* (pp. 176-178).

JUnit. (2012). Retrieved from http://junit.org

Kandel, E. R., Schwartz, J. H., & Jessell, T. M. (2000). *Principles of neural science* (4th ed.). New York, NY: McGraw-Hill.

Kaner, C. (1996). What is a software defect? *Software Q&A, 3*(6). Retrieved April 2, 2011, from http://www.kaner.com/pdfs/defects4.pdf

Kaner, C., Bach, J., & Petticord, B. (2001). *Lessons learned in software testing: A context-driven approach.* New York, NY: Wiley Computer Publishing.

Kanoun, K., Madeira, H., Crouzet, Y., Cin, M. D., Moreira, F., & Garcia, J. R. (2004). *DBench dependability benchmarks.* Retrieved May 1, 2011, from http://www.laas.fr/DBench/Final/DBench-complete-report.pdf

Kanoun, K., & Spainhower, L. (Eds.). (2008). *Dependability benchmarking for computer systems.* Wiley. doi:10.1002/9780470370506

Keller, A., & Ludwig, H. (2003). The WSLA framework specifying and monitoring service level agreements for web services. *Journal of Network and Systems Management, 11*(1), 57. doi:10.1023/A:1022445108617

Kempe, D., Kleinberg, J., & Tardos, É. (2003). Maximizing the spread of influence through a social network. *Proceedings of the Ninth ACM SIGKDD International Conference on Knowledge Discovery and Data Mining KDD 03,* (p. 137). ACM Press. doi:10.1145/956755.956769

Kephart, J., & Chess, D. (2003). The vision of autonomic computing. *Computer, 36*(1), 41–52. doi:10.1109/MC.2003.1160055

Khalidi, Y. (2011, March). Building a cloud computing platform for new possibilities. IEEE Computer Magazine, p. 29.

Kienle, H., & Vasiliu, C. (2008, October). *Evolution of legal statements on the web.* 10th Workshop on Web Systems Evolution, (p. 73). Bejing, China: IEEE Computer Society Press.

Kim, H., Smith, J., & Shin, K. G. (2008). Detecting energy-greedy anomalies and mobile malware variants. *Proceedings of the 6th International Conference on Mobile Systems, Applications, and Services*, (pp. 239-252). ACM Press. doi:10.1145/1378600.1378627

Kim, K. H. (1989). An approach to experimental evaluation of real-time fault-tolerant distributed computing schemes. *IEEE Transactions on Software Engineering, 15*(6), 715–725. doi:10.1109/32.24725

King, T. M. (2009). *A self-testing approach for autonomic software.* Doctoral dissertation. Florida International University, Miami, FL.

King, T. M., & Ganti, A. S. (2010). *Migrating autonomic self-testing to the cloud.*

King, T. M., & Ganti, A. S. (2010). Migrating autonomic self-testing to the cloud. *2nd International Workshop on Software Testing in the Cloud (STITC), 3rd IEEE International Conference on Software Testing, Verification and Validation (ICST)*, (pp. 438-443).

King, J. C. (1976). Symbolic execution and program testing. *Communications of the ACM, 19*(7), 385–394. doi:10.1145/360248.360252

King, T. M., Ramirez, A. E., Cruz, R., & Clarke, P. J. (2007). An integrated self-testing framework for autonomic computing systems. *Journal of Computers, 2*(9), 37–49. doi:10.4304/jcp.2.9.37-49

Klein, G. (2010, November). From a verified kernel towards verified systems. In the *8th Asian Symposium on Programming Languages and Systems* (APLAS 2010) (pp. 21–33). Shanghai, China: Springer.

Klein, G., Elphinstone, K., Heiser, G., Andronick, J., Cock, D., Derrin, P., et al. (2009, October). seL4: formal verification of an OS kernel. In the *ACM SIGOPS 22nd Symposium on Operating Systems Principles* (SOSP 2009) (pp. 207–220). Big Sky, MT: ACM Press.

Korecki, J. (2005). *Sourceforge. Net: Cvs ~ Compile Farm.* Retrieved April 27, 2011, from http://www.nd.edu/~oss/Papers/Korecki_Sourceforge.pdf

Korel, B. (1990). Automated software test data generation. *IEEE Transactions on Software Engineering, 16*(8), 870–879. doi:10.1109/32.57624

Kosmatov, N. (2010). *Online version of the PathCrawler test generation tool.* Retrieved from http://pathcrawler-online.com/

Kosmatov, N., Botella, B., Roger, M., & Williams, N. (2011, March). Online test generation with PathCrawler: Tool demo (Best tool demo award.). In the *3rd Workshop on Constraints in Software Testing, Verification, and Analysis* (CSTVA 2011) (pp. 316–317). Berlin, Germany: IEEE Computer Society.

Kosmatov, N., Williams, N., Botella, B., Roger, M., & Chebaro, O. (2012, May). A lesson on structural testing with pathcrawler-online.com. In the *6th International Conference on Tests and Proofs* (TAP 2012) (pp. 169–175). Prague, Czech Republic: Springer.

Kosmatov, N. (2010). Constraint-based techniques for software testing. In Meziane, F., & Vandera, S. (Eds.), *Artificial intelligence applications for improved software engineering development: New prospects.* Hershey, PA: IGI Global.

Krena, B., Letko, Z., Nir-Buchbinder, Y., Tzoref-Brill, R., Ur, S., & Vojnar, T. (2009). A concurrency testing tool and its plug-ins for dynamic analysis and runtime healing. In *Runtime Verification, Lecture Notes in Computer Science 5779/2009*, (pp. 101-114).

Kruse, P., & Luniak, M. (2010). Automated test case generation using classification trees. In *Proceedings of STAREAST- Software Testing Conference, Analysis & Review.*

Krutchen, P. (2002). *Rational unified process.* Addison Wesley, 2002.

Kumar, V., & Gupta, A. (1994). Analyzing the scalability of parallel algorithms and architectures: A survey. *Journal of Parallel and Distributed Computing, 22*(3), 379–391. doi:10.1006/jpdc.1994.1099

Kundra, V. (2011, February). *Federal cloud computing strategy.* The U.S. CIO. Retrieved April 23, 2011, from http://www.cio.gov/documents/Federal-Cloud-Computing-Strategy.pdf

KVM. (2012). *Website.* Retrieved from http://www.linux-kvm.org/page/Main_Page

Lakhotia, K., McMinn, P., & Harman, M. (2009). Automated test data generation for coverage: Haven't we solved this problem yet? *Testing: Academic and Industrial Conference - Practice and Research Techniques,* (pp. 95–104).

Lanza, M., & Ducasse, S. (2003). Polymetric views – A lightweight visual approach to reverse engineering. *IEEE Transactions on Software Engineering, 29*(9), 782–795. doi:10.1109/TSE.2003.1232284

Laurendeau, C., & Barbeau, M. (2006). Threats to security in DSRC/WAVE. In T. Kunz & S. S. Ravi (Eds.), *Lecture Notes in Computer Science, 4104,* (pp. 266–279). Springer. Retrieved from http://www.springerlink.com/index/232853512q76hgt4.pdf

Lawton, G. (2008). Is it finally time to worry about mobile malware? *Computer, 41*(5), 12–14. doi:10.1109/MC.2008.159

Le Traon, Y., et al. (2007). *Testing security policies: Going beyond functional testing.*

Leavitt, N. (2005). Mobile phones: The next frontier for hackers? *Computer, 38*(4), 20–23. doi:10.1109/MC.2005.134

Leconte, M., & Berstel, B. (2006, September). *Extending a CP solver with congruences as domains for software verification.* In the CP 2006 Workshop on Constraints in Software Testing, Verification and Analysis (CSTVA 2006). Nantes, France: Springer.

Ledeczi, A., Bakay, A., Maroti, M., Volgyesi, P., Nordstrom, G., & Sprinkle, J. (2001). Composing domain-specific design environments. *Computer, 34*(11), 44–51. doi:10.1109/2.963443

Lee, E. A., & Seshia, S. A. (2011). *Introduction To Embedded Systems – A Cyber-Physical Systems Approach.* Retrieved April 27, 2011, from http://LeeSeshia.org

Leroy, X. (2009). Formal verification of a realistic compiler. *Communications of the ACM, 52*(7), 107–115. doi:10.1145/1538788.1538814

Li, A., Yang, X., Kandula, S., & Zhang, M. (2010). CloudCmp: Comparing public cloud providers. *Internet Measurement Conference* (pp. 1-14).

Lienhard, A., Ducasse, S., & Gırba, T. (2009). Taking an object-centric view on dynamic information with object flow analysis. *Computer Languages, Systems & Structures, 35,* 63–79. doi:10.1016/j.cl.2008.05.006

Linthicum, D. S. (2010). *Cloud computing and SOA convergence in your enterprise: A step-by-step guide.* Upper Saddle River, NJ: Addison-Wesley.

Liskov, B., & Guttag, J. (1988). *Abstraction and specification in program development.* New York, NY: MIT Press, McGraw-Hill Books.

Litoiu, M. (2010, September). *A performance engineering method for web services. 12th Symposium on Web Systems Evolution,* (p. 101). Temesvar, Hungary: IEEE Computer Society Press.

Liu, L., Yan, G., Zhang, X., & Chen, S. (2009). VirusMeter: Preventing your cellphone from spies. *Proceedings of the 12th International Symposium on Recent Advances in Intrusion Detection* (pp. 244-264). Berlin, Germany: Springer-Verlag. doi:http://dx.doi.org/10.1007/978-3-642-04342-0_13

Liu, H. H. (2009). *Software performance and scalability.* New Jersey: John Wiley & Sons, Inc. doi:10.1002/9780470465394

Liu, H., & Orban, D. (2010). Remote network labs: An on-demand network cloud for configuration testing. *ACM SIGCOMM Computer Communication Review, 40*(1), 93–101.

Lockheed Martin. (2010). *Awareness, trust and security to shape government cloud adoption.* Retrieved from http://www.lockheedmartin.com/data/assets/isgs/documents/CloudComputingWhitePaper.pdf

Lorenzoli, D., Mariani, L., & Pezzè, M. (2008). Automatic generation of software behavioral models. In *Proceedings of the International Conference on Software Testing* (pp. 501-510).

Loulergue, F., Gava, F., Kosmatov, N., & Lemerre, M. (2012, July). (To appear). *Towards verified cloud computing environments*. In the 2012 International Conference on High Performance Computing and Simulation (HPCS 2012). Madrid, Spain: IEEE. *Computers & Society*.

Lyon, G., Kacker, R., & Linz, A. (1995). A scalability test for parallel code. *Software, Practice & Experience, 25*(12), 1299–1314. doi:10.1002/spe.4380251202

Ma, B., Chen, B., Bai, X., & Huang, J. (2010). Design of BDI agent for adaptive performance testing of web services. *International Conference on Quality Software* (pp. 435–440).

Mann, J. (1996). *The role of project escalation in explaining runaway information systems development projects: A field study*. Atlanta, GA: Georgia State University.

Marchetto, A., Tonella, P., & Ricca, F. (2008). State-based testing of Ajax web applications. In *Proceedings of the International Conference on Software Testing* (pp. 121-130).

Marre, B., & Arnould, A. (2000, September). Test sequences generation from Lustre descriptions: GATeL. In the *15th IEEE International Conference on Automated Software Engineering* (ASE'00) (pp. 229–237). Grenoble, France: IEEE Computer Society.

Marre, B., & Michel, C. (2010). Improving the floating point addition and subtraction constraints. In the *16th International Conference on Principles and Practice of Constraint Programming (CP 2010) (Vol. LNCS 6308*, (pp. 360–367). St. Andrews, UK: Springer.

Martin, E., et al. (2006). Defining and measuring policy coverage in testing access control policies. *Proceedings of the 8th International Conference on Information and Communications Security*, (pp. 139-158).

Martin, B. (1996). Technological vulnerability. *Technology in Society, 12*(4), 511–523. doi:10.1016/S0160-791X(96)00029-2

Martin, R. (2005). The test bus imperative - Architectures that support automated acceptance testing. *IEEE Software Magazine, 22*(4), 65.

Masticola, S., & Gall, M. (2008). Vision: Testing of mechatronics software using agile simulation. In *Proceedings Of The 3rd International Workshop On Automation Of Software Test* (pp. 79 – 84).

Mather, T., Kumaraswamy, S., & Latif, S. (2009). *Cloud security and privacy: An enterprise perspective on risks and compliance (theory in practice)*. O'Reilly.

Matos, V., & Grasser, R. (2010). Building applications for the Android OS mobile platform: A primer and course materials. *Journal of Computing Sciences in Colleges, 26*(1), 23–29. Retrieved from http://portal.acm.org/citation.cfm?id=1858449.1858455

Maybury, M. (2009). *How to protect digital assets from malicious insiders*. Retrieved from http://www.thei3p.org/research/mitremi.html

McCabe, T. (1976). A complexity measure. *IEEE Transactions on Software Engineering, 2*(4), 308. doi:10.1109/TSE.1976.233837

McDonald, M., & Aron, D. (2011, June). *Reimagining IT: The 2011 CIO agenda*. Gartner Technology Research. Retrieved June 26, 2011, from http://www.gartner.com/DisplayDocument?id=1524714

McMinn, P. (2004). Search based software test data generation: A survey. *Software Testing. Verification and Reliability, 14*(2), 105–156. doi:10.1002/stvr.294

Meier, M. W. (1998). Architecting principles for systems-of-systems. *Systems Engineering, 1*(4), 287–384.

Mell, P., & Grance, T. (2009). The NIST definition of Cloud computing. *National Institute of Standards and Technology, 53*(6).

Mell, P., & Grance, T. (2009, August 21). *NIST working definition of cloud computing* (Draft), Vol. 15.

Mell, P., & Grance, T. (2011, January). *The NIST definition of cloud computing* (800-145). National Institute of Standards and Technology. Retrieved April 24, 2011, from http://csrc.nist.gov/publications/nistpubs/800-145/SP800-145.pdf

Mell, P., & Grance, T. (2011). *The NIST definition of cloud computing. (Special Publication 800-145), National Institute of Standards and Technology*. NIST.

Memon, A., Porter, A., Yilmaz, C., Nagarajan, A., Schmidt, D., & Natarajan, B. (2004). Skoll: Distributed continuous quality assurance. *Proceedings 26th International Conference on Software Engineering*, (pp. 459-468). IEEE Computer Society. doi:10.1109/ICSE.2004.1317468

Menasce, D., Ruan, H., & Gomaa, H. (2007). QoS management in service-oriented architectures. *Performance Evaluation, 64*(7), 646. doi:10.1016/j.peva.2006.10.001

Mesbah, A., & van Deursen, A. (2009). Invariant-based automatic testing of AJAX user interfaces. In *Proceedings of the International Conference on Software Engineering* (pp. 210-220).

Mesbah, A., Van Deursen, A., & Lenselink, S. (2012). Crawling Ajax-based web applications through dynamic analysis of user interface state changes. *ACM Transactions on the Web, 6*(1), 3:1-3:29.

Meyer, B. (2008). Seven Principles of Software Testing. *IEEE Transactions on Computers, 41*(8), 99–101.

Meyers, S. (1996). *More Effective C++: 35 New Ways To Improve Your Programs And Designs.* Upper Saddle River, NJ: Addison-Wesley.

Meyers, S. (1997). *Effective C++: 50 Specific Ways To Improve Your Programs And Design.* Upper Saddle River, NJ: Addison-Wesley.

Michael, C. C., & Radosevich, W. (2005). Risk-based and functional security testing. *Build Security In.* microTool. (2010). *in-Step.* Retrieved April 21, 2011, from http://www.microtool.de/instep/en/

Michael, C., McGraw, G., & Schatz, M. (2001). Generating software test data by evolution. *IEEE Transactions on Software Engineering, 12*, 1085–1110. doi:10.1109/32.988709

Michel, C. (2002, January). Exact projection functions for floating point number constraints. In the 7th International Symposium on Artificial Intelligence and Mathematics (AIMA 2002). Fort Lauderdale, Florida, USA.

Mickens, J. W., & Noble, B. D. (2007). Analytical models for epidemics in mobile networks. *Third IEEE International Conference on Wireless and Mobile Computing Networking and Communications WiMob 2007,* (WiMob), (p. 77). IEEE. doi:10.1109/WIMOB.2007.4390871

Microsoft. (2011). *Daytona project.* Retrieved June 9, 2012, from http://research.microsoft.com/en-us/projects/daytona/

Microsoft. (2011). *Windows Azure: Microsoft's Cloud services platform.* Retrieved April 22, 2011, from http://www.microsoft.com/windowsazure/windowsazure/

Microsoft. (2012). *Azure platform.* Retrieved June 9, 2012, from http://www.microsoft.com/windowsazure/

Miller, P. (2010). *Cook-A file construction tool-reference manual.* Retrieved April 27, 2011, from http://miller.emu.id.au/pmiller/software/cook/cook-2.34.rm.pdf

Miller, B. P. (1990). An empirical study of the reliability of UNIX utilities. *Communications of the ACM, 33*(12), 32–44. doi:10.1145/96267.96279

Miller, W., & Spooner, D. (1976). Automatic generation of floating-point test data. *IEEE Transactions on Software Engineering, 2*(3), 223–226. doi:10.1109/TSE.1976.233818

Miluzzo, E., Lane, N. D., Fodor, K., Peterson, R., Lu, H., Musolesi, M., et al. (2008). Sensing meets mobile social networks: the design, implementation and evaluation of the CenceMe application. *Conference on Embedded Networked Sensor Systems* (Vol. 10, pp. 337-350). ACM Press. doi:10.1145/1460412.1460445

Miura, S., Hanawa, T., Yonemoto, T., Boku, T., & Sato, M. (2009). RI2N/DRV: Multi-link Ethernet for high-bandwidth and fault-tolerant network on PC clusters. *The 9th Workshop on Communication Architecture for Clusters (CAC) in IPDPS* (pp. 1–8). IEEE Computer Society.

Mohan, P., Padmanabhan, V. N., & Ramjee, R. (2008). Nericell: Rich monitoring of road and traffic conditions using mobile smartphones. *Proceedings of the 6th ACM Conference on Embedded Network Sensor Systems SenSys 08* (p. 323). ACM Press. doi:10.1145/1460412.1460444

Molyneaux, I. (2009). *The art of application performance testing.* Sebastopol, CA: O'Reilly Media, Inc.

Montemerlo, M., Becker, J., Bhat, S., Dahlkamp, H., Dolgov, D., & Ettinger, S. ... Thrun, S. (2008). Junior: The Stanford entry in the urban challenge. In M. Buehler, K. Iagnemma, & S. Singh (Eds.), *Journal Of Field Robotics, 25*(9), 569–597.

Montemerlo, M., Thrun, S., Dahlkamp, H., Stavens, D., & Strohband, S. (2006). Winning the DARPA Grand Challenge with an AI robot. In *Proceedings Of The National Conference On Artificial Intelligence* (pp. 982–988). Menlo Park, CA: AAAI Press.

Moreno, J. (2010). *A testing framework for cloud storage systems.* Master thesis, Swiss Federal Institute of Technology Zurich.

Mosley, D. J., & Posey, B. A. (2002). *Just enough software test automation.* Upper Saddle River, NJ: Prentice Hall PTR.

Mugridge, R., & Cunningham, W. (2005). *Fit for developing software: Framework for integrated tests.*

Mulliner, C., & Vigna, G. (2006). Vulnerability analysis of MMS user agents. *22nd Annual Computer Security Applications Conference, ACSAC 06* (pp. 77-88).

Myers, C. R. (2003). Software systems as complex networks: Structure, function, and evolvability of software collaboration graphs. *Physical Review E: Statistical, Nonlinear, and Soft Matter Physics, 68.*

Myers, G. (1979). *The art of software testing.* John Wiley & Sons, Inc.

Nanda, S., & Chiueh, T. (2005). *A survey on virtualization technologies.* SUNY at Stony Brook.

Narasimhan, B., & Nichols, R. (2011, March). State of cloud applications and platforms – The cloud adapter's view. *IEEE Computer Magazine,* p. 24.

Naur, P., & Randell, B. (Eds.). *Software engineering: Report of a conference sponsored by the NATO Science Committee.* Garmisch, Germany, 7-11 Oct. 1968. Retrieved from http://homepages.cs.ncl.ac.uk/brian.randell/NATO/nato1968.PDF

Nimbus. (2012). *Website.* Retrieved from http://workspace.globus.org

Nipkow, T., Paulson, L. C., & Wenzel, M. (2002). *Isabelle/HOL — A proof assistant for higher-order logic (Vol. 2283).* Springer.

NIST & RTI. (2002). *The economic impacts of inadequate infrastructure for software testing.* (No. RTI Project Number 7007.011): National Institute of Standards and Technology.

NoMagic. (2011). *MagicDraw.* Retrieved April 21, 2011, from http://www.magicdraw.com/

NSF. (n.d.). *TeraGrid.* Retrieved from https://www.teragrid.org/

Nurmi, D., & Wolski, R. Grzegorczyk, Graziano Obertelli, G., Soman, S., Youseff, L., & Zagorodnov, D. (2009). The eucalyptus open-source cloud-computing system. *IEEE International Symposium on Cluster Computing and the Grid,* (pp. 124-131). Los Alamitos. CA: IEEE Computer Society Press.

OASIS. (2008). *eXtensible access control markup language* (XACML). Retrieved April 21, 2011, from http://www.oasis-open.org/committees/tc_home.php?wg_abbrev=xacml

Oberheide, J., Veeraraghavan, K., Cooke, E., Flinn, J., & Jahanian, F. (2008). Virtualized in-cloud security services for mobile devices. *Proceedings of the First Workshop on Virtualization in Mobile Computing,* (pp. 31-35). ACM. doi:10.1145/1622103.1629656

Object Management Group. (2002). *Lightweight CORBA component model RFP.* Object Management Group.

Office for Civil Rights. (2003, May). *Summary of the HIPAA privacy rule.* US Department of Health and Human Services. Retrieved April 13, 2011, from http://www.hhs.gov/ocr/privacy/hipaa/understanding/summary/privacysummary.pdf

Ofutt, J., & Xu, W. (2004). Generating test cases for web services using data perturbation. *ACM SIGSOFT Software Engineering Notes, 29*(5), 1. doi:10.1145/1022494.1022529

Ojala, A., & Tyrvainen, P. (2011, July). Developing cloud business models. *IEEE Software Magazine, 22*(4), 42.

Olio. (2011). Retrieved from http://incubator.apache.org/olio/

Oliver, E. (2010). The challenges in large-scale smartphone user studies. *Proceedings of the 2nd ACM International Workshop on Hot Topics in Planet-Scale Measurement,* (pp. 1-5). ACM Press. doi:10.1145/1834616.1834623

Oliver, E. (2009). A survey of platforms for mobile networks research. *ACM SIGMOBILE Mobile Computing and Communications Review, 12*(4), 56. doi:10.1145/1508285.1508292

OMG. (2003). *MDA guide version 1.0.1.*

OMG. (2007). *OMG unified modeling language (OMG UML): Superstructure,* V2.1.2.

OpenNebula. (2012). *Website*. Retrieved from http://www.opennebula.org

OpenStack. (2012). *Website*. Retrieved from http://openstack.org/

Oriol, M., & Ullah, F. (2010). YETI in the cloud. *2nd International Workshop on Software Testing in the cloud (STITC), 3rd IEEE International Conference on Software Testing, Verification and Validation (ICST)*, (pp. 434-437).

Oxley. (2002, July). Sarbanes-Oxley Act of 2002. *Sarbanes-Oxley Act Community Forum*. Retrieved April 13, 2011, from http://frwebgate.access.gpo.gov/cgi-bin/getdoc.cgi?dbname=107_cong_reports&docid=f:hr610.107.pdf

Pagden, E. (2003). *The IT utility model—Part I*. Sun Professional Services.

Pagden, E. (2003). *The IT utility model—Part II*. Sun Professional Services.

Page, A., & Johnston, K. (2008). *How we test software at Microsoft*. Microsoft Press.

Pakhira, A., & Andras, P. (2010). *Can we use network analysis methods to discover functionally important method calls in software systems by considering dynamic analysis data?* Paper presented at the PCODA, Beverley,MA.

Parveen, T., & Tilley, S. (2010) When to migrate software testing in the cloud? In *Proceedings Of The 2nd International Workshop On Software Testing In The Cloud* (STITC'10) (pp. 13 – 16). Melbourne, FL: Florida Institute of Technology.

Parveen, T., & Tilley, S. R. (2010, April). When to migrate software testing to the cloud? In the *Third International Conference on Software Testing, Verification and Validation Workshops* (ICSTW 2010) (pp. 424–427). Paris, France: IEEE Computer Society.

Parveen, T., Tilley, S., Daley, N., & Morales, P. (2009). Towards a distributed execution framework for JUnit test cases. In *Proceedings of the 25th IEEE International Conference on Software Maintenance* (pp. 425-428). Los Alamitos, CA: IEEE Computer Society. doi:10.1109/ICSM.2009.5306292

Pettey, C. (2009, October). *Gartner identifies the top 10 strategic technologies for 2010*. Gartner Technology Research. Retrieved April 24, 2011, from http://www.gartner.com/it/page.jsp?id=1210613

Pettey, C. (2010, June). *Gartner says worldwide cloud services market to surpass $68 billion in 2010*. Gartner Technology Research. Retrieved April 24, 2011, from http://www.gartner.com/it/page.jsp?id=1389313

Piercy, M. (2004). Embedded devices next on the virus target list. *Electronics Systems and Software*, *2*(6), 42–43. doi:10.1049/ess:20040612

Porter, A., Yilmaz, C., Memon, A. M., Schmidt, D. C., & Natarajan, B. (2007). Skoll: A process and infrastructure for distributed continuous quality assurance. *IEEE Transactions on Software Engineering, 33*(8), 510-525. IEEE Computer Society. doi:10.1109/TSE.2007.70719

Porter, A. A., Siy, H. P., Toman, C. A., & Votta, L. G. (1997). An experiment to assess the cost-benefits of code inspections in large scale software development. *IEEE Transactions on Software Engineering, 23*(6), 329–346. doi:10.1109/32.601071

Poshyvanyk, D., Gueheneuc, Y. G., Marcus, A., Antoniol, G., & Rajlich, V. (2007). Feature location using probabilistic ranking of methods based on execution scenarios and information retrieval. *IEEE Transactions on Software Engineering, 33*(6), 420–432. doi:10.1109/TSE.2007.1016

Potanin, A., Noble, J., Frean, M., & Biddle, R. (2005). Scale-free geometry in OO programs. *Communications of the ACM, 48*(5), 99–103. doi:10.1145/1060710.1060716

Potter, B., & McGraw, G. (2004). Software security testing. *IEEE Security and Privacy, 2*(5), 81–85. doi:10.1109/MSP.2004.84

Potyra, S., Sieh, V., & Cin, M. D. (2007). Evaluating fault-tolerant system designs using FAUmachine. *Workshop on Engineering Fault Tolerant Systems (EFTS '07)* (p. 9). Association for Computing Machinery.

Pretschner, A., Broy, M., Krueger, I. H., & Stauner, T. (2007). Software engineering for automotive systems: A roadmap. In *Proceedings Of 2007 Future Of Software Engineering* (FOSE'07) (pp. 55 – 71). Washington, DC: IEEE Computer Society.

Provos, N., & Holz, T. (2007). *Virtual honeypots: From botnet tracking to intrusion detection* (1st ed.). Addison-Wesley Professional.

Rajlich, V., & Wilde, N. (2002). *The role of concepts in program comprehension.* Paper presented at the IWPC/ICPC.

Randell, B., & Buxton, J. N. (Eds.). (1969). *Software engineering techniques: Report of a conference sponsored by the NATO Science Committee.* Rome, Italy, 27-31 Oct. 1969. Retrieved from http://homepages.cs.ncl.ac.uk/brian.randell/NATO/nato1969.PDF

Rao, A. S., & Georgeff, M. P. (2000). BDI agents: From theory to practice. *International Conference on Multi-Agent Systems* (pp. 312–319).

Rauskolb, F. W., Berger, K., Lipski, C., Magnor, M., Cornelsen, K., & Effertz, J. ... Rumpe, B. (2010). Caroline: An autonomously driving vehicle for urban environments. In M. Buehler, K. Iagnemma, & S. Singh (Eds.), *The Darpa Urban Challenge - Autonomous Vehicles In City Traffic, Springer Tracts In Advanced Robotics, Volume 56* (pp. 441 – 508).

Reese, G. (2009). *Cloud application architectures: Building applications and infrastructures in the cloud.* O´Reilly Press.

Reference Architecture Working Group. (2011, March). *Cloud computing reference architecture.* National Institute of Standards and Technology. Retrieved May 24, 2011, from http://collaborate.nist.gov/twiki-cloud-computing/pub/CloudComputing/ReferenceArchitectureTaxonomy/NIST_CC_Reference_Architecture_v1_March_30_2011.pdf

Reis, C., & Gribble, S. D. (2009). *Isolating web programs in modern browser architectures.* Paper presented at the Eurosys 2009.

Rensfelt, O., Hermans, F., Gunningberg, P., & Larzon, L. (2010). Repeatable experiments with mobile nodes in a relocatable WSN testbed. *6th IEEE International Conference on Distributed Computing in Sensor Systems Workshops (DCOSSW), 2010* (pp. 1-6).

Rhodes, C. J., & Nekovee, M. (2008). The opportunistic transmission of wireless worms between mobile devices. *Physica A: Statistical Mechanics and its Applications, 387*(27), 6837-6844. Elsevier B.V. Retrieved from http://arxiv.org/abs/0802.2685

Rhoton, J. (2009). *Cloud computing explained: Implementation handbook for enterprises.* Recursive Press. [1]

Ricca, F., & Tonella, P. (2001). Analysis and testing of web applications. In *Proceedings of the International Conference on Software Engineering* (pp. 25-34).

Ricci, R., Alfred, C., & Lepreau, J. (2003). A solver for the network testbed mapping problem. *SIGCOMM Computer Communications Review, 33*(2), 30–44. doi:10.1145/956981.956988

Richardson, D. J., & Wolf, A. L. (1996). Testing at the architectural level. In *Proceedings of the Second International Software Architecture Workshop (ISAW-2)* (pp. 68-71). San Francisco, California.

Rimal, B. P., Choi, E., & Lumb, I. (2009). A taxonomy and survey of cloud computing systems. In *International Joint Conference on Networked Computing, Advanced Information Management & Services, and Digital Content Multimedia Technology and its Applications,* Washington, DC, USA (pp.44-51).

Rings, T., et al. (2010). On the standardization of a testing framework for application deployment on grid and cloud infrastructures. *Proceedings of the 2010 Second International Conference on Advances in system Testing and Validation Lifecycle,* (pp. 99-107). Washington, DC: IEEE Computer Society.

Rittel, H., & Webber, M. (1973). Dilemmas in a general theory of planning. *Policy Sciences, 4,* 155–169. doi:10.1007/BF01405730

Riungu, L. M., et al. (2010). *Research issues for software testing in the cloud.*

Riungu, L. M., Taipale, O., & Smolander, K. (2010). Research issues for software testing in the cloud. *2nd International Conference on Cloud Computing Technology and Science,* (pp. 557-564).

Riungu, L. M., Taipale, O., & Smolander, K. (2010). Software testing as an online service: Observations from practice. In *Proceedings of the 2nd International Workshop on Software Testing in the Cloud* (STITC'10) (pp. 7–12). Melbourne, FL: Florida Institute of Technology.

Riungu, L. M., Taipale, O., Smolander, K., Hanawa, T., Banzai, T., Koizumi, H., et al. (2010). *Software testing in the cloud.* Paper presented at the 2nd International Workshop on Software Testing in the Cloud Co-located with the 3rd IEEE International Conference on Software Testing, Verification, and Validation (ICST 2010).

Riungu-Kalliosaari, L., Taipale, O., & Smolander, K. (2012). Testing in the cloud: Exploring the practice. *Special Issue on Software Engineering for the Cloud. IEEE Software*, 46–51. doi:10.1109/MS.2011.132

Robinson, J. (2009, April). Cloud computing spending leaps 21%. *Information Age*. Retrieved April 24, 2011, from http://www.information-age.com/channels/data-centre-and-it-infrastructure/perspectives-and-trends/1017852/cloud-computing-spending-leaps-21.thtml

Robinson, P., & Ragusa, C. (2011). Taxonomy and requirements rationalization for infrastructure in cloud-based software testing. *IEEE Third International Conference on Cloud Computing Technology and Science,* (pp. 454-461).

Roßner, T. (2010). *Basiswissen modellbasierter Test.* Dpunkt-Verlag.

Rothermel, G., & Untch, R. Chu, C., & Harrold, M. (1999). Test case prioritization: An empirical study. In *IEEE International Conference of Software Maintenance* (pp. 179–188). Los Alamitos, CA: IEEE Computer Society. doi:10.1109/ICSM.1999.792604

Rothermel, G., & Harrold, M. (1997). A safe, efficient regression test selection technique. *ACM Transactions on Software Engineering and Methodology*, *6*(2), 173–210. doi:10.1145/248233.248262

Rothermel, G., Untch, R. H., Chengyun, C., & Harrold, M. J. (2001). Prioritizing test cases for regression testing. *IEEE Transactions on Software Engineering*, *27*(10), 929–948. doi:10.1109/32.962562

Roy, P. (n.d.). *Slimtune.* Retrieved from http://code.google.com/p/slimtune/

Rozinat, A., & van der Aalst, W. M. P. (2007). Conformance checking of processes based on monitoring real behavior. *Information Systems*, *33*(1), 64–95. doi:10.1016/j.is.2007.07.001

Rubinov, M., & Sporns, O. (2010). Complex network measures of brain connectivity: Uses and interpretations. *NeuroImage*, *52*(3), 1059–1069. doi:10.1016/j.neuroimage.2009.10.003

Rugaber, S., Stirewalt, K., & Wills, L. (1995). The interleaving problem in program understanding. In E. Chikofsky, L. Wills, & P. Newcomb (Eds.), *Working Conference on Reverse Engineering*, (pp. 166-175). Los Alamitos, CA: IEEE Computer Society Press.

Rumpe, B., Berger, C., & Krahn, H. (2006). Software engineering methods for quality management of intelligent automotive systems. In *integrierte sicherheit und fahrerassistenzsysteme, no. 1960* (pp. 473 – 486).

Ruth, M., et al. (2007, July). Towards automatic regression test selection for web services. *COMPSAC'07: Proceedings of the 31st Annual International Computer Software and Applications Conference,* Vol. 2, Bejing, (p. 729).

Salesforce Usage Trends. (2011). Retrieved from http://trends.builtwith.com/analytics/Salesforce

Sampath, S., Sprenkle, S., Gibson, E., Pollock, L. L., & Greenwald, A. S. (2007). Applying concept analysis to user-session-based testing of web applications. *IEEE Transactions on Software Engineering*, *33*(10), 643–658. doi:10.1109/TSE.2007.70723

Saucelabs. (2010). *Sauce OnDemand: Cloud testing service.* Retrieved January 27, 2010, from http://saucelabs.com/products/sauce-ondemand

Scalable Network Technologies. (n.d.). *Qualnet.* Retrieved from http://www.scalable-networks.com/

Schabenberger, R. (2007). ADTF: Framework for driver assistance and safety systems. In *vdi wissensforum iwb gmbh (ed.), integrierte sicherheit und fahrerassistenzsysteme* (pp. 701–710).

Schaefer, W., & Wehrheim, H. (2007). The challenges of building advanced mechatronic systems. In *Proceedings Of Fose '07: 2007 Future Of Software Engineering* (pp. 72–84). Washington, DC: IEEE Computer Society. doi:10.1109/FOSE.2007.28

Schmidt, A.-D., Schmidt, H.-G., Batyuk, L., Clausen, J. H., Camtepe, S. A., Albayrak, S., & Yildizli, C. (2009). Smartphone malware evolution revisited: Android next target? *2009 4th International Conference on Malicious and Unwanted Software MALWARE*, (pp. 1-7). IEEE. doi:10.1109/MALWARE.2009.5403026

Schmidt, D. C. (1994). ACE: An object-oriented framework for developing distributed applications. *Proceedings of the 6th USENIX C++ Technical Conference*, USENIX Association.

Schneier, B. (1999). Attack trees. *Dr. Dobb's Journal*, *24*(12), 21–29.

Scholtz, J. (2001). Adaptation of traditional usability testing methods for remote testing. In *Proceedings of the 34th Annual Hawaii International Conference on System Sciences (HICSS-34)*, Volume 5.

Schroeter, A. (2009). *Kiwi Imaging With Opensuse Build Service*. Retrieved April 27, 2011, from http://en.opensuse.org/images/b/be/OBS-Imageing.pdf

Scott, M. (2008). *Tort liability for vendors of insecure software: Has the time finally come?* Retrieved from http://www.law.umaryland.edu/academics/journals/mdlr/print/articles/67-425.pdf

SDTCorp. (2010). *Unified TestPro – Keyword driven automation and manual testing tool*. Retrieved January 25, 2010 from http://www.sdtcorp.com/utp_solution.html

Seaman, C. B. (1999). Qualitative methods in empirical studies of software engineering. *IEEE Transactions on Software Engineering*, *25*, 557–572. doi:10.1109/32.799955

Seeley, D. (1988). *A tour of the worm*. Department of Computer Science, University of Utah.

Sen, K., Marinov, D., & Agha, G. (2005, September). CUTE: A concolic unit testing engine for C. In the *5th Joint Meeting of the European Software Engineering Conference and ACM SIGSOFT Symposium on the Foundations of Software Engineering* (ESEC/FSE 2005) (pp. 263–272). Lisbon, Portugal: ACM Press.

Severance, C., & Dowd, K. (1998). *High performance computing* (2nd ed.). O'Reilly Media.

Shabtai, A., & Elovici, Y. (2010). Applying behavioral detection on Android-based devices. *Mobile Wireless Middleware Operating Systems and Applications*, (pp. 235–249). Springer. Retrieved from http://www.springerlink.com/index/G404U422T1008740.pdf

Shabtai, A., Fledel, Y., Kanonov, U., Elovici, Y., Dolev, S., & Glezer, C. (2010). Google Android: A comprehensive security assessment. *Security & Privacy*, *8*(2), 35–44. doi:10.1109/MSP.2010.2

Shankaran, N., Schmidt, D. C., Chen, Y., Koutsoukous, X., & Lu, C. (2007). *The design and performance of configurable component middleware for end-to-end adaptation of distributed real-time embedded systems*. 10th International Symposium on Object/Component/Service-oriented Real-time Distributed Computing. Santorini Island, Greece: IEEE.

Shannon, C. (1949). A mathematical theory of communication. *The Bell System Technical Journal*, *27*, 379.

Sharp, D. (2011, June). Will cloud computing be the future of IT? *Online Magazine and Writer's Network*. Retrieved June 26, 2011, from http://www.suite101.com/content/will-cloud-computing-be-the-future-for-it-a327753

Shaw, M., & Garlan, D. (1996). *Software architecture: Perspectives on an emerging discipline*. Upper Saddle River, NJ: Prentice Hall.

Shull, F. (2012, March). A brave new world of testing – An interview with Google's James Whittaker. *IEEE Software Magazine*, p. 4.

Siegel, S. (1996). *Object-oriented software testing – A hierarchical approach* (p. 93). New York, NY: John Wiley & Sons.

Siegl, S., Hielscher, K.-S., German, R., & Berger, C. (2011). Formal specification and systematic model-driven testing of embedded automotive systems. In *Proceedings Of The Conference On Design, Automation, And Test In Europe* (DATE 2011), (pp. 1530 – 1591).

Siemens. (2010). *Towards a cloud-specific risk analysis framework*.

Sinofsky, S. (2012, 2 May). *Cloud services for Windows 8 and Windows Phone: Windows Live, reimagined.* MSDN Blog. Retrieved May 31, 2012, from http://blogs.msdn.com/b/b8/archive/2012/05/02/cloud-services-for-windows-8-and-windows-phone-windows-live-reimagined.aspx

Smith, D., & Lewis, G. (2007, March). *Standards for service-oriented systems.* Paper presented at the 11th European Conference on Software Maintenance and Reengineering (CSMR10), Amsterdam.

Smith, C., & Williams, L. (2001). *Performance solutions: A practical guide to creating responsive, scalable software.* Boston, MA: Addison-Wesley Professional.

Sneed, H. (1990). The data-point estimation method. *Online - Zeitschrift für Datenverarbeitung, 5,* 48.

Sneed, H. (2005, March). Testing an egovernment website. *7th IEEE International Symposium on Web Site Evolution* (WSE2005), Budapest, (p. 3).

Sneed, H. (2007, October). *Testing against natural language requirements.* Paper presented at 7th Int. Conference on Software Quality (QSIC2007), Portland.

Sneed, H. (2008, April). Certification of web services. *2nd Workshop on SOA-Based Systems, CSMR2008,* Athens, 2008, (p. 336).

Sneed, H. (2008, Oct.). *Bridging the concept to implementation gap in software testing.* 8th International Conference on Software Quality (QSIC2008), Oxford.

Sneed, H. (2010, Sept.) Measuring web service interfaces. *Workshop on Website Evolution – WSE2010,* Temesvar, Romania, (p. 41).

Sneed, H. (2012, June). *Offering cloud service testing as a service.* Paper presented at Ignite Conference, SQS Ignite-Swiss, Geneva, 2012.

Sneed, H., & Huang, S. (2006). WSDLTest – A tool for testing web services. *Proceedings of WSE-2006,* Sept. 2006, (p. 14). Philadelphia, PA: IEEE Computer Society Press.

Sneed, H. (2009). A pilot project for migrating COBOL code to web services. *International Journal of Software Tools Technology Transfer, 1*(2), 103.

SNIA. (2011). *Cloud data management interface.*

Sobel, W., Subramanyam, S., Sucharitakul, A., Nguyen, J., Wong, H., & Patil, S. … Patterson, D. (2008). CloudStone: Multi-platform, multi-language benchmark and measurement tools for Web 2.0. *Proceedings of the 1st International Workshop on Cloud Computing and its Applications.*

Software Engineering Institute. (2006). *Ultra-large-scale systems: Software challenge of the future.* Pittsburgh, PA: Carnegie Mellon University.

Software Research Associates. (2011). Automated testing of modern Web Applications, *SRA Business White Paper.* SRA Inc., San Francisco

Software Research Associates. (2011). *eValid business description* (white paper). San Francisco, CA: Author.

Sogeti. (2009). *STaaS - Software testing as a service.* Retrieved May 10, 2009, from http://www.sogeti.com/upload/Looking%20for%20Solutions/Documents/STaaS_leaflet%20v%20Feb%202009.pdf

Sogeti. (2010). *STaaS - Software testing as a service.* Retrieved January 25, 2010, from http://www.sogeti.com/looking-for-solutions/Services/Software-Control-Testing/STaaS-/

Sommerville, I. (2001). *Software engineering* (6th ed.). Boston, MA: Addison-Wesley Longman Publishing Co., Inc.

Sommerville, I. (2010). *Software engineering* (9th ed.). Addison Wesley.

Source Insight. (2012). *Website.* Retrieved from http://www.sourceinsight.com/

Spanoudakis, G., & Zisman, A. (2010). Discovering services during service-based system design using UML. *IEEE Transactions on Software Engineering, 36*(3), 371. doi:10.1109/TSE.2009.88

Sridhar, M., & Hamlen, K. (2010). ActionScript in-lined reference monitoring in Prolog. *Proceedings of the 12th International Conference on Practical Aspects of Declarative Languages,* (pp. 149–151). Springer.

Srinivasan, S., & Getov, V. (2011, March). Navigating the cloud computing landscape – Technologies, services and adapters. *IEEE Computer Magazine,* p. 22

SSELab. (2011). *SSELAB*. Retrieved April 27, 2011, from http://sselab.de

StackOps. (2012). *Website*. Retrieved from http://www.stackops.org/

Steen, M. V. Van der zijden, S., & Sips, H. J. (1998). Software engineering for scalable distributed applications. *International Computer Software and Applications Conference* (pp. 285-292).

Steve, G. (2004). Threats looming beyond the perimeter. *Infosecurity Today, 1*(6), 12-14. Retrieved from http://www.sciencedirect.com/science/article/pii/S1742684704001296

Strauss, A., & Corbin, J. (1990). *Basics of qualitative research: Grounded theory procedures and techniques.* Newbury Park, CA: SAGE Publications.

Stylianou, A., & Kumar, R. (2000). An integrative framework for IS quality management. *Communications of the ACM, 43*(9), 99. doi:10.1145/348941.349009

Su, J., Chan, K. K. W., Miklas, A. G., Po, K., Akhavan, A., Saroiu, S., et al. (2006). A preliminary investigation of worm infections in a Bluetooth environment. *Proceedings of the 4th ACM Workshop on Recurring Malcode WORM 06*, (p. 9). ACM Press. doi:10.1145/1179542.1179545

Sun, X. H., & Ni, L. M. (1993). Scalable problems and memory-bounded speedup. *Journal of Parallel and Distributed Computing, 19*(1), 27–37. doi:10.1006/jpdc.1993.1087

Tahvildar, L., & Kontogiannis, K. (2004). Improving design quality using meta-pattern transformations: A metric-based approach: Research Articles. *Journal of Software Maintenance Evolution, 16*(4-5), 331–361. doi:10.1002/smr.299

Taobao. (2011). Retrieved from http://www.taobao.com/

Taylor, S., Schroeder, K., & Doerr, J. (2003). *Inside Intuit: How the makers of Quicken beat Microsoft and revolutionized an entire industry.* Boston, MA: Harvard Business School Press.

Teng, C.-C., & Helps, R. (2010). Mobile application development: Essential new directions for IT. *2010 Seventh International Conference on Information Technology New Generations*, (pp. 471-475). IEEE. doi:10.1109/ITNG.2010.249

Terekhov, I. (2003). Meta-computing at D0. *Nuclear Instruments & Methods in Physics Research. Section A, Accelerators, Spectrometers, Detectors and Associated Equipment, 502*(2-3), 402–406. doi:10.1016/S0168-9002(03)00452-2

TESIS DYNAware GmbH. (2011). *DYNA4*. Retrieved April 27, 2011, from http://tesis-dynaware.com

Tigris.org. (2011). *CXXTEST*. Retrieved April 27, 2011, from http://cxxtest.tigris.org

Tigris.org. (2011). *FSVS*. Retrieved April 27, 2011, from http://fsvs.tigris.org

Tilley, S. (2010). Distinct facets of the Software Testing in the Cloud 2010 workshop. *Proceedings of the 2nd International Workshop on Software Testing in the Cloud*, (p. 1). Retrieved April 17, 2010, from http://www.stitc.org/2010/proceedings/index.html

Tilley, S. R., & Parveen, T. (2010). When to migrate software testing to the cloud? In *Proceedings of Third International Conference on Software Testing, Verification, and Validation Workshops*, (pp. 424-427).

Tillmann, N., & de Halleux, J. (2008, April). White box test generation for. NET. In the *2nd International Conference on Tests and Proofs* (TAP 2008) (pp. 133–153). Prato, Italy: Springer.

Tonella, P. (2004). Evolutionary testing of classes. In *Proceedings of the International Symposium on Software Testing and Analysis* (pp. 119-128).

Tong, L., Zhao, Q., & Adireddy, S. (2003). *Sensor networks with mobile agents. IEEE Military Communications Conference 2003 MILCOM 2003* (Vol. 1, pp. 688–693). IEEE. doi:10.1109/MILCOM.2003.1290187

Torrens, H. (2008, October). Coming to terms with cloud computing. *Application Development Trends* Retrieved April 23, 2011, from http://adtmag.com/articles/2008/10/02/coming-to-terms-with-cloud-computing.aspx

Tosic, V., Pargurek, B., & Patel, K. (2003). WSQL – A language for the formal specification of classes of service for web services. In L. Zhang (Ed.), *International Conference of Web Services*, (p. 375).

Töyssy, S., & Helenius, M. (2006). About malicious software in smartphones. *Journal in Computer Virology, 2*(2), 109-119. Paris, France: Springer. doi:doi:10.1007/s11416-006-0022-0

Troger, P., Meyer, H., Melzer, I., & Flehmig, M. (2007). Dynamic provisioning and monitoring of stateful services. *Proceedings of the 3rd International Conference on Web Information Systems and Technology (WEBIST '07)*, (pp. 434-438). Barcelona, Spain.

Tsai, W. T., Chen, Y., Paul, R., Liao, N., & Huang, H. (2004). Cooperative and group testing in verification of dynamic composite web services. *Workshop on Quality Assurance and Testing of Web-Based Applications* (pp. 170–173).

Tsai, W. T., Paul, R., Song, W., & Cao, Z. (2002). Coyote: An XML-based framework for web services testing. *Proceedings of the 7th IEEE International Symposium on High Assurance Systems Engineering, HASE 2002, October 25-26, 2002; Tokyo, Japan*, (p. 173).

Tsai, W. T., Zhou, X., Chen, Y., & Ai, X. (2008, August). On testing and evaluating service-oriented software. *IEEE Computer Magazine*, p. 40.

Tsai, W. T., Paul, R., Yu, L., Saimi, A., & Cao, Z. (2003). Scenario-based web service testing with distributed agents. *IEICE Transaction on Information and System. E (Norwalk, Conn.), 86-D*(10), 2130–2144.

Tudor, B., & Pettey, C. (2010). *Gartner says worldwide mobile phone sales grew 35 percent in third quarter 2010; Smartphone sales increased 96 percent*. Retrieved from http://www.gartner.com/it/page.jsp?id=1466313

Turner, M., Budgen, D., & Brereton, P. (2003). Turning software into a service. *Computer, 36*(10), 38–44. doi:10.1109/MC.2003.1236470

UKeScience. (n.d.). *National Grid Service(NGS)*. Retrieved from http://www.ngs.ac.uk/

Underseth, M. (2007). The complexity crisis in embedded software. In *Embedded Computing Design* (pp. 31-33).

Utest. (2009). *Case study: Community testing for agile-development web applications*. Retrieved May 10, 2009, from www.utest.com/download/uTestCaseStudyCommunity-TestingForAgileDev.pdf

van der Aalst, L. (2010). *Software testing as a service (STaaS) (Tech. Rep.)*. Vianen, The Netherlands: Sogeti. Retrieved from http://www.leovanderaalst.nl/Software Testing as a Service - STaaS.pdf

van Heesch, D. (2011). *Doxygen*. Retrieved April 27, 2011, from http://www.stack.nl/~dimitri/doxygen/index.html

Varia, J. (2008). Cloud architectures. *AWS Cloud Computing Whitepapers*. Retrieved May 1, 2011, from http://aws.amazon.com/jp/whitepapers/

Verdon, D., & McGraw, G. (2004). Risk analysis in software design. *Security & Privacy, 2*(4), 79–84. doi:10.1109/MSP.2004.55

Verma, A., Llorà, X., Goldberg, D. E., & Campbell, R. H. (2009). Scaling genetic algorithms using MapReduce. In *Proceedings of the 2009 Ninth International Conference on Intelligent Systems Design and Applications*, (pp. 13-18). Washington, DC: IEEE Computer Society.

VMware. (2012). *Website*. Retrieved from http://www.vmware.com/

von Hagen, W. (2008). *Professional Xen Virtualization*. Indianapolis, IN: Wiley Publishing Inc.

von Neumann-Cosel, K., Nentwig, M., Lehmann, D., Speth, J., & Knoll, A. (2009) Preadjustment of a vision-based lane tracker. In *Proceedings On Driving Simulation Conference*.

von Wedel, X. (2011). *Cloud9 Ide Launches Paas For Javascript And Html5*. Retrieved April 27, from http://cloudexpo-europe.com/node/1733520/print

Vos, T., Baars, A., Lindlar, F., Kruse, P., Windisch, A., & Wegener, J. (2010). Industrial scaled automated structural testing with the evolutionary testing tool. In *Proceedings of the 2010 Third International Conference on Software Testing, Verification and Validation* (ICST '10), (pp. 175-184). Washington, DC: IEEE Computer Society.

Vossen, G. (2011). The great mistrust of small and middle-sized enterprises towards cloud computing. *Digital Zetschrift, 23*.

Vouk, M. A. (2008). Cloud computing — Issues, research and implementations. *30th International Conference on Information Technology Interfaces*, (pp. 31-40). Cavtat, Croatia.

Wahl, N. (1999). An overview of regression testing. *ACM SIGSOFT Software Engineering Notes, 24*(1), 69–73. doi:10.1145/308769.308790

Walker, J. (2008). *Open Solaris test farm*. Retrieved May 1, 2011, from http://hub.opensolaris.org/bin/download/Community+Group+testing/files/opensolaristesting.pdf

Walters, L. O., & Kritzinger, P. S. (2002). *Email message interarrival time analysis*. Retrieved April 11, 2011, from http://pubs.cs.uct.ac.za/archive/00000107/01/mailTrace.pdf

Wang, L., Wang, Z., Yang, C., Zhang, L., & Ye, Q. (2009). *Linux kernels as complex networks: A novel method to study evolution*. Paper presented at the ICSM.

Wang, Q., Wang, C., Li, J., Ren, K., & Lou, W. (2009). *Enabling public verifiability and data dynamics for storage security in cloud computing*. European Symposium on Research in Computer Security, Saint Malo, France.

Wang, P., Gonzalez, M., Hidalgo, C. A., & Barabasi, A. L. (2009). Understanding the spreading patterns of mobile phone viruses. *Science, 324*(5930), 1071–1076. Retrieved from http://arxiv.org/abs/0906.4567doi:10.1126/science.1167053

Wei, Y., & Blake, M. B. (2010). Service-oriented computing and cloud computing. *IEEE Internet Computing, 14*(6), 72–75. doi:10.1109/MIC.2010.147

Wheeler, D. (n.d.). *SLOCCount*. Retrieved from http://www.dwheeler.com/sloccount/

White, J., Benavides, D., Schmidt, D. C., Trinidad, P., Dougherty, B., & Ruiz-Cortes, A. (2010). Automated diagnosis of feature model configurations. *Journal of Systems and Software, 83*(7), 1094–1107. http://www.sciencedirect.com/science/article/pii/S016412121000049Xdoi:10.1016/j.jss.2010.02.017

Whittaker, J. A. (2002). *How to break software: A practical guide to testing*. Wiley. Vaquero, L. M., Rodero-Merino, L., Caceres, J., & Lindner, M. (2009). A break in the clouds: Towards a cloud definition. *Computer Communication Review, 39*(1).

Wickremasinghe, B., Calheiros, R. N., & Buyya, R. (2010). CloudAnalyst: A CloudSim-based visual modeller for analysing cloud computing environments and applications. *International Conference on Advanced Information Networking and Applications* (pp. 446-452).

Wikipedia. (2012, May 17). *Endianness*. Retrieved from http://en.wikipedia.org/wiki/Endianness

Williams, N., Marre, B., Mouy, P., & Roger, M. (2005, April). PathCrawler: Automatic generation of path tests by combining static and dynamic analysis. In the *5th European Dependable Computing Conference* (EDCC 2005) (pp. 281–292). Budapest, Hungary: Springer.

Wilson, A., & York, M. (2011). Perceived or real risks using smartphones. *ABIS 2011 Referenced Proceedings* (pp. 79-81).

Wirfs-Brock, R., Wilkerson, B., & Wiener, L. (1990). *Designing object-oriented software*. Prentice-Hall, Inc.

Wolverton, R. W. (1974). The cost of developing large-scale software. *IEEE Transactions on Computers, C-23*(6), 615–636. doi:10.1109/T-C.1974.224002

Woods, S., & Yang, Q. (1996). The program understanding problem: Analysis and a heuristic approach. In T. Maibaum & M. V. Zelkowitz (Eds.), *International Conference on Software Engineering*, (pp. 6-15). Los Alamitos, CA: IEEE Computer Society Press.

Wooldridge, M., & Jennings, N. R. (1995). Intelligent agents: Theory and practice. *The Knowledge Engineering Review, 10*(2), 115–152. doi:10.1017/S0269888900008122

Wordpress.com Weblog. (2008, September). *Life in the cloud, living with cloud computing*. Wordpress.com. Retrieved April 23, 2011, from http://computinginthecloud.wordpress.com/2008/09/25/utility-cloud-computing-flashback-to-1961-prof-john-mccarthy/

World Wide Web Consortium. (2002). *Web service definition*. Retrieved from http://www.w3.org/tr/2002wd-wsa-reqs-20021011

World Wide Web Consortium. (2008) *Web service definition*. Retrieved from http://www.w3.org/tr/wsdl20

World Wide Web Consortium. (2011). *SuperSareware*. Retrieved form http://www.supershareware.com/info/soa-cleaner

World Wide Web Consortium. (2011). *Parasoft SoapTest*. Retrieved from http://www2.parasoft.com

World Wide Web Consortium. (2011). *Web inject*. Retrieved from http://www.webinject.org

Worms, K. (2010). *Experience of a Swiss Bank in migrating to SOA*. Paper presented at 25th International Conference on Software Maintenance – ICSM2010, Temisoara, Romania.

Xen. (2012). *Website*. Retrieved from http://xen.org/

Xie, T., Tillmann, N., Halleux, P., et al. (2012, March). Environmental modelling for automated cloud application testing. *IEEE Software Magazine*, p. 30.

Yan, G., & Eidenbenz, S. (2006). Bluetooth worms: Models, dynamics, and defense implications. *2006 22nd Annual Computer Security Applications Conference ACSAC06*, (pp. 245-256). IEEE. doi:10.1109/ACSAC.2006.18

Yan, G., Cuellar, L., Eidenbenz, S., Flores, H. D., Hengartner, N., & Vu, V. (2007). Bluetooth worm propagation: Mobility pattern matters! *Proceedings of the 2nd ACM Symposium on Information, Computer, and Communications Security*, (pp. 32-44). Retrieved from http://portal.acm.org/citation.cfm?id=1229294

Yan, T., Marzilli, M., Holmes, R., Ganesan, D., & Corner, M. (2009). mCrowd: a platform for mobile crowdsourcing. *Conference on Embedded Networked Sensor Systems* (pp. 347-348). ACM. doi:10.1145/1644038.1644094

Yang, Y., Onita, C., Dhaliwal, J., & Zhang, X. (2009). TESTQUAL: Conceptualizing software testing as a service. *15th Americas Conference on Information Systems*, San Francisco, California, USA, paper 608.

Yau, S., & Ho, G. (2011, October). Software engineering meets services and cloud computing. *IEEE Computer Magazine*, p. 47.

Yigitbasi, N., Iosup, A., Epema, D., & Ostermann, S. (2009). C-Meter: A framework for performance analysis for computing clouds. *IEEE/ACM International Symposium on Cluster Computing and the Grid* (pp. 472-477).

Yoo, S., Harman, M., & Ur, S. (2011). Highly scalable multi objective test suite minimisation using graphics cards. In *Proceedings of the 3rd Symposium on Search Based Software Engineering*, (pp. 219-236).

Yu, L., Tsai, W. T., Chen, X., Liu, L., Zhao, Y., Tang, L., & Zhao, W. (2010). *Testing as a service over cloud*. 5th IEE International Symposium on Service Oriented System Engineering.

Yu, L., Zhang, L., Xiang, H., Su, Y., Zhao, W., & Zhu, J. (2009). A framework of testing as a service. *International Conference on Management and Service Science*, (pp. 1-4).

Zaidman, A., & Demeyer, S. (2008). Automatic identification of key classes in a software system using webmining techniques. *Journal of Software Maintenance and Evolution, 20*(6), 387–417. doi:10.1002/smr.370

Zander, J., et al. (2005). *From U2TP models to executable tests with TTCN-3 - An approach to model-driven testing*.

Zech, P. (2011). Risk-based security testing in cloud computing environments. *Proceedings of the 4th International Conference on Software Testing, Verification and Validation (ICST 2011)*, (pp. 411-414). Berlin, Germany.

Zhang, C., & Jacobsen, H.-A. (2007). *Efficiently mining crosscutting concerns through random walks*. Paper presented at the 6th International Conference on Aspect-Oriented Software Development.

Zhang, S., Ding, Z., Zong, Y., & Gu, N. (2007). Remote software testing system based on grid workflow. In *Proceedings of 11th International Conference on Computer Supported Software Work in Design (CSCWD 2007)* (pp. 577-581). Melbourne, Australia.

Zhang, X., Freschl, J., & Schopf, J. M. (2003). A performance study of monitoring and information services for distributed systems. *Proceedings 12th IEEE International Symposium on High Performance Distributed Computing 2003*, (p. 12). IEEE Computer Society. Retrieved from http://arxiv.org/abs/cs/0304015

Zhang, Q., Cheng, L., & Boutaba, R. (2010). Cloud computing: State-of-the-art and research challenges. *Journal of Internet Services and Applications, 1*(1), 7–18. doi:10.1007/s13174-010-0007-6

Zheng, B., Xiong, Y., Zhang, Q., & Lin, C. (2006). The spread of epidemics on smartphones. In Xiao, Y., Shen, X., & Du, D. (Eds.), *Wireless/mobile network security*. Springer.

Zhu, H. (2006). A framework for service-oriented testing of web services. Paper presented at *COMPSAC '06: Proceedings of the 30th Annual International Computer Software and Applications Conference*, Vol. 2, (pp. 145–150).

Zvegintzov, N. (1997). A resource guide to year 2000 tools. *Computer*, *30*(3), 58–63. doi:10.1109/2.573662

About the Contributors

Scott Tilley is a faculty member at the Florida Institute of Technology, where he is a Professor of Software Engineering in the Department of Computer Sciences, a Professor of Information Systems in the College of Business, and an Associate Member of the Harris Institute for Assured Information. He is also a Visiting Scientist at Carnegie Mellon University's Software Engineering Institute. His current research is in software testing, cloud computing, and system migration. He is Chair of the Steering Committee for the IEEE *Web Systems Evolution* (WSE) series of events, and a Past Chair of ACM SIGDOC. He was General Chair for ICSM 2008 in Beijing, China. He is the lead author of the book *Software Testing in the Cloud: Migration & Execution* (Springer, 2012). He writes the weekly "Technology Today" column for the *Florida Today* newspaper (Gannett). Scott holds a PhD in Computer Science from the University of Victoria.

Tauhida Parveen is an Independent Consultant and Trainer with an emphasis on cloud computing and software testing. She has worked in quality assurance with organizations such as WikiMedia Foundation, Millennium Engineering & Integration, Yahoo!, Sabre, and Progressive Auto Insurance. She has presented at numerous trade conferences, published in several academic journals, and organized workshops at international events. She is an ISTQB Foundation Level Certified Software Tester (CTFL). She is the co-author of the book *Software Testing in the Cloud: Migration & Execution* (Springer, 2012). Tauhida holds a PhD in Computer Science from the Florida Institute of Technology.

* * *

Peter Andras is a Reader in the School of Computing Science at the University of Newcastle upon Tyne, UK. He has published 2 books and over 100 research papers. He works in the areas of complex systems, software engineering, computational intelligence, and computational neuroscience. He is member of the International Neural Network Society and of the Society for Artificial Intelligence and Simulation of Behaviour, a Senior Member of the IEEE, and a Fellow of the Society of Biology. Peter has a PhD in Mathematical Analysis of Neural Networks from Babes-Bolyai University, Romania.

Xiaoying Bai is an Associate Professor in the Department of Computer Science and Technology at Tsinghua University, China. Her major research area is model-driven testing and test automation techniques in various software paradigms, such as distributed computing, service oriented architecture (SOA), and embedded systems. She has led more than 10 projects in China, including projects funded by the National Key Science and Technology program, the National Science Foundation, and the National High

Tech 863 program. She has had international collaborations with IBM, Freescale, and Fujitsu. She is also involved in two Key Projects of Chinese National Programs for Fundamental Research and Development 973 program. She has published over 90 papers and is co-author of the book *Service-Oriented Software Engineering* (Tsinghua University Press). She is the Associate Editor of *IJSEKE*. Xiaoying holds a PhD in Computer Science from Arizona State University.

Christian Berger is an Assistant Professor of Software Engineering in the Department of Computer Science & Engineering at Chalmers University of Gothenburg, Sweden. Previously, he was a research assistant at Technische Universität Braunschweig. He has also worked for two companies of the Volkswagen Group in the field of active safety vehicle functions for passenger and pedestrian protection. He coordinated the interdisciplinary CarOLO project for the development of the autonomously driving vehicle "Caroline." The team participated in the 2007 DARPA Urban Challenge and placed in the final with ten other teams from 89 initial competitors. His team was the best European participant in that international competition. He has published more than 30 peer-reviewed articles in workshops, conferences, journals, and books. Christian holds a PhD in Computer Science from RWTH Aachen University.

Eric Bower is a Senior Software Engineer at ENSCO, Inc. in Melbourne, FL. His current work involves designing and developing a "big data" search application. His past research focused on software testing in a distributed environment. Eric holds an MSE degree in Software Engineering from the Florida Institute of Technology.

Ruth Breu is a Professor in the Institute of Computer Science at the University of Innsbruck, Austria, where she is head of the Quality Engineering research group. Previously, she worked for several years as software engineering consultant for companies in the finance and telecommunication sector. She has extensive experience in the areas of model-driven software development, requirements engineering, quality management, and security engineering. She is co-author of three books and over 100 publications in international journals and conferences. Since 2009 she has been scientific head of QE LaB, a private-public partnership that focuses on continuous quality management of collaborative systems. Ruth holds a PhD in Computer Science from the University of Passau.

Alan Brown is an IBM Distinguished Engineer and the Chief Technology Officer for IBM Rational in Europe. He consults with clients on software engineering strategy related to enterprise solutions, process improvement, and transition to more agile delivery practices. In recent years he has worked in a variety of senior software delivery roles in industry, government, and academic research organizations. He is the author of a number of books and many papers on software engineering principles and practices. In September 2012 he took a leave of absence from IBM and was appointed Professor of Innovation and Entrepreneurship in the Business School at the University of Surrey, UK. Alan holds a PhD in Computer Science from the University of Newcastle-upon-Tyne.

Chia-Chu Chiang is an Associate Professor in the Department of Computer Science at the University of Arkansas at Little Rock. Previously, he worked at Allen Systems Group, Inc. (formerly Viasoft) in Phoenix where he was responsible for developing and maintaining commercial products for reengineering Assembly, COBOL, and PL/I legacy systems. He has published more than 105 referred research papers in IEEE, ACM, and international journals and conferences. He has obtained external funding from ETRI, Syntel™ LLC., Acxiom, CognitiveDATA, the US DoD, and the NSF. His research areas include formal methods, reverse engineering, reengineering, program analysis, component-based software development, middleware, heterogeneous distributed parallel programming, and text extraction from various file formats. He is a member of ABET, ACM, and the IEEE. Chia-Chu holds a PhD in Computer Science from Arizona State University.

Sergio Di Martino is an Assistant Professor in the Department of Computer Science at the University of Naples "Federico II," Italy, where he is also the co-chair of the Knowledge Management and Engineering Lab. His main research interests include empirical software engineering, software metrics, and knowledge discovery from complex datasets. He has published more than 60 refereed papers in international journals, books, and conference proceedings. Sergio holds a PhD in Computer Science from the University of Salerno.

Michael Felderer is a Research Assistant in the Institute of Computer Science at the University of Innsbruck, Austria. He also works as a consultant and speaks at industrial conferences. His research interests are model-driven testing, risk-based testing, model engineering, software evolution, and requirements engineering. Michael holds a PhD in Computer Science from the University of Innsbruck.

Filomena Ferrucci is a Professor of Computer Science at the University of Salerno, Italy. She is Program Co-Chair of the International Summer School on Software Engineering and she was Program Co-Chair of the 14th International Conference on Software Engineering and Knowledge Engineering. Her main research interests include empirical software engineering, search-based software engineering, software development effort estimation, and human-computer interaction. She has published over 150 refereed papers in international journals, books, and conference proceedings. Filomena holds a PhD in Applied Mathematics and Computer Science from the University of Naples "Federico II."

David Froslie is a Software Test Architect working on the Dynamics Enterprise Resource Planning (ERP) product line for Microsoft Corp. He has held multiple roles at Microsoft over the past ten years including Development Lead, Test Manager, and his present role as Test Architect. In addition to being responsible for the development and implementation of automation test strategies for Microsoft Dynamics AX ERP, Dave provides technical leadership to the team of Software Design Engineers in Test that develop the core automated test infrastructure. David holds an MBA from the University of St. Thomas.

José Ángel Galindo is a PhD student at the Virginia Polytechnic Institute (Virginia Tech). His research interests are software product lines, feature models, variability management, packaging systems, dependencies analysis, and software architecture evolution. José holds a graduate degree from the University of Seville, Spain.

Annaji Sharma Ganti is a PhD student in the Department of Computer Science at North Dakota State University in Fargo. He also works at Microsoft Corp. as a Software Design Engineer in Test II, and has over four years of experience in the software industry. His research interests include software testing, cloud computing, virtualization, and Web services. His dissertation focuses on developing a novel approach to support integration testing of cloud application services. Annaji holds an MS degree in Computer Science from North Dakota State University.

Jerry Zeyu Gao is a Professor in the Department of Computer Engineering at San Jose State University. He had over 10 years of industry working experience on software engineering and IT development applications before he joined San Jose State University in 1998. In addition, he has several years of management experience in software engineering R&D in industry. His major research subjects in the past include software engineering, object-oriented software, component-based software engineering, mobile computing and e-commerce. His current research interests include cloud testing and TaaS, cloud computing, and mobile cloud services. He has published widely in IEEE/ACM journals and international conferences. He co-authored three published technical books and edited numerous books in software engineering and mobile computing with IEEE Computer Society Press, Artech House, and Wiley. Jerry holds a PhD in Computer Science from the University of Texas at Arlington.

W. Morven Gentleman is a Consultant in software technology. He retired as a Professor of Computer Science from Dalhousie University in 2008. His career experience was balanced almost equally between industrial research (the National Research Council of Canada, the UK's National Physical Laboratory, and Bell Labs at Murray Hill) and academia (Dalhousie and the University of Waterloo). He has published in areas as diverse as numerical analysis, computer algebra, complexity theory, compiler technology, operating systems, computer architecture, real-time systems, signal processing, and robotics, but for decades his primary focus has been software engineering, including testing and software architecture. He has held management positions, up to Director General of the Institute for Information Technology at NRC. Morven holds a PhD in Mathematics from Princeton University.

Andy Gokhale is an Associate Professor in the EECS Department and a Senior Researcher in the Institute for Software Intensive Systems at Vanderbilt University. As a doctoral student at Washington University, Andy developed benchmarks for CORBA performance over ATM networks. His research contributed many components to TAO -- most notably the various Object Adapter demultiplexing strategies, IIOP optimizations, and the TAO IDL compiler. He previously worked as a member of the research staff for Bell Labs at Murray Hill. Andy holds a DSc in Computer Science from Washington University in St. Louis.

Toshihiro Hanawa is an Associate Professor in the Center for Computational Sciences at the University of Tsukuba, Japan. Previously, he was a member of the "Dependable Operating Systems for Embedded Systems Aiming at Practical Applications" project supported by JST/CREST in Japan (2007-2012), and an Assistant Professor at Tokyo University of Technology, Japan (1998-2007). His research interests include computer architecture, interconnection network, dependable systems, and benchmarking. He is a member of IEEE CS and IPSJ. Toshihiro holds a PhD degree in Computer Science from Keio University.

Mark Harman is Professor of Software Engineering in the Department of Computer Science at University College London, where he directs the Centre for Research on Evolution Search and Testing (CREST) and is Head of Software Systems Engineering. He is widely known for work on source code analysis and testing and was instrumental in founding the field of Search Based Software Engineering (SBSE). SBSE research has rapidly grown over the past five years and now includes over 1,000 authors from nearly 300 institutions spread over more than 40 countries. Mark holds a PhD in Computer Science from the Polytechnic of North London.

James Hill is an Assistant Professor of Computer Science in the Department of Computer & Information Science at Indiana University-Purdue University at Indianapolis (IUPUI), where he is also the co-director of the Software Engineering and Distributed Systems (SEDS) group. He is the co-founder and Chief Technology Officer (CTO) of Sprezzat, Inc, a company that focuses on solutions for mobile marketing. He has published over 45 journal, conference, workshop, and book chapter publications that focus on the areas of enabling early integration testing of large-scale distributed software systems, domain-specific modeling, real-time software instrumentation, techniques for integrating large-scale software systems, and software performance analytics. His research in this area has lead to two open-source projects: the Component Workload Emulator (CoWorkEr) Utilization Test Suite (CUTS), and the Open-source Architecture for Software Instrumentation of Systems (OASIS). James holds a PhD in Computer Sciences from Vanderbilt University.

Philipp Kalb is a Research Assistant in the Institute of Computer Science at the University of Innsbruck, Austria. His research interests are model-driven engineering, model versioning, model evolution, and change-driven processes. Philipp holds an MSc in Computer Science from the University of Innsbruck.

Tariq King is an Assistant Professor in the Department of Computer Science at North Dakota State University in Fargo. He is the Director of the Software Testing Research Group and serves as a Software Test Lead for the WoWiWe Instruction Company. His research and instructional interests include software testing, autonomic and cloud computing, and model-driven engineering. He has published over 20 research papers in the field of software testing and is a principal investigator on a Small Business Innovation Research Phase II grant from the NIH. Tariq holds a PhD in Computer Science from Florida International University.

Nikolai Kosmatov is a researcher with the Software Safety Lab of CEA LIST, France. His research interests have focused on constraint solving, software verification, and automatic test generation. Nikolai has taught various courses in Mathematics and Computer Science at Saint-Petersburg State University, the University of Orléans, the University of Besançon, the University Pierre and Marie Curie in Paris, and RWTH Aachen University in Germany. Nikolai holds a PhD in Mathematics jointly from Saint-Petersburg State University in Russia and the University of Besançon in France.

Valerio Maggio is a PhD student at the University of Naples "Federico II". His research interests are focused on the definition and application of information retrieval and machine learning techniques to software maintenance tasks, such as mining software repositories, software clustering, and clone detection. Valerio holds an MSc degree in Computer Science from the University of Naples "Federico II."

Madhav Marathe is a Professor of Computer Science and Deputy Director of the Network Dynamics and Simulation Science Laboratory at the Virginia Polytechnic Institute (Virginia Tech). Previously, he was team leader in a theory-based advanced simulation program to represent, design, and analyze extremely large socio-technical and critical infrastructure systems at the Los Alamos National Laboratory. He has published more than 200 research articles in peer reviewed journals, conference proceedings, and book, specializing in population dynamics, telecommunication systems, epidemiology, design and architecture of the data grid, design and analysis of algorithms for data manipulation, design of services-oriented architectures, and socio-technical systems. He is the recipient of the 2010 Award for Research Excellence from the Virginia Bioinformatics Institute, and the 2011 Inaugural George Michael Distinguished Scholar at the Lawrence Livermore National Laboratory. Madhav holds a PhD in Computer Science from the University at Albany.

Anjan Pakhira is a PhD student in the School of Computing Science at the University of Newcastle upon Tyne, UK. His research focuses on the application of complex network analysis to large scale software system engineering. Previously, he worked on the UK eScience program, developing large scale grid/cloud-enabled and HPC applications at STFC's Rutherford Appleton Laboratory, supporting e-enablement and e-infrastructure of physical sciences research facilities. Anjan holds an MSc in High Performance Computing from the University of Edinburgh.

Adam Porter is a Professor with the Department of Computer Science at the University of Maryland and is the Associate Director of the Institute for Advanced Computer Studies. He is a winner of an NSF CAREER Award and the Dean's Award for Teaching Excellence in the College of Computer, Mathematical, and Physical Sciences at the University of Maryland. He is currently a member of the editorial board of *IEEE Transactions on Software Engineering* and served previously on the editorial board of *ACM Transactions on Software Engineering and Methodology*. He is a senior member of both the IEEE and ACM. His current research interests include empirical methods for identifying and eliminating bottlenecks in industrial development processes, experimental evaluation of fundamental software engineering hypotheses, and development of tools that demonstrably improve the software development process. Adam holds a PhD in Computer Science from the University of California, Irvine.

Wishnu Prasetya is a Researcher and Lecturer at the Department of Information and Computing Sciences at Utrecht University, The Netherlands. He teaches courses such as Modeling and Systems Development, Software Testing, and Program Verification. His research areas are compositional proofs of distributed algorithms, formalization with theorem provers, software logging, testing of object-oriented programs, testing of Internet applications, and testing of games. Wishnu holds a PhD in Computer Science from the University of Utrecht.

Jeffrey Reed is the Willis G. Worcester Professor in the Bradley Department of Electrical & Computer Engineering and the director of Wireless at the Virginia Polytechnic Institute (Virginia Tech). His areas of expertise are in software radios, smart antennas, and ultra wideband. He is the author of *Software Radio: A Modern Approach to Radio Engineering* (Prentice Hall, 2002) and *An Introduction to Ultra Wideband Communication Systems* (Prentice Hall, 2005). He is a Fellow of the IEEE. Jeff holds a PhD in Electrical Engineering from the University of California, Davis.

Randall Rice is a leading author, speaker, and consultant in the field of software testing and software quality. His recent work is in testing cloud computing and service-oriented architecture projects. Randy is a director on the American Software Testing Qualifications Board and has been published by *Better Software, Crosstalk* and *Enterprise Systems Journal*. He is the publisher of *The Software Quality Advisor* newsletter. He is co-author with William Perry of the books, *Surviving the Top Ten Challenges of Software Testing* and *Testing Dirty Systems*. Randall served as Chair of the Quality Assurance Institute's International Software Testing Conference from 1995–2000 and was a founding member of the Certified Software Test Engineer (CSTE) certification program. As author and trainer of over 60 software testing training courses, he has had the privilege of training thousands of software testers throughout North America. Randy is an ISTQB Certified Tester – Advanced Level (Full).

Leah Riungu-Kalliosaari is a PhD student and Researcher at Lappeenranta University of Technology, Finland. Her research focuses on cloud computing and its impact across different organizational contexts, including testing and quality assurance. She holds an MSc in Information Technology from Lappeenranta University of Technology and a double major BSc in Computer Science and Mathematics from the University of Namibia.

Federica Sarro is a PhD student at University of Salerno, Italy. Her main research area is search-based software engineering, with specific interest in the definition and the empirical evaluation of search-based approaches for predictive modeling in the context of software development effort estimation, and for fault prediction and software testing. Her research interests also include functional metrics for sizing software products and human-computer interaction. Federica holds an MSc degree in Computer Science from the University of Salerno.

Mitsuhisa Sato is a Professor in the Graduate School of Systems and Information Engineering at the University of Tsukuba. He has been Director of the Center for Computational Sciences at the University of Tsukuba since 2007. Previously, he was a senior researcher at the Electrotechnical Laboratory (1991-1996), and a chief of the Parallel and Distributed System Performance Laboratory in Real World Computing Partnership of Japan (1996-2001). In October 2010, Mitsuhisa was appointed to lead the programming environment research team in the Advanced Institute of Computational Science (RIKEN), which is the main body to run Japanese petaflops facility "K" computer. His research interests include computer architecture, compilers, performance evaluation for parallel computer systems, OpenMP, and parallel programming. He is a member of IEEE CS and IPSJ, IEICE, JSIAM. Mitsuhisa holds a PhD in Information Sciences from the University of Tokyo.

Douglas Schmidt is a Professor of Computer Science and Associate Chair of the Computer Science and Engineering program at Vanderbilt University. He has also been the Chief Technology Officer for the Software Engineering Institute at Carnegie Mellon University. In addition, he served as a Deputy Office Director and a Program Manager at DARPA, where he led the national research and development effort on middleware for distributed real-time and embedded (DRE) systems. He has published 10 books and more than 500 technical papers covering a wide range of software-related topics. He has led the development of ACE, TAO, CIAO, and CoSMIC for the past two decades. These technologies are DRE middleware frameworks and model-driven tools used successfully by thousands of companies and agencies worldwide. Doug holds a PhD in Computer Science from the University of California, Irvine.

Bharat Shah is an Engineering Manager for Lockheed Martin Information Systems & Global Solutions (IS&GS)-Civil organization. He has more than 30 years of information systems experience across a broad base of system architectures and technologies. He has presented papers at international conferences on approaches to Internet-based application testing, information systems security testing, cloud computing controls assessment, and critical infrastructure controls assessment. He is certification as a Certified Information Systems Auditor (CISA) and Certified in Risk and Information Systems Controls (CRISC) from Information Systems Audit and Control Association (ISACA). Bharat holds MSC degrees from the University of Maryland and Capella University.

Kari Smolander is a Professor of Software Engineering in the Department of Information Technology at the Lappeenranta University of Technology, Finland. In addition to his long teaching experience, he has worked for several years in industry. In the 1990's he was the main architect in the development of MetaEdit CASE tool. He has more than 100 refereed research papers in international journals and conferences. His current research interests include architectural aspects of systems development and organizational view of software development. Kari holds a PhD in Computer Science from the Lappeenranta University of Technology.

Harry Sneed began working in testing with the Siemens ITS project in 1977. He co-founded the first commercial test laboratory in Budapest in 1978. He has developed more than 20 different test tools. Harry has worked as a project leader and tool designer for the Hungarian IT laboratories, as a reengineering project leader at the Swiss Union Bank, and as a tester and quality assurance specialist in Vienna. He has written 21 books and published more than 400 papers. He lectures at the University of Regensburg, the University of Koblenz, and the University of Szeged. In 2005 Harry was appointed by the German Gesellschaft für Informatik as a GI Fellow and served as general chair for ICSM. In 2008 he received the Stevens Award for his pioneering work in software maintenance. Harry holds a Master's Degree in Information Sciences from the University of Maryland.

Ossi Taipale is a Researcher at the Lappeenranta University of Technology, Finland, where he leads a project on software quality and testing. He has a long career in the IT sector, both in industry and as an entrepreneur. In recent years he has focused on academic research in software testing. From 1994-2000 he worked as the program manager of the "Adaptive and Intelligent Systems Applications" research program, which was funded by the Finnish Funding Agency for Technology and Innovation and participating industry partners. He is Finland's representative on the ISO/IEC WG26, which develops standards related to software testing. Ossi holds a DSc from Lappeenranta University of Technology.

Paolo Tonella is head of the Software Engineering Research Unit at Fondazione Bruno Kessler (FBK) in Trento, Italy. He is the author of the book *Reverse Engineering of Object Oriented Code* (Springer, 2005). He has written over 100 peer reviewed conference/workshop papers and over 40 journal papers. In 2011 he was awarded the ICSE 2001 MIP (Most Influential Paper) award for his paper, "Analysis and Testing of Web Applications." He was Program Chair of ICSM 2011 and ICPC 2007, and was General Chair of ISSTA 2010 and ICSM 2012. He is on the editorial board of *EMSE* and *JSME*. His current research interests include code analysis, web and object oriented testing, and search-based test case generation. Paolo holds a PhD in Computer Science from the University of Padova.

Wei-Tek Tsai is a Professor in the School of Computing, Informatics, and Decision Systems Engineering at Arizona State University. He has published over 300 papers in various journals and conferences, received two Best Paper awards, and several honorable professorships His main research interests are software testing, software engineering, and embedded system development. The US DoD, Department of Education, NSF, EU, and industrial partners such as Intel and Fujitsu have supported his work. His recent efforts focus on software as a service (SaaS) and service-oriented computing. Wei-Tek holds a PhD in Computer Science from the University of California, Berkeley.

Hamilton Turner is a PhD student in the Bradley Department of Electrical & Computer Engineering at the Virginia Polytechnic Institute (Virginia Tech). While pursuing his undergraduate degree at Vanderbilt University he founded a student group to develop mobile applications for university applications. This work was eventually adopted as the first official mobile application for Vanderbilt He has published 3 journal articles, 2 book chapters, and 7 conference publications. Hamilton holds a BE in Computer Engineering from Vanderbilt University.

Shmuel Ur is a Visiting Fellow in the Department of Computer Science at the University of Bristol, UK. He has published in the fields of hardware testing, artificial intelligence, algorithms, software testing, and testing of multi-threaded programs. He has more than 60 professional publications, more than 30 granted patents, and has given numerous talks and tutorials. He was a scientist with IBM Research in Haifa, Israel for 16 years, where he held the title of IBM Master Inventor. He has taught software testing at the Technion and Haifa University. He has also consulted with banks and companies as to how to improve their software development process. After leaving IBM Research, He is active in the area of intellectual property education for computer professionals. Shmuel holds a PhD in Computer Science from Carnegie Mellon University.

Tanja Vos is a Lecturer in the Computation and Information Systems Department (DSIC) at the Technical University of Valencia, Spain. She carries out her research in the Center for Software Production Methods (ProS), where she leads the Software Testing & Quality (STaQ) group. She has more than 10 years of experience with formal methods and software testing. She is involved in many research projects on software testing in an industrial setting. She has successfully coordinated the EU-funded EvoTest proposal from 2006-2009 and is currently coordinating the EU-funded FITTEST project on Future Internet Testing. Tanja holds a PhD in Computer Science from the University of Utrecht.

Anil Vullikanti is an Associate Professor in the Department of Computer Science and in the Virginia Bioinformatics Institute at the Virginia Polytechnic Institute (Virginia Tech). Previously he was a postdoctoral associate at the Max-Planck Institute and a technical staff member at the Los Alamos National Laboratory. His current interests are at the interface of theoretical computer science and modeling and simulation of social and infrastructure systems, epidemiology, and mobile computing. He has published in diverse conferences and journals, including *Nature*, *Journal of the ACM*, *ACM SIGMETRICS*, and *IEEE INFOCOM*. Anil holds a PhD in Computer Science from the Indian Institute of Science.

Joachim Wegener leads the software analysis and testing group at DaimlerChrysler research laboratories, Berlin / Stuttgart. He has been the main software architect for the successful TESSYtesting environment and the CTE classification tree editor. He is a leading researcher in evolutionary test generation and has published more than 30 papers on this subject's foundations and applications. His thesis work received the "Best Dissertation in Software Engineering" award of the Ernst-Denert-Stiftung, 2002. He is chairman of the GI working group "Test eingebetteter Systeme," Fachgruppe TAV (2.1.7), and has twice been program chair of the GECCO Search-Based Software Engineering track. Joachim holds a PhD in Computer Science from Humboldt University.

Jules White is an Assistant Professor in the Bradley Department of Electrical & Computer Engineering at the Virginia Polytechnic Institute (Virginia Tech). His research focuses on applying search-based optimization techniques to the configuration of distributed, real-time, and embedded systems. In conjunction with Siemens AG, Lockheed Martin, IBM and others, he has developed scalable constraint and heuristic techniques for software deployment and configuration. He is the Project Lead of the Eclipse Foundation's Generic Eclipse Modeling System (GEMS). Jules hold a PhD in Computer Science from Vanderbilt University.

Shucheng Yu is an Assistant Professor in the Department of Computer Science at the University of Arkansas at Little Rock. His current research interests include security and privacy in cloud computing, attribute-based cryptography, and wireless networks and their security. He is a member of IEEE, ACM and Sigma Xi. He serves as an editor for *KSII Transactions on Internet and Information Systems* and *International Journal of Research and Reviews in Wireless Sensor Networks*. Shucheng holds a PhD in Electrical & Computer Engineering from Worcester Polytechnic Institute.

Philipp Zech is a Research Assistant in the Institute of Computer Science at the University of Innsbruck, Austria. His research interests are software testing, model-driven testing, security testing, model engineering, services computing, and logic programming. Philipp holds an MSc in Computer Science from the University of Innsbruck.

Index